ICELAND

39 Reykjavík

48

45

DENMARK

50 Aarhus
51 Ballerup
52 Billund
53 Copenhagen
54 Fåreveile
55 Hellebaek
56 Hjørring
57 Kerteminde
58 Kolding
59 Kongens Lyngby
60 Naevsted
61 Odense
62 Rødovre
63 Skagen

NORWAY

40 Ålesund
41 Bergen
42 Geilo
43 Gjøvik
44 Hjerkinn
45 Narvik
46 Oslo
47 Sandnes
48 Tromsø
49 Trondheim

49

40
44

63
56

50
52 57
58
60

61

43

42

41

46

47

55

54

59

51
62
53

MODERN SCANDINAVIAN DESIGN

Charlotte and Peter Fiell are leading authorities on the history, theory and criticism of design and have written and edited over 50 books on the subject, including *Design of the 20th Century*, *The Story of Design*, *Designing the 21st Century* and the bestselling *1000 Chairs*.

Magnus Englund is co-founder of Skandium, the high-end furniture retailer and contract dealer in modern Scandinavian furniture. He has previously written two bestselling books on Scandinavian design, and is a trustee of the Isokon Gallery, a London museum celebrating the 1930s Modernist movement.

LAURENCE KING

Laurence King Publishing
361–373 City Road
London EC1V 1LR
T + 44 (0)20 7841 6900
F + 44 (0)20 7841 6910
enquiries@laurenceking.com
www.laurenceking.com

© Text 2017 Charlotte Fiell, Peter Fiell and Magnus Englund

Charlotte Fiell, Peter Fiell and Magnus Englund have asserted their rights under the Copyright, Designs, and Patents Act 1988, to be identified as the Authors of this Work.

A catalogue record for this book is available from the British Library.

ISBN: 978-1-78627-052-8

Design: Henrik Nygren Design

Printed in China

Cover
Sweden © Felix Odell/Link.

Bellyband (unfolded)

BACK FLAP
top left, interior of Bagsværd Church, Bagsværd, by Jørn Utzon, p.54; *top right*, stained pine stool by Axel Einar Hjorth, p.105; *middle right*, Crux carpet by Pia Wallén, p.497; *middle*, Unikko (Poppy) textile by Maija Isola, p.487; *bottom right*, indoor watering can by Gunnar Anders, p.374; *bottom left*, Etcetera lounge chair and ottoman by Jan Ekselius, p.165.

BACK
top left Ring lounge chairs by Nanna and Jørgen Ditzel, p.155; *top right* textile by Marjatta Seppälä (attributed), p.459; *middle right* stoneware bowl by Axel Salto for Royal Copenhagen, ca. 1947 © Bukowskis [not featured in the book]; *bottom right* Wenge serving platter by Theodor Skjøde Knudsen, p.406; *bottom left* Ultima Thule Model no. 2232 plate by Tapio Wirkkala, p.276; *middle left* AJ cutlery by Arne Jacobsen, p.394; *centre middle* Vivianna Bangle watch by Vivianna Torun Bülow-Hübe, p.520.

FRONT
top left Wonderlamp Model Typ F by Verner Panton, p.229; *top right* Picknick platters and bowl by Marianne Westman, p.347; *centre right upper* Aalto vase by Alvar Aalto, p.248; *centre right lower* model 41 Paimio chair by Alvar and Aino Aalto, p.95; *bottom right* Fuga bowl by Sven Palmqvist, p.260; *bottom centre* elephant toy by Kay Bojesen, p.411; *bottom left* CH28 lounge chair by Hans Wegner, p.143; *centre left* detail of Ant chair by Arne Jacobsen, p.124; *centre middle* Kanna watering can by Carl-Arne Breger, p.442.

FRONT FLAP
top left Tverrfjellhytta (Norwegian Wild Reindeer Centre Pavilion), Hjerkinn, Dovrefjell national park, Norway, by Snøhetta, p.75; *top right* PH Artichoke pendant light by Poul Henningsen, p.204; *centre right* Drop chairs by Arne Jacobsen in room 606 of the SAS Royal Hotel, Copenhagen, p.36; *bottom right* Large Camel floor lamp, model no. 2368, by Josef Frank, p.206; *bottom left* Patronen armchair by Gustaf Axel Berg, p.120.

page 4 Detail of the PH Artichoke pendant light by Poul Henningsen, p.204; *page 6* Wenge serving platter by Theodor Skjøde Knudsen, p.406; *page 9* Series 7 (model no. 3107) chairs by Arne Jacobsen; *pages 10–11* standing stones in Norway; *pages 78–79* Habo, Jönköping, Sweden; *pages 196–197* Åstön, Timrå, Sweden; *pages 236–237* Iceland; *pages 312–313* Hellvi, Gotland, Sweden; *pages 366–367* Norway; *pages 404–405* Aspudden, Sweden; *pages 430–431* Gullfoss Falls, Iceland; *pages 454–455* Kyllej, Gotland, Sweden; *pages 502–503* Iceland; *pages 538–539* Hellvi, Gotland, Sweden.

MODERN SCANDINAVIAN DESIGN

CHARLOTTE FIELL
PETER FIELL
MAGNUS ENGLUND

LAURENCE KING PUBLISHING

Editor's note: The birth and death dates for key individuals and the founding dates of companies and design practices mentioned in the text appear next to their entries in the index.

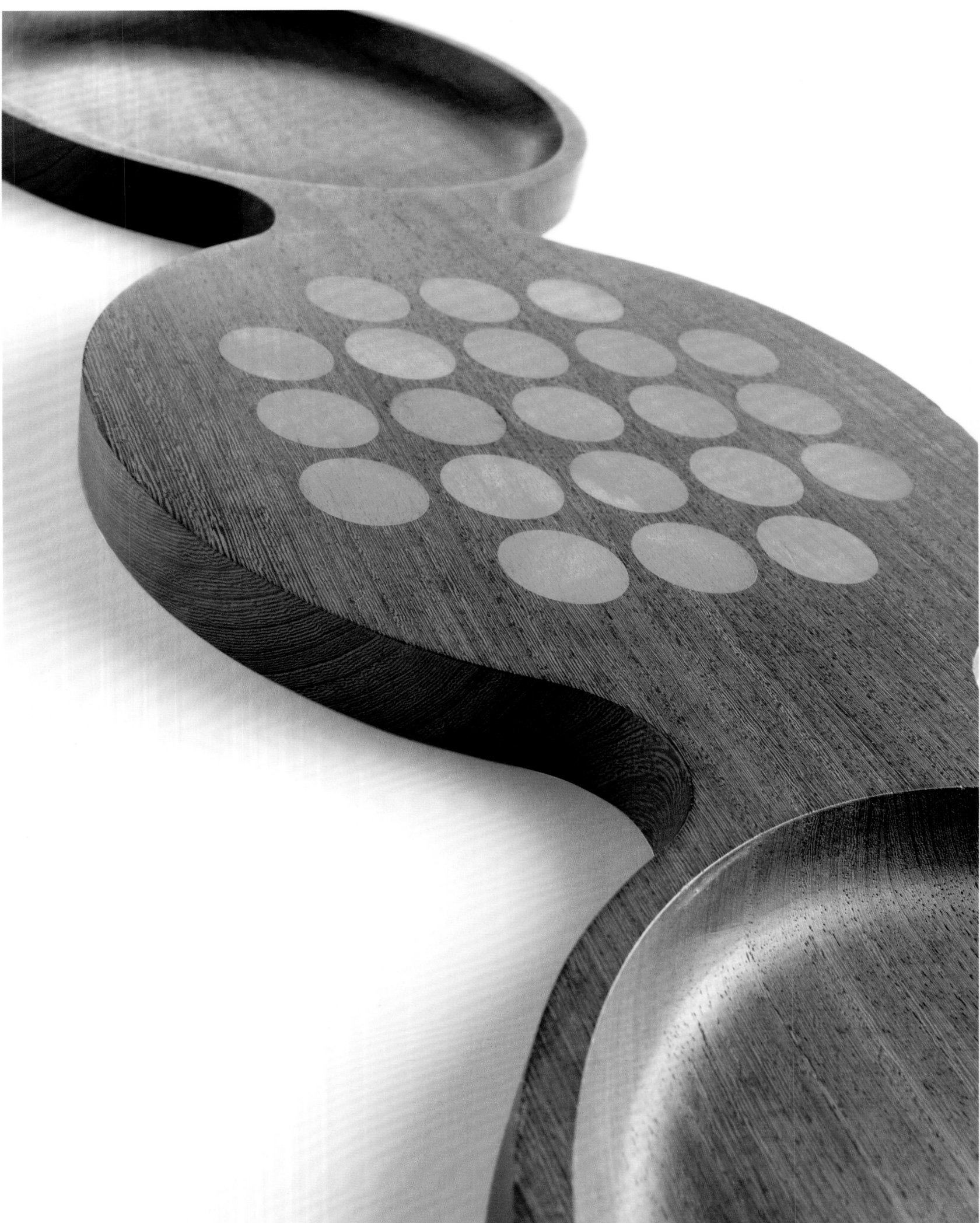

INTRODUCTION

What is Scandinavian design? The term 'Scandinavian design', if used in its most precise definition, refers only to the design output of the countries on the Scandinavian Peninsula: Denmark, Sweden and Norway. Since the 1950s, however, the phrase has also included design from Finland, which in fact played a central role in the postwar development of what we now think of as Scandinavian design. In this survey, we have also included a small amount of work from Iceland, which is likewise part of the Nordic region rather than technically part of Scandinavia. More recently the term 'Nordic design' has begun to gain increasing currency, especially in the auction world. We felt, however, that for clarity's sake we should stick to the more commonly used term, even though Nordic design is perhaps more correct in its etymology, referring as it does to the whole of the Nordic region.

As for the design categories we selected to be featured over the coming pages, we decided to concentrate on architecture (including interior design), furniture design, lighting design, glassware, ceramics, metalware, woodenware, plastics, textiles, jewellery and graphic design primarily for the sake of brevity, but references to both industrial design and fashion are also peppered throughout the book. Further criteria for the selection of individual designs were influence and innovation, which is why you will find so many homewares in this survey, for Scandinavian designers – more than designers anywhere else in the world – have long realized the truth of the saying 'Home is where the heart is'.

To go back to the title of this publication, what do we mean exactly by 'Modern'? For this comprehensive survey we have focused on the period from 1925 to the present, which was marked in the Nordic region by the ascendency of Modernism and the later flowerings of Postmodernism and then Late Modernism. The year 1925 saw the first stirrings of a definable Scandinavian Modern design sensibility in the Swedish Pavilion at the Exposition Internationale des Arts Décoratifs et Industriels Modernes held in Paris. It is well known that the title of this landmark exhibition spawned the term 'Art Deco', but it was also where the term 'Swedish Grace' was coined to describe a new Nordic version of Modern Neoclassicism, which with its formal simplicity would lead to the birth of Nordic Functionalism in the early 1930s. Indeed, many designers and architects in the Nordic countries were influenced profoundly by the new rational approach to design and architecture, known as Modernism, emanating from Germany and France during the 1920s, and – while taking on its form-follows-function goals – they suffused it with a very Scandinavian design sensibility, so that their interpretations of this new movement were less dogmatic and much more human-centric.

In fact, the origins and development of Scandinavian Modernism can be traced through a number of key publications, seminal exhibitions and design-reforming organizations, which are referred to repeatedly over the coming pages. One of the earliest publications that helped to shape the evolution of Modern Scandinavian design was a book of illustrations by the Swedish artist Carl Larsson that depicted his family's simple yet aesthetic life in their summer home, Lilla Hyttnäs, in Sundborn, an idyllic village in the rural and mystic heartland of Sweden. Entitled *Ett Hem* (A Home) and published in 1899, it was a potent expression of Swedishness and as such can be seen as part of the wider National Romantic movement that swept through the Nordic region, as well as elsewhere in Europe, during the latter years of the nineteenth century. But over and above this, Larsson's book provided an inspirational glimpse into an artistic yet simple life of familial domesticity, which was at its heart anti-bourgeois and chimed with the contemporaneous Arts and Crafts sentiments of leading design reformers in Germany, Austria, Britain and America. Larsson's colourful and sentimental depictions of family life fundamentally shaped the Scandinavian notion of home – light-filled everyday spaces furnished simply and tastefully. Indeed, a direct inspirational-lifestyle lineage can be seen to run from Larsson's 'simple life' watercolours to the democratic interiors found in today's IKEA catalogues.

The same year that Larsson's book was published, the Swedish feminist writer Ellen Key wrote her famous pamphlet *Skönhet för Alla* (Beauty for All), which linked ethics with aesthetics, and argued that if design standards could be improved, the lives of ordinary people could be enhanced immeasurably. Her concept of good design as a tool for social change helped to develop a more egalitarian, human focus among Swedish design practitioners, which in turn influenced the reform of design in other Nordic countries over the following decades. In 1919 the director of the Svenska Slöjdföreningen (Swedish Society of Crafts and Industrial Design), Gregor Paulsson, went further by publishing a pamphlet entitled *Vackrare Vardagsvara* (More Beautiful Everyday Objects), which called on manufacturers to focus their efforts on providing well-designed everyday wares to working-class consumers. Like Key's publication, it helped to instil the idea of democratic design values in Scandinavian design circles. Another Swedish publication that had a strong impact on the development of Modern Scandinavian design was the famous *Acceptera!* (Accept!) manifesto of 1931, written by Paulsson with five of the leading Swedish Modernist architect-designers of the day: Erik Gunnar Asplund, Wolter Gahn, Sven Markelius, Uno Åhrén and Eskil Sundahl. This rallying cry for Functionalism in the name of social democracy ultimately provoked the widespread acceptance of Modern design ideals across the Nordic countries.

Yet despite sharing comparable life-enhancing goals and having evolved from similar craft traditions, each of the four main Nordic countries – Denmark, Sweden, Norway and Finland – had a markedly different and distinctive national approach to Modern design. In Denmark and Sweden, the dominance of Neoclassicism in the eighteenth and nineteenth centuries strongly influenced the evolution of Modern design in the twentieth century. Indeed, the design output of both nations tends to rely far more on classical proportions than that from either Norway or Finland. In Denmark, there has also long been a quest among designers for 'ideal forms', which has involved the reworking of age-old vernacular and archetypal forms to create designs of rare aesthetic and functional refinement. Likewise, the Danish lifestyle philosophy of *hygge* – pronounced 'hue-gah' and often credited as one of the main reasons why Denmark is consistently ranked top of the United Nation's World Happiness Report – has similarly had an enormous impact on the focus of Danish design practice. Although there is no direct translation of *hygge*, it is essentially a positive mindset that emphasizes the importance of 'being' rather than 'having', and of living in the present and creating around one an atmosphere of heart-warming cosiness and togetherness. As a means of beating the blues during the long, cold, dark winter months that all Nordic countries endure, the concept stresses the emotional joy to be found in homely surroundings, from the glow of a lit candle to the warmth of a blanket. Indeed, the whole idea of *hygge* as a way of living well helps to explain why so many Danish designers have focused on the creation of thoughtfully designed and beautifully executed Modern wares for domestic use.

In contrast, in Sweden the development of Modern design has been driven by stronger socio-political imperatives, and the social democratic concept of the *Folkhemmet* (the people's home), which is inextricably linked to the founding of the Swedish welfare state. The concept of *Folkhem* was that society should be organized like a family, built on equality and mutual understanding, with the state taking a benevolent yet ultimately controlling role that ensured the increased well-being of Swedish citizens. This, of course, brought not only the eventual introduction of free education, free universal healthcare and generous welfare provisions, but also the design and construction of comprehensive social housing programmes. In fact, Sweden, more than any other nation during the first half of the twentieth century, could be said to have built a modern democratic society through the harnessing of Modern democratic design. The Swedish adoption of Functionalism for the greater social good determined not only the type of model housing estates that were built, but also the type of homewares designed and manufactured to furnish them. This sense of social morality runs through Modern Swedish design, and was for decades expressed through its greater sense of utilitarianism – for example, much Modern Swedish furniture has a more industrial quality than, say, Modern Danish furniture, which relies more on ideal forms and superlative craft skill. Likewise, within the Nordic region, it is not surprising that Postmodernism found its most fertile ground in Sweden in the 1980s, because since the late 1920s the adoption of Modern design values in Sweden has been a political issue. Yet, despite the questioning of these values by the likes of Jonas Bohlin, even to this day Swedish design tends to be guided by ethical considerations. Leading the way in the creation of more affordable good design, Swedish designers also helped to pioneer a more human-centric approach to design, and some are among the greatest pioneers of ergonomic design and inclusive design for disability (which, although not covered in this book, is deserving of a special mention). Today the democratic values of Swedish design have been successfully globalized by IKEA, which attempts to bring good design to everyone's home through five key goals: functionality, aesthetics, high quality, affordability and sustainability.

Throughout much of its history, Norway took on the role of 'little brother' to its Nordic neighbours, being far smaller in terms of population and international influence. Historically, it was also significantly less prosperous, until oil revenues from the North Sea began flowing into the country from the 1960s onwards, making it today one of the world's most affluent nations in terms of GDP. Because for centuries day-to-day survival in Norway had been very hard, with people not only having to endure long, harsh winters but also often living in relative isolation along its fjord-dotted coastline, a can-do self-reliance became an entrenched part of the national psyche. To put it bluntly, if you needed an axe, you just had to make one yourself. Indeed, Norway's centuries-old tradition of tool-making prompted a long-held belief in *brukskunst*, which means 'useful art' or 'applied art'. The Foreningen Brukskunst (Society of Applied Arts) was established in Oslo in 1918 with the intention of bringing artists and manufacturers together in order to create better-designed products for everyday living. Another important aspect of Norwegian culture that also had a direct bearing on the evolution of Modern Norwegian design was its rich folk handicraft traditions, which have been honed over the centuries as a way of whiling away the hours during the long winter evenings. These folk handicrafts traditionally gave Norwegian interiors that all-important Scandinavian warm, homely quality, too. But more than this, the folk arts, which must be seen to include tool-making, engendered an intimate hands-on knowledge of functional form and material properties, which resulted in, among many other things, the beautiful yet practical cutlery designs of Tias Eckhoff, and the iconic cheese-slicer famously invented by Thor Bjørklund – both of which are essentially useful tools for better living.

In comparison, Finnish design has tended to have a more refined quality, often inspired by the raw beauty of nature. Of all the Nordic countries, it is Finland that perhaps best encapsulates the idea of the 'Soul of the North', and its people have a definable stoicism born of living at the edge of human habitability. The country's severe climatic conditions and its history of economic hardship have engendered its people with an emotional reserve as well as a sense of inner fortitude, which is described by them as *sisu* – equating to the North American concept of having 'the right stuff'. This attribute has led some Finnish designers doggedly to pursue optimum functionality in their designs, such as Alvar Aalto's Model no. 60 stool for Artek (1932–33), Kaj Franck's Kilta tableware for Arabia (1948) or Olof Bäckström's classic orange-handled scissors for Fiskars (1967). There is, however, another side to Finnish design that seems to compensate for the emotional reserve found among its people, while also conveying the deep emotional connection they have with nature. Whether it is ice-like glassware by Tapio Wirkkala, bold large-print textiles by Maija Isola or ceramics by Birger Kaipiainen decorated in relief with profusions of berries and fruits, such designs have a strong sense of individual creative expression and are fundamentally celebrations of the natural world.

In 1954 Denmark, Sweden, Norway and Finland co-operated in the staging of a landmark exhibition, 'Design in Scandinavia – An Exhibition of Objects for the Home', organized by the American Federation of Arts in New York. This major three-year touring event was staged in 22 cities across the United States and Canada, and featured 700 homeware designs selected by a panel of 12 Scandinavian design experts from the four nations. There had been earlier exhibitions that featured designs from these individual countries, but this was the first comprehensive international exhibition in which they shared the same platform, and as such it contributed to a huge surge of public interest in Scandinavian design in North America. The influential 'Formes Scandinaves' exhibition held at the Musée des Arts Décoratifs in Paris in 1958 also helped to raise the profile of Scandinavian design across Europe, where it was seen as the epitome of 'good design' as well as 'good taste'.

Scandinavia's promotion of high-quality goods for everyday use had an underlying humanism that offered an alternative understanding of Modernism and ultimately reflected the democratic principles upon which the governance of these Nordic countries is based. In fact, in most people's minds during the postwar period, the term 'Scandinavian' was synonymous with the term 'Modernism'. The liberal openness of Scandinavian societies is mirrored in the inclusive nature of their design output, and the potent message of Scandinavian design is that good design is the birthright of all – regardless of class, gender, age or physical ability. As Alvar Aalto put it, making reference to William Morris, 'Every house, every product of architecture should be a fruit of our endeavour to build an earthly paradise for people.' This social message, which is so entrenched in Scandinavian design ideology, centres on the deeply held belief that all human life has value. The innate essentialism and aestheticism found in so many Scandinavian designs, as featured over the coming pages, can also be seen as an outward expression of Lutheranism – a branch of Protestant Christianity that has shaped Scandinavian culture over the centuries, and which views good works as the fruits of faith.

Today Scandinavian design continues to lead ethically by example, by perpetuating the long-held ideals of good design: practical function, truth to materials, aesthetic refinement, beautiful craftsmanship, emotional connection, social responsibility and democratic affordability.

Ultimately, it is the innate honesty of Scandinavian design, which exemplifies the ideals of good design, that makes it so compelling. Indeed, it is this adherence to truthfulness that has allowed Nordic designers consistently to create designs that not only delight the eye and the hand, but also warm the heart.

ARCHITECTURE

The varying fortunes of the Scandinavian countries around the period of World War I came to shape their individual national identities. Norway had peacefully broken away from its union with Sweden in 1905 after less than 100 years, leaving Sweden the size it is today. Finland, which had made up the eastern part of a Swedish Baltic Empire since early medieval times, had come under Russian rule in 1809. In the chaos of the Russian revolution, Finland seized the opportunity to become its own independent nation. Denmark had already lost its southern provinces to Prussia in the mid nineteenth century, a few decades after the loss of Norway to Sweden, and had settled down as a much smaller nation, albeit with Greenland, Iceland and the Faroe Islands still under the Danish flag.

When these geographically reduced but fiercely independent nations searched for new national identities, the symbolism of buildings became important. While France had been a major cultural influence on Scandinavia until the Napoleonic wars, it was Prussia and later Germany that came to dominate art, design and architecture. The stylistic impact of the Franco-Belgian Art Nouveau style and the British Arts and Crafts Movement was mirrored in the heavier interpretation of the 'New Art' movement found in Germany and Austria, known as Jugendstil, and it was from there that new influences travelled north to the Nordic countries.

In Finland, which had German influences going back to the medieval Hanseatic League, a National Romantic form of Art Nouveau emerged that was known as Finnish Jugend, and which frequently drew inspiration from the national epic poem *Kalevala* by Elias Lönnrot (1835). The Finnish painter Akseli Gallen-Kallela transformed the *Kalevala* into paintings, and in 1900 decorated the Finnish Pavilion at the Exposition Universelle in Paris.

The architects Eliel Saarinen, Herman Gesellius and Armas Lindgren, who had founded a firm together in 1896, created the pavilion. Their most recognized works are Helsinki Central Station and their collective home, Hviiträsk. In 1923 Saarinen moved to the USA with his family, including his son Eero, where he went on to design and subsequently direct the Cranbrook Academy of Art in Michigan, an institution that saw students such as Harry Bertoia, Charles and Ray Eames, Florence Knoll and Ralph Rapson. The Swedish sculptor Carl Milles was sculptor in residence. The profound influence that Eliel Saarinen and his very Finnish interpretation of Art Nouveau had on Art Deco, the

International Style and Modernism in the USA cannot be overstated.

Alvar Aalto also initially worked in the National Romantic style, but swiftly moved on to a form of Modern Classicism and then to the fully fledged International Style. His breakthrough came in 1928 with the Paimio Sanatorium building, which was widely publicized around the world. Early in his career, Aalto had designed furniture for his buildings, including some incorporating tubular steel that was influenced by the designs of Marcel Breuer created at the Bauhaus, but for the Paimio building he designed birch furniture using a laminating and bending technique that he had devised. This softer, more organic tendency found in his modern furniture was also reflected in his architecture, and came to define what in the Nordic countries is known as Functionalism. When Aalto visited the Stockholm Exhibition of 1930 he was already at the top of his profession, and he remains to this day the most internationally celebrated architect of the region. This did not stop a backlash against him in his native Finland from the 1960s onwards, however, and by his death in 1976 he had come to symbolize the 'old school' for a new generation of Finnish architects. Nevertheless, his legacy remains enormous, and when the century-old Helsinki universities of Technology, Economics and Art and Design merged into one in 2010, they were jointly renamed Aalto University.

At the end of World War II, the German army in Finland and the Baltics retreated through northern Finland to still-occupied Norway, burning every building in its way. The Finnish loss of Karelia to the Soviet Union led to a mass movement of Finns fleeing west, into a Finland damaged by the Soviet bombing of Helsinki and other cities. Because Finland had sided with Germany to stop the Soviet invasion, it was excluded from the US Marshall Plan to rebuild Europe (officially named the European Recovery Program), and it was also burdened with large war reparations to the Soviet Union for the same reason. Despite this, Finland managed to start a massive house-building programme after 1945 that kept architects, the timber industry and the makers of sanitaryware and other essential fixtures and fittings busy. The result is Europe's youngest housing stock, in an unusually coherent style of architecture.

When Norway broke free from Sweden in 1905, it was still culturally close to Denmark, since it had been tied into a union with that nation from 1524 until 1814, and before that in the Kalmar Union from 1397. The capital, Oslo, had been renamed Christiania by King Christian IV of Denmark in 1624, and did not get its Norwegian name back until 1924. When Norway tried to find a national style of

Stockholm City Hall, designed by Ragnar Östberg, completed 1923

Finnish Pavilion at the Exposition Universelle in Paris, designed by Eliel Saarinen, Herman Gesellius and Armas Lindgren, 1900

Paimio Sanatorium in Paimio, Finland, designed by Alvar Aalto, completed 1933

Viking Ship Museum in Bygdøy, Oslo, designed by Arnstein Arneberg, completed 1932, further addition 1957

Opposite: Interior of the Norwegian Wild Reindeer Centre Pavilion at Hjerkinn on the outskirts of the Dovrefjell national park, designed by Snøhetta, 2009–11

architecture after its independence in 1905, it was to an earlier age that its artists and architects turned. This was helped by the unique tradition and preservation of Stave churches in Norway, early medieval Christian churches constructed from wood that incorporate runic inscriptions and the carved dragon heads found on the prows of Norse ships. The great fire of Ålesund in 1904, which virtually destroyed the entire city, gave more than 50 Norwegian architects the opportunity to manifest their own Norwegian interpretation of the Jugend style. To this day Ålesund remains one of the most complete Art Nouveau cities in the world, with more than 320 buildings constructed over the course of just a few years.

Among the most recognized Norwegian architects of the early twentieth century were Magnus Poulsson and Arnstein Arneberg. Both studied not only in Norway but also in Stockholm, where they came into contact with Classicist architects, such as Erik Lallerstedt and Sigurd Lewerentz.

Arneberg's Viking Ship Museum in Oslo (begun 1932/1957) shows this Classicist influence, but it is the Oslo City Hall project he co-designed with Poulsson that reveals their rapid change in architectural style. They had originally won the competition as early as 1918 with a proposal within the National Romantic Jugend style, influenced by the design for Stockholm City Hall by Ragnar Östberg.

Owing to lack of money, however, the Oslo project was severely delayed. Building work commenced only in 1931, and in the interim its design was significantly altered, reflecting the rise of the Functionalist style in the Nordic region. By 1940 some parts could be used as offices, but with the German occupation its construction was put on hold; it was not until 1950 that the building was officially opened. It is now known internationally as the location of the Nobel Peace Prize awards ceremony. Arneberg went on to design the interiors of the United Nations Security Council chamber, a gift from Norway to the world.

Arne Korsmo worked for Arneberg and Poulsson before setting up his own practice in 1928. He became one of the strongest Scandinavian proponents of the International Style, or Functionalism as it was known in the region. Korsmo created the Norwegian Pavilion at the Exposition Internationale des Arts et Techniques dans la Vie Moderne in Paris in 1937 and at the 10th Milan Triennial in 1954. From 1950 he was the Norwegian representative of CIAM (the International Congress of Modern Architecture, founded by Le Corbusier), and he went on to marry the celebrated designer Grete Prytz Kittelsen.

There are at least two notable differences between the historical architecture of Denmark and that of Norway: the former's

abundance of castles and rich use of brick. As the political and economic centre of Denmark–Norway, the Danes built their castles at home, and since theirs was a low-lying land filled with soil, they tended to use brick much more than in mountainous and heavily forested Norway. Brick was also less commonly used in Sweden, except the southern flatlands of Scania, which face Denmark. It was there that most of Sweden's important castles and cathedrals were built, rather than in its eastern outpost of Finland. This perhaps explains why the influence of Jugendstil is less prevalent in Denmark and Sweden, for they already had their high-status buildings that celebrated national glory. This meant that they tended towards a more Classical style, and the merging of classical Greek proportion with early Modernist simplicity came to dominate the national architectural styles in the first decades of the twentieth century.

The Swedish architect Erik Gunnar Asplund was the foremost champion of Modernism, and, were it not for his early death, he would have been equally celebrated as a Functionalist. His early work includes some major and internationally known buildings, including the extension of Gothenburg Town Hall, the Woodland Cemetery in Stockholm (now a UNESCO World Heritage Site), Stockholm City Library and the Scandia Cinema, also in Stockholm.

But it was his shaping of the Stockholm Exhibition of 1930 that was Asplund's greatest legacy, because it firmly and definitely rooted the International Style – or Functionalism – as the dominant force within Scandinavian architecture. The exhibition was the creation of the Svenska Slöjdföreningen (Swedish Society of Crafts and Industrial Design), led by Gregor Paulsson, and was inspired by his visit to the Deutscher Werkbund's Weissenhof housing estate exhibition in Stuttgart in 1927. But the Stockholm Exhibition of 1930 – which attracted some 4 million visitors – was far from uncontroversial. One of its fiercest critics was the furniture designer Carl Malmsten, and the furore the exhibition sparked led to the drafting of the *Acceptera!* (Accept!) manifesto in 1931 by Asplund, Gregor Paulsson, Wolter Gahn, Sven Markelius, Eskil Sundahl and Uno Åhrén. In this seminal text, they argued that the production of housing and consumer goods must embrace Functionalism in order to meet the needs of modern society.

In 1932 the Social Democrats came to power in Sweden and adapted Functionalism as a tool to build the welfare state, or, as it was then known, the *Folkhemmet* (the people's home). They realized that the only way to achieve this political concept was to gather industry and the unions around the pursuit of a common goal – the growth of GDP – for they

Oslo City Hall, designed by Arnstein Arneberg and Magnus Poulsson, 1931–50

Skogskyrkogården (Woodland Cemetery) in Enskede, Stockholm, designed by Erik Gunnar Asplund and Sigurd Lewerentz, 1918–40

Swedish Pavilion designed by Carl Bergsten for the Exposition Internationale des Arts Décoratifs et Industriels Modernes in Paris, 1925

Advertising mast on exhibition building at the Stockholm Exhibition, designed by Erik Gunnar Asplund, 1930 (signage by Sigurd Lewerentz)

understood that unity rather than conflict was the way forward. This subsequently became the economic formula adopted by Social Democratic governments across Scandinavia, and after World War II also became the blueprint for Clement Attlee's Labour government in Britain. Even before this, during the interwar period, Swedish architecture – especially social housing projects – had become highly admired in Britain, and many progressive British architects had visited Sweden from the 1930s onwards to see what had been achieved in this realm.

In Denmark, Classicism was manifested in the work of architects such as Kay Fisker, Kaare Klint and Arne Jacobsen. Klint came to influence several generations of Danish furniture designers through his teaching, while Jacobsen managed to make the journey from Classicist via Functionalist to pure Modernist, making him the most internationally known Danish architect today. Of the same generation were Mogens Lassen, his brother Flemming Lassen and Vilhelm Lauritzen, the last of whom designed both the Danish Radio building and Copenhagen airport. Erik Møller worked with Jacobsen on the Aarhus and Søllerød city halls during World War II, and on Rødovre Town Hall in the 1950s. Møller famously described Jacobsen's celebrated SAS Royal Hotel as a 'glass cigar box'.

Jørn Utzon had studied under Fisker and worked for Aalto. Utzon was one of many Danish architects and designers who fled to Stockholm as the German occupation became harsher towards the end of the war, joining Jacobsen, Poul Henningsen and Henning Koppel. His best-known building is, of course, the Sydney Opera House, the construction of which was famously difficult, but he also built the National Assembly in Kuwait and many residential projects in Denmark.

By the 1970s the International Style was coming in for widespread and severe criticism internationally, and this did not escape Scandinavia. In Sweden the 'Million Programme' of 1965–74, with its aim of creating a million new homes, had resulted in new suburbs of dubious architectural merit, often with poor transport links, which soon fell into social decline. The destruction of Stockholm's city centre between the mid 1950s and the mid 1970s to make way for corporate and government offices, wider roads and communal parking garages became a symbol of the political elite being out of touch with the citizens. The final straw came in the spring of 1971 when the government planned to fell 13 elm trees in the Kungsträdgården, a park in central Stockholm, to make way for a new underground station. The ensuing demonstration, which became known as *Almstriden* – The Battle of the Elms – boiled over, and

as a result images of the Swedish police attacking demonstrators with truncheons were broadcast on televisions across the world.

One of the few Swedish architects who managed to escape criticism at the time was actually not Swedish, but British: Ralph Erskine, who had moved to Sweden as early as 1939. Labelling him a Postmodernist because of his work in the 1970s is to oversimplify a long career, and his humane housing developments remain popular with residents. In later years, Gert Wingårdh was the most successful Swedish architect, working both at home and abroad. Even though he was easily labelled a Postmodernist at one point, his style has developed by combining ecological awareness with technological expertise. In recent years, at least in Sweden and Finland, large, faceless architectural practices working hand-in-hand with developers have undertaken most big development projects, and as a result there have been very few spectacular buildings built by 'starchitects' in these countries. The mistakes of the 1960s and 1970s loom large, holding back the political will for daring and potentially controversial projects that could cost votes.

Instead, it is in Norway and Denmark that the most progressive projects have been seen in the new century, with architectural firms that have an international reputation. The growth of the Copenhagen region thanks to the recent Øresund Bridge and the development of the old harbour has catapulted firms such as BIG (Bjarke Ingels Group), Schmidt Hammer Lassen and 3XN (formerly Nielsen, Nielsen and Nielsen) into opening offices abroad. But older Danish architectural firms are still successful internationally, such as C. F. Møller – named after its founder, who worked with Kay Fisker in the 1920s – which worked on the Olympic Village in London, and Dissing+Weitling (the direct continuation of Arne Jacobsen's practice), which designed the spectacular Øresund Bridge in conjunction with engineers from Ove Arup as part of the ASO Group.

Since Norway became an oil-producing nation in the 1970s and has consequently experienced huge growth in GDP, many major infrastructure projects have been undertaken there: not just the tunnels, bridges and airports that help to tie this long and mountainous nation together, but also educational and cultural buildings. Most recently, the architectural firm Snøhetta has made headlines with the library in Alexandria, Egypt, and the Oslo Opera House, which won the office the Mies van der Rohe Award in 2009.

SAS Royal Hotel and Terminal Building in Copenhagen, designed by Arne Jacobsen, 1955–60

House of Sweden (Swedish and Icelandic Embassies Building) in Washington, DC, designed by Gert Wingårdh and Tomas Hansen (with VOA Associates), 2004–6

Øresund Bridge linking Copenhagen with Malmö, Sweden, designed by ASO Group (Georg Rotne of Dissing+Weitling and Jørgen Nissen, Klaus Falbe-Hansen, Kaj Madsen and Niels Gimsing of Ove Arup), 1995–2000

GRUNDTVIG'S CHURCH, COPENHAGEN

This remarkable church in the Bispebjerg district of Copenhagen was built to commemorate the pastor, author, poet, philosopher, teacher, historian and politician Nikolaj Frederik Severin Grundtvig (1783–1872), who is credited with helping to shape a modern national consciousness in Denmark with his socially reforming ideas, the legacy of which ultimately helped to determine the evolution of Danish design. In 1913 a competition was held to design a church dedicated to his memory, and Peder Vilhelm Jensen-Klint's winning entry can be seen as the embodiment of Grundtvig's humanistic ideology and sense of spirituality. Employing the palest creamy-yellow brickwork, Jensen-Klint's soaring design references the Gothic style yet in a thoroughly Modern way. Inside the church there is a remarkable sense of simplicity and serenity thanks to its monotone palette, elegantly attenuated columns and lancet windows of plain glass. On the outside, the structure's remarkable west façade echoes this uplifting feeling with its curious ribs that reach skyward. Jensen-Klint sadly died before its completion, but his son Kaare Klint – himself a noted architect and designer – oversaw the church's completion in 1940.

1–3. Main entrance, side elevation and interior of Grundtvig's Church, Copenhagen, by Peder Vilhelm Jensen-Klint, 1913–26/1940

Opposite: Early photograph of Grundtvig's Church, ca. 1926

1.

2.

3.

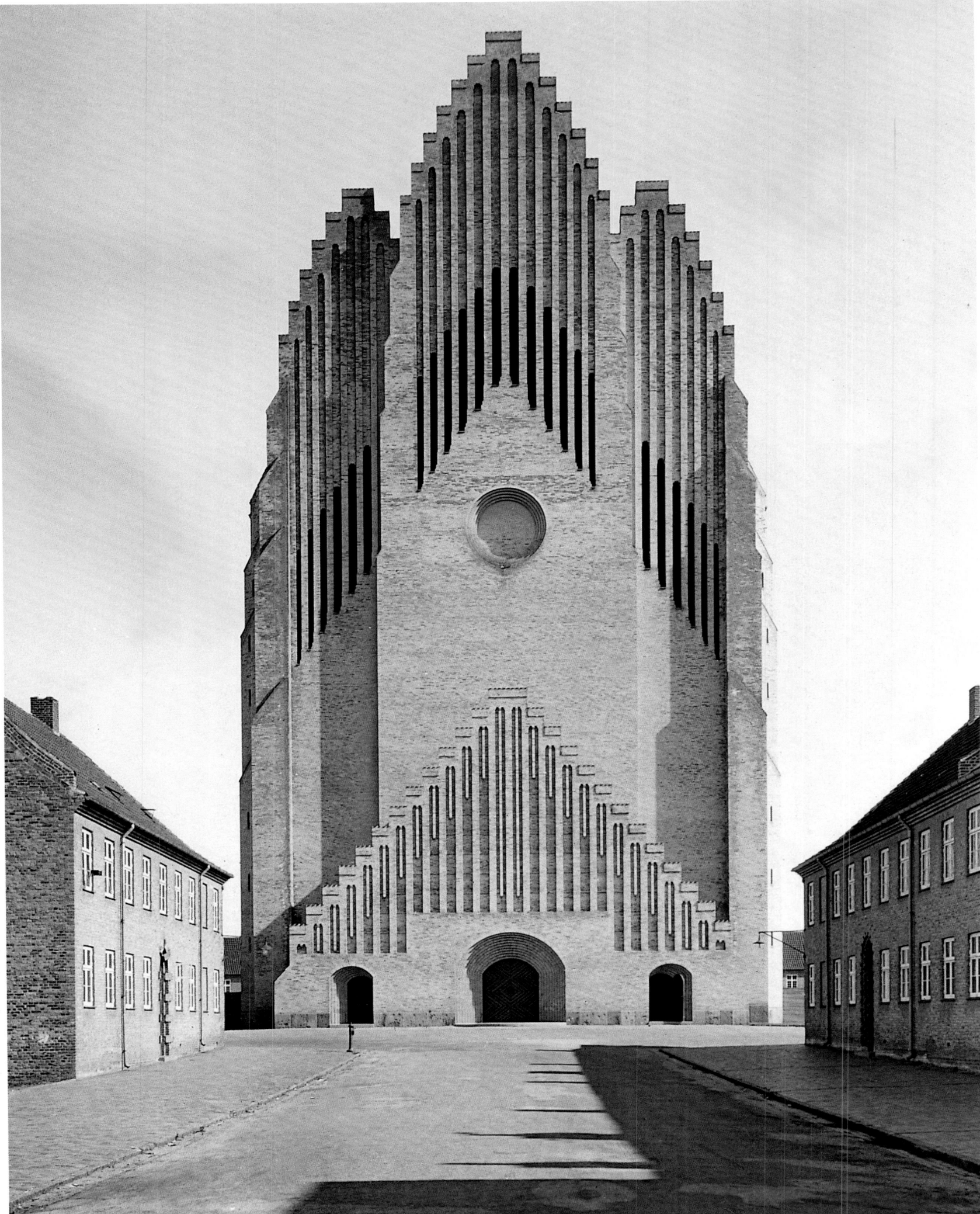

STOCKHOLM EXHIBITION (STOCKHOLMSUTSTÄLLNINGEN), 1930

The Stockholm Exhibition of 1930 was a watershed event in the history of design, for it heralded the emergence of Scandinavian Modernism. It was the brainchild of Gregor Paulsson, the director of Svenska Slöjd-föreningen, who had previously visited the Deutscher Werkbund's landmark exhibition 'Die Wohnung' (The Housing) of 1927 – which featured the Weissenhof estate of model dwellings – and determined that a similar showcase of Modernism should be staged in Sweden. The exhibition's slogan, *Acceptera!* (Accept!), was a plea for architects, designers, manufacturers and the general public alike to embrace Modernism, which was then seen as a panacea to (among other things) the growing crisis of Stockholm's overcrowded slums, which were rife with tuberculosis. Featuring numerous buildings designed by Erik Gunnar Asplund, including the Paradise Restaurant and a stylish entry propylaeum, the exhibition established Functionalism within Scandinavian design circles, swept away all vestiges of the Art Deco style and gave many Swedes their very first tantalizing taste of Modernism.

Below & 2. Views of two different buildings at the Stockholm Exhibition, 1930 – Paradiset (Paradise) restaurant (below) and Lilla Paris park restaurant (far right), both by Erik Gunnar Asplund

1. Advertising tower by Erik Gunnar Asplund for the Stockholm Exhibition, 1930

3. Watercolour-and-pencil perspective sketch by Erik Gunnar Asplund for a building at the Stockholm Exhibition, 1930, ca. 1929

1.

3.

2.

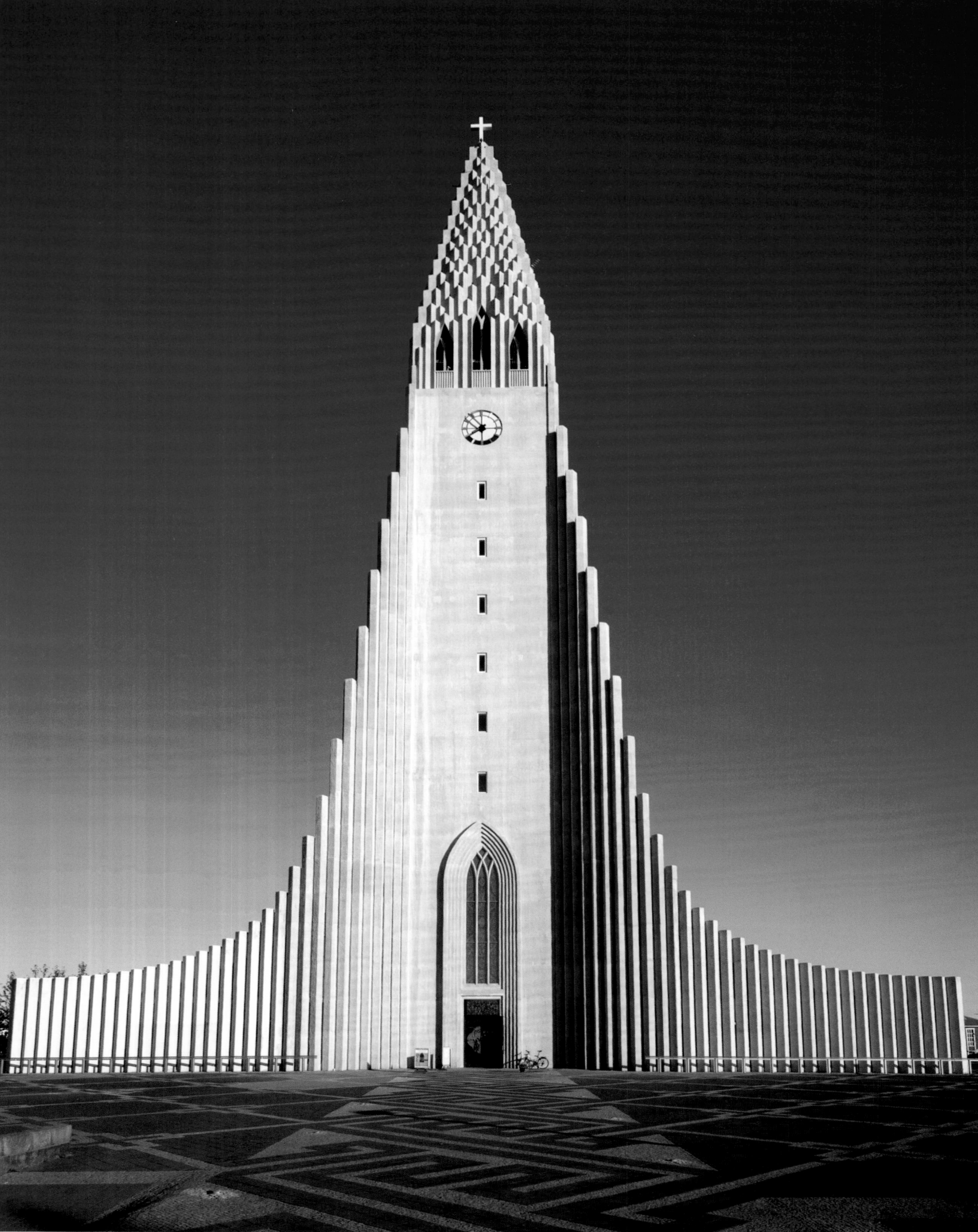

HALLGRÍMSKIRKJA

Any visitor to Reykjavík cannot help but be astonished by the expressive bravado of the Hallgrímskirkja, a proto-Brutalist reinforced-concrete Lutheran church set in the heart of Iceland's windswept capital. Influenced almost certainly by the stepped Expressionist façade of Peder Vilhelm Jensen-Klint's earlier Grundtvig's Church (see pp. 16–17), it was designed in 1937 by Iceland's State Architect, Guðjón Samúelsson, whose buildings were often inspired by the natural geology of this stunningly beautiful land of fire and ice. He was, it is said, especially taken with the basalt columns found at Svartifoss (Black Falls) in the south of the country – incredible columnar jointing formations that must surely have influenced his design of the soaring tower of the Hallgrímskirkja. Having studied architecture at the Kongelige Danske Kunstakadmi (Royal Danish Academy of Fine Arts) in Copenhagen, Samúelsson became a leading proponent of Modernism in Iceland and an early pioneer of reinforced-concrete buildings – a choice prompted by the lack of available local materials. The Icelandic term *Steinsteypuklassík* (concrete classicism) was ultimately coined to reflect the distinctive national style that Samúelsson helped to develop, and unquestionably the Hallgrímskirkja, completed in 1986, marks its high point.

Opposite: Hallgrímskirkja (Church of Hallgrímur), Reykjavík, by Guðjón Samúelsson, commissioned 1937, built 1943–86

1 & 2. Detail of the apse and vaulted ceiling

1.

2.

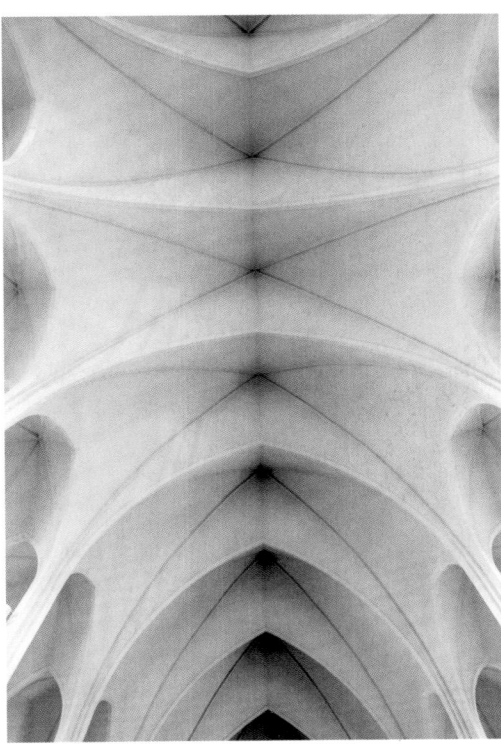

STOCKHOLM CITY LIBRARY

In the early twentieth century the City of Stockholm decided to build a public library, and hired the architect Erik Gunnar Asplund to scope out the requirements of such a building and draft a brief for a design competition that would be open to all architects. At the time the USA had the most advanced public library system in the world, so Asplund began his investigations there. He soon became so well versed in the subject that the project's building committee decided to ditch the idea of a competition, it having become clear to them that he would be the best candidate for the job. The site planned for the library was close to a steep hill and, worried that it might visually overshadow his building, Asplund opted for a compact plan with a strong geometric symmetry. With its orange-painted stucco and monumental massing, the resulting library (designed and built between 1918 and 1927) was a daring exercise in formal abstraction that married Classical form with Modern reductivism – a theme that is repeatedly found in Scandinavian architecture and design.

1. Stockholm City Library by Erik Gunnar Asplund, completed 1927, photographed in the 1930s

2 & 4. Detail of the front entrance and front elevation

3. Main cylindrical reading room, bathed in natural light

5. Watercolour visualization of the library by Erik Gunnar Asplund, ca. 1918

1.

2.

3.

4.

5.

THE WOODLAND CEMETERY

In 1912 Stockholm City Council set aside a 100-hectare plot of land in the district of Enskede for the development of a new cemetery. The idea was to create a resting place that would combine harmoniously architecture and natural landscape. To this end, an international architectural competition was held two years later with the brief that any scheme should take into account the pine-covered ridge of gravel and sand without compromising the buildings' architectural integrity, and that the layout of the grounds should be easy to navigate. The following year, first prize was awarded to Erik Gunnar Asplund and

Sigurd Lewerentz's 'Tallum' entry. In 1920 work began on the careful landscaping of the grounds, most of which was designed by Lewerentz. By 1940 construction of Asplund's Woodland Crematorium and its three chapels – Faith, Hope and the Holy Cross – had also been completed. In addition, Asplund was responsible for the design of the cemetery's Woodland Chapel and Tallum Pavilion. With their thoughtfully devised scheme, which conveyed a strong sense of spirituality, dignity and modernity, Asplund and Lewerentz established an entirely new design format for cemeteries that would influence the development of many similar sites around the world.

Below: Chapel of the Holy Cross, the Woodland Crematorium, by Erik Gunnar Asplund, at the Skogskyrkogården (Woodland Cemetery) in Enskede, Stockholm, 1935–40

1. Skogskapellet (Woodland Chapel) by Erik Gunnar Asplund, 1918–20

2. The colonnade of the Chapel of the Holy Cross, with Resurrection sculpture by John Lundqvist

1.

2.

PAIMIO SANATORIUM

It is difficult to comprehend the devastating impact tuberculosis had on people's lives in the early twentieth century. The spread of this contagious disease had been accelerated by rapid urbanization, and had led governments throughout Europe in the 1920s and 1930s to place increasing emphasis on the notion of health and hygiene. This resulted in a number of modern sanatoriums being built to isolate and treat those afflicted with the disease. One such building in Paimio, Finland, was famously designed by Alvar Aalto, and has since been recognized as a prescient masterpiece of

Modern architecture. A remarkable *Gesamtkunstwerk* (total work of art), Aalto's Paimio Sanatorium (1928–33) employed state-of-the-art reinforced concrete and steel-framed windows in its construction, and was furnished with suitably modern furniture (see pp. 94–95), fixtures and fittings specially created to be both hygienic and comforting to patients. This light-filled hospital with its organically shaped entrance canopy and yellow-painted stairwells was a clean and modern building, yet it was also a very welcoming space that heralded a new, more human Modernism.

Opposite & 1. Stairwell and entrance lobby of the Paimio Sanatorium, Paimio (Finland), by Alvar Aalto, completed 1933

2 & 3. Exterior views of the Paimio Sanatorium, including the main entrance (left)

1.

2.

3.

OTHER ALVAR AALTO BUILDINGS

Over his long career Alvar Aalto worked on all kinds of architectural projects, from small private residences to social housing developments to comprehensive city planning schemes. Within this body of work there was also a wide range of institutional buildings, including town halls, libraries, universities, churches, theatres and government offices. One of his earliest public commissions, the Viipuri Library, strongly reflected his innovative approach to Modernism. For instance, the undulating wave-like ceiling of its lecture hall, designed to enhance acoustics, had an engaging organic quality that was the very antithesis of the sterile white room-cubes so beloved of Modernists in France and Germany. Another project that epitomizes the originality of Aalto's religious buildings is the Lakeuden Risti Church (1957–60) with its soaring cruciform bell tower. It is, however, his last major public commission, Finlandia Hall (1962) – completed after his death – that is his most visible, and arguably most accomplished, landmark building. Located in the heart of Helsinki, this world-class congress centre and events venue, clad in white Carrara marble and local Oulainen granite, possesses an elegant monumentality that is unequivocally Nordic in character.

1. Lecture hall at Viipuri Library, Viipuri (Finland), by Alvar Aalto, 1927–35

2. Bell tower at the Lakeuden Risti Church, Seinäjoki (Finland), by Alvar Aalto, 1957–60

3 & 4. Finlandia Hall, Helsinki, by Alvar Aalto, designed 1962, constructed 1967–72

1.

2.

3.

4.

SVEN MARKELIUS

Sven Markelius was one of the most influential design-reforming architects in Sweden during the interwar period. He helped to promote the cause of Modernism in Scandinavia through not only his exemplary Modern buildings, but also his co-authorship of the famous *Acceptera!* (Accept!) manifesto (1931), which argued that Functionalism must be embraced in order to meet the needs of modern society. Two of his earliest buildings were his own residence, the Villa Markelius (1933), and the Helsingborg Concert Hall (1932), both of which were remarkably forward-looking with their unadorned white stucco façades and bold geometric massing. After World War II, such was Markelius's professional stature, he was nominated by the Swedish government to advise on the design of the United Nations Conference Building in New York. That included responsibility for the interior design of the building's Economic and Social Council chamber (1952), which featured a floor-to-ceiling panel of his brightly coloured and boldly geometric Pythagoras textile (1952; see p. 477). During the latter part of his career he focused increasingly on urban planning, devising the redevelopment scheme of the Norrmalm district of Stockholm (from 1945) and the town plan for the Stockholm suburb of Vällingby (1953).

1. Sven Markelius with a model of his plan for the redevelopment of the Norrmalm district, Stockholm, 1954

2. Villa Markelius in Stockholm, 1933 – a residence Sven Markelius designed for his own use

3. Helsingborg Concert Hall, Helsingborg (Sweden), by Sven Markelius, 1932–34

4. Kollektivhus (social housing) on John Ericcsonsgatan, Stockholm, by Sven Markelius, 1935

5. The United Nations Economic and Social Council chamber, United Nations Headquarters, New York, by Sven Markelius, 1952

1.

2.

3.

4.

5.

H55 PAVILIONS

A number of key exhibitions in the twentieth century were vital to the promotion of the work of Scandinavian designers and to the forging of a collective transnational Nordic design identity. One of these was the H55 International Exhibition of Applied Arts of Housing and the Interior held in Helsingborg, Sweden, in 1955 – often simply referred to as 'H55'. Organized by the Swedish Society of Crafts and Industrial Design, it took as its main theme the efficient use of building materials to meet the postwar need for better-quality modern housing in Europe. To this end, it showcased designs and buildings that demonstrated that if beauty of form were married to practical function, it could be used to create contemporary, life-enhancing living environments. Set directly on the waterfront, on an 800-metre-long, 300-metre-wide windswept breakwater, the exhibition consisted of three main pavilions designed by Carl-Axel Acking, one of which contained Bar 55. This trio of pavilions with their distinctively scooped roofs and T-shaped elevations had a decidedly uplifting nautical air as befitted their location, and cleverly employed modern steel frames hung with wall panels. In addition, each of the ten participating countries had its own specially designed pavilion in which to display its national design output.

1. Carl-Axel Acking with a model of one of his H55 pavilion buildings, ca. 1955

2, 3 & opposite: Various views of the pavilions designed by Carl-Axel Acking for the H55 exhibition, Helsingborg (Sweden), 1955

1.

2.

3.

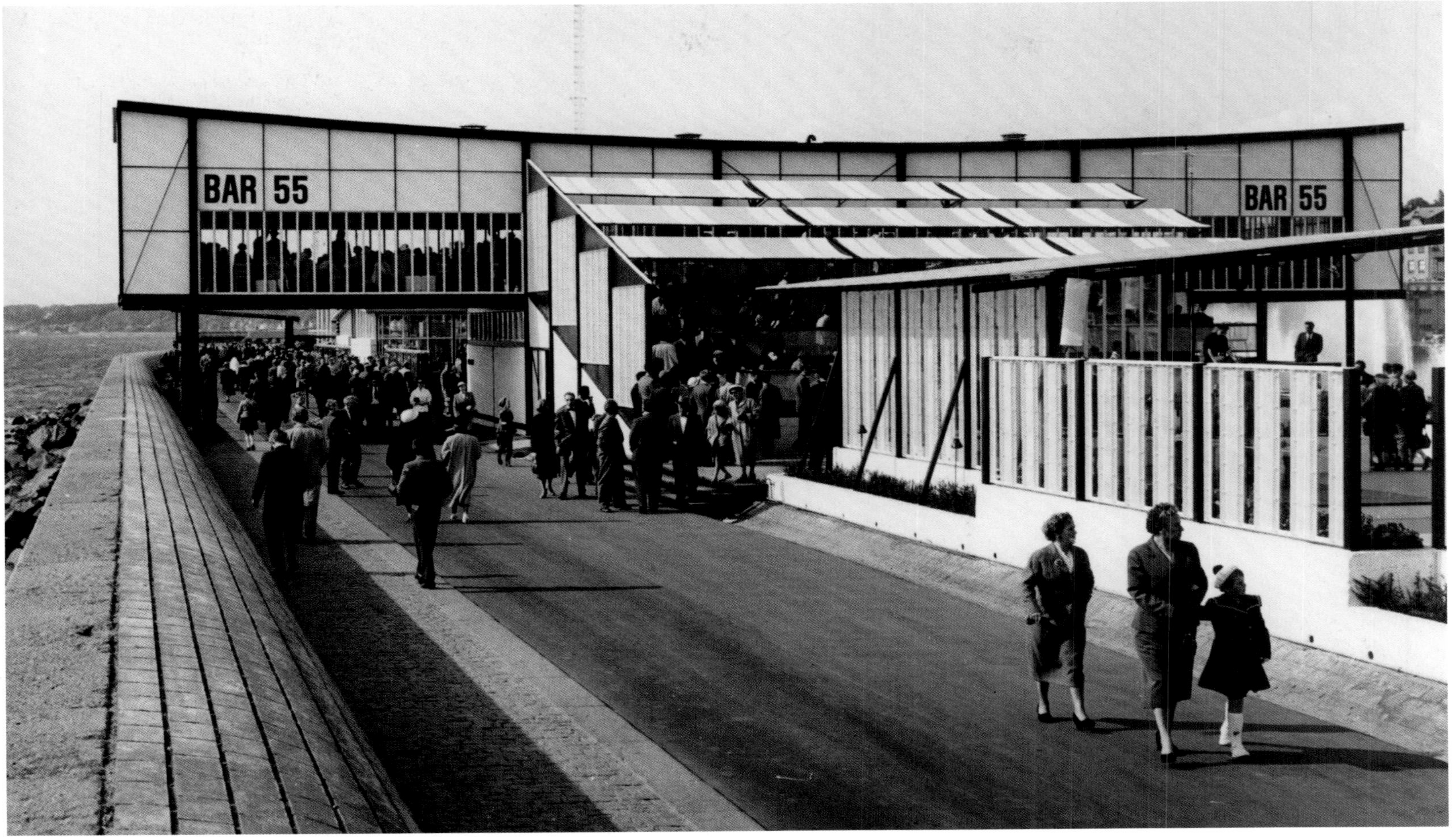
BAR 55
BAR 55

Västra gatan

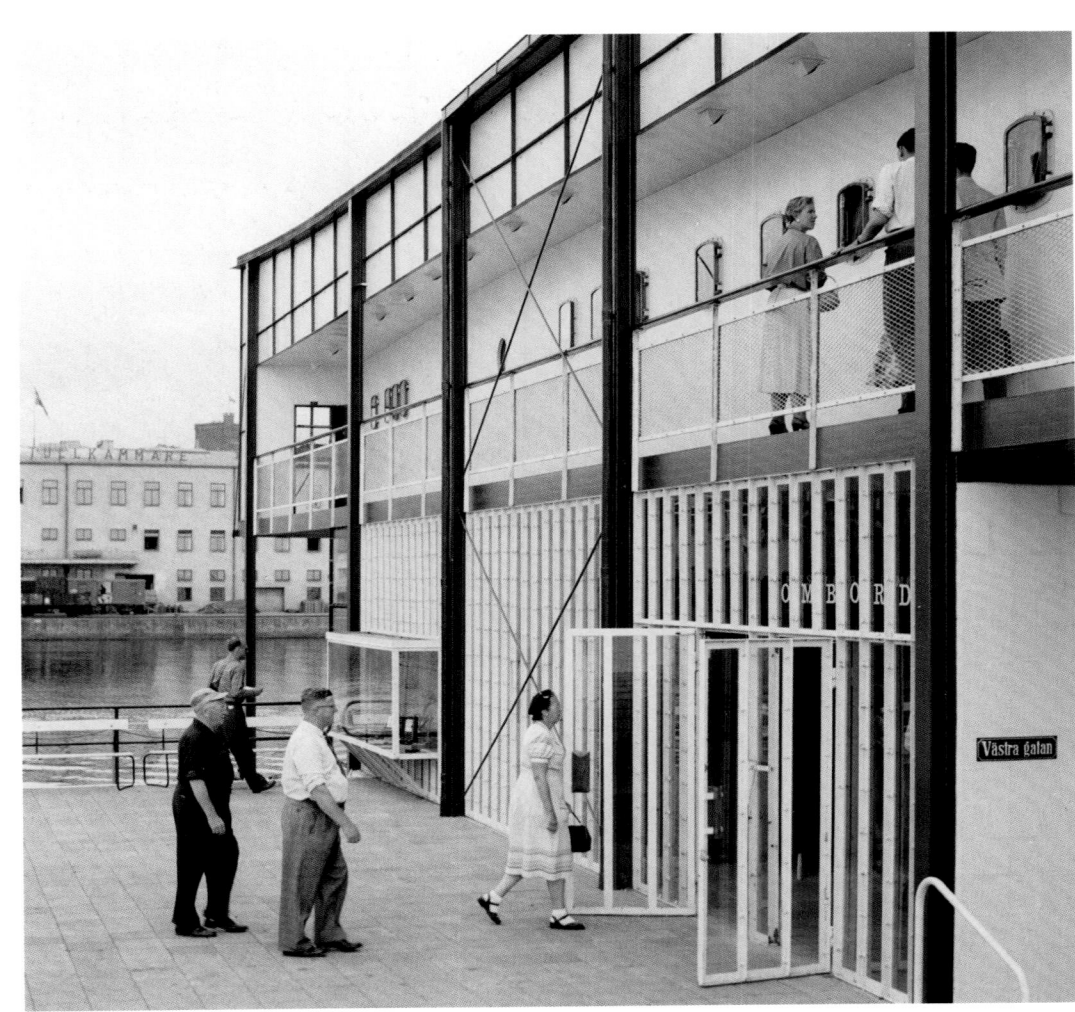

SAS ROYAL HOTEL

The SAS Building in Copenhagen (1955–60) is Arne Jacobsen's acknowledged masterwork. It was designed for the Scandinavian Airlines System (SAS) to incorporate the super-stylish Royal Hotel and to serve as a downtown air terminal for the carrier. Centrally located on one of the city's busiest intersections, the building towers above its neighbours, standing out proudly as an exemplar of International Modernism. Its reinforced-concrete internal structure was cast on site, and incorporates six concealed weight-bearing pillars. Clad in a modular curtain wall of glass and aluminium spandrels, the building's visual mass is broken up by the exterior's reflective qualities, which produce a curious sense of monumentality and, at the same time, lightness. Conceived as a wholly integrated *Gesamtkunstwerk*, Jacobsen also designed the hotel and terminal's interiors, as well as all the furniture, lighting, fixtures and fittings to go in them. This included his famous Swan and Egg chairs (see pp. 128–29), which adorned the hotel's lobby as well as its bedrooms.

1, 3 & opposite: Lobby and exterior view of the SAS Royal Hotel, Copenhagen, by Arne Jacobsen, 1955–60

2. Historic image of the Snack Bar, located behind the Winter Garden on the main floor of the SAS Royal Hotel

1.

2.

3.

ROOM 606

On the sixth floor of the SAS Building in Copenhagen (see pp. 34–35), Arne Jacobsen's *tour de force* of International Modernism, is a light-filled bedroom that has been kept more or less as its architect envisioned it nearly 60 years ago. Room 606 is actually the last surviving original interior in the Royal Hotel, and functions as a visual and aesthetic time capsule. The room itself is a harmonious composition of eau-de-nil walls, oatmeal-coloured carpet, striped bedspreads and sculptural furniture.

The cool, pale turquoise upholstery contrasts elegantly with the visual warmth of the original wood fittings, which include space-saving built-in drawers, hanging space, luggage storage and an integrated vanity table. The room is in many ways the embodiment of Modern at mid-century. Today it has become a place of pilgrimage for the design-savvy traveller, for it can be rented for the night, just like any of the other 274 bedrooms in the hotel, which is now known as the SAS Radisson – you just have to book well in advance.

1. Historic image of a bedroom in the **SAS Royal Hotel,** Copenhagen, by Arne Jacobsen, 1955–60, showing a woman seated in a Drop chair (Model no. 3110) by Jacobsen

2. Pair of Drop chairs by Arne Jacobsen in Room 606 of the **SAS Royal Hotel**

Opposite: Room 606 in the **SAS Royal Hotel**

1.

2.

JACOBSEN'S OTHER MASTERWORK – ST CATHERINE'S COLLEGE, OXFORD

St Catherine's College, Oxford (1959–64), is regarded as one of Arne Jacobsen's key architectural projects. Set amid the ancient buildings of the 'city of dreaming spires', St Catz, as it is nicknamed, incorporates elements of a traditional Oxford college, most notably a 'staircase' format and a rectangular quad, which has at either end the dining hall and library, and student accommodation on the two flanking sides. Yet, unlike traditional college quads, St Catherine's is not closed off, but instead has hedged pathways leading from one building to another and to its extensive landscaped garden. Indeed, one of the most remarkable things about this campus is the harmonious relationship between buildings and grounds, and the fact that it offers a haven of quiet solitude within a seemingly rural landscape, when it is actually only a few minutes' walk from the heart of Oxford. In 1993 the original college buildings were listed Grade I by English Heritage, guaranteeing their careful preservation. While over the years certain buildings have been sympathetically added here and there, this rather austere, minimalist 'new' college remains largely intact and still provides the perfect light-filled learning, teaching and living environment for its students and staff.

Below: Covered walkway at St Catherine's College, Oxford, by Arne Jacobsen, 1959–64

1 & 2. Exterior views of St Catherine's College

1.

2.

INTERIORS OF ST CATHERINE'S COLLEGE, OXFORD

The motto of St Catherine's College is *Nova et Vetera* (Old and New), and that reflects how Arne Jacobsen conceived this *Gesamtkunstwerk*. He essentially updated the established, largely medieval format of the Oxford college by setting Modern buildings of glass and concrete in a traditional quadrangle-based layout. This reworking of tradition was similarly played out in the buildings' interiors. For example, in the college's dining hall the Master's High Table was raised on a platform, as is the age-old custom, yet the specially created high-backed Oxford chairs were anything but traditional. Originally, the students sat on benches in the dining hall, again according to convention, and it was only later, when female students were admitted (in 1974) that they were exchanged for his 3107 chairs, for the sake of decorum. The use of a restricted earth-toned colour palette and exposed 'raw' materials such as concrete and brick produces a strong sense of permanence that belies the uncompromising Modernity of these interiors.

Below: Library at St Catherine's College, Oxford, by Arne Jacobsen, 1959–64

1. Dining hall at St Catherine's College

2. Master's dining room at St Catherine's College

3. Passageway leading to the Senior Common Room at St Catherine's College

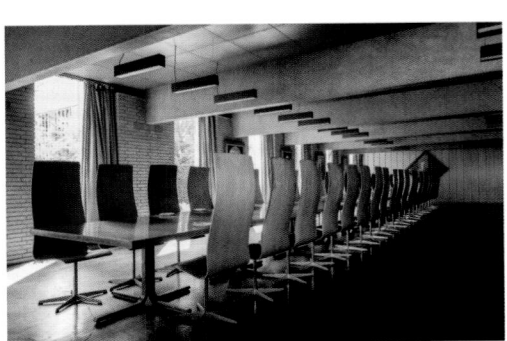

1.

2.

3.

ARNE JACOBSEN + AARHUS CITY HALL

In 1937 Arne Jacobsen won the competition for the design of Aarhus's new city hall with an entry he had devised in collaboration with Erik Møller. The winning proposal comprised three large buildings, each of which had a strong sense of volumetric geometry, and which cleverly overlapped and interconnected in order to break up the overall mass of this Norwegian Porsgrunn marble-clad edifice. The only major difference between what was originally planned and what was actually built was the addition of a soaring clock tower with a curious skeleton structure. This cage-like element not only helped to give the building a distinctive character, but also imbued it with lightness and transparency. Inside the building this feeling of airy modernity was replicated through the use of skylights that bathed the interiors in natural daylight, and staircases with open balustrades and internal balconies with rhythmic contoured lines. Indeed, the whole project was a masterful exercise in how to create a monumental Neoclassical building within a Modern idiom, as well as a refined and thoroughly contemporary expression of Nordic civic pride.

Opposite: The main chamber, the clock tower and the main staircase of Aarhus City Hall by Arne Jacobsen and Erik Møller (Denmark), 1937–42

Below: Full exterior of Aarhus City Hall

OTHER JACOBSEN BUILDINGS

During the late 1920s, as a young architect, Arne Jacobsen spent most of his time designing single-family houses. In 1931, however, he received his first big break, from a consortium that commissioned him to design a brand-new apartment complex in Klampenborg, a suburb of Copenhagen. The resulting Bellavista apartment building (1931–34), with 68 units, was a daring exercise in Modern living with its U-shaped plan and two staggered wings that gave each apartment its own balcony and contributed an appropriately nautical air to this seaside building. Another early building that similarly showed Jacobsen's genius for creating functional yet sculptural buildings was a petrol station (1936) designed for Amoco, which was again extremely forward-looking for its day. In contrast, the buildings he designed towards the end of his career had a greater sense of mass and strict Modernity. For instance, the National Bank of Denmark headquarters in Copenhagen (1961–78) and the Danish Embassy in London (1969–77), as befitting their importance, both have façades that convey a sombre and weighty monumentality, yet even so they are enlivened by the exquisite detailing that gave all his buildings that extra-special Nordic quality.

Below: Bellavista apartment building in Klampenborg, near Copenhagen, by Arne Jacobsen, completed 1934

1. Petrol station on the coastal road at Skovshoved Harbour, north of Copenhagen, by Arne Jacobsen for Amoco, completed 1936

2. Danmarks Nationalbank (National Bank of Denmark), Copenhagen, by Arne Jacobsen, designed 1961, built 1965–71 (Phase I); 1972–78 (Phase II)

1.

2.

FINN JUHL'S HOUSE

In 1942 Finn Juhl and his first wife, Inge-Marie Skaarup, built a simple home for themselves in Charlottenlund, just outside Copenhagen. This off-white stuccoed, brick-built house, which thankfully has been preserved as it was, represents a three-dimensional realization of Juhl's interdisciplinary approach to architecture and design. For Juhl, a house, if it were to function properly, must be built from the inside out, with its internal configuration of rooms dictating how the exterior would ultimately look. The surrounding garden, created by the landscape designer Troels Erstad, was also an integral part of the scheme, with Juhl having carefully positioned the house's windows so that there was a good view over it from every room. Indeed, the house is remarkable for its sense of light-filled space and homely warmth – the overall effect being enhanced by the palest of yellow paint on the ceilings. Inside, it provided the perfect stripped-down setting not only for Juhl's art collection, but also for his many furniture designs (see pp. 112–15). As an early exercise in Scandinavian lifestyle design, the Juhl house is probably matchless and certainly exemplifies the key attributes of Scandinavian interior design: uncluttered simplicity, practical functionality, homely comfort and a natural airiness.

Below: Finn Juhl's study area within the open-plan living space of his house in Charlottenlund (Denmark), 1942

1. Exterior of Finn Juhl's house

2. Table and chairs in the master bedroom of Finn Juhl's house

3. Open-plan living area of Finn Juhl's house

2.

1.

3.

VERNER PANTON

From the late 1950s to the early 1970s the iconoclastic Danish furniture, lighting and interior designer Verner Panton shook up the whole notion of Scandinavian design, which had hitherto been closely associated with the tenets of evolutionary 'ideal' forms and democratic good taste. Panton created revolutionary Pop designs for furniture, lighting and textiles that were saturated with colour and boldly sculptural or patterned. During this period he also created many memorable interior spaces that skilfully combined his designs in breathtakingly daring compositions that were far more than the sum of their individual parts. Whether it was a corridor in a restaurant, a canteen in a publishing house, a hotel dining room or even a small corner in his own apartment, Panton was able to infuse each space with an optimistic sense of time-shifting futurism. These experimental space-age interiors powerfully reflected the optimism and forward-looking zeitgeist of the era in which they were created, and in so doing redefined the aesthetic landscape of Scandinavian design.

1. Corridor of Varna restaurant, Aarhus (Denmark), by Verner Panton, 1971

2. Canteen of Spiegel Verlag publishing house, Hamburg (Germany), by Verner Panton, 1969

3. Dining room of Panton's private apartment in Hasenrain, Basle (Switzerland), by Verner Panton, 1964–72

4. Astoria hotel and restaurant, Trondheim (Norway), by Verner Panton, 1960

1.

2.

3.

4.

VISIONA 2

Between 1968 and 1975 the German chemical giant Bayer hired a pleasure cruiser on the Rhine during the annual Cologne Furniture Fair and transformed it into a floating temporary exhibition space to showcase its latest synthetic materials. Each year a well-known designer was commissioned by the company to create a series of progressive installations. For the first, *Visiona 0* (1968), Verner Panton designed a series of avant-garde room sets that creatively exploited the potential of Bayer's new Dralon fabric. It was, however, Panton's later *Visiona 2* installation of 1970 that took the design world by storm with its psychedelic 'Phantasy Landscape' comprising a series of dream-like 'living cave' spaces that invited playful interaction. Radical and forward-looking, *Visiona 2* tore up all current notions of architecture and interior design, and projected a futuristic vision of soft stretch jersey-covered furniture and bold sculptural lighting where traditional delineations between floors, walls and ceiling dissolved into a sensorial happening of colour, form, sound and smell.

Opposite: 'Phantasy Landscape' installation, part of *Visiona 2* by Verner Panton for Bayer at the Cologne Furniture Fair (Germany), 1970

1. 'Spiralleuchten' (Spiral Lights) installation, part of *Visiona 2*

2. Easy rocking chaises shown as part of *Visiona 2*

2.

1.

AARNO RUUSUVUORI

During the 1960s and 1970s there were a number of Scandinavian architects and designers who worked within a distinctively Nordic quasi-Brutalist style. Among these was the Finnish architect Aarno Ruusuvuori, who designed a number of exposed-concrete buildings, including the Hyvinkää Church (1961) and the Weilin & Göös printworks in Espoo (1964–66), now the WeeGee Exhibition Centre. Having studied at the Helsinki University of Technology, Ruusuvuori became quite a divisive figure within Finnish architectural circles, for as an arch-modernizer during the

1970s he proposed the controversial demolition of a large number of historic buildings to make way for his ambitious (though thankfully largely thwarted) modernization plans for Helsinki City Hall. Ruusuvuori was also a professor and the director of the Museum of Finnish Architecture, and as such an influential pioneer of Scandinavian Brutalism, which is less hard-edged than other national expressions of this controversial architectural style. In 1992 he published a book whose title translates as 'Structure is the Key to Beauty', and certainly it was this concept that guided his own architecture, which is distinguished by a raw and powerful muscularity.

1. Weilin & Göös printworks, Espoo (Finland), by Aarno Ruusuvuori, 1964–66 – converted into the WeeGee Exhibition Centre in 2006

2. Brutalist concrete detail of the Weilin & Göös printworks

3 & 4. Hyvinkää Church (also known as the New Church of Hyvinkää), Hyvinkää (Finland), by Aarno Ruusuvuori, 1961

1.

2.

3.

4.

JØRN UTZON

Throughout his career, the Danish architect Jørn Utzon always shunned publicity, despite having designed one of the world's most celebrated modern buildings: the Sydney Opera House (designed 1957). An architectural visionary, Utzon was fascinated by structures found in the natural world, especially those of a cellular nature, and his pioneering approach to building design, which he called 'Additive Architecture', was based on organic growth patterns. In his manifesto *Additive Architecture* of 1970 he argued that buildings should not be conceived as identical boxes, but instead be designed more freely using repeating elements that could be added over time depending on functional need, imbuing them with an inherent 'naturalness'. Whether it was his own house sympathetically nestling in the forest of Hellebæk in Denmark, which had a strong Frank Lloyd Wright quality, or his Bagsværd Church with its simple, unassuming, cellular exterior and dramatic organic interior form, Utzon's buildings always expressed a close and very Scandinavian connection to nature.

1. Jørn Utzon's own house, Hellebæk (Denmark), 1950–52

2. Interior of Bagsværd Church, Bagsværd, Copenhagen, by Jørn Utzon, 1968–76

Opposite: Sydney Opera House (Australia) by Jørn Utzon, designed 1957, completed 1973

1.

2.

HOUSES OF THE FUTURE

In 1954 the plastics manufacturing company Polykemi was established in Vantaa, Finland, to produce (among other things) acrylic sanitaryware, Perspex bubble-like dome-lights, plastic door handles, and roof and façade panels. Given its expertise in the mass-manufacture of innovative plastic products, it is not surprising that Polykemi eventually expanded its operation into product architecture, famously producing the Futuro house designed in 1968 by Matti Suuronen. This pod-shaped space-age dwelling made of fibreglass was so lightweight that it could be airlifted into remote regions by helicopter. The Futuro, which received enormous international press attention when it launched, still has a loyal following of aficionados, who proactively work to conserve the few examples that remain. Polykemi also made another mass-produced dwelling, the Venturo house by Hannu Vilho Sakari Laitinen, which was patented in Sweden in 1970. Intended as a go-anywhere summer cabin, it was cleverly based on the idea of modularity, so a number could be linked to suit living requirements. The 1970s oil crisis and the consequential rise in the cost of plastics, however, meant that these futuristic pod-like dwellings were produced in very limited numbers.

Below: Venturo house by Hannu Vilho Sakari Laitinen for Polykemi (Finland), 1971 – this example is now used as a cafe at the Kivik Art Centre in Kivik (Sweden)

1. Futuro house by Matti Suuronen for the Futuro Corporation (USA), 1968

2 & 3. Plans of the Futuro house

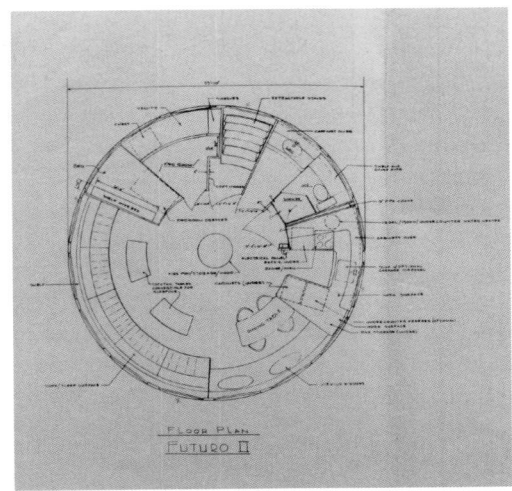

2.

3.

1.

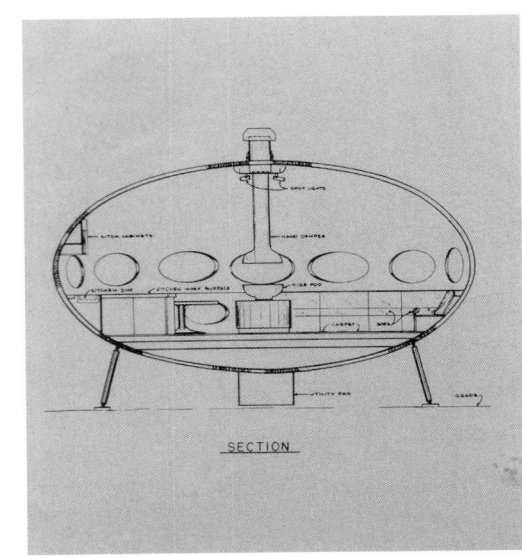

THE ROCK CHURCH

No trip to Helsinki is complete without a visit to the Temppeliaukion kirkko, or Rock Church, designed by two architect brothers, Timo and Tuomo Suomalainen, for a competition held in 1961. Their plan for this stone-hewn Lutheran place of worship was for economic reasons eventually scaled back to a quarter of its intended size. Even so, it is a very impressive building, set directly into solid bedrock and bathed in natural light from a circle of window lights that support its domed copper roof. Its internal rough, unworked rock walls were not part of the brothers' original plan, being deemed by them too radical for the competition's jury; however, after consulting the conductor Paavo Berglund and the acoustic engineer Mauri Parjo, it was determined that the sound requirements of the church could be met by leaving the walls unplastered – and so they were. Located in the heart of the city, the Rock Church was completed in 1969 and has become a much-visited tourist destination. Perhaps more than any other building, the Rock Church reflects the deep-rooted connection found in Nordic countries between design and landscape.

1 & 3. Interior and exterior of Temppeliaukion kirkko (Rock Church), Helsinki, by Timo and Tuomo Suomalainen, designed 1961, built 1968–69

2. Detail of the Rock Church, showing how it has been built into the granite bedrock

4. Detail of the wall-mounted candleholders in the Rock Church

1.

2.

3.

4.

ERIK ASMUSSEN

Guided by a holistic approach to design based on the teachings of Rudolf Steiner, Erik 'Abbi' Asmussen designed buildings that were contemporary interpretations of Nordic vernacularism in modern industrial materials. As a young man, Asmussen was inspired to study architecture at Copenhagen Technical College (KTS) after seeing Erik Gunnar Asplund's buildings at the Stockholm Exhibition in 1930. Following his studies, he apprenticed at the architecture practice of Flemming Lassen and Kay Fisker. The latter, having rejected the bland universalism of the International Style, was developing his own

form of functionalism, which was rooted in Danish building traditions. Asmussen would build on Fisker's legacy in his own work. He also worked at other architecture practices in Stockholm, where he spent the war years. His 'Eureka!' moment came when he visited Rudolf Steiner's Goetheanum building at Dornach, Switzerland, in 1947, which led him over the next decade to reassess his architectural priorities. In the late 1950s he began developing an anthroposophical architectural approach based on Steinerian philosophy, which he subsequently put into glorious practice in his design of the Steiner buildings in Dornach and in Järna, Sweden.

1. Robygge training centre with restaurant and shop by Erik Asmussen at the Rudolf Steiner Seminary (now the Järna Kulturcentrum) (Sweden), completed 1979

2. Almandinen Music Building by Erik Asmussen at the Rudolf Steiner Seminary (now the Järna Kulturcentrum) (Sweden), completed 1974

3. Auditorium of the Hall of Culture by Erik Asmussen at the Rudolf Steiner Seminary (now the Järna Kulturcentrum), completed 1992

4. Library building by Erik Asmussen at the Rudolf Steiner Seminary (now the Järna Kulturcentrum), completed 1973 – now used as offices

1.

2.

3.

4.

ARCTIC ARCHITECTURE

Situated inside the Arctic Circle, Tromsø in Norway is famous as a place for viewing the Northern Lights, which illuminate the night sky spectacularly at certain times of the year. It is also a major cultural hub for the far north, and boasts a number of interesting buildings, both historic and contemporary. Among these, the Ishavskatedralen (Arctic Cathedral) designed by Jan Inge Hovig in 1965 is by far the best known. An acknowledged masterpiece of Nordic architecture, the building was cleverly constructed from 22 aluminium-coated concrete panels that are stepped so that glazed sections could be interspersed between them, thereby providing a light-filled interior. The jagged structure of the building also makes reference to its Arctic location, being reminiscent of the heaving forms found in ice-packed waters. The steep roofline of the building is functional, too, being perfectly suited to cope with heavy snowfalls in winter. JAF Arkitektkontor's stunning Polaria aquarium (1996–98), also in Tromsø, similarly makes reference to ice formations with its domino-like sections that give the appearance of being just about to slip into the freezing waters of the Norwegian Sea.

Below: Arctic Cathedral, Tromsø (Norway), by Jan Inge Hovig, completed 1965

Opposite: Polaria, Tromsø (Norway), by JAF Arkitektkontor, 1996–98

1.

2.

ICONIC WATER TOWERS

The Swedish architect Sune Lindström studied at the Kungliga Tekniska Högskolan (Royal Institute of Technology) in Stockholm from 1926 to 1931, during which time he also spent one semester at the Staatliches Bauhaus in Dessau, Germany. After graduating he worked for KFAI – the Co-operative Association's Architectural and Engineering Office – and then, from 1937 to 1939, was the director of HSB, Sweden's largest housing co-operative. It was, however, while working as the chief architect for Vattenbyggnadsbyrån (VBB), an engineering firm that had long specialized in the construction of water buildings, that Lindström designed his mushroom-shaped water tower in Örebro (1955–57). Incorporating a cafe and conference centre at its top, this landmark structure is a soaring 58 metres high and can hold an impressive 9 million litres of water. After the critical success of his first 'fungus' tower, Lindström became the go-to architect for such structures, and notably built 30 more towers in Kuwait, including the iconic Kuwait Towers (1971–76) in Kuwait City, which he designed in collaboration with his wife, the designer Malene Bjørn.

1. Kuwait Towers, Kuwait City, by Sune Lindström and Malene Bjørn, 1971–76 (opened 1979)

2. 'Mushroom' water towers, Kuwait City, by Sune Lindström, 1970–76 – one of five groups of water towers constructed in Kuwait City by VBB

Opposite: Svampen ('the mushroom') water tower, Örebro (Sweden), by Sune Lindström, 1955–57 (opened 1958)

1.

2.

ØRESUND BRIDGE

Connecting Copenhagen in Denmark to Malmö in Sweden, the Øresund Bridge dramatically spans the Øresund Strait and is nearly 8 kilometres long. The idea for the bridge was first proposed in 1936, but, owing to World War II and then subsequent disagreements over the bridge's precise placement and breadth of function, the commencement of the project was delayed. Eventually, in 1973, the governments of Denmark and Sweden signed an agreement to go ahead with this massive infrastructure project. Five years later, however, because of the economic situation and growing ecological concerns,

the project was shelved. It was only in 1991 that the idea was given the green light again, and a new bridge was designed by the architect Georg Rotne of Dissing+Weitling in conjunction with the Ove Arup engineers Kaj Madsen, Niels Gimsing, Jørgen Nissen and Klaus Falbe-Hansen. Building work began in 1995 and this stunning cable-stayed bridge, which carries a railway and a motorway, was finally completed in 2000 to mark the new millennium. Apart from providing a vital link between the two countries, carrying people, goods and telecommunications, the Øresund Bridge also provides an important symbol of Scandinavian international co-operation.

Opposite: Øresund/Öresund Bridge, Malmö–Copenhagen, by ASO Group Georg Rotne, Kaj Madsen, Niels Gimsing, Jørgen Nissen and Klaus Falbe-Hansen), 1995–2000

Below: Øresund/Öresund Bridge lit up in the evening

BIG = BJARKE INGELS GROUP

No architecture practice currently in Scandinavia is bigger in terms of influence or profile than the Bjarke Ingels Group. Often referred to as BIG, the office was founded by Bjarke Ingels in 2005 and now has over 400 employees, including architects, designers and builders, working on a variety of projects, from individual buildings and developments – including residential, commercial and industrial – to vast urban-planning initiatives. The firm also undertakes a lot of research and development into energy-efficient building solutions with its BIG IDEAS lab, which was set up in 2014. The two projects shown here are innovative developments in Ørestad, a new suburb of Copenhagen. The VM Houses (2004–5) are so named because the plans of the two adjacent apartment buildings look like the letters V and M when seen from above, and were chosen as a way of opening up the buildings to ensure that they provided good views of the surrounding town and landscape. The mixed-use 8 House development, also known as Big House (2010), likewise has an interesting plan, based on a looping yet angular figure of eight. It incorporates external sloping walkways that cleverly connect housing, offices, shops and a kindergarten to a central hub-like courtyard.

Opposite: 8 House (Big House) mixed-use development, South Ørestad, Copenhagen, by BIG (Bjarke Ingels Group), 2010

Below: VM Houses residential apartment blocks, South Ørestad, Copenhagen, by BIG (Bjarke Ingels Group), 2004–5

DANISH PAVILION + LEGO HOUSE

Bjarke Ingels's spiralling Danish Pavilion for Expo2010 in Shanghai and his block-like LEGO House headquarters reflect his rare ability to create distinctive statement buildings that have a playful quality as well as a strongly sculptural look. As one of the most inspiring architects of his generation, Ingels takes an enthusiastic 'Yes Is More' approach to the potential of architecture and design, and has an infectious can-do attitude that enables his architectural visions to be realized despite their often extraordinarily inventive nature. Essentially a utopian pragmatist, Ingels takes a highly personal analytical approach to design and architecture, inspired by both Darwinian evolutionary theory and Nietzschean philosophy as it relates to the transformative nature of creative power. Through his buildings he demonstrates unequivocally this latter postulation with uplifting architectural virtuosity.

Above & below: Danish Expo Pavilion by BIG (Bjarke Ingels Group) for Expo2010, Shanghai (China), 2010

Opposite: Renderings of LEGO House, Billund (Denmark), by BIG (Bjarke Ingels Group), 2014–16

SNØHETTA – OSLO OPERA HOUSE

Situated on the Bjøvika Peninsula and overlooking the Oslo Fjord, Snøhetta's Oslo Opera House is a glittering white jewel set in the heart of a comprehensive urban-renewal project. A monumental building, in both senses of the word, the opera house is a landmark that symbolizes the Norwegian capital's growing influence, both economically and culturally, thanks to the oil and gas revenues that have seen the country grow from 'little brother' status to the other Nordic nations to being one of the wealthiest places per capita in the world. Snøhetta's opera house is as much an exercise in architectural narrative as it is a functional building for the staging of opera and ballet. With its clear glass exterior and white marble sloping roof, which provides a deck from which to view the fjord, this stunningly beautiful and architecturally exciting monument to Nordic culture is symbolically suggestive of Norway's snow-covered mountains and heaving icebergs. This is perhaps not so surprising when one considers that the architectural practice that designed it takes its name from the towering Snøhetta mountain – the highest peak of the Dovrefjell range in central Norway.

Below: Interior of Oslo Opera House by Snøhetta, 2008

1. Entrance of Oslo Opera House

2. Sloping viewing roofs of Oslo Opera House

1.

2.

SNØHETTA – TVERRFJELLHYTTA

The traditional buildings found in the Nordic region have always been firmly rooted in their surrounding landscapes, thanks to the use of local materials, be it wood or stone. Indeed, Norway has a long and proud tradition of remarkable wooden buildings that stretches back centuries to intricate Stave churches and turfed-roof log houses and barns. In the Nordic region, the ability to make strong buildings out of wood was a primary means of survival in years gone by. Snøhetta's Tverrfjellhytta (Norwegian Wild Reindeer Centre Pavilion) at the edge of the Dovrefjell national park is a tribute to this age-old tradition of wooden buildings, and takes the form of a simple square timber box. One side is glazed to provide a viewing platform for visitors inside the building, and the other side comprises a sculpted wooden-block wall with an organic form that echoes the shapes of the neighbouring mountains. This wooden element, like the one found inside, cleverly integrates seating for visitors and helps visually and symbolically to connect the building with the awe-inspiring landscape.

Below & opposite: Interior and exterior views of Tverrfjellhytta (Norwegian Wild Reindeer Centre Pavilion), Hjerkinn, Dovrefjell national park (Norway), by Snøhetta, 2009–11

STUDIO GRANDA – NORDIC CONTEMPORARY

Studio Granda has designed some of the most interesting buildings in Reykjavík and the surrounding Icelandic countryside. The practice was founded in 1987 by the Icelandic-born Margrét Harðardóttir and British-born Steve Christer, who had met while studying at the Architectural Association in London. This team first came to prominence in the late 1980s, when they won the international competition to design the Ráðhús Reykjavíkur (Reykjavík City Hall). The resulting landmark building (completed 1992) with its barrel-vaulted roof appears almost to float, with its front colonnade disappearing into the reflective waters of Tjörnin Pond. It is, however, two later residential projects that best exemplify the practice's uncompromising Nordic Contemporary aesthetic, and both boast traditional Icelandic turfed roofs. The B14 villa (2007–12) has a Neo-Brutalist quality thanks to its use of bold geometry and raw concrete. Similarly, the Hof house, though timber-clad, has internal walls of in-situ concrete to divide the living space. The stark, elemental nature of concrete, which has long been a favoured building material in Iceland because of the lack of local stone and wood, is perfectly suited to the rugged landscapes that surround these two very distinctive Nordic residences.

Below: B14 villa, Garðabær (Iceland), by Studio Granda, designed 2007–12, built 2010–12 – bordering a lava field, with views over the Bláfjöll mountain ridge

Opposite: Hof house in Höfðaströnd (Iceland) by Studio Granda, designed 2003–7, built 2004–7 – less than 100 kilometres from the Arctic Circle

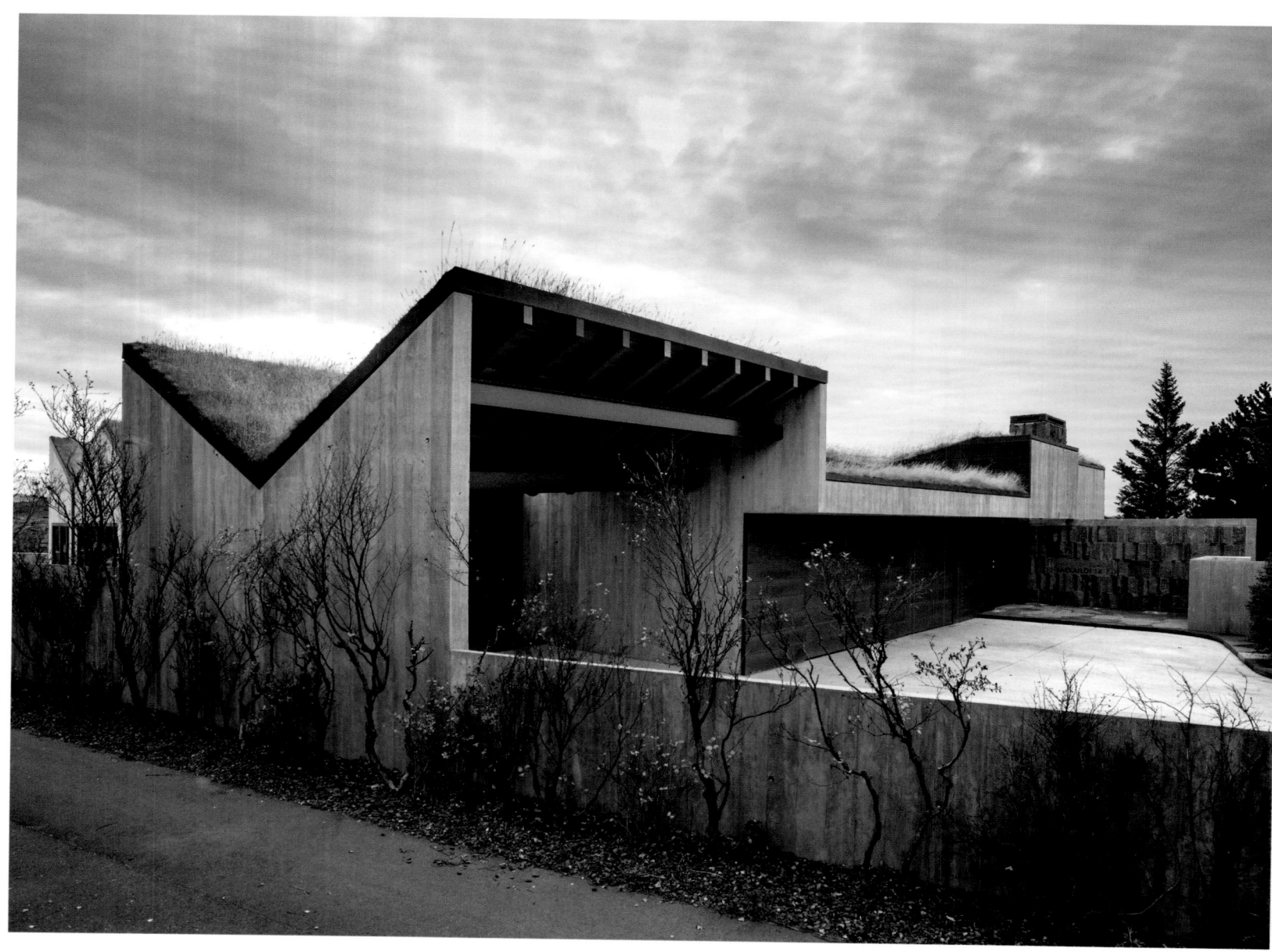

FURNITURE

Just as architecture evolved differently in each of the Nordic countries, so did furniture design, with each nation focusing on the use of different materials and stylistic elements. Yet numerous influences and technical developments were also shared across the region.

The Austrian architect Josef Frank moved to Stockholm in 1933 and began designing Modern furniture, often based on historic archetypes, for Svenskt Tenn that is still seen in Sweden as the epitome of good taste. Svenskt Tenn, founded by Estrid Ericson, exhibited Frank's designs at the Paris Exposition Internationale des Arts et Techniques dans la Vie Moderne of 1937 and at the New York World's Fair of 1939. During his career Frank designed some 2,000 pieces of furniture, and today Svenskt Tenn still manufactures a wide range of his designs. Carl-Axel Acking, like Frank, also designed Modern archetypal furniture that possessed a definable Swedish elegance.

Nordiska Kompaniets Verkstäder (Nordic Company's Workshops) similarly played a leading role in the development of Modern Swedish furniture design. It was set up in 1904 to supply furniture to Sweden's leading department-store group, Nordiska Kompaniet (also known as NK). By the 1930s it had some 400 employees. Carl Malmsten, Erik Gunnar Asplund and Axel Einar Hjorth all worked as designers for the company; the last acted as its design director from 1927 to 1938. In 1947 Knoll Associates became the US distributor of NK furniture, including designs by Elias Svedberg, who developed the affordable Trivia series from the mid 1940s onwards, including a knock-down safari chair. The NK workshop closed in 1973, however, being unable to compete with the lower-priced furniture being manufactured by the likes of IKEA.

Bruno Mathsson, a fifth-generation Swedish furniture-maker, also helped to shape the evolution of Swedish furniture design. He studied what he described as the 'mechanics of sitting', and famously sat in a snowdrift in order to analyse his own seated imprint. Mathsson's work was shown at the Exposition Internationale des Arts et Techniques dans la Vie Moderne in Paris in 1937, where it won a Grand Prix and drew much international interest. Indeed, Edgar Kaufmann Jr of the Museum of Modern Art (MoMA), New York, was so impressed with Mathsson's designs that in 1939 he ordered a number of his chairs for the museum's new extension. That same year, Mathsson's furniture was also displayed at the New York World's Fair and at the Golden Gate Exhibition in San Francisco.

After World War II, Mathsson's popularity increased in the USA, and he later also enjoyed some success in Japan. Today, his furniture is a standard feature in Swedish institutions thanks to its practical function and timeless aesthetic.

Without question, however, the person who managed to turn Modern Swedish furniture into a global phenomenon was Ingvar Kamprad, who founded IKEA in 1943. Initially, IKEA sold pens, picture frames and nylon stockings through mail order. Furniture was introduced in 1948, and three years later the first IKEA catalogue was published. Gillis Lundgren, who joined IKEA as its fourth employee in 1953, designed some of its all-time furniture classics, including the Impala chair (1972) and the bestselling Billy bookcase (1979), which has sold well over 40 million units. Lundgren is also credited with the introduction of flat-pack self-assembly at IKEA, when he removed the legs of his Lövet table (1956) so it could fit into his car. The first IKEA store opened in Älmhult, Sweden – where the company's headquarters remain – in 1958, and later stores opened in Norway (1963), Denmark (1969), Switzerland (1973) and West Germany (1974). Rapid expansion ensued, and today IKEA operates 267 stores in 25 countries and publishes about 250 million copies of its catalogue annually. Through its phenomenal success, it has spread the very Swedish concept of democratic design around the world.

During the 1960s and 1970s a number of Swedish designers worked in a Neo-Functionalist style, while designing furniture that was suitable for use mainly in public spaces. Among the most prominent of these were Åke Axelsson, Börge Lindau and Bo Lindekrantz. The 1980s, however, were difficult for the Swedish furniture industry: IKEA had moved its production abroad, while Italian design, in the full throes of Postmodernism, was attracting all the attention. But at the graduation show of the Konstfack (University College of Arts, Crafts and Design) in Stockholm in 1981, Jonas Bohlin showed a chair that was unergonomic, expensive and made of concrete – indeed, the very antithesis of everything Swedish design had stood for since the 1930s. The functionalist design community was horrified, but for the younger generation the chair signalled a new direction for not only Swedish furniture, but also Scandinavian design in general.

The Swedish manufacturer Källemo (est. 1965) helped to forge this new Postmodern direction by producing designs not only by Bohlin, but also by Mats Theselius and other progressive designers. Källemo's lead was followed in the late 1980s and early 1990s by the firms Asplund, Box Design,

Haga chest-of-drawers by Carl Malmsten for Nordiska Kompaniet (Sweden), 1920s

Model no. 652 armchair by Josef Frank for Svenskt Tenn (Sweden), 1936

Cabinet by Carl-Axel Acking for Svenska Möbelfabrikerna Bodafors (Sweden), 1940s

Pernilla Three lounger with bookrest by Bruno Mathsson for Karl Mathsson (Sweden), 1940s

The first IKEA catalogue (Sweden), 1951, featuring the MK wing-backed chair

Opposite: Nobody chairs by Komplot Design for Hay, 2007 – made from thermo-pressed PET felt

CBI and David Design. During this period the Milan furniture fair became an important meeting place for Swedish designers such as Thomas Eriksson, Thomas Sandell and Björn Dahlström to share ideas with their British peers, such as James Irvine, Jasper Morrison and Tom Dixon. They also met Italian designers and manufacturers including Giulio Cappellini, who famously produced Eriksson's iconic Cross medicine cabinet (1992). Today, Eriksson and Sandell are internationally renowned designers, who design for a wide range of manufacturers both at home and abroad, while a new generation of Swedish designers is undoubtedly benefitting creatively from the increasing interest worldwide in all things Scandinavian.

While Swedish furniture was largely driven by ideas of democracy and functionalism, Danish furniture came from an entirely different tradition: fine cabinetmaking, which has been practised in Denmark for generations. In 1924 the Kongelige Danske Kunstakademi (Royal Danish Academy of Fine Arts; KADK) in Copenhagen established a lectureship in furniture design and appointed Kaare Klint. The list of students under Klint's tutelage is a who's who of Danish designers. Early Danish furniture classics include Klint's Faaborg chair (1914) and Safari chair (1933), Mogens Koch's Folding chair (1932) and Ole Wanscher's Egyptian stool (1957).

An important catalyst for the development of Danish Modern furniture design was the annual exhibitions held by the Copenhagen Cabinetmakers' Guild from 1927 to 1966. Likewise, Den Permanente – a collective-run shop that had a 'permanent' exhibition of Danish arts and crafts – opened by, among others, Kay Bojesen, helped to generate interest in contemporary Danish design during its years of operation (1931–89). This torch-bearing role was later taken up by the department store Illums Bolighus (est. 1925). By the 1960s, some 25 per cent of all Danish furniture sales went to the UK, and sales to the USA peaked in 1963. The increasing popularity of wood-grained Formica as a substitute for real wood in the mid 1960s, however, damaged exports to the USA, and the Danish furniture industry began to wane. Similarly, changing fashions in the late 1960s and early 1970s favoured the Pop aesthetic of Italian design, and by the 1980s Danish design seemed in terminal decline.

In the late 1980s and early 1990s, however, design galleries and collectors specializing in postwar furniture led a reappraisal of Danish Modern furniture, which eventually prompted manufacturers such as Carl Hansen & Søn (est. 1908) and Fritz Hansen in Allorød (est. 1872) to reissue designs from their back catalogues. At the same time, new Danish companies emerged to produce contemporary furniture that channelled the spirit of mid-century Danish Modernism. Today, the Danish furniture industry employs some 15,000 people, and its 400 manufacturing companies produce goods worth around €1.75 billion each year. Over 80 per cent of the furniture is sold abroad, making furniture Denmark's fifth most important export industry. As a result, Denmark has maintained its place as the world's leading furniture producer in relation to its population.

One of the first Danish designers to receive international recognition after World War II was Finn Juhl, who made his furniture debut in 1937 with the cabinetmaker Niels Vodder. His designs were at first controversial, with his Pelican chair (1939) being described as a 'tired walrus'. Despite this, Juhl's work became celebrated abroad. In 1948 MoMA's Edgar Kaufmann Jr toured Scandinavia and wrote an article about Juhl. Juhl participated in the 'Good Design' exhibition in Chicago in 1951, and during the 1950s he exhibited at the Milan Triennials. Apart from his furniture pieces, Juhl also designed interiors for the United Nations Trusteeship Council chamber, SAS aeroplanes and Georg Jensen shops.

Arne Jacobsen was foremost an architect, each of whose buildings was a *Gesamtkunstwerk*. This meant that he designed everything that went into them: door handles, clocks, furniture, lighting, carpets, cutlery and vases. He began working with the furniture manufacturer Fritz Hansen in 1934, but his real commercial breakthrough came with the Ant chair in 1952. The Ant, or Model 3100, originally had three legs to keep materials to a minimum and to increase the number of chairs that could be placed around a table. The narrow waist that gave the chair its name eliminated the areas prone to deformation in the plywood moulding process. Model 3107 followed in 1955, with a wider seat and four legs. This design was copied from the start, the most famous forgery being straddled by the model Christine Keeler in a photograph from 1963. Jacobsen subsequently developed variants of these two chairs: the Tongue chair (1955), the Munkegaard or Mosquito chair (1955), the Grand Prix chair or Model 3130 (1958) and the Lily or Model 3208 (1970). His famous Egg and Swan chairs of 1958 were both created for the SAS Royal Hotel, together with the Giraffe chair, which was used in the dining room but never mass-produced. Jacobsen also designed sofa versions of the Egg and Swan. In 1962 he designed the tall-back wooden Oxford chair for the High Table at St Catherine's College, Oxford. He also designed the Ox lounge chair and footstool (1966–67), a very masculine answer to the Eameses' famous Model 670 lounge chair.

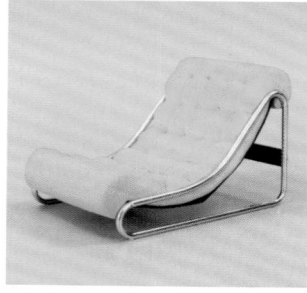

Impala chair by Gillis Lundgren for IKEA (Sweden), 1972

Billy bookcase by Gillis Lundgren for IKEA (Sweden), 1979 – more than 40 million units have been sold since its launch

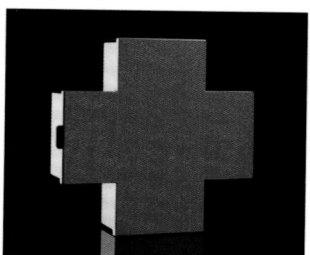

Cross medicine cabinet by Thomas Eriksson for Cappellini (Italy), 1992

Faaborg chairs by Kaare Klint for the Faaborg Museum on the island of Funen (Denmark), 1914

Pelican armchair by Finn Juhl for Niels Vodder (Denmark), 1939 – reissued by House of Finn Juhl

In contrast, Hans Wegner was first and foremost a furniture designer, having apprenticed with master cabinetmaker H. F. Stahlberg aged only 17. He subsequently studied cabinet-making at the Teknologisk Institut and later enrolled at the School of Arts and Crafts, where he specialized in furniture design and making. In 1938 Wegner joined the practice of Erik Møller and Flemming Lassen, and in 1940 he moved on to work for Møller and Jacobsen. At about this time he began working with the master cabinetmaker Johannes Hansen, which played a major role in introducing Modern furniture design to Denmark. Wegner established his own studio in 1943, and the following year he designed the China series inspired by Ming dynasty chairs. It was, however, his Wishbone chair (1949) for Carl Hansen & Søn that became Wegner's most commercially successful design. He also designed furniture for FDB (the Danish Co-op) and, in his later years, for P. P. Møbler, which now produces pieces originally designed for Johannes Hansen. Like Jacobsen, Wegner also designed a very masculine leather-padded armchair, similarly titled the Ox chair (1960).

In a similar vein, Børge Mogensen trained as a cabinetmaker and then studied at the School of Arts and Crafts before attending KADK in Copenhagen. He subsequently worked for various studios in the city, including Kaare Klint's. From 1942 to 1950 he led FDB's studio, designing affordable Modern furniture. Along with Wegner, Mogensen participated in the International Competition for Design in Low-cost Furniture of 1948, run by MoMA. Inspired by the exhibition, he experimented with plywood and began producing furniture that had a more contemporary spirit. In 1952 he began collaborating with Andreas Graversen, who acquired Fredericia Furniture (est. 1911) in 1955. Over the years the two men developed a strong friendship fuelled by the common goal of creating simple, high-quality furniture. Mogensen also worked with Grethe Meyer on the Boligens Byggeskabe (Construction Cupboards of the House) project (1954), which was based on analytical studies of the standard measurements of common objects and how many of these items the average person owned. Between 1954 and 1968, with Karl Andersson & Söner, Mogensen developed the Øresund storage furniture range, which aimed 'to solve every storage need that could arise in the modern home'. In 1971 he and Graversen jointly received the Danish Furniture Prize for their contribution to the Danish furniture industry, and in 1972 Mogensen became an Honorary Royal Designer for Industry at the Royal Society of Arts in London.

Poul Kjærholm belonged to a younger generation of Danish furniture designers.

His influences came mainly from outside Denmark, not least from the Modernist work of Ludwig Mies van der Rohe. Like many Scandinavian designers, however, he took an essentialist approach and tried to pare down his designs to their most minimal form. Kjærholm's career began as a cabinetmaker's apprentice, but he later studied at the School of Arts and Crafts in 1952. From the mid 1950s he designed for the manufacturer Ejvind Kold Christensen, who provided him with a large degree of creative freedom. In 1958 his work attracted acclaim at the 'Formes Scandinaves' exhibition held in Paris, and the same year he was awarded the Lunning Prize. While his contemporaries opted for wood as their primary material, Kjærholm chose steel, combined with wood, leather, cane or marble. He noted: 'Steel's constructive potential is not the only thing that interests me; the refraction of light on its surface is an important part of my artistic work. I consider steel a material with the same artistic merit as wood and leather.'

Grete Jalk also trained as a cabinetmaker, then studied at the Danish Design School and under Kaare Klint at KADK's furniture school. Experimenting with plywood, she developed a series of highly sculptural chairs in the 1960s. For the manufacturer Poul Jeppesen, she designed numerous comfortable furniture pieces that were distinguished by clean lines and were popular in both Denmark and the USA.

Verner Panton, the most revolutionary Danish furniture designer, graduated from KADK and briefly worked in Jacobsen's office, where he was charged with devising the first colour scheme for the Ant chair. During the 1960s he produced numerous innovative and playful designs for furniture, lighting and textiles. His earliest furniture designs were the Bachelor chair (1953) and Tivoli chair (1955), put into production by Fritz Hansen. Like other designers, Panton experimented with the development of a one-piece moulded plastic chair, and famously became the first to have such a piece successfully injection-moulded (1971), having initially been put into production in fibreglass by the Swiss company Vitra in 1967. Over the following years he designed a number of radical interior schemes, each conceived as a *Gesamtkunstwerk*, which included his numerous furniture designs.

Another Danish designer who found international success was Jens Risom, who was a graduate of the Royal Danish Academy of Fine Arts. In 1939 he moved to the USA, and two years later he began working for Knoll Associates, producing 15 designs for its first catalogue. One of his most successful pieces for Knoll was the Model no. 654W (1943) – now called the Risom lounge chair – which originally incorporated rejected parachute

Oxford high-backed chair by Arne Jacobsen for Fritz Hansen (Denmark), 1962–65

Ox chair by Hans Wegner for A.P. Stolen (Denmark), 1960 – now made by Erik Jørgensen

Øresund storage range by Børge Mogensen for Karl Andersson & Söner (Sweden), from 1955 and still in production – showing 852 cabinets and 892 wall brackets, with matching table and chairs

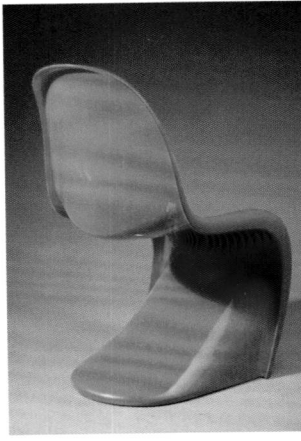

Panton chair by Verner Panton for Vitra (Switzerland) – first produced in 1967

Model no. 654W lounge chair by Jens Risom for Knoll (USA), 1943 – now called the Risom lounge chair

straps made of fabric webbing. After completing wartime service Risom set up his own furniture company, which did much to modernize furniture design in postwar America. Other designers who also helped to shape the evolution of Danish furniture in the 1960s and 1970s included Preben Fabricius, Jørgen Kastholm and Nanna Ditzel.

The name of Alvar Aalto will forever dominate the story of Finnish furniture in the twentieth century. Following the design of the Paimio Sanatorium (1928–33), for which he designed site-specific furniture, Aalto developed numerous other furniture pieces. Initially, most were specially created for architectural commissions and only later put into mass-production, such as his Model no. 60 stacking stool for Viipuri Library. Although Aalto designed some early experimental chairs with tubular-metal frames, it was his furniture designs constructed entirely of wood, developed in Otto Korhonen's furniture factory in Turku, that sold in higher numbers. The British architectural critic and champion of Modernism Philip Morton Shand got to know Aalto through the CIAM (International Congress of Modern Architecture), and in 1933 staged an exhibition of Aalto's furniture entitled 'Wood Only' at the department store Fortnum & Mason in London. The following year Shand founded Finmar, which imported Aalto's furniture into Britain. The relative cheapness of Aalto's furniture was a draw, as was the fact that he used wood rather than steel in its construction, since many customers considered tubular metal too radical.

In 1935 Aalto founded Artek with his wife and design collaborator, Aino, Maire Gullichsen (whose grandfather was one of Finland's wealthiest businessmen) and the art historian Nils-Gustav Hahl. The name of this new furniture manufacturing and retailing enterprise was a contraction of 'Art' and 'Technology'; its aim was 'to sell furniture and to promote a modern culture of living by exhibitions and other educational means'. After World War II Aalto focused mainly on architecture and left the running of Artek to Aino. After her untimely death in 1949, it was his second wife, Elissa, who managed Artek. Eventually Vitra acquired Artek, in 2013, and the following year Artek purchased the Korhonen factory, where Aalto's furniture is still made today.

Like Aalto, the Finnish architect Pauli Blomstedt initially worked in the Nordic Classical style, but soon turned to Modernism. After studying architecture at Helsinki University of Technology, he first worked for Armas Lindgren – a colleague of Eliel Saarinen – and later for Bertel Jung and Gunnar Taucher. During the 1920s Blomstedt took part in a number of building competitions, including one for the design of the Liittopankki (Union Bank) headquarters in Helsinki, which he won; it was built in 1929. He went on to design a number of other buildings in a modernistic style, as well as several tubular-steel furniture pieces that similarly bridged the gap between Art Deco and Bauhaus Functionalism. Today the Finnish manufacturer Tetrimäki produces a number of Blomstedt's 'Post-Deco' furniture designs, including his streamlined Model 1300 credenza (ca. 1932).

While Aalto set the standards for pre-war furniture design in Finland, it was Ilmari Tapiovaara who developed the first successful postwar Finnish furniture, while the country was still suffering severe shortages. After studying furniture design at Helsinki's Taideteolliseen Keskuskouluun (Central School of Industrial Arts), Tapiovaara worked briefly in Le Corbusier's office in Paris. In 1937 he began work as artistic director at Asko, then the biggest furniture company in Finland. In 1941 he joined the furniture company Keravan Puuteollisuus, and between 1946 and 1947 he designed interiors for the Domus Academica student housing complex in Helsinki. For that project he created the plywood Domus chair, which could be stacked into small crates and was exported in large numbers to America. In 1951 he established his own office, and the following year he taught at the Illinois Institute of Technology, working under Mies van der Rohe. Apart from his elegant furniture, he also designed graphics and lighting as well as interiors for Olivetti stores, banks, hotels, offices and bars.

Eero Aarnio has long enjoyed being the *enfant terrible* of Finnish furniture design, holding a role similar to that of Verner Panton in Denmark. He studied at the Institute of Industrial Arts, Helsinki, before undertaking an apprenticeship with Tapiovaara and a stint with the Asko furniture company. In 1962 he set up his own design practice to explore new furniture ideas. One resulting design was the iconic Ball (or Globe) chair of 1963. Its use of fibreglass and its bold form were so radically new for the furniture industry that Aarnio had to acquire the material from the Finnish boat industry. He had his own Ball chair fitted with a telephone, while some of his customers had the cocoon-like chair fitted with audio speakers. In 1968 Aarnio designed the hanging Bubble chair in transparent acrylic and chromed steel, and the same year he won a US Industrial Design Award for his pill-like, fibreglass Pastilli chair (1967).

Terence Conran has often claimed that the Karuselli (Carousel) fibreglass chair (1964) by Yrjö Kukkapuro is his favourite chair. Indeed, in 1974 the *New York Times* nominated it as the most comfortable chair in the world. Having graduated as an interior architect from the Institute of Industrial Arts in Helsinki, Kukkapuro founded his own practice in 1959. Apart from designing furniture, which was always distinguished by strong graphic profiles, Kukkapuro was also an influential design academic. With his wife, Irmeli Kukkapuro, and the engineer Eero Paloheimo, he built a house and studio in Kauniaslainen in 1968, inspired by the curved roofline of Eero Saarinen's TWA terminal at John F. Kennedy airport in New York.

More recently, innovative Finnish furniture design has been the preserve of Ilkka Suppanen, who studied architecture at Helsinki University of Technology and interior and furniture design at Helsinki University of Art and Design. He has designed furniture for Avarte, Cappellini, Fornasarig, Vivero, Woodnotes and Zanotta. In 1997, with three colleagues, Suppanen founded the design co-operative Snowcrash, which won the Young Designer of the Year Award in Germany that same year. In 2000 Suppanen and Harri Koskinen were jointly named Young Designer of the Year by Design Forum Finland. Koskinen had likewise studied design at Helsinki University of Art and Design, and similarly now works in a wide range of product areas, although glass and furniture design are his specialities. His designs include furniture for Artek, Cassina, Finlayson, Fornasarig, Meetee, Montina, Nikari, Skandium, Woodnotes and Zanat. He also designs products for HarriKoskinenWorks, his own furniture and lighting collection. He has received numerous awards, including a Compasso d'Oro in 2004, the Pro Finlandia medal in 2007 and the Torsten & Wanja Söderberg Prize in 2009.

The country that is least known in terms of Scandinavian furniture design is Norway, many of whose companies fell victim to cheap imports in the 1960s and 1970s. But from the 1940s until the 1960s Norway produced beautiful, well-made and well-designed furniture, often with a formal language that was akin to both Danish and Brazilian mid-century furniture, using dark and exotic woods.

Bendt Winge was one of the first to create Modern designs for the Norwegian furniture industry. Trained as a cabinetmaker and interior designer, he established his own studio in 1934. One of his early bestsellers was the Klaffebord no. 2 gateleg dining table (ca. 1952), produced by Kleppe Møbelfabrikk. Later, for Romo fabrikker, Winge designed the R-48 plastic chair (1970), which is very similar in form and material to Robin Day's Polypropylene side chair (1962–63) but which had a hole in its seat section and is normally seen in its upholstered version. Some 5 million units of this comfortable yet utilitarian design have been sold, and it is still in production.

Arne Tidemand Ruud followed in the footsteps of his father, who managed furniture factories in Oslo and Gjøvik in Norway as well as Odense, Denmark. He apprenticed in his father's factories and received a craftsman's diploma in 1935 while studying at the National Academy of Arts and Design in Oslo. Upon his father's death he assumed the management of the Inventar factory in Gjøvik with his wife, Solveig, a textile designer. For three decades they designed and produced furniture and interiors for cafes, restaurants, banks and hotels. Ruud's best-known design is the reclining teak-and-leather Holmenkollen lounge chair (1959), which received first prize at the Cologne furniture fair in 1960. Both its name and its form were inspired by the Holmenkollen ski jump in Oslo, and it was exported to the USA, Germany and Sweden.

Jan Lunde Knutsen, one of Norway's most outward-looking furniture designers, came to prominence in the 1960s after living for most of the 1950s in the USA. Returning to Norway in the early 1960s, he worked for Sørlie Møbler, which produced the elegant Rondo chair of 1961.

The Norwegian furniture manufacturer Rastad & Relling functioned ostensibly as a creative incubator for emerging designers, including Arne Halvorsen, Sigurd Ressell and Ingmar Relling. In 1954 Relling designed the Nordic chair for Vestlandske Møbelfabrikk, while his well-known Siesta armchair (1964) for Westnofa won first prize in the Norwegian Furniture Council Competition in 1965. Fredrik Kayser also worked for Rastad & Relling, designing the Kamin (1946) and Kryss (1955) chairs. He later designed the plain yet elegant Hertug sideboard (1960) for Viken Møbelfabrikk, and during the latter part of his career worked with Vatne Lenestolfabrikk.

Another Norwegian designer of innovative furniture was Gerhard Berg, a graduate of the Statens Håndverks- og Kunstindustriskole (Norwegian National Academy of Craft and Industrial Art; SHKS) in Oslo. His designs were distinguished by their soft, organic forms, as exemplified by his Nor and Tyrol chairs and his Varia sectional sofa (all 1955). Berg also experimented with new materials, such as fibreglass. He designed furniture for L. K. Hjelle and P. I. Langlo, but it is his work for Stokke that is probably the best known, such as his Aksla (1961) and Kubus (1964) armchairs.

Øyvind Iversen designed the City dining chair in 1955 as a diploma project while studying at SHKS in Oslo. A Norwegian answer to Arne Jacobsen's 3107 chair, this design with its moulded plywood seat section became a bestseller and triggered several spin-offs. Another successful Norwegian design was the 1001 chair (1959) by Sven Ivar Dysthe, who had studied industrial design at the Royal College of Art, London.

It was, however, the Scandia chair (1957) by Hans Brattrud that was most innovative of all the seating designs developed in Norway during the 1950s. The chair started life as a student project while Brattrud was studying at SHKS. With horizontal metal ribs that cleverly support a series of two-dimensional vertical elements in moulded plywood, the chair was put into production in 1960, and further models were developed using the same constructional concept. In 1967 it was awarded a gold medal at the international arts and crafts fair in Munich, and that same year it also received the Award for Design Excellence from the Norwegian Design Council.

The Norwegian designer who has had the greatest long-term influence, however, is Peter Opsvik, one of the world's leading pioneers of ergonomic seating. Having studied at the Statens Høgskole for Kunsthåndverk og Design in Bergen (National College of Applied Art and Design; now Bergen Academy of Art and Design) and SHKS in Oslo, he initially worked as an industrial designer for the Tandberg Radio Factory in Oslo from 1965 to 1970, while also working as a freelance furniture designer. Since 1970 Opsvik has dedicated himself to the design of ergonomic seating, mainly for Stokke and HÅG. Among his many ingenious designs are the adjustable Tripp Trapp children's high chair (1972) and the Variable Balans sitting tool (1979) and Capisco chair (1984), all of which have sold extremely well around the world.

During the 1980s and 1990s Norwegian furniture fell out of fashion, but the design collective Norway Says changed that. Founded in 2000 by Andreas Engesvik, Torbjørn Anderssen and Espen Voll, the group gained international attention with designs that were both functionally and formally interesting. In 2009 Engesvik went solo and founded his own studio, while the other two continue to co-operate as Anderssen & Voll. The trio have been instrumental in creating the 'New Nordic' style. Engesvik has worked for, among others, Muuto, Fontana Arte and Asplund; Anderssen & Voll has designed for various manufacturers, including Kvadrat, Erik Jørgensen and Hay. The Nordic furniture industry is well placed in today's global marketplace, thanks to its continuing focus on simple yet thoughtful designs and their high-quality manufacture.

Stack of Model no. 60 stools by Alvar Aalto for Artek (Finland), 1932–33

Model no. 8160 armchair and Model no. 8161 ottoman by Pauli Blomstedt (Finland), 1932–33 – this example is a reissue by Adelta, ca. 1990

Bubble hanging chairs by Eero Aarnio for Asko (Finland), 1968 – later reissued by Eero Aarnio Originals

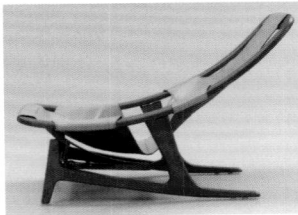

Holmenkollen lounge chair by Arne Tidemand Ruud for Inventar (Norway), 1959

Variable Balans sitting tool by Peter Opsvik for Stokke (Norway), 1979 – later manufactured by Varier (Norway)

SWEDISH GRACE

The influential British architecture critic Philip Morton Shand, on visiting the Swedish Pavilion at the Exposition Internationale des Arts Décoratifs et Industriels Modernes in Paris in 1925, famously coined the term 'Swedish Grace' to describe a new current within Scandinavian design, which was a Neoclassical form of the Art Deco style. Of the many pieces he would have seen in the Swedish Pavilion, perhaps the most striking were two gilded cabinets designed by the architect Carl Hörvik and executed by NK (Nordiska Kompaniet). They were displayed in the pavilion's reception hall flanked by matching armchairs. The pieces shown here, which were recently acquired by the Nationalmuseum in Stockholm, reveal not only a strong classicism but also a proto-modern austerity, especially when the cabinet's doors are closed and its stunning gilded interior hidden. As the German writer Armand Weiser noted in *Deutsche Kunst und Dekoration* (Vol. 57, 1925–26), 'there was something very special which separated this [Swedish] pavilion from all the others: the surprising and convincing relationship between function and pure design, between simplicity and exquisite workmanship, between delicacy and solidity.' Indeed, the same could be said of Hörvik's pieces, which won a prestigious Grand Prix at this landmark exhibition.

1. The reception hall in the Swedish Pavilion at the Exposition Internationale des Arts Décoratifs et Industriels Modernes in Paris, 1925, showing Carl Hörvik's cabinets and matching armchairs as well as Simon Gate's famous Parispokalen (Paris Cup, see p. 239), produced by Orrefors

2 & opposite: Gilded cabinet and matching pair of small armchairs designed by Carl Hörvik for NK (Sweden), for the Swedish Pavilion, 1925

1.

2.

SENNA LOUNGE CHAIR

Best remembered for his International Style buildings designed for the Stockholm Exhibition of 1930, Erik Gunnar Asplund – like so many of his Scandinavian architect peers – began working in a stripped-down Neoclassical Art Deco style during the 1920s. Asplund had initially proposed the design of his Senna chair for inclusion in the Swedish Pavilion at the Exposition Internationale des Arts Décoratifs et Industriels Modernes in Paris in 1925, but it was rejected. Despite this, examples of the design were executed for a 'studio' installation displayed at the exhibition, and won a Diplôme d'honneur. Inspired by Greek and Egyptian antecedents, the design, with its tooled leather upholstery, sinuous walnut frame and carved ivory roundels emblazoned with a man's and a woman's face, was the apotheosis of Swedish Grace refinement. It was not, however, a commercially viable design, and at first only the examples shown at the exhibition were made. Asplund later helped to initiate the design's reissue by the Italian manufacturer Cassina in 1983, but again very few examples were produced owing to the high cost of its manufacture.

Below & 2. Senna lounge chair by Erik Gunnar Asplund, originally executed by David Blomberg (Sweden), 1925; this is an original example

1. Detail of Senna lounge chair – a later re-edition by Cassina in 1983

1.

2.

ASPLUND + MARKELIUS

By the late 1920s and early 1930s a more stridently Modernist approach had begun sweeping through Swedish design and architecture circles. Indeed, this movement, known as Funkis (Functionalism), would become de rigueur after the Stockholm Exhibition of 1930, which was a hugely influential showcase for this new forward-looking direction. Among its leading proponents were Erik Gunnar Asplund and Sven Markelius, both of whom created furniture that exemplified the influence of the new International Style. Inspired by the pioneering tubular-metal furniture designed by their peers in Germany,

these two Swedish architect-designers also created chairs with tubular-metal frames: Markelius designed a cantilevered model for Stockholms Nya Järnsängsfabrik in about 1930, while Asplund designed his well-known leather and tubular-metal office chair for the boardroom of the Swedish Society of Crafts (Hemslöjdföreningen) in 1931. Indeed, Markelius had visited the Bauhaus in 1927 and met Walter Gropius, whose theories had a profound influence on his development as a designer. Like Alvar Aalto, Markelius took on board the egalitarian intention of German Functionalism but adapted it to a more human Scandinavian sensibility.

Below: Tubular-metal cantilevered chair by Sven Markelius for Stockholms Nya Järnsängsfabrik (Sweden), ca. 1930

1. Unique macassar ebony desk by Sven Markelius executed by NK (Sweden), 1932 – originally created for his own home, Markelius later gave this desk to the designer Vicke Lindstrand.

2. Orchestra stacking chairs by Sven Markelius for Bodafors (Sweden), 1932 – a child-sized version was also produced

3 & 4. Office chair by Erik Gunnar Asplund for NK (Sweden), ca. 1931 – originally designed for the Swedish Society of Crafts office and later reissued by Källemo (this example believed to be a prototype)

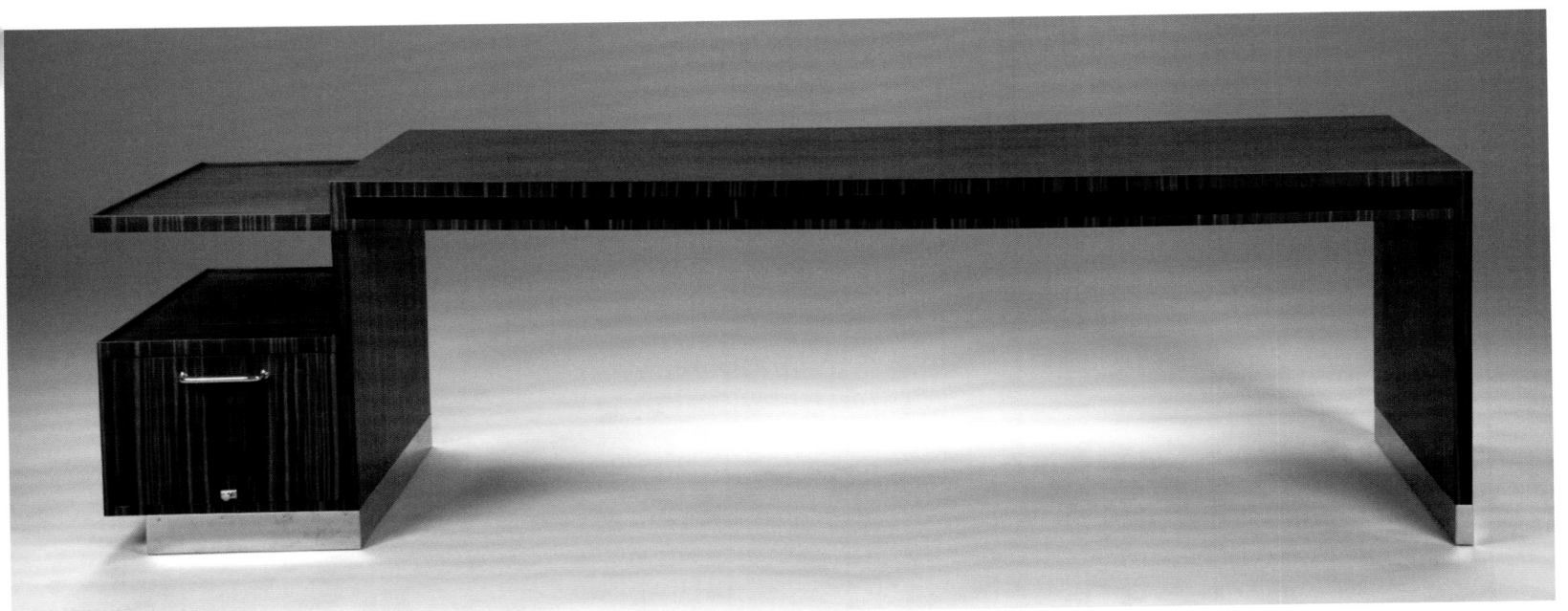

1.

2.

3.

4.

SCANDINAVIAN ART DECO

Art Deco was a truly international style, which, having emerged in France during the early 1920s, reached its streamlined Art Moderne zenith in America during the Depression-laden 1930s. In Scandinavia, the style was particularly popular in Sweden. Indeed, as we have seen, the term 'Swedish Grace' was coined by the critic Philip Morton Shand in 1925 to describe a distinctly Nordic Neoclassical interpretation of Art Deco. By the 1930s, however, a number of Swedish designers, such as Bo Wretling, Axel Einar Hjorth and Uno Åhrén, had moved on stylistically and were designing furniture with a much more Modernistic flavour, although still within an Art Deco idiom. The five pieces of furniture shown here were manufactured by Svenskt Tenn, NK (Nordiska Kompaniet) or Otto Wretling and reveal a robust geometric vocabulary of form, which reflects the Nordic tendency towards designs that have a strong graphic outline – one of the central reasons why so many designs from Scandinavia have over the years been deemed iconic.

Below: Armchair by Bo Wretling for Otto Wretling (Sweden), 1930s

1. Lemon-wood and walnut cabinet by Axel Einar Hjorth, manufactured by NK (Sweden), 1930 – exhibited at the landmark Stockholm Exhibition of 1930

2. High-backed wing armchair attributed to either Uno Åhrén or Björn Trägårdh, manufactured by Svenskt Tenn (Sweden), 1930s

3. Lacquered wood bookcase by Axel Einar Hjorth (attributed), manufactured by NK (Sweden), 1930s

4. Three-tiered side tables by Axel Einar Hjorth for NK (Sweden), 1930 – created specially for the Stockholm Exhibition

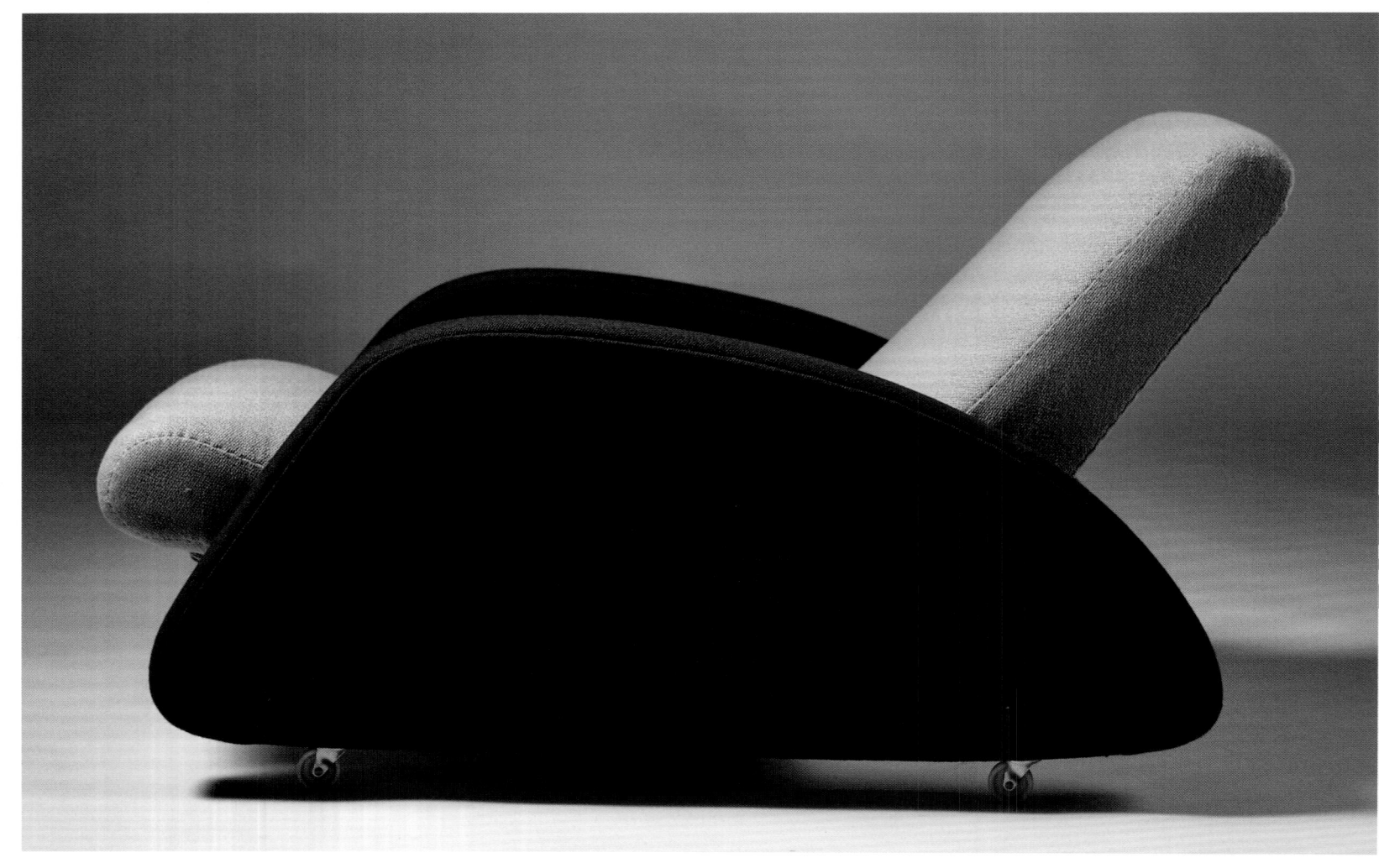

1.

2.

3.

4.

AALTO CHAIRS

During the late 1920s and 1930s, while architect-designers in France and Germany explored the formal and functional possibilities of tubular steel as a material for Modern furniture, Alvar and Aino Aalto in Finland preferred to experiment with two other man-made materials that were arguably better suited to the task in hand. These two 'new' materials were plywood and laminated wood, both made by gluing layers of wood veneer together to form what are essentially glue-and-wood composite materials; the direction of the veneers' grain determines whether the resulting material is laminated wood or plywood. Using stronger laminated constructions for the chairs' supporting frames and thinner, more mouldable plywood for their seating sections, the two designers were able to create sculptural seat forms that provided ergonomic comfort without the need for traditional springing or padded upholstery. In this way they introduced a new organic sensibility to Modern design, as the chairs shown here so elegantly demonstrate. The Aaltos' chair designs became hugely influential not only in Scandinavia but also abroad, especially in postwar Great Britain and America.

1. Model 51/403 armchair by Alvar and Aino Aalto for Artek (Finland), 1932

2. Model 21 cantilevered side chair by Alvar and Aino Aalto for Artek (Finland), ca. 1933

3. Model 41 Paimio chair by Alvar and Aino Aalto for Huonekalu-Ja Rakennustyötehdas (Finland), 1930–31 – later produced by Artek

4. Model 31/42 cantilevered armchair by Alvar and Aino Aalto for Artek (Finland), 1932

1.

2.

3.

4.

1.

2.

3.

AALTO: STOOLS + TROLLEY

Apart from designing numerous chairs, Alvar Aalto also created three important stools that reflected his ongoing research into the bending of laminated wood and plywood. Model 60 (1932–33) was a simple stacking design with three L-shaped legs bent from laminated birch, around a circular seat. This 'bent-knee' stool can be viewed as a quintessential example of early Scandinavian Functionalism. The later Model Y61 stool (1947), however, with its four Y-legs and canvas-webbed seat, was a less utilitarian design, being intended more for domestic use. Its ingeniously simple design comprises just four inverted U-shaped elements bent from laminated wood, which provide the supporting frame for its woven seat. In contrast, the Model X602 fan-legged stool (1954), which had either three or four legs, was a much more technically sophisticated design in that it involved the splicing of an L-shaped section of laminated wood and the subsequent reconnection of the pieces into a fan-like configuration. Another landmark Aalto design was the Model 98/901 tea trolley (1936), which – like the Model X – used the minimum amount of material to the maximum functional effect; at the same time, its soft, undulating lines reflected Aalto's more human approach to Modernism.

1. Model X602 fan-legged stool by Alvar Aalto for Artek (Finland), 1936

2. Model 60 L-legged stacking stool by Alvar Aalto for Artek (Finland), 1932–33

3. Model Y61 stool by Alvar Aalto for Artek (Finland), 1947 – also known as the Y-legged stool

Below: Model 98/901 tea trolley by Alvar Aalto for Artek (Finland), 1936

OTHER AALTO FURNITURE

Unlike his Modernist counterparts in France and Germany, Alvar Aalto understood that there was no point in creating Modern furniture out of tubular steel and glass if people did not find these materials physically or psychologically comforting. In any case, wood was in far more plentiful supply in his native Finland than were these modern industrial materials. By pioneering his own techniques of laminating and moulding wood, Aalto was able to produce furniture every bit as innovative as anything designed by the likes of Le Corbusier or Marcel Breuer. In fact, his work was arguably more radical because, rather than being

designed primarily for efficient mass-production, it was conceived from the point of view of the user. That is not to say that Aalto's European peers did not influence him, because they most certainly did: earlier tubular-steel designs, for example, inspired his use of cantilevered frames in the Model 39 chaise (ca. 1937) and Model 37 lounge chair (1936). In contrast, however, his Model 71 table (1933) with its useful hanging shelf redefined the two-tier configuration seen in contemporaneous Art Deco pieces thanks to his mastery of simplification, which allowed him to create this useful and attractive piece of furniture from just two circular pieces of wood and four L-shaped legs.

1. Model 39 chaise by Alvar Aalto for Artek (Finland), ca. 1937

2 & 4. Model 71 tiered occasional table by Alvar Aalto for Artek (Finland), 1933

3. Model 37/400 upholstered armchair by Alvar Aalto for Artek (Finland), 1936

1.

2.

3.

4.

IDEAL FORMS

The concept of ideal forms based on the study of historic paradigms is a powerful theme in Scandinavian design, especially in that of Denmark and Sweden. One of the most influential advocates of this theme was Kaare Klint, who taught his students at KADK in Copenhagen to analyse the construction, form and measurements of antique furniture in order to create their own highly refined modern interpretations of it (see pp. 106–7).

Indeed, one of Klint's most famous students was the architect-designer Ole Wanscher, who wrote several books on furniture history and designed the folding stool shown opposite, inspired by ancient Egyptian models. Another designer who studied antique antecedents carefully and channelled their ideal forms into his own work was the Austrian-born Swede Josef Frank (see pp. 102–3). But, although he took his ideas from earlier archetypes, he did so in a stripped-down design language that renders his pieces timeless.

1. Mahogany side table by Josef Frank for Svenskt Tenn (Sweden), ca. 1940s

2. Model 997 Shaker rocking chair by Josef Frank for Svenskt Tenn (Sweden), 1940

3. Egyptian-style Thebes stool by Josef Frank for Svenskt Tenn (Sweden), 1941

Opposite: Egyptian stool by Ole Wanscher for A.J. Iversen (Denmark), 1957

2.

3.

1.

JOSEF FRANK + SVENSKT TENN

Regarded as one of the most influential Swedish designers of all time, the Austrian-born Josef Frank was an internationally acclaimed designer even before he fled to Stockholm in 1933 to escape Nazism. The following year he began working as a designer for Svenskt Tenn, Sweden's most fashionable interior design shop, which had been founded by Estrid Ericson a decade earlier. There he was able to explore a freer, more artistic form of Modernism, which rejected the sterile standardization and hard-edged aesthetic espoused by Le Corbusier and other members of the Modern Movement. Instead, Frank focused on creating contemporary furniture, lighting, textiles and housewares that would imbue interiors with comfort, colour and an all-important sense of home. Many of his furniture designs were modern reworkings of traditional pieces, which he would embellish with burr-walnut veneers or cover with varnished botanical prints. With such designs Frank was at the forefront of forging a very Scandinavian, evolutionary rather than revolutionary approach to Modernism.

Below: Flora cabinet by Josef Frank for Svenskt Tenn (Sweden), 1930s

1. Flora chest of drawers by Josef Frank for Svenskt Tenn (Sweden), 1940s

2. Model 881 cabinet by Josef Frank for Svenskt Tenn (Sweden), 1938 – sometimes referred to as the Nationalmuseiskåpet (National Museum Cabinet)

3. Pair of sideboards by Josef Frank for Svenskt Tenn (Sweden), 1951

JOSEF FRANK + SVENSKT TENN

1.

2.

3.

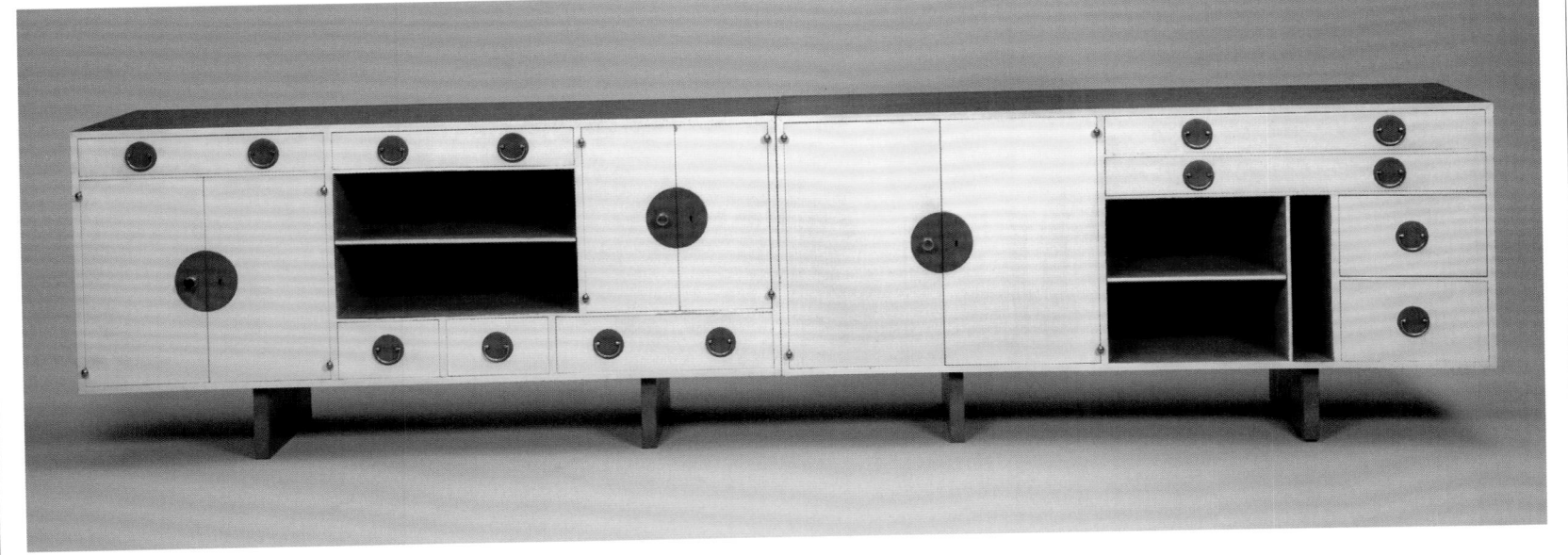

1.

2.

AXEL EINAR HJORTH

Axel Einar Hjorth led the furniture design department of the famous Nordiska Kompaniet (NK) department store from 1927 to 1938, and was a key figure in the evolution of Modern furniture design in Sweden. At first his furniture designs were influenced by the French Art Deco style, in that they often employed luxury materials and were boldly geometric in form. Soon, though, he began to create furniture with a more Modernistic flavour, such as the three-tiered side tables shown on p. 93. During the mid 1930s, however, Hjorth's work took on a completely different stylistic direction when he set about creating simple furniture with an engaging Scandinavian rustic appearance perfectly suited to the austerity of the Depression era. With their basic yet bold forms and use of inexpensive pine, such pieces referred to their Swedish antecedents, radically updating them with their stripped-down simplicity.

1. Chairs by Axel Einar Hjorth for NK (Sweden), 1932

2. Console table by Axel Einar Hjorth for NK (Sweden), 1932

3. Lovö rocking chair by Axel Einar Hjorth for NK (Sweden), 1930s

4. Stained pine stool by Axel Einar Hjorth for NK (Sweden), 1930s

5. Occasional table by Axel Einar Hjorth for NK (Sweden), 1932

3.

4.

5.

KAARE KLINT + MOGENS KOCH

Kaare Klint's Safari chair and Mogens Koch's MK-16 folding chair epitomize the desire among Danish designers for ideal forms based on the modern refinement of historic archetypes. Both chairs followed earlier models: Koch's was a reworking of a folding director's chair invented by the Gold Medal Camp Furniture Company of Racine, Wisconsin, in the 1890s; Klint's was inspired by a collapsible campaign chair used by British explorers, travellers and military officers, manufactured by Maple & Co. in the early years of the twentieth century. Working as a professor from 1924 to 1954, Klint's influence on his students at the furniture school of KADK in Copenhagen is legendary. Indeed, his teaching methodology, based on ergonomics and the analysis of earlier typologies, set the agenda for Danish furniture designers throughout most of the twentieth century. Koch worked with Klint from 1925 to 1930 and was also an influential professor at KADK. By stripping down his designs to their functional essentials, Koch – like Klint – always sought to achieve a refined balance of comfort and aesthetics.

Below: Safari chair by Kaare Klint for Rud. Rasmussen (Denmark), 1933

1. MK-16 folding chair by Mogens Koch for Rud. Rasmussen (Denmark), 1932 – also manufactured by Interna (Denmark)

2. Six folded MK-16 chairs in matching storage stand

3. Set of 12 modular bookcases by Mogens Koch for Rud. Rasmussen (Denmark), 1928

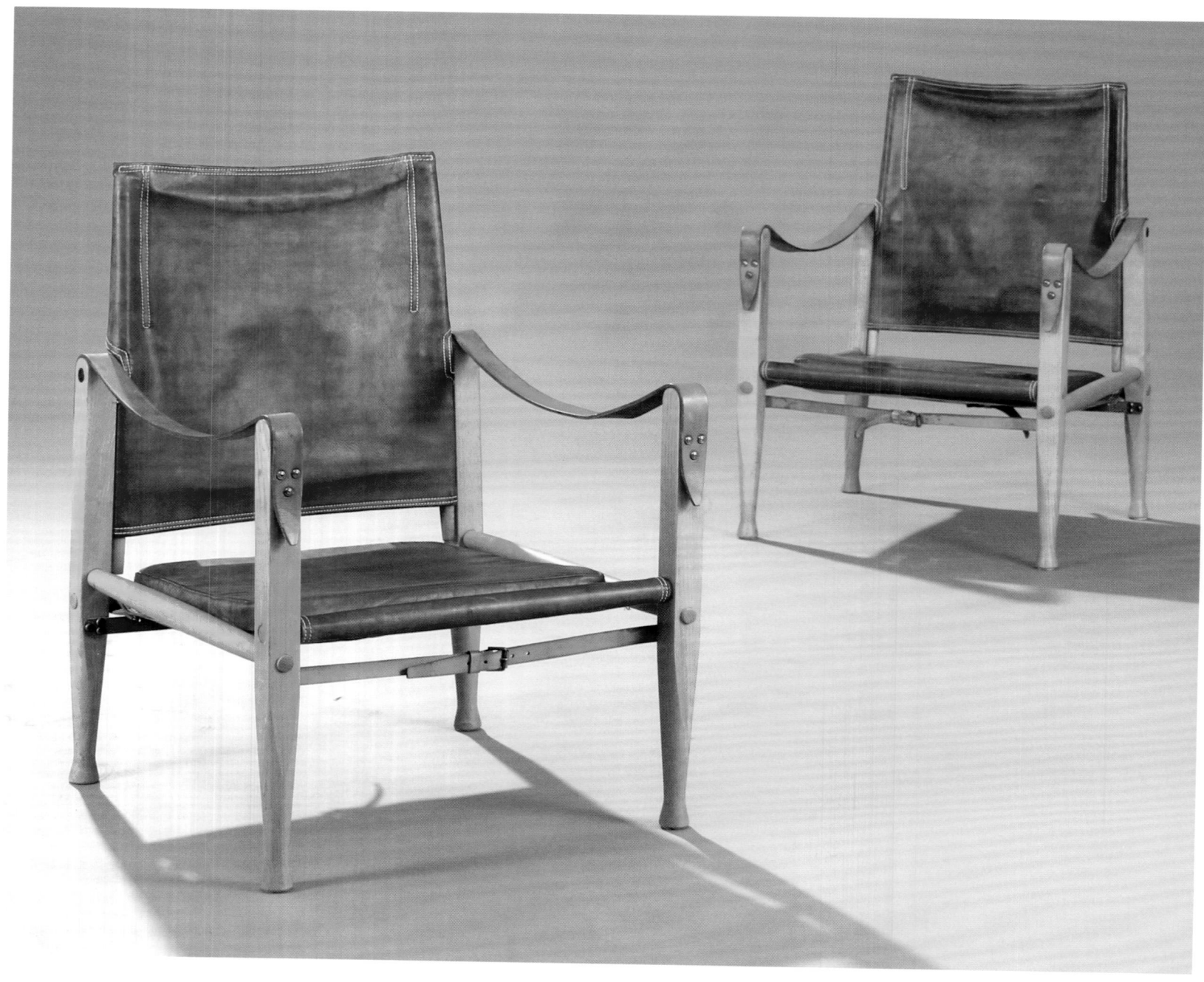

2.

1.   3.

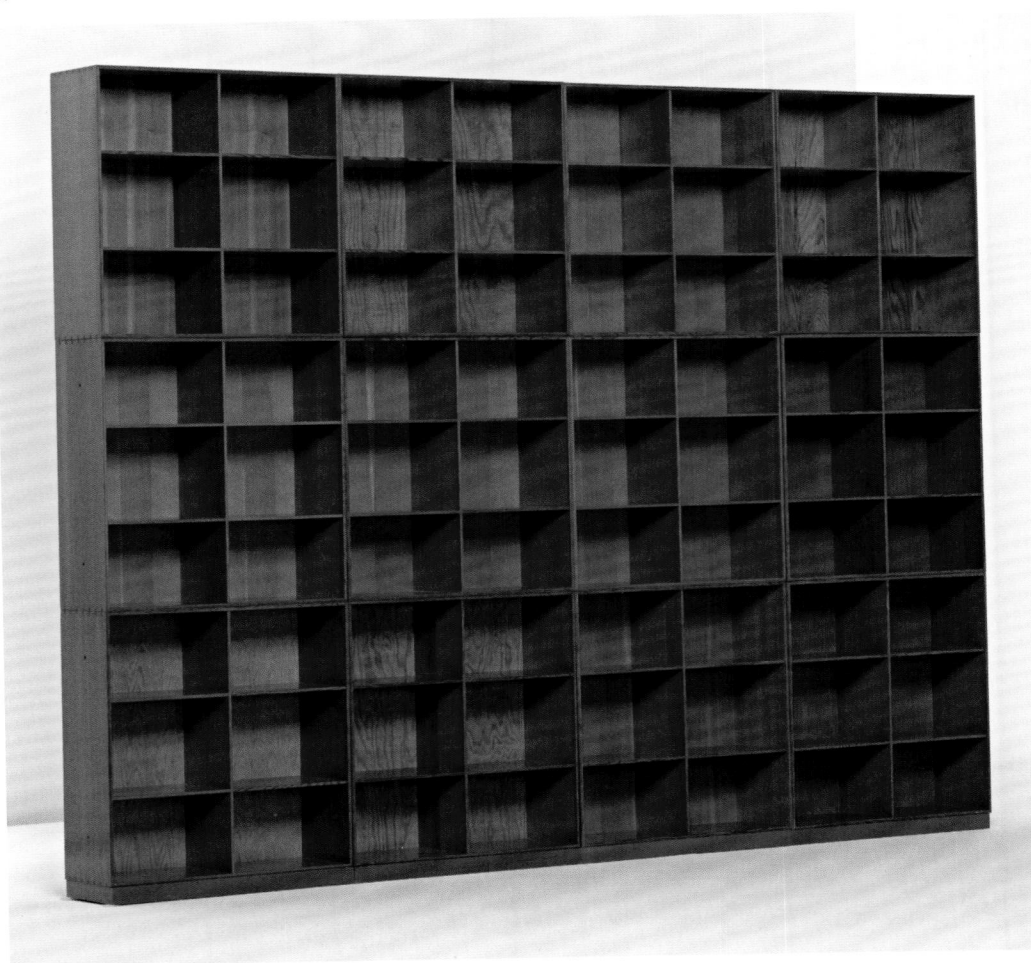

PEDER MOOS

Peder Moos was more a furniture sculptor than a furniture designer, and his pieces possess a distinctive woodcraft bravado. They were normally only made to order, and he executed them himself. A farmer's son, Moos had initially trained as a joiner at Askov Højskole, a folk school in Southern Jutland. He subsequently worked as a cabinetmaker in Paris and in the Swiss cities of Geneva and Lausanne, then studied at KADK from 1935 to 1938 under two important furniture masters, Kaare Klint and Einar Utzon-Franck. He then

established his own workshop in the Bregade district of Copenhagen, and ran it for the next two decades. Moos participated in the annual Cabinetmakers' Guild exhibitions in Copenhagen, displaying furniture that always revealed a strong attention to detail and craftsmanship. With their elegant, undulating lines, Moos's designs – now prized by collectors for their rarity – not only evoked Art Nouveau organicism, but also possessed very strong and distinct Scandinavian qualities, born of exacting craft skills and an almost magical ability to transform wood into lively biomorphic forms.

Below: Chair executed in Peder Moos's own workshop (Denmark), 1978 – the chair's textile was designed by Moos's sister, Marie

1. Occasional table executed in Peder Moos's own workshop (Denmark), ca. 1948

2 & 3. Armchair executed in Peder Moos's own workshop (Denmark), 1949

1.

2.

3.

FRITS HENNINGSEN

Frits Henningsen was known as an uncompromising designer who crafted furniture of
exemplary quality. Unlike most Danish designers, Henningsen made his own furniture,
with the help of skilled assistants, rather than
having other workshops execute it for him.
He learned his practical furniture-making
skills as an apprentice to the master cabinetmaker I. P. Mørck. He also studied at the
Danish Academy of Fine Arts in Copenhagen
under Kaare Klint, who taught him to appreciate antique furniture of various periods and
styles. Henningsen also broadened his knowledge of contemporary design through travel,
and worked in Germany, France and Britain
for a number of years before returning to
Copenhagen in 1915 and setting up his own
workshop there. From 1927 he was an active
member of the city's Cabinetmakers' Guild
and participated in its exhibitions, showing
designs that often incorporated exotic woods,
such as Cuban mahogany or Brazilian rosewood. His furniture has a rather curious
hybrid quality, being influenced both by traditional furniture types, such as the historic
wing chair, and by the emerging contemporary trend for more organic forms.

1. Leather and oak armchair by Frits Henningsen
(Denmark), ca. 1939

2. Armchair by Frits Henningsen (Denmark), ca. 1940

Opposite: Lounge chair by Frits Henningsen (Denmark),
1947

1.

2.

FINN JUHL: SCULPTING FUNCTIONAL FORM

The gifted Danish designer Finn Juhl once noted: 'A chair is not just a product of decorative art in a space, it is a form and a space in itself.' Certainly, his seating designs had a distinctive sculptural presence that was as much about their inherent form as it was about the effect that form had on the surrounding space. His NV-45 lounge chair (1945) with its lively, undulating lines reveals not only Juhl's rare ability to transform wood into flowing organic forms, but also the mastery of Niels Vodder's cabinetmaking skills, which enabled him to sculpt Juhl's sketches and drawings into beautiful pieces of 'living' furniture. Juhl's Chieftain armchair and sofa (1949) possess an even bolder aspect. As their title suggests, these pieces, with their shield-shaped back sections, convey a strong sense of masculine power, thanks in large part to the sculptural virtuosity of their designer's organic lines (see also pp. 114–15).

Below: Chieftain sofa by Finn Juhl for Niels Vodder (Denmark), 1949 – reissued by Niels Roth Andersen (Denmark) ca. 1985

1. NV-45 lounge chair by Finn Juhl for Niels Vodder (Denmark), 1945

2. Finn Juhl relaxing in a Chieftain armchair outside his own house (see pp. 46–47), ca. 1950

3. Chieftain armchair by Finn Juhl for Niels Vodder (Denmark), 1949

1.

3.

2.

FINN JUHL: ARTFUL PROPORTIONS + EXQUISITE DETAILING

Throughout his career, Finn Juhl designed furniture that transmuted wood into seductive organic forms, and in doing so he helped to revitalize the skill-intensive woodcraft traditions of Danish cabinetmaking. His famous sofa with its distinctive 'floating' backrest, designed for Baker (1951), and his later NV-53 two-seater sofa both have a strongly sculptural bearing, as has his NV-48 chair (1948) with its segmented backrest, which recalls the contemporaneous sculptures of Hans Arp and Alexander Calder. Other pieces by Juhl, such as his Egyptian chair (1949) and Judas dining table (ca. 1950), similarly reveal his almost obsessive attention to proportion and detailing; the latter has a 'constellation' of silver circles inlaid in its richly figured rosewood top. Juhl once observed: 'One cannot create happiness with beautiful objects, but one can spoil quite a lot of happiness with bad ones', which is probably why he always went the extra mile to create the most attractive yet functional designs he could.

Below: NV-53 sofa by Finn Juhl for Niels Vodder (Denmark), 1953

1. NV-48 armchair by Finn Juhl for Niels Vodder (Denmark), 1948

2. Sofa by Finn Juhl for Baker (Denmark/USA), 1951

3. Judas dining table by Finn Juhl for Niels Vodder (Denmark), ca. 1950

4. Egyptian dining chair by Finn Juhl for Niels Vodder (Denmark), 1949

1.

2.

3.

4.

PREBEN FABRICIUS + JØRGEN KASTHOLM

Preben Fabricius and Jørgen Kastholm met at the School of Interior Design in Copenhagen, where they studied under Finn Juhl. They later established a studio together in Gentofte, eastern Denmark, and developed a number of interesting furniture designs together between 1961 and 1968. Most were produced by Danish manufacturers, but some were also manufactured by Alfred Kill, a German design entrepreneur who had a furniture factory in Fellbach, near Stuttgart. In many ways, the two designers were following in the footsteps of Juhl, who had designed for the US market in the 1950s, and the fact that their designs were produced by a German company reflected the growing international reach of Scandinavian design. However, their Scimitar chair (1962), manufactured by Ivan Schlechter of Denmark, is their undeniable masterwork. At the beginning of the 1960s, Kastholm worked in Lebanon, and it was the sweeping lines of the Middle Eastern swords he had seen there that inspired the sculptural form of this design. Two seating designs that possessed similarly evocative, poised forms are the Grasshopper (1968) and Bird (1964), both of which reflected their designers' desire for simplicity, which they saw as the key to producing ideal timeless forms.

Opposite: Scimitar chair Model IS 63 by Preben Fabricius and Jørgen Kastholm for Ivan Schlechter (Denmark), 1962

1. Bird high-backed chair Model FK6726 by Preben Fabricius and Jørgen Kastholm for Alfred Kill (Germany), 1964

2. Grasshopper chaise longue by Preben Fabricius and Jørgen Kastholm for Alfred Kill (Germany), 1968

1.

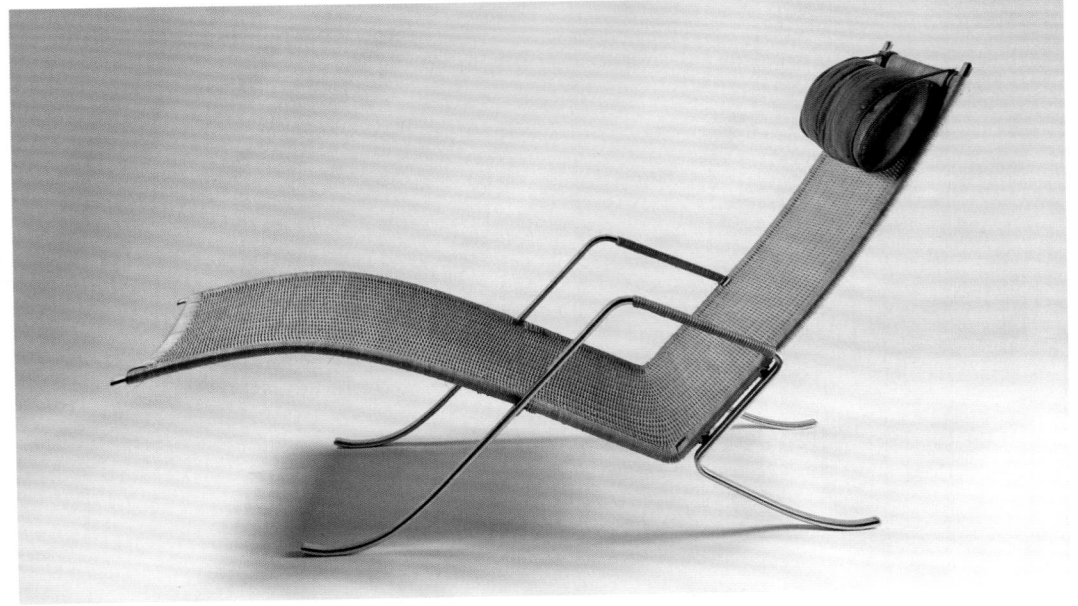

2.

BRUNO MATHSSON

While Alvar Aalto is often credited with forging in the 1930s a more human Scandinavian variation of Modernism, it would be a mistake to think he did this single-handedly, for in Sweden at the same time another designer, Bruno Mathsson, was creating furniture that was equally pioneering and within a similar 'organic design' vein. A fifth-generation cabinetmaker, Mathsson had learned joinery early on in his father's furniture workshop. The crucial skills gleaned from this hands-on experience – involving ten years standing at a lathe making Baroque chairs – allowed him later to develop not only a revolutionary technique for fabricating laminated-wood furniture components, but also a method of bending them using heat, water and pressure. Apart from experimenting with new materials and moulding techniques, Mathsson was also fascinated by the mechanics of sitting, and studied it carefully, with the aim of coming up with seating that provided comfort whether at work or at rest. And that is exactly what he achieved by using ergonomically contoured frames and cradling seating sections made from hemp webbing for, among other designs, his Grasshopper armchair (1931), his Eva chair (1934) and his Pernilla lounge chair (1944) and lounger (1943/44).

1. Pernilla One lounge chair by Bruno Mathsson for Karl Mathsson (Sweden), 1934

2. Eva chair by Bruno Mathsson for Karl Mathsson (Sweden), 1933 – introduced 1941

3. Bruno Mathsson relaxing at his home on a Pernilla Three lounger, designed 1943/44

4. Pernilla Two lounge chair and ottoman by Bruno Mathsson for Karl Mathsson (Sweden), 1944

1.

2.

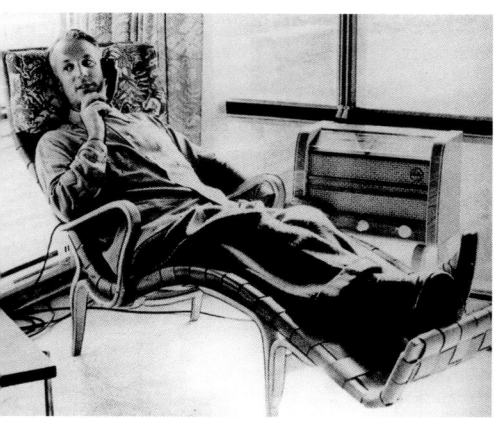

8.

9.

LARSSON + BERG

In the mid 1930s Bruno Mathsson designed a range of seating that incorporated ergonomic laminated-wood frames and woven hemp-webbing seats that cradled the body in comfort without the use of padding (see pp. 118–19). Such was the influence of Mathsson's designs that two other Swedish furniture designers also created similar models. Axel Larsson notably employed a woven webbed seat for an elegant solid-wood-framed armchair that was manufactured by the Svenska Möbelfabrikerna about 1937, while in the early 1940s Gustaf Axel Berg designed a range of chairs with not only woven webbed seats but also ergonomically contoured frames of laminated wood. These included his cantilevered Patronen (Boss), Torparen (Farmer), Husmodern (Housewife) and Tösen (Girl) chairs, and were even more ergonomically refined than Mathsson's earlier designs, being based on Berg's extensive anatomical research into forms that would provide comfortable and healthful support in all the right places. This interest in ergonomic seating became a defining feature of Swedish design, especially in the 1970s, when the country led by example in the field of socially inclusive design.

1. Patronen armchair by Gustaf Axel Berg for G. A. Berg (Sweden), 1942

2. Early photograph of a low-back variant of the Torparen (Farmer) chair by Gustaf Axel Berg for G. A. Berg (Sweden), ca. 1942

3. Early photograph of the Patronen armchair by Gustaf Axel Berg for G. A. Berg (Sweden) – shown in profile

Opposite: Armchair by Axel Larsson for Svenska Möbelfabrikerna (Sweden), ca. 1937

1.

2.   3.

BØRGE MOGENSEN

The 1950s was truly a golden period for Danish furniture, and it is remarkable just how many prodigiously talented designers were working in the Copenhagen area at the time. This was thanks to the excellent training most had received from the likes of Kaare Klint, and was helped by the Danish Cabinetmakers' Guild, which held regular exhibitions that encouraged creative innovation. But what is so striking about these designers is that each had his own distinctive style, and none more so than Børge Mogensen. One of his earliest designs was the Shell chair (1949), which with its sturdy frame and strong profile expressed the robust, no-nonsense masculinity that became his signature style. His Model no. 2229 Hunting chair (1950) was the first of his designs to combine an exposed wooden frame with seat and back slings made of thick saddle leather. This was followed by his similarly constructed Spanish armchair and Model no. 2225 armchair in 1958 and 1959 respectively. These designs typify Mogensen's formal vocabulary, which was often imitated by other designers but never equalled in its sheer bravado.

1. Shell chair by Børge Mogensen for Jeppesen (Denmark), 1949

2. Hunting chairs, Model no. 2229, by Børge Mogensen, executed by Erhard Rasmussen (Denmark), 1950

Opposite: Spanish chair by Børge Mogensen for Fredericia (Denmark), 1958

1.

2.

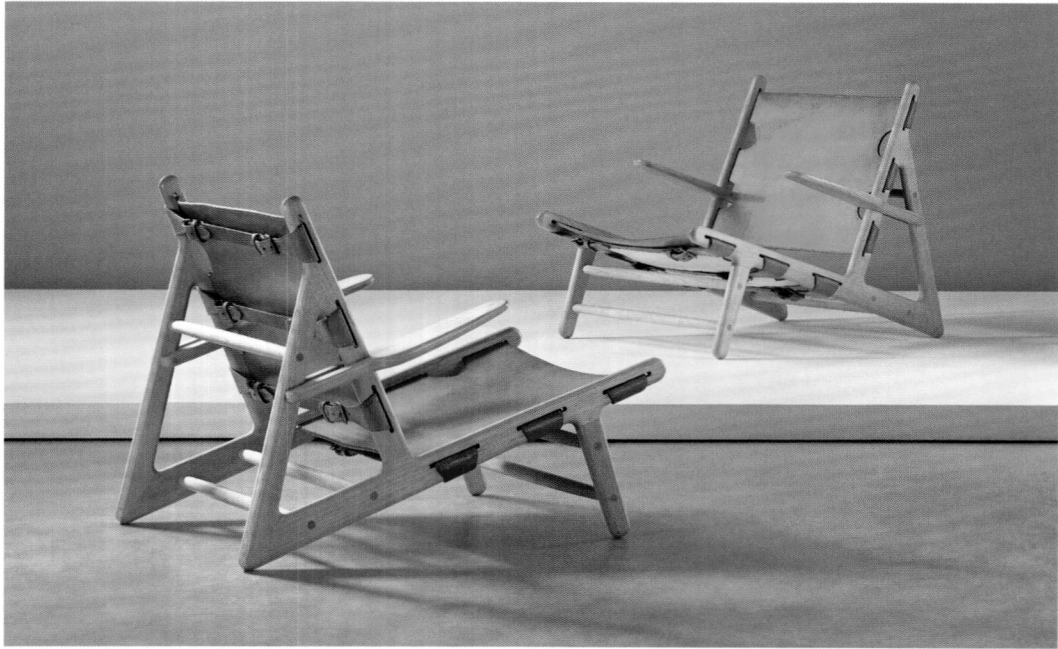

THE ANT CHAIR

The Danish pharmaceutical company Novo Industri was an important client of Arne Jacobsen, and repeatedly commissioned him to design laboratories, administrative buildings and extensions over the decades. One of these extensions incorporated a staff canteen, for which a lightweight, stackable chair was needed. This offered Jacobsen the perfect opportunity to develop his own model in conjunction with the furniture manufacturer Fritz Hansen. The resulting Model no. 3100 stacking chair was initially designed with a three-legged tubular-steel base, on to which a single-piece compound-moulded plywood seat and back section was attached with rubber bumpers and screws. Because the design required the seat to follow the contours of the human body, the continuous plywood shell had to be moulded three-dimensionally. This technique was fraught with complication, as the plywood easily distorted when bent over three planes. Jacobsen, however, got around the problem by giving the shell a waisted form that removed any deformation caused by the critical 90-degree bend where the seat becomes the back. It also meant that no hidden slits were needed, as had been used on an earlier design by the American Ray Komai. Model no. 3100 was, therefore, the first chair to be put into mass-production that actually achieved this great technical leap in seating design. Its biomorphic form also gave the design an endearing character, and today it is affectionately known simply as 'The Ant'.

Below and opposite: Ant chairs and matching table by Arne Jacobsen for Fritz Hansen (Denmark), 1952

JACOBSEN'S PLYWOOD CHAIRS

Like the Ant chair of 1952 (see pp. 124–25), these sculptural seating designs by Arne Jacobsen broke new ground within Danish furniture circles, for they were neither based on historic 'ideal' precedents, nor relied on exquisite craft. Indeed, this series of chairs met the challenges of large-scale mass-production head on by incorporating standardized compound-moulded plywood seat shells that could be attached to a wide variety of bases, depending on the functional requirements. Of this comprehensive range of seating designed by Jacobsen from 1955 to 1970, it was his

Model no. 3107 chair (1955) and its numerous variants from the Series 7 range that became one of the most commercially successful seating programmes ever produced. Inexpensive, lightweight and strong, Jacobsen's iconic plywood 3107 chair brought him widespread international recognition, and since its launch a staggering 7 million have been sold. The longevity of its appeal and its remarkable global success, however, must surely be attributed as much to its characterful, friendly form as to its practical function, since the curved front edge of its seat has a radius that makes it look as though it is smiling.

Below: Series 7 (Model no. 3107) chairs by Arne Jacobsen for Fritz Hansen (Denmark), 1955

1. Grand Prix Model no. 4130 chair by Arne Jacobsen for Fritz Hansen (Denmark), 1957

2. Model no. 3105 chairs by Arne Jacobsen for Fritz Hansen (Denmark), 1955

3. Model no. 3208 armchair by Arne Jacobsen for Fritz Hansen (Denmark), 1970

4. Model no. 3103 chair by Arne Jacobsen for Fritz Hansen (Denmark), 1957

5. Model no. 3207 armchair by Arne Jacobsen for Fritz Hansen (Denmark), 1955

1.

2.

3.

4.

5.

ARNE JACOBSEN: THE EGG + THE SWAN

Between 1957 and 1958 Arne Jacobsen designed two of the most iconic Scandinavian designs of all time, the Egg (Model no. 3316) and Swan (Model no. 3320) chairs, specifically for the SAS Royal Hotel in Copenhagen (see pp. 34–37). These designs can be seen as evolutions of his Ant chairs and Series 7 range (see pp. 124–27) in that they employed in their construction sculptural, ergonomic seat shells, albeit made from Styropor (an expanded polystyrene invented by the plastics firm BASF) rather than moulded plywood. This new synthetic polymer had a greater plasticity, which enabled more fluid forms to be produced. The insides of the self-supporting plastic seat shells were upholstered with a layer of foam rubber that was thinned towards the outer edges. The entire shell was then covered in either a textile or leather. By twinning ergonomically contoured seat shells with foam-rubber upholstery, Jacobsen was able to provide a high degree of comfort without traditional springs, thus reducing overall weight and bulk. This meant that the seat sections could be supported on slender, swivelling pedestal bases, giving the Egg and the Swan a visual lightness that was quintessentially forward-looking.

1. Swan chair, Model no. 3320, by Arne Jacobsen for Fritz Hansen (Denmark), 1957–58

2. The Swan chair being made at Fritz Hansen's factory in Denmark

Opposite: Egg chair, Model no. 3316, and ottoman by Arne Jacobsen for Fritz Hansen (Denmark), 1957–58

1.

2.

ARNE NORELL

The Swedish furniture designer and maker Arne Norell established his own workshop in Sundbyberg, near Stockholm, in 1954, and four years later moved the enterprise to Småland, where it developed into Möbel AB Arne Norell (later Norell Möbel). Norell was a versatile designer who always kept up with the latest trends. He was also very skilled at combining different materials, using turned wood, bentwood, leather, upholstery, textiles and steel in ingenious ways to create constructionally innovative furniture. His Tummen (Thumb) lounge chair (1950–52), with its asymmetrical form, expressed the biomorphic sculptural tendency found in Scandinavian design in the 1950s, while his later chairs and sofas, which included the Sirocco (1964), Ilona (1971), Inca (ca. 1970) and Indra (ca. 1970), incorporated solid wooden frames held together with self-supporting strapped leather covers that were absolutely on-trend for their day. A similar padded-leather seating sling was used for his most celebrated chair, the steel-framed Ari (1966). This quintessential 1960s Scandinavian design received the British Furniture Manufacturers' Showpiece of the Year award in 1973, and has been Norell Möbel's flagship model for more than 40 years.

1. Sirocco armchair by Arne Norell for Möbel AB Arne Norell (Sweden), 1964 – still in production with Norell Möbel

2. Ari chair and footstool by Arne Norell for Möbel AB Arne Norell (Sweden), 1966 – still in production with Norell Möbel

Opposite: Tummen (Thumb) lounge chair by Arne Norell for Möbel AB Arne Norell (Sweden), 1950–52

1.

2.

MOGENS + FLEMMING LASSEN

The Danish brothers Mogens and Flemming Lassen were among the most influential Modernist architect-designers in Scandinavia between and after the wars. Mogens, an acclaimed pioneer of Danish Functionalism inspired by the form-follows-function ideology of the Bauhaus, famously designed the ML42 stool for an exhibition at the Danish Museum of Art and Design (Kunstindustrimuseet) in Copenhagen in 1942. This classic Mid-century design was an elegant Modern reworking of the three-legged stools traditionally used by Danish cobblers. Mogens also designed the stylish leather-slung Saxe folding chair for the Copenhagen Cabinetmakers' Guild competition of 1955. Flemming similarly designed a number of interesting furniture pieces, including a very Modern interpretation of a wing chair that he created as a one-off for himself. Flemming also designed the wonderfully titled Tired Man armchair for the Copenhagen Cabinetmakers' Guild competition of 1935. Flemming noted that he wanted anyone sitting in this easy chair, which was offered in a sheepskin-upholstered option, to feel 'as warm and safe as a polar bear cub in the arms of its mother in the middle of the ice cap'. Today, the Lassen brothers' designs are being painstakingly reissued to the same exacting manufacturing standards as when they debuted, by the Copenhagen-based company By Lassen, founded in 2008 by the brothers' descendants.

Below: ML42 stool by Mogens Lassen for K. Thomsen (Denmark), 1942 – reissued by By Lassen

1. ML10097 Egyptian table by Mogens Lassen for Rud. Rasmussen (Denmark), 1940

2. Mogens Lassen in the gardens of the Danish Museum of Art and Design, Copenhagen, with his Saxe chair (1955) and ML42 stool (1942)

3. Den trætte mand (Tired Man) armchair by Flemming Lassen for A. J. Iversen (Denmark), 1935 – reissued by By Lassen

1.

2.

3.

POUL KJÆRHOLM

Unlike most Danish furniture designers, Poul Kjærholm came to favour steel over wood, and as a result his designs bear a stronger Modernist aesthetic. Having trained as a joiner in the town of Hjørring, he continued his studies at the Kunsthåndværkerskolen in Copenhagen (School of Arts and Crafts; now KADK). Even as a young designer he was interested in the constructional potential of materials, especially steel, which he felt offered the same artistic fineness as any natural material. His earliest furniture was made of wood, however, most notably the sculptural PK0 prototype armchair (1952) he designed while working briefly for Fritz Hansen. Indeed, it was not until Kjærholm started working for his friend Ejvind Kold Christensen in the mid 1950s that he was able to experiment properly with ready-made strips of steel. The resulting range of designs, which included the PK22 lounge chair (1956), PK71 nesting tables (1957) and PK24 hammock chaise longue (1965), exemplified Kjærholm's rare ability to create elegant furniture with simple flowing lines and perfect proportions that humanized modern industrial materials by marrying them harmoniously with natural materials, such as leather and woven cane.

Below: PK0 chair by Poul Kjærholm for Fritz Hansen (Denmark), 1952 – produced as a limited edition of 600 pieces in 1997

1. PK24 chaise longue by Poul Kjærholm for E. Kold Christiansen (Denmark), 1965 – later manufactured by Fritz Hansen

2. PK9 chairs by Poul Kjærholm for E. Kold Christensen (Denmark), 1960 – later manufactured by Fritz Hansen

3. PK71 nesting tables by Poul Kjærholm for E. Kold Christensen (Denmark), 1957 – later manufactured by Fritz Hansen

4. PK22 lounge chairs by Poul Kjærholm for E. Kold Christensen (Denmark), 1956 – later manufactured by Fritz Hansen

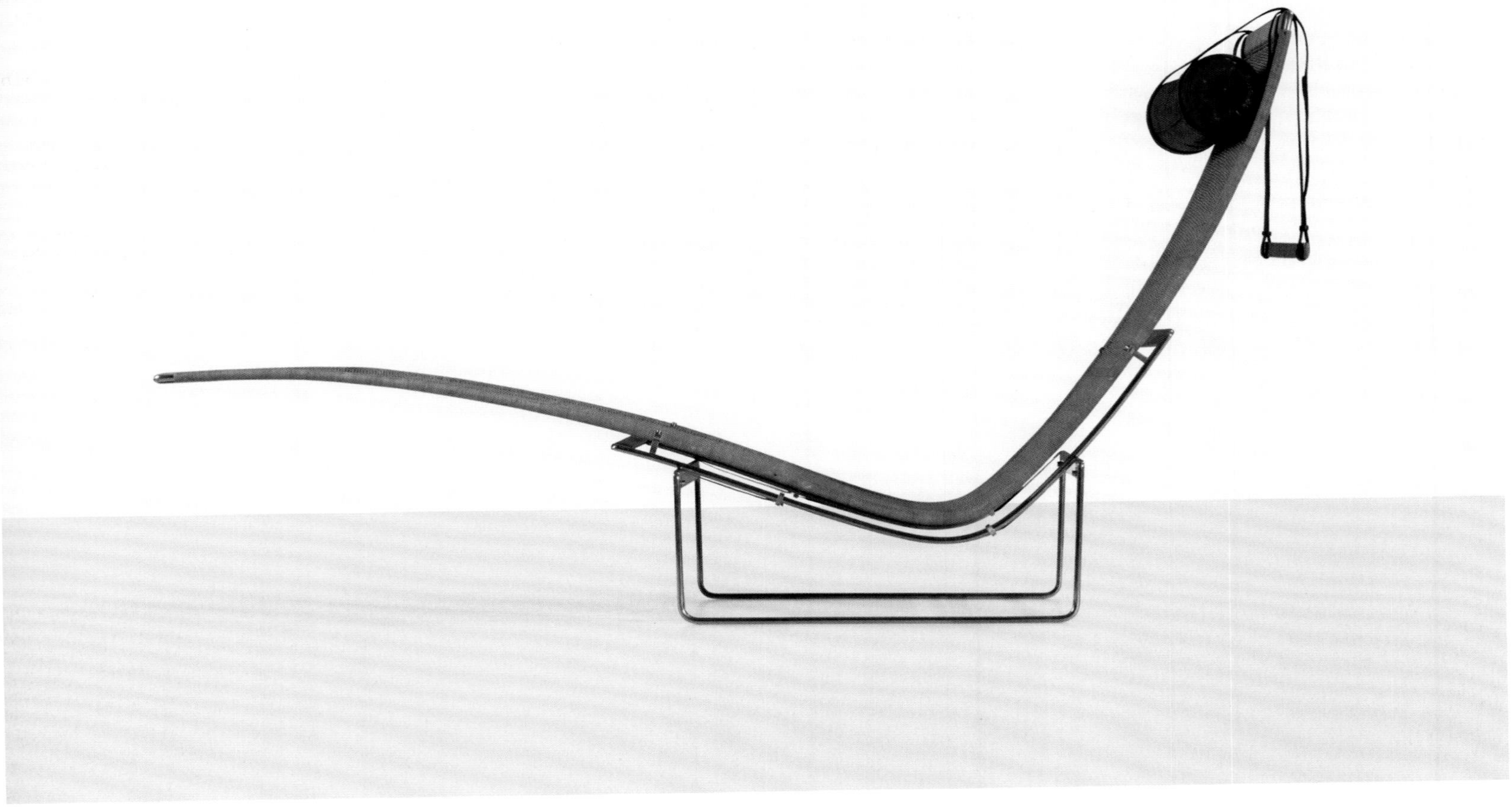

1.

3.

4.

2.

PETER HVIDT +
ORLA MØLGAARD-NIELSEN

Both Orla Mølgaard-Nielsen and Peter Hvidt studied cabinetmaking at the School of Arts and Crafts in Copenhagen; the former continued his studies under Kaare Klint at KADK in Copenhagen, and the latter established his own design practice in 1942. From 1944 to 1965 they worked in partnership, designing furniture for various Danish manufacturers. Their best-known design is the AX chair (1947), which was developed in collaboration with the manufacturer Fritz Hansen. This design pioneered a new manufacturing technique known as 'lamella-gluing', which involved glue-laminating layers of beech

veneer around a solid teak core – in much the same way wooden tennis rackets used to be made. This technique, which provided very great structural strength, was also used to construct Hvidt and Mølgaard-Nielsen's matching AX table (1954) with its distinctive crutch-like legs, and also the X chair (1960). The two men also designed the six-segment Model no. 523 table (ca. 1960) for France & Søn; it could be configured as a round table or, as shown, in a dramatic snaking form. Like other Danish designers, Hvidt and Mølgaard-Nielsen used their cabinetmaking skills to great effect in the design of stylish sideboards, but it is the pioneering AX chair for which they are best remembered.

1. AX chair, Model no. 6020, by Peter Hvidt and Orla Mølgaard-Nielsen for Fritz Hansen (Denmark), 1947

2. AX coffee table, Model no. 6950, by Peter Hvidt and Orla Mølgaard-Nielsen for Fritz Hansen (Denmark), 1954

3. X chair, Model no. 6103, by Peter Hvidt and Orla Mølgaard-Nielsen for Fritz Hansen (Denmark), 1960

4. Model no. 523 table by Peter Hvidt and Orla Mølgaard-Nielsen for France & Søn (Denmark), ca. 1960

5. Model no. 26025 cabinet by Peter Hvidt and Orla Mølgaard-Nielsen for Søborg Møbelfabrik (Denmark), 1965

1.

2.

3

5.

HANS WEGNER

Hans Wegner was the undisputed 'King of Chairs' – the chair aficionado's chair designer of choice. His design-and-making genius was derived from his great skill in cabinet-making, which he acquired as a young apprentice from the German master cabinet-maker H. F. Stahlberg in his native Jutland. He also became well versed in the design-teaching methods of Kaare Klint when he trained under Orla Mølgaard-Nielsen at the School of Arts and Crafts in Copenhagen. It was there that he acquired an analytical approach to problem-solving in design through the precise study of human proportions and the careful assessment of historical furniture. This approach, which centred on the concept of 'ideal forms', acted as a springboard for such later designs as his Peacock chair (1947), the form and construction of which were based closely on a traditional English design known as the Windsor chair. Throughout his career Wegner was also obsessive when it came to the detailing of his designs, believing that 'there is never one damn thing that cannot be made better.'

Below: Hans Wegner with a model of one of his chair designs

Opposite: Peacock chair by Hans Wegner for Johannes Hansen (Denmark), 1947

THE CHAIR

Throughout his career, Hans Wegner was obsessed with the idea of creating 'just one good chair'. In fact, that impetus led him to design over 3,500 chairs, of which a staggering 500 made it into production. Many are now rightfully regarded as design masterpieces that epitomize Danish Modernism – such as the Peacock (pp. 138–39) or Valet chairs. Despite his relentless quest, though, Wegner believed firmly that there was no such thing as

the definitive chair. Nevertheless, and to his great disquiet, his Round chair of 1950 came to be regarded as such. After being selected as the chair to be used by John F. Kennedy and Richard Nixon for the first ever televised presidential election debate, in 1960, the design acquired the moniker 'The Chair' in America. Yet, for all that it encapsulated the very essence of Danish woodcraft and Scandinavian design philosophy, Wegner – with characteristic modesty – always preferred to refer to it as 'The Round One'.

Below: John F. Kennedy sitting in 'The Chair' during the recording of the first US presidential election television debate, 1960

Opposite: Round chair by Hans Wegner for P. P. Møbler (Denmark), 1950 – also known as 'The Chair'

JUST ONE GOOD CHAIR

Constantly experimenting with form, function and material, Wegner tirelessly pursued his goal of creating 'just one good chair'. The result was that he actually created many, spanning the spectrum of seating design, from bespoke art furniture to simple mass-produced models. Yet, whether he was designing a one-off 'throne' or a humble kitchen chair, Wegner was able to give his designs 'a touch of spirit' – a character that helped to engender emotional engagement – and to imbue them with a naturalness that meant, as he put it, that 'they could only be what they were and nothing else'.

Chairs by Hans Wegner:

1. China chair, Model no. 4283, for Fritz Hansen (Denmark), 1944

2. J16 rocking chair for F.D.B. Møbler (Denmark), 1944

3. Wishbone (Y-back) chair for Carl Hansen & Søn (Denmark), 1950

4. Papa Bear chair, Model no. AP19, for A. P. Stolen (Denmark), 1950–51

5. Model no. 1936 lounge chair for Fritz Hansen (Denmark), 1948

6. Dolphin armchair, Model no. JH510, for Johannes Hansen (Denmark), 1950

7. CH28 lounge chair for Carl Hansen & Søn (Denmark), 1951

8. Heart chair for Fritz Hansen (Denmark), 1952

9. Valet chair for Johannes Hansen (Denmark), 1953

10. CH33 chair for Carl Hansen & Søn (Denmark), 1957

11. Ox chair for A. P. Stolen (Denmark), 1960

12. CH07 Shell chair for Carl Hansen & Søn (Denmark), 1963

1.

2.

3.

4.

5.

6.

10.

7.

11.

8.

9.

12.

HALYARD

As well as being the Danish capital, Copenhagen is a busy port with numerous canals intersecting its historic centre. In fact, the whole place has a strongly nautical air, and it is therefore unsurprising that a number of Danish designers incorporated halyard – the hemp or Manila rope used for ships' rigging – into their furniture designs. Good weight-bearing characteristics meant that halyard could provide a comfortable seating cradle without the bulkiness of traditional padded upholstery. It also provided interesting optical qualities. Hans Wegner's Flag Halyard armchair of 1950 is thought to be the first design to incorporate this material in its construction. A year later, Poul Kjærholm designed his elegant PK25 lounge chair, which incorporated a length of halyard line wound around a steel frame. During the 1960s both Peter Karpf and Jørgen Høvelskov also experimented with halyard: the former designed a chair in the form of a giant cat's cradle; the latter one whose form was inspired by the bow of a Viking ship. Wegner returned to halyard later, in the 1980s, this time with his hoop-shaped Circle lounge chair (1986).

1. PK25 chair by Poul Kjærholm for E. Kold Cristiansen (Denmark), 1951 – later manufactured by Fritz Hansen

2. Harp chair by Jørgen Høvelskov for Christensen & Larsen (Denmark), 1968

3. PP130, Circle lounge chair by Hans Wegner for P. P. Møbler (Denmark), 1986

4. Wing lounge chair by Peter Karpf for Christensen & Larsen (Denmark), ca. 1966

5. Flag Halyard ring-chair by Hans Wegner for Getama (Denmark), 1950 – later manufactured by P. P. Møbler

1.

2.

4.

3.

5.

MID-CENTURY IKEA

In 1943 Ingvar Kamprad established a mail-order company called IKEA – the name of which derived from his initials and the first letters of Elmtaryd (the name of the farm on which he grew up) and Agunnaryd (its parish) – that sold pencils, postcards and other small items. Five years later Kamprad began exploring the possibility of selling furniture, since many local farmers made furniture in their spare time to bolster their income. In 1951 the first IKEA furniture catalogue was issued, and four years later the first IKEA-designed furniture was launched. After joining IKEA in 1953, Gillis Lundgren created many of the company's designs in the 1950s, including the Tema bookcase (1955). He is also credited with inspiring the company's adoption of flat-pack, self-assembly furniture, when, after a photo shoot of his Lövet table for the catalogue, he removed its legs so that he could fit it into a car. His Regal bookshelf (1959) was one of the first products sold by IKEA in flat-pack form. And while IKEA was not the first company to sell this kind of furniture, it was the first to develop it commercially in a highly systematic way. (See also pp. 190–91.)

1. Lövet table by Gillis Lundgren for IKEA (Sweden), 1956 – reissued as the Lövbacken table in 2013

2. IKEA advertisement promoting the Lövet table, ca. 1953

3. Winni chairs, manufactured by IKEA (Sweden), 1956

4. Tema bookcase/shelving unit by Gillis Lundgren for IKEA (Sweden), 1955

5. Korsör sideboard, manufactured by IKEA (Sweden), 1967

2.

1.

3.

4.

5.

'NORWEGIAN' MODERN

Although Norway's design output is less well-known than that of its Nordic neighbours, a few years ago certain Mid-century furniture pieces by Norwegian designers – or thought to be by Norwegian designers – began realizing impressive prices at auction. The phenomenon was fuelled by the massive oil revenues Norway has enjoyed since the 1970s, and especially since the turn of the millennium, which have transformed this small nation into the fifteenth biggest oil producer in the world. When a previously overlooked design, now better known as the Clam chair, was mistakenly attributed to a little-known Norwegian designer called Martin Olsen – and because the sheepskin-covered piece was thought to be 'Norwegian-designed' – it started making waves in the international auction market, as Norway's cash-rich oil executives vied with one another to acquire an example of this home-grown 'design classic'. It transpired, however, that the chair was actually by the Danish architect Philip Arctander – whose reputation has since risen considerably with the help of the prices his misattributed pieces achieved at auction. Nevertheless, other designs of solid Norwegian origin are worthy of special mention, notably a range of chairs by Hans Brattrud, cleverly constructed from strips of plywood, and the Falcon chair by Sigurd Ressell, which epitomizes the wood-and-leather look of the 1970s.

Below: Clam chair by Philip Arctander for Nordisk Staal- & Møbler Central (Denmark), 1944

1. Scandia Senior lounge chair by Hans Brattrud for Hove Möbler (Norway), 1957 – later manufactured by Fjordfiesta

2. Cabinet by Philip Arctander for Nordisk Staal- & Møbler Central (Denmark), ca. 1950

3. Falcon lounge chairs and matching table by Sigurd Ressell for Vatne Möbler (Norway), ca. 1969–70

2.

.

3.

1.

2.

MODERN ICELANDIC FURNITURE

Icelandic furniture designers have always suffered from a lack of local raw materials, for, unlike their Nordic neighbours, they do not have a plentiful supply of timber to hand, nor ready access to materials such as steel. In fact, virtually everything must be imported. Despite this considerable drawback, there has still been a local need for furniture, and Icelandic designers have risen to the task in innovative ways. In the 1950s and 1960s the government banned the importation of furniture, which led to the founding of several indigenous small-scale manufacturers to supply the home market. The results of this initiative included Helgi Hallgrímsson's stylish rocking chair (1958) for FHI and Gunnar Magnússon's Apollo lounge chair and matching table (1967) for Kristján Ásgeirsson. The cylindrical staging sections of the *Saturn V* moon rocket used by NASA for its Apollo space missions inspired the latter design, as its name suggests. Another Icelandic design that has become something of a classic is the Fuzzy stool of 1972 by Sigurður Már Helgason. Upholstered in shaggy, long-stranded Icelandic sheepskin, this charming footstool was originally designed by Helgason, who had trained as a woodcarver at the Icelandic School of Arts and Crafts in Reykjavík, as a confirmation gift for girls.

1. Rocking chair by Helgi Hallgrímsson for FHI (Iceland), 1958

2. Apollo lounge chair by Gunnar Magnússon for Kristján Ásgeirsson (Iceland), 1967

Below: Fuzzy stools by Sigurður Már Helgason for Fuzzy (Iceland), 1972

GRETE JALK

Grete Jalk designed numerous pieces of solid wood furniture, but it is for her sculptural plywood pieces that she is now best remembered. Having trained as a joiner at the School of Arts and Crafts in Copenhagen, she later studied at the furniture school of KADK under Kaare Klint, who taught his students the importance of anthropometrics and the analysis of seminal furniture archetypes. In 1946, having completed her studies, Jalk won first prize in the annual Cabinetmakers' Guild competition in Copenhagen. She opened her own studio in 1953 and began designing elegant Modern pieces based on traditional furniture types, notable for their invisible joints and subtle organic lines. In the early 1960s, however, inspired by the furniture of Alvar Aalto and Charles Eames, Jalk began experimenting with laminated wood and moulded plywood. This led to some very innovative and sculptural furniture, such as her well-known two-piece chair (1963). As a prominent member of the Danish design community, Jalk also helped to publicize Scandinavian design internationally through her editorship of *Mobilia* magazine (see pp. 562–63) and with her design of several government-sponsored travelling exhibitions.

Below: Laminated chair by Grete Jalk for P. Jeppesens Møbelfabrik (Denmark), 1963

Opposite: Lounge chairs by Grete Jalk for France & Søn (Denmark), 1968

NANNA + JØRGEN DITZEL

Nanna Hauberg and Jørgen Ditzel met in 1943 while they were both studying furniture design in Copenhagen, and, as Nanna later recalled, it was love at first sight. The following year they exhibited together at the Cabinetmakers' Guild exhibition, and in 1946 they married and established their own design studio. For the next 15 years they worked side by side, designing numerous pieces of furniture as well as jewellery (see pp. 514–15). In 1954 they were asked by Poul Kold, who owned a sawmill in Kerteminde, to create furniture designs for his company. This resulted in, among other things, the Ditzels' well-known

Ring lounge chair (1958) and an elegant armchair and ottoman – unofficially called the 'Nursing' chair (1956), both of which incorporated then state-of-the-art latex foam upholstery. Sadly, however, in 1961 this fruitful design partnership came to an abrupt end, when Jørgen died after a stomach operation, leaving Nanna to pursue her design career alone, which she did with remarkable grace and flair. Over four-and-a-half decades she forged a reputation as 'The First Lady of Danish Furniture Design' by creating not only upholstered furniture, but also children's furniture, wicker furniture and experimental plywood furniture, always pushing material, technological and aesthetic boundaries.

Below: 'Nursing' chair with ottoman by Nanna and Jørgen Ditzel for Kolds Savværk (Denmark), 1956

1. Ring lounge chairs by Nanna and Jørgen Ditzel for Kolds Savværk (Denmark), 1958

2. Chair by Nanna Ditzel for Poul Christiansen (Denmark), 1962

3. George Tanier Inc., advertisement for the Ring chair by Nanna and Jørgen Ditzel, ca. 1958

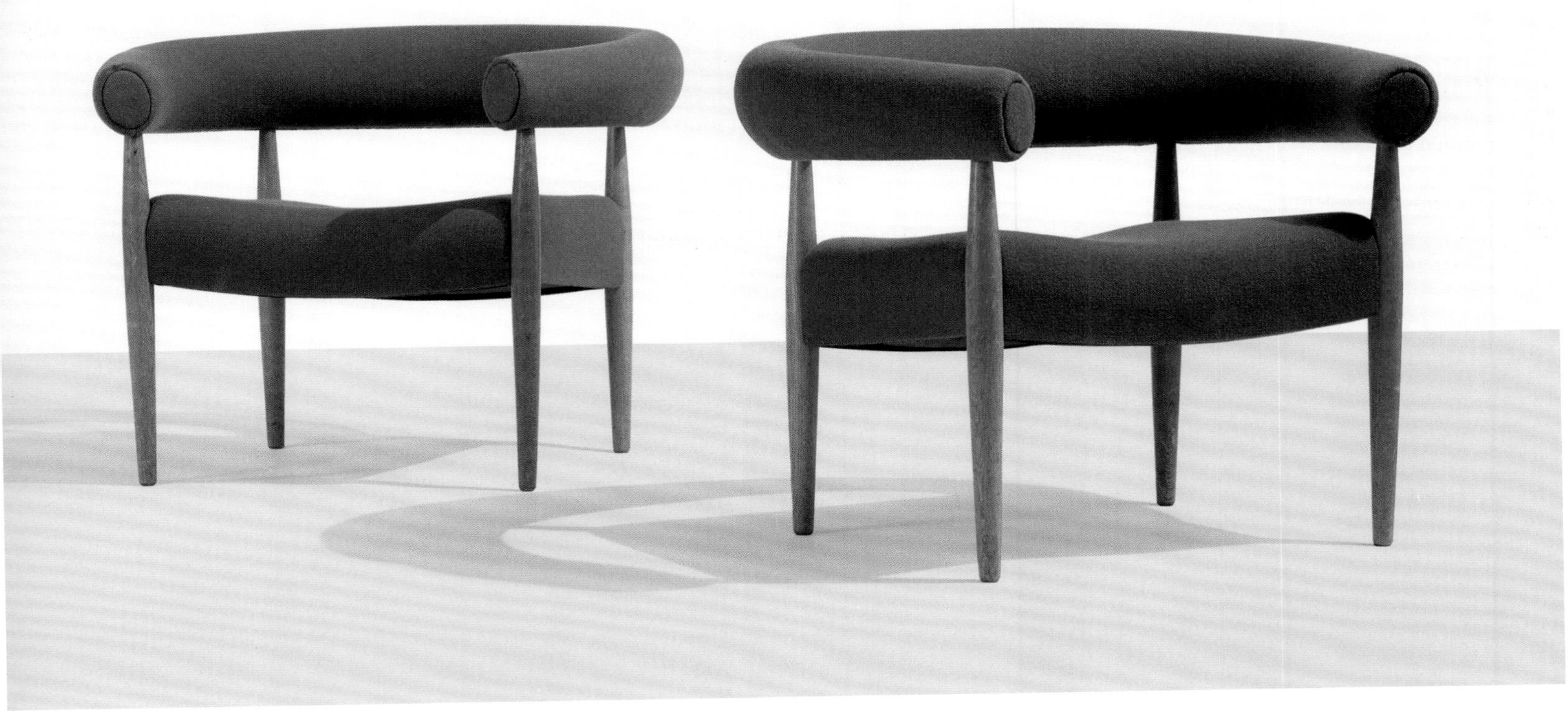

1.

2.

3.

RING CHAIR
DESIGNED BY Nanna + Jørgen Ditzel
SELECTED IN DENMARK BY
GEORGE TANIER INC
521 MADISON AVE., NEW YORK 22, N.Y. THROUGH DEALERS, DECORATORS, ARCHITECTS

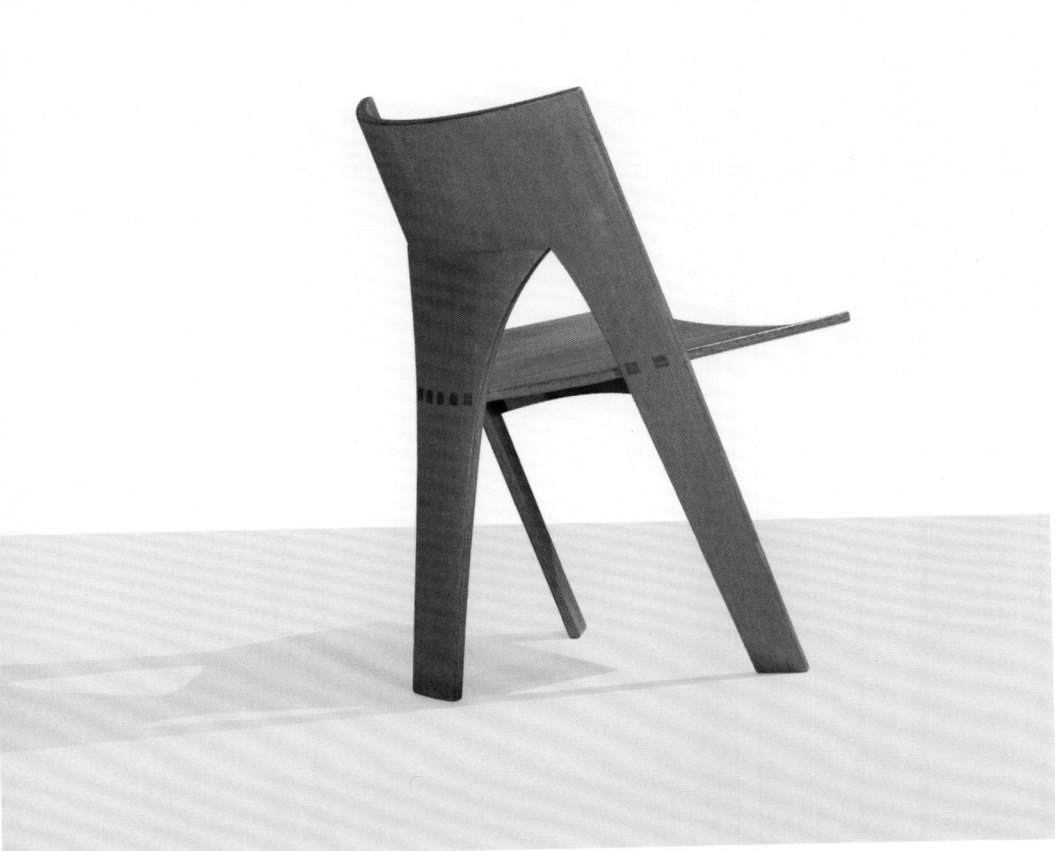

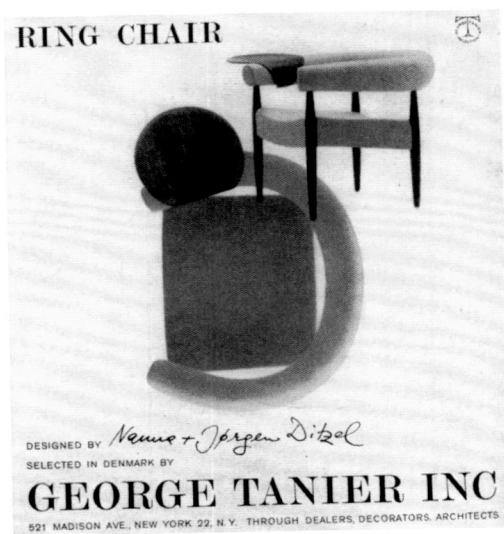

DITZEL'S DESIGNS FOR CHILDREN

In 1955 Nanna and Jørgen Ditzel designed an oak high chair, which was manufactured by Kolds Savværk and subsequently enjoyed a large amount of attention from the international design press. It is not surprising, therefore, that when Ditzel found herself suddenly widowed in 1961, and looking after three infants by herself, she again turned her attention to the design of children's furniture. In 1962 she designed her famous Trisser (Toadstool), inspired by her observations that 'children never sit still for two minutes; they get up, stand on the chair and subsequently it tips over.' Her design allowed a child to turn while remaining seated, and the stools could also be stacked like a toy. Following on from this, Ditzel created more children's furniture for Kolds in 1963. This new collection included a bunk bed, an indoor climbing frame and her Lulu cradle (named after one of her twin daughters), all of which were made from Oregon pine. *Mobilia* magazine noted in its review of these designs: 'Nanna Ditzel belongs to the few independent and untraditional furniture designers … her designs show her ideas and way of work, which is both human and natural.'

Below: Children's high chair by Nanna and Jørgen Ditzel for Kolds Savværk (Denmark), 1955

1. Nanna and Jørgen Ditzel's neighbour's daughter photographed with the Toadstool children's stools designed by Nanna Ditzel for Kolds Savværk (Denmark), 1962

2. Lulu cradle by Nanna Ditzel for Kolds Savværk (Denmark), 1963

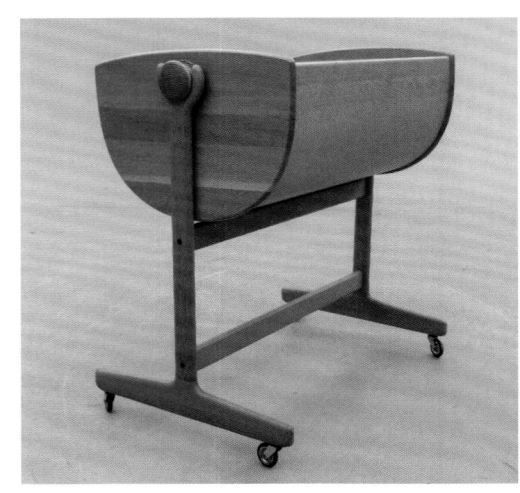

2.

ILMARI TAPIOVAARA

Ilmari Tapiovaara was a leading designer in Finland, who also enjoyed international recognition for his innovative furniture designs. He graduated as an interior architect from Helsinki's Central School of Industrial Arts in 1937. He then spent six months working in Le Corbusier's office in Paris before being appointed art director of Asko, then the largest furniture manufacturer in Finland. In 1941 Tapiovaara joined the firm's rival Keravan Puuteollisuus, and it was there that he created one of his best-known designs, the stacking Domus chair (1946). In about 1950 Tapiovaara founded a design office with his architect wife, Annikki, and subsequently worked as a freelance furniture designer. A slew of stylish seating designs ensued, notably the Lukki chair (1951), the Pirkka chair, stools and bench (1955), the Mademoiselle lounge chair (1956) and the Crinolette armchair (1962). Incorporating solid wood elements, these remarkable designs – although thoroughly Modern – were all based on earlier ideal furniture forms. By contrast, Tapiovaara's Wilhelmiina stacking chair of 1959 employed a laminated-wood frame that was totally original in form. Throughout his career, spanning four decades, Tapiovaara relentlessly pursued the goal of the universal multipurpose chair, and in the process created many excellent seating solutions that have gone on to stand the test of time both aesthetically and functionally.

1. Pirkka chair by Ilmari Tapiovaara for Laukaan Puu (Finland), 1955

2. Mademoiselle lounge chair by Ilmari Tapiovaara for Laukaan Puu (Finland), 1956

3. Domus stacking chairs by Ilmari Tapiovaara for Keravan Puuteollisuus (Finland), 1946 – originally exported as the Finnchair and later produced by Wihl. Schauman

4. Domus lounge chair by Ilmari Tapiovaara for Keravan Puuteollisuus (Finland), 1946

1.

2.

4.

YNGVE EKSTRÖM

In 1999 the Swedish design magazine *Sköna Hem* (Sweet Home) asked its readers to vote for their favourite twentieth-century piece of furniture. They chose the Lamino lounge chair (1956), a piece that encapsulates the essence of Mid-century Scandinavian Modernism with its graceful form and practical human-centric functionality. Its creator, Yngve Ekström, was born in Småland in southern Sweden and began working in the local furniture factory when he was just 13 years old. His natural talent for carpentry and this early on-the-job experience gave him an in-depth understanding of materials and techniques, which he later put to good use as a designer. In 1945 Ekström co-founded Swedese in Vaggeryd, and he led the firm for more than four decades. During this period he designed over 150 different pieces of furniture, lighting and textiles that made it into production. Crucially, Ekström was able to transfer the values of quality and beauty associated with traditional craftsmanship into Modern designs suitable for industrial production. But beyond this, it was his commitment to simplicity that set his furniture apart, for, as he once observed, 'He who has already matured to appreciate great simplicity does not need a large apparatus to lead a good life, neither for his body nor for his soul.'

Below: Lamino lounge chair and ottoman by Yngve Ekström for Swedese (Sweden), 1956

1. Arka chair by Yngve Ekström for Stolab (Sweden), 1955

2. Pinocchio chairs by Yngve Ekström for Stolab (Sweden), ca. 1955

1.

2.

1.

2.

3.

WOODCRAFT DESIGN

One of the greatest defining attributes of Mid-century Modern Scandinavian furniture is its exemplary craftsmanship, which has imbued many designs with a sense of both enduring quality and timeless beauty. Because of the centuries-old tradition of handcraftsmanship in the Nordic countries, and the fact that industrialization came relatively late to the region, many Scandinavian designers learned crucial woodworking skills from master craftsmen in local workshops. But, over and above this, these countries (except Iceland) also had a very strong and pervasive woodcraft culture, being so densely forested. Certain mid-century designers, such as Jens Quistgaard and Niels Vodder in Denmark and Tapio Wirkkala in Finland, became virtuoso masters of woodcraft, who skilfully created furniture from many different timbers, including imported varieties such as teak. Their designs radically pushed the aesthetic and technical boundaries of traditional Nordic furniture-making to create what can only be described as a design-led art form.

Valhalla bar stool by Jens Quistgaard for IHQ (Denmark), 2001

Stick lounge chairs by Jens Quistgaard for Richard Nissen (Denmark), 1966

Rosewood and laminate sideboard by Arne Vodder for Sibast Møbler (Denmark), 1950s

X-frame table by Tapio Wirkkala for Asko (Finland), 1958 – this example came from Wirkkala's own studio

Nikke chairs by Tapio Wirkkala for Asko (Finland), 1958

Laminated table by Tapio Wirkkala for Asko (Finland), 1958

4.

5.

6.

SCANDI-SCULPTURAL CONFIDENCE

In the 1950s Scandinavian design was seen as the embodiment of good taste, and the refined furniture designs by Arne Jacobsen and Hans Wegner, for example, held up as shining exemplars of good design. Inspired by the biomorphic forms coming out of the USA, however, a much more sculpturally expressive tendency began to emerge in the middle of the decade in Scandinavian design circles. One of the earliest designs to reveal this new direction was the three-legged Arabesk lounge chair (1955) by the Swedish designer Folke Jansson, with its dramatically sweeping back rail arcing from one leg to another.

In Denmark, this emerging sculptural confidence was exemplified in Poul Volther's Corona chair (1961) with its 'floating' segmented back that was reputedly inspired by time-lapse photographs of a lunar eclipse. By the late 1960s and early 1970s, Scandinavian furniture designers, like their peers in Italy, were fully exploring the expressive potential of foam rubber and other new materials in order to create body-hugging seating forms with strong biomorphic character. Gösta Berg and Stenerik Eriksson's Seagull armchair and ottoman (1968) and Jan Ekselius's Etcetera lounge chair and ottoman (1970) are perhaps the most visually stunning examples of them all.

Below: Seagull armchair and ottoman by Gösta Berg and Stenerik Eriksson for Fritz Hansen (Denmark), 1968

1. Etcetera lounge chair and ottoman by Jan Ekselius for J. O. Carlsson (Sweden), 1970 – also known as the Jan chair

2. Corona chair by Poul Volther for Erik Jørgensen (Denmark), 1961

3. Arabesk lounge chair by Folke Jansson for S. M. Wincrantz (Sweden), 1955

3.

THE PANTON CHAIR

The culmination of years of research, the Panton chair was the world's first single-material, single-form chair to be produced in injection-moulded plastic. Verner Panton designed its progenitor, the cantilevered S-chair made from a single piece of moulded plywood, in 1955, and in the late 1950s, in collaboration with the manufacturer Dansk Akryl Teknik, he began developing a prototype of a similarly S-formed chair made of vacuum-formed Polysteron. The goal was to mass-produce it in injection-moulded plastic, but because of its high development costs none of the manufacturers Panton approached were prepared to take the risky investment. In 1963, however, he contacted the owners of Vitra – Willi and Rolf Fehlbaum – who immediately saw the chair's potential and decided to underwrite its development. For the next four years Panton worked with Vitra's technicians to hone the design, making it sleeker and better able to stack. When launched in 1967 it was made in cold-pressed fibreglass, and the following year it was produced in polyurethane hard foam using a new reaction injection-moulded (RIM) process, but both these plastics were too rigid for comfort. In 1971, after slight modification, the Panton chair was finally able to be injection-moulded in an ASA thermoplastic that proved to be the ideal material for its mass-manufacture, and also provided enough springy resilience for comfort.

1 & opposite: Panton chair by Verner Panton for Vitra (Switzerland), first released in 1967

2. Early publicity photograph of the Panton chair, ca. 1967

1.

2.

PANTON'S CONE CHAIRS

In the late 1950s Verner Panton designed his revolutionary Series K range of 'cone' chairs, stools and tables, which powerfully presaged his bolder and more sculptural designs from the 1960s (see pp. 170–71) and cemented his credentials as one of the most radical furniture designers of his generation. His K1 Cone chair (1958) was designed for the restaurant of the Komi-gen (Come Again) inn on the island of Funen, where his father was the publican. The distinctive foam-upholstered inverted-cone form of this novel design, tapering down to a simple X-shaped metal base, radically eliminated the need for traditional chair legs, giving the piece an extraordinarily futuristic aesthetic. The chair was subsequently put into production by Plus-Linje, as were three other variations of it: the K2 Wire Cone chair, the K3 Heart Cone chair and the K4 Pyramid Cone chair. All were designed in 1958–60 and were just as sculptural and eye-catching as the K1.

1. Publicity photograph of the Heart Cone chair, Model no. K3, by Verner Panton for Plus-Linje, ca. 1960

2. Pyramid Cone chair, Model no. K4, by Verner Panton for Plus-Linje (Denmark), 1958–60

3. Cone chairs, Model no. K1, by Verner Panton for Plus-Linje (Denmark), 1958–60

Opposite: Heart Cone chair, Model no. K3, by Verner Panton for Plus-Linje (Denmark), 1958–60

1.

2.

3.

PANTON + EXPERIMENTATION

In the 1960s and 1970s Verner Panton developed numerous groundbreaking seating designs that pushed aesthetic, functional and technical boundaries, and that were the antithesis of Danish design tradition, which for decades had been guided by the notion of ideal archetypal forms. His Living Tower (1968–69), for example, comprised two highly sculptural foam-upholstered elements that when placed together provided four seating levels. This design reflected the 1960s interest in the idea of 'interior landscapes', and as such speculated on new ways of living. His later Pantonova and

1-2-3 System ranges, both manufactured by Fritz Hansen, might have been less radical in terms of their function, but they were arguably just as revolutionary aesthetically and technically. Panton explained: 'The main purpose of my work is to provoke people into using their imagination. Most people spend their lives living in dreary, grey-beige conformity, mortally afraid of using colours. By experimenting with lighting, colours, textiles and furniture and utilizing the latest technologies, I try to show new ways, to encourage people to use their "phantasy" imagination and make their surroundings more exciting.'

Below: Living Tower by Verner Panton for Herman Miller/Vitra (Switzerland), 1968–69 – also sometimes referred to as the Pantower

1. Pantonova chairs, Model 113T, by Verner Panton for Fritz Hansen (Denmark), 1971

2. Pantonova reclining chair and ottoman, Models 125T and 126S, by Verner Panton for Fritz Hansen (Denmark), 1971

3. 1-2-3 System chairs, Model A, by Verner Panton for Fritz Hansen (Denmark), 1973

4. Page from a *Mobilia* issue dedicated to the work of Verner Panton, showing chairs from his 1-2-3 System range, 1970s

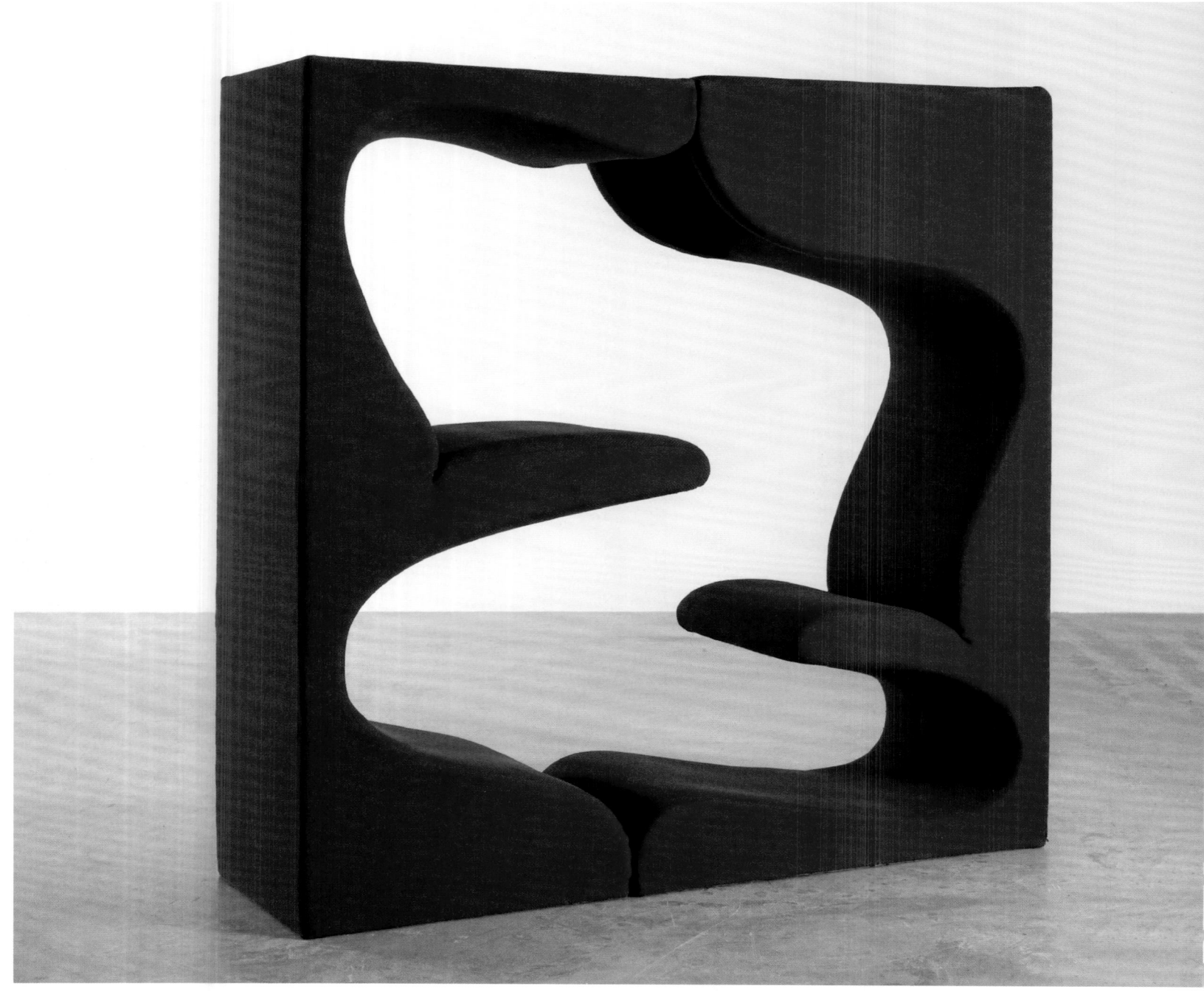

1.

2.

3.

4.

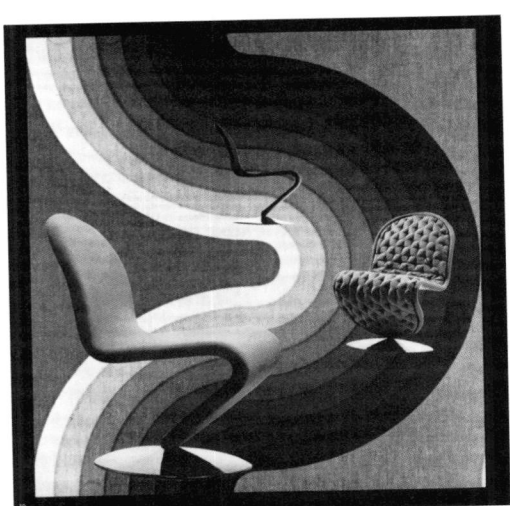

STEEN ØSTERGAARD

After World War II, new plastics began coming on to the market that offered designers the tantalizing potential to create what is essentially the holy grail of chair design: a single-form, single-material unit. Over the years, many designers tried unsuccessfully to achieve this goal of total structural unity, but Verner Panton eventually made the breakthrough with his iconic S-shaped Panton chair, which was famously launched by Vitra in 1967 (see pp. 166–67). Three years later, however, his fellow Dane Steen Østergaard launched another single-form, single-material chair – the Model no. 290. In a number of important ways it was a more resolved design: it used less material, stacked more efficiently and was far more comfortable. It was the first chair to be injection-moulded entirely in glass-filled nylon, a composite material with remarkable strength and resistance to wear and weather. Lightweight yet with enough springy resilience for comfort, Østergaard's Model no. 290 and his related range of seating for CADO, which included ever-so-stylish tub chairs and a lounge chair and ottoman, were elegant examples of how state-of-the-art plastics were being used by Scandinavian designers to create durable, high-quality designs that were the very antithesis of the Pop throwaway culture of the 1960s.

1. Model no. 265 lounge chair by Steen Østergaard for CADO (Denmark), ca. 1970

2. Model no. 290 stacking chair by Steen Østergaard for CADO (Denmark), 1966–68

3. Early promotional photograph of Model no. 290 stacking chairs by Steen Østergaard grouped around a table, ca. 1970

Opposite: Model no. 291 armchairs by Steen Østergaard for CADO (Denmark), ca. 1970

1.

2.

3.

CADOVIUS + STRINNING

Poul Cadovius's Royal System shelving (1948) was developed as a means of freeing up living space from unwanted clutter. His rationale was that 'if we were to use the walls in the same way we use the floor, we would get more space to live in.' Functional and flexible, the elegant Royal System was a highly efficient design that became an instant international success. In fact, its Danish creator had to establish his own manufacturing company, CADO, in the late 1950s in order to meet demand. The year after Cadovius had designed his Royal System, the Swedish designer Nils Strinning came up with a very Swedish shelving solution that had an even more functionalist edge with its ladder-like metal supports. This ingenious solution was originally developed for a bookshelf-design competition held by the Swedish media group Bonnier in 1949. It won the competition and was put into production the same year. In 1950 the String shelving system was specified for the newly built United Nations building in New York, cementing for all time its international design credentials.

1 & 2. String shelving system by Nils Strinning for String Design (Sweden), 1949

3 & opposite: Royal System shelving by Poul Cadovius for CADO (Denmark), 1948

1.

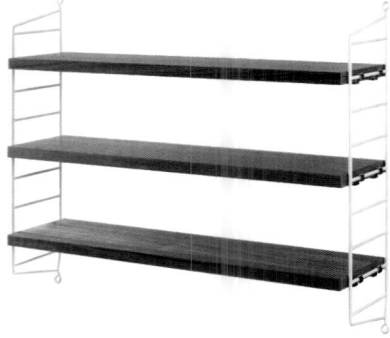

3.

2.

EERO AARNIO

Eero Aarnio's famous Ball chair (1963) made its debut at the Cologne Furniture Fair in 1966, and proclaimed a new direction for Finnish design that was both forward-looking and futuristic. It was followed in 1967 by another fibreglass design, the low-slung Pastillichair, which was intended for both indoor and outdoor use. But perhaps the most curious and quirky of all Aarnio's designs is the Pony (1973), which took the cartoonized form of an animal and was more interactive sculptural plaything than serious seating solution.

This design reflected the blurring of boundaries between art and design, which – while common in Italy – was less of a tendency in Scandinavian design. Aarnio acknowledges that sometimes his designs come from his dreams or imagination, but at other times they are prompted by the desire to solve a real problem, which explains why certain of his pieces have a rather curious, whimsical quality: 'I began to design furniture, because a piece of furniture is the most important and most prominent product of an interior, and a chair is the most difficult and most fascinating thing to design.'

Below: Tomato lounge chair by Eero Aarnio for Asko (Finland), 1972

1. Pony chair by Eero Aarnio for Asko (Finland), 1973 – reissued by Adelta in 1990

2. Pastilli chair by Eero Aarnio for Asko (Finland), 1967 – later manufactured by Adelta

3. Eero Aarnio in the Ball (Globe) chair, ca. 1962

4. Ball (Globe) chair by Eero Aarnio for Asko (Finland), 1962 – later manufactured by Eero Aarnio Originals

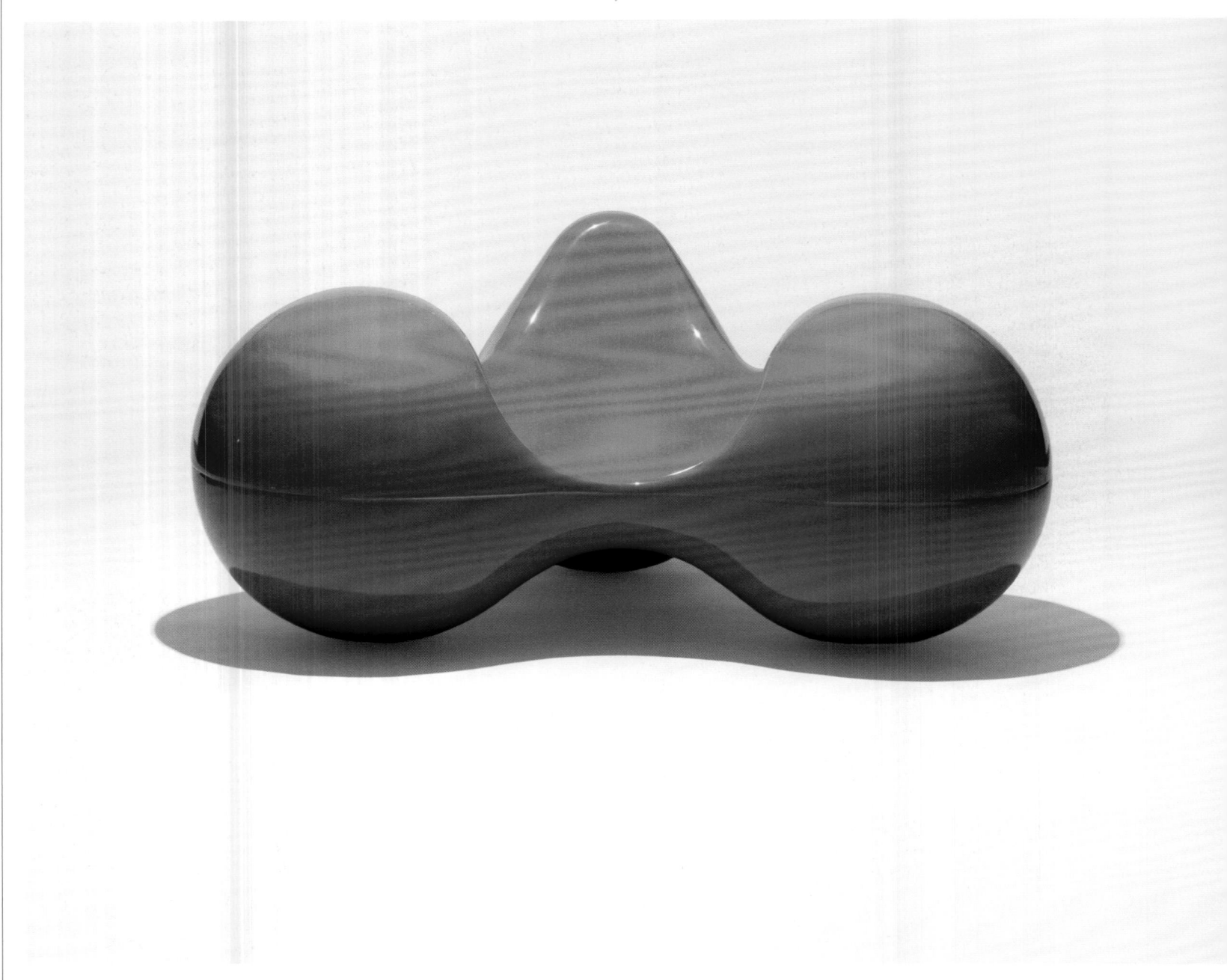

2.

4.

YRJÖ KUKKAPURO

Throughout his long career, Yrjö Kukkapuro has been one of the great innovators of Finnish furniture design. In 1956, while studying interior design at the Institute of Industrial Arts in Helsinki, he co-founded the furniture company Moderno, which produced his Lokki and Lukku chairs that year. The following year the latter design was selected by the designer Antti Nurmesniemi for display at the exhibition 'Tulevaisuuden Koti' (Home of the Future) in Helsinki, and that helped to establish Kukkapuro's reputation in Finland as an up-and-coming designer. In 1959 he established his own design studio, and during the

1960s he produced designs that were as notable for their pioneering ergonomics as for their state-of-the-art plastic construction, including the fibreglass-shelled Karuselli (Carousel) lounge chair (1964–65). The spineline of this landmark design was famously based on the imprint Kukkapuro's body made in the snow. After the oil crisis of 1973, Kukkapuro began using moulded plywood instead of synthetic polymers in his seating designs, leading to the development of various innovative office chairs including the Fysio (1976). In the 1980s he also produced a number of Postmodern seating designs with a strongly graphic outline – a trait that is characteristic of Finnish design in general.

Below: Karuselli rocking lounge chair with ottoman by Yrjö Kukkapuro for Haimi (Finland), 1964–65

1. Haimi brochure featuring the Model nos. 414 and 415 chairs by Yrjö Kukkapuro, ca. 1964

2. Model no. 415 side chairs by Yrjö Kukkapuro for Haimi (Finland), 1964

2.

ANTTI NURMESNIEMI

A pioneer of modern 'Finnish Form', Antti Nurmesniemi was not only a skilled designer working in the fields of interiors, furniture and products, but also an influential design educator. After graduating from the University of Art and Design in Helsinki, he worked as a furniture designer for Stockmann before joining the architecture practice of Viljo Revell as a furniture and interior designer in 1951. The following year Nurmesniemi designed his well-known horseshoe-shaped Sauna stool for the Palace Hotel in Helsinki. In 1954–55 he worked in the Milanese architectural practice

of Giovanni Romano, which undoubtedly had a formative influence on his development as a designer of stylishly modern furnishings – such as his 001 chair (1960), also known as the Triennale chair because it was specially created for display at the 12th Milan Triennial. Sometimes he would upholster his furniture with textiles designed by his wife, Vuokko Nurmesniemi, as seen on the chaise longue below. One of the great international ambassadors of twentieth-century Finnish design, Antti Nurmesniemi once declared: 'Design is a language of cultural policy that has reached a material form.'

Opposite: 001 Triennale side chair by Antti Nurmesniemi for J. Merivaara (Finland), 1960 – later manufactured by Piiroinen

1. Sauna stools by Antti Nurmesniemi for G. Soderstrom (Finland), 1952

2. Chaise longue by Antti Nurmesniemi for Vuokko (Finland), ca. 1970

2.

NEO-RATIONALISM

In the late 1960s a Neo-Rationalist style appeared in Swedish and Danish furniture design that coincided with the international emergence of the High-Tech style in architecture. Indeed, these two trends would eventually intertwine completely, as this new kind of furniture from Scandinavia became a ubiquitous feature of many High-Tech interiors in the early 1970s. Together the designers Börge Lindau and Bo Lindekrantz developed one of the most successful furniture ranges exemplifying this new back-to-modern-design-basics movement; it incorporated thick-gauge tubular metal and was manufactured by Lammhults. The design team of Jan Dranger and Johan Huldt, likewise, used industrial processes to create lightweight and functional furniture under their Innovator Design label, which was retailed by the likes of Roche Bobois and Habitat. The two men also designed enamelled tubular-metal furniture with washable seat covers for IKEA. This type of furniture, although essentially channelling the spirit of 1930s Swedish Functionalism, was very much of its time, and hugely influential. In Denmark the Neo-Rationalist style was expressed in the work of Erik Magnussen, whose ingenious Z-Down folding lounge chair (1966) also employed a lightweight yet sturdy tubular-metal frame.

Below: Z-Down folding lounge chairs by Erik Magnussen for Torben Ørskov & Co. (Denmark), 1966

1. S70-3 bar stool by Börge Lindau and Bo Lindekrantz for Lammhults (Sweden), 1968

2. Armchair by Jan Dranger and Johan Huldt (attributed) for IKEA (Sweden), ca. 1970

3. S70-5 sofa by Börge Lindau and Bo Lindekrantz for Lammhults (Sweden), 1968

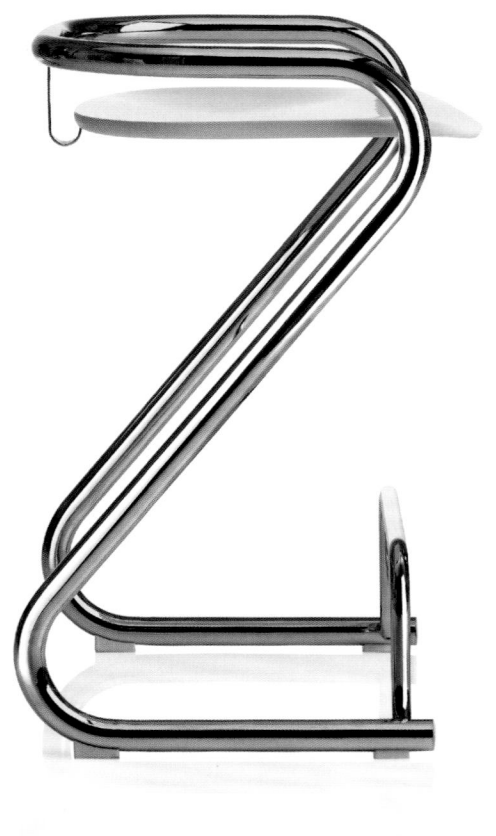

1.

2.

3.

PETER OPSVIK

The Norwegian designer Peter Opsvik has spent the whole of his career – spanning more than 45 years – creating designs based on the idea of dynamic sitting. One of his first successes was the ingenious Tripp Trapp child's chair, devised in 1972, which has adjustable seat and footplate positions so that it can effectively grow with the child. This wooden high chair revolutionized the concept of children's seating by providing comfortable and ergonomic sitting positions for a range of ages. Likewise, Opsvik's Variable Balans stool (1979) introduced a whole new category of seating into the furniture market: the kneeling chair. Designed to promote movement when seated for prolonged periods, this 'sitting tool' ensures many good sitting postures and makes it easy to change between them. Opsvik observes: 'My theory about sitting is very simple; if we're allowed to move, we move.' And it is this belief that has led him to design various other seating solutions, notably the Gravity Balans rocking chair, as well as a number of interesting prototypes that allow the body to move freely while being cradled by padded supports.

Below: Gravity Balans rocking chair by Peter Opsvik for Stokke, 1983 – later manufactured by Varier (Norway)

Opposite: Globe Garden sitting-tree by Peter Opsvik for Moment (Sweden), 2014 – original design concept for this seating design dates from 1984

JONAS BOHLIN

In the 1980s and early 1990s Jonas Bohlin was the high-profile *enfant terrible* of Swedish design, his idiosyncratic work far more akin to the contemporaneous British Creative Salvage movement than to the work of earlier Swedish designers. While studying as an interior architect at the Konstfack in Stockholm, he created the Concrete chair (1981) – a Neo-Brutalist design that heralded a new direction in Scandinavian design. Debuted at his degree show,

it rocked the Swedish design establishment, as Ulf Beckman, the editor of *Form* magazine, noted: 'We never quite recovered from the shock of his chair.' It was intended to function as a piece of design-art, and came to epitomize Swedish Postmodernism. Bohlin subsequently created other pieces of furniture from industrial materials such as concrete, steel and plywood that also had a strong sculptural quality, and which similarly challenged the pervasive legacy of Swedish Functionalism.

Opposite and below: Concrete chair by Jonas Bohlin for Källemo (Sweden), 1981

KÄLLEMO

Having been involved in the furniture industry since World War II, Sven Lundh founded his own company, Källemo, in Värnamo, southern Sweden, in 1965. His goal was to produce innovative furniture to the highest standards, but also with a strong artistic quality. Lundh felt that design in Sweden was being stultified by the pervasive conservatism of the furniture establishment, which included the Furniture Institute (Möbelinstitutet) in Stockholm and the VDN labelling scheme (later known as Møbelfakta), and that the quality criteria being laid down by such organizations must be countered. He finally discovered the perfect Postmodern design to fulfil this purpose: the

Concrete chair (1981) by Jonas Bohlin, who had recently graduated from the Konstfack in Stockholm (see pp. 186–87). Källemo first exhibited this radical design-art piece at the Stockholm Furniture Fair in 1981, and put it into limited production the following year. Although this iconoclastic design was initially difficult to sell, it provoked endless reaction and debate in Swedish design circles, helping to establish Källemo's 'dare to question' design credentials. Since then Källemo has produced numerous quirky design-art pieces that have – like Bohlin's design – pushed aesthetic, symbolic, functional and technical boundaries, and that are ultimately the result of Lundh's belief in creativity over commercialism.

Below: Anno chair by Sigurdur Gustafsson for Källemo (Sweden), 2001

1. National Geographic bookcase by Mats Theselius for Källemo (Sweden), 1990

2. Tango chairs by Sigurdur Gustafsson for Källemo (Sweden), 1997

3. NON chairs by Komplot Design for Källemo (Sweden), 2000

1.

2.
3.

IKEA PS RANGE

In 1994 IKEA launched its first PS collection, which was intended for a more design-orientated audience, one that wanted something a little more stylish than the 'classic' furniture staples the retail giant was renowned for producing. This first collection comprised 40 different products by 20 designers, and its name reflected the fact that it was viewed as an add-on to the company's main product line. Although the pieces were more expensive than other IKEA products, they were still a lot more affordable than most contemporary 'designer furniture' then available, and they introduced an interesting platform for more experimental designs within IKEA. Since then, a new range of IKEA PS designs has been launched annually; some of the pieces are available only for a short time, while others remain in production for a number of years. Many of these stylish yet functionally practical pieces have been created by leading Scandinavian designers, including Thomas Sandell, Nicholai Wiig Hansen and Thomas Eriksson, and have enjoyed extraordinary success, selling in the millions and thereby bringing a little bit of cutting-edge contemporary Scandinavian design into ordinary people's homes across the world.

Below: IKEA PS sofa bed by Thomas Sandell, Chris Martin and the IKEA of Sweden design team for IKEA (Sweden), 1999

1. IKEA PS cabinet/locker by Nicholai Wiig Hansen for IKEA (Sweden), 1998

2. IKEA PS Vågö easy chair by Thomas Sandell for IKEA (Sweden), 2000

3. IKEA PS 1995 clock by Thomas Eriksson for IKEA (Sweden), 1995

4. IKEA PS Gullholmen rocking chair by Maria Vinka for IKEA (Sweden), 2001

1.

2.

3.

4.

1.

2.

NORDIC CONTEMPORARY – LATE TWENTIETH CENTURY

Having shaken off the pervasive influence of Postmodernism in the late 1980s and early 1990s, Nordic designers began to create furniture that went back to their regional design roots. Caroline Schlyter's self-produced Lilla H. chair (1993), for instance, recalled the earlier plywood experiments of Alvar Aalto, as did Peter Brandt's simple yet clever Bimbo stool (1993) for Blå Station. Likewise, the comprehensive Snow range of multifunctional storage cabinets and drawer units designed by Jonas Bohlin and Thomas Sandell in 1994 echoed the aesthetic refinement, practical functionality and high-quality manufacture that had for so long been associated with Scandinavian furniture design. The Snow case furniture system also expressed the inherent values of the New Simplicity movement that emerged in Europe in the early 1990s. This not only established the reputation of its manufacturer, Asplund, as a progressive design-led company, but also helped to focus the international design spotlight once again on the Nordic countries.

1. Lilla H. high-backed chair by Caroline Schlyter (self-produced) (Sweden), 1989

2. Snow cabinet by Jonas Bohlin and Thomas Sandell for Asplund (Sweden), 1994

Below: Bimbo stool by Peter Brandt for Blå Station (Sweden), 1993

NORDIC CONTEMPORARY – EARLY TWENTY-FIRST CENTURY

Since the millennium, Nordic furniture design has undergone something of a renaissance. Companies such as Hay, Asplund, Normann Copenhagen, Design House Stockholm and Versus successfully produce for the international market pieces by Scandinavian designers notable for their formal, functional and technical innovation. For instance, the Brick (2010) came about because the Danish architect Bjarke Ingels could not find 'the right architect's sofa' for his apartment. With his KiBiSi design group partners, Jens Martin Skibsted and Lars Larsen, he developed a modular furniture-building system made out of upholstered brick-like cushions. Likewise, Louise Campbell's Prince chair (2002) has a laser-cut powder-coated steel frame with a felt-covered, water-cut neoprene covering, while the Rock rocking chair (2012) by Fredrik Färg and Emma Marga Blanche has an ingenious knock-down flat-pack construction comprising just four elements held together with simple wooden pegs. The Form chair (2014) by Simon Legald and the Vass sideboard (2007) by Claesson Koivisto Rune, however, perhaps best express the new Nordic Simplicity of the early 2000s, which channels the long-held Scandinavian design values of high-quality manufacture and functional practicality.

1. Vass sideboard by Claesson Koivisto Rune for Asplund (Sweden), 2007

2. Brick sofa by KiBiSi (Bjarke Ingels, Lars Holme Larsen and Jens Martin Skibsted) for Versus (Denmark), 2010

3. Prince chair by Louise Campbell for Hay (Denmark), 2002

4. Rock rocking chair by Fredrik Färg and Emma Marga Blanche for Design House (Sweden), 2012

5. Form chair by Simon Legald for Normann Copenhagen (Denmark), 2014

1.

2.

3.

4.

5.

LIGHTING

Poul Henningsen was without doubt the most influential Scandinavian lighting designer of the twentieth century. What Alvar Aalto was to Nordic architecture, Henningsen was to Scandinavian lighting, and it is no coincidence that both represented their respective nations at the CIAM (International Congress of Modern Architecture). Henningsen's name will forever be synonymous with the Copenhagen lighting company Louis Poulsen, for which he created the vast majority of his designs. He joined the company in 1924, and the following year his first designs were shown at the landmark Exposition Internationale des Arts Décoratifs et Industriels Modernes in Paris, where they earned him a gold medal. However, his breakthrough came with his invention of the PH three-bowl shading system, patented in 1926, which cleverly screened the light source, reducing glare while still allowing the emitted light to be scattered. The legend is that Henningsen came up with this novel idea while in his kitchen looking at a stack of bowls. Although it is a good story, his approach to lighting design was in fact much more scientific, and during his career he expounded various far-reaching theories on light emission, which are still used to this day.

Although Henningsen studied architecture, he never graduated, and instead turned to painting and writing. In the late 1920s he edited the satirical periodical *Kritisk Revy* (Critical Review) and also wrote plays that mocked old-fashioned, conservative values. His book *Hvad med Kulturen?* (What About Culture?; 1933) did more of the same, as did his *Danmarksfilmen* (Film of Denmark; 1935). He never joined the Communist party, but criticized the Social Democrats for not being radical enough. Following the German occupation of Denmark in 1940, he used Louis Poulsen's magazine – *NYT* – for political propaganda, often through poetry. When the German occupation became harsher in 1943, he fled with his wife, Inger, together with Arne Jacobsen, who was Jewish, and his wife, crossing the water to Sweden at night in a small rowing boat. Like so many Danish intellectuals and Scandinavian Jews, he spent the rest of the war in neutral Stockholm. After the war he became more sceptical about the Soviet Union, but continued to debate and write; the maxim 'All political art is bad – all good art is political' is one of his best-remembered *bons mots*.

Henningsen's best-known lighting designs are the PH 5 and Artichoke globe (both late 1950s). He did, however, create dozens of other designs throughout his four-decade

career, many of which are still in production. In Denmark, PH lights were used widely in shops, factories, offices and homes, and they were also admired by a number of 'foreign' architects, most notably those associated with the Bauhaus. Aalto was also a fan of Poul Henningsen's designs, and largely based his own lighting designs on Henningsen's theories.

While in Stockholm, Henningsen experimented with lampshades made of intricately folded paper. On his return to Denmark in 1945, he realized that Tage Klint had already developed the same idea and had set up the lighting manufacturing company Le Klint two years earlier. The Le Klint folded-paper shade concept actually goes back to 1901, when the architect Peder Vilhelm Jensen-Klint began to make simple lampshades this way. Tage Klint named the company after his daughter Lise Le Charlotte Klint, who was involved with the business in the early days. His well-known architect brother, Kaare Klint, also contributed designs, as did his son Esben Klint and the architect-designer Mogens Koch. Today, the most popular Le Klint designs are those by Poul Christiansen, who designed for the company from 1967 to 1987. Christiansen later set up with Boris Berlin the innovative Danish design company, Komplot Design (est. 1987), which has produced a number of other lighting designs for various manufacturers.

Another designer closely associated with Louis Poulsen was Arne Jacobsen, who created for many of his buildings site-specific lighting designs that were then put into production by the Copenhagen-based lighting company. For example, in 1946 Jacobsen collaborated with Erik Møller to design the Aarhus glass globe to light the new Aarhus City Hall; and his minimalist Eklipta wall light was originally designed for Rødovre City Hall. A smaller version of this simple yet functional design was also later created for St Catherine's College, Oxford. It is, however, the AJ floor, wall and table lamps, originally devised for the SAS Royal Hotel in Copenhagen in 1960, that are unquestionably Jacobsen's most accomplished lighting designs.

The highly innovative Danish designer Verner Panton also famously designed numerous spectacular lamps during his career, the first being the Topan (1959) and Moon (1960) pendant lights. In 1964 he developed the Fun lamp for J. Lüber in Switzerland, originally made out of metal foil cut by his Swedish wife, Marianne. Panton's other notable lighting designs include the Flowerpot pendant lights (1968) and the Panthella table lamp (1971), both of which are still in production. Like Panton, Hans Wegner is chiefly remembered as a furniture designer, but he too designed a number of innovative lamps, including the L37 Pendant (1962) with its ingenious rise-and-fall

Early example of the PH 4 pendant light by Poul Henningsen for Louis Poulsen (Denmark), 1930s

105 pendant light by Mogens Koch for Le Klint (Denmark), 1945

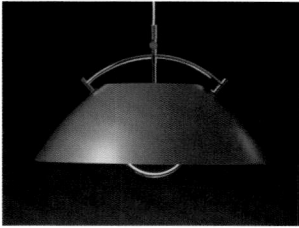

L37 'The Pendant' light by Hans Wegner for Johannes Hansen (Denmark), 1962 – production continued by Louis Poulsen, and since 1989 by Pandul

IQ light by Holger Strøm (self produced) (Denmark), 1973

Caravaggio pendant light by Cecilie Manz for Lightyears (Denmark), 2005

Opposite: Octo and Secto pendant lights by Seppo Koho for Secto Design (Finland) – shown in a private residence in Siuntio, Finland

function, and the Opala range (1973) for Hotel Scandinavia in Copenhagen. Both are still in production with Pandul.

The 1960s and 1970s brought an explosion of Danish lighting brands producing innovative designs in bright plastics, space-age shapes and shiny metals, with Fog & Mørup, Kemp & Lauritzen, LYFA and Lyskaer being among the most prominent. Glass and ceramics brands such as Holmegaard and Royal Copenhagen also began developing lighting collections during this period. Likewise, many designers better known for their contributions to furniture design turned their hands to lighting, most notably Finn Juhl, Michael Bang and Henning Koppel. Cheap imports, however, eventually took their toll on most of these brands, leaving Louis Poulsen and, on a far smaller scale, Le Klint the standard-bearers of modern classic Danish lighting. In recent years, however, there has been something of a resurgence in Danish lighting: Lightyears has found success with its Caravaggio pendant (2005) by Cecilie Manz, and design-led lifestyle brands such as Muuto, Normann Copenhagen and Hay are manufacturing a number of interesting lights.

Sweden has never had a flagship lighting brand like Louis Poulsen, nor a major lighting designer like Poul Henningsen. Instead, it was often the Swedish glassworks that developed lighting collections. Pukeberg glassworks merged with Arvid Böhlmark's lighting company in Stockholm in 1894, and was the first Swedish semi-automated producer of glass globes. In the 1930s they had great success with lit glass tops for petrol pumps. After World War II, Orrefors glassworks expanded its lighting division and hired the designer Carl Fagerlund. He remained head of lighting design there from 1946 until 1980, and was later successful internationally with lighting installations at the head office of General Motors and the Kennedy Center in the USA. Boda glassworks (est. 1942) also had a lighting division, notably producing designs by Erik Höglund in the 1960s.

There are also a number of dedicated lighting companies in Sweden, of which Fagerhult is the largest lighting manufacturer in Scandinavia today. Its Fabian light (1969) for domestic use is still in production, but the vast majority of its designs are manufactured for the contract market. Fagerhult has bought up several lighting brands over the years. One of them, Falkenberg, collaborated with the architect Helge Zimdahl, who designed the modernist Sveaplans Flickläroverk school building (1936) in Stockholm. The company Ateljé Lyktan is also part of the Fagerhult group – it was founded in 1934 by Hans and Verna Bergström in Helsingborg, and the former was its sole designer until the 1960s.

In the early 1950s Hans Bergström experimented with spray-on plastic webbing to create innovative lampshades, and he subsequently patented this novel production process and used it to create a range of globe-like pendants. In 1954 he won a gold medal at the Milan Triennial for his Struten pendant, which is still in production. In the early 1960s Anders Pehrson, head of design for Philips in Sweden, took over the company, and his Bumling pendant (1968) is the closest thing Sweden has had to a lighting design classic. Ateljé Lyktan also took over the production of Erik Gunnar Asplund's 1922 pendant for his famous Skandia cinema in 1965, and this is still part of the company's collection.

Other Swedish lighting companies include Örsjö Belysning, which has collaborated with Orrefors, Pukeberg and IKEA. Today the firm works with a newer generation of Swedish designers, including Matti Klenell, Folkform, Claesson Koivisto Rune and Jonas Bohlin. Another firm, Zero, is in Nybro, near the Pukeberg glassworks. Initially Börge Lindau was its chief designer, but it now collaborates with various contemporary designers and design studios, including Thomas Sandell, Thomas Bernstrand, Fredrik Mattson, Front and Broberg & Ridderstråle, to name but a few. The company Wästberg similarly works with Swedish designers and design groups, such as Jonas Lindvall and Claesson Koivisto Rune, while also collaborating with international names such as Inga Sempé and Ilse Crawford.

Norway's most internationally successful lighting company is Luxo, which was founded in 1934 by Jacob Jacobsen. Jacobsen worked in the textile industry, but when he received two Anglepoise lamps in a delivery of textile machines from England, he became intrigued by their metal sprung-arm construction and eventually acquired a licence to manufacture and distribute his own version. This led to the launch in 1937 of his L-1 lamp, which became a huge commercial success – selling over 25 million units worldwide since its launch – and was the springboard from which Luxo became one of the world's leading contract lighting suppliers. In recent years the Swedish architect Olle Anderson has been Luxo's most prolific designer.

Two other notable Norwegian lighting designs are the S-10053 or Dokka lamp (1954) and the S-30016 or Birdy lamp (1952), both of which were designed by Birger Dahl for Sønnico and won medals at the Milan Triennial in 1954. Having been a student of the well-known Norwegian architect-designer Arne Korsmo, Dahl became an acknowledged pioneer of Scandinavian lighting while working as head designer for Sønnico, and his designs were typified by their simple yet

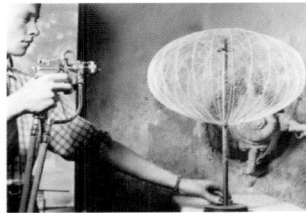

Plastic is sprayed on to a wire frame to create a lampshade at Ateljé Lyktan (Sweden), ca. 1952

Bumling pendant light by Anders Pehrson for Ateljé Lyktan (Sweden), 1968

L-1 task light by Jac Jacobsen for Luxo (Norway), 1937

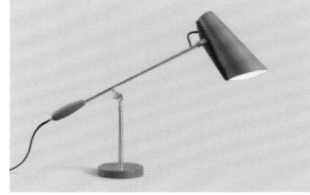

Birdy table light by Birger Dahl for Sønnico (Norway), 1952 – reissued by Northern Lighting

Ricochet lighting installation by Daniel Rybakken for the gallery Spazio Rossana Orlandi (Italy), 2012

striking geometric forms. Today, Dahl's two key designs – Dokka and Birdy – are manufactured by the Oslo firm Northern Lighting, which also produces contemporary lighting by a new generation of Norwegian designers, notably Atle Tveit, Morten Skjærpe Knarrum and Jonas Norheim.

Daniel Rybakken is another Norwegian designer who has made waves in the lighting industry, having created several products for the Italian manufacturer Luceplan. After studying at the Arkitektur- og Designhøgskolen i Oslo (Oslo School of Architecture and Design) and the Högskolan för Design och Konsthantverk (School of Design and Crafts) in Gothenburg, Sweden, Rybakken opened his own design studio, which has branches in both cities. He has since received numerous awards, including a 'Best of the Best' Red Dot Award in 2007 and a Design Report Award at the Salone Satellite, Milan, in 2009. Rybakken's work bridges the worlds of art and design, comprising limited editions, art installations and prototypes for serial production. His focus is on daylight and how to artificially re-create both its appearance and subconscious effect.

Like its Nordic neighbours, Finland has also boasted some formidable lighting designers. For instance, Alvar Aalto – who frequently used Poul Henningsen's lights for his earlier projects – went on to design his own unique fixtures. The most memorable of these is the brass Golden Bell or Model no. A330, created for the interior of the Savoy restaurant in Helsinki in 1937. Aalto's Hand Grenade or Model no. A110 light (1952) was initially created for the Finnish Engineers' Association Building, and its title reflects the impact of World War II on Finnish culture. Another design known as the Bilberry (Model no. A338) was originally created for the Villa Carré in France, which Aalto built for the renowned French gallerist Louis Carré in 1958. Its unusual side opening was devised for the illumination of artworks.

Lisa Johansson-Pape was the undisputed master of postwar Finnish lighting design. After graduating in 1927 from Taideteolliseen Keskuskouluun (Central School of Industrial Arts) in Helsinki, she worked for the Kylmäkoski furniture factory. In 1933 she joined the Suomen Käsityön Ystävät (Friends of Finnish Handicraft), and from 1937 she designed furniture for the department store Stockmann. She began designing for Stockmann's lighting factory, Orno, in 1942, and eventually became its artistic director. During her tenure there she produced numerous lighting designs that were notable for their sculptural forms and Mid-century Modern elegance. In the 1950s she also began to collaborate with the glass-blowers at the

Iittala glassworks, and her resulting bulbous glass lamps received awards at the Milan Triennials of 1951 and 1954.

A colleague of Johansson-Pape at Orno, Yki Nummi, worked as a designer for the factory from 1950 to 1975, during which period he created dozens of light fixtures. His best-known luminaires are the Modern Art table lamp (1955) – so called because the Museum of Modern Art in New York purchased an example for its permanent collection – and the Lokki (Seagull) pendant (1960), also known as the Skyflyer, for obvious reasons. Many of his lighting designs reflect his studies in mathematics and physics at university, which he undertook before taking a degree in decorative painting at the Institute of Industrial Arts in Helsinki. Like other Scandinavian lighting designers, Nummi was awarded gold medals at the Milan Triennial, in 1954 and 1957. His countryman Tapio Wirkkala also designed numerous lights with similar geometric forms and strong, highly identifiable graphic profiles.

Several decades later, the Finnish designer Harri Koskinen created his famous glass Block lamp (1997) for Design House Stockholm, and it was an immediate international success. Koskinen has since designed many other lamps and numerous other products, but it is this brick-like light that will be forever associated with him and with the generation of new Finnish designers that emerged in the 1990s.

Another classic from that decade was the inflatable Globlow lamp (1996) by Markus Nevalainen, Rane Vaskivuori and Vesa Hinkola for their design collective Snowcrash (in existence 1997–2002). The Finnish architect Seppo Koho has also enjoyed great success with his series of laminated-birch plywood lamps for the Finnish company Secto Design, starting with the conical Secto lamp (1995) and adding to the range with the Victo, Octo, Atto and others. The sheer quality and diversity of lighting designs produced in the Nordic countries over the decades has undoubtedly been prompted by the region's long, dark winters and the realization that the quality of light can profoundly affect both physical and emotional well-being.

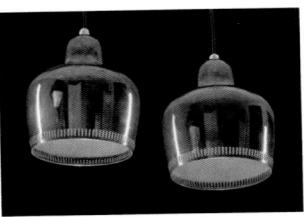
Golden Bell (Model no. A330) pendant lights by Alvar Aalto for Louis Poulsen (Denmark), 1937 – reissued by Artek

Acrylic pendant light by Yki Nummi for Orno (Finland), ca. 1960s

Big and Mini Block lights by Harri Koskinen for Design House Stockholm (Sweden), 1997

Globlow lamp by Markus Nevalainen, Rane Vaskivuori and Vesa Hinkola for Snowcrash (Finland), 1996

POUL HENNINGSEN

Since Thomas Edison's invention of the commercially viable electric light bulb in 1879, lighting designers have sought to find a way of eliminating glare without reducing the amount of emitted light. This seemingly insurmountable problem captured the imagination of the Danish designer-inventor Poul Henningsen, and led him to spend some ten years methodically investigating how to diffuse and control light. Eventually, in the winter of 1925–26, while having a cup of coffee, he had what can only be described as a 'Eureka!' moment that led to a design breakthrough in the form of the first three-shaded PH lamp (1926). His realization was that if he configured a series of lampshades like a stack of differently sized bowls, he could effectively bounce the light from the internal light source and thus reduce glare without compromising the amount of light emitted. This earliest PH light was the first of many lighting designs by Henningsen that used his ingenious louvred shades to produce warm-hued, glare-free light that prompted the formation of so-called harmonic shadows.

1. PH 5/3 ceiling light by Poul Henningsen for Louis Poulsen (Denmark), ca. 1926 – the example shown is a very early one, produced between 1926 and 1928

2. Poul Henningsen in the 'demonstration room' he designed for Louis Poulsen's showroom in Nyhavn, Copenhagen, in 1939

Opposite: PH 3½–2½ table light by Poul Henningsen for Louis Poulsen (Denmark), 1928 – this specific version has been only recently reissued by Louis Poulsen

1.

2.

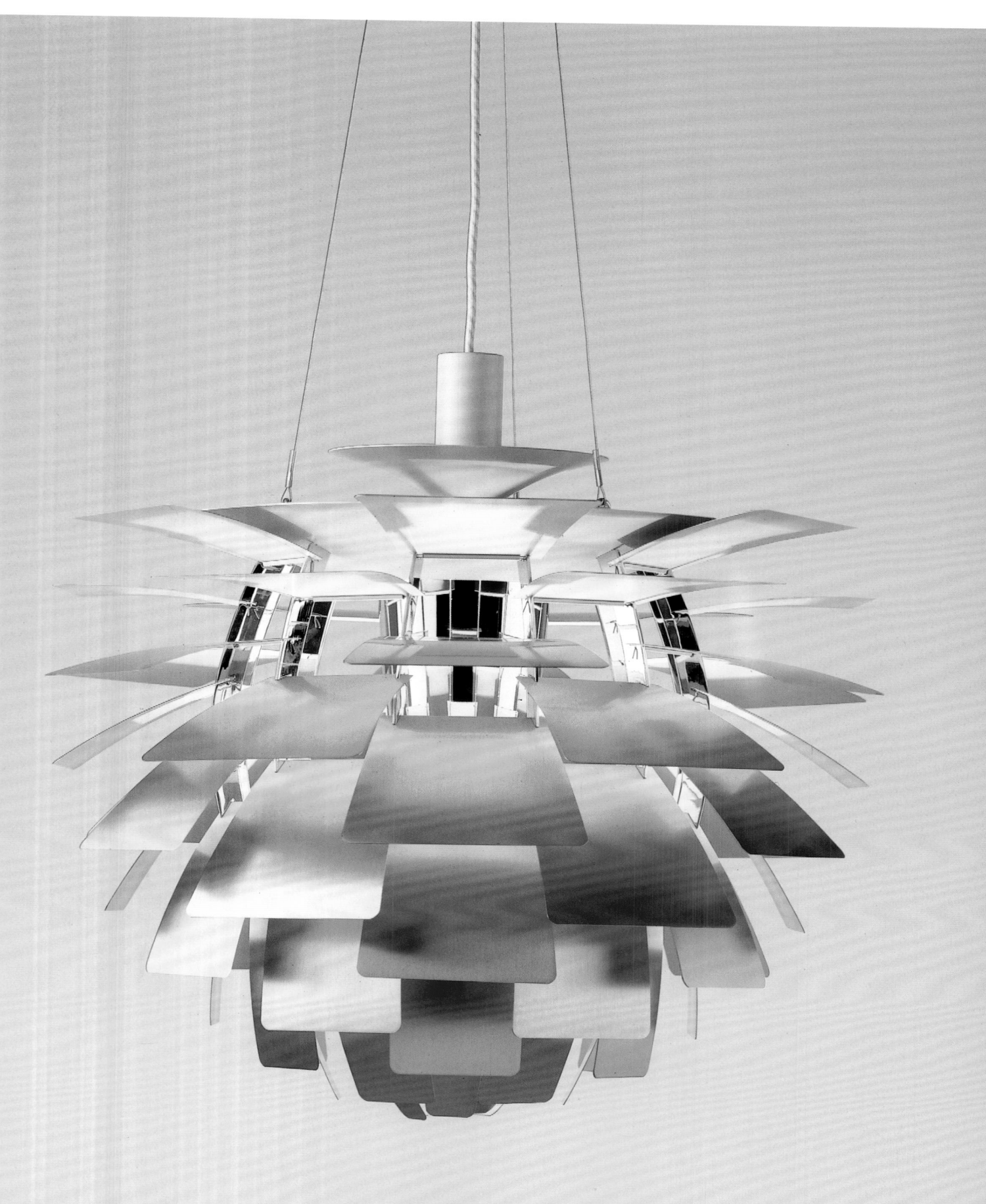

HENNINGSEN: LIGHT YEARS AHEAD

Poul Henningsen was one of the most influential lighting designers of all time, and an important pioneer of Modern Danish design. By taking a scientific approach to lighting and spending some 30 years researching the physics behind the diffusion of light, he was able to create a series of multi-shaded pendant lamps that were far ahead of the other lighting designs that were then being developed. Among his best-known designs are the Spiral ceiling light for the main hall at the University of Aarhus in 1942, and the Artichoke, created for the Langeline Pavilion in Copenhagen in 1957. The latter was originally manufactured in copper, but a white version was introduced in 1980. With its pine cone-like configuration of light-reflecting 'petals', this design has a more organic quality than others by Henningsen, a fact that perhaps explains its enduring appeal. Another piece by Henningsen that deserves special mention is the Snowball, which was shown for the first time in the exhibition 'Glass, Light and Colour' at the Danish Museum of Decorative Art in Copenhagen in 1958. Eventually manufactured posthumously, from 1983 onwards, this eye-catching eight-shaded lamp does exactly what Henningsen always set out to achieve: it provides glare-free light that produces soft shadows, while being easy on the eye – both functionally and aesthetically.

Opposite: PH Artichoke pendant light by Poul Henningsen for Louis Poulsen (Denmark), 1957

1. Spiral pendant light by Poul Henningsen for Louis Poulsen, 1942

2: PH Snowball pendant light by Poul Henningsen for Louis Poulsen (Denmark), 1958

2.

JOSEF FRANK

The Austrian-born designer Josef Frank had a profound impact on the development of Swedish design, despite the fact he was already 50 years old when he emigrated to Sweden in 1933 to escape persecution by the Nazis. While living in Vienna, he had been an associate of the Wiener Werkstätte and also a member of both the design-reforming Deutscher Werkbund and its Austrian equivalent, the Österreichischen Werkbund. He was therefore well aware of the latest developments in design and architecture, and had already begun questioning Modernism's growing puritanical streak, which he felt was too doctrinal. Instead, he sought to produce designs that could be mixed and matched and were compatible with existing domestic wares, which would better enable people to create a relaxing ambience in their homes. Joining Svenskt Tenn as a designer in 1934, he created numerous lighting designs that were unequivocally modern yet also possessed a timeless, graceful elegance that allowed them to fit easily into any interior scheme. Lampshades in gold, red and green constituted one of his preferred combinations, and reflected his love of rich, warm colours.

1. Large Camel floor lamp, Model no. 2368, by Josef Frank for Svenskt Tenn (Sweden), 1939

2. Three-branch table light, Model no. 2468, by Josef Frank for Svenskt Tenn (Sweden), 1930s – this early example dates from the 1950s

3. Table lamp by Josef Frank for Svenskt Tenn (Sweden), 1930s – this early example dates from the 1940s

4. China floor light by Josef Frank for Svenskt Tenn (Sweden), 1950s

5. Three Spirals floor light, Model no. 2431, by Josef Frank for Svenskt Tenn (Sweden), 1938 – shown at the Golden Gate Exhibition in San Francisco in 1939, it is also sometimes referred to as the San Francisco lamp

2.

1.

3.

4.

5.

ALVAR AALTO

Although best remembered for his landmark architecture, groundbreaking furniture and innovative glassware, Alvar Aalto was also an accomplished lighting designer who produced numerous innovative designs that were intended to eliminate glare and emit a soft, warm-toned light. Many were designed specifically for his buildings, and put into industrial production later. For instance, his brass A330S pendant light (1937), often referred to as the Golden Bell, was designed initially for the Savoy restaurant in Helsinki. The design evolved in 1954 into the larger A330 model – shown opposite – which was itself initially created for the staff canteen at the University of Jyväskylä in central Finland. For the same project, Aalto designed what is probably his best-known light, the A331, also known as the Beehive in tribute to its nest-like, stepped form, which efficiently diffuses emitted light. Another well-known Aalto lighting design, the A110 pendant light (1952), was nicknamed the Hand Grenade thanks to its likeness to a German Model 24 *Stielhandgranate* (stalk hand grenade) used during World War II. This ingeniously simple cylinder-on-a-pole design was designed specially for the headquarters building of the Finnish Engineers' Association. Today, Artek continues to manufacture 13 of Aalto's lighting designs, testifying to their remarkable functional and aesthetic longevity.

Below: Beehive pendant lamp, Model no. A331, by Alva Aalto for Artek (Finland), 1953

1. Model no. A111 pendant lamp, nicknamed the Hand Grenade, by Alvar Aalto for Valaistustyö (Finland), ca. 1958

2. Model no. A335 B pendant light by Alvar Aalto for Valaistustyö (Finland), 1950s

3. Golden Bell pendant light, Model no. A330, by Alvar Aalto for Valaistustyö (Finland), 1954

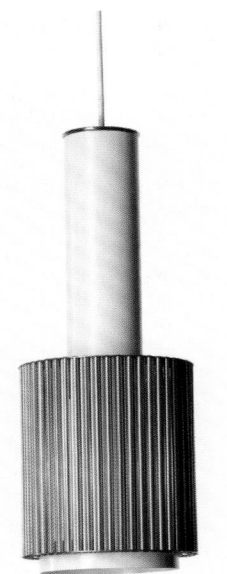

1.

2.

3.

PAAVO TYNELL

Paavo Tynell studied metalworking at the Central School of Industrial Arts in Helsinki and later married Helena Tynell (neé Turpeinen), an accomplished glassware designer (see pp. 306–7). In 1918 Paavo set up his own metalworking venture, Taito, specializing in the production of architectural lighting and fittings. During the 1940s he designed numerous lights that were inspired by natural forms. For instance, a chandelier might reference a loosely clustered bouquet of flowers, while a wall light might take the form of a branching stem terminating in bell-shaped shades. One of his best-known designs is a desk lamp with a shade in the form of a scallop shell. In 1948 Tynell began exporting his products to the USA, where they were sold by Finland House, New York, an influential showcase of Scandinavian design. In 1950 Taito merged with Idman, and as a result Tynell's work become less fantastical and more suited to industrial production, typified now by the use of simple yet sculptural brass shades that were often delicately perforated in order to produce a pleasing effect of scattered light.

Below: Model no. 9029/4 chandelier by Paavo Tynell for Taito (Finland), ca. 1950

1. Table lamp by Paavo Tynell for Taito (Finland), 1941

2. Three-shade chandelier by Paavo Tynell for Taito (Finland), ca. 1950

3. Wall sconce by Paavo Tynell for Taito (Finland), ca. 1947

2.

1.

3.

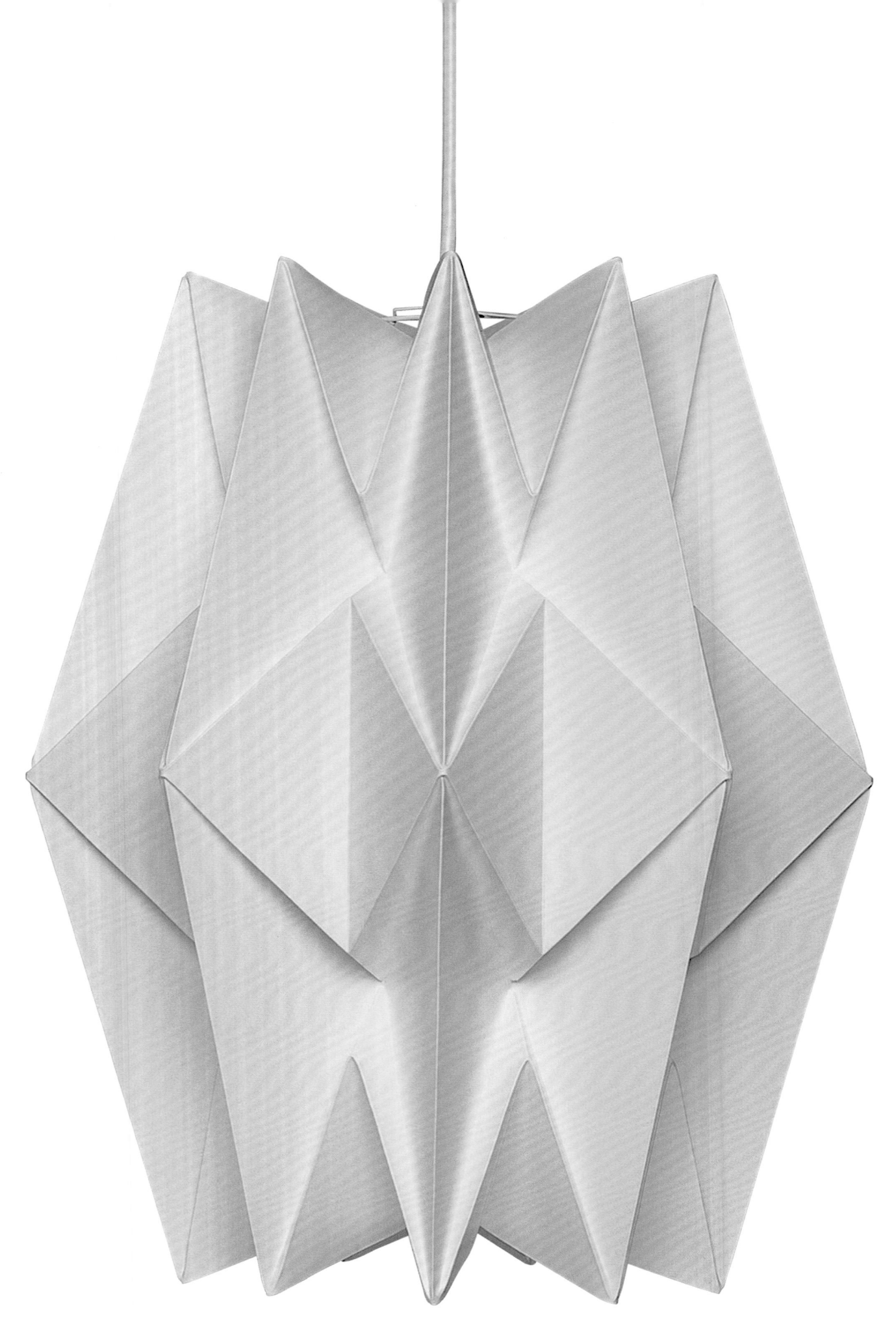

LE KLINT

The well-known Danish lighting manufacturer Le Klint has turned the hand-pleating of paper lampshades almost into an art form. The history of the company goes back to 1901, when the architect Peder Vilhelm Jensen-Klint designed a simple stoneware oil lamp for which he made a shade from pleated parchment, having been unable to find anything suitable to purchase. Other members of his family subsequently tried their hand at making pleated paper lampshades, and this popular family pastime eventually became a small home-run business. In 1943 Klint's eldest son, Tage, founded the Le Klint company and opened a shop in central Copenhagen to sell the family's products. The following year his architect brother, Kaare, designed the Lantern lamp (also called the Fruit lamp), which incorporated cross-pleating, giving it a much more modern look. Relatively inexpensive to produce, this light, together with a Mid-century Modern design by the architectural duo of Peter Hvidt and Orla Mølgaard-Nielsen, became almost ubiquitous in interior-design magazines during the 1950s. In 1965 Andreas Hansen updated the look of Le Klint's paper shades with his design of the Model no. 157 pendant light, which heralded a more sculptural Pop aesthetic for the company.

Opposite: Organ Pipe pendant light, Model no. 152, by Peter Hvidt and Orla Mølgaard-Nielsen for Le Klint (Denmark), 1952

1. Model no. 1-27 pendant light by Tage Klint for Le Klint (Denmark), ca. 1943 – the ancestry of this design can be traced back to the pleated shades created by Tage's father, Peder Vilhelm Jensen-Klint, for his own stoneware table lights in 1901

2. Model no. 157 pendant light by Andreas Hansen for Le Klint (Denmark), 1965

3. Lantern pendant light, Model no. 101A, by Kaare Klint for Le Klint (Denmark), 1944

1.

2.

3.

POUL CHRISTIANSEN

Poul Christiansen, one of Denmark's leading contemporary designers, founded Komplot Design with Boris Berlin in 1987. Before that, however, he had made quite a name for himself as a lighting designer working for Le Klint (see pp. 212–13). In 1967 he produced his first design for the Odense-based firm, the Model 167. It marked the beginning of an impressive series of pendant lights that took the company's famous paper-folding technique to another level of mathematical and formal sophistication. Rather than employing straight plissé folds, as his predecessors Kaare Klint and Mogens Koch had done with

their designs for the company, Christiansen used sine curves as his point of departure. The resulting range of lights designed over a 20-year period, from 1967 to 1987, was far more sculptural and spectacular than anything previously produced by Le Klint. Some models, such as the iconic Model 172 (1971) have remained in continuous production for decades thanks to their timeless appeal. Christiansen notes modestly: 'My work for Le Klint has been inspired by the company's unique key competency: pleating paper. I have tried to transcend some of the barriers for the sculptural shapes you can create simply by pleating.'

1 & 3. Model no. 178 pendant light by Poul Christiansen for Le Klint (Denmark), 1975

2. Model no. 167 pendant light by Poul Christiansen for Le Klint (Denmark), 1967

4. Model no. 172 pendant light by Poul Christiansen for Le Klint (Denmark), 1971

5. Model no. 169 pendant light by Poul Christiansen for Le Klint (Denmark), 1970

1.

2.

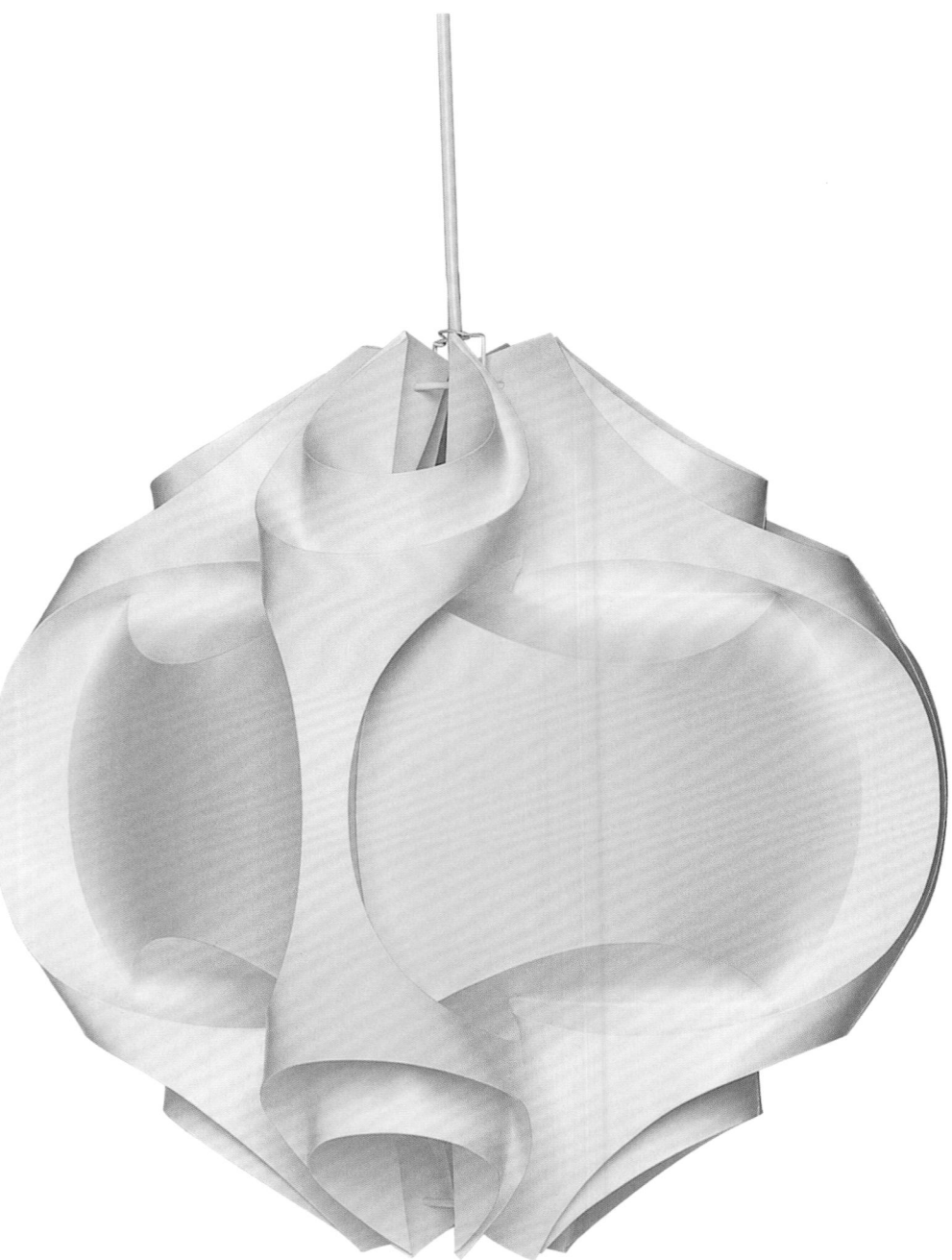

4.

3.
5.

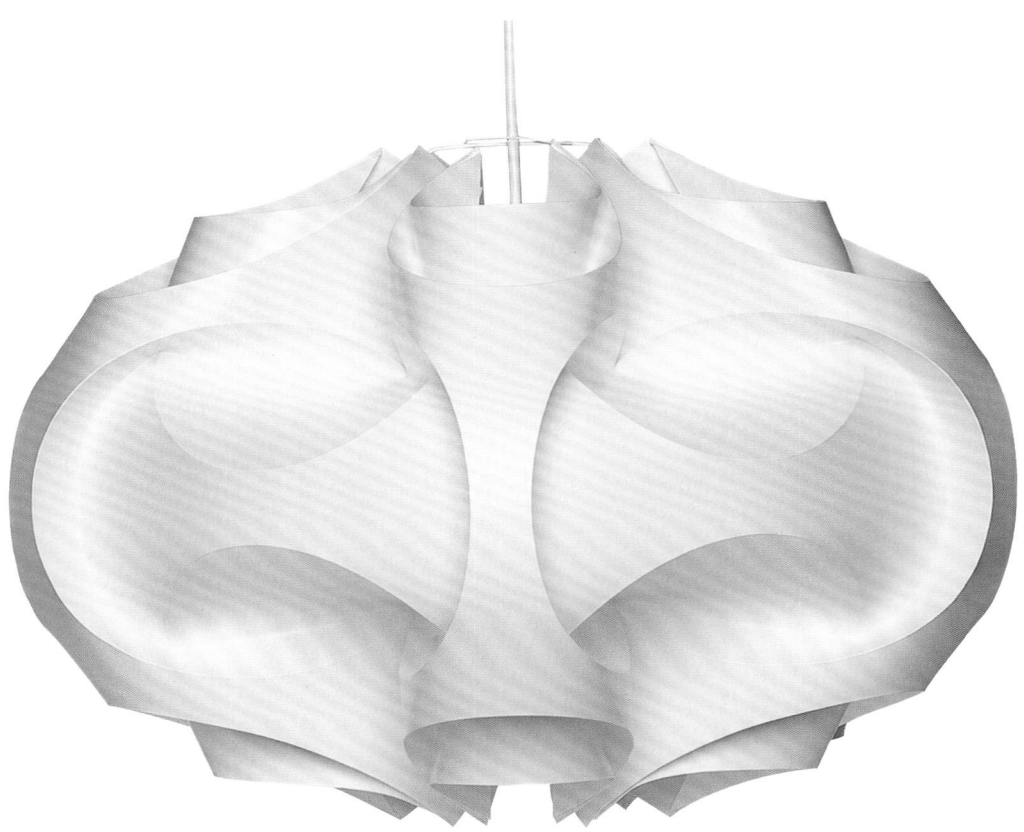

TAPIO WIRKKALA

A master form-giver, Tapio Wirkkala was an exceptional talent and a creative genius who worked in a wide variety of design disciplines. Whatever kind of product he turned his hand to, he was able to imbue it with a distinctive sculptural flair born out of a profound understanding of materials. He produced about 75 different lighting designs, many of which combined mould-blown glass diffusers in various subtle hues with minimalistic metal fittings. These pieces were produced by Idman or the Iittala glassworks, or in some cases by both. Wirkkala designed not only the lights themselves, but also special bulbs to be used with them, and those were manufactured by Airam. A Scandinavian Airlines advertisement from 1963 featured three of Wirkkala's pendant models, each with a differently shaped bulb. Tellingly, the ad featured the byline: 'Scandinavian Modern is a Wirkkala lamp' – which pretty much sums up Wirkkala's extraordinary contribution to the development of Modern Scandinavian design.

1. Pair of Model no. K2-140 pendant lights by Tapio Wirkkala for Iittala/Idman (Finland), 1960

2. Scandinavian Airlines advertisement showing lighting designs by Tapio Wirkkala, 1963

3. Model no. K10-11 floor light by Tapio Wirkkala for Idman (Finland), 1958

4. Model no. 4614 pendant light by Tapio Wirkkala for Iittala/Idman (Finland), 1962

5. Model no. 4619 pendant light by Tapio Wirkkala for Iittala/Idman (Finland), 1962

1.

2.

3.
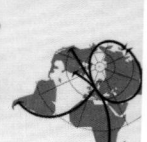

4.

5.

YKI NUMMI

Between 1950 and 1975 the Finnish designer Yki Nummi produced numerous lighting designs for Orno (Stockmann's lighting factory) that were notable for their use of 'new' acrylic polymers. For instance, the base of his Modern Art table lamp (1955) was made from a wide-gauge tube of transparent acrylic on which rested a simple, translucent white shade. This clever proto-minimalist design got its name from its acquisition in 1958 by New York's Museum of Modern Art for its permanent collection. Nummi also created a number of equally progressive suspension lights with interesting space-age forms, such as the Skyflyer (1960), which looked like a hovering flying saucer when aglow in a darkened room. Nummi received widespread international recognition during his lifetime, not only winning two gold Milan Triennial medals, but also having his work included in various landmark exhibitions, including the touring show 'Design in Scandinavia' (1954–57) and the H55 exhibition in Helsingborg, Sweden (1955; see p. 32).

1. Modern Art table light by Yki Nummi for Stockmann-Orno (Finland), 1955 – later reissued by Adelta

2. Skyflyer pendant light by Yki Nummi for Orno (Finland) (later Adelta), 1960 – originally known as Lokki (Seagull)

Opposite: Pendant light by Yki Nummi, ca. 1960

1.

2.

LISA JOHANSSON-PAPE +
GRETA MAGNUSSON-GROSSMAN

The Finnish architect-designer Lisa Johansson-Pape (neé Johansson) worked for the Stockmann department store and designed numerous lighting products for its manufacturing company, Orno. Her designs were distinguished by their practical functionality, simple basic forms and use of brass, acrylic or glass. Johansson-Pape's range of opaque-glass lights (1954), shown below, brought her international recognition and was highly influential for later lighting designers. The Swedish architect-designer Greta Magnusson-Grossman was a similarly important female figure in the world of Scandinavian design who likewise specialized in the creation of innovative lighting as well as furniture and interiors. In 1940 she moved to Los Angeles, where she opened a studio-shop with her husband on Rodeo Drive, catering to a fashionable Hollywood clientele. She also designed for a number of manufacturers, including Barker Brothers, Ralph O. Smith and Glenn of California. Her well-known Grasshopper floor light (1947) and Cobra table light (1948) epitomized her stylish 'Swedish Modern' look; the latter won a coveted Good Design Award in 1950.

1. Pendant light by Lisa Johansson-Pape for Orno (Finland), 1950s

2. Three opaque-glass pendant lights by Lisa Johansson-Pape for Orno (Finland), 1954 – this range of lights won a gold medal at the 10th Milan Triennial in 1954

3. Double Cobra table light by Greta Magnusson-Grossman for Ralph O. Smith (Sweden/USA), 1948

4. Grasshopper floor light by Greta Magnusson-Grossman for Ralph O. Smith (Sweden/USA), 1947

1.

2.

3.

4.

O HAMMERBORG + HANS BERGSTRÖM

The Danish lighting company Fog & Mørup began making international design waves when it appointed Johannes 'Jo' Hammerborg head of design in 1957. He had previously spent eight years working for Georg Jensen as a silversmith and designer, and in this new role he brought a fresh, modern look to Fog & Mørup's product line. His Lento table light (1967) and his spun-aluminium Vega pendant light (1968), for example, had a strongly contemporary feel through their very pure, pared-down forms. In contrast, the lighting created by the Swedish designer Hans Bergström for his own lighting company, Ateljé Lyktan, in the 1950s and early 1960s had a much more exuberant Mid-century Modern quality that reflected the continuing influence of Italian design on Scandinavian designers. His Model no. 711 table light (ca. 1953) and chandelier (1953), shown here, stylistically recall contemporaneous designs produced by the likes of Stilnovo and Arredoluce in Italy.

Opposite: Chandelier by Hans Bergström for Ateljé Lyktan (Sweden), 1955

1. Lento table light by Jo Hammerborg for Fog & Mørup, 1967

2. Vega pendant light by Jo Hammerborg for Fog & Mørup, 1968

3. Model no. 711 table light by Hans Bergström for Ateljé Lyktan (Sweden), ca. 1953

1.

3.

2.

ARNE JACOBSEN

Louis Poulsen still manufactures a number of lighting designs by Arne Jacobsen, some of which have been in production for more than half a century. The AJ Royal pendant light, AJ floor light and AJ table light being a case in point, having all been designed for the SAS Royal Hotel in Copenhagen in 1960 (see pp. 34–37). Similarly, a cube-like pendant light made from four interlocking sheets of acrylic was also originally designed for the hotel's snack bar, and has recently been re-issued by another lighting manufacturer. But perhaps the most versatile and enduring of all Jacobsen's many lighting designs is the discus-shaped AJ Eklipta. Designed as part of an integrated scheme for Rødovre City Hall in 1959, it was initially produced in two sizes (35 and 45 centimetres), one model being used indoors to illuminate the dramatic staircase, and the other outdoors as wall lighting. A smaller version (22 centimetres) of this minimalistic design was later developed for St Catherine's College, Jacobsen's extraordinary *Gesamtkunstwerk* in the heart of historic Oxford (see pp. 38–41). Today, this understated yet beautiful light is still used around the world in a wide range of architectural contexts. As Jacobsen once observed, 'The primary factor is proportions,' and certainly the AJ Eklipta bears out this sentiment, for its simple yet precise essentialist form gives it enormous functional application and a timeless appeal.

1. AJ Royal pendant light by Arne Jacobsen for Louis Poulsen (Denmark), 1960 – originally designed for the bar and restaurant of the SAS Royal Hotel in Copenhagen

2. AJ Eklipta wall light by Arne Jacobsen for Louis Poulsen (Denmark), 1959 – originally designed for Rødovre City Hall, and later incorporated into the design scheme for St Catherine's College, Oxford

3. AJ table light by Arne Jacobsen for Louis Poulsen (Denmark), 1960 – originally designed for the SAS Royal Hotel in Copenhagen

Opposite: AJ table light and AJ floor light by Arne Jacobsen for Louis Poulsen (Denmark), 1957 – originally designed for the SAS Royal Hotel in Copenhagen

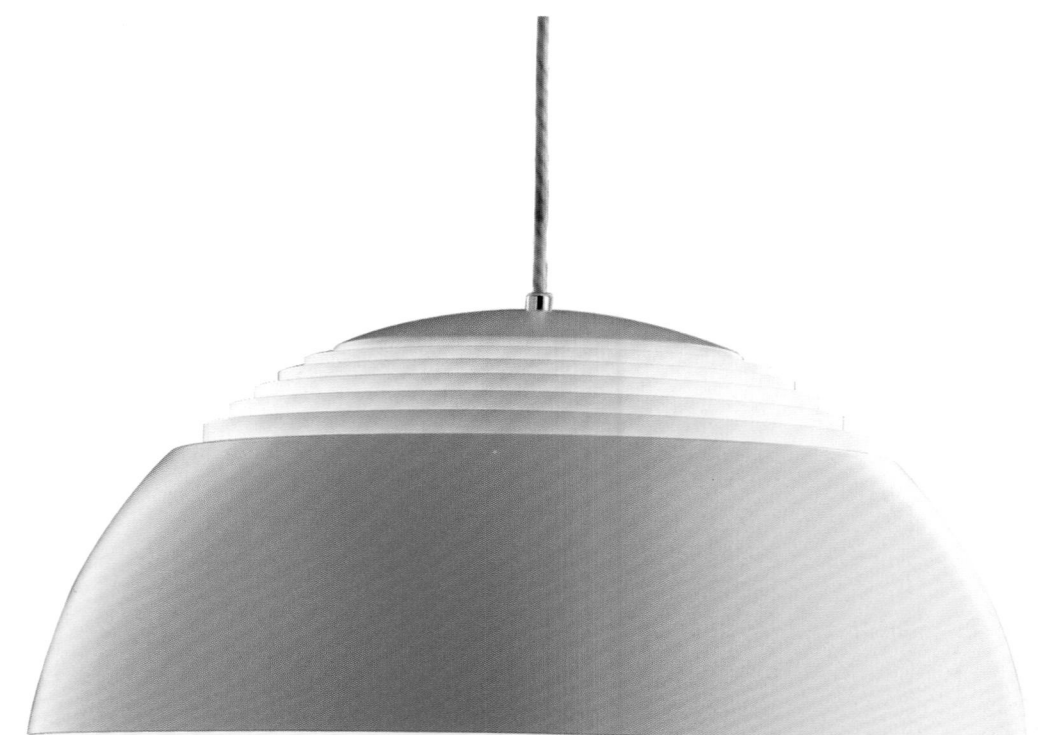

1.

2.

3.

ANTON – THE LIGHTING MAGICIAN

erner Panton's forward-looking and futuris-
c lighting designs rejected the refined good
aste of Danish Modernism completely, and
nstead gave exuberant expression to a new
nd youthful Pop sensibility. The Flowerpot
ange of lights (1968), manufactured by Louis
oulsen, cleverly incorporated two enamelled
netal hemispherical elements, which were
ositioned facing each other so that the larger
ne functioned as a shade, while the smaller
ne acted as a reflector. This ingeniously
imple yet visually impactful configuration

meant that the Flowerpot lights, which came
in two sizes, emitted a soft, diffused light with
a warm glow. Panton revisited the idea of using bowl-shaped reflectors in his design of the
VP-Globe (1969–70), which took the form of
a giant acrylic bubble enclosing an innovative
arrangement of five light-diffusing elements.
His later Fun range of pendant lights incorporated discs of aluminium or shell that filtered
and scattered the rays from the hidden light
bulb. Indeed, no other Scandinavian designer created lighting that produced such an
atmospheric, almost magical, effect.

Opposite: Big Flowerpot pendant light by Verner Panton
for Louis Poulsen (Denmark), 1968

1. VP-Globe pendant light by Verner Panton for Louis
Poulsen (Denmark), 1969–70

2. VP-02 Fun shell pendant light by Verner Panton for
J. Lüber (Switzerland), 1964

2.

PANTON – TRIPPING THE LIGHT FANTASTIC

Verner Panton was a prolific, multitalented designer who loved exploring and experimenting with new materials and technology. He produced many highly innovative lighting designs that used state-of-the-art polymers to spectacular effect. In 1964, for the Swiss manufacturer J. Lüber, Panton designed his impressive Fun lighting range, which employed a series of metal rings from which discs of aluminium and translucent shell were suspended (see p. 227). From this influential series Panton went on to evolve two sculptural lighting ranges, the Ball and Spiral lights (both 1970). Instead of using metal or shell discs, these lights incorporated plastic balls and spirals of varying size and colour, made of Cellidor, a newly developed cellulose-based thermoplastic. These extraordinarily innovative lights featured heavily in Panton's out-of-this-world *Visiona 2* installation for Bayer at the Cologne Furniture Fair in 1970 (see pp. 50–51), and were also used extensively in his space-age psychedelic interiors for the Varna restaurant (1971) in Aarhus, Denmark (see p. 48).

Below: Wonderlamp, Model Typ H, by Verner Panton for J. Lüber (Switzerland), 1970

1. SP2 Spiral lamp by Verner Panton for J. Lüber (Switzerland), 1970

2. Wonderlamp, Model Typ F, by Verner Panton for J. Lüber (Switzerland), 1970

1.

2.

LYFA

In the 1920s the Københavns Lampe- og Lysekronefabrik (Copenhagen Lamp and Chandelier Factory) was established in Ballerup, and in 1930 its name was simplified to LYFA. Throughout the early years of the firm's operation it was more a follower than a leader, for example producing lights that were inspired by those designed by Poul Henningsen for its competitor, Louis Poulsen. Between the 1950s and the 1970s, however, LYFA commissioned innovative lighting from leading Danish design practitioners of the day, including Finn Juhl, Piet Hein, Bent Karlby, Louis Weisdorf, Acton Bjørn

and Simon Henningsen (the son of Poul). During this golden period, LYFA earned an international reputation for producing some of the most interesting and experimental lighting in the world, let alone Scandinavia. Indeed, it won nine iF (International Forum) awards during this time. Among its most eye-catching designs were the diminutive but stunning Divan-2 pendant light by Simon Henningsen – as innovative as anything his father had designed – and the Pantre and Pan-Opticon lights by Bent Karlby, which, although extremely simple in their tubular construction, possessed a stylish, on-point Op Art aesthetic.

1. Pantre pendant light by Bent Karlby for LYFA (Denmark), ca. 1965

2. Pan-Opticon wall appliques by Bent Karlby for LYFA (Denmark), ca. 1965

Opposite: Divan-2 pendant lamp by Simon Henningsen for LYFA (Denmark), 1962 – sometimes called the Tivoli lamp

1.

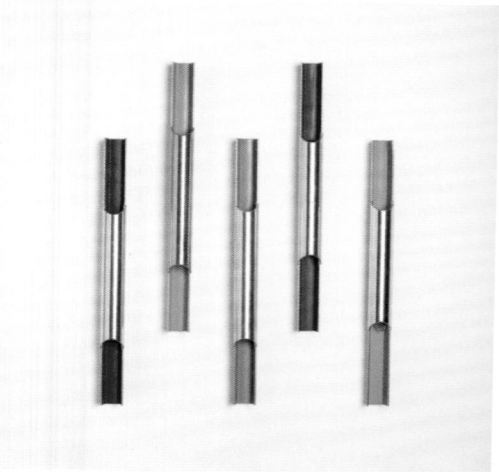

2.

CONTEMPORARY NORDIC LIGHTING
1990s–2010s

The power of electric light to brighten and visually warm a home during the long, grey months of a Scandinavian winter has meant that Nordic designers have always been much more interested than those from most other countries in the creation of innovative lighting and the quality of the light it emits. Today, Scandinavia continues to benefit from a vibrant lighting design sector, with many home-grown talents designing for both native and foreign manufacturing companies. For example, the renowned Danish-Icelandic installation artist Olafur Eliasson designed his modular Starbrick pendant light in 2009 for the well-known German manufacturer Zumtobel. Another design that deserves special mention is the Block lamp (1997) by the Finnish designer Harri Koskinen, in which an ordinary light bulb is simply but innovatively encased in a thick-walled glass box. This was one of the most acclaimed lighting designs of the 1990s, and helped to catapult its creator into the rarefied ranks of international design stardom. The other two designs shown here, the Work lamp (2009) by Form Us With Love and the Mutatio table light (2014) by Christian Troels, likewise demonstrate how Scandinavian designers love to come up with inventive lighting that looks good and functions well.

Below: Block lamp by Harri Koskinen for Design House Stockholm (Sweden), 1997

1. Starbrick pendant light by Olafur Eliasson for Zumtobel (Germany), 2009

2. Mutatio table light by Christian Troels for Le Klint (Denmark), 2013

3. Work lamp by Form Us With Love for Design House Stockholm (Sweden), 2009

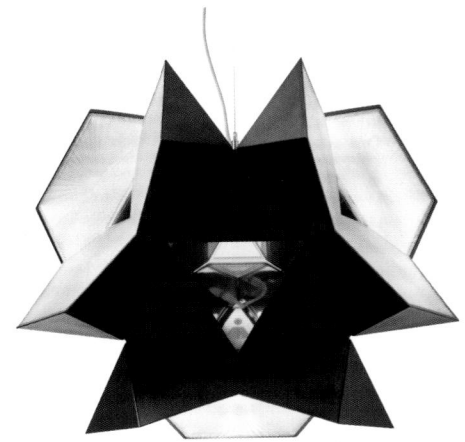

1.

2.

3.

LOUIS POULSEN CONTEMPORARY

Over the last 90 years the Copenhagen-based manufacturer Louis Poulsen has been guided by a lighting philosophy initiated by the pioneering scientific research into light diffusion and reflection undertaken in the late 1920s by its legendary chief designer, Poul Henningsen. To put it simply, the company is interested in producing only 'human-friendly' lighting that provides pleasant, healthful, non-glaring illumination. In fact, the firm has codified this philosophy with the acronym FCA: function, comfort, ambience. It is this human-centric approach to lighting design that has driven

the development of its contemporary lighting designs by the Copenhagen-based designer Louise Campbell, which feature cleverly louvred light-screening elements. Likewise, the recently launched, colourful and shapely Cirque range by the Swedish designer and graphic artist Clara von Zweigbergk also provides a warm, soft light, which accords with the Poulsen philosophy. Looking like multi-hued spinning tops, the three Cirque pendants reflect the emitted light off their polished internal copper surfaces, softening it. The design was inspired by a trip to the Tivoli Gardens, which is a short walk from the firm's headquarters and showroom in Copenhagen.

1. Snow floor light by Louise Campbell for Louis Poulsen (Denmark), 2009

2. Collage pendant light by Louise Campbell for Louis Poulsen (Denmark), 2005

3. LC Shutters pendant light by Louise Campbell for Louis Poulsen (Denmark), 2012

Opposite: Cirque pendant lights by Clara von Zweigbergk for Louis Poulsen (Denmark), 2016

1.

2.

3.

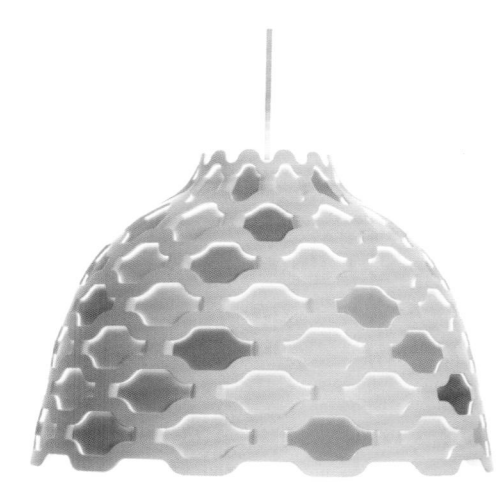

GLASSWARE

he manufacturing of glass has always been ed to nature. Before the harnessing of gas nd electricity for power, some 40 cubic metres f timber per day were needed to keep the furaces going at a single glassworks in order to nelt sand into glass. Scandinavian glassworks ere therefore founded in densely forested egions. The growth in the number of Nordic lassworks during the nineteenth century was artly caused by a shift within iron manufacuring away from extracting the metal from ogs and lakes to the more efficient mines. his meant that the glassworks no longer had o compete for timber in the areas they had reviously shared. The most common products made by glassworks before the twentieth entury were bottles, drinking glasses, jars nd windowpanes. However, in the latter half f the nineteenth century the arrival of gas ghting created a need for light fittings.

The oldest surviving Scandinavian glassorks is Kosta, which was founded in 1742 by nders Koskull and Georg Bogislaus Staël on Holstein, two officers of the Swedish king harles XII's army. (The name Kosta derives om their surnames.) The glassworks is in he Småland district of southern Sweden, hisorically a poor area, where the production of ar, coal and iron were the main industries and arming was difficult, owing to the dense forsts and poor soil. The success of Kosta meant hat various entrepreneurial staff left to set up heir own glassworks. As late as 1965 there ere still 50 such firms in Sweden, of which 8 were in Småland.

But it was not Kosta that brought Swedish lass the long period of fame and success it njoyed during the twentieth century, but he firm's main competitor, Orrefors, also in måland. Founded in 1898 on the site of an oldr ironworks, the company produced mainly indow glass and bottles until 1913. When the actory changed hands in that year, Orrefors egan to produce drinking glasses, vases and ther homewares, some inspired by the Art louveau glassware of the French designer mile Gallé. The turning point came in 1916, hen Orrefors employed the artist Simon ate. The following year, Gate was joined by dward Hald, who had studied under Henri latisse in Paris. These gifted designers explored the 'Graal' technique developed by he master blower Knut Bergqvist in 1916, its ame inspired by the legend of the Holy Grail San Graal in Old French), which was said to ave contained the blood of Christ.

No exhibition was more important in romoting the Art Deco style than the xposition Internationale des Arts Décoratifs et Industriels Modernes in 1925, also known as the Paris World's Fair. The entry requirements stipulated that all designs be 'modern'. It was a huge international success and attracted more than 16 million visitors. The Neoclassical Swedish Pavilion designed by Carl Bergsten and furnished by, among others, Erik Gunnar Asplund, drew considerable praise; its centrepiece was the colossal Parispokalen (Paris Cup) by Gate. In the Grand Palais, another display of Swedish design included glassware by Hald, decorated with engraved scenes of contemporary city life. Together, the two men's work helped to win Orrefors a gold medal, and Sweden won more medals in Paris than any other nation except the host. One of the many visitors was the British design critic Philip Morton Shand. In an article in *Architectural Review*, he used the term 'Swedish Grace' to describe what he had seen in Paris, making particular reference to Swedish glassware. Swedish Grace has become the standard term to describe the Neoclassic style found in Sweden in the 1920s, and which acted as a bridge between Art Deco and Modernism.

Another pioneering glassware designer, Edvin Örhström, joined Orrefors in 1936. He and the designer Vicke Lindstrand developed the Ariel technique (named after the character in Shakespeare's *The Tempest*), by which air bubbles are trapped within the glass. Nils Landberg and Sven Palmqvist, two engravers who had worked in the drawing office at Orrefors, were also promoted and became designers. Landberg created the elegant Mid-century Modern Tulip goblets (1957) with their slender stems, while Palmqvist became one of the great innovators of Swedish glass. He invented several new techniques, including Fuga, Kraka and Ravenna. Ingeborg Lundin joined the firm in 1947, and her large glass Apple vase of 1955 has become an icon of Swedish design. Gunnar Cyrén, a silversmith, joined the company in 1959. His colourful, stripy Pop glasses would come to epitomize Scandinavian design in the Swinging Sixties. In the 1970s Eva Englund joined Orrefors and was trained in the Graal technique by Hald. Her work was so popular that, at an exhibition in the NK department store in Stockholm, she allegedly sold 50 pieces in two minutes. During the 1970s and 1980s Olle Alberius, Lars Hellsten, Jan Johansson, Anne Nilsson, Erika Lagerbielke and Helén Krantz also designed for Orrefors, and in the 1990s and 2000s Lena Bergström and Ingegerd Råman produced memorable glassware for the company.

The Kosta glassworks also played a pivotal role in the development of Scandinavian glassware. It had changed hands in 1936, being taken over by the owners of Åfors glassworks.

Triton vases by Simon Gate for Orrefors (Sweden), 1923

Simon Gate with his famous Parispokalen (Paris Cup) for Orrefors (Sweden) – originally designed for the Paris World's Fair in 1925

Ariel vase, Model no. 304, by Edvin Öhrström for Orrefors (Sweden), 1944

Tulpan (Tulip) goblets by Nils Landberg for Orrefors (Sweden), 1957

Ravenna bowl by Sven Palmqvist for Orrefors (Sweden), ca. 1948 – technique developed in 1948

Opposite: Model 1379 vase by Erkkitapio Siiroinen for Riihimäen Lasi, Riihimäki (Finland), 1970

At this stage Kosta was in poor shape, and the former manager of the Emmaboda window glassworks, Alfred Rosén, was recruited as the venture's new director (a role that later passed to his son Lennart). In 1942 Kosta celebrated its 200th anniversary, but its main product was still a humble storage jar used during the war to conserve food. Things improved after the war, and the highly talented Vicke Lindstrand joined Kosta as a designer in 1950; he was such a forceful personality that eventually Lennart Rosén resigned and instead bought the old Reijmyre glassworks. In 1947 the owners of Åfors and Kosta bought Boda glassworks, where Alfred Rosén's son Erik became manager at the age of 23. In 1958 Åfors was added to his responsibility, and from 1964 he was also in charge of Boda. This is significant because by the 1960s the Swedish glass industry was in crisis owing to competition from cheap imports; without the talent of Erik Rosén, it would not have survived as long as it did.

The most important new designer recruited for Boda by Erik Rosén was Erik Höglund, who arrived in 1947 when only 23 years old. With his big, chunky pieces of coloured glass, often containing random air bubbles, he initially shocked the workers at Boda, but over time he became a favourite with the public. Another notable figure was Mona Morales-Schildt, who began working for Kosta in 1958, having previously assisted Wilhelm Kåge at the Gustavsberg porcelain factory and designed ceramics for the Finnish company Arabia. She stayed until 1971 at Kosta, where she created a series of beautiful cased-glass vases. Other well-known names who had their breakthrough in glass design at Kosta or Boda in the 1960s and early 1970s include Bertil Vallien, Monica Backström, Göran Wärff, Ann Wärff, Signe Persson-Melin, Kjell Engman and Ulrica Hydman-Vallien. The silversmith Sigurd Persson also worked for Kosta during this period.

Sadly, however, the Swedish glass industry was on the wane by the mid 1970s. The ceramics company Upsala-Ekeby – which had bought the porcelain producer Rörstrand in 1964 – went on to acquire Kosta and Boda in 1975, merging them into Kosta Boda in 1977. In 1982 an investment company bought Upsala-Ekeby and the group was split up. Kosta Boda was sold to another investment company, which merged it with Orrefors to form Orrefors Kosta Boda in 1990. In 1997 the company was sold to the Danish group Royal Scandinavia, which also numbered in its portfolio Holmegaard, Georg Jensen, Royal Copenhagen and Venini. Production at Boda eventually ceased in 2003, and in 2005 – with production remaining only at Åfors, Kosta and Orrefors – the group was sold yet again.

In 2013 the new owner closed manufacturing operations at Åfors and Orrefors, leaving only Sweden's oldest glassworks, Kosta, still operating on home soil. Some historic glassworks in Småland still carry on, notably Pukeberg, Skruf and Nybro, but the golden age of glass production in Småland – once known as the 'Kingdom of Glass' – is now most definitely in the past.

Finnish glass did not attain the international success of Swedish glass during the 1920s, but it more than made up for that in the decades that followed. In 1932 Karhula glassworks (established in 1888 in the village of Karhula, and later merged with Iittala) held a competition that both Alvar Aalto and his first wife, Aino, entered independently, he under a pseudonym since he was well known. Aino beat him with her design Bölgeblick (Wave View), winning second prize. The Aaltos had visited the Stockholm Exhibition of 1930, where one of Erik Gunnar Asplund's buildings by the sea was named Böljeblick, its roof covered with corrugated steel, similar in shape to the rippling rings on water. The glass series is made to this day, now by Iittala as the 'Aino Aalto' collection.

The second Aalto design to put Finnish glass on the map was also for Karhula, created this time by Alvar, with the intriguing title Eskimoerindens Skinnbuxa (Eskimo Woman's Leather Trousers). The name derives from the notion that the vase's shape was reminiscent of the form created by an Eskimo woman leaving her leather trousers in a heap outside her igloo, where they subsequently freeze into a stiff mass. The vase was first shown at the Exposition Internationale des Arts et Techniques dans la Vie Moderne of 1937 in Paris, for which Aalto had designed the forest-inspired Finnish Pavilion, Le Bois est en Marche (The Wood Is on the March). That same year he designed the Savoy restaurant in Helsinki – still in existence with its original interior – incorporating this undulating vase, which as a consequence is often referred to as the Savoy vase.

The painter Göran Hongell became the first designer to be employed full-time by Karhula-Iittala. In 1949 he created Aarne, the first glassware range with an integrated single-stage stem. Aarne won a gold medal at the Milan Triennial of 1954, and remains Hongell's best-known glassware design, having been put back into production by Iittala in 1981.

The biggest leap forwards in Finnish glass design, however, came in the aftermath of World War II with the work of Timo Sarpaneva and Tapio Wirkkala. Both were multitalented geniuses who worked in a wide range of design disciplines and materials, but they are most widely known for their work in glass. In 1946 Wirkkala won a competition

held by Iittala and began designing for th glassworks. Over the next five years h produced many designs for Iittala, of whic more than 120 were put into productio He was awarded three gold medals at th Milan Triennial in 1951 for his glass design Like Sarpaneva, Wirkkala created both a glass and everyday glassware, including th hugely popular and influential Ultima Thu glassware range (1968). In the late 1960s h designed the new Finlandia vodka bottle, als based on a surface structure made to loo like melting ice.

Sarpaneva began working for Iittala i 1951, and that year received a silver med at the Milan Triennial, followed by sever gold medals for his sculptural glassware. F the introduction of his colourful i-linja (i-lin glassware range (1956), he also designed sty ish packaging and a new logotype for Iittala, white 'i' in a red circle, that is still in use toda Sarpaneva was a friend of the Finnish pres dent Urho Kekkonen, who awarded him th Pro Finlandia Medal in 1958 (Wirkkala ha been the recipient of this prestigious Finnis art award three years earlier). Sarpanev also designed textiles, ceramics and cas iron cookware, but it was his work in glas that brought him widest acclaim, especial his bark-like Finlandia series of glasswar (1964–70) and his iconic icicle-like Festiv candlesticks (1966).

Kaj Franck, who had initially worke at the Arabia ceramics factory in 1945, wa also a key figure in the development Modern glassware in Finland. The followin year, however, he was awarded second an third prizes in the Iittala competition tha was won by Wirkkala, and that led Franc to join the glassworks as a designer. In 19 he moved to the Nuutajärvi glasswork continuing to work concurrently as artist director of Arabia. His simple and function Kartio series (1958) would become his bes selling glassware design, and today, near six decades after its launch, it remains i production.

Nanny Still worked as a designer f the Riihimäen Lasi glassworks in Riihimä from 1949 until 1976. She also designe glassware for Val Saint Lambert in Belgiun where she lived for some time. From 197 she likewise created glass and ceramic de signs for Rosenthal in Germany. Alway formally inventive and a superb colouris she won the Diplôme d'honneur at the Mila Triennial of 1954. Two other well-know female glass designers who worked f Riihimäen were Gunnel Nyman and Helen Tynell. Riihimäen was at one point the larg est glassworks in Finland, but, as were s many Nordic glassworks, it was sadly force to close its doors in 1990. Today, however, i vocative old buildings contain the Finnish Glass Museum, which testifies to the rich artistry found in Finnish glassware during its golden period.

The museum's collection features heavily the work of Oiva Toikka, who introduced the Pop aesthetic to Finnish glassware when he began designing for Iittala in the 1960s, having first worked in ceramics. His Kastehelmi (Dewdrop) series of 1964 was a great commercial success and has recently been put back into production, but his most famous body of work is without question his series of glass birds, launched in 1973. The multitalented Toikka has also created textile designs for Marimekko and worked as a stage and costume designer.

In more recent times, Harri Koskinen has forged an international reputation with his glassware for Iittala, the first of which was introduced in 1996. Since then he has contributed both to Iittala's product line and to those of its sister brands Arabia and Hackman. He has also acted more recently as Iittala's design director, while working for many other companies on a wide range of products.

Any survey of Nordic design must include the output of Hadeland glassworks in Norway, the country's oldest surviving industrial company. In 1928 it employed Sverre Pettersen as head of design, and he stayed until 1949. The master glass-blower Johan Wilhelm Johansson's son Willy Johansson became a designer there in 1947 and soon became head of design, having been an apprentice since 1936; he worked there until he retired in 1988. He won a gold metal at the Milan Triennial in 1957. Arne Jon Jutrem, who had studied under the painter and sculptor Fernand Léger in Paris, joined Hadeland in 1950. He won a gold metal at the Milan Triennial in 1954 and later designed for Holmegaard in Denmark (1963–66). After a period as a painter in Paris in 1968–72, Jutrem returned to Hadeland in 1984. Another Hadeland designer who picked up medals in Milan during the 1950s was Hermann Bongard.

The most famous Danish glassworks, Holmegaard, was founded in 1823. Its golden era stretched from the 1930s to the 1980s with the work of Jacob Bang, Per Lütken and Bang's son Michael. Jacob Bang, who started at the company in 1928, introduced Modernist designs. Lütken worked there from 1942 until his death in 1998, creating over 3,000 different designs. The company's speciality was bi-coloured glass, often white inside with strong colours on the outside, as in the Gulvvase (floor vase) by Otto Brauer (1962), based on a design by Lütken from 1958. The strong colours and forms continued in the 1960s with the Carnaby series, inspired by Swinging London. The Danish design

company Rosendahl now owns Holmegaard, and in 2009 production was moved abroad.

There was another notable pioneer of Modern glassware in Denmark during the 1950s and 1960s: the Kastrup glassworks. After a number of mergers, it came to own Hellerup glassworks, Aarhus glassworks and United glassworks in Odense. Several prolific designers worked for Kastrup, including Jacob Bang, Nanna and Jørgen Ditzel, Grethe Meyer and Sigvard Bernadotte. It was merged with Holmegaard in 1965 and closed in 1979.

Although the Nordic glassware industry is a shadow of its former self in both creative and manufacturing terms, the brands that have survived – particularly Iittala and Orrefors – are enjoying renewed interest. Design excellence in glassware has long been found in Scandinavia, and that will undoubtedly continue to be so, for no other medium expresses the quality of light better. As anyone who has spent time in the North will explain, light, even if it takes the form of a votive candleholder, is highly prized during the dark days and long nights of winter.

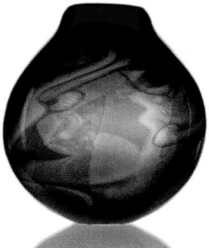

Graal bowl by Eva Englund for Orrefors (Sweden), 1988

Zebra vase by Vicke Lindstrand for Kosta (Sweden), 1950s

Bottle, vases and drinking glasses by Erik Höglund for Boda (Sweden), 1960s

Viktigt glassware by Ingegerd Råman for IKEA (Sweden), 2016

Bölgeblick jug and tumblers by Aino Aalto for Karhula (Finland), 1932 – later produced by Iittala

SWEDISH GRACE – ART DECO

The breakthrough for Swedish design came at the Exposition Internationale des Arts Décoratifs et Industriels Modernes in Paris in 1925, when the designs on show in the Swedish Pavilion led to the coining of the phrase 'Swedish Grace' to describe a distinctive Scandinavian Art Deco style. The pavilion, designed by Carl Bergsten, took the form of a white Neo-Greek temple with Ionic columns, but inside was intricately engraved,

Neoclassically inspired glassware, including Simon Gate's specially designed Parispokalen (Paris Cup) for Orrefors glassworks, an enormous Baroque-inspired urn. The use of refined engraving continued to evolve at Orrefors over the next decade or so, but during the late 1920s and the 1930s it became much bolder, as reflected by Vicke Lindstrand's Pearl Diver vase. It was, however, a later vase by Lindstrand, featuring intertwining female nudes, that perhaps marked the artistic and technical apotheosis of glass engraving in Sweden.

1. Pearl Diver vase by Vicke Lindstrand for Orrefors (Sweden), 1930s

2. Engraved glass bowl with stand by Simon Gate for Orrefors (Sweden), 1928

Opposite: Cut and sandblasted vase by Vicke Lindstrand for Orrefors (Sweden), ca. 1937

1.

2.

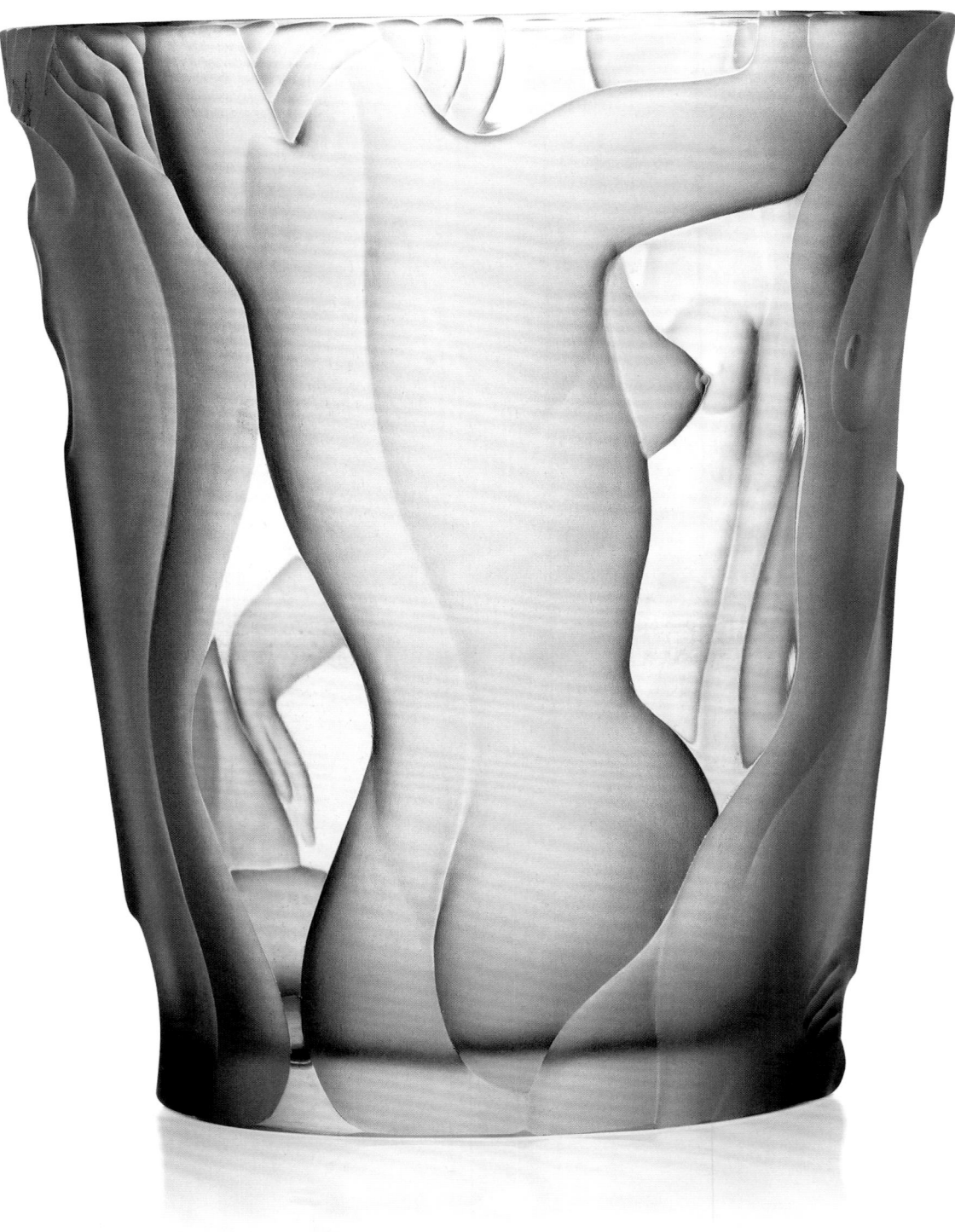

SIMON GATE

Having studied painting in Stockholm, Simon Gate was an accomplished fine artist when in 1916 he became the first artist-designer to be recruited by Johan Ekman, owner of the Orrefors glassworks. The appointment was prompted by Ekman's desire to develop glassware designs that had a greater sense of artistry. In fact, Gate had the creative breadth to design both functional, everyday wares (which were produced by Orrefors' sister company Sandvik) and more artistic pieces, which were often engraved with Neo-Baroque pictorial scenes; his Parispokalen (Paris Cup) for the Paris Exposition Internationale des Arts Décoratifs et Industriels Modernes in

1925 was the most celebrated of such pieces. At Orrefors, with the master glass-blower Knut Bergkvist, Gate also developed an important new technique, which was named Graal after the Holy Grail. It involved covering glass blanks with thin layers of coloured glass that were then incised with motifs and encased in another layer of clear glass. The technique could be used to create an interesting mosaic-like effect, as can be seen in the blue bowl shown below. During the 1930s Gate created bolder designs that were simpler in form and decoration, reflecting the growing influence of Modernism in Scandinavia. As experimental as his earlier work, many of these weighty pieces featured square-cut geometric motifs that gave a faceted, jewel-like effect.

Below: Graal bowl by Simon Gate for Orrefors (Sweden) 1928 – executed by Knut Bergqvist

1. Model no. SP14 vase by Simon Gate for Orrefors (Sweden), ca. 1930 – designed for the Stockholm Exhibition of 1930

2. Vase by Simon Gate for Orrefors (Sweden), late 1920s

3. Model no. 1506 vase by Simon Gate for Orrefors (Sweden), 1931

1.

2.

3.

1.

2.

3.

AINO AALTO

Aino Marsio began working in Alvar Aalto's architecture practice in 1924. The couple fell in love and married the following year. In 1935 they founded their own manufacturing company, Artek, to produce their furniture designs (see p. 84). Before this, however, Aino had forged a reputation as an innovative designer in her own right by winning second prize in a glassware competition held by Karhula in 1932. Her prize-winning Bölgeblick (Wave View) range of pressed glassware embodied

the Functionalist spirit that emerged in Scandinavian design in the early 1930s. Its concentric, ribbed forms were inspired by ripples of water as they spread outwards, and it takes its name from the Norwegian word for this phenomenon. This versatile, stackable, space-saving product range was well suited to industrial production and heralded a forward-looking Modern aesthetic in Finnish glassware. Produced in a number of colours, the Bölgeblick glassware was awarded a gold medal at the 6th Milan Triennial in 1936.

1. Bölgeblick jug by Aino Aalto for Karhula (later Iittala; Finland), 1932

2. Early example of a bowl from the Bölgeblick glassware range by Aino Aalto for Karhula (Finland), 1930s/1940s

3. Competition design drawings for the Bölgeblick range by Aino Aalto, ca. 1932

Below: Bölgeblick tumblers by Aino Aalto for Karhula (later Iittala; Finland), 1932

THE AALTO VASE

Alvar Aalto designed a range of glassware, including vases in various shapes, sizes and colours, for a competition organized by Karhula-Iittala in 1936 to find designs suitable for display at the Exposition Internationale des Arts et Techniques dans la Vie Moderne to be held the following year in Paris. Of these competition-winning models, the Aalto vase (also sometimes referred to as the Savoy vase) went on to become one of the most iconic Scandinavian designs ever created. It also adorned the tables of the up-market Savoy restaurant in Helsinki, designed by Aalto in 1936–37 (see also pp. 208–9). The Aalto vase was revolutionary because its undulating biomorphic shape

meant that flowers fell away from one another when placed in it, rather than being kept in an upright, posy-like formation, meaning that they were more naturally positioned. The organic form of this seminal design was based on sketches that Aalto rather intriguingly entitled Eskimoerindens Skinnbuxa (Eskimo Woman's Leather Trousers); but, since Aalto was the son of a cartographer, it could be that the vase's asymmetrical outline was actually inspired by the Finnish landscape, which is famously dotted with lakes. Interestingly, *aalto* means 'wave' in Finnish, so this design may also have been intended as a play on his surname. It certainly evokes the ebb and flow of water along a shore.

Below: Aalto vase by Alvar Aalto for Karhula (later Iittala Finland), 1936

1 & 2. Two early examples of the Aalto vase by Alvar Aalto, manufactured by Karhula (Finland), late 1930s – first shown at the Exposition Internationale des Arts et Techniques dans la Vie Moderne, Paris, in 1937, the design is also often referred to as the Savoy vase

3. Alvar Aalto's sketches (coloured pencil and collage) for the Karhula glassware competition, 1936

1.

2.

3.

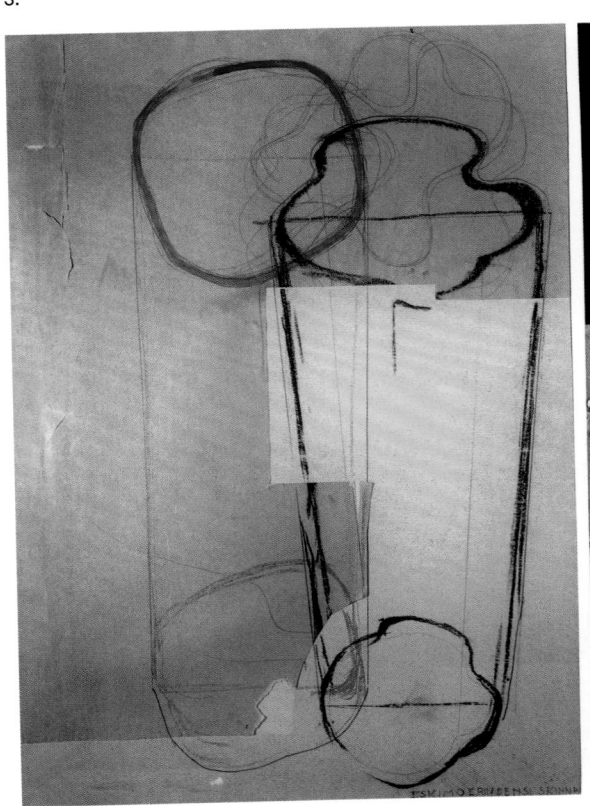
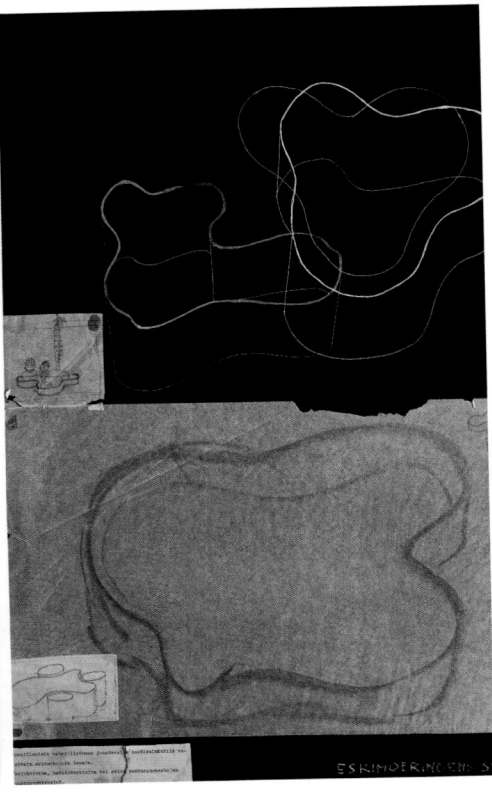

ALVAR AALTO GLASSWARE

In 1933 Alvar Aalto designed a five-part nesting glassware set for a competition held by the Riihimäen Lasi glassworks, and won second prize. This early nesting set was based on a series of simple concentric forms, but Aalto revisited the concept of nesting glassware six years later using a much more fluid and organic language of form, when he co-designed with his wife Aino the stunning Aalto-kukka (Aalto Flower) set, which comprised four stacking size-gradated vases/bowls. This new design was developed specifically for the New York World's Fair of 1939, its free-form shape echoing the extraordinary outward-sloping, undulating form of the Finnish Pavilion that Aalto designed for the event. That year Aalto also designed a set of stackable bowls, Model no. 9769 A-B-C-D, which were also subtly asymmetrical and had a strongly sculptural quality. These early glassware pieces by Aalto, including his famous 'Savoy' range of 1936, presaged the innovative organic-form art-glass vessels designed by Tapio Wirkkala and Timo Sarpaneva for Iittala in the 1950s and 1960s.

1. Aalto-kukka (Aalto Flower) set of four nesting vases/bowls by Alvar and Aino Aalto for Karhula-Iittala (later Iittala; Finland), 1939

2. Aalto vase by Alvar Aalto for Karhula (later Iittala; Finland), 1936 – this low-sided version of Aalto's famous design was also intended to function as a serving dish

Opposite: Model nos. 9769 A-B-C-D stackable bowls for Iittala (Finland), 1939 – these examples were produced in 1956

1.

2.

EDWARD HALD

Between 1908 and 1912, Edward Hald trained in France under the Post-Impressionist artist Henri Matisse, an experience that had a profound stylistic influence on his work as an innovative designer of artistic glassware. In 1917 Hald was employed by Orrefors to create 'beautiful things for everyday life', and began designing pieces of engraved glassware that revealed the Expressionist influence of his French mentor. By the late 1920s and the 1930s, however, he had moved away from the Swedish Grace style and was creating bolder vessels that had a modernistic quality. In 1933 he was appointed managing director of Orrefors, and under his leadership the glassworks continued production throughout the war, despite a severe decrease in exports and a shortage of materials. It was during this period that Hald invented two innovative techniques, Slip Graal and Fish Graal. The former involved carving ridges into a sandwich layer of coloured glass, which was then encased in clear glass; the latter produced a painting-like scene trapped within the vessel's thick glass walls. The lively designs shown here, which were created in the mid 1950s using these techniques, demonstrate Hald's mastery of glass as an expressive medium.

1. Fish Graal vase by Edward Hald for Orrefors (Sweden), 1936

2. Slip Graal bowl by Edward Hald for Orrefors (Sweden), 1954

Opposite: Slip Graal vase by Edward Hald for Orrefors (Sweden), 1954

1.

2.

GUNNEL NYMAN

On graduating from the Taideteolliseen Keskuskouluun (Central School of Art), Helsinki, in 1932, Gunnel Nyman became a designer for the Riihimäen Lasi glassworks. She subsequently pioneered an innovative technique that involved blowing molten glass into a pin-studded mould in order to create an even distribution of tiny indentations. The resulting pricked-glass body was then encased in thick glass, producing an attractive pattern of minuscule trapped bubbles. Her designs were

also distinguished by the use of soft, organic forms, such as the twisted shape of her stunning GN27 vase of 1947. Although Nyman is known best for her encased-bubble vases, she also created another well-known design, the Calla vase (1946), which took the abstract form of a lily. Sadly, Nyman's untimely death at the age of 39 meant that she was unable to build on these early achievements, but her innovative pricked-bubble technique became highly influential both at home and abroad, and her designs remained extremely popular throughout the 1950s.

Below: Model no. GN17 bubble-cased glass vase by Gunnel Nyman for Nuutajärvi Notsjö (Finland), ca. 1943

1. Model no. GN27 bubble-cased glass vase by Gunnel Nyman for Nuutajärvi Notsjö (Finland), 1947

2. Model no. GN25 bubble-cased glass vase by Gunnel Nyman for Nuutajärvi Notsjö (Finland), ca. 1945 – this example executed 1955

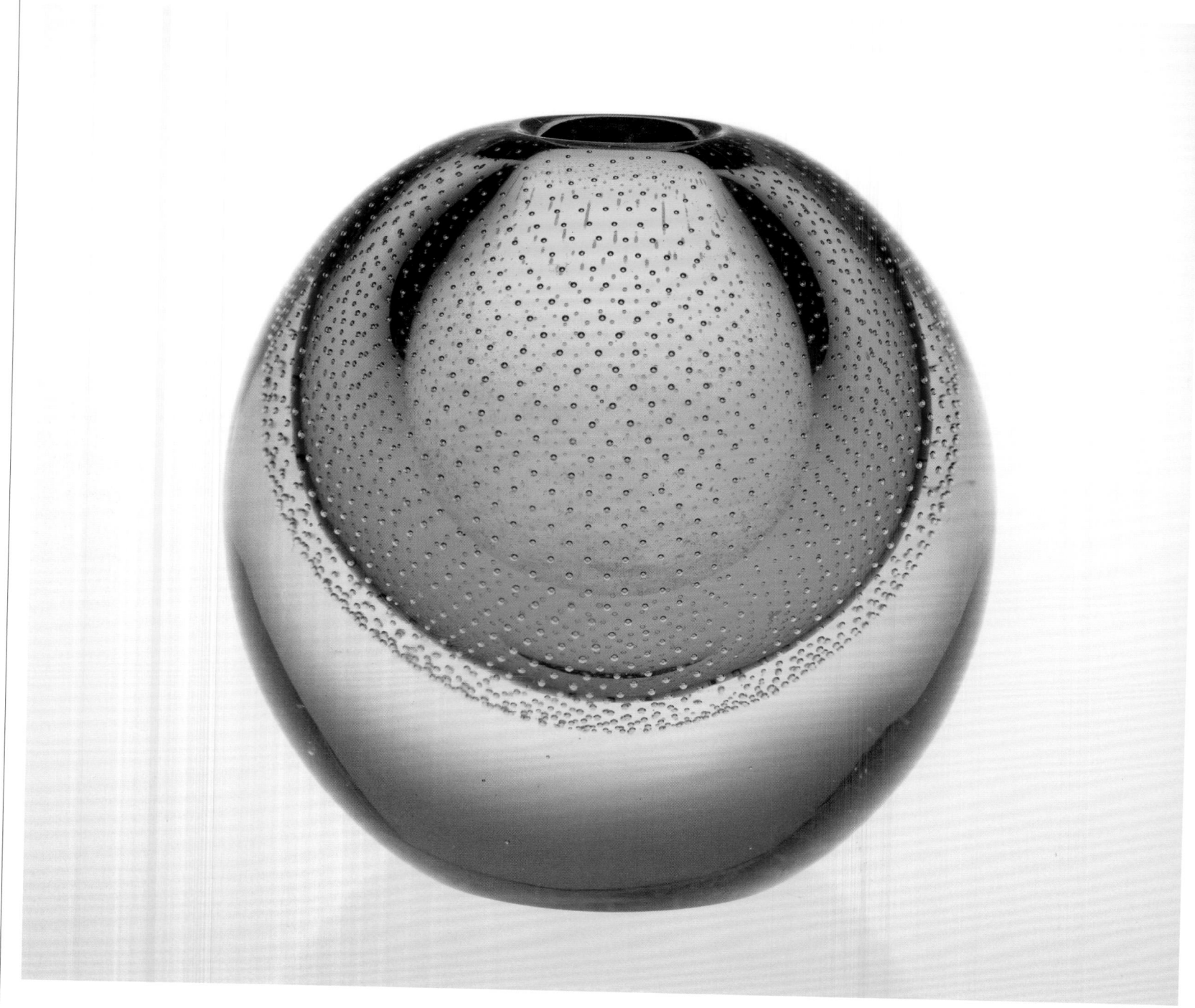

1.

2.

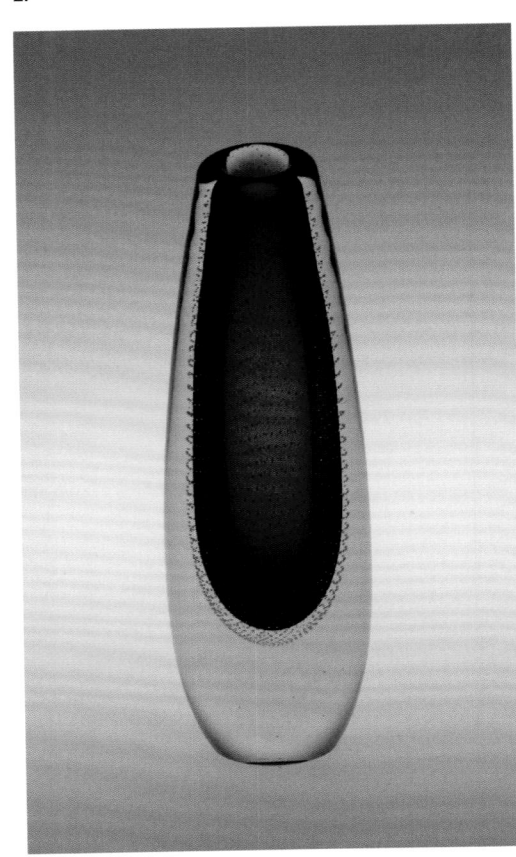

PER LÜTKEN

An acknowledged master of Danish glassware design as well as an accomplished glass-blower, Per Lütken is credited with having designed over 3,000 pieces of glass for the Holmegaard glassworks. He worked there as a designer for more than half a century, joining the firm in 1942 and remaining there until his death in 1998. During the 1950s he created two seminal designs, the Provence bowl (1955) and the Selandia dish (1957), both of which remain in production thanks to the timeless appeal of their soft-edged sculptural forms. Lütken was by all accounts a perfectionist, and when

glass-blowers complained about the technical difficulties involved in making his designs, he would famously retort: 'Well, who said things were supposed to be easy?' It was this tireless can-do spirit that led him to experiment constantly and was ultimately responsible for a number of other successful designs, including the free-form Flamingo series (1953), which incorporated the *sommerso* technique; the colourful Pop-inspired Carnaby series (1968); and various elegant drinking-glass ranges, including Ship's Glass (1971) and Charlotte Amelie (1981) – both of which reflected the Danish obsession with ideal forms.

Below: Provence bowl by Per Lütken for Holmegaard (Denmark), 1955

Opposite: Selandia shallow dish by Per Lütken for Holmegaard (Denmark), 1957

VICKE LINDSTRAND

Vicke Lindstrand consistently developed new techniques and pioneered new forms during his long career. He first made a name for himself as a glass designer in the 1930s with his Art Deco vessels for Orrefors, incorporating delicately engraved figurative motifs. Having left Orrefors in 1940, Lindstrand spent the next decade working for the ceramics manufacturer Upsala-Ekeby, for which he produced a number of free-form designs. In 1950 he was appointed art director of the Kosta glassworks (a position that he would hold for 23 years), and began designing glassware with similarly abstracted forms, which were technically and decoratively much more interesting than anything he had done before. His Abstracta series epitomized his output during this period and revealed the influence of Abstract Expressionism, the internal 'trapped' decoration of the vases recalling the dripped lines of Jackson Pollock's action paintings of the late 1940s and early 1950s. The free-form black vase (ca. 1954) shown below similarly reveals the influence of the then-fashionable biomorphic trend. As one of the most formidably gifted glassware designers of the twentieth century, Lindstrand was, time and again, able skilfully to channel the progressive spirit of the era in his remarkably accomplished designs.

Opposite & 1. Abstracta (Abstract) vases by Vicke Lindstrand for Kosta (Sweden), 1950s

2. Free-form pierced vase by Vicke Lindstrand for Kosta (Sweden), ca. 1954 – this design was included in the landmark 'Design in Scandinavia' US travelling exhibition of 1954–57

3. Winter vase by Vicke Lindstrand for Kosta (Sweden), 1950s

3.

SVEN PALMQVIST

Sven Palmqvist trained at the Orrefors glass-works' engraving school before joining the firm's design team in 1930. Encouraged by Simon Gate, and while still working for the glassworks, Palmqvist continued his studies at the Konstfack (University College of Arts, Crafts and Design) and the Konstakademien (Academy of Art) in Stockholm. He later took study trips to Germany and Czechoslovakia, and studied at the Académie Ranson in Paris under Paul Cornet and Aristide Maillol. During World War II Palmqvist returned to Sweden and resumed his design career at Orrefors, staying there until 1972 and then working as a freelance designer for the glassworks.

During this long tenure he invented various influential glass techniques, including Kraka (1944), Ravenna (1948) and Fuga (1954), which cemented his reputation as one of the most innovative glass artists of his generation. His Ravenna technique, inspired by a trip to the northern Italian town famed for its Byzantine mosaics, involved a pattern being engraved into a coloured ground, layered with differently hued crushed glass and encased in a layer of clear glass so as to produce a mosaic-like effect. It was, however, Palmqvist's centrifugally moulded Fuga range of glassware, comprising basic utilitarian forms and produced in a variety of sizes, that ultimately won him a prestigious Grand Prix at the 11th Milan Triennial, in 1957.

1. Print advertisement by Anders Beckman for Orrefors (Sweden), 1956 – showing sculptural vessels similar to those designed by Sven Palmqvist for the glassworks

2. Fuga bowl by Sven Palmqvist for Orrefors (Sweden), 1954

3. Ravenna bowl by Sven Palmqvist for Orrefors (Sweden), 1959

4. Ravenna bowl, Model no. 7194, by Sven Palmqvist for Orrefors (Sweden), 1950s/1960s

5. Ravenna bowl, Model no. 1685, by Sven Palmqvist for Orrefors (Sweden), 1960

1.

2.

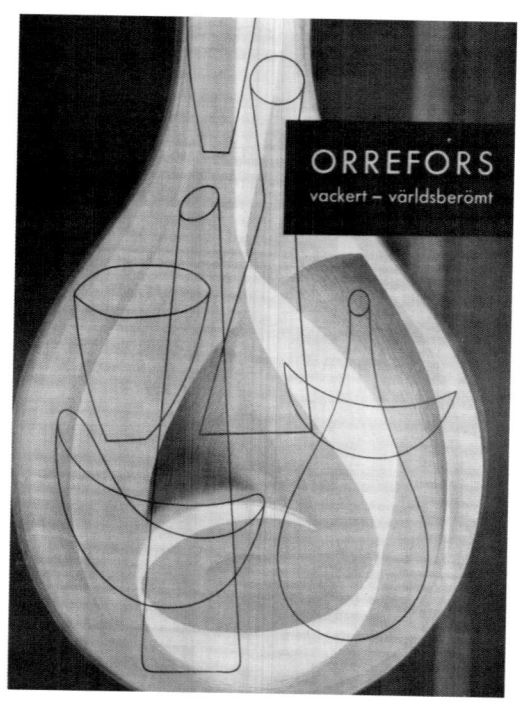

3.

4.

5.

ERIK HÖGLUND

Often credited with revitalizing Swedish art glass, Erik Höglund was an exceptionally gifted glassware designer who pioneered his own very distinct craft-orientated and artful style. His collaboration with the Boda glassworks spanned two decades – 1953 to 1973 – and over this period he created numerous everyday glassware designs that were infused with sculptural bravado. His pieces emphasized the intrinsic material properties of glass, often employing free-blown techniques and thick-walled bubbled soda glass. Inspired by historic glassware, he also frequently employed 'impressed' seal-like motifs to decorate his pieces for a charming folk-art quality. In fact, this type of rustic decorative device – mainly depicting animals or naked women in a primitive style – became a signature of his work, and was widely copied by other designers.

Below: Bull ashtray/bowl by Erik Höglund for Boda (Sweden), ca. 1960

1. Decanter, bowl, vases and goblet by Erik Höglund for Boda (Sweden), ca. 1953–1960s

2. Seven different ashtrays and bowls by Erik Höglund for Boda (Sweden), ca. 1960

1.

2.

TIMO SARPANEVA – FORM-GIVER

In the 1950s Finnish design was reaching its zenith in terms of sheer creativity and international influence. There were few designers in Finland whose work was more exciting than that of Timo Sarpaneva, who was able to create sculptural yet functional glassware designs that captured the abstract essence of nature with their seductive organic forms. A remarkably talented form-giver, Sarpaneva produced for the Iittala glassworks numerous designs, such as those shown here, that blurred the long-established boundaries between art and design, and that evoked that special, almost mystical, connection with nature that most Finns believe they possess. Many of his pieces had either an icy or a frosted look, which is testament to the skill of Iittala's glass-blowers: the pieces appear to have been formed from frozen water, rather than blown from red-hot molten glass.

Below: Lancet III art object/vase by Timo Sarpaneva for Iittala (Finland), 1955

1. Devil's Churn sculptural free-form plate by Timo Sarpaneva for Iittala (Finland), 1950

2. Orchid vases by Timo Sarpaneva for Iittala (Finland), 1954

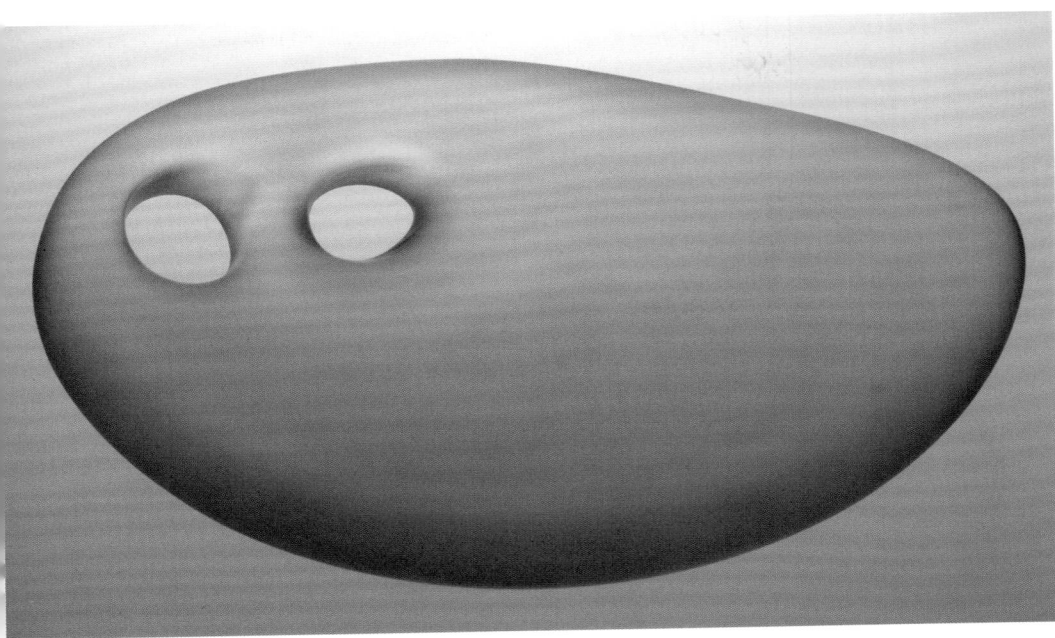

1.

2.

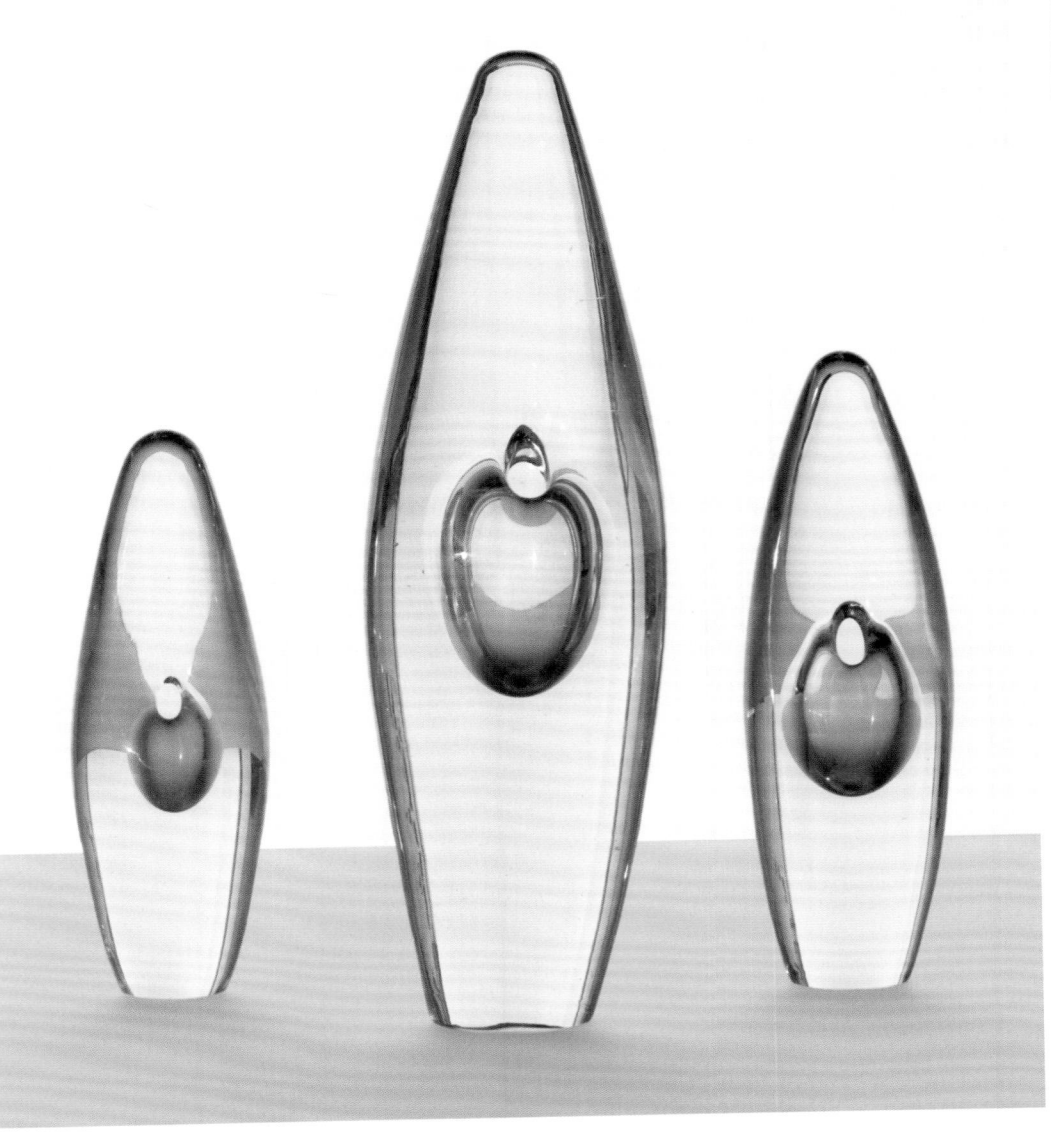

TIMO SARPANEVA – DESIGN FROM NATURE

Having designed exquisite, organic-inspired glassware in the 1950s, Timo Sarpaneva developed in the 1960s an influential range of art glass, known as Finlandia (1964), which took an even more emphatic step towards designing from nature. Indeed, the bark patterns that distinguish this series of vases and bowls were made by nature itself, in that Sarpaneva lined the moulds into which molten glass was blown with charred pieces of tree trunk. The textured patterns that resulted from this process mirrored the unique and irregular bark of the wood. Sarpaneva eventually abandoned the use of wood-lined moulds, which burned further and further every time they were used, in favour of imprinted metal moulds, which were better suited to his higher-volume glassware designs. Sarpaneva's innovative textured pieces, including his well-known Festivo candlesticks (1966), heralded a completely new frosted-ice aesthetic in glassware, which became hugely influential on glass design in the 1970s, both in Scandinavia and elsewhere.

1. Finlandia (Crack on the Ice) vase by Timo Sarpaneva for Iittala (Finland), 1964

2. Festivo candlesticks by Timo Sarpaneva for Iittala (Finland), 1966

3. Finlandia vase, Model no. 3356, by Timo Sarpaneva for Iittala (Finland), 1964

4. (From left) Nardus, Crassus and Krookus vases by Timo Sarpaneva for Iittala (Finland), 1960s/1970s

1.

2.

3.

4.

OIVA TOIKKA

Oiva Toikka, a well-known and much-loved designer in his native Finland, has perhaps pushed the technical and aesthetic boundaries of Scandinavian art glass further than any other design practitioner. Having trained as a ceramicist and then worked for a decade as a designer at Arabia, Toikka held his first exhibition of glassware at the Wärtsilä showroom in Helsinki in 1963. The following year, for Nuutajärvi Notsjö, he designed his famous Kastehelmi (Dewdrop) range of moulded glassware, which was relaunched by Iittala in 2010. However, it is his colourful studio art-glass pieces from the mid to late 1960s, such as the examples shown here, that best demonstrate his imaginative Pop aesthetic. These led to his development of two comprehensive collections of art glass, intended for collectors. In 1972 he modelled a flycatcher bird in glass, the first of over 400 bird sculptures designed by him for Iittala. Five years later he introduced the first of his Annual Cubes – paperweight-like blocks of glass that tested the skill of Iittala's glass-blowers severely with their beautiful but technically difficult internal decorations.

Opposite: Lollipop art-glass object by Oiva Toikka for Nuutajärvi Notsjö (Finland), 1968

1. Pompom art-glass vase by Oiva Toikka for Nuutajärvi Notsjö (Finland), late 1960s

2. Flower art-glass object by Oiva Toikka for Nuutajärvi Notsjö (Finland), 1960s/1970s

3. Oiva Toikka at Nuutajärvi Notsjö, 1966

2.

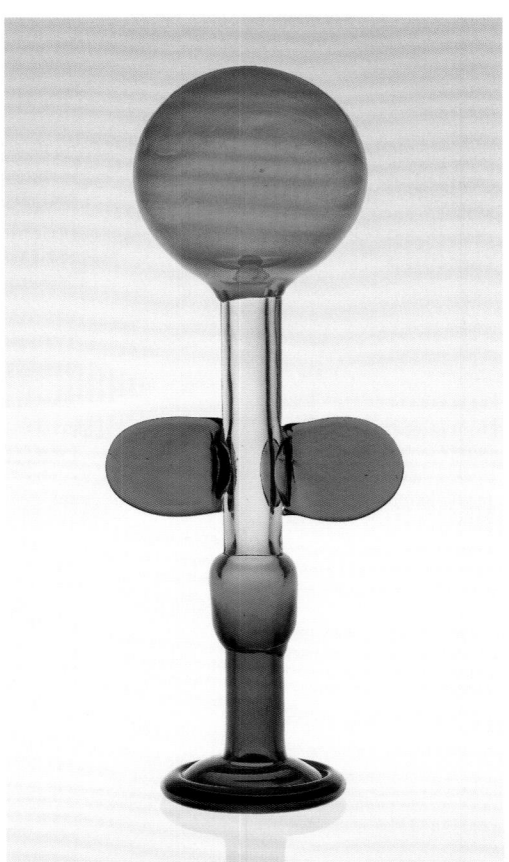

3.

KAJ FRANCK

The ceramicist and glassware designer Kaj Franck is often described as 'the conscience of Finnish design', for throughout his career he designed aesthetically pure objects, eliminating anything superfluous. His mass-produced Kartio glassware (1958) and Kilta and Teema china ranges (1948–52 and 1977–80) most notably embody this restrained approach to design. He did, however, produce other pieces, similarly formally refined but with a more playful spirit, which were manufactured in far lower numbers. For instance, his Prisma range of faceted vases (1954), his Kremlin Kellots (Kremlin Bells) double decanter (1957) and his colourful and chunky Pop goblets (1969) all reveal his skill as both a rational form-giver and a gifted colourist. Franck once noted: 'Colour is the only decoration needed.'

1. Prisma (Prism) vase by Kaj Franck for Nuutajärvi Notsjö (Finland), 1954

2. Pop goblets by Kaj Franck for Nuutajärvi Notsjö (Finland), 1969

3. Tupa jug with matching drinking glasses by Kaj Franck for Iittala (Finland), 1948

Opposite: Kremlin Kellots (Kremlin Bells) double decanters and Model no. KF 1500 decanter by Kaj Franck for Nuutajärvi Notsjö (Finland), 1957

1.

2.

3.

TAPIO WIRKKALA – NATURE AS INSPIRATION

The Finnish designer Tapio Wirkkala had a deep spiritual connection to nature, as many of his fellow countrymen do, and that was expressed time and again in his work. Indeed, the forms found in his work were almost entirely inspired by the natural world – a leaf, a bird, a whirlpool, a seashell, a tree trunk and a frozen puddle were all points of reference for his designs. Sometimes he was inspired by half-forgotten memories that provoked an abstract sense of nature's essence, the origin of which could not be directly identified. Having won first prize in a competition held by the Iittala glassworks in 1946, Wirkkala began working for the firm that year. Importantly for his development as a designer of glassware, he was given creative free rein there, and was actively encouraged to experiment, with the assistance of the company's skilled glass-blowers and technicians. The resulting body of work, which spanned more than four decades and includes the three designs shown here, was truly awesome in its comprehensiveness, inventiveness and sheer originality. Here we see, for instance, the forms of a delicately veined leaf, a chanterelle mushroom and an iceberg translated with breathtaking virtuosity into bowls and vases that were quite simply unlike any other glassware that had gone before.

Below: Model no. 3337 glass object/bowl by Tapio Wirkkala for Iittala (Finland), 1952

1. (From left) Model no. 3523 vase, ca. 1951; Lehti (Leaf) bowl, Model no. 3307, 1946; and Kantarelli (Chanterelle) vase, Model no. 3200, ca. 1952, by Tapio Wirkkala for Iittala (Finland)

2. Jäävuori (Iceberg) vase, Model no. 3525, by Tapio Wirkkala for Iittala (Finland), ca. 1951

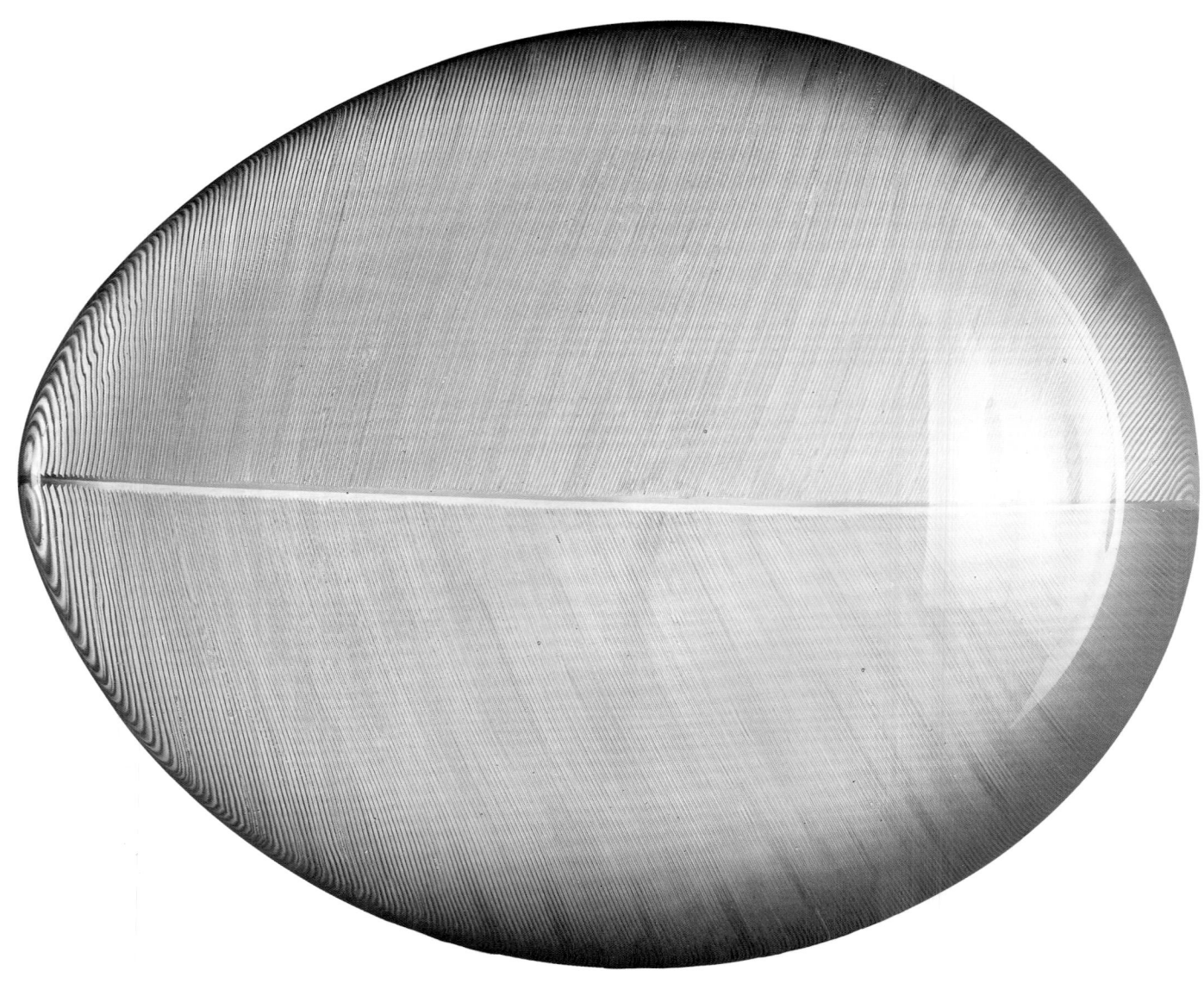

1.

2.

1.

2.

WIRKKALA + COLOUR FIELD GLASS

The famous Venini glassworks in Venice had over the decades earned an international reputation for its innovative, experimental, stunning glassware. Having worked exclusively with Italian designers, in the 1950s and early 1960s Venini decided to cast its design net beyond its national boundary. In the mid 1960s Tapio Wirkkala, like a number of other celebrated international designers, was invited to work as a freelance designer for the Venetian glassworks. Over the next two decades or so he designed a number of glass pieces that were totally different from the industrially produced glassware and

art glass he was concurrently designing for Iittala. Wirkkala's Venini pieces incorporated glass-blowing techniques that had been perfected by the Italian company's glass-blowers, most notably the famous *incalmo* method, which allowed different blown-glass elements to be fused precisely and seamlessly. The result was that Wirkkala's Venini pieces were not only technically more sophisticated than his work for Iittala, but also more delicate and formally refined. In addition, many incorporated multicoloured bands or patchworks of subtly contrasting shades of glass, which gave them a sense of gem-like preciousness and essentially made them the art-glass equivalent of Colour Field painting.

1. Model nos. 3584 and 3594 vases/art objects by Tapio Wirkkala for Iittala (Finland), 1955

2. Bolle bottle-vases by Tapio Wirkkala for Venini (Italy), 1966

Below: Free-blown glass charger by Tapio Wirkkala for Venini (Italy), 1967–68

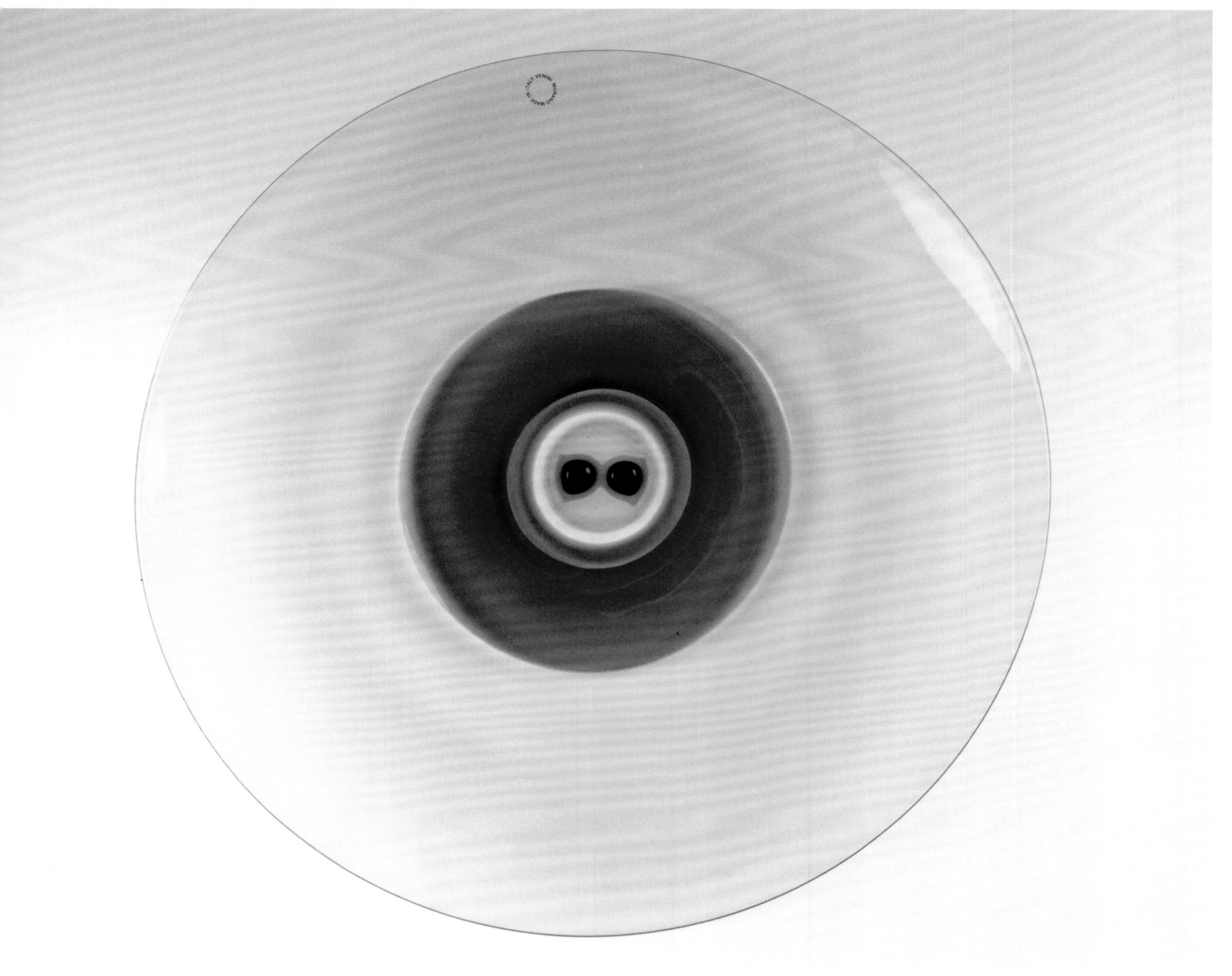

WIRKKALA'S ICE FORMS

As so often happens in Scandinavian in-house
design departments, Tapio Wirkkala's experimental studio art-glass pieces for Iittala
informed the development of less expensive,
serially manufactured products. In the
mid 1960s, with the help of Iittala's skilled
glass-blowers and technicians, both Wirkkala
and Timo Sarpaneva were exploring the production of textured glass pieces, the shapes
of which were inspired by forms found in
nature. While Sarpaneva experimented with
charred wooden moulds that gave his pieces
a bark-like texture (see pp. 266–67), Wirkkala
explored textured, frosted surfaces inspired
by the melting ice of Lapland, which he was
able to mimic skilfully by painstakingly carving patterns into moulds. His best-known
ice-form range is Ultima Thule (1968), named
after the designation used on medieval maps
to show northern lands that were beyond the
borders of the known world. So revolutionary
was this series of glasses, plates, jugs and so
on that it took thousands of hours to perfect
the necessary glass-blowing techniques for
its manufacture. Another Wirkkala design
that was also serially produced, albeit using a
mould blown-glass technique, was the Pinus
vase (1973), which is so strikingly realistic
that it is hard to believe it is not hewn from a
naturally formed block of melting ice.

1. Ultima Thule Model no. 2232 plate by Tapio Wirkkala
for Iittala (Finland), 1968

2. Ultima Thule glassware range by Tapio Wirkkala for
Iittala (Finland), 1968

Opposite: Pinus Model no. 2784 vase by Tapio Wirkkala
for Iittala (Finland), 1973

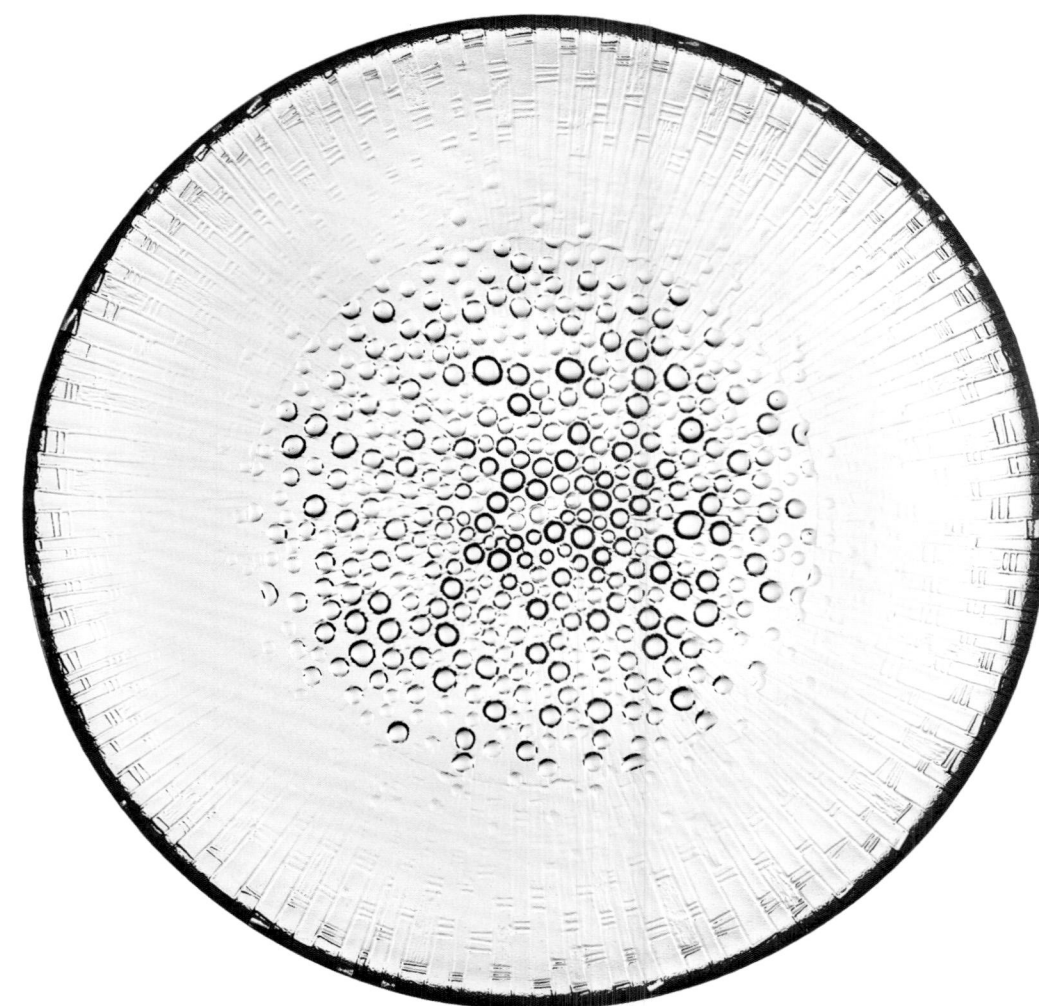

1.

2.

HOLMEGAARD DECANTERS

In 1825 Countess Henriette Danneskiold-Samsøe established a glassworks at Holmegaard Mose (Holmegaard Moor), having received royal assent from King Frederick VI. The location was chosen because its peat bog would provide fuel to operate a high-temperature glass kiln. The glassworks produced green bottles at first, but it soon diversified into making tableware with the assistance of Bohemian glass-blowers. From the 1840s Holmegaard produced a very specific type of spirit decanter known as a *klukflaske* (gurgling bottle), which was popular in Scandinavia for the pouring of ice-cold *snaps* or aquavit. In 1928 Holmegaard's first in-house designer, Jacob Bang, designed a modern interpretation of this traditional decanter, entitled Kluk Kluk (Glug Glug). Over the succeeding decades Holmegaard produced more decanter designs of note, including the Viking carafe designed by Ole Winther in 1955, inspired by historic 'onion bottles', and Tom Nybroe's elegant Perfection carafe (2010–12), the shape of which provides efficient oxidization for any wine that is swirled along its narrow neck.

1. Perfection decanter by Tom Nybroe for Holmegaard (Denmark), 2010–12

2. Kluk Kluk (Glug Glug) decanter by Jacob Bang for Holmegaard (Denmark), 1928

Opposite: Viking decanter by Ole Winther for Holmegaard (Denmark), 1955

1.

2.

HOLMEGAARD GOES POP

In 1962 Otto Brauer designed his famous bottle-shaped Gulvvase (floor vase) for Holmegaard, based on a model by fellow Holmegaard designer Per Lütken from 1958. This distinctive object became a ubiquitous feature in 'designer' interiors throughout the 1960s and 1970s. With its simple but bold silhouette, the Gulvvase is truly timeless, and essentially a skilful distillation of the archetypal bottle form. Brauer's classic was also turned into a decanter with the addition of round, bubble-like stoppers, and was later produced in various colourful cased-glass options. In 1968 Holmegaard launched its Carnaby range of glassware by Lütken and Christer Holmgren, which can be seen as an evolution of Brauer's bottle vase, but had a much bolder Pop aesthetic. Youthful, sculptural and colourful, this glassware captured the optimistic zeitgeist of the 'Age of Aquarius' period (roughly 1967–72), and at the same time marked one of the creative high points of Scandinavian design.

Opposite: Gulvvase (floor vase) by Otto Brauer for Holmegaard (Denmark), 1962

1. Carnaby vases by Per Lütken (bulbous orange vase and yellow vases) and Christer Holmgren (tall orange vase) for Holmegaard (Denmark), 1968

2. Decanters by Otto Brauer for Holmegaard (Denmark), ca. 1962

1.

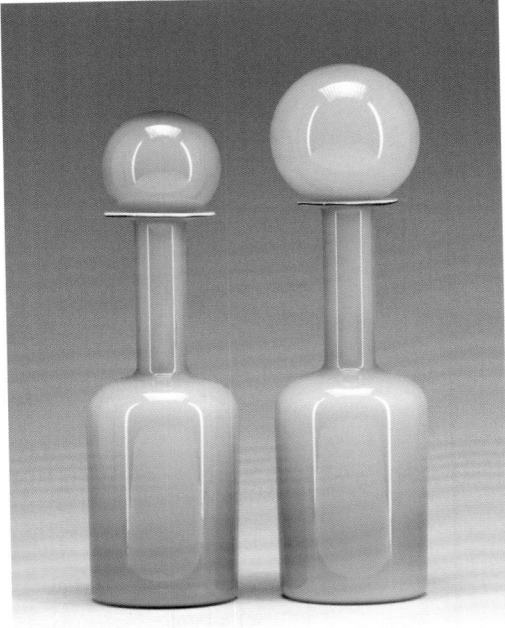

2.

POPGLAS KOLLEKTION

One of the most famous glassware ranges of the Swinging Sixties was Gunnar Cyrén's Popglas Kollektion (Pop Glass Collection) for Orrefors in 1966. Having studied at the Stockholm Konstfack and then the Kölner Werkschule (Cologne Arts and Crafts School) in Germany, Cyrén was apprenticed as a goldsmith and silversmith. This extensive hands-on training enabled him to create highly refined objects, yet he was not stuck in the Swedish Modernist design tradition, preferring instead to explore colour, form and technique, rather than the development of mass-producible functional objects. Working for Orrefors from 1959 to 1970, he designed numerous one-off and limited-edition pieces, most notably his Pop glasses, which featured distinctive banded glass stems in bright, contrasting colours that made them time-consuming and technically difficult to make. Cyrén recalled that about 100 different stem variations were made for this range, and that the colours he selected for them were inspired by the vivid hues of fish he encountered at the aquarium in Copenhagen.

Right & 2. Pop goblets by Gunnar Cyrén for Orrefors (Sweden), 1964–69

1. Design drawing for Pop goblet by Gunnar Cyrén for Orrefors (Sweden), 1967

1.

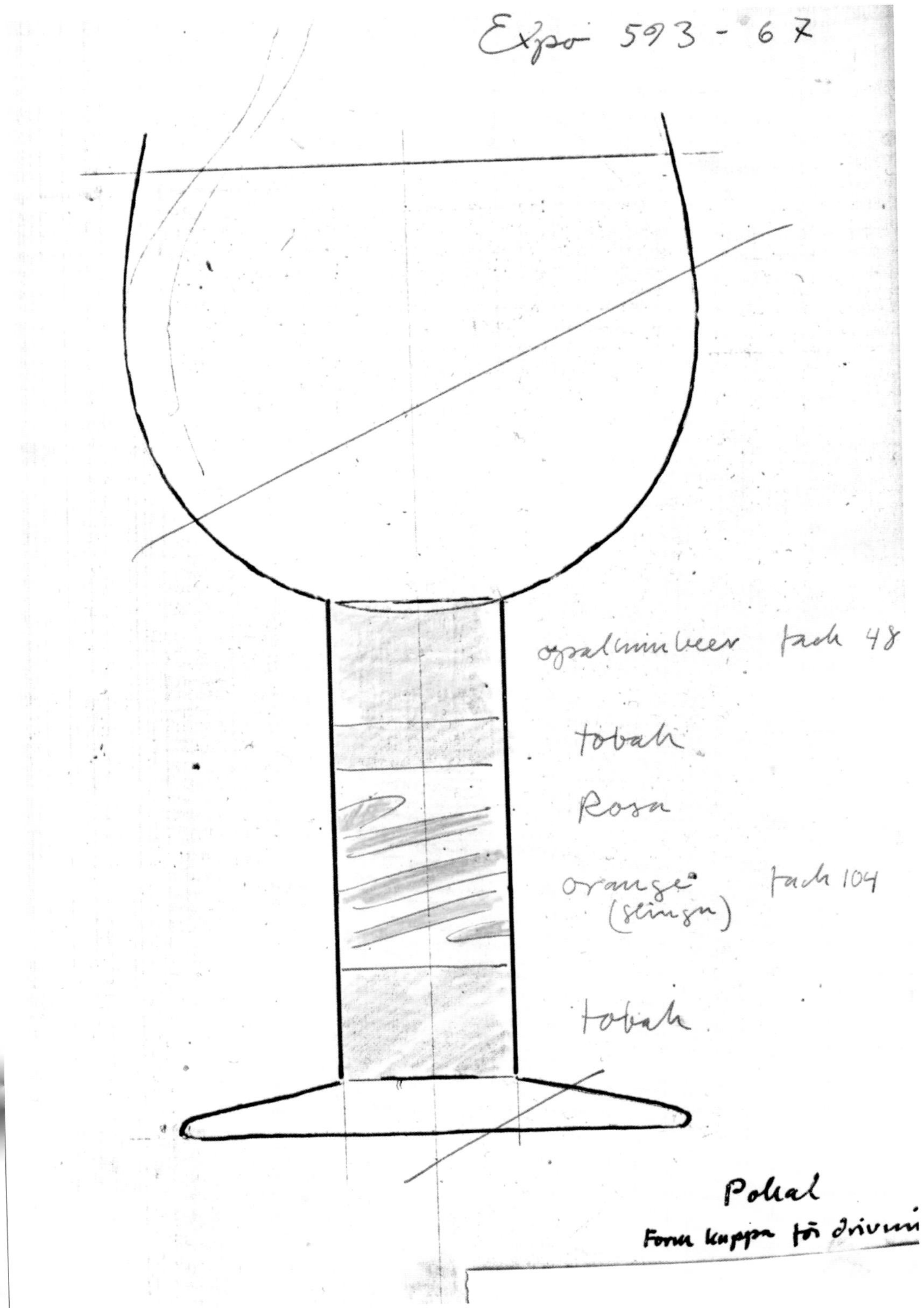

Expo 593 - 67

2.

opalwinlueer   fach 48

tobak.

Rosa

orange°
(slingn)   fach 104

tobak.

Pokal
Form kuppa för driven

EDVIN ÖHRSTRÖM

Edvin Öhrström initially trained at the Konstfack in Stockholm and later studied sculpture under Carl Milles and Nils Sjögren at the Kungliga Konsthögskolan (Royal Institute of Art) in the same city. Moving to Paris in 1932, he continued his studies at the Académie Scandinave, which was run by Nordic artists and regularly staged exhibitions of Scandinavian art. He returned to Sweden, and established his own glass studio in 1936. From then until 1957 he spent two months a year at Orrefors, where he developed the Ariel technique with Vicke Lindstrand and the master glass-blower Gustav Bergkvist. The technique involved covering a blank with layers of coloured glass that were then engraved; the body of the vessel then had another layer of molten clear glass carefully pulled over it, thereby creating internal air bubbles where any recesses might exist. Öhrström used this method to create richly coloured designs that had an innate sense of artistry, functioning more as glass sculptures than as practical vessels. As a testament to his contribution to the artistic development of Swedish glass design, Öhrström was awarded the Prins Eugen Medal in 1979.

Below: Flickan och duvan (The girl and the pigeon) Ariel vase, Model no. 560L, by Edvin Öhrström for Orrefors (Sweden), 1948

1. Ariel bowl by Edvin Öhrström for Orrefors (Sweden), 1952 – seen from above

2. Model no. 86 vase by Edvin Öhrström for Orrefors (Sweden), 1948

3. Model no. 358F Ariel bowl by Edvin Öhrström for Orrefors (Sweden), ca. 1950

1.

2.

3.

NANNY STILL

After graduating from Helsinki's Central School of Industrial Arts, Nanny Still joined the design team at the Riihimäen Lasi glassworks in Riihimäki, about 70 kilometres north of the Finnish capital, in 1949. The glassworks employed designers including Aimo Okkolin, Helena Tynell and Tamara Aladin during its 'golden period', which lasted from about 1949 to 1976. But it was Still's work that arguably had the greatest creative breadth, ranging from her famous multicoloured decanters, to her strongly graphic profiled Pompadour vases,

to her later chunkier and boldly patterned Grapponia and Fenomena ranges. Throughout her time at Riihimäki (which lasted until 1976), Still always managed successfully to channel the latest design trends into her glasswork, and even helped to define them. A gifted colourist, she felt 'a special urge to create colour', and worked closely with the chemists at Riihimäki to develop glass in new hues, including a bright turquoise that was inspired by a sand-polished shard of glass found on a beach in Capri; it was later used as the colour for her Harlekiini range (1958; see p. 292).

1. Portrait of Nanny Still holding one of her glassware designs, taken by Aarne Pietinen, 1956

2. Pompadour vases by Nanny Still for Riihimäen Lasi (Finland), 1945

Opposite: Decanters/bottles by Nanny Still for Riihimäen Lasi (Finland), ca. 1950

1.

2.

INGEBORG LUNDIN

The Äpplet (Apple) vase (1955) by Ingeborg Lundin for Orrefors is one of the most iconic Scandinavian glassware designs of all time. Having studied at the Konstfack and the Kungliga Tekniska Högskolan (Royal Institute of Technology) in Stockholm, Lundin had joined Orrefors in 1946, when Sven Palmqvist and Edvin Öhrström were busy pioneering the Ravenna and Ariel techniques respectively. In contrast, Lundin preferred to focus on pure form rather than the development of virtuoso techniques. Her Apple vase, like her Timglas (Hourglass) vase of two years before, possessed an understated refinement that reflected the postwar desire for less fussy pieces. Taking the form of a giant glass bubble, the Apple vase was produced in a number of subtle tints – green, blue and grey – as well as in clear uncoloured glass. The sculptural purity of its simple fruit-inspired form helped to emphasize the lightness and transparency of the medium from which it was made. Indeed, it was this ability to express the intrinsic qualities of materials that came to define postwar Scandinavian design.

Opposite: Äpplet (Apple) vase by Ingeborg Lundin for Orrefors (Sweden), 1955

1. Orrefors advertisement showing the Äpplet (Apple) vase by Ingeborg Lundin, 1963 – the drinking glasses shown were also designed by Lundin

2. Timglas (Hourglass) vases by Ingeborg Lundin for Orrefors (Sweden), 1953

1.

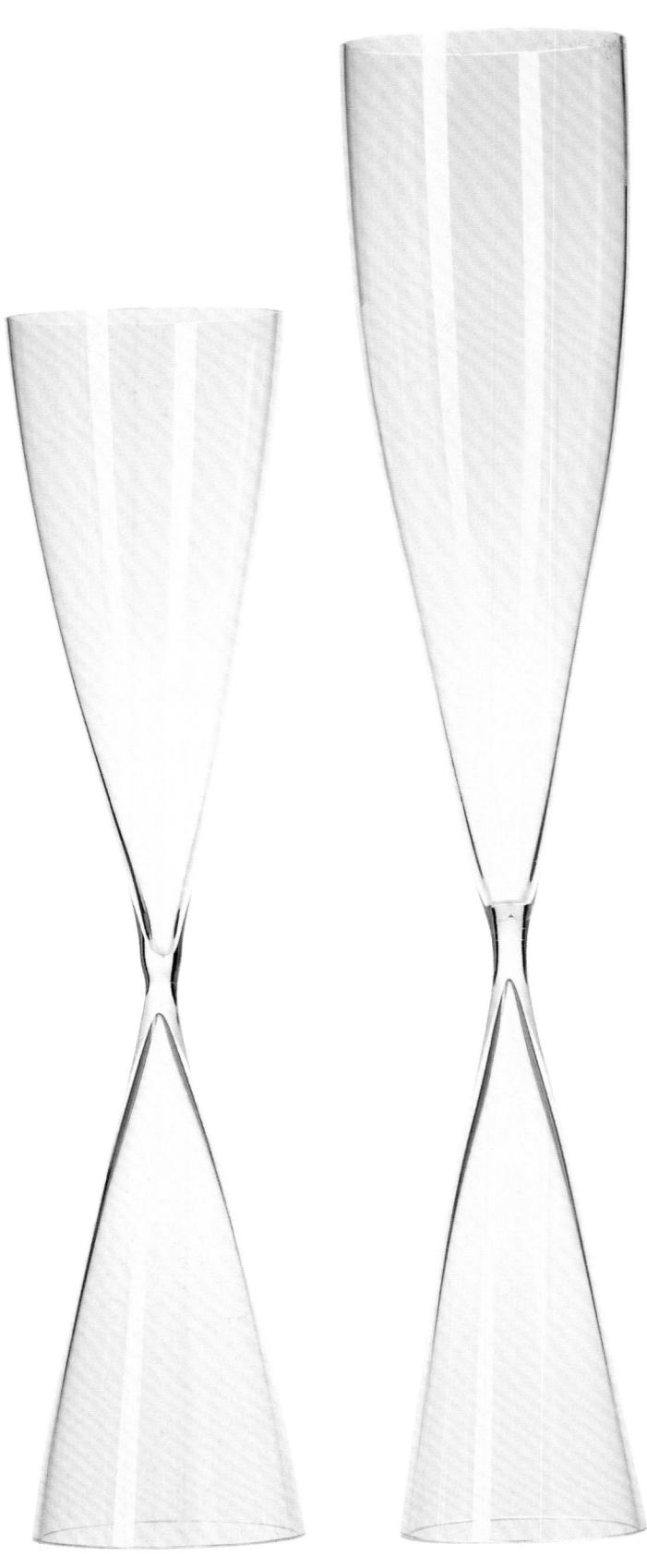

NILS LANDBERG

The Swedish glassware designer Nils Landberg studied at the Högskolan för Design och Konsthantverk (School of Design and Crafts) in Gothenburg before undertaking two years of training at the Orrefors glassworks' engraving school. He also took study trips to France and Italy before being hired by Orrefors in 1927, working at first as an engraver and as an assistant to Edward Hald (see pp. 252–53). In 1935 he began producing his own designs for the glassworks, including several engraved pieces that were shown at the Paris Exposition of 1937 and the New York World's Fair of 1939. In the early 1950s Landberg began experimenting with both form and colour, which resulted in a number of dusky-hued vases and bowls with sculptural, organic forms that exploited the *sommerso* technique. It was, however, his series of Tulpan (Tulip) glasses from 1957, with their delicate, attenuated stems supporting differently shaped organic-formed bowls, that ultimately brought him the greatest acclaim. Winning a gold medal at the 11th Milan Triennial, in 1957, the Tulpan goblets testify not only to Landberg's form-giving talent, but also to the technical virtuosity of the highly skilled Swedish glass-blowers who made them.

Right: Tulpan (Tulip) goblet by Nils Landberg for Orrefors (Sweden), 1957

1 & 3. Tulpan (Tulip) goblets by Nils Landberg for Orrefors (Sweden), 1957

2. Orrefors advertisement showing the Tulpan (Tulip) goblets by Nils Landberg, 1961

1.

2.

3.

FORM + COLOUR

In the 1950s and 1960s only the Italian designers working with the glassworks on the Venetian island of Murano could equal the sheer artistry and technical virtuosity of the Scandinavian glass factories, of which there were many scattered throughout the Nordic region thanks to plentiful supplies of wood and sand. But while much Italian glassware of this period relied on complicated techniques and was very colourful, most Scandinavian glassware was subtly hued and possessed understated sculptural forms. Indeed, the examples shown here, which were produced in Finland and Sweden during the 1950s and 1960s, reflect the casual yet contemporary Mid-century Modern look that was so quintessentially Scandinavian. But, over and above this, in Scandinavia it was about not just the look of the object itself, but how it would function. For example, the vases by Arthur Percy (below) and Bo Borgstrom (opposite) were designed so that they would look beautiful when flowers were arranged in them – a consideration not generally found in the design of Italian vases, which were often intended to function more as *objets d'art*. The same can be said for Nanny Still's wonderful turquoise double decanter (below left), which, while sculptural in form, was first and foremost intended as a functional object.

1. Harlekiini (Harlequin) double decanter by Nanny Still for Riihimäen Lasi (Finland), 1958

2. Blomglas (Bulb vase) by Arthur Percy for Gullaskruf (Sweden), 1952

Opposite: Model no. 4807 vase and Bamboo vase, Model no. B5/80, by Bo Borgstrom for Aseda (Sweden), 1960s

1.

2.

FLYGFORS

Flygfors Glasbruk was founded in 1888 by Ernst Wiktor Lundqvist and August Zeitz in a small village of the same name in the Swedish region of Kalmar. At first the company concentrated on the production of window glass, but in 1930 it diversified into the manufacture of tableware, and two years later began producing glass light fixtures. From 1939 to 1942 Willem de Moor was art director there, and during his tenure he designed bowls and vases with simple forms made from thick-walled bubbled glass. Paul Kedelv, who had been taught by Edvin Öhrström at the Konstfack

in Stockholm and then worked for Orrefors and Nuutajärvi Notsjö, joined Flygfors in 1949. He introduced a new contemporary spirit into the glassworks' product line with a range of designs that were both colourful and sculptural. His Coquille range came in a dazzling array of hues, shapes and sizes, and featured numerous bowls and vases that consisted of a distinctive core of coloured and white glass encased in a layer of clear glass and blown into free-form sculptural shapes. This innovative glassware was utterly in tune with the fashionable biomorphic look of the 1950s, and consequently spawned a plethora of imitations, both at home and abroad.

Opposite: Coquille Fantasia art object/vase by Paul Kedelv for Flygfors (Sweden), 1956

1. Coquille vase by Paul Kedelv for Flygfors (Sweden), 1954

2. Coquille bowl by Paul Kedelv for Flygfors (Sweden), 1950s

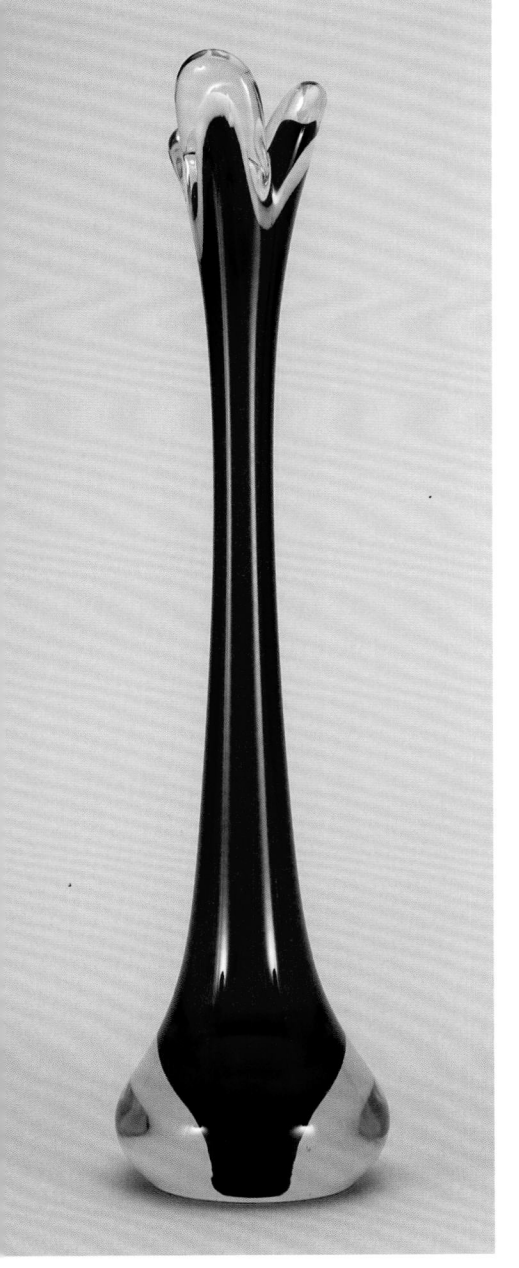

2.

GÖTE AUGUSTSSON + RUDA GLASBRUK

From the late 1960s to the mid 1970s, a new, Brutalist-inspired style came to the fore in Scandinavian design, perhaps best expressed in the realm of glassware by the uncompromising work of Göte Augustsson. Born in the Kalmar region of Sweden, Augustsson was a self-taught designer who initially worked for the Jungner glassworks. When the firm took over the Ruda glassworks in 1947, he became Ruda's works manager and chief designer. In fact, it would appear that he designed practically all the glassworks' products in the 1950s, 1960s and early 1970s. During his tenure, Augustsson designed an extensive range of thick-walled glassware with a distinctive, chunky, Brutalist aesthetic. The original moulds for these pieces used a traditional technique known as *kolsnittsteknik*, which involved carving the required forms into soft, carbonized wood. These carbon moulds did not last long, however, so production costs were high. This popular series of glassware, including bowls, vases, flasks and drinking vessels, was for the most part produced in an inky cobalt blue, although other then-fashionable colour options – forest green, amethyst and smoky grey – were also available. Local myth has it that the range sold for less than it cost to produce, which, if correct, goes some way in explaining the closure of the Ruda glassworks in 1972.

1. Vase by Göte Augustsson for Ruda (Sweden), 1960s

2 & 3. Detail and full image of bottle vase by Göte Augustsson for Ruda (Sweden), 1960s

Opposite: Vase by Göte Augustsson for Ruda (Sweden), 1960s

1.

2.

3.

GÖRAN WÄRFF + KOSTA

The Swedish glassware designer Göran Wärff and his German-born wife, Ann (neé Wolff), both studied at the famous HfG design school in Ulm, Germany, before becoming designers at the Pukeberg glassworks in Sweden. After spending five years there, they both became in-house designers for Kosta Boda. Göran held this position for a decade, then worked as a freelance designer for the company. Over the years he created numerous

highly priced one-off and limited-edition art-glass pieces for the firm, as well as more mainstream pieces that were serially manufactured, such as those shown here. Melting polar ice inspired the curious icicle-like and rutted forms of these designs, while their use of different internal colours gave them a shimmering, almost rainbow-like quality that was highly original and testified to the skill of the glass-makers working in the Småland region, honed over generations.

1. Art glass/paperweight by Göran Wärff for Kosta (Sweden), 1960s/1970s

2. Göran Wärff at Kosta's glassworks, 2000s

3. Polar candleholder by Göran Wärff for Kosta, 1960s

4. Vase by Göran Wärff for Kosta (Sweden), 1967

1.

2.

3.

4.

1.

2.

THE TEA LIGHT

There are two theories about how the type of votive candle known as a tea light got its name. One contends that it comes from the fact that they were originally used in tabletop warmers to keep food and drinks warm; the other asserts that it comes from the fact that small candles were used in tea ceremonies in Japan to create a warm ambience. Whatever the origin of their name, there is no disputing that tea lights in beautifully designed glass holders are ubiquitous in Nordic interiors, especially during the winter months, when they give that important feeling of *hygge*, a Danish word (of old-Norse origin) that means homely, cheery warmth. The Scandinavian glass tea light, however, really came into being only in the 1970s with designs such as Ann Wärff's ever-popular Snowball tea-light holder (1973) for Kosta, and Tapio Wirkkala's icy-looking centrifugally cast Stellaria tea-light holder (1978). Other tea-light-holder designs that have enjoyed much international success are Torben Jørgensen's Lotus (1993) for Holmegaard, and Heikki Orvola's multi-hued Kivi (1988) for Iittala, both of which have become timeless favourites thanks to their beauty and simplicity.

1. Stellaria tea-light holders, Model no. 2656, by Tapio Wirkkala for Iittala (Finland), 1978

2. Snowball tea-light holders by Ann Wärff for Kosta Boda (Sweden), 1973

3. Lotus tea-light holder by Torben Jørgensen for Holmegaard (Denmark), 1993

4. Kivi tea-light holder by Heikki Orvola for Iittala (Finland), 1988

3.

4.

MONA MORALES-SCHILDT

Daughter of a renowned Spanish-Swedish composer and wife of an acclaimed Swedish travel writer, Mona Morales-Schildt studied in Stockholm and Paris before joining the ceramics manufacturer Gustavsberg to work as Wilhelm Kåge's assistant. She later became a designer at the Arabia ceramics manufactory in Finland. There she designed various collections, including a dinner service for the 1940 Summer Olympic Games, which were supposed to be held in Helsinki but were cancelled owing to the outbreak of war. After returning to Sweden, Morales-Schildt worked as a designer for the Kosta glassworks in Småland from 1958 to 1971. During this period she

nurtured a deep interest in glass production and collaborated with the master glass-blower Bengt Heintze to develop a number of glassware ranges, including her Ventana series of vases, bowls and other items, which was introduced in 1959 and extended over the succeeding years. This stunningly beautiful range, with its distinctive faceted look and bold colour combinations, was inspired by the work of the Venetian glass designer Paolo Venini, for whom Morales-Schildt had worked briefly. Her designs are notable for reflecting the strong ties that existed between Scandinavian designers and their Italian counterparts in the 1950s, with each design culture helping to enrich the other immeasurably.

Below & opposite: Ventana vases by Mona Morales-Schildt for Kosta (Sweden), 1950s/1960s

NUUTAJÄRVI

In 1793 the famous Notsjö glassworks was founded in Nuutajärvi, some 150 kilometres northwest of Helsinki, by Major Jacob Wilhelm de Pont, whose father had been an ironmaster at the Åviks glassworks. At first the factory produced window glass and bottles, but it diversified into pressed glassware in 1851. Two years later Adolf Törngren purchased the glassworks and instigated a programme of modernization. In 1895 the firm opened its own shop in Helsinki, named after its account-ant, G. F. Stockmann, and it grew over the years into the city's premier department store. In 1950 the Nuutajärvi glassworks was acquired by the Wärtsilä Group, which appointed Kaj Franck (see pp. 270–71) its art director. Under Franck's enlightened guidance from 1950 to 1976, it evolved into a powerhouse of innova-tive glassware production. During this golden period it manufactured not only numerous interesting ranges by Franck, but also aesthet-ically and technically innovative designs by, among others, Oiva Toikka, Heikki Orvola, Saara Hopea, Runar Engblom and Kerttu Nurminen. In the 1980s Toikka, Orvola and Nurminen continued to create experimental art-glass pieces alongside designs more suita-ble for higher-volume production. Eventually, however, it was decided to merge Nuutajärvi with Iittala in 1988, which effectively closed the chapter on what had been one of the most interesting and longest-running centres of Nordic glass production.

Below: Lumikuru (Snow Canyon) by Kerttu Nurminen fo Nuutajärvi Notsjö (Finland), 1985

1. Two bottles/vases and a dish by Kerttu Nurminen for Nuutajärvi Notsjö (Finland), 1991

2. Pantteri (Panther) vase by Saara Hopea for Nuutajär Notsjö (Finland), ca. 1956

3. Model no. KF 245 vases by Kaj Franck for Nuutajärvi Notsjö (Finland), 1957

1.

3.

HELENA TYNELL

The Finnish designer Helena Tynell is best known for the many innovative and stylistically diverse glassware designs she produced for the Riihimäen Lasi glassworks in Riihimäki. Tynell had studied at the Central School of Industrial Arts in Helsinki, and then spent three years working as a designer at the Arabia ceramics factory, before joining the Riihimäki glassworks in 1946. She remained a designer there for 30 years, and created a number of blow-moulded chunky Pop-style vases during the 1960s, including her well-known Aurinkopullo (Solar Bottle). It was, however, her series of art-glass studio pieces, including her rainbow-hued Revonlulet (Northern Lights) vases (1960) and her architectonic Castello vase (ca. 1960), that revealed her true mastery of both form and colour. With their strongly graphic profiles and distinctive sculptural presence, this extraordinary body of work marked a high point in Finnish glass design.

1. Glass sculpture/vase by Helena Tynell for Riihimäen Lasi (Finland), 1960s/1970s

2. Castello glass sculpture/vase by Helena Tynell for Riihimäen Lasi (Finland), 1960s

Opposite: Revonlulet (Northern Lights) vase by Helena Tynell for Riihimäen Lasi (Finland), 1960

1.

2.

1.

2.

3.

TWENTY-FIRST-CENTURY SCANDINAVIAN GLASS

Since the millennium, the Nordic tradition of exemplary glassware design has been kept alive by the likes of Ingegerd Råman at Orrefors (see pp. 310–11) and Harri Koskinen at Iittala. Despite the fact that today there are considerably fewer Nordic glassworks in operation than in decades gone by, those that have managed to survive have in recent years seen their international reputation grow exponentially. For instance, Iittala is now a major design-led brand that is recognized around the world. Experimental low-volume art glass is still being created, too, but not in the quantities it once was. For instance, the Finnish interior architect Pertti Metsälampi self-produces his Fons II and Fons III bowls (2000) in small numbers, while also devising one-off art-glass installations. Over the years Råman has also managed to revitalize Scandinavian glassware production by creating serially manufactured designs such as her evocative Drop of Water decanter (2000) alongside higher-priced, limited-edition art glass. Iittala's Pro Arte line has similarly helped to keep alive the culture of art-glass production in Finland, and Koskinen's Alue bowl (2000) in that range is a stunning example of contemporary Finnish glassware. Meanwhile, Anu Penttinen's Vitriini box (2010), which is part of Iittala's main range, reveals the continuing excellence of Nordic glassware design for industrial mass-production.

1. Alue bowl by Harri Koskinen for Iittala (Finland), 2000 – an Iittala Pro Arte limited-edition piece

2. Vitriini box by Anu Penttinen for Iittala (Finland), 2010

3. Drop of Water decanter by Ingegerd Råman for Orrefors (Sweden), 2000

Below: Fons II and Fons III bowls by Pertti Metsälampi (self-produced) (Finland), 2000

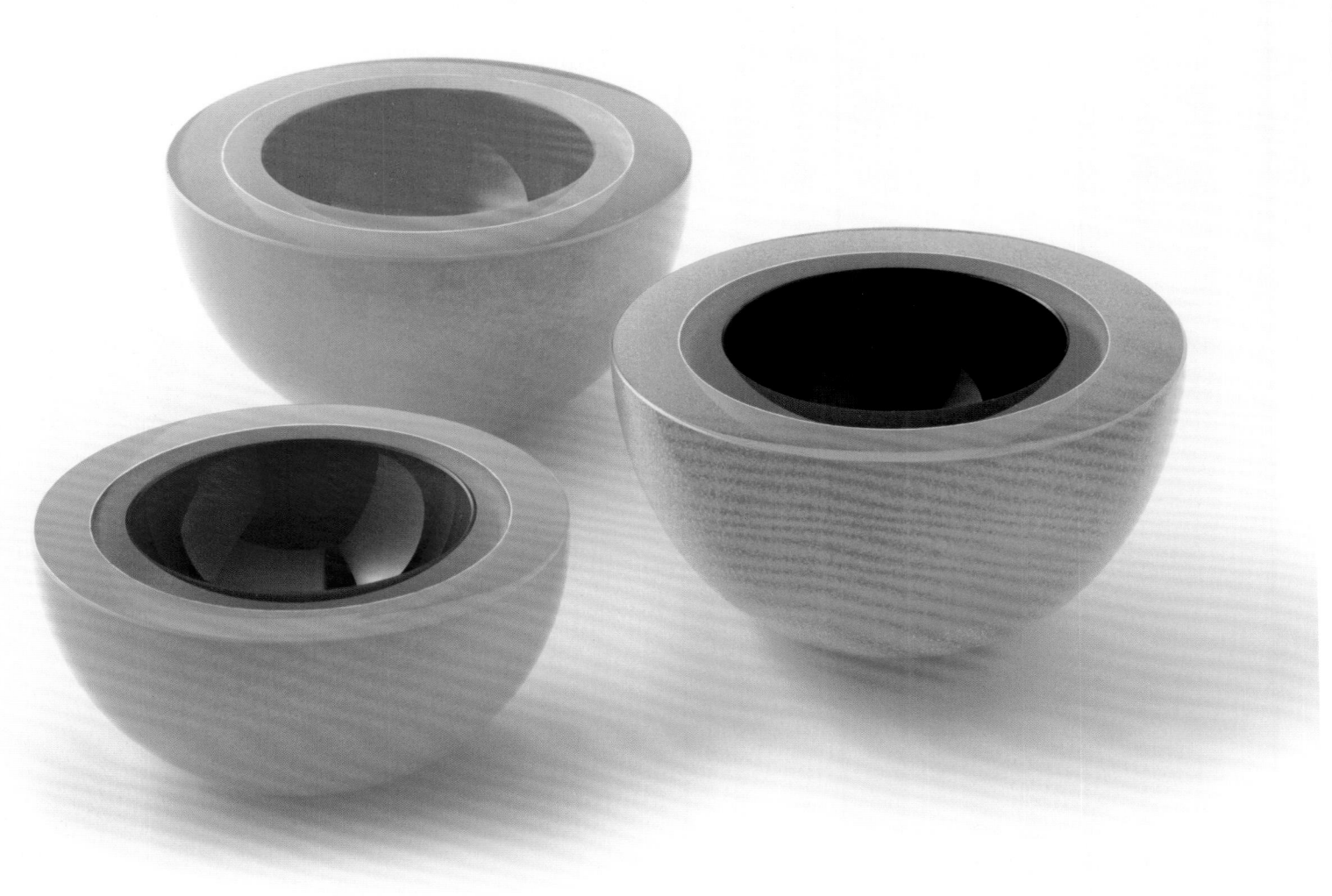

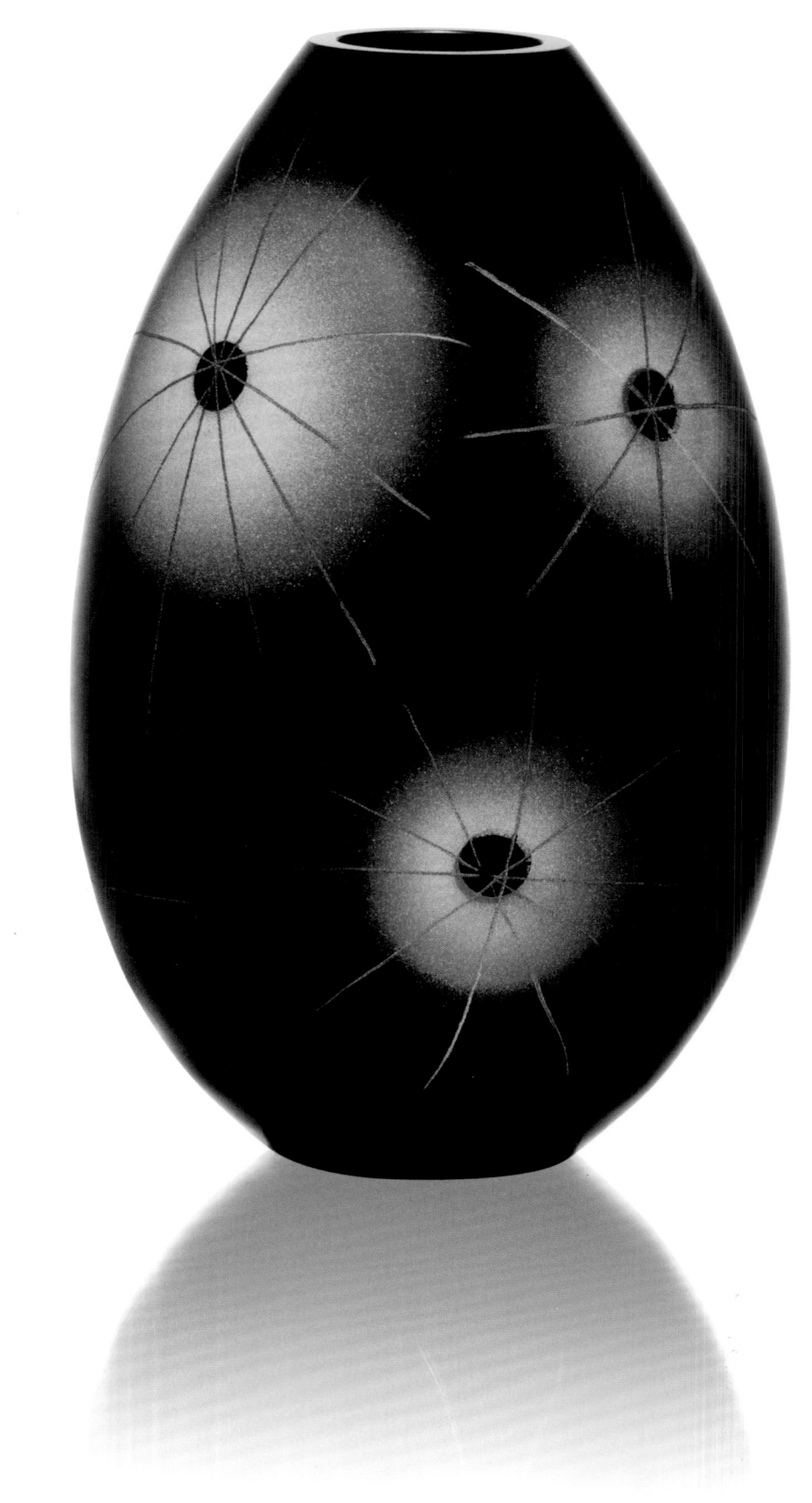

INGEGERD RÅMAN

One of Sweden's most prominent designers, Ingegerd Råman is regarded as a national treasure in her native country, for over the years she has honed her design skills to such an extent that her glassware and ceramics transcend the everyday. Whether intended for mass-production or as limited editions, her work exemplifies the very best of Scandinavian design. Her utilitarian glassware produced by Orrefors, Skruf and IKEA is distinguished by a timeless simplicity and artistry, for, as she notes, 'A jar with a lid is a jar with a lid, but there has to be warmth, thought, an idea and poetry behind it.' It is, however, her studio art glass that reveals her ability to create glassware infused with an almost spiritual presence. Having initially worked for the Johansfors glassworks, Råman joined the Skruf glassworks in 1981, and found success there with her Bellman range, which is still in production. Since 1999 she has worked for Orrefors, designing not only several ranges of drinking glasses, but also limited-edition art-glass pieces. Among the latter is her Bon Bon range of vases (2009), which celebrated her tenth anniversary working with Orrefors' skilled glassworkers and incorporated various hands-on techniques, including blasting, painting, cutting and engraving.

Opposite: Bon Bon vase by Ingegerd Råman for Orrefors (Sweden), 2009

1. Ingegerd Råman with one of her large-scale art-glass pieces at the Orrefors glassworks, 2000s

2. Pond Black Tangle bowl by Ingegerd Råman for Orrefors (Sweden), 2006

2.

1.

CERAMICS

When it was announced that the Arabia factory in Helsinki would close down in 2015, and that all production would be moved to Thailand, many saw it as the end of an era. Arabia was the last major Scandinavian ceramics factory still to be manufacturing locally. Many brands, such as Royal Copenhagen, Bing & Grøndahl, Kähler, Rörstrand, Gustavsberg, Höganäs, Upsala-Ekeby and Stavangerflint had already either ceased trading or moved production abroad. Indeed, today only Norway's Figgjo maintains local production on any sizeable scale.

The oldest of all these factories was Rörstrand, founded in Stockholm in 1726. By 1900 the factory had some 1,100 employees, but as the city expanded the factory's land was needed for housing, so the facility was demolished in 1926. Production was moved to Gothenburg, where Rörstrand had acquired the Gothenburg porcelain factory in 1914; the factory later relocated to Lidköping, southern Sweden, in 1941. One of its most popular ranges was the traditional Gron Anna (Green Anna), made 1898–1943 and again 1966–2002, its latter incarnation containing pieces by the designer Carl-Harry Stålhane.

Gunnar Nylund was born in Paris to artistic parents, his mother a Danish ceramist and his father a Finnish painter and sculptor. Originally trained as an architect, Nylund first worked at the Grankulla earthenware factory near Helsinki and then moved to Denmark in 1924 to work for Bing & Grøndahl. In 1928 he left to set up Nylund & Krebs with the Danish ceramist Nathalie Krebs, who experimented with glazes as Nylund experimented with forms. At an exhibition held at Svenskt Tenn, Stockholm, in 1930, Nylund's work was discovered by Rörstrand. The following year he left his partnership with Krebs (it was subsequently renamed Saxbo Stentøj) and began designing wares for Rörstrand. During the 1930s Nylund created graceful Modernist pieces in richly glazed stoneware and rough chamotte ware. Parallel with creating one-off designs, he also designed everyday porcelain. Nylund remained creative director of Rörstrand until 1958, when he became creative director at the Nymølle pottery in Denmark. He left after a few years, however, to continue working freelance for Rörstrand.

Having a similar formal sensibility to Nylund, Carl-Harry Stålhane also created numerous designs for Rörstrand. He had trained as a painter and sculptor before joining the team at Rörstrand in 1939, when he was only 19 years old. One of his first assignments was to paint earthenware under the guidance of the Swedish expressionist painter Isaac Grünewald. Stålhane was soon invited to exhibit at the Nationalmuseum in Stockholm with Nylund, and was promoted to art director of Rörstrand when Nylund left in 1958. In the early 1960s Stålhane created larger, more rugged forms with thick glazes. He experimented with the different clays found in the rich soil near the factory, although he did not throw his own pieces, so was dependent on the factory's master throwers. In 1973 Stålhane ended his long career at Rörstrand to open his own studio, Designhuset, with his master thrower Kent Ericsson, and he continued to produce studio ceramics in the Chinese and Japanese styles that had always fascinated him.

Founded in 1826 in a suburb of Stockholm, the Gustavsberg factory expanded rapidly during the nineteenth century so that by 1900 it had a workforce of 800. Central to the company's history is Wilhelm Kåge, who had studied painting in Stockholm, Gothenburg, Copenhagen and Munich before embarking on a career as a commercial artist. In 1917 he exhibited his Arbetarservisen (Worker's Dinner Service) with its Liljeblå (blue lily) decoration at the influential Hemutställningen or Home Exhibition organized by the Swedish Society of Crafts and Industrial Design and held at the Liljevalchs gallery in Stockholm. The exhibition brought him to the attention of Gustavsberg, which hired him as its art director later that year. Gustavsberg also put this practical dinnerware into mass-production. However – despite being in accord with the Society's catchphrase, *Vackrare vardagsvara* (better everyday goods), and having democratic 'good design' intentions – because of World War I and the ensuing national famine, widespread poverty and dire housing shortages, it was far too expensive for most workers. Kåge did, however, create a more commercially successful follow-up design, the Pyro service of 1929, which was Gustavsberg's first ovenproof dinnerware.

The 1930s were a period of decline for Gustavsberg, and the Swedish Cooperative Union (Kooperativa förbundet; known as Coop) acquired the factory in 1937. Coop attempted to modernize the product line radically, sold the ceramics through its large national network of stores, and even had buses visiting remote villages, which functioned as mobile co-operative ceramic shops. The factory also became Sweden's largest producer of porcelain sanitaryware, and its anchor logo was visible in countless bathrooms installed during the postwar building boom. During this period, Kåge found success with his mottled green Argenta earthenware range of vases, bowls, tobacco jars, ashtrays and so on, with its stylized Art Deco motifs picked

Serpent Carolina vase and two handled ewers/vases by Gunnar Nylund, and bowl by Carl-Harry Stålhane, all for Rörstrand (Sweden), 1950s

Chamotte stoneware vase by Gunnar Nylund for Rörstrand (Sweden), 1930s

Arbetarservisen (Worker's Dinner Service) by Wilhelm Kåge for Gustavsberg (Sweden), 1917 – decorated with Liljeblå pattern

Argenta vase by Wilhelm Kåge for Gustavsberg (Sweden), 1930s – with mermaid motif picked out in silver

Praktika storage jars by Wilhelm Kåge for Gustavsberg (Sweden), 1933

Opposite: Unico Moss vase by Anders Arhoj for Kähler (Denmark), 2015

out in silver. But his Praktika series (1933), a basic Modernist design of stackable tableware aimed at working-class families, failed commercially because the intended buyers preferred more traditional, ornate products.

Kåge's successor at Gustavsberg, Stig Lindberg, was the youngest of five children from a working-class family in Umeå, northeastern Sweden. After graduating from the Konstfack (University College of Arts, Crafts and Design) in Stockholm, he managed to secure a position at Gustavsberg in 1936. Taller and slimmer than most, the 20-year-old Lindberg had been wandering around the forecourt when the factory manager, Axel Odelberg, spotted him and asked why he was there. 'I'm looking for a job,' replied Lindberg. 'Well, there aren't any,' said Odelberg, the 1930s recession having taken its toll on sales. 'If you employ me I'll make sure there will be plenty of work here at the factory,' came the quick answer. Instead of throwing him out, Odelberg brought him to the artistic director, Kåge. From then on, Lindberg worked for Gustavsberg on and off for the rest of his life, and in 1949 he became artistic director. Lindberg not only designed household crockery, but also hand-painted studio pottery. He designed for other companies, too, and worked in a wide range of disciplines, creating among other things television and radio sets, children's book illustrations, various glass and plastic objects, textiles and graphics.

The Swedish designer Arthur Percy studied art in Paris in the 1910s, and was made creative director of the Gefle porcelain factory in Gävle in 1923. His breakthrough, however, came two years later at the Paris Exposition Internationale des Arts Décoratifs et Industriels Modernes of 1925, where he displayed his Art Deco ceramics. He also participated in the Stockholm Exhibition of 1930, the New York World's Fair of 1939 and the H55 exhibition in Helsingborg in 1955. During his tenure at Gefle, he designed numerous Art Deco-style ceramics, including a stylishly modern scallop-edged, all-black lustre dinner service (1927). Percy also worked for the Karlskrona porcelain factory in southern Sweden (1942–51), and designed glassware for the Gullaskruf glassworks.

Another key Swedish ceramics manufacturer was Upsala-Ekeby, founded in 1886 on a plot of land with suitable clay. At first it made bricks, various ceramic goods and ovens, relying – like most ceramics and glass factories – on copying foreign designs. The Svenska Slöjdföreningen (Swedish Society of Arts & Design) called for the better design of everyday wares with its Hemutställningen (Home Exhibition) in 1917, and many companies heeded its advice and began to employ artists as designers. At Upsala-Ekeby,

Anna-Lisa Thomson and Sven-Erik Skawonius were among the first artist-designers to be engaged, and Vicke Lindstrand later acted as the firm's artistic director (1942–50). Upsala-Ekeby acquired Rörstrand in 1964, and around this time also added Reijmyre glassworks, the Kosta and Boda glassworks and the Gense metalware factory to its growing portfolio. The increasing threat from cheap imports, however, finally brought down the company, and the original site was sold off in 1973. Today only Rörstrand remains, now owned by the Fiskars Group; much of its production has long since been moved overseas.

In Finland, the most important ceramics manufacturer was, and still is, Arabia. Rörstrand established the firm in Helsinki in 1873, when Finland was still a Grand Duchy under imperial Russian rule. The initial purpose was to export into the large Russian market, but in 1916 Rörstrand sold the company and, in a later twist of fate, Arabia instead came to own Rörstrand between 1927 and 1932. In common with many other ceramic factories and glassworks, the owners of Arabia came to the realization that they needed an artistic director, and in 1932 they appointed Kurt Ekholm, who remained until he moved to Sweden to teach in 1948. In 1941, despite the war, Arabia was given permission to extend the factory; a nine-storey building was completed by 1947. Ekholm's most important contribution was the Arabia Art Department, which he started in 1932. He also established a museum on the ninth floor of the factory building in 1948. Arabia's longest-lasting artist was the Austrian-born designer Friedl Holzer-Kjellberg, who worked there 1924–70 and took over as manager of the museum when Ekholm left. She developed very thin, transparent 'rice' porcelain, as well as new glazes.

Over time, the Arabia factory had become a giant, employing more than 2,000 people by the outbreak of World War II. Owing to wartime shortages and the need to maintain the export operation for income, domestic trade was subject to sales quotas until 1949. Most goods sold in Finland were seconds, since the prime-quality products were reserved for export. In 1945 Arabia appointed Kaj Franck to develop its product design. He had previously studied furniture design at the Taideteolliseen Keskuskouluun (Central School of Industrial Arts) in Helsinki, illustrated catalogues for the Riihimäki glassworks and worked as an interior designer, decorator and textile designer. He was also a leading propagandist for democratic design for the masses, in tune with Modernist ideas. According to Franck, to be good and beautiful an object must be durable, robust, easy to clean, functional and indispensable, and remain true to the materials being used – and, of

course, any superfluous decoration should b[e] eliminated. In 1946 he designed tableware fo[r] the Family Welfare Association of Finland, an[d] the following year he participated in a desig[n] competition run by Iittala, in which he share[d] first prize with Tapio Wirkkala. He went on t[o] design the functional and affordable Karti[o] glassware range (1946–50) for Iittala, and i[n] 1952 he designed for Arabia its ceramic equiv[-] alent: the Kilta range. Stridently modern, i[t] constituted a radical break from tradition[al] ceramics in that each item was conceived sep[-] arately according to its function. The idea wa[s] that individual pieces could be combined fo[r] multiple uses. One of Franck's last project[s] was to redesign Kilta. The resulting Teem[a] range (1977) for Arabia comprised 19 piece[s] based on the elementary Bauhaus forms o[f] the circle, square and cone. Franck said: 'Th[e] only possibility for resolving the technica[l] aspects of utilitarian wares consists in bein[g] both radical and socially committed.'

Esteri Tomula worked at Arabia unde[r] Franck from 1947 to 1984. Having graduate[d] from the Central School of Industrial Arts i[n] Helsinki in 1947, she became best known fo[r] her decorative work that was often inspire[d] by nature. Her most celebrated designs ar[e] the Fennica vases, Krokus tableware an[d] Botanica wall plates, which usually combin[e] printing and hand-painting. None of her wor[k] is still in production, but her vintage piece[s] have become very collectible – especially ex[-] amples decorated with her Tatti mushroo[m] pattern, which was also used by Arabia on [a] line of enamelware.

Arabia dominated Finnish ceramics fro[m] the beginning, but in 1918 another compan[y,] Kupittaan Savi, started up in Kuppis, a dis[-] trict of Turku in the southwest of the countr[y.] It was awarded a medal at the Expositio[n] Internationale des Arts et Techniques dan[s] la Vie Moderne, Paris, in 1937 and at th[e] Milan Triennial of 1954, and at one poin[t] had 600 employees. Its designers include[d] Marjukka Paasivirta-Pääkkönen, Linnea Leh[t]onen, Orvokki 'Okki' Laine, Heidi Blomste[dt] and Laila Zink. However, this once-thrivin[g] business struggled increasingly with over[-] seas competition and changing tastes, an[d] ceased trading in 1968.

The fortunes of Danish ceramics manu[-] facturers were significantly brighter, howeve[r.] Den Kongelige Porcelænsfabrik (Royal Porce[-] lain Factory) had been founded in Copenhage[n] in 1775 under the protection of Queen Julian[e] Maria of Brunswick-Wolfenbüttel-Bevern. It[s] three-wave logo represents the three majo[r] waterways surrounding Denmark: Øresund[,] Storebælt (Great Belt) and Lillebælt (Littl[e] Belt). In 1882 the venture was bought by th[e] Aluminia ceramics factory, but in 1969 De[n] Kongelige Porcelænsfabrik swallowed u[p] he Aluminia brand. The firm was renamed Royal Copenhagen after merging with the Holmegaard glassworks in 1985.

Den Kongelige Porcelænsfabrik entered its first era of international success under the design guidance of the architect and painter Arnold Krog, its artistic director from 1891 to 1916. Krog was succeeded by Christian Joachim, who became artistic director at Aluminia in 1911, and then at Den Kongelige Porcelænsfabrik in 1922 – a tenure that lasted until 1933. Nils Thorsson subsequently took up this key position at Aluminia in 1933 and at Den Kongelige Porcelænsfabrik in 1949; he oversaw the design output of both factories until 1969. During this period Thorsson, who encouraged the use of modern production techniques and experimentation with glazes and abstract patterns, introduced a more modern style. The two factories worked with numerous artists, including Axel Salto and Grethe Meyer. The former became renowned for his organic vessels inspired by forms found in nature, while the latter created Modernist wares, notably the Blåkant (Blue Edge) range in 1965 and the Whitpot (White Pot) series in 1972.

An important moment for Royal Copenhagen came in 2000, when the 26-year-old Karen Kjældgård-Larsen created her Blå Mega Mussel Riflet (Blue Fluted Mega) dinner service, a blown-up version of the classic hand-painted Blue Fluted Plain or Musselmalet (clam-painted) service. Some believe the name results from the fluted shape being reminiscent of a clam, but the service is actually based on chrysanthemum and cinquefoil motifs imported from China in the eighteenth century. Its blue colour and distinctive fluting have long been associated with Royal Copenhagen, and Kjældgård-Larsen's clever updating of this classic Danish design freshened it for a younger generation.

Another important Danish ceramics manufacturer was Kähler Keramik, which began in 1839 when the Holstein potter Herman Kähler opened a small workshop in Naestved, eastern Denmark. Early production included stoves and cookware, but in 1880 the company began making art pottery. Early designers included Thorvald Bindesbøll, Karl Hansen Reistrup and Laurits Andersen Ring. Kähler had its international breakthrough at the Exposition Universelle in Paris in 1889 with a red vase glazed with metallic lustre for a copper-like effect. The Kähler family's era ended in 1975 when the Næstved municipality took over the factory, and it was later bought by Holmegaard. Although Kähler was declared bankrupt in 2008, the architect Frantz Longhi has since relaunched the brand. Kähler continues to produce beautiful ceramics – including Anders Arhøj's exquisite

Unico vase (2015) – and recently acquired the old Naestved workshop, which will be re-opened as an office and museum.

The Fuurstrøm factory was founded in Denmark shortly before World War II to produce inexpensive earthenware goods. After the war, the company began to produce more artistic lines under the name Nymølle, most of them designed by Bjørn Wiinblad. In the mid 1970s Fuurstrøm went bankrupt, but Nymølle struggled on for a couple of years before being bought out by Wiinblad himself. A Danish painter, designer and artist, he worked in a wide range of design disciplines, from metalware to graphics, but it is for his ceramics that he is best known. Typical of his work in this field are decorative motifs of whimsical round-faced people, dressed in vaguely nineteenth-century costumes, sometimes almost psychedelic, often with gold or silver details. Wiinblad was also an important designer of ceramics for the German company Rosenthal, which relaunched some of his designs in 2013. The firm is actively supporting the preservation of his home and studio, the Blue House in Kongens Lyngby, to the north of Copenhagen, as a museum.

Norway's most high-profile ceramics firm, Figgjo, was founded in Sandnes in 1941. In 1946 Ragnar Grimsrud was employed as its design director. He had previously worked at two other Norwegian ceramics factories, Graverens and Egersund Fayancefabrik, and during his tenure at Figgjo came to dominate product development at the factory for several decades. In 1961 he launched his very plain, functional white Figgjo 35 series, which is still in production. After Grimsrud retired, in the 1970s, Olav Joa took over as design director. In recent years Figgjo has focused almost exclusively on the development of hardwearing yet innovatively shaped wares for the restaurant and catering trade.

Stavangerflint began production in Stavanger in 1949 as Stavanger Fajansefabrikk, but soon added the word 'flint', hoping to enhance perception of the quality of its products. Its most internationally successful designer was Inger Waage, who had studied at the Statens Håndverks- og Kunstindustriskole (Norwegian National Academy of Craft and Industrial Art) in Oslo from 1943. After graduating, she moved to Stavanger and set up her own workshop. Waage became the first design director at Stavangerflint in 1953. By 1955, the company had to establish a new department with ten assistants in order to cope with the orders of her hand-painted ceramics destined for Britain, America and other markets. In 1968 Stavangerflint merged with its competitor, Figgjo; it closed in 1979, when production was transferred to Figgjo.

Lustre bowl by Arthur Percy for Gefle (Sweden), 1927

Pastoraali (Pastoral) range by Esteri Tomula for Arabia (Finland), 1965

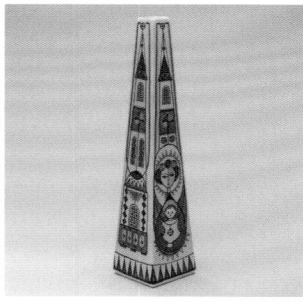

Vase by Laila Zink for Kupittaan Savi (Finland), ca. 1960

Marselis vases by Nils Thorsson for Aluminia (Denmark), 1950s

Blåkant (Blue Edge) teapot by Grethe Meyer for Royal Copenhagen (Denmark), 1965

Bowl by Inger Waage for Stavangerflint (Norway), ca. 1950s/1960s

LOUISE ADELBORG + SWEDISH GRACE

Louise Adelborg is sometimes referred to as 'Rörstrand's grand old lady' because her work is so synonymous with the ceramics factory. Born into a Swedish aristocratic family, she grew up on the Öster Malma estate in Södermanland in southeastern Sweden, and studied at the Tekniska Skolan (Technical School) in Stockholm. She also made study trips to Italy and France, and in 1916 her ceramic and textile designs were exhibited for the first time at the Gummerson Gallery, Stockholm – an influential showcase of modern art. Around this time she began designing

for the Rörstrand factory, where she remained working for 57 years. In 1923 she made a name for herself with a vase decorated with a simple wheat-ear motif, but it was a porcelain service with the same decorative device that can be seen as her real breakthrough design. Exhibited in 1930 at the landmark Stockholm Exhibition, where it was displayed as Sweden's 'National Service', this simple, functional, yet classically inspired design brought Adelborg widespread international acclaim. The design reflected the softer Scandinavian approach to Modernism, and was put into production in 1932, renamed 'Swedish Grace', the phrase coined by Philip Morton Shand (see p. 86).

Below: Swedish Grace bowls for Rörstrand (Sweden), 1930

1. Louise Adelborg with various pieces of her Swedish Grace service designed for Rörstrand, ca. 1930s/1940s

2. Pieces from the Swedish Grace range by Louise Adelborg for Rörstrand (Sweden), 1930

EARLY ARABIA

Arabia was established in 1873 but did not become a design innovator until Kurt Ekholm's appointment as art director in 1932. Prompted by the economic depression of the 1930s, the factory studied its production processes scientifically, automated them as much as possible and strove for more rational designs. Ekholm's simple and practical Sinivalko (White-Blue) tableware range (1936) reflected this new form-follows-function ethos, yet was not too utilitarian in its aesthetic for general acceptance. In 1945 Kaj Franck joined the firm, and the following year, in response to a discussion between the Family Welfare Association of Finland and Arabia about the need for tableware that would meet the demands of large families living in rural areas, he was made director of Arabia's model-planning department. The resulting RA range (1946) in plain white earthenware was perfectly suited to its requirements, but was if anything a little too plain. Three years later Franck evolved its forms into a more sculptural porcelain range. Known as the RN tea and coffee service (1949), it was produced in white and a number of fashionable pastels. Likewise, Friedl Holzer-Kjellberg's delicate FK rice-porcelain series (1943) signalled a more artistic mid-century direction for Arabia.

1. Sinivalko (White-Blue) range by Kurt Ekholm for Arabia (Finland), 1936

2. FK rice-porcelain bowls by Friedl Holzer-Kjellberg for Arabia (Finland), 1943

Opposite: RN Sointu tableware by Kaj Franck for Arabia (Finland), 1949

1.

2.

EWALD DAHLSKOG

The Swedish ceramicist and painter Ewald Dahlskog joined Bobergs Fajansfabrik (Bo Fajans) in Gävle in 1929 and set about creating distinctive earthenware designs in a chunky architectural style that reflected the new and emerging Functionalist tendency in Swedish design circles. These bold, geometric pieces, many of which featured bands of surface ribbing, can also be seen as a Modernistic expression of the then-fashionable international Art Deco style. Dahlskog's work was exhibited in 1930 at the Stockholm Exhibition, a fittingly forward-looking showcase for his work, which was described by the Swedish press as 'functionalist'. The following year his designs were included in the exhibition 'Swedish Applied Arts' held at Dorland House in Regent Street, London, where they inspired the New Zealand-born designer Keith Murray to come up with similar geometric ceramics for the English firm Wedgwood.

Below: Kulvasen vases by Ewald Dahlskog for Bobergs Fajansfabrik (Sweden), 1930–48

1. Lava jug by Ewald Dahlskog for Bobergs Fajansfabrik (Sweden), 1930s

2. Golvvas vase by Ewald Dahlskog for Bobergs Fajansfabrik (Sweden), 1930s–1940s

3. Tellus planters by Ewald Dahlskog for Bobergs Fajansfabrik (Sweden), 1930s–1940s

1.

2.

3.

AXEL SALTO

A uniquely talented ceramics artist and formidable clay modeller, Axel Salto looked to nature as his primary source of design inspiration, and the shapes of gourds, seed pods, budding cones and leaf veins all influenced the evocative organic forms and incised motifs he employed in his sculptural stoneware vessels. Salto brought an artistic sensibility into play in the design of ceramics, having trained as a painter at the Kongelige Danske Kunstakademi (Royal Danish Academy of Fine Arts; KADK) in Copenhagen. He began his career in 1923 as a ceramicist at Bing & Grøndahl, and two years later his work was singled out for special mention by the French press when he exhibited at the Exposition Internationale des Arts Décoratifs et Industriels Modernes in Paris. At about the same time he began working with Nathalie Krebs at Saxbo Stentøj (Saxbo Stoneware), and he continued to do so until 1933, when he joined the design team at Royal Copenhagen. There, he designed some of his best-known pieces, notable for their bold modelling and for the rich, earth-hued 'Solfatara' mottled glazes that helped to heighten the sense that his work was inspired deeply by nature. In 1951 Salto was awarded a Grand Prix for his distinctive designs at the 9th Milan Triennial, and his work continues to be highly sought after by collectors, thanks to its enduring 'natural' appeal.

1. Large stoneware vase by Axel Salto in 'Knoppig' style for Royal Copenhagen (Denmark), ca. 1950s – this impressive piece recently sold for 1.2 million Danish krona

2. Stoneware vase by Axel Salto for Royal Copenhagen (Denmark), 1951

Opposite: Large stoneware vase by Axel Salto for Royal Copenhagen (Denmark), 1951

1.

2.

WILHELM KÅGE

At the Gustavsberg porcelain factory, Wilhelm Kåge designed a wide range of ceramics that always seemed to capture the spirit of the age in which they were created. Having studied painting in Gothenburg under the painter Carl Wilhelmson, Kåge later learned about three-dimensional design at Johan Rohde's studio-school in Copenhagen. He also learned about typography and graphic composition at the Plakatschule (Poster School) in Munich. Being well grounded in both fine and applied arts, Kåge was appointed art director of Gustavsberg in 1917, ostensibly to create a new range of tableware to be included that year in the Home Exhibition in Stockholm. The resulting Liljeblå service, with its folk-inspired motif, was one of the first open-stock ranges created specifically for the working classes. ('Open stock' could be purchased piecemeal, making it much more affordable than traditional services.) Kåge subsequently designed a more utilitarian tableware range, Praktika (1933), which when launched was acclaimed for its easy-to-store compactness and easy-to-clean forms. Although it was a commercial failure, importantly it reflected the increasing influence of Functionalism in Sweden during the 1930s. In about 1940 Kåge, ever the design chameleon, changed stylistic tack and began creating a series of vessels entitled Surrea, which were inspired by Surrealism. These quirky vessels with their split-in-half-and-joined-back-together forms heralded a brave new sculptural tendency at Gustavsberg, one that became hugely influential both in Scandinavia and elsewhere.

Below & opposite: Surrea vases by Wilhelm Kåge for Gustavsberg (Sweden), ca. 1940

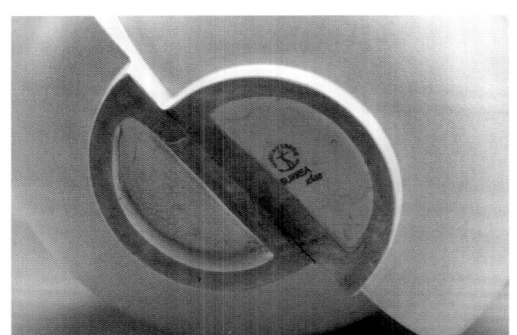

TOINI MUONA

Toini Muona created distinctive designs that balanced interesting forms and decoration with sublimely beautiful glazes. She had studied ceramics under the talented Belgium-born designer Alfred William Finch at the Central School of Industrial Design in Helsinki, graduating in 1926. From 1929 she regularly participated in the annual exhibitions held by the Suomen Taideteollisuusyhdistyksen (Finnish Society of Crafts) and Ornamo (another leading Finnish association established for the promotion of art and design). In 1931 Muona began working for Arabia, and in 1933 she was made a member of its famed design studio, a position she held until 1970. In 1944 she had a joint exhibition with fellow Arabia designer Birger Kaipiainen, whose work possesses a similar experimental freshness and sense of artistry. Over the course of her illustrious career Moana won numerous awards for her forward-looking designs, including two gold medals at the Milan Triennials of 1933 and 1951, a Diplôme d'honneur at the Milan Triennial of 1954, and a Pro Finlandia medal in 1957. She also briefly designed for Nuutajärvi in the 1960s, producing glassware that, like her ceramic pieces, was interesting in both form and technique.

1. Vase by Toini Muona for Arabia (Finland), 1940s

2. Dish by Toini Muona (self-produced) (Finland), 1950s – signed TM

Opposite: Plaque by Toini Muona for Arabia (Finland), 1950s

1.

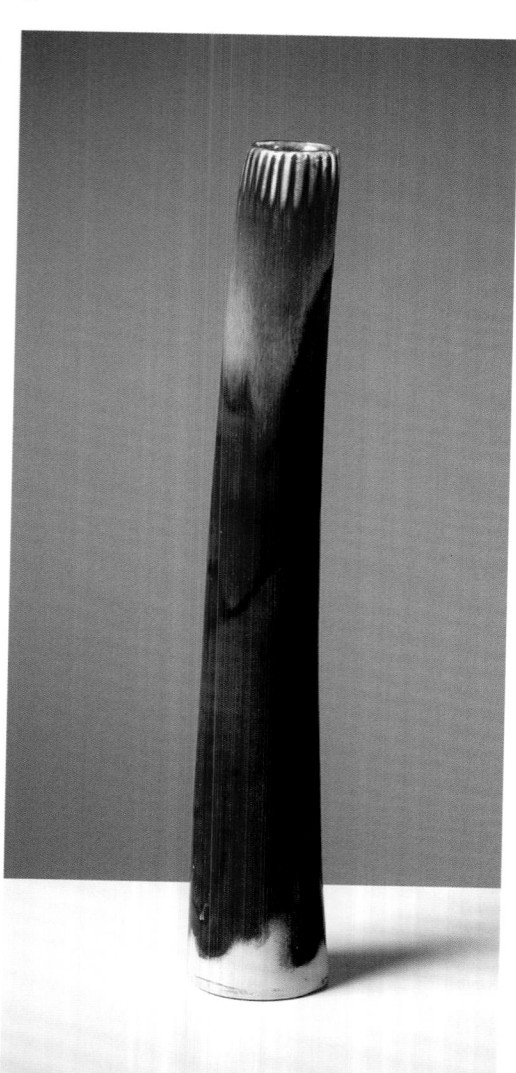

2.

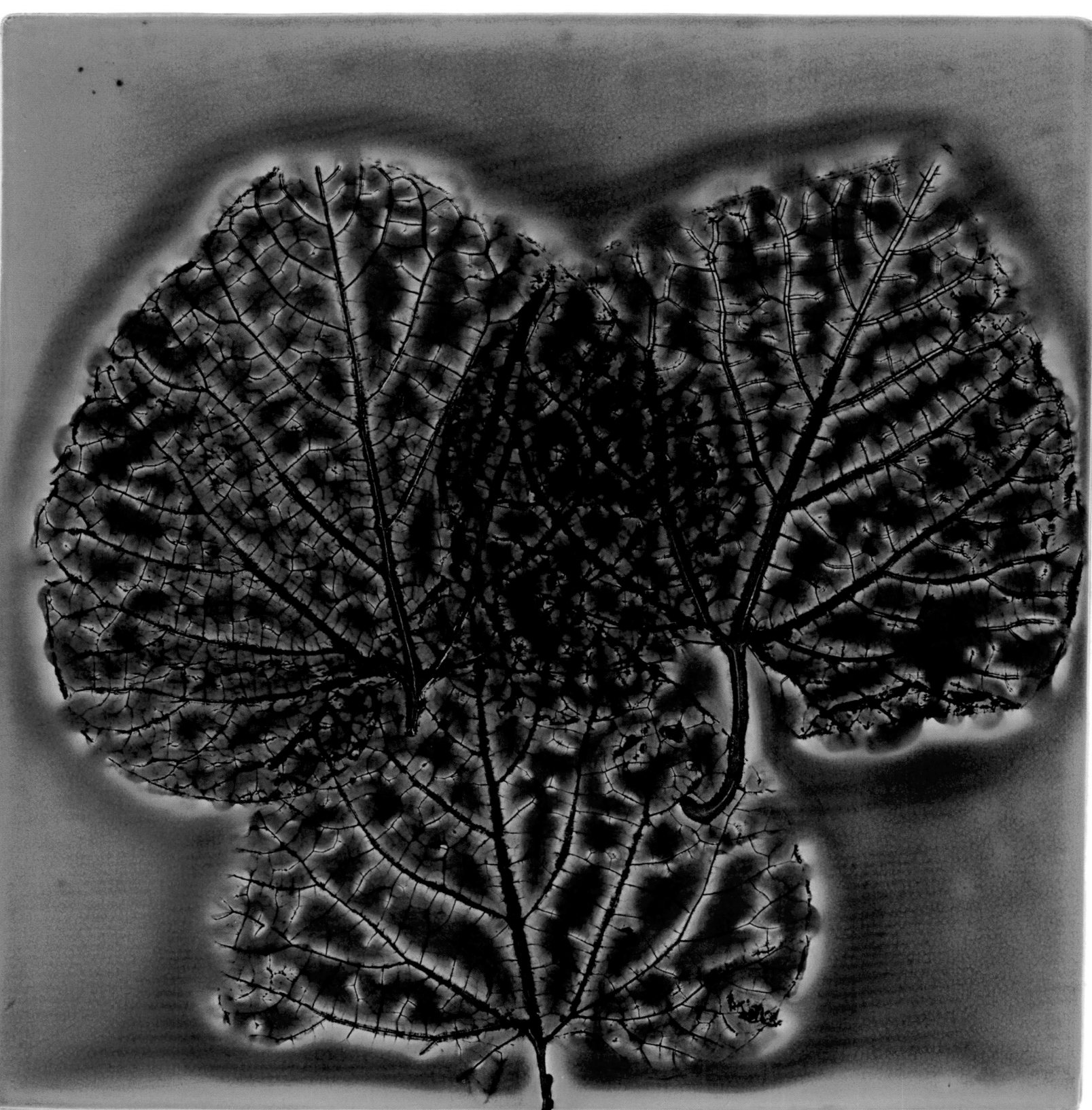

GUNNAR NYLUND

The ceramicist Gunnar Nylund was born in Paris into a highly creative family (his Danish mother was an artist, while his Swedish–Finnish father was a sculptor), who subsequently moved to Copenhagen and later to Helsinki. Following the outbreak of the Finnish Civil War in 1918, Nylund and his mother moved back to Denmark. After his schooling he studied ceramics in Helsinki before training as an architect at KADK in Copenhagen. During this period he helped his father with his sculptures, becoming an accomplished modeller in the process, and also began designing for Bing & Grøndahl. In 1928, with Nathalie Krebs, he set up Nylund & Krebs, which manufactured stoneware pieces designed by him and Krebs, as well as other designers. Two years later he was appointed Rörstrand's art director, a position he held until 1958. During his tenure he produced numerous designs for the factory, distinguished by their updated archetypal forms or undulating organic shapes that were exquisitely glazed in richly mottled earth tones.

1. Three vases by Gunnar Nylund for Rörstrand (Sweden), 1950s

2 & 3. Bowls by Gunnar Nylund for Rörstrand (Sweden), 1950s

Opposite: Vase by Gunnar Nylund for Rörstrand (Sweden), 1950s

1.

2.

3.

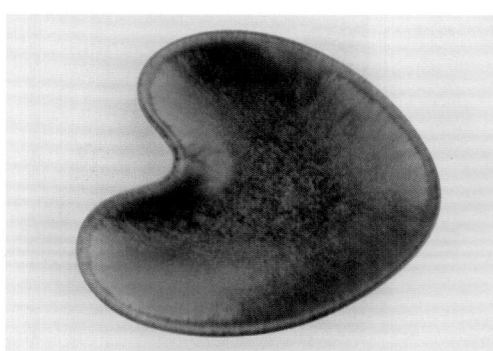

ULLA PROCOPÉ

In the late 1940s Kaj Franck assembled a formidable design team at Arabia, and Ulrika 'Ulla' Procopé was one of its most gifted members. She had trained at the Central School of Industrial Design in Helsinki, then worked for Arabia from 1948 until 1967, the year before her untimely death at the age of 47. Yet despite her relatively short career, Procopé designed an impressive number of ceramics that were notable for their beautifully proportioned sculptural forms. She also had the skill to design both tableware and ovenware that retained a handmade craft quality, despite being industrially manufactured. Her Oriental-inspired GA teapot (1953), which was launched by Arabia in 1957, is perhaps her best-known design; with its woven cane handle and subtly mottled glaze it certainly evokes a sense of handcraftsmanship. Likewise, her Valencia service (ca. 1960), inspired by traditional hand-painted Spanish blue-and-white ceramics, employed simple forms yet was decorated with a vibrant folk-style pattern that harked back to Finland's rich craft tradition.

1. GA teapot by Ulla Procopé for Arabia (Finland), 1953

2. Ruska tea service by Ulla Procopé for Arabia (Finland), 1960

3. Liekki cookware by Ulla Procopé for Arabia (Finland), 1957

4. Valencia dinnerware by Ulla Procopé for Arabia (Finland), ca. 1960

2.

1.

4.

HERTHA BENGTSON

Having studied at the Gerlesborgsskolan (Gerlesborg School of Fine Art) in Sweden and also at the Académie de la Grande Chaumière in Paris, Hertha Bengtson initially worked as a pattern designer for the Hackefors porcelain factory in Lidköping. In 1941, however, at the age of 24, she joined the Rörstrand factory as a ceramics artist and designer. She soon became one of the most accomplished shape designers working there, memorably creating two influential tableware ranges, Blå Eld (Blue Fire; 1949) and Koka Blå (Boil Blue; ca. 1950). Both are now widely recognized in Sweden as design classics. The earlier of the two ranges, Blå Eld, best exemplifies the Swedish goal of creating products with the intention of, in the words of the Swedish feminist writer Ellen Key, bringing about 'a more beautiful everyday life'. With its distinctive, almost biomorphic forms and its simple repeating wheat-ear pattern, Bengtson's Blå Eld service cleverly presaged the new, more casual spirit that came to define lifestyles in the 1950s, but in an understated yet stylish way.

1. Hertha Bengtson in her studio, ca. 1950s

2. Blå Eld (Blue Fire) teapot by Hertha Bengtson for Rörstrand (Sweden), 1949

3. Rörstrand mark on the base of a teapot

Opposite: Blå Eld (Blue Fire) coffee pot, jugs and dish by Hertha Bengtson for Rörstrand (Sweden), 1949 – produced between 1950 and 1970

1.

2.

3.

JENS QUISTGAARD

Jens Quistgaard created a number of notable ceramic designs that, like his better-known woodenwares and cast-iron pieces, expressed his distinctive 'signature' style. One early design was for a Japanese-inspired teapot (1949–50) made of natural stoneware, with a brass-and-cane handle. This perfectly proportioned design (opposite, below) reveals Quistgaard's mastery of form and decoration, and his innate sympathy for materials. Through skilful handling and carefully considered designs, he let materials express their inherent natural qualities. The overall shape and repeating leaf pattern of this early design, produced by Palshus, was later echoed in his popular caramel-coloured Relief stoneware service (1959–60), produced by Kronjyden Nissen and also by Bing & Grøndahl. It was, however, Quistgaard's fluted Flamestone oven-to-table range (1958) that unequivocally demonstrated his ability to create new shapes loosely inspired by evocative archetypal forms (in this case those drawn from North Africa) that were on trend yet also inherently timeless because they were so beautifully conceived and executed.

Below: Flamestone tableware by Jens Quistgaard for Dansk (Denmark/USA), 1958

1. Relief tableware by Jens Quistgaard for Kronjyden Nissen/Bing & Gröndahl (Denmark), 1959–60

2. Stoneware teapot by Jens Quistgaard for Palshus (Denmark), 1949–50

1.

2.

BIRGER KAIPIAINEN

In Finland, there is a tradition of designers creating items for industrial production alongside one-off or limited-edition studio pieces, a practice that allows them to experiment with materials, techniques, forms and colour. One such designer was Birger Kaipiainen, who, after studying at the Central School of Applied Arts in Helsinki, joined the art department of the Arabia ceramics factory when he was just 22 years old. He went on to become one of the most renowned Finnish ceramicists of all time.

Although he is probably best remembered for his sumptuously decorated Paratiisi tableware for Arabia, which is still in production, he also designed numerous studio pieces in Arabia's workshops during his 50-year career at the factory. These highly decorative, colourful wares were inspired not only by nature – flowers, berries, fruits – but also by Byzantine art. A melancholic character, Kaipiainen escaped everyday reality through his work, which had a poignant, nostalgic quality that revealed an almost pantheistic reverence for nature in all its multi-hued splendour.

1. Carnations and berries dish by Birger Kaipiainen for Arabia (Finland), 1950s

2. Pansy dish by Birger Kaipiainen for Arabia (Finland), 1950s

3. Birger Kaipiainen hand-decorating one of his ceramic pieces in the Arabia studio, 1960s

Opposite: Large dish by Birger Kaipiainen for Arabia (Finland), 1950s

1.

2.

3.

KAJ FRANCK

In 1948 Kaj Franck designed his Kilta tableware range, which introduced the concept of mix-and-match. It was also available to buy as 'open stock', making it much more affordable. Key to its success, however, was the fact that this minimalist oven-safe range was available in a variety of attractive colours – white, black, yellow, green, brown and cobalt blue – that were intended to be combined. Franck also designed the individual pieces so that the plates and bowls stacked efficiently, while the rational rectangular or square forms adopted for the serving platters and vegetable dishes meant that they were space-saving. In 1951 he designed for Arabia another colourful mix-and-match earthenware range, FA, which had a softer organic line that was more in keeping with the tastes of the time. Kilta was discontinued in 1975, being deemed too old-fashioned, but a couple of years later the managing director of Arabia asked Franck to create a 'new Kilta'. The resulting 19-piece Teema range essentially updated this landmark design by softening its rather utilitarian aesthetic, without compromising any of its functionality.

Below: Kilta range by Kaj Franck for Arabia (Finland), 1948, 1951–52

1. Arabia advertisement for the Kilta range, 1956

2. Teema teapot by Kaj Franck for Arabia (Finland), 1977–80

3. FA jug and mugs by Kaj Franck for Arabia (Finland), 1950s

2.

CARL-HARRY STÅLHANE

One of the primary distinguishing features of Scandinavian design has been the search for ideal forms through a honing of historic archetypes. Carl-Harry Stålhane's extraordinary stoneware vessels created for Rörstrand in the early 1950s are among the most beautiful outcomes of this evolutionary approach to design. Inspired by Oriental paradigms, Stålhane's soft-edged designs were essentially modern evolutions of 'classical' ceramic forms. With their subtly mottled matt glazes, these beautiful yet understated pieces reflected the

emergence of a new sculptural refinement that would come to define Scandinavian design in the mid twentieth century. In 1951 Stålhane received a gold medal at the 9th Milan Triennial, testifying to the influence of these graceful studio ceramics as well as to his status as a design innovator. An extremely versatile designer, he also created a number of decorated ceramics, ranging from pieces embellished with painterly representations of native flora, as seen below, to his much more elaborate Cubist-influenced Torro range (1955–56), which was inspired by the work of Pablo Picasso.

1. Stoneware plate by Carl-Harry Stålhane for Rörstrand (Sweden), ca. 1950

2. Carl-Harry Stålhane in his studio, with blank vessels behind him awaiting glazing and decoration, 1950s

3. Nine vases and a bowl by Carl-Harry Stålhane for Rörstrand (Sweden), ca. 1950

4. Ten vases and a stemmed bowl by Carl-Harry Stålhane for Rörstrand (Sweden), ca. 1950

1.

2.

BERNDT FRIBERG

The Swedish ceramicist Berndt Friberg began his career as a thrower at the Höganäs stoneware factory, where he worked until 1918. That year he travelled to Denmark and was employed in the art ceramics workshop of Møller & Bøgely. The following year he returned to Sweden and found work at the Raus stoneware factory, south of Helsingborg. Eventually, in 1934, he joined the Gustavsberg porcelain factory, where he worked for ten years as a thrower for Wilhelm Kåge and Stig Lindberg. In 1944 he joined the design team of the famous Gustavsberg studio, and three years later he received his first gold medal at the 8th Milan Triennial. Two more gold medals followed, in 1951 and 1954. Being a highly accomplished maker as well as a skilful designer enabled Friberg to create beautiful studio ceramics that combined refined 'ideal forms' with exquisite glazing techniques. Many of his designs reflect the influence of the Japanese ceramic tradition, especially in their mottled glazes and perfectly proportioned shapes, and as such possess an engaging, timeless beauty that invites quiet contemplation.

Below: Two stoneware vases by Berndt Friberg for Gustavsberg (Sweden), 1971 and 1957

1. Three stoneware vases by Berndt Friberg for Gustavsberg (Sweden), 1971–75

2. Stoneware teapot by Berndt Friberg for Gustavsberg (Sweden), 1966

2.

MARIANNE WESTMAN

Marianne Westman is best remembered for the ceramics she created for Rörstrand, most notably Mon Amie (1952), Picknick (1956) and Pomona (1956), although she also designed equally accomplished textiles and glassware. Having studied pottery under Edgar Böckman at the Konstfack in Stockholm, as a newly graduated 22-year-old, Westman was initially reluctant to join Rörstrand, for her dream had always been to set up her own ceramics studio in her home town, Falun in Dalarna county.

However, a simple naïve sketch of a flower marked her design debut when it was transformed into the decoration for her Mon Amie range. This fresh, daisy-like pattern perfectly captured the postwar zeitgeist and the desire for more casual everyday wares and brighter, lighter living spaces. According to Rörstrand, 'Marianne was often quick to identify new trends and production methods. Her distinctive, light-hearted designs for household items in the 1950s and 1960s have earned her a lasting place in Swedish design history.'

Below: Mon Amie coffee service by Marianne Westman for Rörstrand (Sweden), 1952

1. Picknick platters and bowl by Marianne Westman for Rörstrand (Sweden), 1956

2. Ägghöna egg holder by Marianne Westman for Rörstrand (Sweden), 1950s

3. Marianne Westman alongside some of her ceramic designs, 1950s

1.

3.

2.

WIRKKALA + ROSENTHAL

In 1879 Philipp Rosenthal founded his eponymous porcelain factory in Selb, Bavaria, but it was his son (also Philipp) who would transform the enterprise by modernizing its product line during the 1950s. In 1961 he introduced the design-led Rosenthal Studio-Line range, which was intended for a more discerning and design-savvy clientele. Various acclaimed German designers were commissioned to create pieces for this new line, as were a number of internationally renowned foreign designers, including Tapio Wirkkala.

In fact, Wirkkala became one of Rosenthal's most prolific designers, creating well over 100 Studio-Line products. Among these, the best-known is the bird-shaped Pollo vase (1970), which came in two sizes and in either matt white or black porcelain. With this sculptural rocking form, so delicately decorated with concentric bands of raised spots, Wirkkala redefined how a bud vase could look. Wirkkala also designed pieces for Rosenthal's main product line, including the Variation tableware range (1962), which was perhaps more functional than his Studio-Line pieces, yet every bit as refined in aesthetic.

Below: Aphrodite art object/vase for Rosenthal Studio-Line (Germany), 1973

1. Variation coffee pot, coffee cup and saucer by Tapio Wirkkala for Rosenthal (Germany), 1962

2. Pollo vase by Tapio Wirkkala for Rosenthal (Germany), 1970

1.

2.

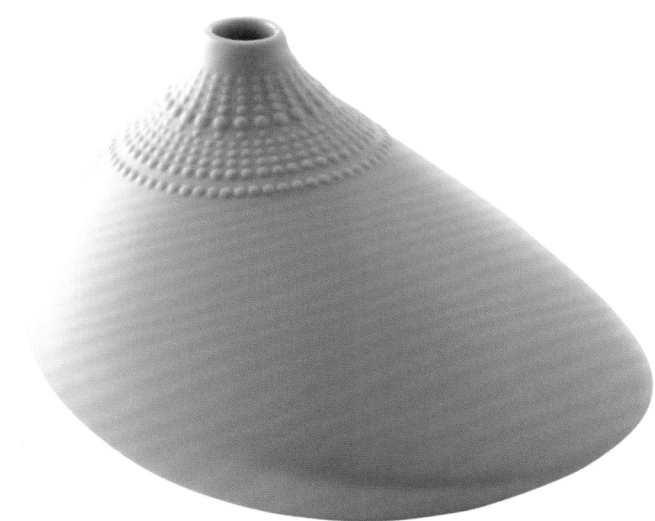

STIG LINDBERG: THE FORM-GIVER

In Sweden the word for a designer is *form-givare*, which translates literally as 'form-giver'. In the 1950s Stig Lindberg became the greatest Swedish form-giver of them all, whose influence spread way beyond the Nordic region. Prodigiously talented, Lindberg was able to design sculptural, organic shapes for ceramics that captured the abstract essence of nature. And, while it could be argued that some of Wilhelm Kåge's designs from his Carrara range (1940s) introduced a biomorphic language of form to Gustavsberg's product line, these pieces with their wavy rims did not have the sculptural refinement of Lindberg's. His free-form Veckla vessels (launched by Gustavsberg in 1951), although eminently functional, were also tabletop exercises in sculptural form-giving, evoking through their soft, undulating lines recollections of branches, shells and the like. Lindberg's stoneware Pungo vases and bowls (ca. 1950), with their matt, colourless glazed surfaces, similarly reveal his ability to create ceramic forms that need no decorative embellishment – although on occasion they were painted with the distinctive gold-and-black motif shown opposite.

Below: Seven Veckla vessels by Stig Lindberg for Gustavsberg (Sweden), 1951

Opposite: Pungo vase and bowl by Stig Lindberg for Gustavsberg (Sweden), ca. 1950 – shown with Veckla bowl, 1951

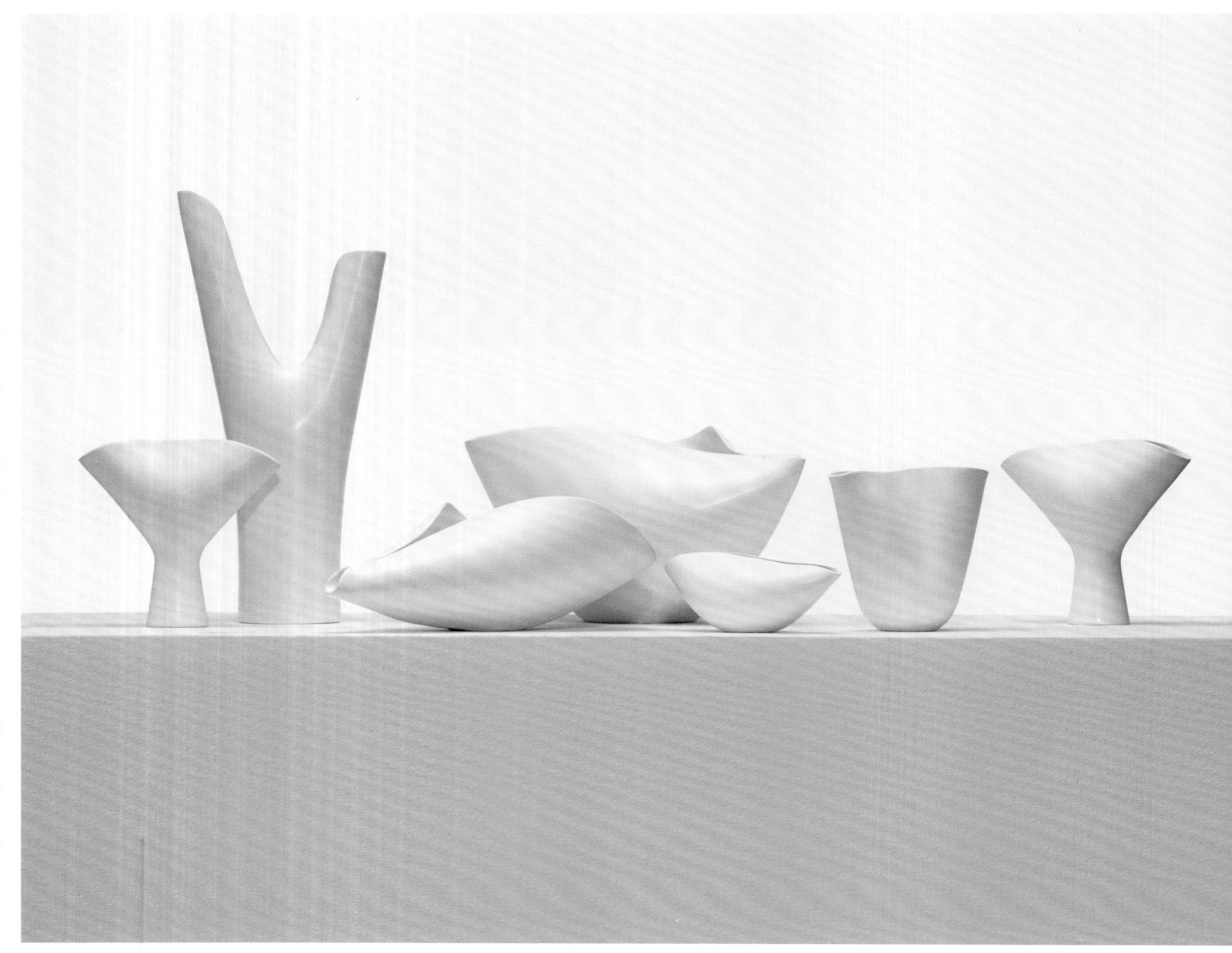

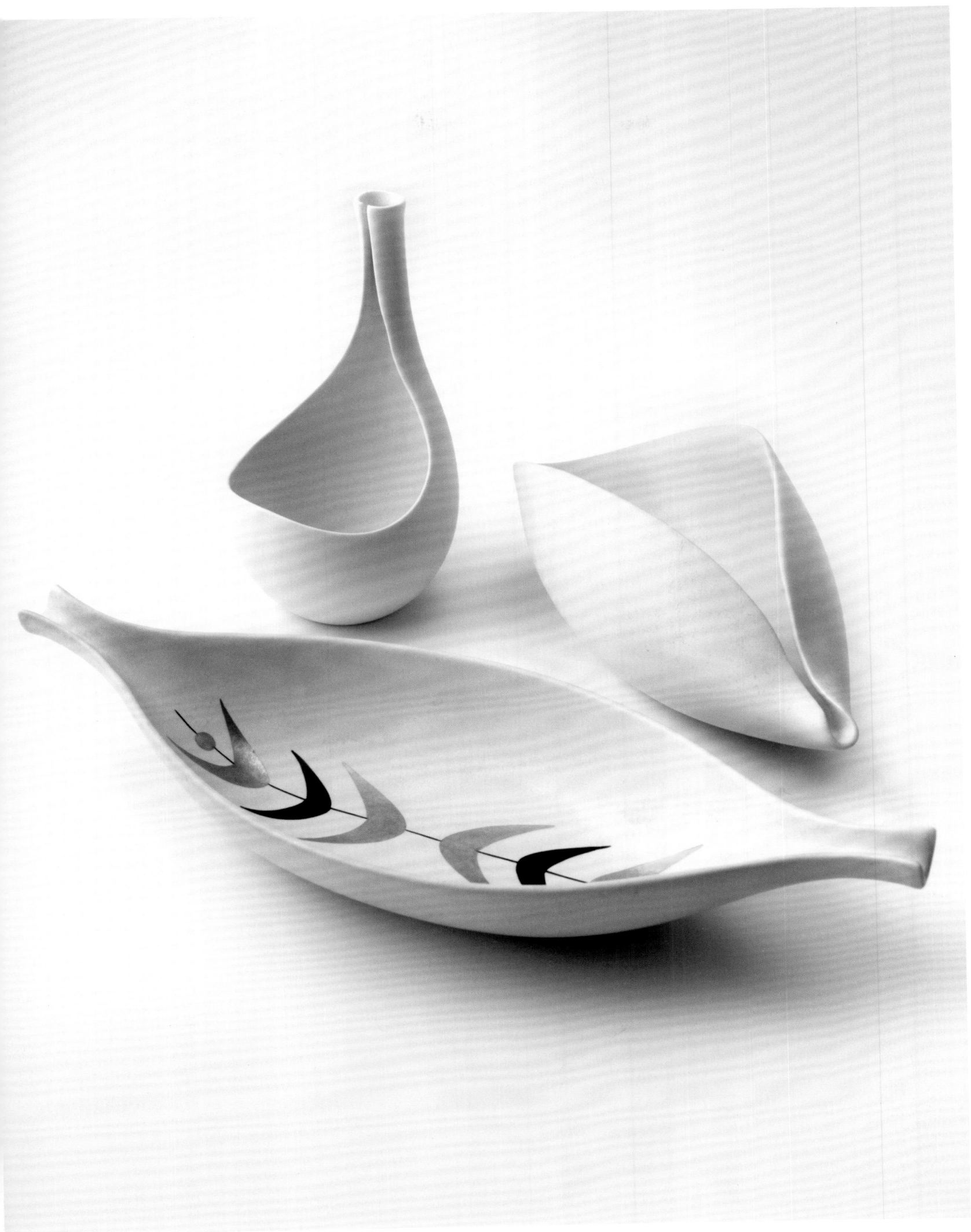

STIG LINDBERG + GUSTAVSBERG

During his illustrious career Stig Lindberg produced hundreds of ceramic designs, some of which were decorated with colourful hand-painted patterns or figurative depictions. These pieces reveal not only Lindberg's form-giving talent, with their free-flowing sculptural shapes, but also his remarkable ability as a pattern maker and decorative artist. Giving more than a passing nod to Scandinavia's decorative folk-art traditions, these pieces were nevertheless very much of their own time, and as such possess a strong Mid-century Modern sensibility. Decorated by highly skilled craftspeople in the painting studio of the Gustavsberg factory, these objects reflect the willingness of some Scandinavian companies to manufacture lower-volume studio pieces alongside industrially mass-produced wares.

1. Faience plate by Stig Lindberg for Gustavsberg (Sweden), 1950s

2. Faience vase by Stig Lindberg for Gustavsberg (Sweden), 1950s

3. Snurran triple vase by Stig Lindberg for Gustavsberg (Sweden), 1950s

Opposite: Faience vase by Stig Lindberg for Gustavsberg (Sweden), 1950s

1.

2.

3.

STIG LINDBERG: FROM ORGANIC TO GEOMETRIC

The creative genius Stig Lindberg worked in a wide variety of design disciplines, from glassware and product design to textiles and graphic design. His work was also stylistically broad, ranging from highly decorated designs to pieces that had a remarkable sculptural purity. The reason he was able to produce such varied work was that he was both an accomplished form-giver and a gifted graphic artist. The four pieces from the Terma stoneware range (1955) shown below demonstrate Lindberg's ability to create sculptural yet functional objects with soft, ergonomic lines, while the two vases and the boat-shaped bowl shown opposite are exercises in pure organic sculptural form. In contrast, the four Domino ashtrays with their Op/Pop art patterning reveal how Lindberg was equally at home with a strictly geometric vocabulary.

Below: Terma stoneware ice bucket, frying pan, saucepan and coffee pot by Stig Lindberg for Gustavsberg (Sweden), ca. 1955

1. Pungo bowl and Endiv (Endive) vases by Stig Lindberg for Gustavsberg (Sweden), ca. 1950 and 1950s

2. Domino ashtrays by Stig Lindberg for Gustavsberg (Sweden), ca. 1955 – one incorporates the Volkswagen logo, since it was made as a promotional gift for the car manufacturer

1.

2.

LINDBERG: FUNCTIONAL + DECORATIVE

In stark contrast to his exquisite undecorated vessels for Gustavsberg, in the 1950s Stig Lindberg also produced a number of ceramic designs that were highly decorative. For example, his playful Karneval (Carnival) range was introduced as part of Gustavsberg's studio line in 1957, and added to over the years (below). This remarkable series of faience wares comprised cylindrical and rectangular slab-like vases, shallow bowls, ashtrays and plates decorated with faux-naïve scenes of (among other things) fanciful townscapes, curious buildings and yellow-skinned characters riding fish and chickens, sailing in boats or taking the form of the Minotaur or mermaids. Beautifully composed and exquisitely drawn, these folk-inspired scenes had a strong pictorial quality that reflected Lindberg's mastery of book illustration. Their light-hearted, humorous aspect is in fact very Scandinavian in flavour; designs like these were meant to bring a little joy into people's lives. The same uplifting quality is also seen in Lindberg's Berså tableware range (1960; opposite), also for Gustavsberg, with its eye-catching, highly stylized leaf motif reflecting the Scandinavian love of simplicity and of nature.

Below: Karneval (Carnival) vases by Stig Lindberg for Gustavsberg (Sweden), 1957–1960s

Opposite: Berså dinnerware by Stig Lindberg for Gustavsberg (Sweden), 1960

BJØRN WIINBLAD

Having initially trained as a graphic designer at KADK, Bjørn Wiinblad found himself pulled towards fine art and over the years perfected his drafting skills by, as he put it, 'just drawing'. Although he was born and bred in Copenhagen, the decorative, whimsical style he evolved was the antithesis of the functional purity that had become so firmly associated with contemporary Danish design. It was while he was working on illustrations for a new edition of *Arabian Nights* that he was first inspired to decorate ceramic objects with themes from these famous stories.

He taught himself various ceramic techniques, and opened his own studio in 1952. Five years later Wiinblad was hired by Rosenthal, the German porcelain manufactory, as one of its chief designers. Over the succeeding decades he produced countless designs for the firm, joyfully decorated with round-faced figures wearing old-fashioned clothing and surrounded by swirling flora. Indeed, his gilt-rimmed Zauberflöte (Magic Flute) tableware series (1989) was one of his more restrained designs. Despite being a controversial figure in Scandinavian design circles, Wiinblad was undoubtedly one of the region's most original designer-artists.

1. Footed bowl by Bjørn Wiinblad (self-produced) (Denmark), 1984

2. Zauberflöte (Magic Flute) porcelain service by Bjørn Wiinblad for Rosenthal (Germany), 1989

1.

2.

FIGGJO

While the illustrious design output of ceramic factories in Denmark, Sweden and Finland is well documented, the Norwegian manufacturing company Figgjo, founded by Harald Lima and Sigurd Figved in 1941, also produced some notable if less well-known designs. In 1946 the firm invested in the building of a tunnel kiln to increase productivity, and in 1951 it began exporting its wares to Denmark and England. Crucially for its international standing, the designer Turi Gramstad Oliver joined its design team in 1960, and over the next 20 years – even after the factory merged with her former employer, Stavangerflint, in 1968 and became Figgjo Flint – she created some of the firm's most famous ranges, including Arden, Clupea, Elvira, Lotte, Market, Oliver, Saga and Tor Viking. Capturing the optimistic spirit of the 1960s and early 1970s, Gramstad Oliver's charming designs had an endearingly childlike quality that proved popular around the world. Today, thanks to their whimsical aesthetic, which evokes the carefree innocence of an earlier and less complicated age, these retro designs continue to be highly sought after by vintage collectors in many countries.

1. The Family platter by Turi Gramstad Oliver for Figgjo (Norway), ca. 1960s

2. Lotte serving dish by Turi Gramstad Oliver for Figgjo (Norway), 1960s – reissued in 1972

2.

INGER PERSSON
+ SIGNE PERSSON-MELIN

The Swedish ceramicists Inger Persson and Signe Persson-Melin both trained at the Konstfack in Stockholm, though some years apart. Persson-Melin had previously trained under Nathalie Krebs at the Kunsthåndværkerskolen (School of Arts and Crafts; now KADK) in Copenhagen. In 1955 she participated in the H55 exhibition in Helsingborg, where she had a 'breakthrough' with a range of rustic spice jars. She was awarded the Lunning Prize three years later, and throughout the rest of her career she continued to design simple, functional wares, such as the teapots shown opposite, that had a strong craft aesthetic. In contrast, Persson is best remembered for a teapot that took the form of a cartoonized Aladdin's Lamp, part of her Pop tableware range (1968) for Rörstrand. This teapot perfectly encapsulated the Pop spirit of the Swinging Sixties with its funky globular form and bold colours – pure white, sunflower yellow, poppy red, cobalt blue or lime green. The designs of both these talented ceramicists reflect the Scandinavian desire for beautiful homewares that enhance everyday life – in this case, the simple ritual of tea making.

Below: Pop teapot by Inger Persson for Rörstrand (Sweden), 1968

1. Teapot by Signe Persson-Melin for Höganäs (Sweden), 1980s

2. Kinesen teapot by Signe Persson-Melin for Rörstrand (Sweden), ca. 1980

1.

2.

ARABIA: 1960S + 1970S CASUAL CHINA

By the mid 1960s a number of leading Scandinavian manufacturers had begun producing ceramics intended specifically for informal use. The Finnish firm Arabia, a trailblazer of this new phenomenon, produced designs that featured simple shapes emblazoned with bold transfer-printed graphic motifs. For example, its Pomona range of storage jars, the forms of which had been designed by Ulla Procopé (see pp. 332–33) in the 1950s, was revitalized for a new generation of homemakers with eye-catching fruit-inspired motifs designed by

Raija Uosikkinen in 1965. Similarly, the form of the Kuutamo (Moonlight) dish featured below was created by Kaarina Aho in 1957, but Hilkka Liisa Ahola's wonderful inky-blue sunflower pattern was added in 1971. The same happened with the Valpuri range: the shapes had been designed by Aho in 1963, but the range was updated five years later with a striking bull's-eye decoration devised by Gunvor Olin-Grönqvist. 'On-trend' designs such as these by Arabia, which were intended for kitchen use and for friends-and-family dining, reflected the more casual lifestyle patterns that began emerging in the 1960s.

Below: Kuutamo (Moonlight) dish by Kaarina Aho (shape) and Hilkka Liisa Ahola (decoration) for Arabia (Finland), 1957/1971

1. FC/Valpuri jugs and mugs by Kaarina Aho and Gunvor Olin-Grönqvist (decoration) for Arabia (Finland), 1963/1968

2. Pomona storage jars by Ulla Procopé (shape) and Raija Uosikkinen (decoration) for Arabia (Finland), 1950s/1965

1.

CONTEMPORARY CERAMICS

Building on the long and proud legacy of innovative ceramic production in the Nordic countries, a number of contemporary designers in Scandinavia continue to create wares for everyday use, based on the honing of beautiful and functional ideal forms. Lovisa Wattman's Collection serving bowl (1996) and Claesson Koivisto Rune's stacking nest of five bowls (including a ceramic one; 2014) are prime examples. Likewise, Anna Kraitz's

Alba vase (2015), with its distinctive buckled leather belt, reveals the very Scandinavian obsession with evolving historic forms – in this case, those found in Oriental ceramics – into something new and fresh. The Scandinavian tendency to whimsical decoration is similarly being kept well and truly alive in the fairy-tale ceramics designed by Klaus Haapaniemi for Iittala, pieces that powerfully evoke the folk traditions of the Nordic region yet in a very twenty-first-century manner.

Below: Collection serving bowl by Lovisa Wattman for Höganäs (Sweden), 1996 – black version introduced in 2000

1. Set of bowls by Claesson Koivisto Rune for Design House (Sweden), 2014 – featuring not only a ceramic bowl, but also others in stainless steel, plastic, wood and glass

2. Taika (Magic) serving plate by Klaus Haapaniemi for Iittala (Finland), 2006

3. Alba vase by Anna Kraitz for Design House (Sweden), 2015

1.

3.

2.

METALWARE

Sweden is famous for its high-quality iron ore deposits, and its long tradition of iron and later steel manufacturing. Sandviken Ironworks (later Sandvik), founded in 1862, was the first company in the world to succeed in using the Bessemer method, which was invented by the British engineer Sir Henry Bessemer for steel production on an industrial scale. It led to a number of Swedish inventions in the realm of steel tools, such as the modern adjustable spanner, invented by Johan Petter Johansson in 1891. Indeed, in some countries this handy tool is still called the 'Swedish key'.

Swedish iron production played a dark role during World War II, however, when the metal was exported to Germany via the ice-free Norwegian port of Narvik. This was a major contributing factor in the German occupation of Norway and Denmark, and possibly the main reason why Sweden was not occupied. The war also played a role in the further development of stainless steel, having previously been developed by the British metallurgist Harry Brearley as a corrosion-free metal for gun barrels in 1912. Brearley came from Sheffield, the centre of the British cutlery industry, and it was not long before his invention was used for kitchen utensils. This new wonder material became popular at the same time as Modernism made its breakthrough in Scandinavia. It was, however, pewter (an alloy of tin and various other metals) that was used in the 1920s and 1930s by the Stockholm-based design-led company Svenskt Tenn – which actually means 'Swedish pewter' – to produce some of the first truly Modern pieces of Scandinavian metalware, including the remarkably progressive Pipes vase (1931) by Nils Fougstedt and the Wave vase (1933) by Björn Trägårdh.

It was, however, the Swedish manufacturing firm Gense that would be at the forefront of the stainless-steel revolution in Scandinavia in the early-to-mid twentieth century. Founded in 1856 in Eskilstuna, a little to the west of Stockholm, the company originally manufactured metal doors for ceramic stoves, as well as coffee roasters. It began to manufacture nickel and silverware in 1885, albeit focusing on coffee pots and candlesticks. In 1915 it began to make silver cutlery, a substantial part of which went to the restaurant trade. In the 1930s Gense began to manufacture stainless-steel cutlery, which turned out to be a momentous step forwards. Sales boomed, and only a few years later a larger factory was established.

The painter, silversmith and metalware designer Folke Arström belonged to the first generation of Swedish industrial designers. From 1936 to 1940 he designed in silver and pewter for Guldsmedsaktiebolaget (GAB) in Stockholm. He joined Gense in 1940, and worked for the next 20 years as the firm's artistic director. The company also collaborated with many freelance designers, such as the sculptor-designer Henning Seidelin. Educated at the Kongelige Danske Kunstakademi (Royal Danish Academy of Fine Arts; KADK) in Copenhagen, Seidelin established his own design company in 1937. As well as his work for Gense, he also designed hollowware and cutlery for the silversmiths Hans Hansen and Poul Lütken Frigast respectively.

The Swedish professor, silversmith and sculptor Sigurd Persson was also closely associated with Gense. In fact, metalware design ran in his blood: his father had opened a gold smithy in 1912, and it was there that Sigurd learned his craft. Having taken his journeyman's examination in 1938, he opened his own studio workshop in Stockholm in 1942, and from then until his death he was actively involved in the design of homewares and jewellery. Much of his work had a strongly geometric quality, and such was the excellence of its design and manufacture that it is now represented in numerous museums across the world, including the Victoria and Albert Museum in London, the Musée des Arts Décoratifs in Paris and the Museum of Modern Art in New York.

One of Gense's main competitors was the Swedish metalware company Ystad-Metall (founded in 1833 as Ystads Metallindustri), which initially made metal fittings for wagons as well as church candelabras. From the 1920s, the factory's production expanded to include pewter, brass and copper. It worked with a long list of prominent designers, notably Hans Bergström, Carl-Einar Borgström and Ulla Fogelklou-Skogh, the last of whom designed a sundial for Ystad-Metall that was shown at the Exposition Internationale des Arts et Techniques dans la Vie Moderne in Paris in 1937. Another Ystad-Metall designer, Ivar Ålenius Björk, also worked as a sculptor, and his public artworks can be found in many Swedish towns. His series of Mid-century-chic brass candlesticks for Ystad-Metall included his Liljan (Lily) candleholder, created for the New York World's Fair of 1939. With the agreement of his descendants, the well-known brass company Skultuna has now rekindled the production of this famous candleholder. Skultuna has also reintroduced the ever-popular Guardian Angel candlestick by Borgström, which was first made for Ystad-Metall in the 1940s.

Skultuna can date its history as far back as 1607, when King Karl IX decided that the eponymous village was a suitable location for a brass foundry: the Svartån brook

Pewter teapot by Nils Fougstedt (attributed) for Svenskt Tenn (Sweden), ca. 1924

Pipes vase by Nils Fougstedt for Svenskt Tenn (Sweden), 1931

Folke Arström holding a set of his Facette cutlery designed for Gense (Sweden), ca. 1949

Candlesticks by Sigurd Persson for Sigurd Persson Design (Sweden), 1963

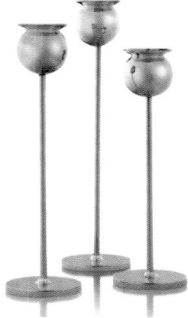

Tulip candlesticks by Pierre Forssell for Skultuna (Sweden), 1970s

Opposite: Maya cutlery by Tias Eckhoff for Norstaal (Norway), 1962 – now manufactured by Stelton

provided water power, charcoal was available from the surrounding woods, there was a harbour in nearby Västerås and the copper mine at Falun was also close. The company's pre-twentieth-century production was centred on the manufacture of brass chandeliers for churches. In the 1920s it manufactured Art Nouveau-style designs by Carl Hjalmar Norrström, but it was the silversmith Pierre Forssell who was the first to add to the firm's product line designs that were unequivocally Modern. A design prodigy, Forssell had become a teacher at the Konstfack (University College of Arts, Crafts and Design) in Stockholm at just 17, and later became a designer and eventually art director for Gense. Between 1955 and 1986 he was employed as a designer at Skultuna, where he created some of his best-loved pieces. Sigvard Bernadotte, an industrial designer and son of King Gustav VI Adolf, also designed for Skultuna in the 1980s. Today the company continues to collaborate with leading Scandinavian designers and design groups, such as Thomas Sandell, Claesson Koivisto Rune, Folkform and Monica Förster.

Another Swedish company notable for its output of design-led metalware was Nilsjohan (founded as Nilsson & Johansson in 1888). From the 1950s Nilsjohan became a major supplier of kitchen products to Swedish households; one of its most iconic products was the Is-Sissi ice bucket by Adam Thylstrup. The sculptor Sonja Katzin designed the Soraya (1965) and Sessan (1960s) cutlery ranges for the company. At its peak, Nilsjohan boasted 3,000 designs in its product line, 700 staff and 1.2 million members in its Köksklubben (Kitchen Club). The Swedish television celebrities Lasse Lönndahl, Sigge Fürst and Lennart Hyland even toured Sweden demonstrating Nilsjohan products in shopping centres. In the 1980s, however, the popularity of the firm's wares declined as women increasingly entered the workplace. Today, although the brand name is owned by the Fiskars Group, it is not currently in use.

The Finnish metalware company Hackman, which was founded in 1790 by the émigré Johan Friedrich Hackman from Bremen, would also become renowned for its manufacture of stylish metalware during the twentieth century. In the early 1800s Hackman had bought Sorsakoski, a small community in eastern Finland. The purchase included a sawmill, a flourmill and a brick factory. Hackman's cutlery-manufacturing business began in the neighbouring Finnish city of Vyborg (now in Russia) in 1876, when Johan Friedrich Hackman the younger was head of the company. Hackman eventually moved its cutlery-manufacturing business to Sorsakoski in the early 1890s.

After the sawmill was destroyed by fire in 1897, Hackman focused its efforts on metalware, and in 1902 it began manufacturing new low-cost cutlery. It was, however, the introduction of stainless steel in the 1920s that revolutionized its business. In the 1950s the Sorsakoski factory also began manufacturing coffee pots, saucepans and other kitchen accessories, as well as making pipes and containers. By the 1960s Kaj Franck and the silversmith Bertel Gardberg were both designing cutlery for Hackman. The company also famously produced Tapio Wirkkala's Puukko hunting knife (1961). In the early 2000s Hackman relaunched itself with the internationally acclaimed Hackman Tools collection, which included designs by Harri Koskinen, Björn Dahlström, Renzo Piano and Antonio Citterio. Now part of the Iittala Group, Hackman is ultimately owned by the Fiskars Group, and to this day it continues to produce beautifully designed, high-quality premium cookware and cutlery.

It is Fiskars, however, that is the dominant metalware manufacturer in Finland. The company was founded in 1649, when a Dutch merchant named Petter Henriksson Thorwöste was given a charter to establish a blast furnace and forging operation in the small Finnish village of Fiskars. In the early years Fiskars made nails, wire, hoes and metal-reinforced wheels from wrought iron. As industrial and economic development accelerated, Fiskars expanded its knife-manufacturing works to become a steel and iron company that manufactured agricultural machinery, steam engines and household utensils, including candlesticks, forks and scissors. The first Fiskars scissors were created 130 years ago, but it was not until 1967 that the firm's famous O-Series orange-handled scissors designed by Olof Bäckström were launched. The choice of plastic for the contoured handles of this early ergonomic design came about because a quantity of orange ABS had been left over from the production of a juicer. It was a fortuitous colour choice in that it gave Bäckström's design a distinctive identity; to date, over a billion of these scissors have been sold worldwide, making it one of the most democratic Scandinavian designs of all time.

Norway also has a proud tradition of metalware manufacture, albeit not quite as historic as that found in Sweden or Finland. Norway's two most famous early contributions to metalware design were a type of paperclip and a popular cheese slicer: the former first patented in 1899 by Johan Vaaler; the latter invented in 1925 by Thor Bjørklund. It was, however, Norsk Stålpress – a cutlery manufacturer founded by Finn Henriksen in 1947 – that heralded the stainless-steel revolution in Norway. The company was originally

based in a former World War II German bunker on the waterfront in Bergen. After moving to larger premises in 1956, it started making stainless-steel cutlery. For many years its largest customer was the airline SAS (Scandinavian Airlines System), and its main designers Erik Herløw and Tias Eckhoff.

Herløw studied architecture at KADK and went on to design many public and industrial buildings, including the American Embassy in Copenhagen (1954) with Ralph Rapson and John van der Meulen. The title of Herløw's book Good Things for Every Day Use (1949) sums up succinctly the guiding aim of Scandinavian design. He also designed many official Danish exhibitions, including the Danish stand at the 1951 Milan Triennial, the famous travelling exhibition 'Design in Scandinavia' which visited 25 museums across North America between 1954 and 1957, and the exhibition 'Formes Scandinaves' (1958) at the Musée des Arts Décoratifs in Paris. As well as designing for Norsk Stålpress, he worked as a designer for A. Michelsen, Kløverblad and Georg Jensen, and notably created the popular and very stylish Obelisk pattern (1954) for Copenhagen Cutlery.

It was, however, Tias Eckhoff's sculptural work that came to epitomize the high-quality and beautiful design of Norwegian metalware in the mid twentieth century. Having worked from 1949 as a ceramics designer for Porsgrunds Porselænsfabrik, he later became an accomplished cutlery designer for Norsk Stålpress; his two best-known patterns were Maya (1961) and Una (1973). Such was the innovative nature of his cutlery designs that he won gold medals at the Triennial in Milan in 1954, 1957 and 1960. Even today, many of his designs are still in production, and some are manufactured by the Danish design-led company Stelton.

The origins of Stelton can be traced back to 1960, when Niels Stellan Høm and Carton Madelaire established a trading company (named with a contraction of their forenames). They first tried selling sports shoes and furniture, but the business did not take off until they heard about a small factory in Fåreveile, which was called Danish Stainless and produced stainless-steel tableware. After establishing an agreement with Danish Stainless, Stelton began marketing a stainless-steel gravy boat that not only sold well in Danish hardware stores, but was also popular abroad. In the USA, Stelton products came to epitomize the Danish Modern style, and as a result sold considerably higher prices than in Denmark.

Peter Holmblad, who joined the company in 1963 as managing director, introduced new catalogues, packaging and graphic design. He was convinced that Stelton could survive only through designing new products since too many companies produced the same types of goods. As the stepson of the architect Arne Jacobsen, it was natural for Holmblad to approach his famous relative and try to convince him to design for the company. He succeeded only after showing his stepfather a design drawing of his own creation, which Jacobsen thought was so poor that he began scribbling designs himself. The brief was to create a comprehensive range of stainless-steel hollowware that could be used domestically as well as in the hospitality sector, and which would include a tea and coffee service, various bowls, an ice bucket and jugs. From a few simple sketches drawn on a napkin, the Cylinda-Line product group was developed over the next three years. This influential range was characterized by the minimalistic simplicity of its cylindrical shapes and its plastic handles, which, along with its brushed-steel surfaces, stood in striking contrast to the highly polished curves of its day. The Cylinda-Line was awarded the ID Prize by the Danish Society of Industrial Design in 1967, and has remained in production ever since.

Stelton's next big success was the now classic stainless-steel EM77 vacuum jug designed in 1977 by Erik Magnussen (which is also produced in colourful ABS). Although Magnussen had trained as a ceramicist at the KADK in Copenhagen, and later designed furniture for Fritz Hansen, door handles for Franz Schneider Brakel, tabletop items for Royal Selangor, lamps for Licht + Form and furniture for Paustian, it is this simple insulated jug that remains his best-known design. In 2004, after a period of challenges, Holmblad sold Stelton to Michael Ring, previously managing director of Georg Jensen. Ring initiated a renaissance at Stelton by not only trimming its product line, but also inviting new designers, such as Prince Carl Philip Bernadotte, Oscar Kylberg and Troels Seidenfaden, to revitalize the firm's range.

Georg Jensen is predominately known for its jewellery, but its ranges of stainless-steel and sterling-silver household items are of unequalled design quality. Sigvard Bernadotte designed a number of pieces for the firm, but it was Henning Koppel who became the company's key designer in this field in the mid twentieth century. He had shown early talent for drawing as a child, and trained as a draughtsman and watercolourist under the painter Bizzie Høyer. He later studied sculpture under Anker Hoffmann at KADK and then at the Académie Ranson in Paris. His outstanding skills as a draughtsman helped him to execute superb renderings of his design concepts. Like many Danish Jews, he fled to Sweden during World War II, and while here he worked for Svenskt Tenn, where

he developed his metal-casting skills. On returning to Denmark, thanks to the knowledge he had gained, he joined Georg Jensen as a designer not only of jewellery, but also of hollowware and flatware. His work was organic in form and inspired by the sculptures of Alexander Calder, Jean (Hans) Arp and Constantin Brâncusi. Many of Koppel's best-known designs were first modelled in clay, which explains the oozing sculptural quality of his work. Supported by a generous father, he never understood the relationship Modernism had with function, affordability and production-friendly design. In fact, he was openly critical of Modernism and unmoved by those critics who encouraged him to design more affordable products. He frequently observed that 'functionalism has nothing to do with the art of forming silver.' Most of his work for Georg Jensen was serially manufactured in relatively low numbers; for example, only 500 examples of his famous silver jug were produced – which in comparison to his other Georg Jensen designs was, for Koppel, an exceptionally high number.

Today Georg Jensen continues its tradition of producing high-quality metal homewares, although non-Scandinavian designers now create most of its products. This reflects the increasing internationalism of design over the last couple of decades, during which many Scandinavian design-led companies have become global brands. However, all the work produced by firms such as Georg Jensen retains strongly Scandinavian core design values.

Soraya cutlery range by Sonja Katzin for Nilsjohan (Sweden), 1965

Puukko hunting knife by Tapio Wirkkala for Hackman (Finland), 1961

All-round cheese slicer by Thor Bjørklund for Thor Bjørklund & Sonner (Norway), invented in 1925; this version redesigned ca. 1950s

Obelisk cutlery by Erik Herløw for Copenhagen Cutlery (Denmark), 1954

Kubus 8 candlestick by Mogens Lassen (Denmark), 1962 – reissued by By Lassen

1.

2.

SYLVIA STAVE

Born in Växjö, Sweden, Sylvia Stave (neé Gadd) was an early, enigmatic female pioneer of Scandinavian Modernism, who created designs in a bold Art Deco style. In 1929, at the age of 21, she ran away to Stockholm to escape her father and stepmother, and adopted her remarried mother's new surname. That year she was hired as a designer by the Stockholm goldsmith C. G. Hallberg, and she became its artistic director two years later. Her silver and pewter designs were influenced by the form-follows-function minimalism of the Bauhaus, but they were never intended for industrial production. Stave took part in several group exhibitions in Sweden, but it was her participation in the Exposition Internationale des Arts et Techniques dans la Vie Moderne, held in Paris in 1937 – when her work was praised for its 'elegant simplicity' – that marked a turning point in her life. She enrolled at the École des Beaux-Arts in Paris the following year, fulfilling her long-held artistic ambitions; but two years later she married a French doctor and abandoned her flourishing career.

1. Vodka cooler by Sylvia Stave for C. G. Hallberg (Sweden), 1930s

2. Silver-plated jug by Sylvia Stave for C. G. Hallberg (Sweden), 1930s

Below: Silver-plated jug by Sylvia Stave for C. G. Hallberg (Sweden), 1930s

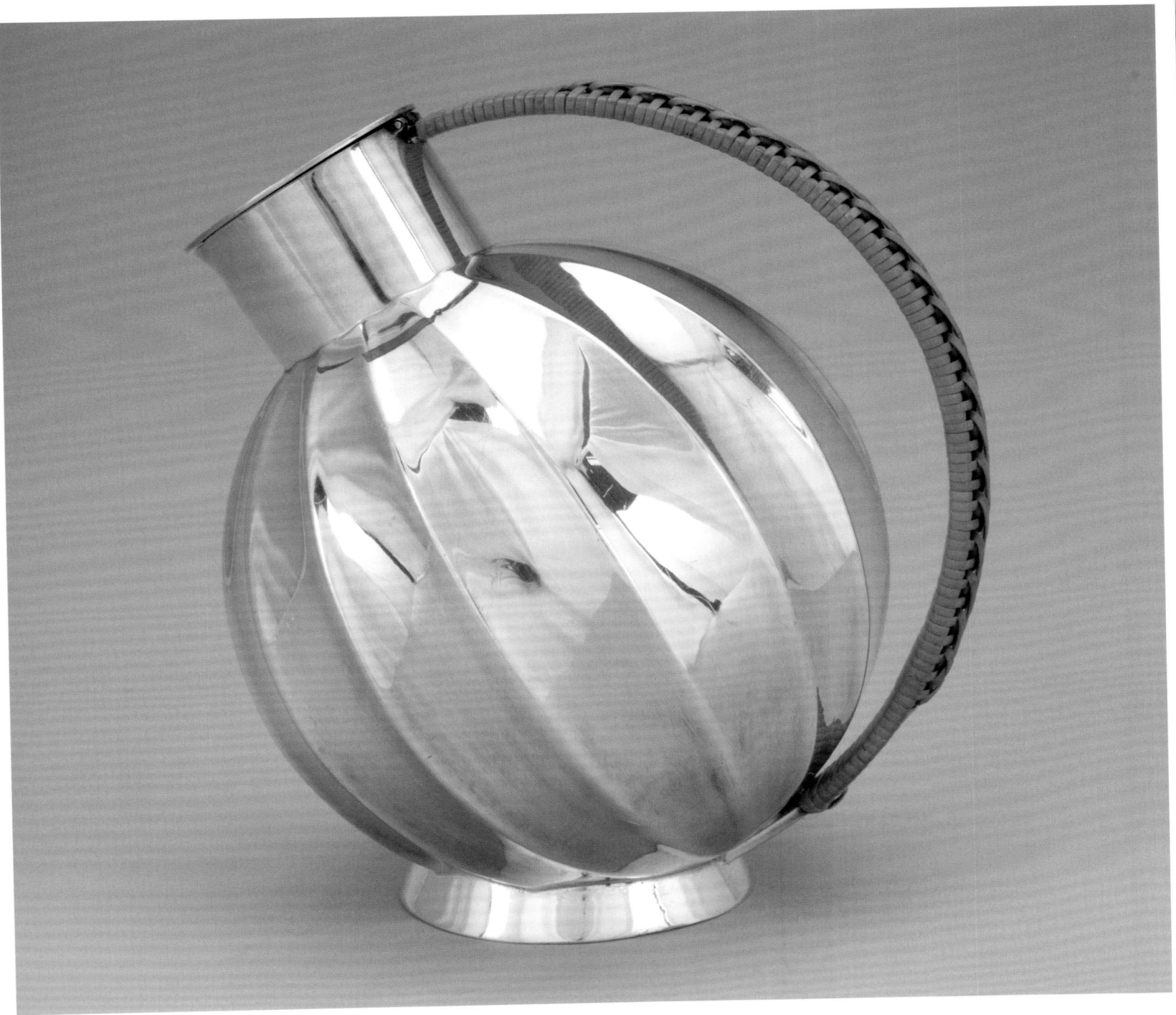

YSTAD-METALL

The history of Ystad-Metall can be traced back to 1833, when a foundry was established in the Skåne region of Sweden for the manufacture of church chandeliers and other objects, such as photograph frames, in brass and copper. In the early twentieth century the foundry began to make pewter wares and also larger pieces in bronze. The company opened a shop in Stockholm in 1927, and King Gustav V famously visited it and purchased a bowl and a vase. In the 1930s Ystad-Metall manufactured pieces by Ivar Ålenius Björk, metalware designs that were some of the most innovative to be found anywhere in Scandinavia at the time. In testament to this is Björk's Lilja (Lily) candlestick, originally designed for the 1939 New York World's Fair but still manufactured by Skultuna, and looking as fresh today as it did some 75 years ago. In the 1950s Ystad-Metall also produced designs by Gunnar Ander with simple yet ingenious construction and strong, sculptural presence.

1. Candelabra by Gunnar Ander for Ystad-Metall (Sweden), 1950s

2. Indoor watering can by Gunnar Ander for Ystad-Metall (Sweden), 1950s

3. Lilja (Lily) candlesticks by Ivar Ålenius Björk for Ystad-Metall (Sweden), 1939

4. Vases by Ivar Ålenius Björk for Ystad-Metall (Sweden), 1930s

1.

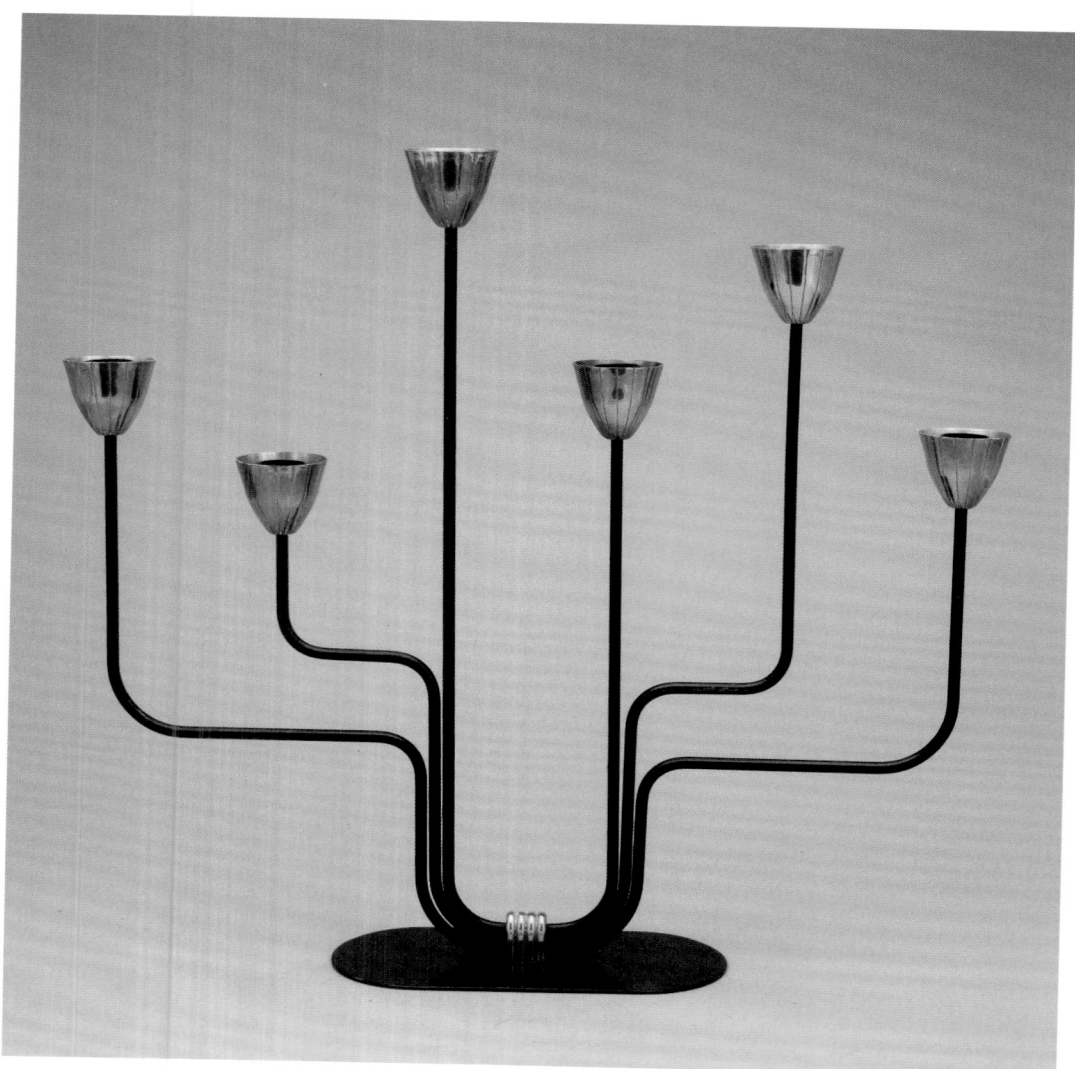

2.

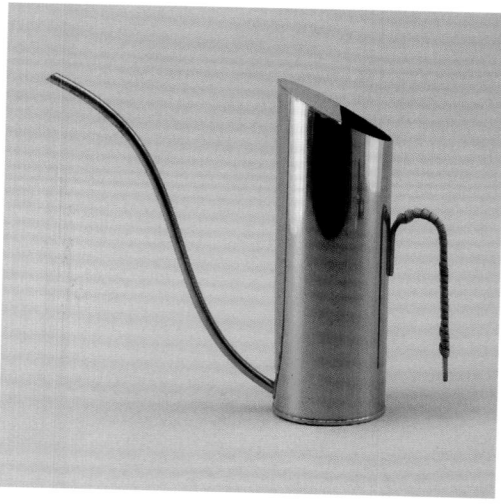

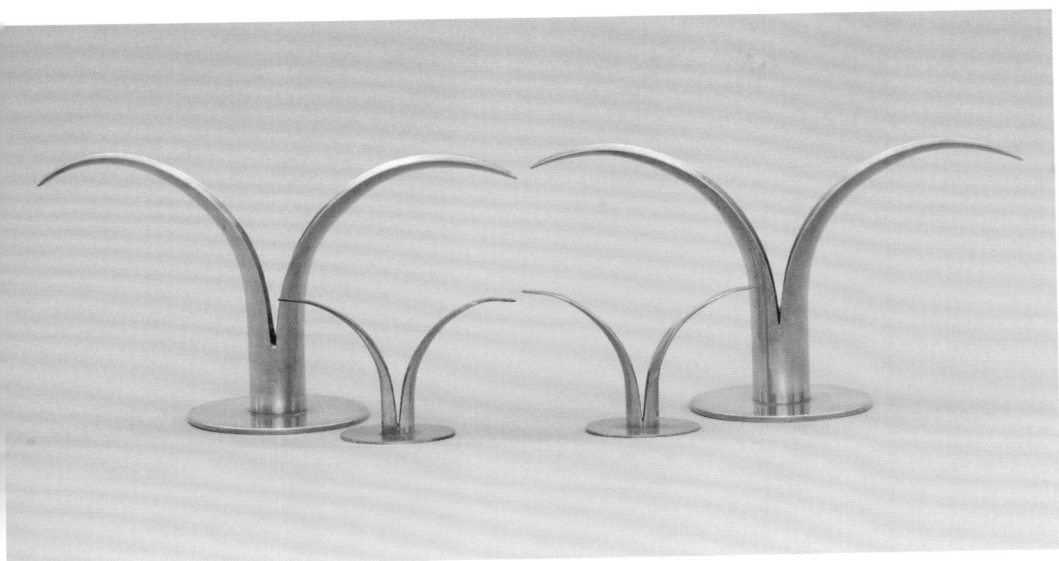

3.

4.

GENSE

In the 1950s a stainless-steel revolution occurred in homeware design, spearheaded by a number of Scandinavian companies and designers. At the forefront was Pierre Forssell's work for Gense, which stands out for its creative exploitation of this seeming wonder material that allowed the mass-production of affordable yet stylish 'New Look' products. Notable for their crisp, contemporary lines, Forssell's designs were far removed stylistically from the silver-plated wares of earlier generations. His simply constructed yet attractive cone-shaped salt, pepper and sugar shakers drew much interest at the 1955 H55 exhibition in Helsingborg, the influential showcase of Swedish mid-century design. Interestingly, the two other Gense serving dishes shown here, the design of which is attributed to Forssell, were sold under the Viners brand in the UK, showing just how influential these Scandinavian stainless-steel wares were at the time.

Below: Stainless-steel serving dishes by Pierre Forssell for Gense (Sweden), 1950s

1. Stainless-steel hors d'oeuvre dish by Pierre Forssell (attributed) for Gense (Sweden), 1950s

2. Salt, pepper and sugar shakers by Pierre Forssell for Gense (Sweden), 1950s

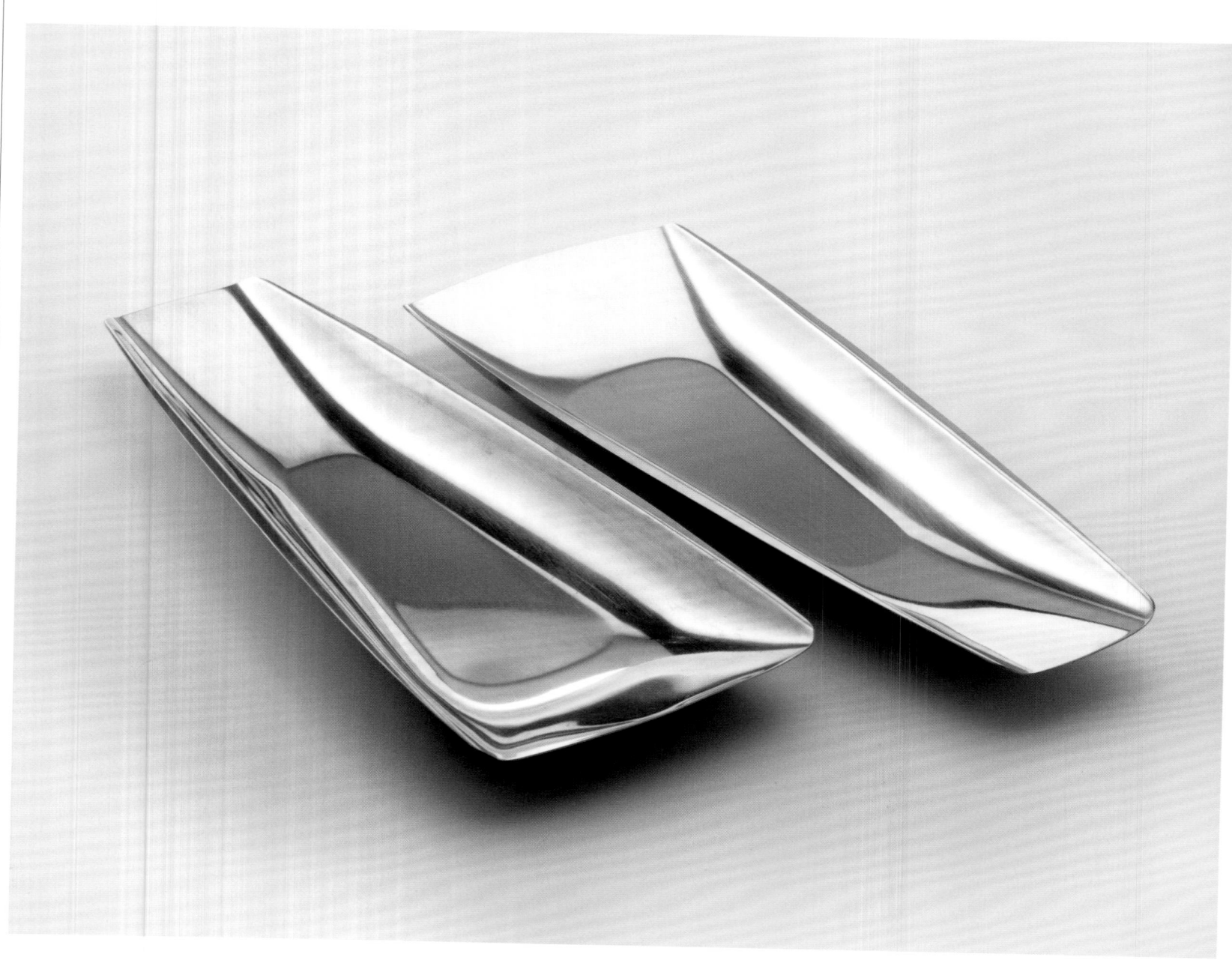

1.

2.

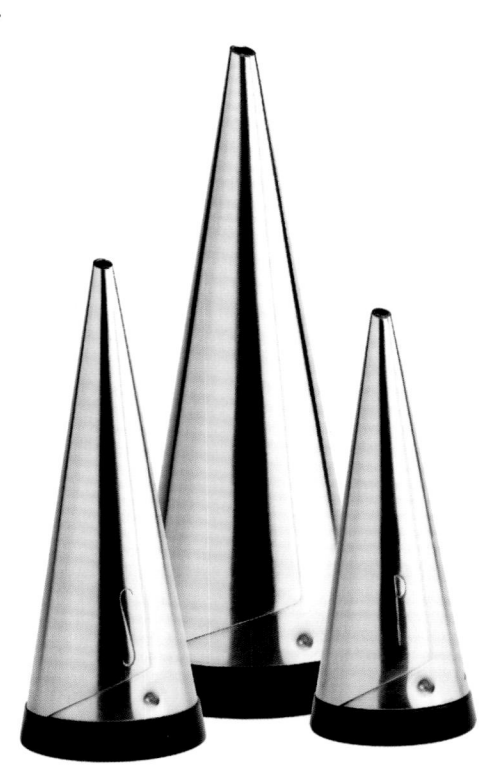

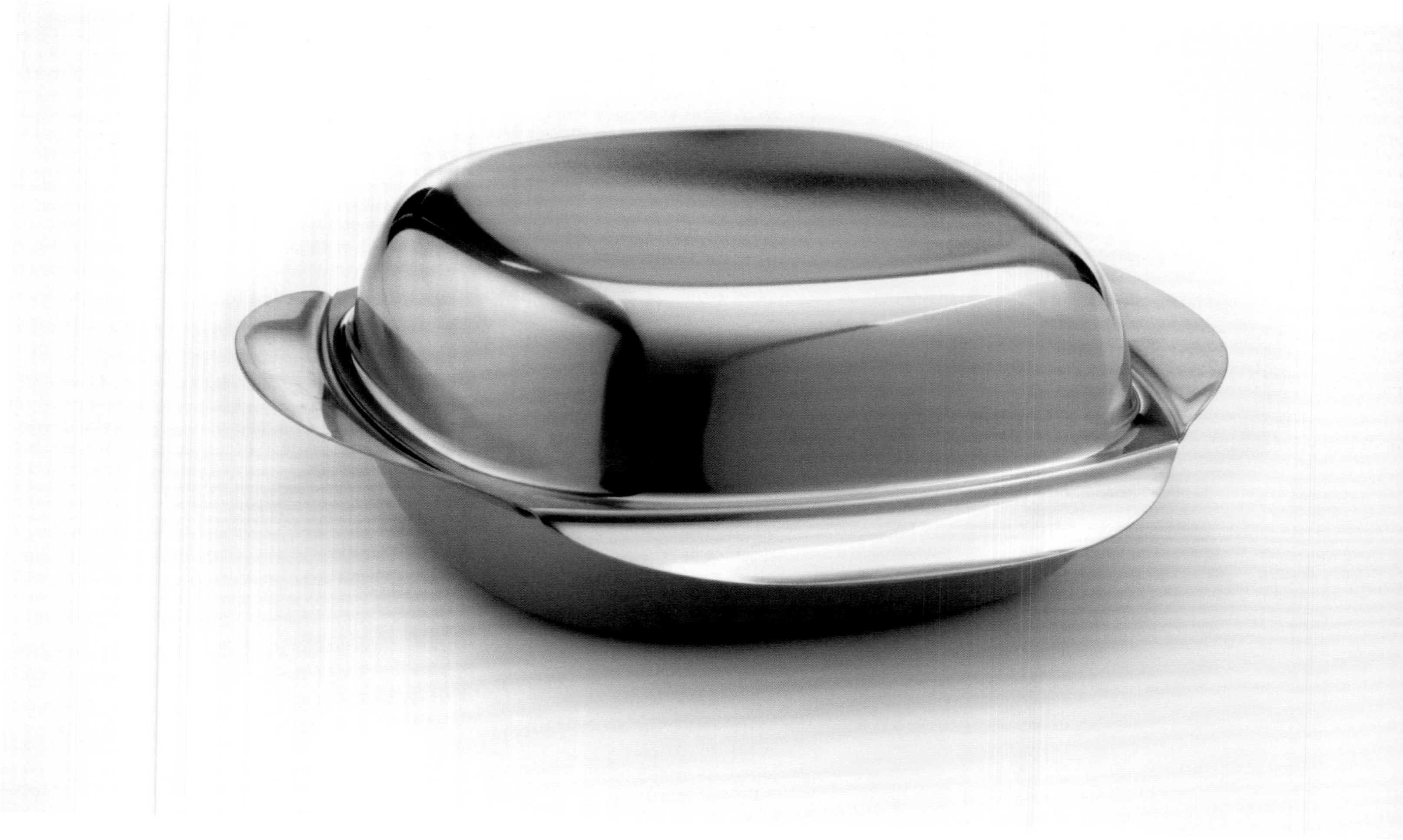

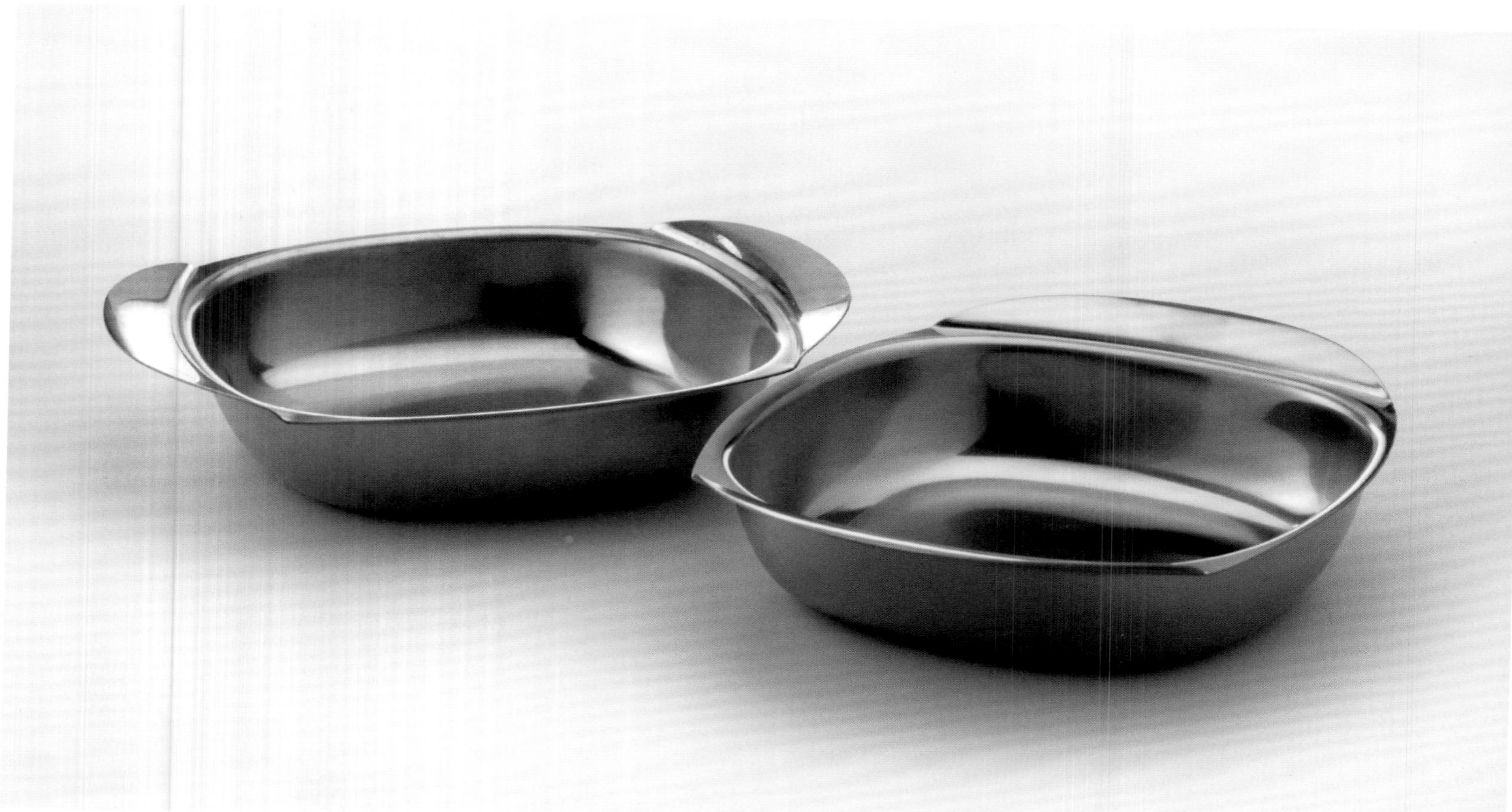

SIGURD PERSSON

Sigurd Persson was at the forefront of the postwar stainless-steel revolution, which began in Sweden and rippled out across the world. Indeed, it was a display of Persson's work that prompted the famous British designer Robert Welch to work in stainless steel as a student at the Royal College of Art, London. The son of a silversmith, Persson was apprenticed with his father before working with the silversmith and court jeweller Anders Nilsson. After taking his journeyman's examination, he travelled to Germany and trained at the Academy of Fine Arts in Munich, but his studies were cut short by the outbreak of war and were completed at the Konstfack in Stockholm. In 1942 he opened his own workshop in the city, producing silverware that was notable for its formal simplicity and lack of embellishment. Seven years later, as an innovative form-giver, Persson was approached by Sune Walldén, the director of Silver & Stål, to design a range of stainless-steel wares that would be suitable for the contract market, especially hospitals and restaurants. The resulting range, which included the Cultura double serving dish shown opposite (1953), presaged a new 'contemporary look' within metalware and was hugely influential on stainless-steel design throughout the 1960s.

Opposite: Cultura double serving dish by Sigurd Persson for Silver & Stål (Sweden), 1953

1. Sigurd Persson working in his studio, ca. 1954

2. Pair of silver-plated metal and porphyry Silverne Stakar (Silvery Poles) candlesticks by Sigurd Persson (self-produced) (Sweden), 1963

2.

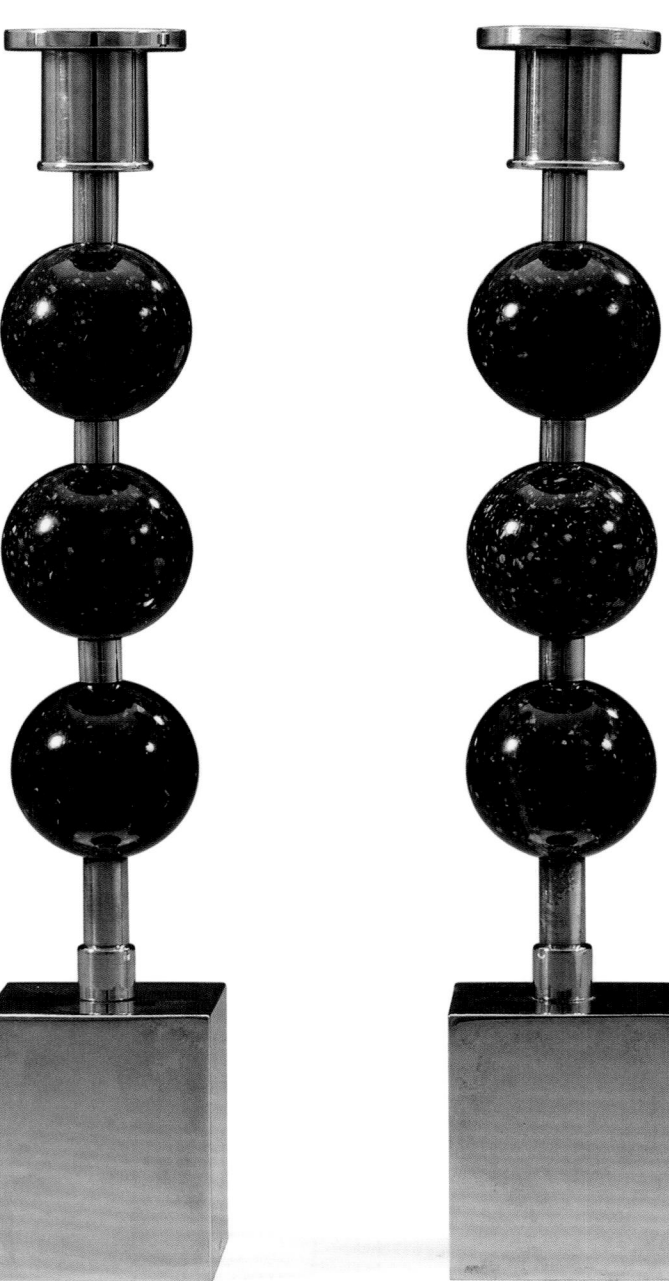

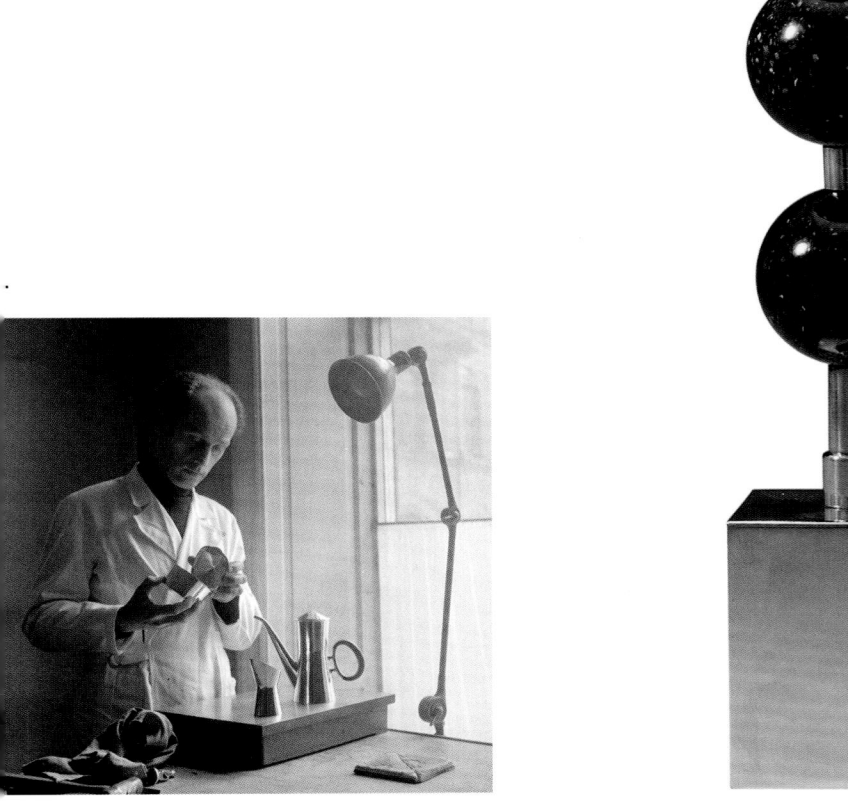

PIET HEIN + POUL KJÆRHOLM

Piet Hein was an intriguing figure, being a scientist, mathematician, inventor, writer and poet as well as an accomplished designer. He had studied at the Institute of Theoretical Physics at the University of Copenhagen (now the Niels Bohr Institute), and was actively involved during the war with the Danish resistance, for which he penned subversive aphoristic poems that he called 'grooks'. After the war he developed a novel circle-cum-square hybrid shape, which he christened the superellipse, and also devised numerous innovative games and puzzles (see also pp.422–23). One of his best-known designs, the Ursa Major (Great She-Bear) candelabra (ca. 1953), is based on the northern hemisphere's constellation of the same name; he designed it while on a trip to Argentina, to remind him of home. Likewise, Poul Kjærholm's elegant, kinetic PK101 chandelier (1956) reflects an interest in mathematical symmetry and cutting-edge science, for its spiralling form was surely inspired by James Watson and Francis Crick's discovery of the double-helix structure of DNA in 1953.

1. Ursa Major (Great She-Bear) candelabra by Piet Hein (self-produced) (Denmark), ca. 1953

2. Super Egg amulet/puzzle by Piet Hein for Skjøde Skjern (Denmark), 1960s – also known as the 'anti-stress' egg, its form was based on the superellipse formula

Opposite: PK101 chandelier by Poul Kjærholm for E. Kold Christensen (Denmark), 1956

1.

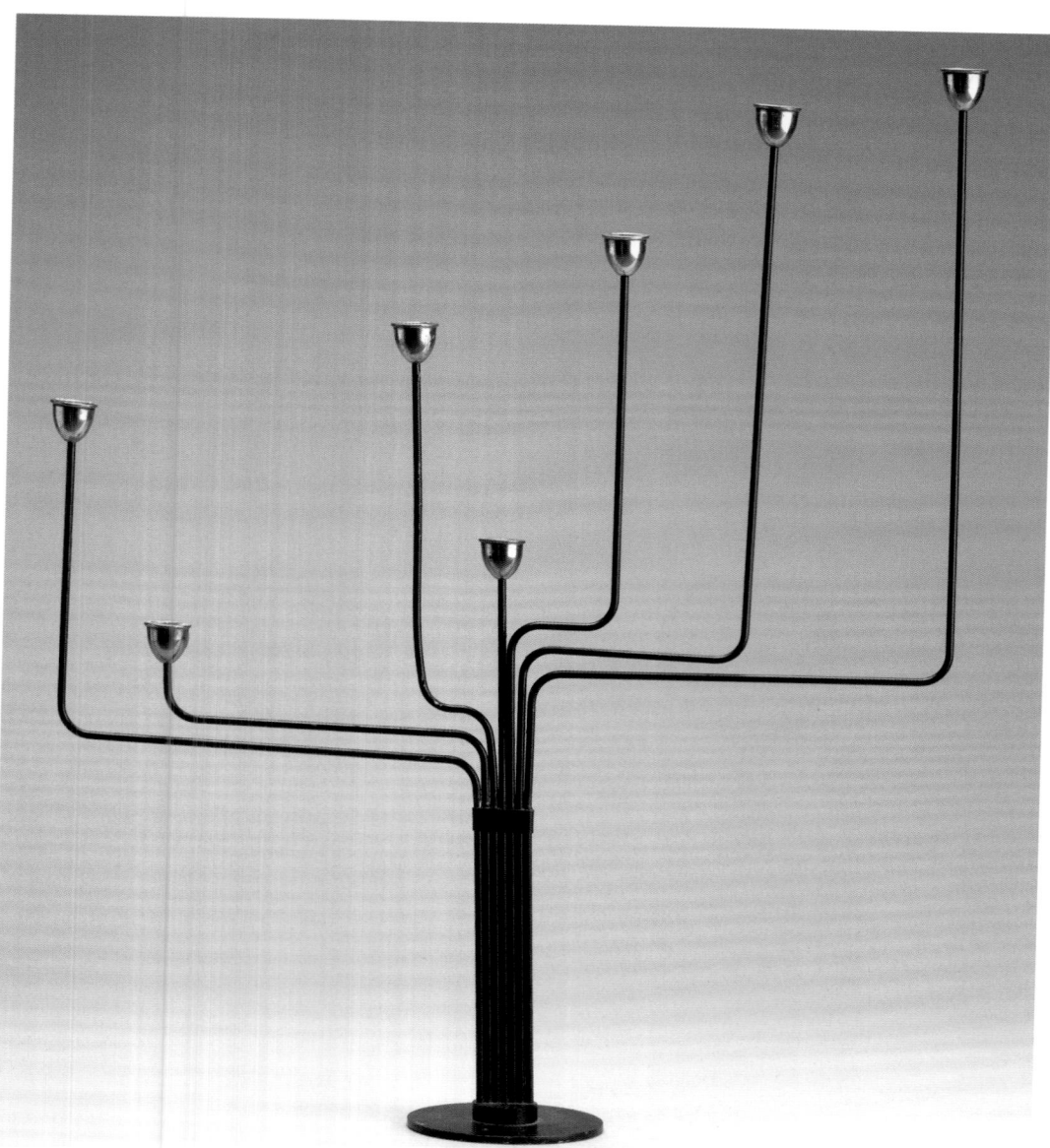

2.

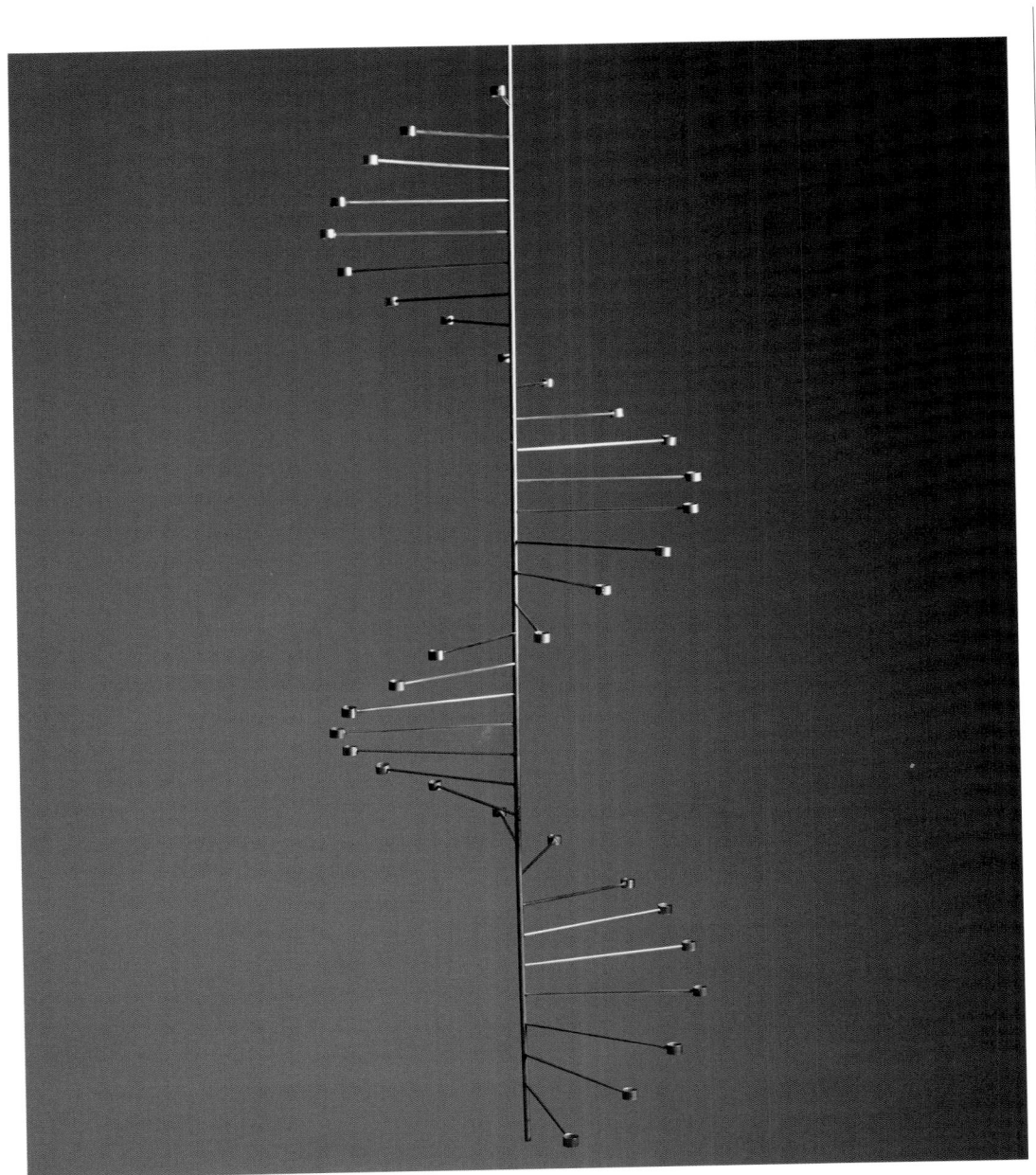

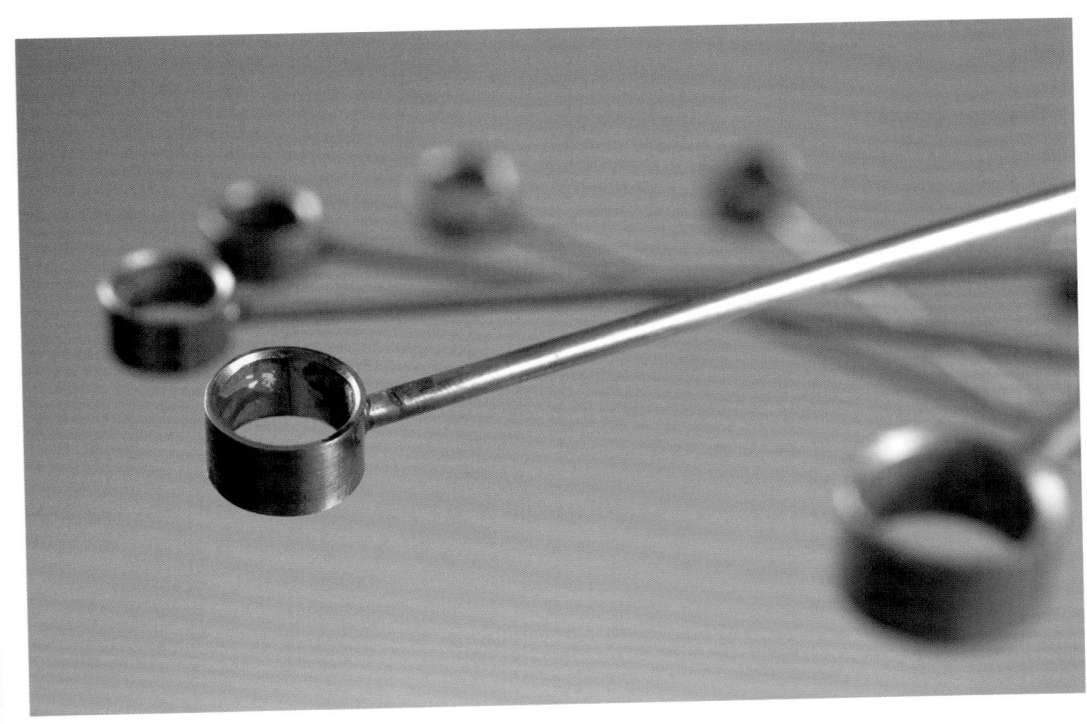

TAPIO WIRKKALA

According to the catalogue raisonné published in 2000 to accompany the landmark retrospective exhibition of his work, Tapio Wirkkala produced nearly 150 different metalware designs. The vast majority were executed in silver by the Suomen Kultaseppien Keskus (Finnish Goldsmiths' Centre; later Kultakeskus) in Hämeenlinna in southern Finland. The various pieces shown here are typical of silverware serially produced by Kultakeskus to Wirkkala's exacting designs

in the 1950s and 1960s. While being perfectly functional, they also possess a very distinctive sculptural bravado, which visually accentuates the inherent physical properties of silver – its form-giving malleability and gleaming reflective surfaces. Sometimes Wirkkala would also incorporate wooden handles or bases into his silverware. These elements were made of tightly grained chocolate-brown Brazilian rosewood, a richly hued exotic timber that perfectly complements the glowing warmth of shimmering precious metal.

Below: Silver vases by Tapio Wirkkala for Suomen Kultaseppien Keskus (Finland), 1954

1. Silver dish by Tapio Wirkkala for Kultakeskus (Finland), 1965

2. Silver and jacaranda vases by Tapio Wirkkala for Kultakeskus (Finland), 1960

3. Sugar bowl, coffee pot and milk jug by Tapio Wirkkala for Kultakeskus (Finland), 1961

1.

2.

3.

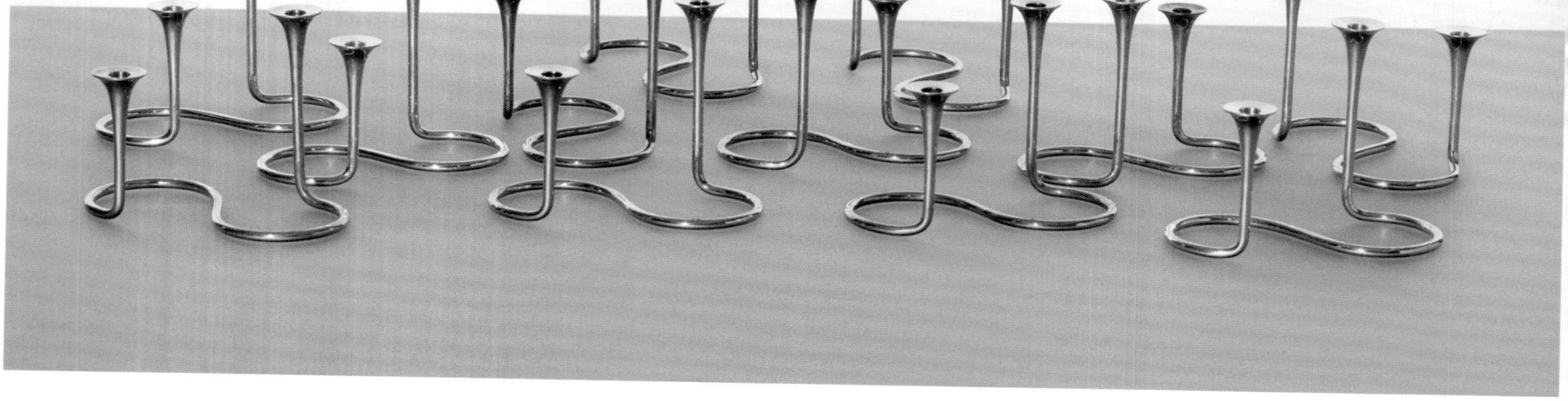

1.

2.

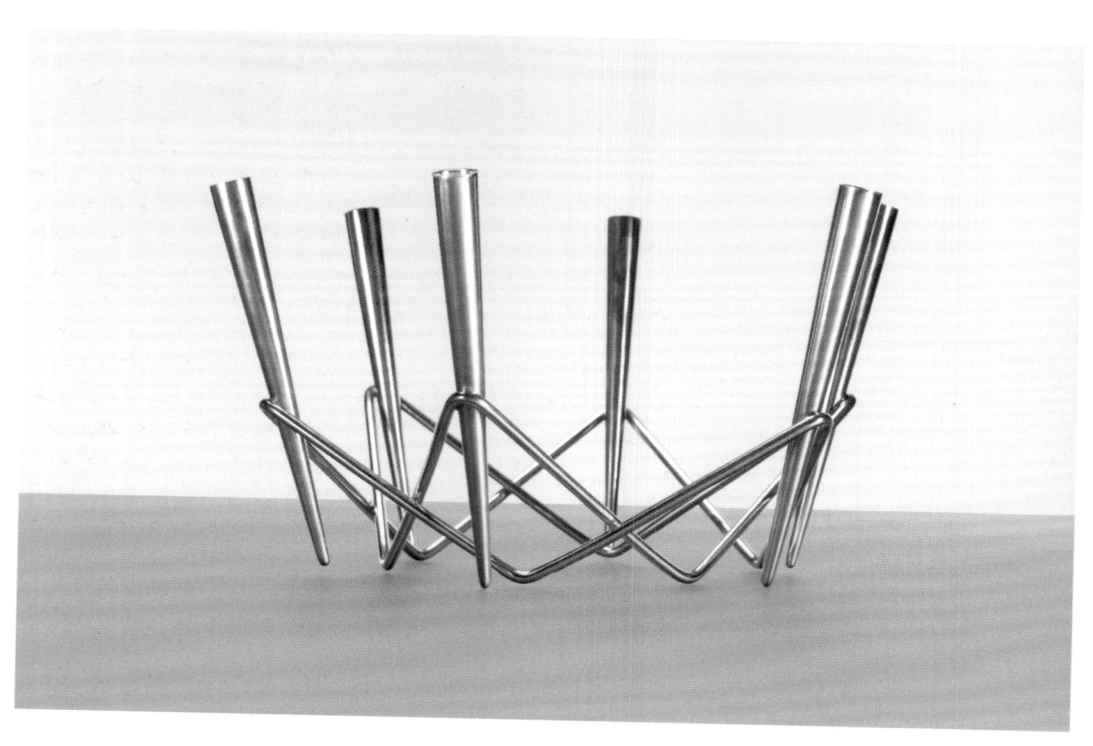

A. MICHELSEN

Having trained as a master silversmith in Copenhagen, Berlin and Paris, Anton Michelsen set up his own gold and silver manufactory in Copenhagen in 1841, and became Goldsmith and Maker of Orders to the Royal Danish Court in 1848. During the nineteenth century, the firm of A. Michelsen was especially known for its beautifully executed Baroque and Rococo Revival wares, which were then the height of fashion. Later, around the turn of the twentieth century, it also manufactured silverware designs by Thorvald Bindesbøll that were in the so-called Skønvirke style, the Danish equivalent of the British Arts and Crafts Movement. In the 1920s the company also produced silverware pieces by Johan Rohde, among others. The firm's creative zenith came in the 1950s, however, and it was during this decade that the firm produced arguably its most innovative silverware designs. These included Søren Sass's elegant Mid-century Modern coffee set (shown below), Eigil Jensen's snaking candlesticks and his three-branched candleholders that interlinked to form a star (opposite). These were designs that, while upholding the craft ideals of traditional Danish silverware, exemplified the 'New Look' of postwar Danish Modernism, which was boldly sculptural and playfully contemporary.

1. Twelve candlesticks by Eigil Jensen for A. Michelsen (Denmark), ca. 1950

2. Pair of interlocking candlesticks by Eigil Jensen for A. Michelsen (Denmark), ca. 1954

Below: Coffee and tea service by Søren Sass for A. Michelsen (Denmark), 1954

HENNING KOPPEL

The son of a journalist, Henning Koppel was sent to a progressive co-educational school run by his aunt Hanna Adler in Copenhagen. There, rather than concentrating on academic subjects, he perfected his drawing skills in the margins of textbooks, managing to become an accomplished draughtsman in the process. When he was 15 he left school determined to become an artist and got into KADK, studying under Einar Utzon-Franck. He subsequently moved to Paris, where he trained as a sculptor under Charles Malfray at the Académie Ranson. He eventually returned to Denmark, but the increasing persecution of Danish Jews during World War II prompted him to flee in 1943 to neutral Sweden with his wife and young daughter. While there, to make ends meet, he traded his art for food and other goods his family needed. This led to an even greater honing of his drafting skills, and he used it to good effect after the war as a designer at the Georg Jensen silversmithy in Copenhagen. His bold, organically formed silver pieces swept away all vestiges of the Art Nouveau and Art Deco styles that had been so prevalent in the firm's output up to this point, and heralded a new sculptural confidence that would come to define Scandinavian design in the 1950s.

1. Model no. 1026 covered fish dish by Henning Koppel for Georg Jensen (Denmark), 1954

2. Henning Koppel sketching in his studio, ca. 1950s

Opposite: Model no. 992 jug by Henning Koppel for Georg Jensen (Denmark), 1952

1.

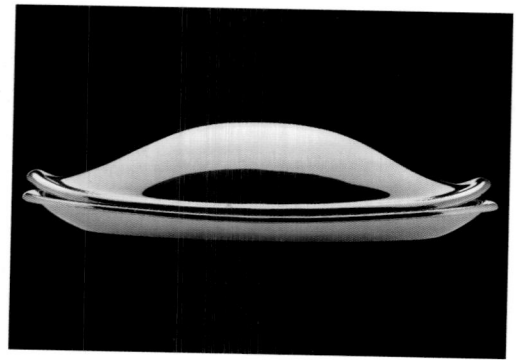

2.

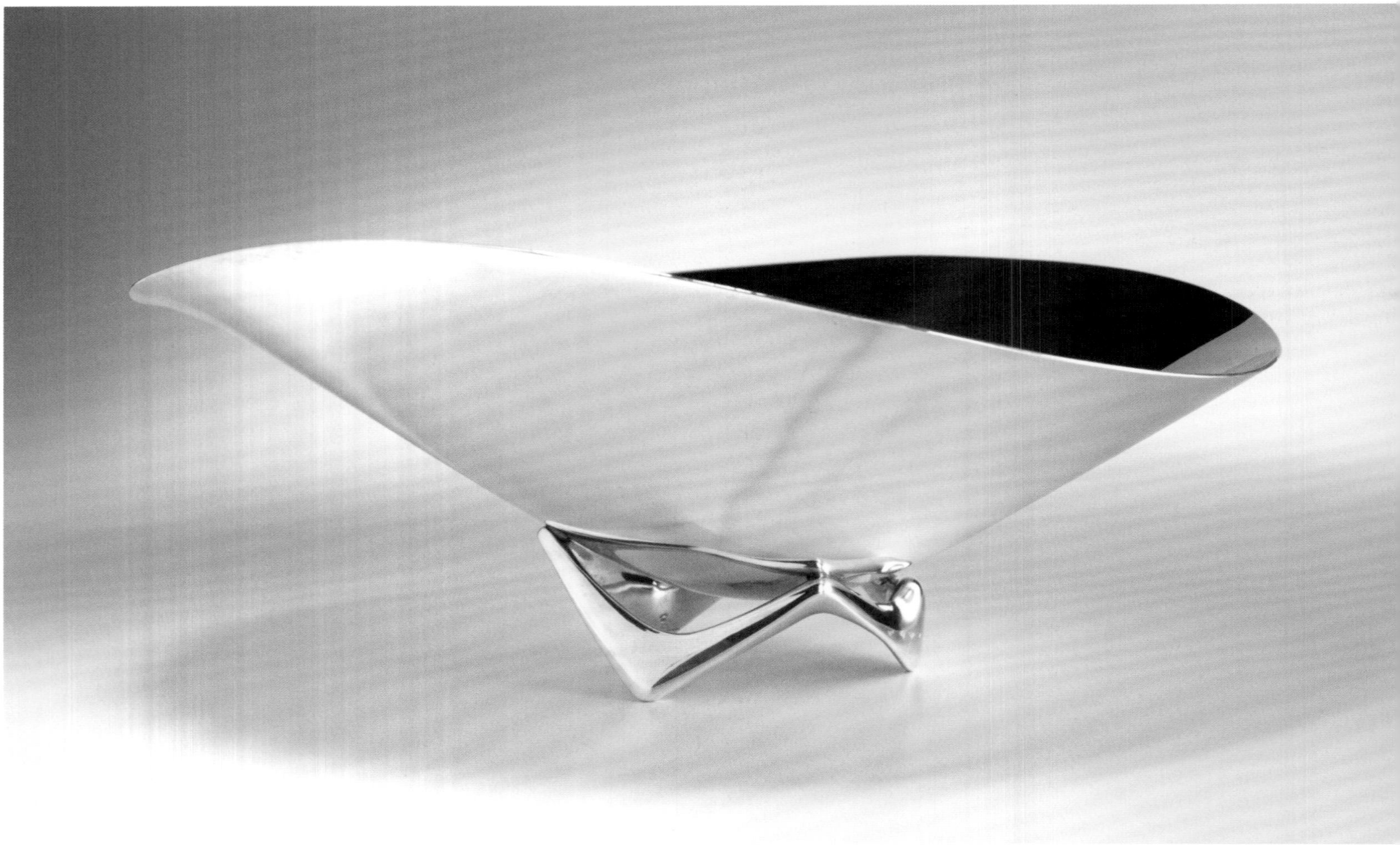

1.

2.

KOPPEL: A FORM-GIVING GENIUS

In the mid twentieth century, in his quest to create metalwares that were both useful and beautiful, Henning Koppel helped to define Danish Modernism. His training as a sculptor in Copenhagen and Paris had endowed him with exceptional modelling skill as well as a mastery of form-giving, which he applied to the design of contemporary silver and stainless-steel wares. His work was distinguished by the use of swelling organic forms that were also functionally thoughtful. He started working for Georg Jensen in 1946 and designed an impressive body of silverware for the Copenhagen-based silversmithy, including the exquisite gold medal-winning Model no. 1017 tea set (1952). The other two pieces shown here, with their strongly asymmetrical, organic forms, demonstrate Koppel's shape-shifting genius, which enabled him to transform a fruit bowl into a stunning sculptural *tour de force*.

1. Model no. 980a bowl by Henning Koppel for Georg Jensen (Denmark), 1948 – awarded the gold medal at the 9th Milan Triennial, 1951

2. Model no. 1017 silver and guaiacwood tea set for Georg Jensen (Denmark), 1952 – awarded the gold medal at the X Milan Triennial, 1954

Below: Model no. 1068 bowl by Henning Koppel for Georg Jensen (Denmark), 1958

PIERRE FORSSELL

As well as notable stainless-steel designs for Gense (see pp. 376–77), Pierre Forssell produced numerous interesting brassware pieces for the Skultuna foundry, where he worked as a designer from 1955 to 1986. These included various wall sconces, candlesticks and flask-and-cup sets, some of which were gold-plated. The designs shown here are typical of his work for Skultuna and reveal his complete mastery of geometric proportion and his ability to channel the spirit of Scandinavian design purity into sleekly fashionable homewares. Although designed in the 1950s and 1960s, they were in fact so forward-looking that they can be seen to presage the bold architectonic forms found in Postmodern designs from the 1980s. Skultuna still manufactures three of Forssell's designs – two sconces and a candlestick set – testifying to the time-defying appeal of his arresting designs.

Below: Gold-plated grog decanter with matching cups by Pierre Forssell for Skultuna (Sweden), 1960s

1. Pair of candlesticks by Pierre Forssell for Skultuna (Sweden), 1950s

2. Eight candleholders by Pierre Forssell for Skultuna (Sweden), 1950s

1.

2.

SCULPTURAL SERVING WARE + CUTLERY

During the postwar period and into the early 1960s, Scandinavian designers led the way in the design of stylish and progressive cutlery and serving sets. The examples shown here reveal how designers such as Henning Koppel, Tias Eckhoff and Pierre Forssell were able to transform the design of these objects into exercises of sculptural modelling. In fact, the design of cutlery and serving wares is notoriously difficult because such products must function almost as prosthetic extensions of the hands using them, and thus must be carefully contoured for comfort and perfectly balanced for functional stability. Given the human-centric nature of Scandinavian design in general, it is not so surprising that Nordic designers were the ones to set new contemporary standards for cutlery and serving utensils after World War II, and to become the acknowledged masters in this exacting design field.

1. Caravel salad servers by Henning Koppel for Georg Jensen (Denmark), 1957

2. Salad servers by Pierre Forssell for Gense (Sweden), 1950s

3. Maya salad servers by Tias Eckhoff for Norsk Stålpress (Norway), 1961 – later produced by Stelton

4. Fuga cutlery by Tias Eckhoff for Gense (Sweden), 1962

1.

2.

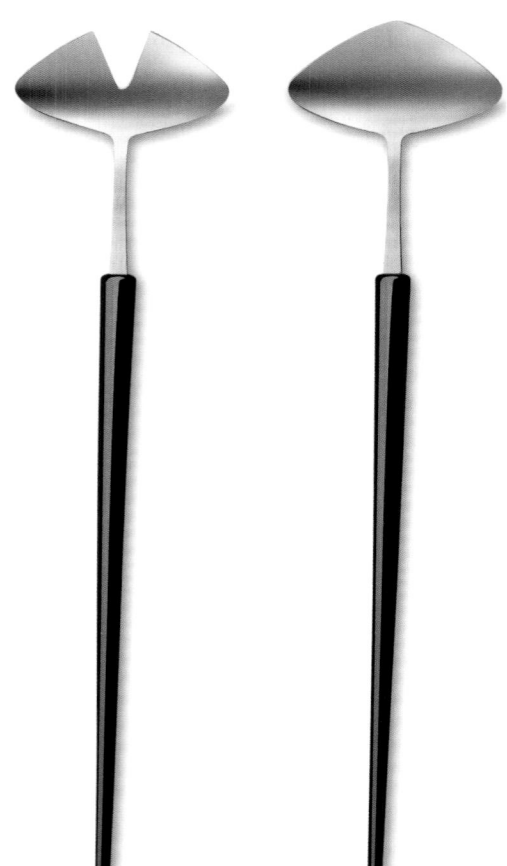

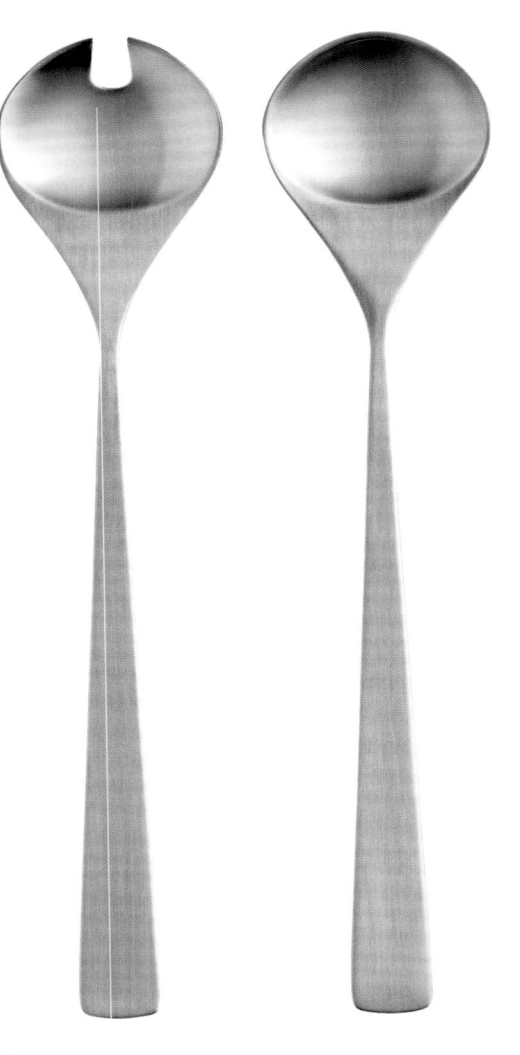

3.

4.

1.

2.

ARNE JACOBSEN

Arne Jacobsen's International Style buildings and product designs always had an innate classicism in their mathematically precise proportions. Indeed, that is what has given them such longevity of appeal. More often than not, Jacobsen's architectural projects were conceived as *Gesamtkunstwerks* (total works of art), meaning that beyond the actual buildings he also designed their interiors, furniture, lighting, fixtures and fittings. For example, his City Hall wall clock (1955; right) was originally designed for Rødovre City Hall, while his elegant AJ candleholder (1958) was designed for the SAS Royal Hotel in Copenhagen (see pp. 34–35), as was his sleek AJ cutlery (1957; opposite). In fact, Jacobsen often stipulated in his contracts with clients that his product designs must be used in a building, in perpetuity. It was, however, his Cylinda-Line stainless-steel hollowware range (1967–1970s; below right) for Stelton, famously sketched out on a napkin (see p. 371), that became his most enduring metalware design, thanks to a classical architectonic quality that has made it impervious to the whims of fashion.

3.

1. AJ candleholder by Arne Jacobsen for Georg Jensen (Denmark), 1958

2. AJ cutlery by Arne Jacobsen for A. Michelsen (Denmark), 1957 – later manufactured by Georg Jensen

3. City Hall wall clock by Arne Jacobsen for Louis Poulsen (Denmark), 1955 – later manufactured by Georg Christensen

4. Cylinda-Line tea and coffee service by Arne Jacobsen for Stelton (Denmark), 1967–1970s

4.

CAST IRON

The craft revival of the 1960s sparked a somewhat unexpected nostalgia for industrial heritage, which in turn prompted designers such as Timo Sarpaneva in Finland and Jens Quistgaard in Denmark to look to the 'old' industrial materials of the past, most notably cast iron. Unlike moulding plastic, for example, casting iron is low-tech and therefore it is much easier and less expensive to amass the necessary production tools. Quistgaard designed numerous candlesticks and trivets using this ancient material, which were mass-produced by Dansk and sold internationally. Of these, his

Model 1706 Star candleholder (ca. 1960) and Spider Model 1724 (ca. 1960) candleholders were perhaps the most spectacular (opposite), especially when lit up with slender, tapering candles, which were also sold by Dansk in vivid colours. Sarpaneva similarly used cast iron for his functional yet sculptural range of cookware, which included his famous cooking pot (1960) with a detachable wooden handle that could be used to lift the lid (below). Countering the buy-it-today-sling-it-tomorrow ethos of Pop culture, these designs had a reassuringly weighty permanence and a timeless beauty inspired by industrial craft.

Below: Cast-iron cooking pot with teak handle by Timo Sarpaneva for W. Rosenlew (Finland), 1960 – later reissued by Iittala

1. Star candleholder, Model no. 1706, by Jens Quistgaard for Dansk (USA), 1960s

2. Spider candleholders, Model no. 1724, by Jens Quistgaard for Dansk (USA), 1960s

1.

2.

ENAMELLED DESIGN-ART WARES

In the late nineteenth and early twentieth century, Norway was famous for its superbly enamelled jewellery and *objets d'art*. It is not surprising, therefore, that one of the country's most eminent silver- and goldsmith firms, David-Andersen, revived this art form in the postwar period with not only Modernist jewellery pieces but also designs, such as the stunning enamel and bronze dish shown below, decorated with abstract forms from nature. These mid-century designs were never intended to be functional, but rather to be used as wall-mounted decorative pieces. The same could also be said of the gloriously hued and patterned enamelled dishes by the Finnish designer Saara Hopea in the 1960s, featuring layer upon layer of semi-transparent colour skilfully combined into stunning abstract compositions. These enamelled art wares crucially helped to keep age-old skills alive and reflected the Scandinavian reverence for craftsmanship at the highest level.

Below: Bronze enamelled wall plate manufactured by David-Andersen (Norway), 1950s

Opposite: Enamelled dishes by Saara Hopea (self-produced) (Finland), 1960s

ENAMELLED HOMEWARES

In the 1950s homemakers were looking for colour to brighten up their living spaces: they had endured a pervasive drabness during the war, and subdued earth tones had been all the rage in the 1930s, especially in Scandinavia. Consumer plastics were still in their infancy, and although colourful plastic homewares were produced during this period, most manufacturers could not justify the huge tooling and equipment costs associated with manufacturing in this synthetic material. Vitreous enamelling, however – coating a metal object with powdered glass and heating it in a high-temperature furnace so that it forms a hard and shiny coating – was a less expensive production method, at least in terms of set-up. Among the most commercially successful Scandinavian designs to employ this technique was a range of bowls designed in 1953 by Herbert Krenchel, a Danish engineer and materials scientist. These simple enamelled-steel bowls, matt black on the outside with a layer of glossy colour inside, won a gold medal at the 10th Milan Triennial, in 1954 (opposite). The Finnish designer Antti Nurmesniemi also found international success in this field with his colourful stove-top coffee pots (1957) for Arabia (below), while the Danish designer Jens Quistgaard's Kobenstyle stacking cookware range (1955), with its distinctive X-shaped lid handles, proved a huge hit in the USA (opposite, below).

1. Krenit bowls by Herbert Krenchel for Torben Ørskov (Denmark), 1953 – later reissued by Normann Copenhagen

2. Kobenstyle casseroles by Jens Quistgaard for Dansk Designs (USA), 1955

Below: Coffee pots by Antti Nurmesniemi for Arabia (Finland), 1957

1.

2.

CONTEMPORARY METALWORK

Keeping the tradition of high-quality metal-work design well and truly alive in Scandinavia, companies such as Stelton, Iittala and Design House Stockholm continue to produce homewares in high-grade stainless steel and cast iron. Intelligently designed from a function-first perspective, these are essentialist products that have been stripped of all superfluous decoration. Indeed, such designs as Björn Dahlström's Tools cookware range (1998; opposite) possess an inherent rightness and express an undoubted purpose, attributes that have long been key to Scandinavian design. Pia Törnell's Night Light (2011; opposite) and Søren Refsgaard's One (2015; below) are ingenious reworkings of archetypal forms – another defining characteristic of Scandinavian design – in this case a chamber candlestick and a bowl-shaped candleholder, both of which have been used for centuries throughout the Nordic region. Although simple in form, these designs are materially highly refined and project a distinctly Scandinavian aesthetic.

Below: Naked candelabra and One candleholders by Søren Refsgaard for Stelton (Denmark), 2015

1. Night Light candleholder by Pia Törnell for Design House Stockholm (Sweden), 2011

2. Tools saucepan by Björn Dahlström for Hackman (Finland), 1998 – later manufactured by Iittala

3. Tools barbecue set by Harri Koskinen for Hackman (Finland), 2000

1.

2.

3.

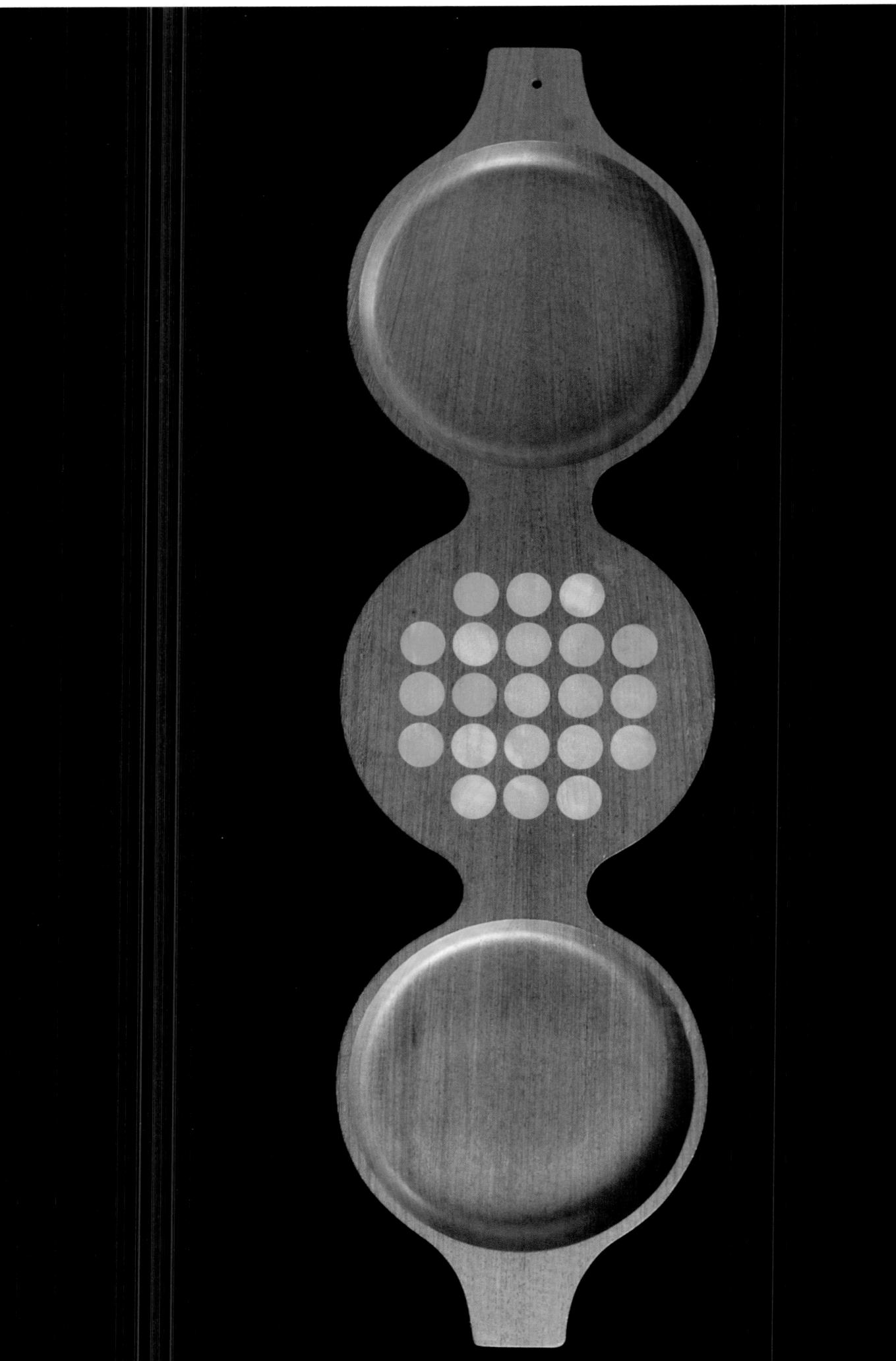

WOODENWARE

Carving in wood is not unique to the Scandinavian countries, but vast forests combined with late industrialization made wooden objects common well into the twentieth century. Bowls, spoons, knife handles, boxes and decorative items were often made in wood, and many survive in the attics and outbuildings of old farms. The hand-carved Dala horse, a national symbol of Sweden, is still made in small workshops in the Dalarna region, and the Mora knives used to carve them still have wooden handles. It is typical of the Scandinavian approach to Modernism that wood was still used in the postwar period, when other countries embraced plastics and metals. Wood was used for furniture, such as teak sideboards and oak chairs, but also for smaller household and decorative objects. In the 1950s and 1960s it was cheap to buy hardwoods such as teak because of deforestation in Asia caused by the wars in Korea and Vietnam. The Americans sold off the wood they had cut down to make room for landing strips and the infrastructure required for the war. Denmark was the world's largest importer of teak in the 1950s, but once restrictions on this hardwood came into force in the 1980s, its popularity waned. Currently, Danish manufacturers use only certified teak.

The Danish silversmith and designer Kay Bojesen was famous for wooden toys. With more than 2,000 designs to his name, Bojesen was one of Denmark's most prolific twentieth-century designers. He is known best for his Monkey, Guardsman and other wooden toys, but his wide-ranging production also includes jewellery, cutlery, teapots and silver goblets. He graduated as a silversmith in 1910 after completing his apprenticeship with Georg Jensen. He travelled to the Research Institute for Precious Metals and Metal Chemistry in Schwäbisch Gmünd in Germany and then on to Paris, where he worked for a period as a silversmith. The birth of his son Otto in 1919 sparked Bojesen's fascination with children's toys and wood. It also brought back memories of his own childhood, when his father, Ernst Bojesen – the publisher of the Danish satirical annual *Blæksprutten* (The Octopus) – made wooden figures and encouraged his children to be creative and playful.

In 1922 the Landsforeningen Dansk Arbejde (Danish Work Association), set up to promote Danish handmade products, organized a toy-design competition. Kay Bojesen entered a painted beech toy drum, a wooden ship, a rideable dragon and a seesaw, and won an award. As one of the first Danish designers to embrace Modernism, he was a founder of Den Permanente, an artists' co-operative with its own shop and exhibition space, which over the decades came to represent the best of Scandinavian design. As well as manufacturing his own range of wooden toys, Bojesen also made wooden bowls by Finn Juhl – including his famous sculptural teak bowl – and sold them in his shop on Bredgade, Copenhagen. Today the Rosendahl Design Group oversees the manufacture of Bojesen's wooden designs, while a company owned by one of his grandchildren produces his steel and silver pieces. As well as his wooden bowls, Juhl also designed a very attractive wall clock in lacquered wood for the chamber of the Trusteeship Council of the United Nations in New York, with a forward-looking, minimal, sculptural aesthetic.

Kristian Vedel, another Danish designer of wooden animals, was best known for his family of characterful Bird toys (1959). Having completed an apprenticeship to a cabinetmaker, Vedel studied under Kaare Klint in the Department of Furniture at the Kongelige Danske Kunstakademi (Royal Danish Academy of Fine Arts; KADK) in Copenhagen. He also trained in the Furniture Design Department of the city's Konstfack (University College of Arts, Crafts and Design) in 1946. He served as chairman of the Danish furniture designers' organization from 1947 to 1949, and was instrumental in setting up the Danish industrial designers' organization, serving as its first chairman (1966–68). As well as designing wooden toys and adult furniture, Vedel also designed award-winning children's furniture and a series of stackable melamine dishes and containers. A worthy recipient of the prestigious Lunning Prize in 1962, he was the subject of a major retrospective held at the Trapholt Museum near Kolding in 2007.

A family of ducks waddled into the rush-hour traffic in the Copenhagen neighbourhood of Frederiksberg in 1959, prompting a policeman to stop all cars and pedestrians so that the ducks could cross the street unharmed. This moment made newspaper headlines and inspired the designer Hans Bølling. His Duck and Ducklings were born after he won an award and received a carpentry machine, which gave him the opportunity to carve wooden figures. The Duck also makes obvious reference to Hans Christian Andersen's 'Ugly Duckling' – a story well known by every Dane. Bølling had originally considered a career as a commercial artist in the advertising world, but eventually followed his passion for architecture, studying at KADK. He subsequently created a plethora of designs, ranging from dolls and furniture to villas, apartment blocks and even town halls.

The Danish designer Paul Anker Hansen is also known for a characterful toy figure, in his case a wooden owl. This classic Danish

Traditional Dala or Dalecarlian horse – the making of this simple painted wooden toy became a popular cottage industry in the nineteenth century. Today it is a high-profile national symbol of Sweden

Rocking Horse by Kay Bojesen for Kay Bojesen (Denmark), 1936

Wall clock by Finn Juhl for the UN Trusteeship Council chamber, New York, 1950

Bird wooden toys by Kristian Vedel for Torben Ørskov (Denmark), 1959 – now produced by Architectmade

Opposite: Wenge serving platter by Theodor Skjøde Knudsen for Skjøde Skjern (Denmark), ca. 1963

toy with its tilting head was produced from 1960 to 1977, when the workshop went out of business; Hansen subsequently made the owls as gifts for friends and family. His children encouraged him to find a new producer, and the company Architectmade now makes his wooden toys in Denmark. Another Dane to turn his hand to toymaking was Jacob Jensen, the world-renowned industrial designer who developed the influential 'house' design language for Bang & Olufsen with his numerous sleek electronic products. What is less well-known is that in 1958 he created a set of toy Viking figures for IGC (International Gift Corporation), handcrafted in Denmark from teak and birch. They were sold as a set of three with interchangeable, modular parts, making them hugely popular with tourists visiting Denmark.

As well as wooden toys, in the 1960s and early 1970s a number of Danish companies began producing high-quality wooden board games for the adult market, the most notable such firm being Skjøde Skjern. Most of its board games were devised by the mathematician-designer Piet Hein and went on to huge international success, being sold under licence by Parker Brothers in the USA. Skjøde Skjern also produced Hein's ingenious SOMA (1936), a solid dissection puzzle made of teak – a classic 'executive' desktop design. The firm made some beautiful homewares, too, from magazine racks, candlesticks and ice buckets to carving boards and serving platters. Most were designed by the company's founder, Theodor Skjøde Knudsen, and were made in interesting combinations of woods, including teak and wenge. The exceptional quality of Skjøde Skjern's output, in terms of both design and manufacture, marked a high point in Danish woodcraft in the second half of the twentieth century.

Immediately after World War II and into the 1950s, 1960s and 1970s, many Danish homewares companies were producing salad bowls and servers, cutting boards, salt and pepper grinders, fondue sets and trays in wood – usually teak, owing to its resistance to moisture. These products were exported in large numbers and can still be found for sale secondhand in many countries. Manufacturers included Digsmed, with its Viking helmet logo, and Lundtofte, which produced elegant designs that combined exotic hardwoods with stainless steel. There were also various companies in the USA that employed Danish designers or designed in a Danish style, and sold the pieces under various trademarks, such as Kalmar, Dolphin, Goodwood and Dansk.

The story of how Dansk came into being is an interesting transatlantic one. In 1954 the American entrepreneur Ted Nierenberg and his wife, Martha, visited the Danish Museum of Art and Design in Copenhagen and saw there a set of teak-handled cutlery by Jens Quistgaard. Impressed with this Mid-century Modern design, the Nierenbergs contacted Quistgaard and offered to manufacture it. This led to Dansk's first product, the Fjord cutlery, which became a bestseller. By 1958 Nierenberg and Quistgaard had expanded Dansk's assortment to include teak magazine racks and stools, stoneware casseroles, salt and pepper grinders and ice buckets. By 1982 Quistgaard had created over 2,000 different designs for Dansk. As a company, Dansk was instrumental in bringing Danish design excellence into countless homes across America and elsewhere, and, thereby, in the internationalization of Nordic design in general.

Several manufacturers in Norway used sculptural wooden handles for their products. Skaugum was founded in 1946 when Herman Solhaug went to the English city of Sheffield to learn about the production of cutlery. After returning to his home village of Geilo, he founded the cutlery factory Geilo Jernvarefabrikk. In the early years the company made Märtha, a cutlery series that combined either rosewood or plastic handles with steel. When Geilo's sales manager resigned to begin working for a competitor, he took with him the name Märtha, which was not a protected trademark. The director of Geilo Jernvarefabrikk, Jens Christian Hauge, who had been Norway's minister of defence (1945–52), telephoned King Haakon VII and asked if Geilo Jernvarefabrikk might call its cutlery Skaugum, after the king's summer residence in the district of Asker, near Oslo. Hauge had known the king since 1944, having been a member of the resistance while the latter was living in exile in London. The king consented, provided the company was run in a proper manner. In 2011 the factory officially changed its name to Skaugum to reflect its most famous product. Skaugum now uses Kebony wooden handles for its cutlery, a Norwegian invention in which softwood is hardened using a chemical process.

Norwegian designers, like their Danish counterparts, also continued the long Nordic tradition of wooden toymaking. Støa Leketøyfabrikk (founded in 1928 by Olav Fidjestøl) has for decades made simple wooden toys in the same workshop in the small village of Marnardal, Norway, many of them designed by the toymaker Olav Øen. A more contemporary Norwegian wooden toy innovator is the design collective Permafrost, which created the oil rig-themed Offshore set (2012) for the exhibition 'New Nordic Architecture and Identity' at the Louisiana Museum of Modern Art, near Copenhagen, in 2012. The components are reduced to their most elemental form and are intended symbolically

Teak bowl by Finn Juhl for Kay Bojesen (Denmark), 1950

Duck and Duckling toys by Hans Bølling for Torben Ørskov (Denmark), 1959

Palisander and stainless-steel salt and pepper shakers manufactured by Lundtofte (Denmark), ca. 1950s

Skaugum cutlery by Herman Solhaug for Geilo Jernvarefabrikk (now Skaugum) (Norway), 1946

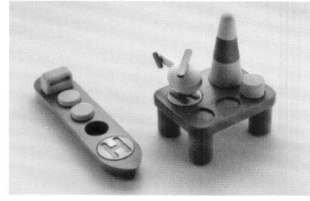

Oil Rig wooden toy by Permafrost (Norway), 2012

to question Norway's national identity and craft heritage.

Perhaps the most famous Scandinavian wooden toy manufacturer of all is BRIO, which can trace its history back to a workshop founded in 1884 by Ivar Bengtsson, a basket-maker, in the small village of Boalt in southern Sweden. It later moved to nearby Osby, and in 1908 the founder's three sons took over the enterprise, naming it BRIO, which is short for Bröderna (the brothers) Ivarsson Osby. BRIO is known best for the wooden toy trains it has made since 1958. In the 1960s and 1970s it also manufactured the Mobilia doll's house with Modern interiors furnished with miniature replicas of furniture designed by Arne Jacobsen. In 2004 the Ivarsson family sold the company, and its new owners moved production to the Far East. BRIO was sold to the well-known German toy group Ravensburger in 2015, yet to this day it remains true to its Nordic design roots.

Well-designed wooden homewares were also to be found in Sweden during the mid twentieth century. Having started out in the 1920s as a supplier of furniture to the likes of the NK department store, by the 1950s the firm of Karl Holmberg in Götene boasted some 20 employees. After the founder's sons took over the company, the focus switched entirely to the design and manufacture of contemporary homewares made from imported teak. Popular items included cutlery, wastepaper baskets, bowls and trays. Success followed, and by the mid 1960s the company had almost 100 staff and was the largest teak manufacturer in Scandinavia. When teak finally became unfashionable in the late 1960s, however, sales slowed, and the company ceased trading in 1973.

The Swedish sculptor and craftsman Johnny Mattsson also created a series of stylish Mid-century Modern designs in pine, teak and mahogany, often using wood from the sixteenth- and seventeenth-century houses that were being demolished in the 1950s and 1960s. His father was also a woodworker and was known locally as Ski-Mattsson, since he crafted wooden skis. In 1941 Johnny established Gävleslöjd (Gävle Crafts), which produced handmade lamps and trays. In 1945 he started to focus on sculptures, particularly those of animals. He also had great early success with a wooden beer beaker based on historical models. Unusually for someone who was so much a 'local' craftsman, Mattsson began to receive orders from across the country from the late 1940s onwards, and his work began to be reviewed in national newspapers. In 1951 a curator at the Gävleborg county museum visited Mattsson and described his work as similar to that of Henry Moore, Jean (Hans) Arp and Constantin Brâncusi. This led to exhibitions both at the museum in Gävle and at the NK department store in Stockholm, which marked his breakthrough. A large number of national exhibitions ensued, as well as exhibitions in Denmark, Norway, the USA, Venezuela and Japan, and at the Milan Triennial of 1954, where he won a medal. Besides his domestic woodenwares, Mattsson also made exquisite organically shaped wooden sculptures, many of them for churches.

To date, little has been written about the use of teak and other hardwoods in Finland. Denmark and Sweden had bigger markets and therefore much larger production, but a few Finnish companies did work in hardwood. One was Noormarkun Käsityöt (Noormarkku Handicraft), which was established in 1961 by the Artek founder Maire Gullichsen and the silversmith Bertel Gardberg in one of the buildings at the Noormarkku ironworks. The idea was to improve the state of handicrafts in the region, and the company engaged the designer Nanny Still with this aim. At first it made turned-wood objects, but later on rugs and furniture were also produced. Many pieces were sold through the Artek shop in Helsinki. The wooden objects are all marked with the Noormarkku/Norrmark N and with the brand name Finnmade. Likewise, the company Lindholm made trays, bowls, serving plates and other household items in its factory in Dragsfjärd, in the very south of Finland, from the 1960s into the 1970s. Its objects are marked 'Lindholm Bangkok Teak Made in Finland'.

The Finnish designer Tapio Wirkkala also made solid teak objects for Asko, where he worked as a freelance designer. But it is undoubtedly his exquisite leaf-shaped bowls and dishes sculpted from blocks of laminated birch plywood that are his most accomplished woodenware designs, and as such they are now highly prized by collectors. His countryman Yki Nummi sometimes incorporated teak elements into his lighting designs for Orno, Stockmann's lighting factory. He also created wooden household objects for Sanka, such as trays and bowls that combined acrylic with teak or rosewood. Likewise, the Danish designer Bertel Gardberg, who opened a shop in Helsinki in the late 1940s to sell his work, created pieces that combined wood with other materials. He especially favoured palisander and teak to use as handles and knobs for his stainless steel and silver designs. Today in Finland cutting-edge woodenware designs are far less common, though the traditional Kuska wooden cups are still extensively made, mainly as souvenirs.

Condiment set produced by Karl Holmberg in Götene (Sweden), 1960s

Teak bowl by Johnny Mattsson (self-produced) (Sweden), ca. 1960s

Rocking Rabbit by Björn Dahlström for Playsam (Sweden), 1987

Detail of laminated birch-leaf dish by Tapio Wirkkala for Soinne & Kni (Finland), 1950s

Laminated birch dish by Tapio Wirkkala for Soinne & Kni (Finland)

KAY BOJESEN

There is something magical about Copenhagen, which was home to the greatest
fairytale-teller of all, Hans Christian Andersen,
and still has the famous Tivoli Gardens pleasure park at its heart. It is not surprising, then,
that the Danish capital is also the birthplace of
the greatest Danish toymaker of all time: Kay
Bojesen. In the early 1920s, while in his mid
thirties, he began designing wooden toys with
articulated limbs, and never looked back. His
most famous toys, the monkey, elephant and
bear, date from the 1950s and were made from
a combination of different woods, either oak
and maple, or teak and limba. Bojesen's characterful monkey, which was included in an
exhibition at the Victoria and Albert Museum
in London in the 1950s, is today considered
a classic of Danish design and is probably
more popular now than ever, thanks to the
current widespread re-evaluation of postwar
Scandinavian design.

Right: Monkey toy by Kay Bojesen for Kay Bojesen
(Denmark), 1951

1. Kay Bojesen with his iconic wooden monkeys, 1950s

2. Bear toy by Kay Bojesen for Kay Bojesen
(Denmark), 1952

3. Elephant toy by Kay Bojesen for Kay Bojesen
(Denmark), 1953

4. Horse toy by Kay Bojesen for Kay Bojesen
(Denmark), 1930s

1.

2.

4.

3.

THE MASTER TOYMAKER

Although Kay Bojesen is best known for his teak animal toys (see pp. 410–11), he also created a number of painted designs that remain in production decades after they were launched, testifying to their enduring appeal. Working at first as a silversmith for Georg Jensen, he turned his attention to toymaking when his son was born, in memory of his father, who had made wooden toys for *his* children. In 1922 Bojesen started designing his own toys, and in 1932 he opened his legendary shop in Copenhagen's Bredgade, which was his window on the world for the next two-and-a-half decades. During this period, he produced numerous solid wooden toys, including those shown here, that have become design classics. With his very Scandinavian child-centric approach to design, his toys were never intended to look remotely lifelike, but rather to have a characterful simplicity that would inspire imaginative play.

Opposite: Painted wooden Puffin toy by Kay Bojesen for Kay Bojesen (Denmark), 1954

1. Painted wooden Zebra toy by Kay Bojesen for Kay Bojesen (Denmark), 1935

2. Painted wooden Guardsman toy by Kay Bojesen for Kay Bojesen (Denmark), 1942

3. Kay Bojesen standing outside his toyshop in Copenhagen, 1950s

1.

2.

3.

FINN JUHL + JOHNNY MATTSSON

In the 1950s the Danish designer Finn Juhl and the Swedish designer Johnny Mattsson both designed wooden bowls with organic forms that beautifully accentuated the graining of the woods from which they were made. For his bowl Juhl used warm-toned, dark honey-coloured teak; it was the wood of choice for most Danish designers in the 1950s, thanks to it being in cheap and plentiful supply because of the widespread forest-clearance programmes being undertaken by the US Army in Southeast Asia during the Korean and Vietnam wars. In contrast, Mattsson, who also worked as a sculptor, employed for his bowls native Karelian birch, which has a distinctive and attractive burl grain. Through their designs, both men essentially revitalized the long-held Nordic craft tradition of carving wooden bowls and cups, and elevated it to art-object status.

Below: Teak bowl by Finn Juhl for Kay Bojesen (Denmark), 1950

Opposite: Karelian birch bowls by Johnny Mattsson (self-produced) (Sweden), 1950s

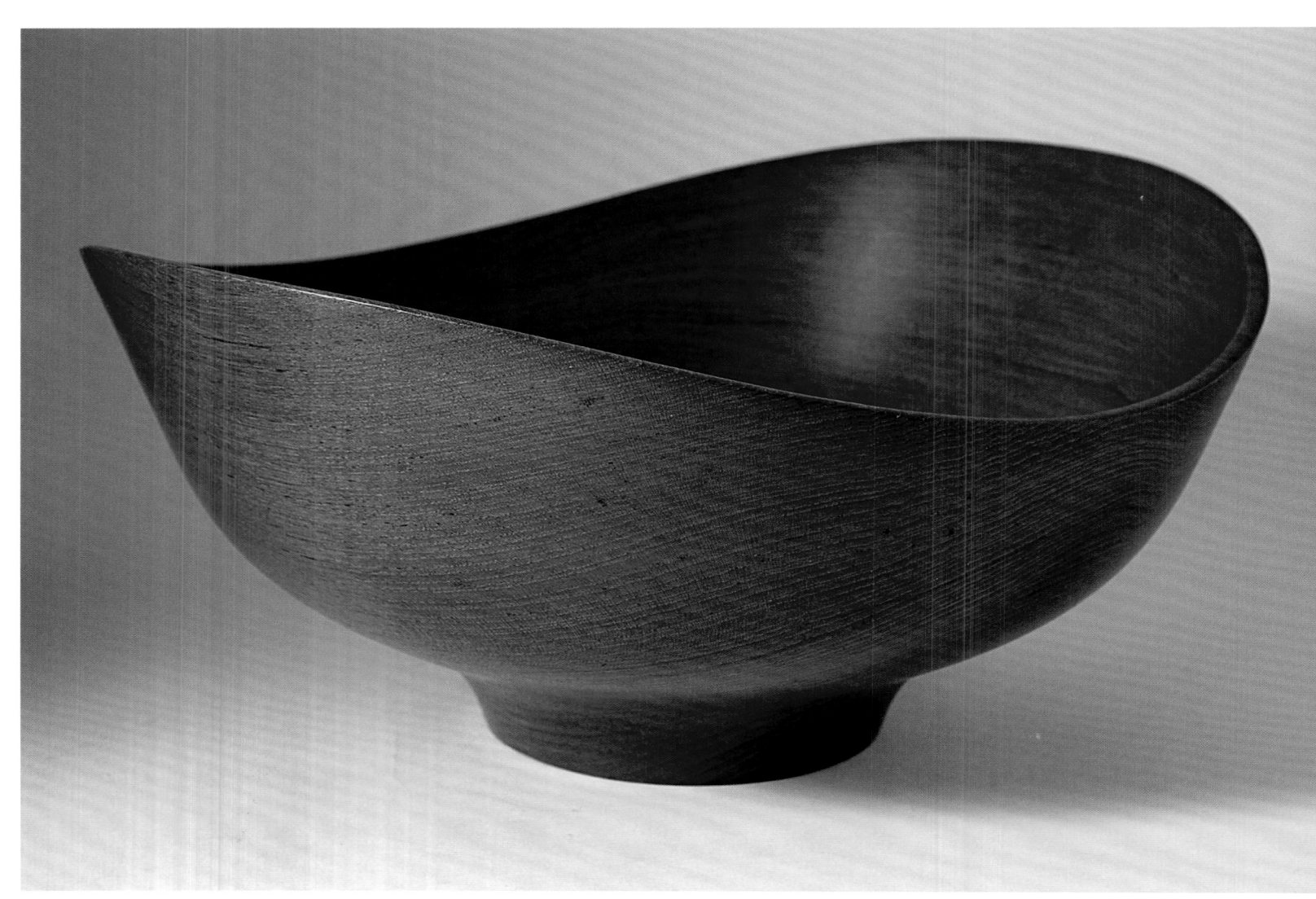

1.

2.

TAPIO WIRKKALA

Tapio Wirkkala conducted his first experiments in knot-free birch plywood in 1948, having been introduced to this new material by the Soinne family, who owned a factory that used it to make aircraft propellers. Wirkkala was especially interested in how blocks of this striated plywood could be carved and ground into sculpted shapes that resembled forms found in nature. These formal experiments eventually led him to design a series of leaf-shaped platters, starting in 1951, which included the three basic leaf shapes shown here. It is testament to Wirkkala's form-giving genius that he was able to use this man-made composite material to evoke so eloquently the abstract essence of nature. Functioning more as tabletop sculptures than as practical designs, Wirkkala's platters are some of the most sought-after objects among collectors of Scandinavian design, and no wonder, for they epitomize the sculptural refinement of postwar Finnish design. Employing the techniques he had used to make these simple yet beautiful pieces, Wirkkala went on to create a number of large-scale free-form plywood sculptures in the 1950s and 1960s.

1. Laminated plywood bowl by Tapio Wirkkala (self-produced) (Finland), 1950s

2. Leaf-shaped laminated plywood dish by Tapio Wirkkala (self-produced) (Finland), 1951

Below: Group of laminated plywood bowls by Tapio Wirkkala (self-produced) (Finland), ca. 1951

JENS QUISTGAARD

The son of a sculptor, Jens Quistgaard learned how to chisel, model, cast and cut stone from an early age, eventually becoming an adept model-maker. He began designing in earnest as a young adult, and eventually, in the late 1940s, some of his designs were put into production by the knife-manufacturing company Raadvad: a cutlery pattern, a range of kitchen tools and a shark-shaped can-opener. It was, however, another cutlery design, Fjord, that precipitated a turning point in his life. Shown in 1954, it caught the eye of the American businessman Ted Nierenberg, who was on the lookout for new designs to market in the USA. He immediately sought out its creator and subsequently set up a new company, Dansk, installing Quistgaard as its chief designer. Over the decades Quistgaard created hundreds of designs for Dansk, of which his teak pieces are the best known. With its staved construction inspired by Viking ships, and its handle reminiscent of those found on traditional Japanese buckets, Quistgaard's ice bucket of 1960 embodied the core attributes of Danish Modernism: beautiful craftsmanship twinned with an ideal form.

1. Staved teak ice bucket by Jens Quistgaard for Dansk (USA), ca. 1960

2. Staved teak tray by Jens Quistgaard for Dansk (USA), ca. 1960

Opposite: Staved teak ice bucket by Jens Quistgaard for Dansk (USA), 1960

1.

2.

MID-CENTURY WOODENWARE

In the mid twentieth century a large number of Nordic manufacturers were making beautifully crafted woodenwares from teak and various other tropical hardwoods that had been felled by the American military in Korea and Vietnam as part of their forest-clearing activities. Indeed, Scandinavian-produced 'Teak Look' homewares were not only hugely popular in the Nordic countries, but also exported successfully in large numbers to other European countries and to North America. In fact, many Scandinavian designers who are best known for their furniture, metalware or glassware design also created wooden homewares, such as Nanna Ditzel, Nanny Still and Bertel Gardberg. The huge variety of wooden homewares produced in the Nordic countries in the 1950s and early 1960s is astonishing, ranging from magazine holders and wastepaper baskets to salad servers and ice buckets. Once plastics had gained a foothold in the homewares market, in the mid to late 1960s, however, the popularity of beautifully crafted wooden products waned considerably, because they simply could not compete on price.

Below: Magazine holder with moveable handle by Jens Quistgaard for Dansk (Denmark/USA), ca. 1953

1. Palisander salad servers by Nanny Still (self-produced) (Finland), 1953

2. Palisander-veneered plywood wastepaper bin by Einar Barnes for P. S. Heggen (Norway), 1960s

3. Teak ice bucket by Bertel Gardberg for Finnmade/ Norrmark (Finland), ca. 1950

4. Oregon pine bowl by Nanna Ditzel for Kolds Savværk (Denmark), 1960s

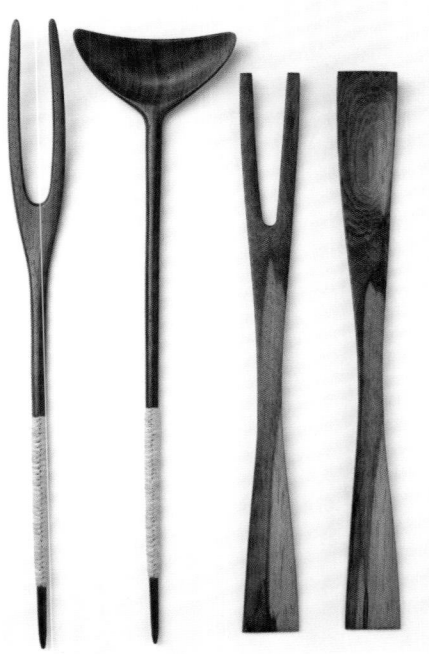

1.

2.
3.

4.

SKJØDE SKJERN

In the 1960s and early 1970s a number of Scandinavian companies found international success with high-end wooden homewares. Some also manufactured characterful wooden toys, as well as board games and puzzles. One of the leaders in this last field was Skjøde Skjern, founded by Theodor Skjøde Knudsen, who designed most of its products. It was, however, the brilliant Danish scientist, mathematician, inventor, designer and poet Piet Hein who was responsible for the creation of the firm's comprehensive range of wooden games. In the early 1940s, at the Institute of Theoretical Physics (now the Niels Bohr Institute) in Copenhagen, Hein had conceptualized a board game while pondering the then-unsolved four-colour problem; he called his game Polygon and wrote about it in 1942 in the Danish newspaper *Politiken*. Skjøde Skjern subsequently put the game, which used a rhomboid board, into production. As well as designing various modern reworkings of traditional games such as roulette, Chinese checkers and solitaire, Hein devised ingenious new games for the company, including Tarnspil (Tower), Pyramystery, Qrazy Qube and the ever-popular SOMA cube, all of which were beautifully crafted from a range of different woods. Sold by Parker Brothers in the USA, Hein's designs reflected the short-lived craze in the late 1960s and 1970s for 'executive' games and puzzles, and helped to perpetuate the renowned woodworking skills of Danish craftsmen.

Below: Old Fox and Tower board games by Piet Hein for Skjøde Skjern (Denmark), 1960s and 1966

1. Roulette board game by Theodor Skjøde Knudsen for Skjøde Skjern (Denmark), 1960s

2. Chinese Checkers board game by Piet Hein for Skjøde Skjern (Denmark), 1960s

1.

2.

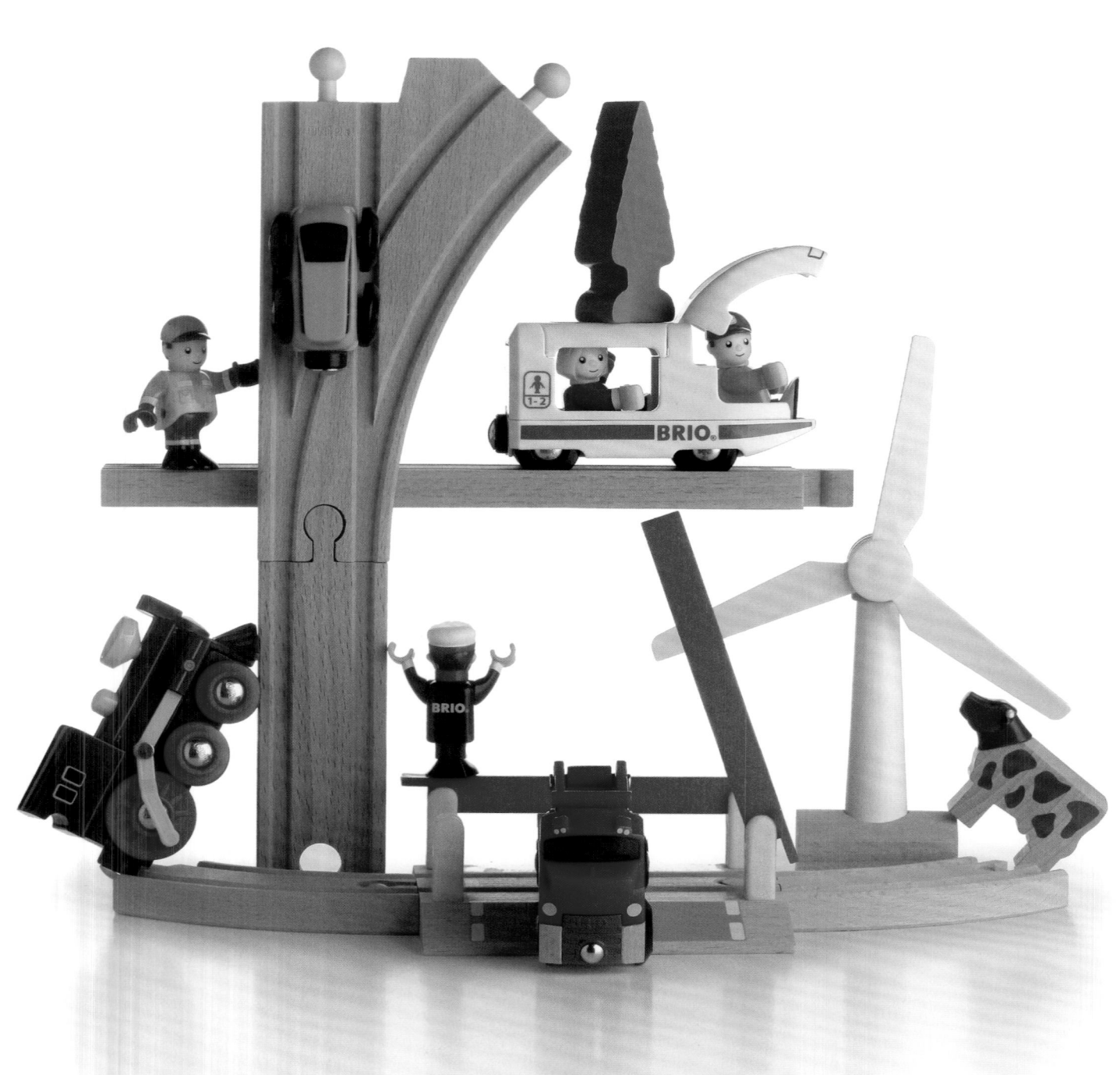

BRIO

In 1909 the Swedish social theorist and feminist Ellen Key published her hugely influential international bestseller *The Century of the Child*. This seminal publication focused on the importance of free education as a key driver of personal development, and it had an enormous bearing on the development of educational theory during the twentieth century. The rallying cry of this high-profile advocate

of child-centred learning was especially taken to heart in the Nordic countries, resulting in Scandinavia becoming a pioneering centre of design for children. This is seen in the design not only of children's furniture, but also of toys, in which the Swedish company BRIO is an acknowledged leader. BRIO is today one of the best-loved Nordic brands, thanks to its exacting manufacture of design-led wooden toys that invite learning through play in the best Scandinavian tradition.

Opposite: Various wooden pieces from a BRIO train set – first Brio train set introduced in 1958

1. Stacking Clown toy by BRIO, 1958

2. Mini Ant toy with bobbing head by BRIO, ca. 1960

3. Train set with a figure-of-eight track – BRIO's first wooden train set was introduced in 1958. This classic example is an evolution of the original BRIO train set

1.

2.

3.

1.

2.

3.

PLAYSAM

Carl Zedig founded Playsam in Kalmar, Sweden, in 1984 with the aim of producing wooden toys that were not only of exceptional quality but also imbued with an 'unforgettable playfulness'. To this end, Playsam acquired the manufacturing rights to a range of toys previously designed by Ulf Hanses for disabled children in the early 1980s. Hanses's Streamliner Classic Car (1984), created specifically for Playsam, fitted perfectly with Zedig's desire for designs that were not only archetypal in form but also possessed a sense of visual 'poetry'. A long-standing favourite among children and adults alike, this bold and simple wooden toy car has since been selected as a Swedish Design Classic by the Nationalmuseum in Stockholm. Zedig notes of Hanses's designs for Playsam's Streamliner range: 'Most important is the simplicity. When you look at a Streamliner, your imagination adds details.' As Scandinavia's leading manufacturer of executive toys, Playsam's playful designs encapsulate the inherent charm and simplicity of Nordic design, while giving a nod to the region's craft heritage, too.

1. Jetliner toy plane by Ulf Hanses for Playsam (Sweden), ca. 1985

2. Sailboat toy boat by Ulf Hanses for Playsam (Sweden), 1986

3. Streamliner Classic toy car by Ulf Hanses for Playsam (Sweden), 1984

Below: Streamliner F1 toy car by Ulf Hanses for Playsam (Sweden), 1984

CONTEMPORARY WOODENWARE

The long-held craft traditions of Scandinavian woodworking are still being upheld by a few Nordic companies, which are making wooden household objects that are intended to enhance daily life. The Finnish company Iittala, for instance, although best known for its glassware, also manufactures woodenwares that are both beautiful and functional. Its Tools salad servers (1998) designed by Carina Seth-Andersson not only have a stunning sculptural form but also are so beautifully balanced that they are a joy to use. Iittala's more recent woodenware designs – such as the Kerros double-decker tray (2014) and the Plektra stool/side table (2015) – similarly have a thoughtful practicality. The Swedish company Iris Hantverk has also attracted widespread acclaim for its beautifully designed woodenwares, including various wooden-handled brushes for household cleaning and personal care. These are made by hand by visually impaired craftsmen 'according to an old Swedish tradition' – thereby helping to preserve craft traditions, while at the same time giving meaningful work to those who are less able-bodied.

Below: Lovisa body brush and Lovisa nail brush by Lovisa Wattman for Iris Hantverk (Sweden), 2002

1. Plektra stool/side table by Ineke Hans for Iittala (Finland), 2015

2. Vakka box container by Elina and Klaus Aalto for Iittala (Finland), 2013

3. Tools birch salad servers by Carina Seth-Andersson for Hackman (Finland), 1998 – later manufactured by Iittala

4. Kerros two-storey tray by Matti Klenell for Iittala (Finland), 2014

1.

2.

3.

4.

PLASTICS

The history of plastics is complex, since it includes a plethora of synthetic polymers with different chemical compositions and physical properties, and its numerous inventions span a multitude of nations. One of the earliest man-made polymers was Bakelite, which was invented by the Belgian-American chemist Leo Baekeland in New York in 1907. It was used extensively for, among other things, radios, telephones and jewellery – indeed, it was marketed as 'the material of a thousand uses'. One of the earliest Bakelite products designed by a Scandinavian-born designer was the Ribbonaire table fan (1931), which was manufactured by the Singer Sewing Machine Company in America. Its creator was Fredrik Ljungström, one of Sweden's foremost design-engineers.

The Swedish electronics company L. M. Ericsson used Bakelite for its DBH 1001 telephone of 1931, which set the standard for the design of modern telephones. This compact model with its integrated dial was actually a Swedish-Norwegian collaboration, being designed and developed in Oslo by Ericsson's sister company Elektrisk Bureau. The Norwegian engineer Johan Christian Bjerknes worked out its internal layout, while the Norwegian artist Jean Heiberg devised its sculptural housing. Commentators praised it for its pure, functional form, and it became a ubiquitous feature of homes provided by the Swedish welfare state. Ericsson also succeeded in licensing the design to several foreign networks, notably the British General Post Office system in 1936. It was the inspiration for the US giant Bell Group's new Model 300, launched in 1937. Bolstered by this early success, Alpha, which had supervised its development for Ericsson, went on to become a leading plastics manufacturer in Sweden. After the war, the firm continued its production of melamine light switches and the like under its Pello trademark, at the same time as manufacturing vinyl records for Metronome.

Other early Swedish plastics manufacturers included Skånska Ättiksfabriken (later Perstorp), Fundator, Wäsby Verkstäder (later Mplast) and Konstharts. By the late 1930s, there were about 25 manufacturers of plastic products in Sweden, yet total output was still less than 1,000 tons. After the war, however, production increased, and Bakelite was gradually replaced by melamine and various thermoplastics, including acrylic, nylon and polypropylene. By 1948, Sweden boasted 50 manufacturers of plastic products, but what to call these new synthetic polymers officially in Swedish was still being debated.

It was only after the establishment of the Svenska Plasttillverkare (Swedish Plastic Manufacturers) trade association in 1948 that the word *plast* (plastic) was adopted. The association also started the magazine *Plastvärlden* (Plastic World), which helped to publicize the efforts of the fledgling Swedish plastics industry. During the 1950s the spread of plastic household products coincided with Sweden's building boom and growing welfare state. In fact, plastics were a godsend for manufacturers because they could be used to produce modern homewares that everyone could afford. Indeed, there seemed to be no limit to the products that could be made from them: combs, toothbrushes, buckets, pens, dinnerware, kitchen utensils, water jugs, butter dishes, bread boxes, egg cups, motorcycle helmets, toys, watering cans, trays, picnic sets, and so on.

Another acknowledged plastic design classic by Ericsson was the one-piece Ericofon, the first telephone to incorporate dial and handset into a single unit. Because of its influence on future telephone design, the Ericofon is considered to be one of the most significant industrial designs of the twentieth century, and as a consequence is in the permanent collections of design museums around the world. In Sweden, it is known as the Cobra telephone, thanks to its upwards-sweeping hooded form. Crucially, the one-piece design anticipated the evolution of cordless and mobile telephones by several decades. Launched in 1954, it was produced in 18 colours that appealed to homemakers wanting to create cheerful living spaces. An evolution of this model, the Model 700 (1976), was designed by Carl-Arne Breger and is easily distinguished from the earlier Ericofon thanks to its more angular design.

There were a number of significant plastic manufacturers in Sweden from the 1950s onwards, but one of the first, Skånska Ättiksfabriken (Scania Vinegar Factory), is particularly interesting. This enterprise grew out of carp-breeding activities undertaken in medieval times by monks at the Herrevad monastery near Perstorp, which led to a carp-breeding venture in the 1860s, which precipitated the founding of a vinegar factory by Wilhelm Wendt. With the help of the Indian chemist Dr Innanendra Das Gupta, the factory developed its own version of Bakelite, which was branded Isolit and launched in the 1920s. Among the early products made from this new material were lavatory seats, electrical components, laminated boards and bathroom and office products. It could not be used for the production of kitchenwares or tablewares, however, because of its unpleasant plastic taste. The company also established its own furniture factory, which made cabinets

Ribbonaire table fan by Fredrik Ljungström for Singer Sewing Machine Company (USA), 1931

Clay model of the DBH 1001 telephone by Jean Heiberg for L. M. Ericsson (Sweden), 1931

DBH 1001 telephone by Jean Heiberg and Johan Christian Bjerknes for L. M. Ericsson (Sweden), 1931

Taffel picnic set by Sigvard Bernadotte for Husqvarna Borstfabrik (Sweden), 1959

VirrVarr laminate board by Sigvard Bernadotte for Perstorp (Sweden) and Formica (USA), 1960

Opposite: EM77 vacuum jugs (1 litre) designed by Erik Magnussen for Stelton (Denmark), 1977

for radios and later on television sets, and ran a glassworks, while all the time the carp-breeding operation continued.

Wendt died in 1924, but his son Otto took over the running of the business until 1955. By that time the company had grown exponentially. One of its most successful products was Perstorpsplatta (Perstorp Board), a laminated board coated in Isolit that had first been developed in the 1920s for the electrical industry, which needed non-conductive surfaces. Isolit could be made only in dark brown or black, so those were the colours offered. An early customer was the Swedish national railway, which used Perstorp boards as railway-carriage tables. After World War II this product, which was effectively the Swedish equivalent of Formica, was developed further, and new colours and patterns introduced. The most famous is the VirrVarr pattern by Sigvard Bernadotte (1960), which was also produced in the USA by Formica. In the 1950s and 1960s Perstorp board became a standard component for new homes, being cheap, hardwearing and easily cleaned. It was also exported widely, not least for use in the interiors of cruise liners. In 1966 the company changed its name to Perstorp in tribute to its most successful product. Besides Bernadotte, Perstorp also worked with Hugo Lindström, Anna-Lena Bergström and Arne Darnell, all skilled industrial designers. In 1970 the company acquired two of its competitors, Hammarplast and Skaraplast.

Gustavsberg is best known for its ceramics and for the work of its most famous artistic director, Stig Lindberg. But by 1945, the company had realized that it needed to add plastic pieces to its product line in order to remain competitive. It identified a number of potential sectors: sanitaryware, office equipment and kitchenware. Lindberg was the first Gustavsberg designer to explore the potential of plastics, creating designs for, among other things, spice jars, a citrus press, trays and mugs. Another Gustavsberg designer who worked successfully in plastic was Carl-Arne Breger, who designed a large number of objects including his famous watering can, which eloquently translated the sculptural organic forms of the factory's ceramics into a synthetic polymer. Breger later became head of the Stockholm office of the industrial-design consultancy Bernadotte & Bjørn, headquartered in Copenhagen. After Breger's departure from Gustavsberg, Peter Pien, Karin Björquist and later Sven-Eric Juhlin carried on producing innovative plastic designs for the company.

Husqvarna Borstfabrik (Husqvarna Brush Factory) grew out of the Husqvarna Steel and Machine Factory in the late nineteenth century, initially to provide brushes to

clean the metal moulds at the local weapons factory. In the 1930s toothbrushes with bone handles were added to its product line, and after World War II nylon replaced the traditional brush heads. Another new product was a plastic washing-up brush, since research had revealed that wooden brushes held large quantities of bacteria. Acton Bjørn and Sigvard Bernadotte were commissioned by Husqvarna to design brushes for hair, teeth and washing dishes. After the successful launch of these products, the company diversified into the production of mugs, carafes and food containers. After leaving Gustavsberg, Carl-Arne Breger also produced designs for Husqvarna Borstfabrik.

Another successful product line was a plastic crate for beer bottles; unlike Denmark and Norway, both Sweden and Finland had standardized beer-bottle sizes, so the brewers were able to agree on a standardized crate in 1967. The size also happened to be perfect for storing vinyl LP records, so the beer crates became a popular feature in many teenage rooms when albums started to outsell 7-inch singles in the late 1960s. During that decade, Husqvarna Borstfabrik also began collaborating with Italian designers, and with the Italian plastics company Kartell. Attempts were made to interest Swedes in plastic furniture designed by Joe Colombo and Anna Castelli Ferrieri, but these models proved difficult to sell into Scandinavia markets. After the oil crisis of the early 1970s, after which the cost of raw plastics rocketed, Husqvarna found market conditions extremely difficult, and by the middle of the decade the company had been taken over by Hammarplast.

The major Swedish plastics manufacturer Skaraplast had begun life in the early twentieth century as Svenssons Träförädling (Svenssons Wood Processing), primarily a manufacturer of wooden lavatory seats. Competition from Perstorp's Isolit models, however, led the firm to manufacture its own plastic lavatory seats, and after World War II the company changed its name to Industri AB Plastics, then in the 1950s to Skaraplast. It made a wide variety of plastic products, including toys, but its focus was household products. During the 1950s and 1960s Skaraplast commissioned designs from Bernadotte & Bjørn, as well as Jan Ostwald and Hans-Erik Persson, but it found it difficult to turn a profit, presumably because of the high tooling and equipment costs. As a result, in 1967 it was taken over by Hammarplast, adding to that firm's growing stable of companies.

Hammarplast (originally Hammargrens Industri) was founded in 1947. Initially, its products were marked 'Made In Sweden', but from 1957 the brand name Hammarplast was used. At about this time the company also

began to credit its designers, who include Bernadotte & Bjørn, as well as Huberth Nilsson, Peter Dreyer and Odd Andersen of it in-house design team. Hammarplast bough Husqvarna Borstfabrik and Skaraplast in th 1960s, and in the 1970s it was acquired b Perstorp, giving it 50 per cent of the Swedis plastics market. Hammarplast bought Nil johan in 1987, and the following year was itse acquired by the Finnish company Hackma Eventually, in 2011, Hammarplast was resol to the Orthex Group, a leading Finland-base group of companies that specializes in plasti household products.

One early plastics manufacturer i Finland was Sarvis, which began in 1921 b making buttons out of casein. Bakelite manu facturing in Finland started in the 1930s, bu it was not until after World War II that pr duction boomed with manufacturers such a Strömfors Bruk, a subsidiary of the large Ah ström Group. In the late 1950s and throughou the 1960s the firm produced designs by Tap Wirkkala, including his melamine Caravel tableware (1959–64), which was used as an i flight service by the airline Finnair. Anothe notable plastic design from Finland was Ol Bäckström's orange plastic-handled scisso (1960), which set ergonomic standards an were produced in the millions from 1967 b Fiskars.

Because the manufacture of plast products requires the making of expensiv steel moulds, and because Finland has a re atively small population, it was difficult fo Finnish companies to sell enough produc to recoup their initial tooling investment To get around this problem, several Finnis manufacturers swapped moulds with Swed ish manufacturers. Sarvis and the Swedis firm Perstorp collaborated in this way, simpl changing the branding for their local market This arrangement continued until Perstor bought Hammarplast in 1970, after which no longer needed access to external mould

An important designer for Sarvis wa Olavi Arjas, who designed a range of succes ful products including a rectangular bucke In 1967 Sarvis hired Tauno Tarna, a forme pupil of Kaj Franck, and this led to Franc himself designing his plastic Pitopöytä tabl ware range for Sarvis in 1977. After Hackma bought Hammarplast to acquire the Nilsjoha brand, it also bought Sarvis, but it soon be came obvious that the Scandinavian mark was too small for it to own two plastic ma ufacturers, and so in 1990 Sarvis was close down. The company's moulds were subse quently sold to manufacturers in Russi Romania and the USA.

In contrast, Denmark was one of th first countries to manufacture and sell Ba kelite products, albeit focusing at first o he production of electrical components. A key figure in the story of Danish plastics is Marius Mulvad, who – after visiting the Bakelite Corporation and Western Electric on a trip to the USA in the 1910s – set up his own plastics manufacturing company in Copenhagen. In 1947 he co-founded the Danish Plastic Collaboration trade organization. Dansk Bakelit Industri (renamed DBI Plastics in 1945) was established in 1935 to make a wide variety of household products from various plastics, including components for the Danish vacuum-cleaner company Nilfisk. Nordisk Kamfabrik (Nordic Comb Factory, founded in 1933) was another early Danish plastics manufacturer.

By far the most internationally known Danish manufacturer of plastic homewares during the postwar period, however, was Rosti, founded by Rolf Fahrenholz and Stig Jørgensen in 1944, its name deriving from the first letters of their first names. The venture started by making Bakelite electrical components, as well as pipes, window scrapers and buttons, but from 1946 it focused on the manufacture of melamine homewares, which were sold under the Mepal brand. Its most famous design was a range of stacking mixing bowls commissioned from the industrial design consultancy Bernadotte & Bjørn. The design firm's principals charged one of their young employees with finding a suitable design; his name was Jacob Jensen, famously to become the design director of Bang & Olufsen. Jensen's elegant and thoughtful mixing-bowl set (1950) was called Margrethe after the Danish princess (and later queen), who was a relative of Sigvard Bernadotte. Another Rosti classic was the Style Copenhagen series by Bjørn Christensen (late 1960s). The company also made kitchenwares designed by Falle Uldall and Erik Lehmann, among others.

In the 1970s the young Danish hollowware company Stelton decided to diversify into the manufacture of plastic homewares, which would be more affordable than its high-end stainless-steel designs, but just as good-quality. To that end, Erik Magnussen designed for it a number of stylish, modern pieces in colourful, hard and shiny acrylonitrile butadiene styrene (ABS), most notably his EM77 vacuum jug (1977). This simple cylindrical design is still in production some 40 years after its launch, and looks as fresh as ever. Another company that has kept up the Danish tradition of producing innovative high-quality homewares made from plastics is Normann Copenhagen. Two of its earliest successes in this field were its fold-up washing-up bowl (2002) and space-saving collapsible funnel (2004) designed by Ole Jensen and Boje Estermann respectively. More recently, its Geo collection (2012) by Nicholai

Wiig Hansen has scooped both a Red Dot Award and a German Design Award, showing that groundbreaking plastic design is still a preserve of Danish design.

Of course, no survey of Danish plastic design is complete without a mention of LEGO, famously founded in 1932 by Ole Kirk Christiansen. Since 1949 it has been producing its ubiquitous plastic toy bricks in ever-increasing numbers, introducing its ingenious interlocking system in 1958. Since then the firm has diversified its product line to keep up to date with toy trends. In 2015 the brand valuation consultancy Brand Finance named the Billund-based company 'the world's most powerful brand'. LEGO continues to expand its global reach as more and more children experience what the company describes as LEGO play, and at the same time get a hands-on understanding of the high-quality values of Scandinavian design.

Model 1456 jug by Sven-Eric Juhlin (attributed) for Gustavsberg (Sweden), ca. 1970

Caravelle tableware by Tapio Wirkkala for Strömfors Bruk (Finland), 1959–64

Classic O-Series scissors by Olof Bäckström for Fiskars (Finland), 1960

Margrethe stacking mixing bowls by Bernadotte & Bjørn (Jacob Jensen) for Rosti (Denmark), 1950

Geo service by Nicholai Wiig Hansen for Normann Copenhagen (Denmark), 2012–15

Publicity image of LEGO bricks, 2016

1.

2.

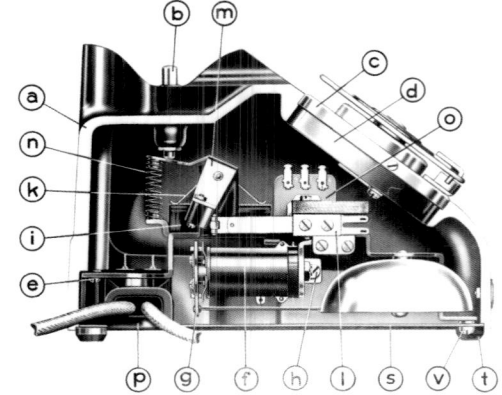

EAN HEIBERG

Although Bakelite was first developed in 1907, it was not until the late 1920s or early 1930s that this new synthetic material came into its own. Marketed as 'the material of a thousand uses', it was easy to mould, very durable, waterproof and non-conductive. One of the first appliances in which Bakelite was exploited was the landmark DBH 1001 telephone designed by the Norwegian artist Jean Heiberg in 1931 with a Bakelite casing. Heiberg had trained at the Statens Håndverks- og Kunstindustriskole (Norwegian National Academy of Craft and Industrial Art) in Oslo, and then studied in Paris. On his return to Oslo he was commissioned to create a Bakelite housing for this new telephone, while the Norwegian engineer Johan Christian Bjerknes devised its internal layout. The development of the DBH 1001 was a joint venture between the Swedish telephone company L. M. Ericsson and its Oslo subsidiary, Elektrisk Bureau. Heiberg created its complex sculptural shape using plaster models, making it far more ergonomically resolved than earlier telephone designs and perfectly suited to being moulded in Bakelite. This influential model set new standards for modern telephone design and was subsequently used across the world.

1. L. M. Ericsson publicity photograph showing the DBH 1001 telephone in use, ca. 1932

2. Cross-section diagram of Jean Heiberg and Johan Christian Bjerknes's DBH 1001 telephone, showing its internal layout, ca. 1931

Below: DBH 1001 telephone by Jean Heiberg and Johan Christian Bjerknes for Elektrisk Bureau (Norway) and L. M. Ericsson (Sweden), 1931

ROSTI MEPAL

The Danish plastics company Rosti (now Swedish-owned) was founded in 1944 and six years later established a sister company, Rosti Mepal, to commercialize a newly developed, hard and durable styrene-acrylonitrile. This melamine polymer, known as Mepal, could be coloured easily, making it perfect for the manufacture of homewares. One of Rosti Mepal's first successes was the Margrethe set of mixing bowls, designed by Jacob Jensen of Bernadotte & Bjørn in 1950. These stylish nesting bowls were named after Sigvard Bernadotte's niece, Queen Margrethe II of Denmark. Another hugely popular Rosti design was a colourful stacking egg cup variously attributed to Bjørn Christensen and Erik Lehmann. In 1965 Rosti launched an extensive range of plastic kitchen spoons, including salad servers that were notable for their forward-looking soft, organic contours. During the 1960s and 1970s, thanks to such stylish designs, Rosti's products became ubiquitous in homes not just in Scandinavia, but also in Europe and America.

1. Salad servers by Rosti Mepal (Denmark), 1965

2. Rosti plastic factory in Roskilde, Denmark, 1971 – showing the hand-finishing of designs made from Mepal melamine

3. Egg cups by Rosti Mepal, 1960s

4. Margrethe mixing bowls by Bernadotte & Bjørn (Jacob Jensen) for Rosti Mepal (Denmark), 1950

1.

2.

3.

4.

ERICOFON

Launched in 1954, the Ericofon was a truly revolutionary telephone that reflected the strength and innovation of Scandinavian industrial design during the postwar period. This ingenious product, designed by Hugo Blomberg and Ralph Lysell of L. M. Ericsson's in-house design team in conjunction with the company engineer Gösta Thames, cleverly integrated the telephone's earpiece, mouthpiece and dial into a single-piece streamlined form moulded in a newly developed and lightweight thermoplastic – ABS. Sculptural and shiny, this ergonomic design was initially marketed for institutional use, in particular for convalescing patients in hospital. Two years after its debut, however, Ericsson recognized its domestic potential and began producing it in a wide range of attractive colours. It subsequently became an international commercial success, selling especially well in Europe, America and Australia.

1. Prototype of the cobra-shaped Ericofon telephone, ca. 1953

2. Rotary dial set within the base section of the Ericofon telephone

3. Press photograph showing the American actress Adrienne Bourbeau with the one-piece Ericofon, 1959

Opposite: Ericofon telephone by Hugo Blomberg, Ralph Lysell and Gösta Thames for L. M. Ericsson (Sweden), 1954

3.

1.
2.

CARL-ARNE BREGER

In Sweden the word for 'designer' is *form-givare* – which directly translates as 'form-giver', probably explaining why in Scandinavia the form of an object is so carefully considered. It is not surprising, then, that a number of mid-century Scandinavian designers explored the formal potential of the newly developed plastics that were coming on to the market. Cheap, colourful and easy to mould, these new materials were suited to the production of high-quality yet democratically affordable housewares. The Swedish designer Carl-Arne Breger was one of the great pioneers in this field, and his Kanna watering can (1957–58) demonstrated how new materials could be employed to create sculptural yet functional forms. Its design skilfully translated the kind of organic form found in Gustavsberg's ceramics of the period into synthetic materials. Crucially, this early design helped Breger to forge a reputation as a specialist in the design of plastics, and he subsequently created many other plastic products, including the Duett jug and citrus press (1967) for Gustavsberg and the Ericofon 700 (1976 see also pp. 440–41) for Ericsson. In fact, he was so closely identified with this area of design that he became widely known in Scandinavia as 'Mr Plastic'.

Opposite: Kanna watering can by Carl-Arne Breger for Gustavsberg (Sweden), 1957–58

1. Ericofon 700 telephone by Carl-Arne Breger for L. M. Ericsson (Sweden), 1976

2. Duett citrus press and jug by Carl-Arne Breger for Gustavsberg (Sweden), 1967

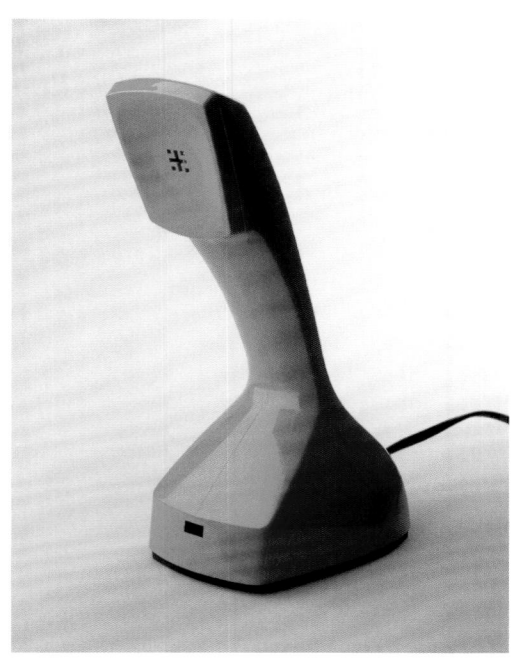

1.

2.

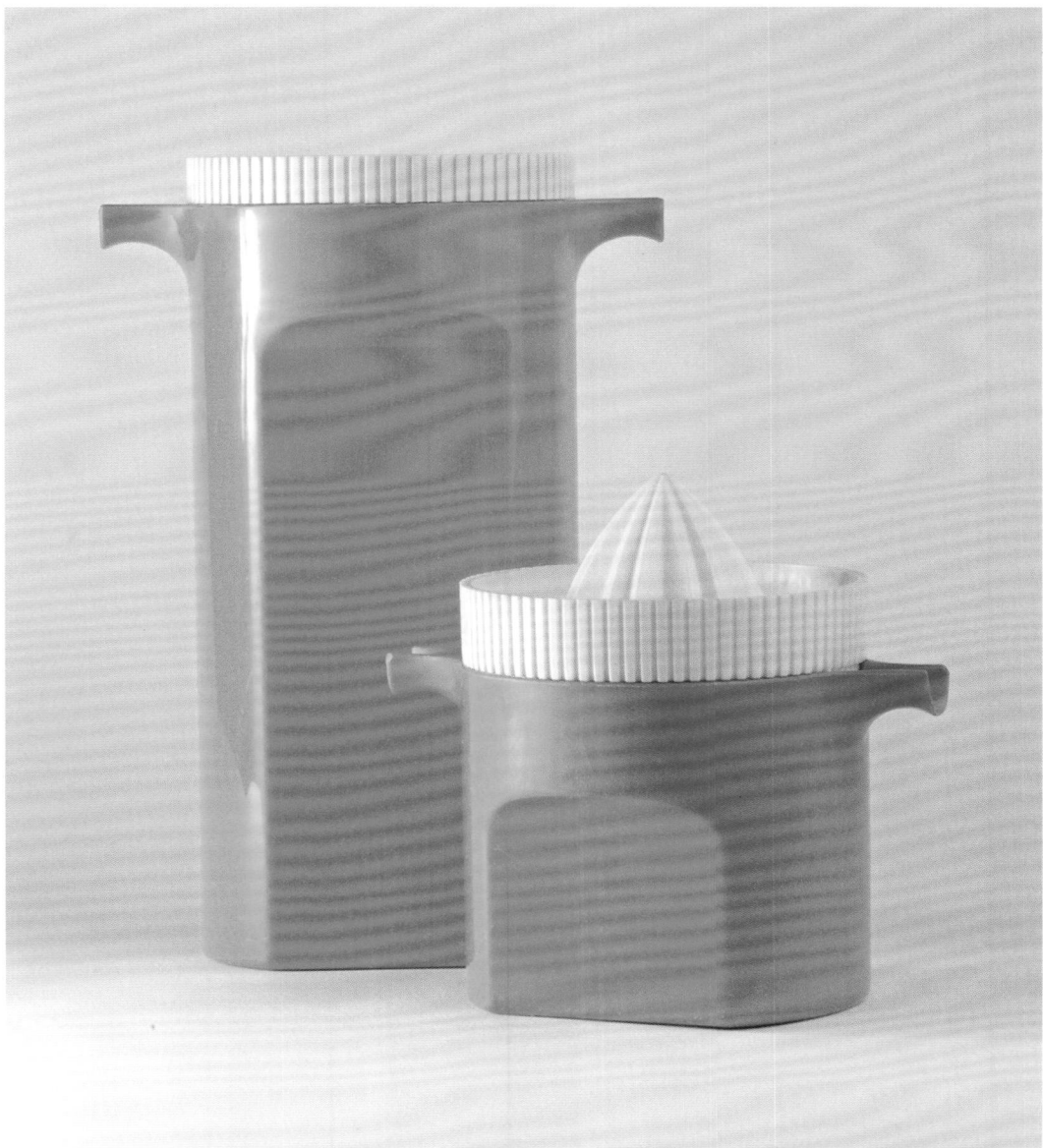

PLASTIC SCANDTASTIC

From the mid 1950s until the mid 1970s a number of Swedish companies focused on the mass-manufacturing potential of new synthetic polymers, which were viewed as modern, democratic materials that could be harnessed to shape the future of the nation's progressive welfare state. For decades the belief had been widely held in Sweden that well-designed everyday wares were the birthright of all, regardless of status, and that 'good design' was ultimately a tool for life-enhancing social change. Companies such as Gustavsberg, Husqvarna and Hammarplast subscribed to this belief, and accordingly developed high-quality plastic housewares for the masses, such as Hans Skillius's Prydan bowls (1974) made of hard and shiny ABS. In fact, most well-known Nordic designers turned their hand to designing in plastics; for instance, the Danish designer Henning Koppel, better known for his exquisite silverware, designed an elegant jug for G. Heskou in the 1960s, while the Finnish designer Kaj Franck, who was renowned for his glassware and ceramics, designed a practical yet stylish tableware range for Sarvis (1977). Indeed, the golden period of Scandinavian design coincided with a plastic design revolution in the Nordic nations, where plastics were seen as noble materials that could be used to produce democratizing designs of real intrinsic value.

Below: Prydan bowls, Model nos 4075 and 4077, by Hans Skillius for Hammarplast (Sweden), 1974

1. Plastic jug by Henning Koppel for G. Heskou (Denmark), 1960s

2. Svanen (Swan) watering can by Knut Brinck (Sweden), 1958–59

3. Pitopöytä (Easy Day) tableware set by Kaj Franck for Sarvis (Finland), 1977

1.

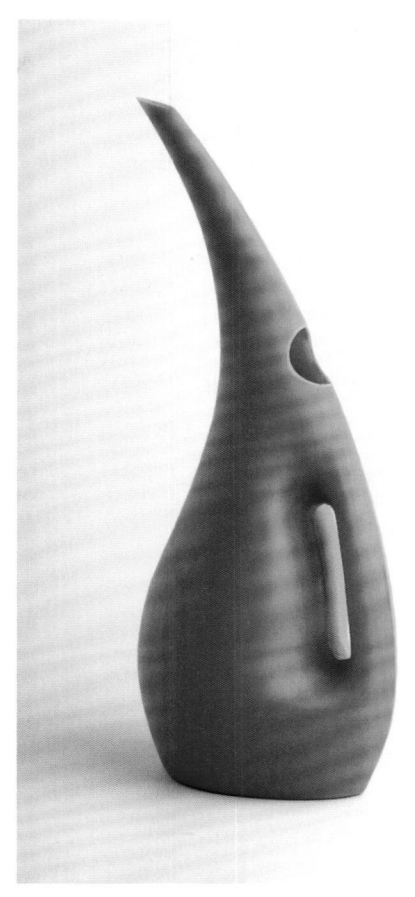

2.

STIG LINDBERG

As a consummate form-giver, Stig Lindberg explored the formal possibilities of the new plastic 'wonder' materials, which were becoming commercially available for the first time during the 1950s and 1960s. One of his earliest designs in plastic was for Gustavsberg, a citrus press with an innovative oval boat-like shape and an integrated handle that made it easy to pour the juice out. Made in tomato-red or lemon-yellow, high-impact polystyrene, it was a bright and cheerful design that was very inexpensive. A few years after its introduction, an example famously broke while being demonstrated on a Swedish television programme because the plastic could not withstand the type of pressure being exerted on it. While this must have been embarrassing for Lindberg at the time, it was the fault of the material rather than any design shortcoming. Nevertheless, he went on to design other plastic products that were more successful, most notably his Simon money box (1961, named after his own dog, also known as Skotte or Scottie), which he created for the Swedish bank Handelsbanken to commemorate its sixtieth anniversary.

Opposite: Simon/Skotte (Scottie) money boxes by Stig Lindberg for Handelsbanken (Sweden), 1961

Below: Citrus presses by Stig Lindberg for Gustavsberg (Sweden), 1953

LEGO

The origins of LEGO can be traced to a small toymaking workshop founded by the master carpenter Ole Kirk Christiansen in 1932. A couple of years later, Christiansen gave both his wooden toys and the workshop a new name: LEGO – a contraction of the Danish phrase *leg godt*, 'play well'. The venture expanded, and in 1940 it manufactured its first plastic toys. Seven years later it became the first Danish company to acquire its own injection-moulding machines, enabling much higher volumes of production. In 1949 LEGO's Automatic Binding Bricks were launched, with raised studs on their tops that fitted on to corresponding hollows on their undersides. The playability of LEGO bricks, however, was dramatically improved with the development in 1957 of a new 'stud-and-tube' coupling system, which was patented the following year. This improved interlocking design made the connections between the bricks extremely stable, allowing more ambitious constructions. Over the succeeding decades LEGO's universal toy-building system has been expanded and diversified to include roof tiles (1958), wheels (1961), Duplo bricks (1969) and minifigures (1978), as well as a host of other components. Today LEGO products are sold in more than 140 countries, making it not only one of the world's most successful toymakers, but also one of the leading Scandinavian brands.

1. LEGO Minifigure, introduced 1978

2. Duplo brick system, introduced 1969

3. The first LEGOLAND theme park in Billund (Denmark) opened 1968

4. The first LEGO Automatic Binding Brick, introduced 1949

Opposite: LEGO bricks with 'stud-and-tube' coupling system, 1957

2.

1.

3.

4.

ERIK MAGNUSSEN + STELTON

Having completed his training as a ceramicist in 1960, Erik Magnussen worked as an in-house designer for the Danish firm Bing & Grøndahl for several years. During this period he designed a tableware range, known as Hank, which – rather curiously – had snap-on plastic handles. The series, one of Magnussen's first forays into designing in plastic, won the Danish Design Prize in 1972. In 1976 he began working for Stelton, a Copenhagen-based company specializing in contemporary stainless-steel hollowware, and the following year he designed his EM77 vacuum jug, which was made of state-of-the-art ABS in a variety of colours. It remains one of Stelton's bestsellers, thanks to its simple, timeless form and high-quality manufacture. In fact, Magnussen became a polymeric specialist, designing various other homewares in plastic for Stelton during this period, including salad servers, a salad bowl and an ice bucket, all of which exemplified his guiding design principles: functional and aesthetic durability, formal simplicity, ease of use and cost-effective manufacture. Crucially, in a very Scandinavian way, Magnussen was able to demonstrate the nobility of plastics through the design of elegant, affordable and long-lasting products.

1. Ice bucket by Erik Magnussen for Stelton (Denmark), late 1970s

2. Salad servers by Erik Magnussen for Stelton (Denmark), late 1970s

Opposite: EM77 thermal jug (½ litre) by Erik Magnussen for Stelton (Denmark), 1977

1.

2.

NORMANN COPENHAGEN

Jan Andersen and Poul Madsen founded Normann Copenhagen in 1999, and three years later the company received widespread acclaim for its Norm 69 lamp. It was, however, the introduction of its ingenious foldable washing-up bowl (2002) by Ole Jensen, made of synthetic rubber, that really announced the firm's cutting-edge design credentials. More space-saving ideas followed in the form of Boje Estermann's award-winning funnel and strainer (2004), both made of flexible Santoprene elastomer that can be folded flat. More recently, the minimalist Geo collection (2012–14), which includes a striking plastic-housed thermal jug by Nicholai Wiig Hansen, has won both a Red Dot Award and a German Design Award 'Special Mention'. With its strongly geometric lines and fashion-inspired colour combinations, this range has been purged of all decorative detail, yet retains a strong sense of character. Hansen notes: 'I've worked with the lines, circles and shapes of the products to create a geometric harmony. The very shapes give the Geo range an edgy and graphic look, and the combined use of classic and light colours helps to soften the masculine appearance.' Normann Copenhagen is one of very few Danish firms still producing high-quality plastic designs that are not only stylish and innovative, but also democratically affordable in the best Scandinavian tradition.

1. Funnel by Boje Estermann for Normann Copenhagen (Denmark), 2004

2. Washing-up bowl and brush by Ole Jensen for Normann Copenhagen (Denmark), 2002

Opposite: Geo vacuum flask by Nicholai Wiig Hansen for Normann Copenhagen (Denmark), 2012

1.

2.

TEXTILES

Any survey of Scandinavian design must include the pioneering work of Märta Måås-Fjetterström, who revitalized the craft-weaving tradition of Sweden with her modern rug designs. In 1914 she exhibited at the Baltic Exhibition in Malmö, where Alfred Nobel's nephew saw her work. Ludvig Nobel subsequently invited her to create textiles for his Skånegården hotel in Båstad and to open a workshop, which remains in operation.

Another major force in Swedish textile design was Josef Frank, a Jewish-Austrian architect-designer who became a Swedish citizen in 1939. For many years he was head designer at the interior-design firm Svenskt Tenn. His highly patterned, richly coloured textiles were the antithesis of the simple fabrics that most Modernists were advocating. He noted: 'The monochromatic surface appears uneasy, while patterns are calming.'

Agda Österberg produced similarly colourful textiles, albeit using abstracted rather than figurative motifs. She studied at the Tekniska Skolan (Technical College; now Konstfack, University College of Arts, Crafts and Design), then at Handarbetets Vänner (Friends of Handicraft; now HV Skola), both in Stockholm. The turning point in her career came in 1920, when she received a grant from Svenska Slöjdföreningen (now Svensk Form; Swedish Form) to spend five weeks in Germany and Italy, including studies at the Bauhaus in Weimar. Österberg exhibited at the Exposition Internationale des Arts Décoratifs et Industriels Modernes in Paris in 1925, and a year later was appointed creative director of Libraria, a company owned by the Swedish Church. In 1933 she moved to Varnhem in central Sweden and bought the Axevalla-Varnhems Slöjd studio, where she continued to create wall hangings and rugs well into the 1980s.

The most well-known Swedish textile designer, however, was Astrid Sampe, who trained at the Tekniska Skolan in Stockholm and the Royal College of Art in London In 1937 she began working as a designer in the Nordiska Kompaniet (NK) department store's Textilkammare (Textile Chamber), and the following year she was made head of this influential studio, a position she retained until 1971. She exhibited at both the Exposition Internationale des Arts et Techniques dans la Vie Moderne, Paris, in 1937 and the New York World's Fair in 1939. She was also employed by Arne Jacobsen, and later commissioned Stig Lindberg to create textiles for NK. In 1946 she helped to arrange the exhibition 'Modern Swedish Home' in London, an event that did much to promote contemporary Scandinavian design in Britain.

In 1954 Sampe launched the Signed Textiles collection for NK with pieces by some of the leading Swedish designers of the time. She also designed textiles for the fabric manufacturer Almedahls and rugs for the carpet factory Kasthall. At the H55 exhibition in Helsingborg in 1955 she introduced the Linen Line for Almedahls, which included Perssons Kryddskåp (Persson's Spice Rack), named after the ceramicist Signe Persson-Melin. Sampe later designed for Knoll International in New York and Donald Brothers in Dundee. She famously designed the carpets for the Dag Hammarskjöld Library at the United Nations Headquarters in New York in 1961, and was one of the first Swedish designers to experiment with computer-aided design.

The Swedish sisters Lisbet and Gocken Jobs made a notable contribution to the development of Scandinavian textile design. They initially worked as ceramicists, but, owing to a wartime shortage of ceramic glaze, Sampe suggested that they transfer their design skill to textiles. This led to an exhibition in 1945 at the NK department store entitled 'När Skönheten Kom till Byn' (When Beauty Came to the Village). Although NK's Textile Chamber produced some of their textiles, most were manufactured by Jobs Handtryck, a company set up by their brother Peer Jobs and still run by their descendants.

Another designer who worked for Jobs Handtryck was Dagmar Lodén (née Henning). In 1944, after the death of her husband, the artist Karl Lodén, she moved to the Dalecarlia district of central Sweden. It was there in 1949 that she began designing textiles, her most popular design being Tistlar (Thistles). She later worked as creative director for Alice Lund Textilier, which specializes in ecclesiastical textiles.

Born in Scania, Ingrid Dessau was well versed in the Swedish handicrafts from an early age, and studied at the Tekniska Skolan in Stockholm. In 1948 she received a grant that enabled her to travel to the USA, Canada and Mexico with her husband, Kaj, who later became Georg Jensen's manager in New York. Inspired by modern jazz and Native American motifs, Dessau's designs were exhibited at the Galerie Moderne in Stockholm in 1953. The following year she became head designer at Kasthall, and between 1970 and 1984 she worked for Kinnasand. She received many awards and continued designing into her late sixties, her last major commission being textiles for the Nobel Prize dinner in 1991.

Hans Krondahl also studied at the Tekniska Skolan. In 1962 he set up his own weaving studio, where he created textiles for NK's Textile Chamber, Borås Wäfveri and

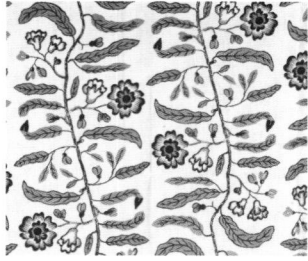

Chianti textile by Josef Frank for Svenskt Tenn (Sweden), ca. 1933

Oxelösunds Skärgård (Oxelösund Archipelago) rug by Dagmar Lodén for Alice Lund Textilier (Sweden), 1969

Randig Banan (Striped Banana) textile by Inez Svensson of 10 Gruppen for IKEA (Sweden), 1986

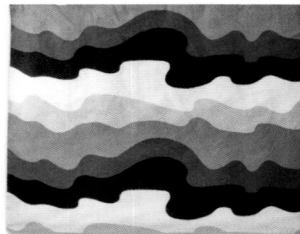

Aalto (Wave) textile by Eine Lepistö for Finlayson (Finland), 1971

Jokapoika (Every Boy) shirt by Vuokko Nurmesniemi for Marimekko (Finland), 1956

Opposite: Marimekko prints (top to bottom): Unikko by Maija Isola (1964), Tiiliskivi by Armi Ratia (1952), Juhla-Raita by Fujiwo Ishimoto (1981) and Pirput Parput by Vuokko Nurmesniemi (ca. 1960)

Katja of Sweden. He was awarded the Lunning Prize in 1965, and from the early 1960s taught textile design in Sweden and elsewhere. From 1979 to 1980 he was a textile-design expert for the United Nations Industrial Development Organization in Indonesia. An influential teacher, Krondahl eventually led the craft department at the University of Gothenburg, and in 1988 he became Professor of Textile Art there.

An interest in perpetuating the craft traditions of developing nations led to the establishment of the Afroart foundation in the 1960s. Its aim was to support, develop and disseminate knowledge about handicrafts in Africa, Latin America and Asia. The first Afroart shop opened in Stockholm in 1967. This social initiative, the brainchild of Jytte Bonnier, had grown out of another project: the founding of an art school by a group of Swedish artists at Rorke's Drift in South Africa. Objects made at the school had provoked international interest, which in turn generated a need for sales outlets outside South Africa. In 2003 the venture changed ownership, and now the Afroart Studio belongs to six Swedish textile designers, who continue to create textiles that are ethically produced in various developing countries.

The hugely influential Swedish design collective 10 Gruppen (Group of 10), also known as 10 Swedish Designers, was founded in 1970 as a reaction to a perceived crisis in the Swedish textile industry. The group included some of the most progressive Swedish designers of the time, often with crossover into Pop art and left-wing politics. The designs were rooted in the geometric Op Art of the 1960s, but also presaged the Postmodern textile patterns of the Memphis design group in Italy. For many years the three remaining members, Birgitta Hahn, Tom Hedqvist and Ingela Håkansson Lamm, led 10 Gruppen and operated their own shop in Stockholm. In 2015, however, they decided that 45 years was enough and sold the company to IKEA, which is relaunching the brand that is famous for its bold, bright textiles.

Finland's history of textile production stretches back to its age-old folk traditions, as well as to the Finlayson cotton mill established in Tampere in 1820. Its founder, the engineer James Finlayson, sold the company in 1836, when he moved back to his native Scotland. In 1934 the Finlayson mill merged with the Forssa mill, another early Finnish textile company, founded by the Swedish-born Axel Wilhelm Wahren. In 1952 Finlayson established a design office, which in the 1960s produced colourful Pop-inspired fabrics by Pirkko Hammarberg, Helena Perheentupa and Mirja Tissari. Eine Lepistö also designed the firm's classic Aalto (Wave) pattern in 1971.

Marimekko, however, has for decades been the highest-profile Finnish textile company, and has grown into a brand recognized around the world. It was established by Armi Ratia and her husband, Viljo, in 1951 – she had studied textile design at the Taideteolliseen Keskuskouluun (Central School of Industrial Arts) in Helsinki, while he had owned a textile factory in Vyborg. When the Red Army overran Vyborg in 1944, the couple moved to Helsinki. After the war ended, they founded the textile company Printex, with Armi at first acting as designer but gradually becoming involved in its administration. In 1949, after poor sales, Armi suggested that they produce more modern textiles. To that end, she engaged Maija Isola as the firm's first full-time designer, and in 1951 a fashion show, 'The Marimekko Project', was held to promote the resulting textiles. (*Marimekko* means 'Mary's dress' in Finnish; Mari is an anagram of Armi.) To keep the venture separate from Printex, Ratia registered it as a new company; the show's designer, Riitta Immonen, was the only other shareholder. In 1953 Ratia hired a second designer, Vuokko Nurmesniemi, to produce fashion and furnishing textiles for the company.

The American architect Ben Thompson had admired Printex fabrics at Expo '58 in Brussels in 1958, and the following year Ratia visited him in Cambridge, Massachusetts, armed with two boxes of Printex fabrics and some Marimekko clothes. That year Thompson held a Finnish-themed exhibition at his influential shop Design Research, and it was a great success. Around this time John F. Kennedy was campaigning for the US Presidency against Richard Nixon, and his wife, Jacqueline, appeared in *Life* magazine wearing Marimekko dresses that she had bought from Thompson. This boosted Marimekko and Printex exports to the US, and soon Marimekko was the preferred label of American intellectuals, architects and liberals.

At about this time Ratia and Nurmesniemi argued over crediting, leading the latter to resign in 1960. The early success of Marimekko, however, was largely caused by the latter's bestselling Jokapoika (Every Boy) shirt of 1956. Fortunately Annika Rimala, who had been hired in 1959, managed to fill the creative gap left by her departure.

In the early 1960s Ratia became so inspired by Marshall McLuhan's idea of the Global Village that she set up the Marikylä (Mari Village) Project, which functioned as a design laboratory for Printex and Marimekko, while also housing staff and developing new ways of living. Marimekko and Printex merged in 1966 in order to keep track of the village's escalating costs. In 1969 the infamous Finnish businessman Jaakko Lassila was appointed

Marimekko's chairman and the Marikylä project was subsequently abandoned, while stock levels, staff numbers and product ranges were reduced in order to improve profitability.

During this period Rimala designed the successful Tasaraita (Even Stripe) range of easy-to-wear jersey clothing for men, women and children, while the Kuski (Coachman) clothing range (1972) by Pentti Rinta became the de facto uniform of young radicals in Finland. The Japanese designer Fujiwo Ishimoto arrived in the early 1970s and brought calmer on-trend designs. By 1981 Marimekko was the most successful company on the Helsinki Stock Exchange in terms of return on capital. After changing hands a couple of times, it was acquired by the banker Mika Ihamuotila in 2007, and since then the focus has been on developing its fashion collection.

Inspired by the success of Marimekko, a number of other Finnish textile manufacturers began producing similarly bold and colourful prints. One such was Helenius, founded by Erkki Helenius, who had worked for Marimekko. Another was Porin Puuvilla, which had Timo Sarpaneva as its creative director from 1955 to 1965, and which merged with Finlayson in 1973.

Sarpaneva also worked with the firm Tampella, as did Olli Mäki, Marjatta Metsovaara and Marjatta Seppälä. Until 1963 the company was named Tampereen Pellava- ja Rauta-Teollisuus Osake-Yhtiö (Flax and Iron Industry of Tampere Stock Company). In later years its core business became iron and steel, but the company continued to produce textiles for historic reasons. In 2010 the jacquard-weaving company Lapuan Kankurit took over the production of designs by Dora Jung that had previously been made by Tampella, where she worked as a designer. The historic Finnish textile mill Jokipiin Pellava, meanwhile, established an in-house design department in the 1970s.

The textile designer Marie Gudme Leth was one of the earliest pioneers of Modern textile design in Denmark. Having studied at the Industrial Arts and Crafts School for Women and then at the Kunsthåndværkerskolen (School of Arts and Crafts; now the Kongelige Danske Kunstakademi or Royal Danish Academy of Fine Arts) in Copenhagen, she travelled in 1921 to Java, where she spent three years learning batik. In 1930 she moved to Frankfurt am Main to study at the Kunstgewerbeschule (School of Arts and Crafts), where she learned about screen-printing. In 1935 Leth co-founded the Dansk Kattuntrykkeri (Danish Calico Printing) factory, and five years later she opened her own design studio. From 1931 to 1948 she taught textile printing at the

Kunsthåndværkerskolen in Copenhagen, and she was awarded gold medals at the Exposition Internationale des Arts et Techniques dans la Vie Moderne in Paris in 1937 and at the 9th Milan Triennial in 1951. Over time her work became increasingly abstract, yet her patterns had a distinctive clarity, being almost mathematical in construction. One of her pupils, Helga Foght, also taught in Germany and later became highly involved with the artists' co-operative Den Permanente. Foght subsequently became a member of the Executive Committee of the National Association of Danish Crafts.

Georg Jensen Damask was directed from 1947 by Bent Georg Jensen, after he had completed his studies at the Textile Institute in Borås, Sweden. He hired as a designer Vibeke Nielsen, who became better known as Vibeke Klint when she married one of Kaare Klint's sons. Other designers who worked for the firm included Karen-Margrethe Naver and Bodil Bødtker-Næss. Jensen also designed patterns himself, including Hexagon, Kubus and Harlekin. He sold the company in 1999, but kept designing for it until 2011. Today the firm continues to produce a mix of classic designs by Arne Jacobsen and Nanna Ditzel alongside newer designs by Andreas Engesvik and Cecilie Manz.

The most renowned Danish textile company is Kvadrat – Danish for 'square'. Founded in 1968 by Poul Byriel and Erling Rasmussen, it has worked with Ditzel, Finn Juhl, Nina Koppel and Gunnar Aagaard Andersen, among others, to create a comprehensive portfolio of upholstery textiles. The 'classic' mainstay of the collection is Ditzel's Hallingdal fabric (1965), which is still made in its original colour palette. New designs are constantly added to Kvadrat's collection, which has become the standard for most design-led furniture companies.

Denmark's neighbour Norway has a long tradition of producing wool: today there are 2.3 million sheep in the country, against a human population of only 5 million. In 1872 Peder Jebsen, having studied modern wool-processing methods in England, determined that the village of Dale, near Bergen, was an ideal place to set up a similar venture thanks to its access to hydropower and a plentiful supply of wool. He subsequently secured usage rights to the local waterfalls, and imported machines from England. His factory was completed in 1879 and remains in the village today as Dale of Norway. Its most famous product is the unisex Cortina sweater, originally designed for the 1956 Winter Olympics in Cortina d'Ampezzo, northern Italy.

Other Norwegian producers include Gudbrandsdalens Uldvarefabrik of Lillehammer. In the 1960s it ended production of its fashion fabrics and rugs, and the focus is now on the manufacture of upholstery textiles, including Ditzel's Hallingdal fabric for Kvadrat. National costumes are still a strong tradition in Norway, and Gudbrandsdalens is also one of the leading manufacturers of fabrics for them. Innvik Sellgren (originally Indvikens Uldspinderi) has likewise focused on upholstery fabrics since the 1960s, and also co-operates with Kvadrat. Mandal Veveri also manufactures blankets and various national costume fabrics. A more recent Norwegian export success was the Bunadspledd (Bunad blanket; 2012) designed by Engesvik and manufactured by Mandal Veveri, inspired by the historical clothing of rural Norway.

Rauma Ullvarefabrikk, which has spun wool since 1927, has over the decades developed into a modern weaving business that today produces mainly Røros blankets and textiles for national costumes. Røros Tweed has also become a renowned Norwegian brand through working with well-known designers, including Inga Sempé and Anderssen & Voll.

Lastly, the designer Sigrun Berg must be mentioned in the context of Norwegian textile design. Having studied at the Arts and Crafts School and the Statens Håndverks- og Kunstindustriskole (Norwegian National Academy of Craft and Industrial Art) in Oslo, she established her own weaving workshop in the city in 1948, making rugs, tapestries, clothes and shawls. Berg also designed textiles for Tele Tweed, De Forenede Ullvarefabrikker, Røros Tweed, Halden Bomuldspinderi & Væveri and Solberg Spinderi. She received awards at the Milan Triennials of 1954 and 1960, and undertook many public commissions, including the interior textiles for the yacht KS *Norge*, the Norwegian people's gift to King Haakon VII in 1947. Crucially, Berg helped to protect the weaving traditions of the region by creating modern designs that employed age-old techniques.

Today, design-led companies such as Hay and Design House Stockholm are producing textiles and carpets that keep alive the spirit of invention and craft that has so long defined textile design and production in the Nordic region.

Tasaraita (Even Stripe) textile by Annika Rimala for Marimekko (Finland), 1968

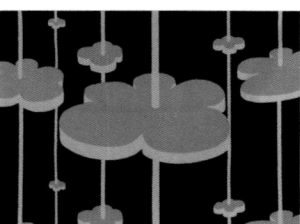

Textile by Marjatta Seppälä (attributed) for Tampella (Finland), ca. 1972

Pigeons linen damask panel by Dora Jung (Denmark), ca. 1973

Cortina sweater by Dale of Norway, 1956

Pleece throw by Marianne Abelsson for Design House Stockholm (Sweden), 1997

IMPI SOTAVALTA

During the 1920s and 1930s the textile art-ist Impi Sotavalta revitalized the Finnish and Swedish tradition of making hand-knotted long-pile rugs, known as *rya*. Historically these rugs had been used as bedcovers, wall hangings or prayer mats, and had often formed part of a bride's dowry. Many were decorated with patterns of animals and flowers, as well as symbolic motifs. Having studied the applied arts in Helsinki and Munich, Sotavalta built on this rich craft tradition, working from 1917 to 1939 as a designer for the Suomen Käsityön Ystävät (Friends of Finnish Handicraft), founded in 1879 by the artist Fanny Churberg to preserve the production of handmade rugs in the face of industrialization. Unusually for the time, Sotavalta travelled extensively, mak-ing annual summer trips to Germany, Austria, France and Italy, while also visiting Egypt, Turkey, Morocco and the Canary Islands. She also went to the landmark Stockholm Exhibi-tion of 1930. As a result of all this she drew inspiration for her own *rya* from a variety of sources – from traditional Arabic carpet weav-ing to the latest trends in European art and design, such as Cubism and Functionalism – giving her work an engaging hybrid quality that was essentially a very Scandinavian ex-pression of the Art Deco style.

1. Evening Song flat-weave carpet by Impi Sotavalta (self-produced) (Finland), 1930s

2. Flat-weave carpet by Impi Sotavalta for Kikan Kutomo (Finland), 1930s

Opposite: Flat-weave carpets by Impi Sotavalta (self-produced) (Finland), 1930s

1.

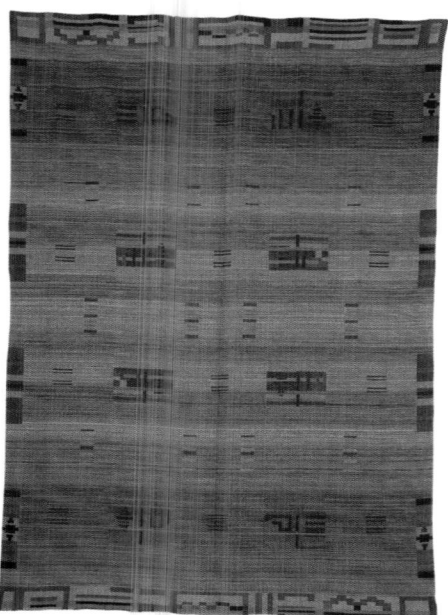

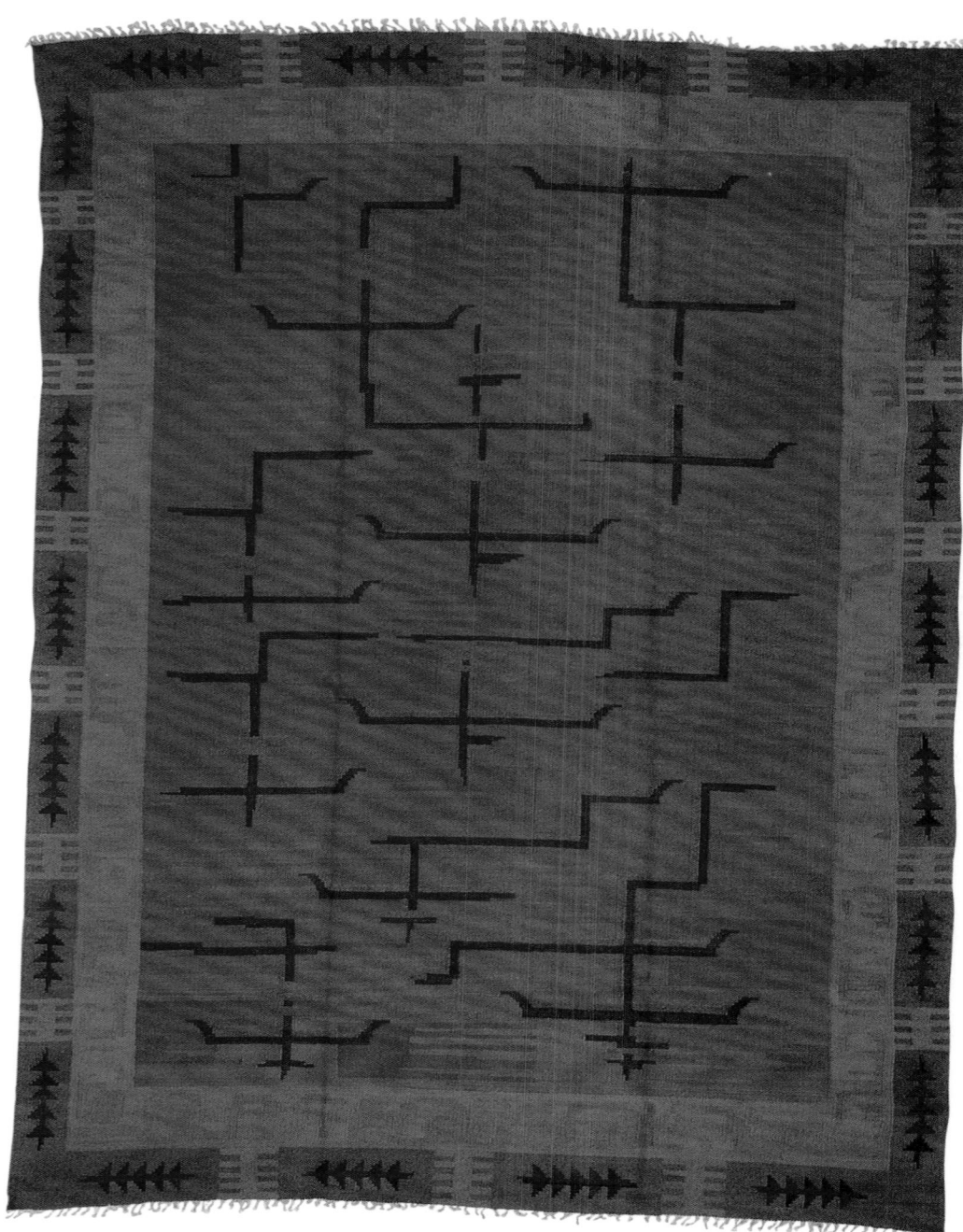

2.

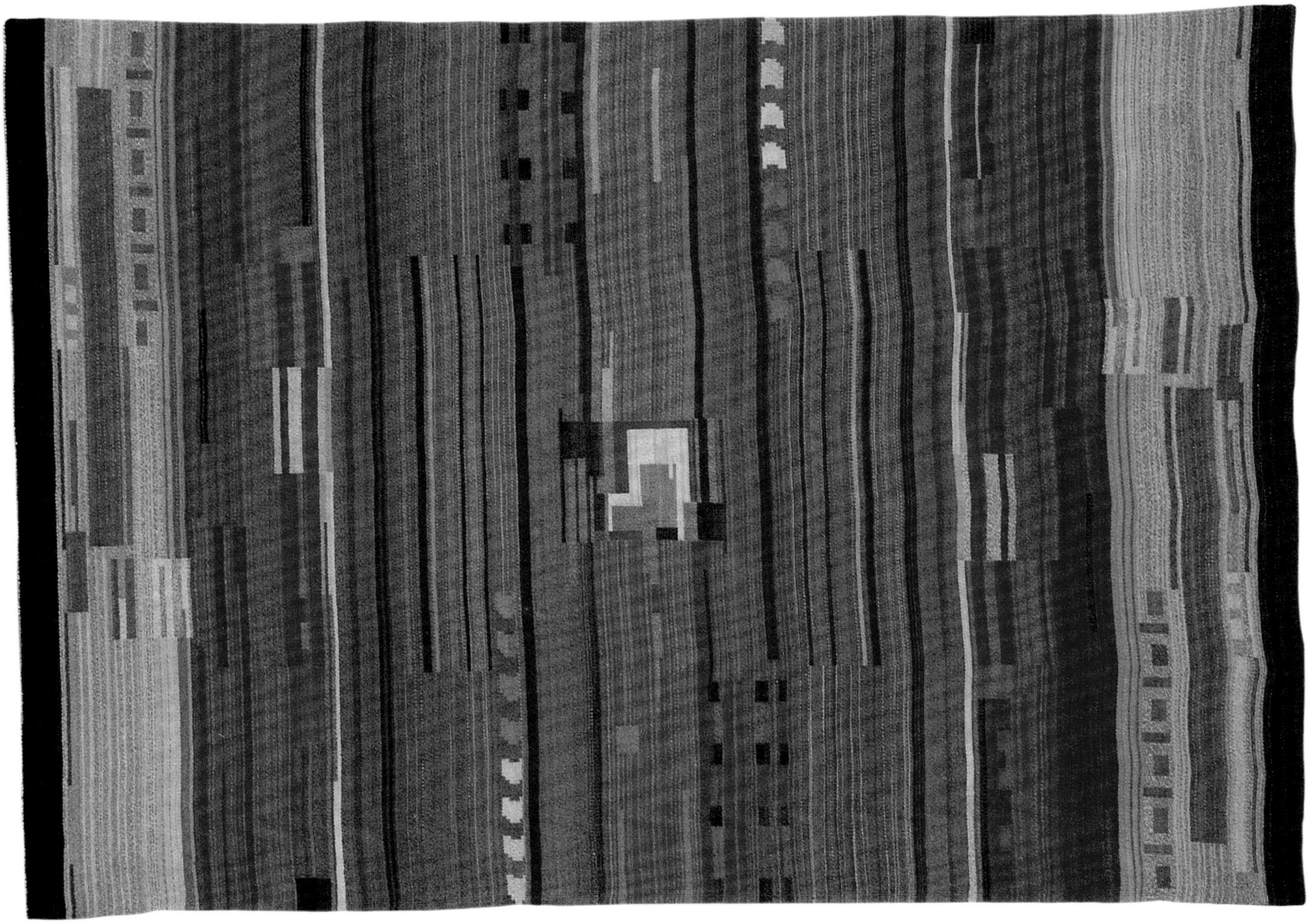

MÄRTA MÅÅS-FJETTERSTRÖM

Märta Måås-Fjetterström was interested in preserving traditional craft skills, in particular the strong weaving traditions found in Sweden. After studying in Stockholm she became an art teacher and then, in 1905, director of the Malmöhus handicraft association. She first showed her hand-woven textiles in an exhibition held by the Svenska Slöjdföreningen (Swedish Society of Crafts and Industrial Design) in 1909. A decade later she set up her famous weaving workshop in Båstad, and it became the most influential Swedish producer of woven textiles, manufacturing not only her own richly coloured and patterned wall hangings and rugs, but also designs by, among others, Barbro Nilsson, Marianne Richter, Ann-Mari Forsberg and Barbro Sprinchorn. Måås-Fjetterström's own modern-folk textile designs, of which she created more than 700, were typified by the use of simplified floral motifs and inspired by her close observation of nature as well as by traditional Swedish and Oriental weaving techniques. The Swedish museum director and curator Erik Wettergren noted in 1934: 'She is a remarkable storyteller … who finds her inspiration in legends and meadows, in the Orient and the North, in ancient beliefs and fresh green leaves, in the Bible and buildings.'

1. Rutmattan hand-woven wool rug by Märta Måås-Fjetterström (self-produced) (Sweden), 1931

2. Röda Åttan (Eight Red) hand-woven wool carpet by Märta Måås-Fjetterström (self-produced) (Sweden), 1928

Opposite: Täppan (Garden Plot) woven tapestry panel by Märta Måås-Fjetterström (self-produced) (Sweden), 1931

1.

2.

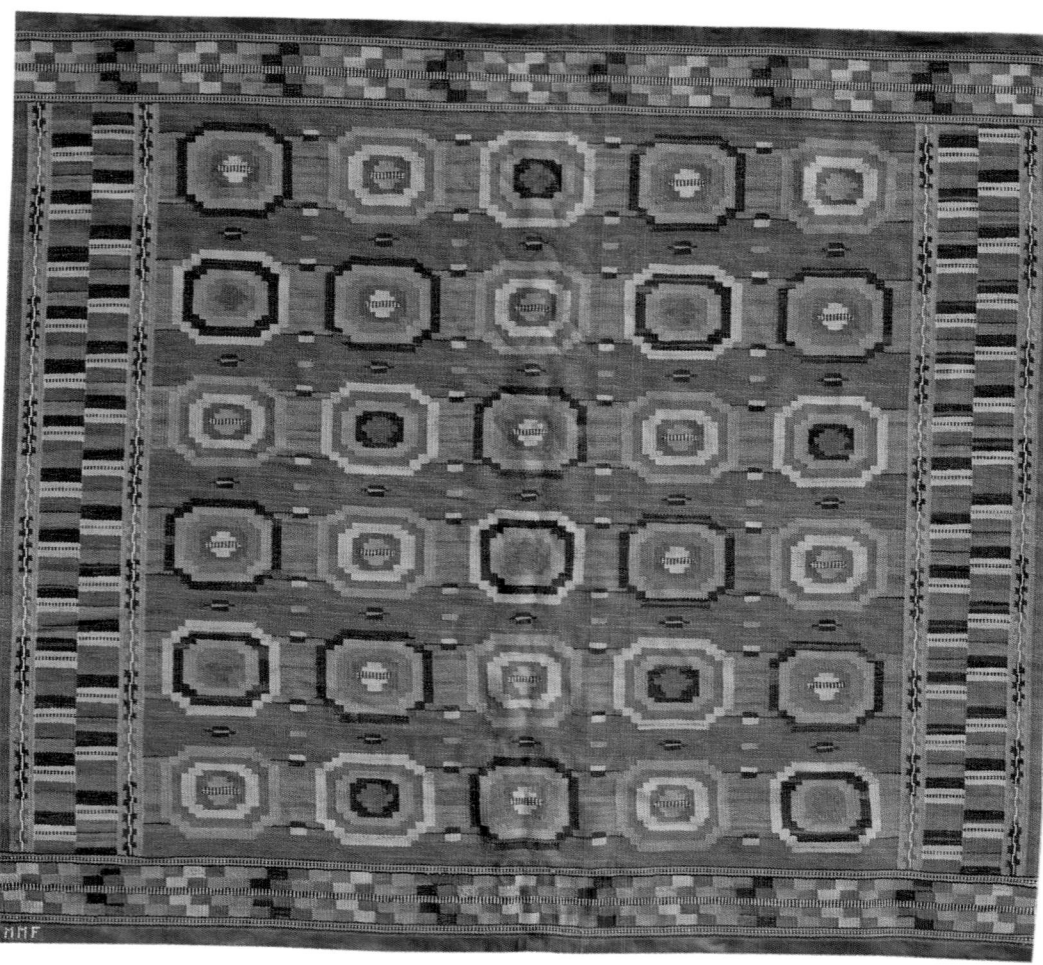

BARBRO NILSSON

Having undertaken extensive training as a textile designer and weaver, Barbro Nilsson taught at the Konstfack in Stockholm from 1934 to 1947, while also working as a textile designer, creating rugs and wall hangings for Märta Måås-Fjetterström's workshop (see pp. 462–63). In 1941, after the death of its founder, she became the workshop's director, and in the 1950s and 1960s she produced numerous designs for tapestries and various kinds of rug that were vibrantly coloured and boldly patterned with highly abstracted motifs inspired by natural flora and fauna. She also developed new weaving techniques. For example, for one of her most famous rug designs – Tånga (Seaweed), which was designed for the H55 exhibition in Helsingborg in 1955 – she devised a pattern of diamonds rhythmically ordered on a background of repeating verticals that gave the design an interesting surface relief. Many of her designs came in different colourways; her Nejlikan (Pimpernel) rug, for instance, was woven not only in vibrant reds, as shown opposite, but also in combinations of muted greys and dusky blues.

Opposite: Röda Nejlikan (Red Pimpernel) hand-woven wool carpet by Barbro Nilsson for Märta Måås-Fjetterström (Sweden), 1950

1. Tånga (Seaweed) hand-woven wool tapestry panel by Barbro Nilsson for Märta Måås-Fjetterström (Sweden), 1955

2. Paula Röd (Red Paula) hand-woven wool rug by Barbro Nilsson for Märta Måås-Fjetterström (Sweden), 1964

1.

2.

MID-CENTURY TEXTILES

During the postwar period, Swedish textile design underwent rather a Renaissance, thanks to the general desire among a new generation of homemakers for contemporary living spaces that were light-filled, bright and cheerful. And what better way to achieve this than with a bold patterned and vividly coloured handcrafted wall hanging or rug? During this period the Måås-Fjetterström workshop, under the gifted directorship of Barbro Nilsson (see pp. 464–65), produced numerous hand-woven textiles with a strongly contemporary flavour, such as Ann-Mari Forsberg's Melon tapestry (1950), which reflected the influence of abstract fine art with its blocking of form and colour. Indeed, the production of handcrafted textiles such as these had for centuries been a thriving cottage industry in Sweden, and it continued to be so after World War II, with designers such as Sofia Widén and Agda Österberg self-producing their designs by hand using various techniques, from embroidery to weaving to silk-screen printing.

1. Hand-embroidered linen panel by Sofia Widén (self-produced) (Sweden), 1958

2. Hand-woven flat-weave carpet by Agda Österberg (self-produced) (Sweden), 1950s

Opposite: Melon hand-woven tapestry panel by Ann-Mari Forsberg for Märta Måås-Fjetterström (Sweden), 1950

1.

2.

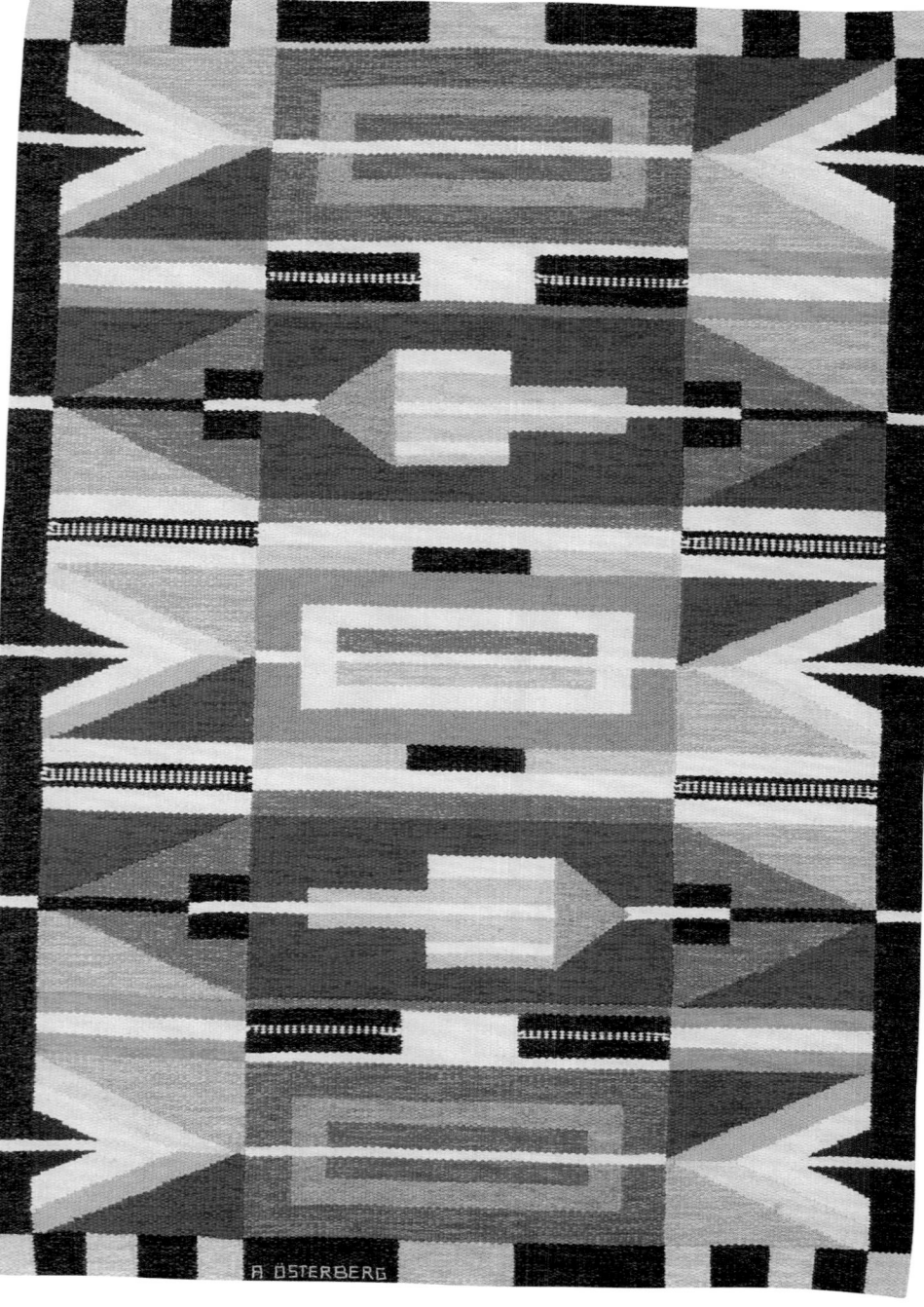

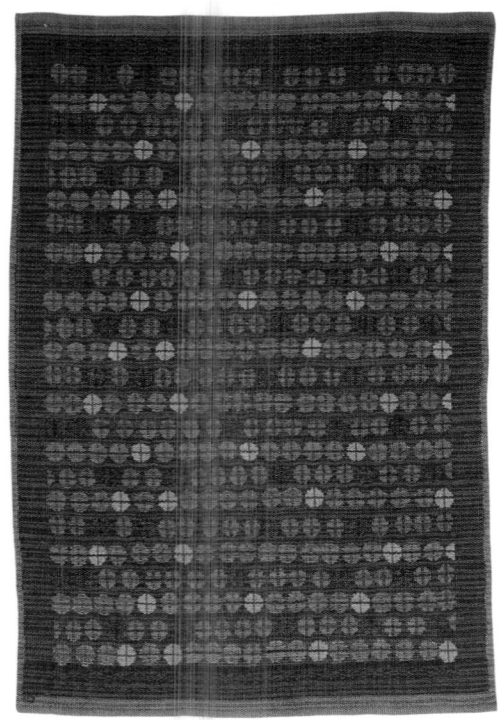

1.

2.

INGRID DESSAU

The Swedish textile designer Ingrid Dessau studied, like so many of her Swedish design contemporaries, at the Konstfack in Stockholm, graduating in 1945. That year she was hired by the Kristianstads Läns Hemslöjd (Handcraft Society for Kristiansen County), and for four years she helped to document the region's textile heritage through watercolour studies. During this period, she also designed rugs and carpets for the organization, such as the flat-weave and tapestry red-ground and diamond-patterned carpet shown below, which dates from the early 1950s. From 1953

she worked as a designer-maker creating exquisite hand-knotted and hand-woven rugs and carpets, while also working as a freelance designer for the carpet manufacturer Kasthall (1954–78) and the textile company Kinnasand (1970–84). She was awarded the Lunning Prize in 1955 for her design work, much of which featured bold geometric patterns, a refined palette of restricted colours and interesting weaving techniques, including a method known as 'basket weaving'. Over the years, as Dessau's confidence grew as a designer, her patterns became bolder, so that they almost functioned as woven fields of pure colour.

1. Hand-woven rug by Ingrid Dessau (self-produced) (Sweden), ca. 1960

2. Hand-woven carpet by Ingrid Dessau (self-produced) (Sweden), 1960s

Below: Flat-weave and tapestry carpet by Ingrid Dessau for Kristianstads Läns Hemslöjd (Sweden), ca. 1953

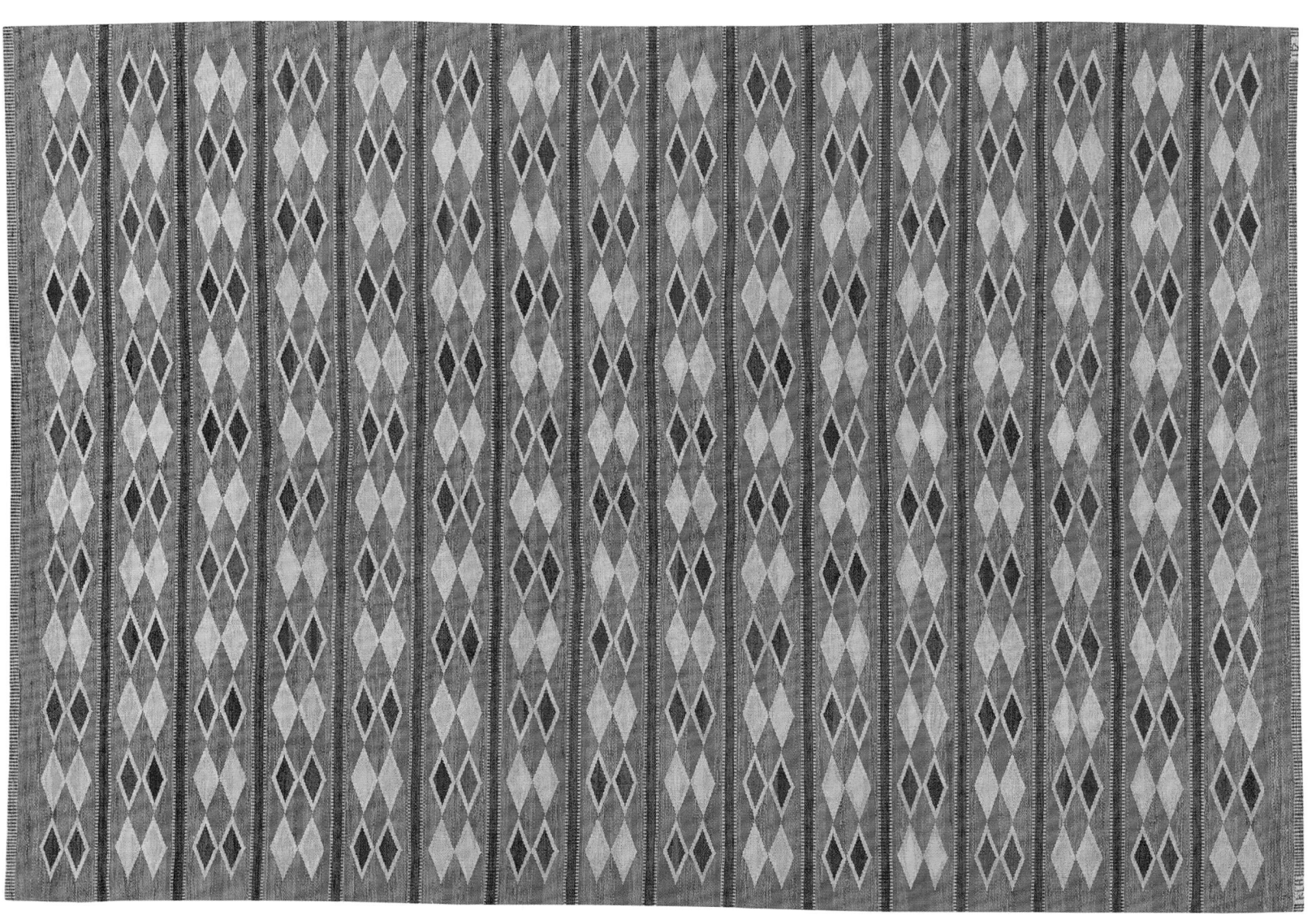

JOSEF FRANK

The Viennese émigré Josef Frank fled to Stockholm in 1933 and the following year began working as a designer for Estrid Ericson's interior-decorating firm, Svenskt Tenn, in central Stockholm. It was there that he established a reputation as a gifted designer of furniture, lighting and textiles. His distinctive contemporary style was quintessentially Scandinavian and completely at odds with the Modern Movement's doctrinal elimination of decoration. Instead, Frank built on the Arts and Crafts tradition of pattern-making inspired by nature, and created stunning fabric designs that had a vibrant gaiety both in line and in colour. His use of eclectic influences imbued his work with stylistic freshness. One of his textiles, for instance, takes inspiration from antique maps, another from Italian terrazzo flooring. The inspiration for his stunning Gröna Fåglar (Green Birds) textile (1943–45), shown opposite, came from *The Green Book of Birds* (1931) by the American naturalist Frank G. Ashbrook, a book that he had come across while staying in Manhattan as a guest lecturer at the New School for Social Research.

Below: Josef Frank in front of one of his many textile designs created for Svenskt Tenn (Sweden), 1950s

Opposite: Gröna Fåglar (Green Birds) textile by Josef Frank for Svenskt Tenn (Sweden), 1943–45

JOSEF FRANK + ACCIDENTISM

While living in Vienna, Josef Frank had been at the forefront of the Modern Movement, but he subsequently rejected the dogmatism that grew up around this new style. Instead, he formulated his own philosophical approach to design and architecture, which he termed 'Accidentism'. Its central tenet was that a home should reflect the personality of its owner, and not the other way around. Rather than designing 'form-follows-function' room sets, Frank sought to create emotionally engaging contemporary interiors that exuded comfort and homeliness. One of the ways in which he achieved this was through his colourful and lively textile designs, many of which featured fantastical flora and fauna. These designs were essentially a Scandinavian evolution of the richly patterned textiles that had been manufactured by the Wiener Werkstätte, of which Frank had been a member, and powerfully reflected the Swedish love of nature. Even on the shortest days of the dark Nordic winter, Frank's vibrant textiles bring the cheering promise of spring's renewal and summer's harvest.

Opposite: Butterfly textile by Josef Frank for Svenskt Tenn (Sweden), 1943–45

1. Tehran textile by Josef Frank for Svenskt Tenn (Sweden), 1943–45

2. Brazil textile by Josef Frank for Svenskt Tenn (Sweden), 1943–45

1.

2.

JOSEF FRANK CARPETS

A prodigiously talented colourist and pattern maker, Josef Frank did not subscribe to the idea of static *Gesamtkunstwerk* (total work of art) interiors, created by designers for their clients and never changed. He had a far freer approach to interior design, and loved homes that were bathed in natural light and that conveyed a sense of warm congeniality and creative spontaneity. For him, designing a room was about making it as liveable as possible for the people who would be using it.

Indeed, he was one of the first to grasp the concept of lifestyle design properly, and his designs for Svenskt Tenn exemplify this, for they can be mixed and matched easily. As well as his upholstery textiles, Frank also designed a number of richly hued and lively patterned carpets that similarly reflected a range of sources, from antique tiger-skin rugs to contemporary mosaic floors. Indeed, many of Frank's designs possessed a quasi-surrealistic proto-Postmodern quality that was decades ahead of its time.

1. Monster carpet, Model no. 19, by Josef Frank for Svenskt Tenn (Sweden), ca. 1950

2. Frank No. III carpet by Josef Frank for Svenskt Tenn (Sweden), 1930s

Opposite: Mosaik (Mosaic) carpet by Josef Frank for Svenskt Tenn (Sweden), late 1940s

1.

2.

SVEN MARKELIUS

One of Sweden's leading proponents of Modernism, Sven Markelius not only designed progressive International Style 'Funkis' buildings and avant-garde tubular-steel furniture (see p. 90), but also turned his hand to designing textiles that were equally forward-looking. He produced the three textiles shown here between the early 1950s and the early 1960s, and they reflect his love of geometric forms, which can perhaps be traced back to his training in the Swedish Neoclassical tradition. The colourways he chose for his textiles also suggest more than a passing interest in colour theory, and give his patterns a strongly contemporary feel. His colour-blocked textiles were manufactured not only in Sweden, but also by Knoll Textiles in New York. Indeed, in 1957 he was awarded first prize in the printed textile category of the American Institute of Decorators' annual competition for designs he had produced for Knoll. His spectrum-inspired Pythagoras textile was famously used to make an eye-catching wall hanging in the United Nations Economic and Social Council chamber in New York.

Opposite: Timmer textile by Sven Markelius for Nordiska Kompaniet (Sweden), 1958

1. Prisma textile by Sven Markelius for Ljungbergs Textiltryck (Sweden)/Knoll Textiles (USA), 1961

2. Pythagoras textile by Sven Markelius for Nordiska Kompaniet (Sweden), 1952 – originally designed for the United Nations Headquarters in New York

1.

2.

SIGVARD BERNADOTTE

Today, Scandinavian Modern rugs and carpets can command high prices in the collectors' market, especially those by Sigvard Bernadotte, who was born a Swedish prince but lost his title when he married a commoner. The reason for these high values is that despite being designed decades ago, Bernadotte's distinctive flat-weave and relief-pile carpets and rugs, which incorporated a host of different weaving techniques, have a remarkable contemporary freshness. A leading industrial designer during the Folkhemmet period, which ran from the 1930s to the mid 1970s,

Bernadotte designed all kinds of household product, including a lawnmower, a venting fan, a plastic picnic set, a kettle, tableware, cutlery, a typewriter and even a tin opener. He was an accomplished designer of silverware and jewellery, too. However, what is less well known is that as well as being a formidably talented product designer, Bernadotte was also a gifted pattern maker and colourist – as his harmoniously balanced and beautifully composed rugs and carpets attest. In the 1950s he also famously applied this skill to the design of the VirrVarr pattern, which was used to decorate laminate board manufactured by Formica (see p. 434).

Below: Flat-weave and relief-pile carpet by Sigvard Bernadotte (Sweden), ca. 1930s

1. Hand-woven flat-weave carpet by Sigvard Bernadotte (Sweden), 1950s

2. Relief-pile carpet by Sigvard Bernadotte for Nils Nessim (Sweden), 1940s

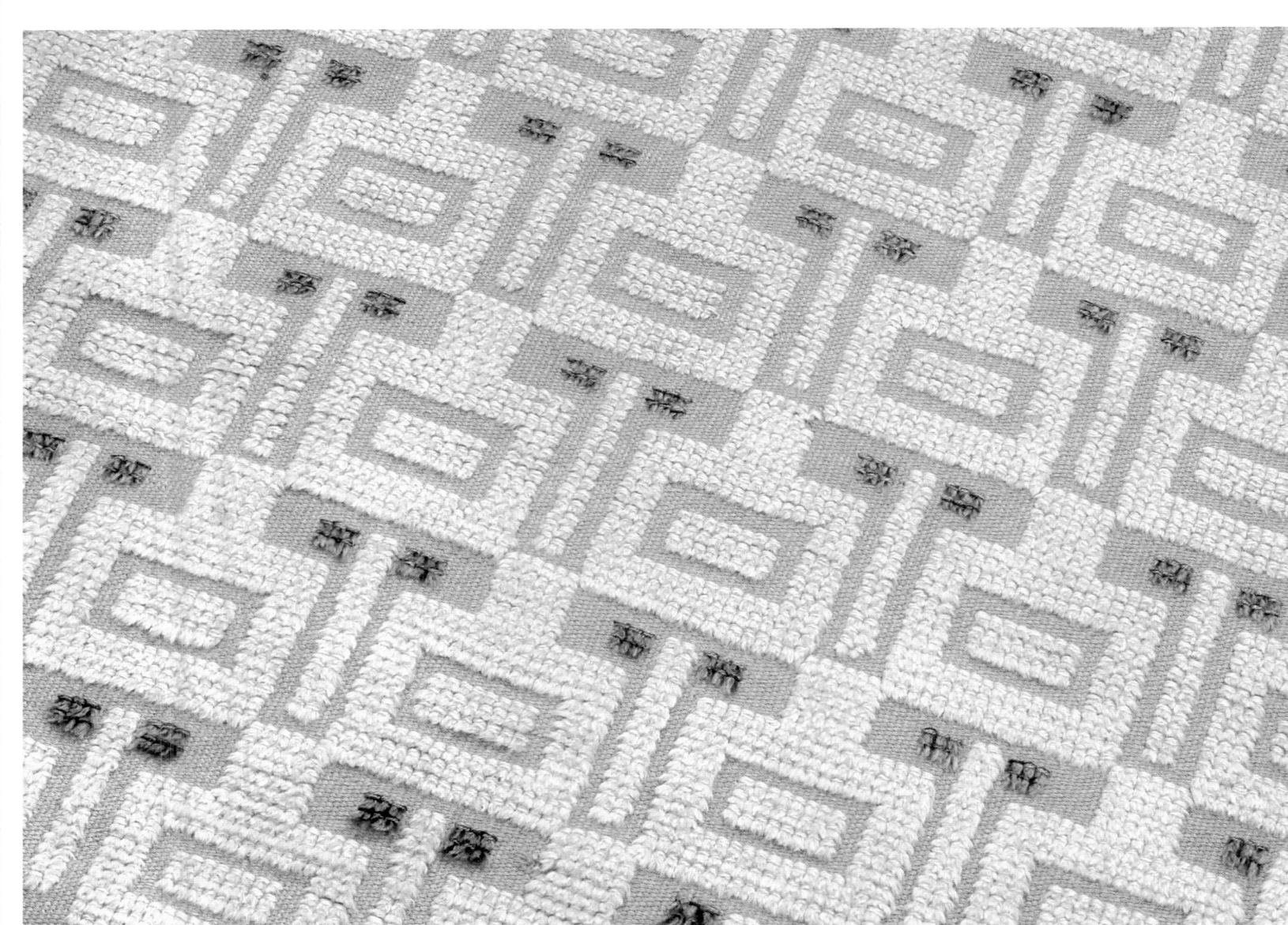

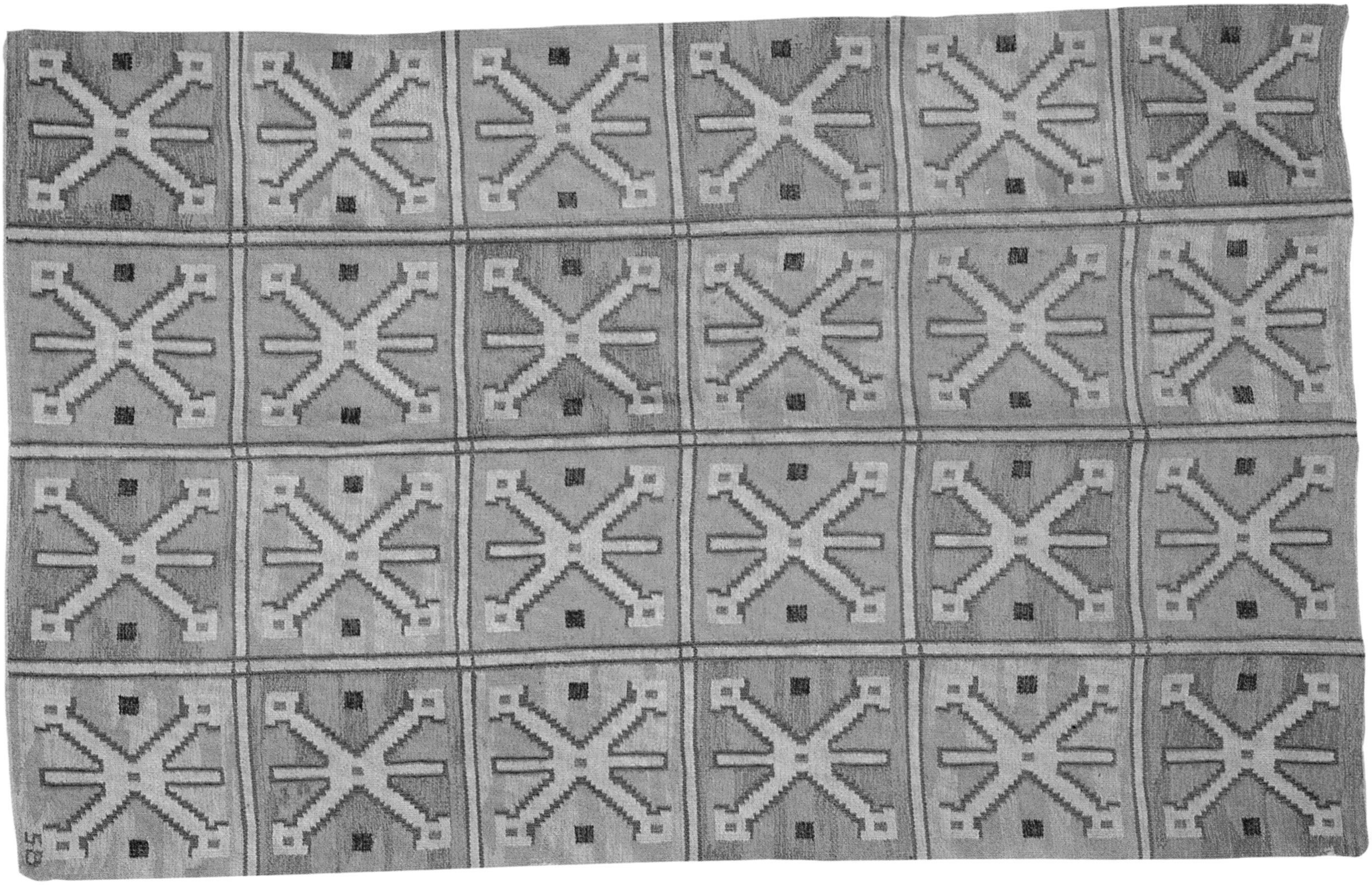

1.

2.

1.

2.

GOCKEN JOBS

Gocken Jobs was the younger sister of the ceramicist and textile designer Lisbet Jobs, and followed in her footsteps by training at the Tekniska Skolan in Stockholm. The sisters opened a ceramics workshop in 1931, but during the war, at the suggestion of Astrid Sampe, turned their attention to textile design. Their breakthrough in this field came in 1945 with their Stockholm exhibition 'När Skönheten Kom till Byn' (When Beauty Came to the Village), its name taken from a poem by Nils Ferlin. Gocken's colourful floral textiles shown here are representative of the Jobs sisters' work, and are still being produced by the textile company established by their brother Peer. As anyone who has ever had the privilege of experiencing high summer in Scandinavia will concur, Gocken's designs, with their stylistic representations of blossoming and swirling flora, ripened fruits and berries, and buzzing insects, capture the short-lived but bounteous nature of this wonderful season in the Nordic region.

1. Stugrabatt (Cottage Flowerbed) textile by Gocken Jobs for Jobs Handtryck (Sweden), 1951

2. Sommar (Summer) textile by Gocken Jobs for Jobs Handtryck (Sweden), 1954

Below: Rabarber (Rhubarb) textile by Gocken Jobs for Jobs Handtryck (Sweden), 1969

ALMEDAHLS

The Swedish industrialist Hans Wesslau acquired a textile mill in Gothenburg in 1840, and six years later, in the same city, purchased the Almedahl estate, where he built a state-of-the-art textile factory. The venture was one of the first Swedish mills to employ steam-driven mechanical looms for the production of linens and damasks. A highly enlightened employer, Wesslau was also an early adopter of corporate social responsibility, and provided housing for his workers as well as free medical care and free education for their children. In the late 1920s Almedahl merged with other mills, and by 1945 the Almedahl-Dalsjöfors Group had about 2,000 employees. In the 1950s it became renowned for progressive textile designs with a remarkable sense of contemporary freshness, such as Marianne Westman's Frisco (1952) and Pomona (ca. 1956) with their abstracted repeating patterns (see also pp. 346–47). In 1955 Astrid Sampe famously designed the revolutionary Linnelinjen (Linen Line) range, which was produced by Almedahls for Nordiska Kompaniet's Textilkammare and launched at the H55 exhibition in Helsingborg. That year Sampe also designed a printed tea towel in the well-known Perssons Kryddskåpp (Persson's Spice Rack) pattern, a tribute to the ceramicist Signe Persson-Melin (pp. 352–53), who had recently designed cork-stoppered spice jars that had attracted a vast amount of attention when shown at H55.

Below: Perssons Kryddskåpp (Persson's Spice Rack) textile by Astrid Sampe for Almedahls (Sweden), 1955 – initially designed as a printed tea towel, this pattern is now produced as a home textile

1. Frisco textile by Marianne Westman for Almedahls (Sweden), 1952

2. Pomona textile by Marianne Westman for Almedahls (Sweden), ca. 1956 – this pattern related to her Pomona ceramics range for Rörstrand, designed at about the same time

2.

STIG LINDBERG

In Sweden, the concept of the people's home – or *folkhemmet* – has not only long guided the country's social democratic politics, but also had an enormous impact on how Swedish designers view their role in society. Stig Lindberg was Sweden's most original and quintessential *folkhemmet* designer, for he focused tirelessly on creating designs that would enliven domestic interiors and help people to turn their houses into homes. His stylishly artful designs – from ceramics to textiles – unequivocally captured the widely held Swedish belief in the life-enhancing value of 'beautiful everyday things'. For example, his Mid-century Modern textile designs, which ranged from colourful and highly graphic repeating patterns to intricate pictorial wall hangings, have a charmingly naïve folk quality that was intended to give any domestic interior a feeling of homely warmth.

Opposite: Lustgården (Paradise) textile by Stig Lindberg for Nordiska Kompaniet (Sweden), 1950s

1. Pottery textile by Stig Lindberg for Ljungbergs Textiltryck, 1950s

2. Livets Träd (Tree of Life) printed velvet wall panel by Stig Lindberg for Nordiska Kompaniet (Sweden), 1950s

2.

1.

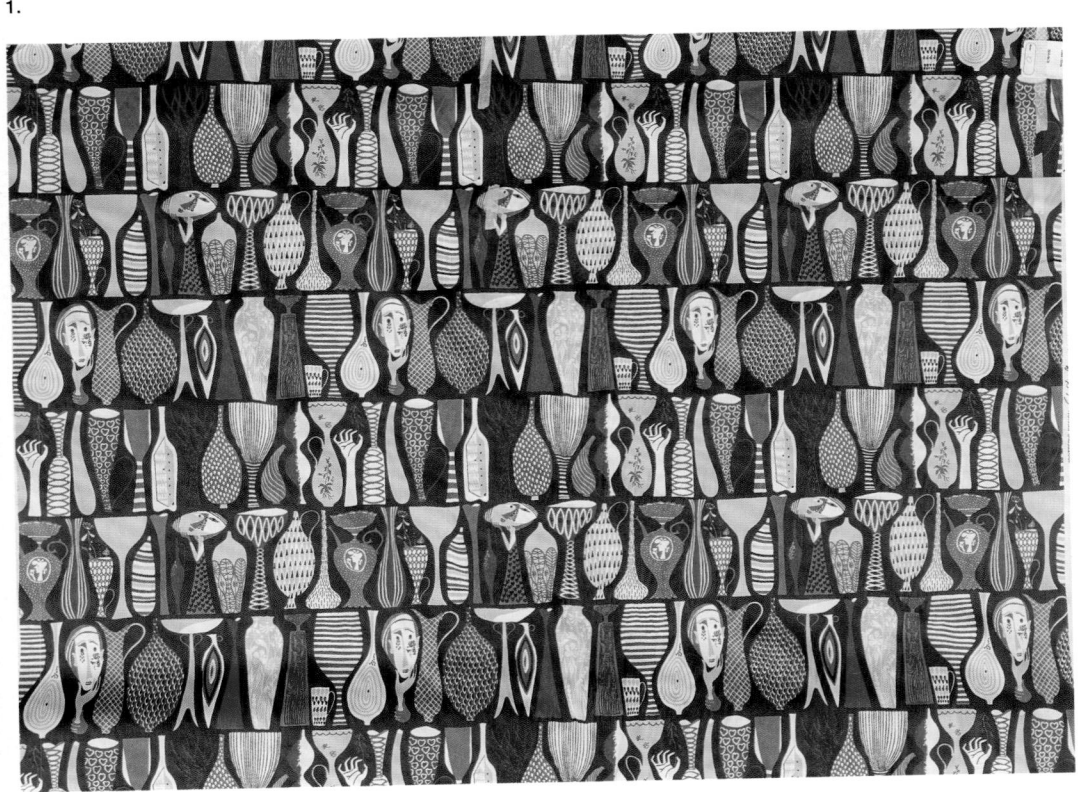

MAIJA ISOLA

Maija Isola designed a number of iconic textile patterns that captured the youthful and optimistic spirit of the Golden Age of Scandinavian design. Her earliest textiles, those from the 1950s, were inspired by African art and Slovakian folk motifs, but by the early 1960s she was designing silk-screen-printed textiles that increasingly reflected the Finnish love of strongly graphic pattern. Many of her designs were inspired by her surroundings: for instance, the twirling wheel-like motifs found in Joonas (1961) – Finnish for Jonah, the biblical figure who was swallowed by a whale – were based on shapes made by sunlight on salt water, which she had observed while holidaying in the Mediterranean. It was, however, her Kaivo (Well) textile, launched in 1964, that unleashed a new era of extra-large patterned textiles. It was part of her revolutionary Arkkitehi (Architects) series for Marimekko, conceived by that company's founder, Armi Ratia, as a means of encouraging architects and interior designers to use large-scale textile hangings in public and commercial buildings. Another bold macro-pattern from the same series was Unikko (Poppy), also designed in 1964. This fresh, vibrant floral textile became Isola's most enduring design, and is almost certainly more popular today than when it was introduced more than 50 years ago.

1. Lokki (Seagull) by Maija Isola for Marimekko (Finland), 1961

2. Joonas (Jonah) textile by Maija Isola for Marimekko (Finland), 1961

3. Kaivo (Well) textile by Maija Isola for Marimekko (Finland), 1964

Opposite: Unikko (Poppy) textile by Maija Isola for Marimekko (Finland), 1964

1.

2.

3.

VERNER PANTON

During his prolific career as one of Scandinavia's most daring design progressives, Verner Panton produced numerous colourful textile and carpet designs that featured strong geometric patterning. Among these, his Mira-X-Set Decor I range (1969), launched in 1971, is probably his most interesting, for it was based on an ingenious mathematical system. The patterns featured five basic motifs – square, circle, stripe, curve and checkers – divided into eight sections, and either manufactured in eight rainbow-like colours (turquoise, blue, violet, mauve, pink, dark red, bright red and orange) or produced in eight shades of a single colour. Each pattern was also produced in three different sizes, which were proportional in a ratio of 1:3:9. In 1975 Panton's more rhythmic Onion textile (1969–75), which possessed an even stronger Op Art aspect in a wide range of colourways, was added to the Decor I collection. These vibrant and distinctive textiles were an integral part of Panton's interior schemes, and were produced in two weights, suitable for using as curtains or upholstery; some of the patterns were also translated into carpet designs.

Below: Kurve textile from Decor 1 collection by Verner Panton for Mira-X (Germany), 1969 – introduced 1971

1. Onion textile from Decor 1 collection by Verner Panton for Mira-X (Germany), 1969 – introduced 1975

2. Square textile from Decor 1 collection by Verner Panton for Mira-X (Germany), 1969 – introduced 1971

3. Checkers textile from Decor 1 collection by Verner Panton for Mira-X (Germany), 1969 – introduced 1971

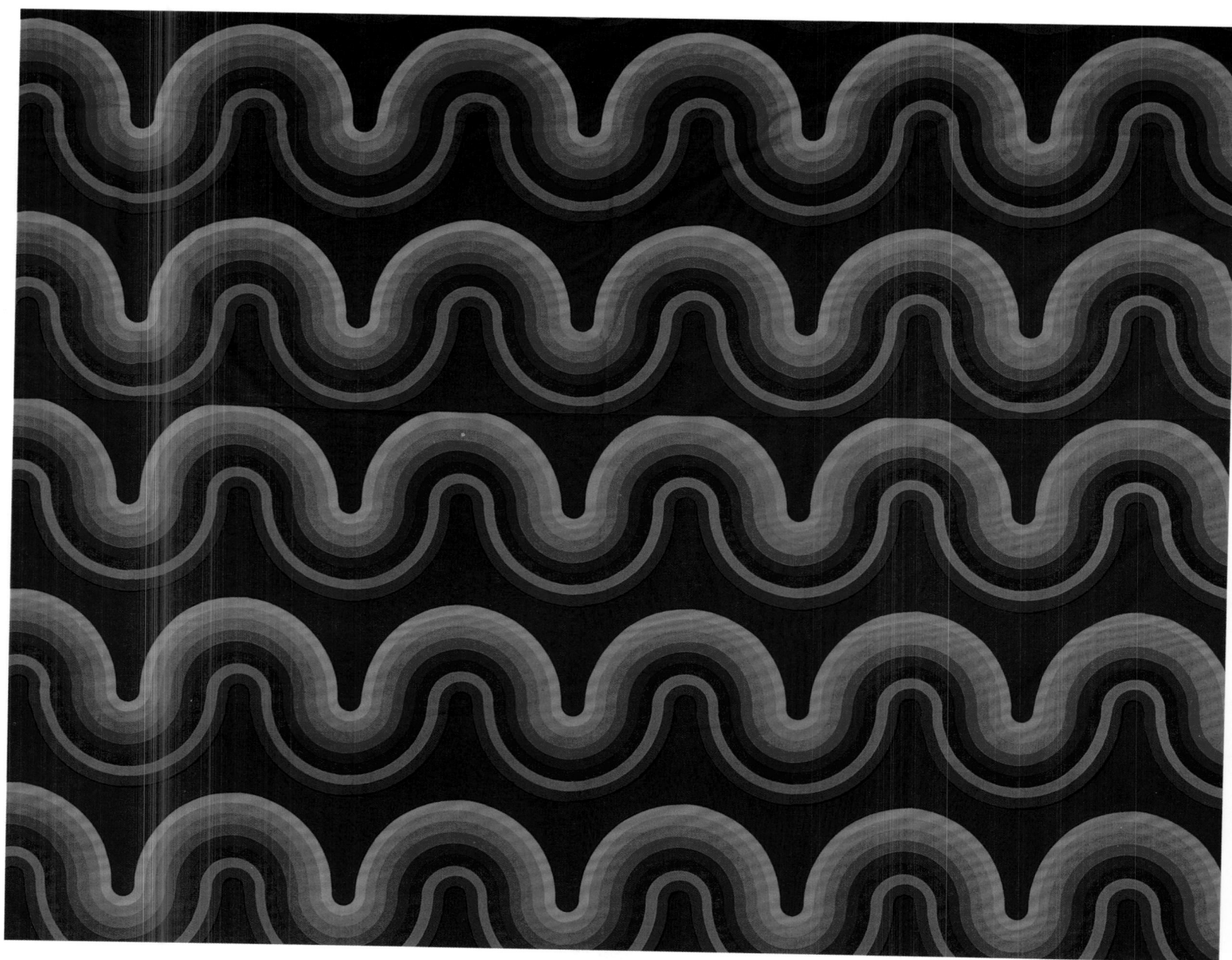

1.

2.

3.

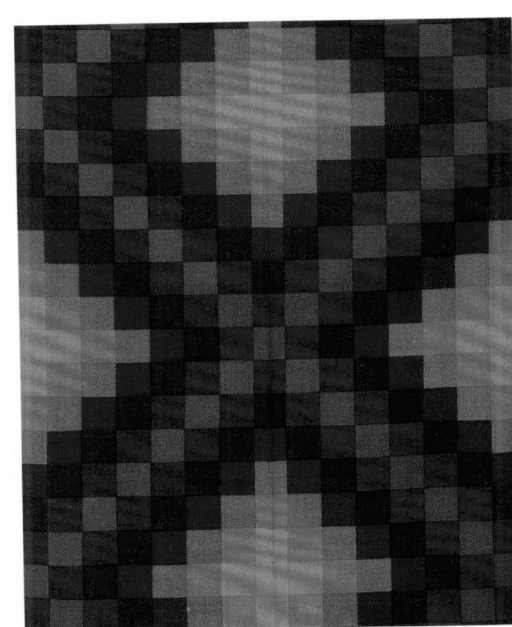

BORÅS

The Swedish city of Borås was an established centre for handcrafted textiles and textile dyeing even before the first weaving mill was founded there, in 1834. It was, however, Borås Wäfveri (Borås Cotton) that would make the city's name synonymous with Modern Swedish textiles. The firm's design zenith was from the 1950s to the 1980s, when it manufactured boldly patterned textiles by the likes of Gunila Axén, Vuokko Nurmesniemi, Sven Fristedt, Lisa Gustafsson, Birgitta Hahn, Lotta Hagerman, Hans Krondahl, Kerstin Persson, Saini Salonen, Ritwa Wahlström and

Helene Wedel – often adorned with large-scale, highly abstracted Pop-naïve motifs. Fristedt, who started working for the firm in 1965, is still employed there as a designer. His first textile for the company was Plexus (1958), which he drew with thick coloured crayons; it could not be printed using the production methods available at Borås, so its silk-screen printing was subcontracted to Ljungbergs Textiltryck, making it the first of many Borås silk-screen-printed textiles. Wedel, the creator of the bestselling Rio pattern (1960s), likewise designed a number of silk-screen-printed patterns for the company, produced in various vivid colour options.

Below: Plexus textile by Sven Fristedt for Borås (Sweden), 1958

Opposite: Rio textile by Helene Wedel for Borås (Sweden), 1960s – two different colourways

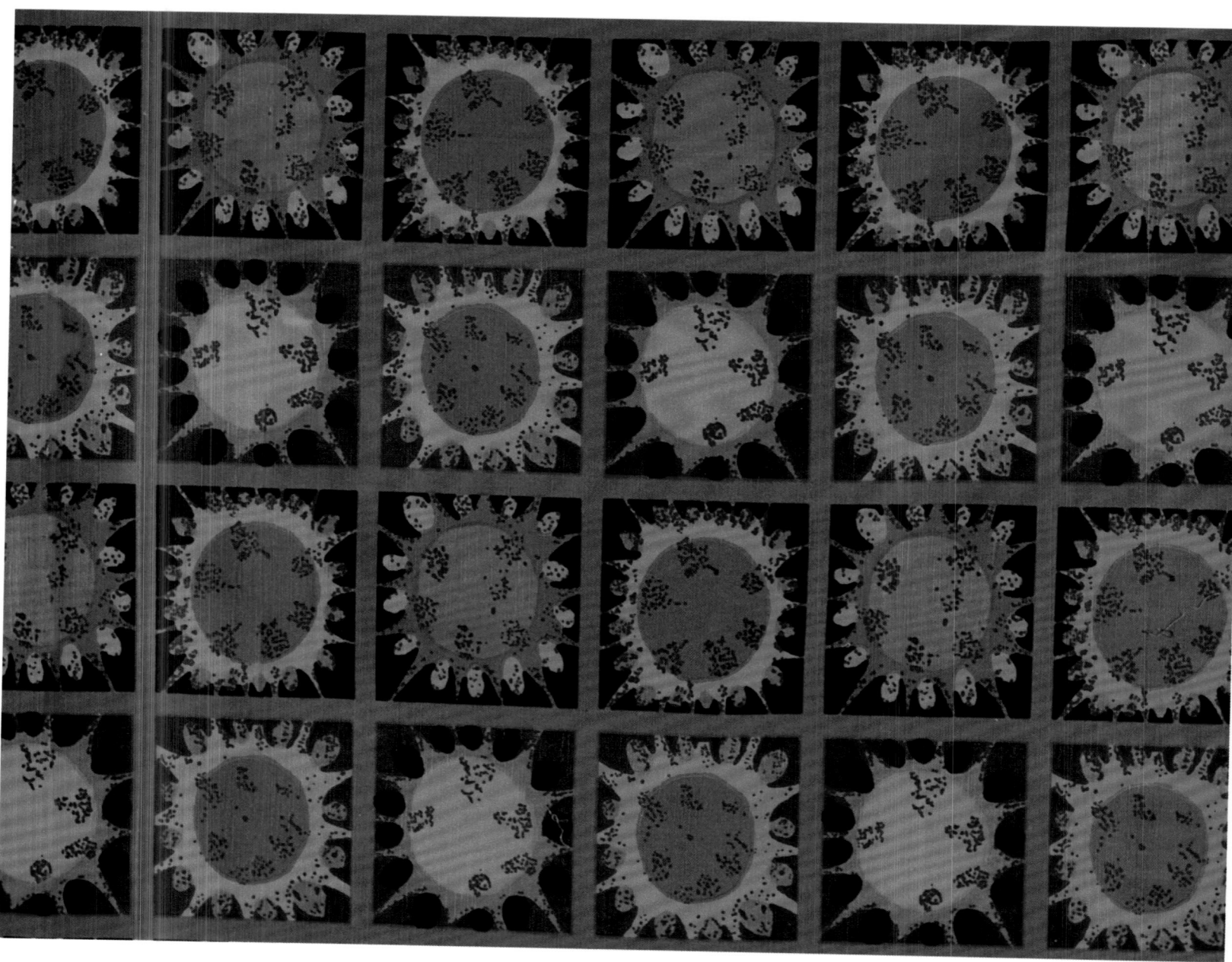

SAINI SALONEN

The Finnish textile designer Saini Salonen was a gifted colourist and skilled pattern maker. She created numerous designs for the renowned Swedish textile manufacturer Borås (see pp. 490–91) in the late 1960s and early 1970s, as brightly colourful as they were boldly patterned. She often incorporated highly abstracted, painterly representations of flowers into her large-print designs – as, for example, in her Sipuli and Lago textile designs, shown here, which came in an impressively wide range of colourways. At times her designs also exhibited an almost naïve, doodle-like quality, as with her exotic, floral Ekero and Mykero patterns and the gloriously multicoloured textile attributed to her, shown below, that takes the form of a gigantic psychedelic butterfly. Salonen's fantastically patterned and vibrantly hued textiles had a forthright Pop aesthetic and a striking graphic bravado that is characteristic of Finnish design in general.

Opposite: Lago textile by Saini Salonen for Borås (Sweden), 1970s

1. Butterfly textile by Saini Salonen (attributed) for Borås (Sweden), 1970s

2. Sipuli (Onion) textile by Saini Salonen for Borås (Sweden), 1970s

1.

2.

10 GRUPPEN

As a means of circumventing the Swedish textile industry, which they felt was strangulating innovative design, ten young and idealistic Swedish designers founded the 10 Gruppen (Group of 10) co-operative in 1970. The idea was that if they retained control of the production of their designs, they could perpetuate the innovation that had so long been associated with good Swedish design, but which they felt was now thin on the ground. The venture became the highest-profile design co-operative in Sweden, and the boldly coloured and patterned textiles created by its members – which included Birgitta Hahn, Tom Hedqvist

and Ingela Håkansson Lamm – helped to define the look of Swedish design in the 1970s and 1980s. Their work was even exhibited around the world. The collective opened its own destination shop on Stockholm's ever-so-trendy Södermalm island, selling all kinds of object made from its distinctive prints and textiles, which are now considered to be part of the Swedish design canon; it also created textiles for Borås Wäfveri and IKEA. The three textiles shown here, Kyoto (1972), Pinta (1992) and Circum (2002), were all produced by Borås, and are highly representative of the co-operative's distinctive work, being playful, bold and bright, and with a touch of Scandinavian quirkiness, too.

Opposite: Pinta textile by Birgitta Hahn as part of 10 Gruppen for Borås Wäfveri (Sweden), 1992

1. Kyoto textile by Tom Hedqvist as part of 10 Gruppen for Borås Wäfveri (Sweden), 1972

2. Poster for the 'Sea Collection' by 10 Gruppen (Sweden), 1975

3. Circum textile by Ingela Håkansson Lamm as part of 10 Gruppen for Borås Wäfveri (Sweden), 2002

1.

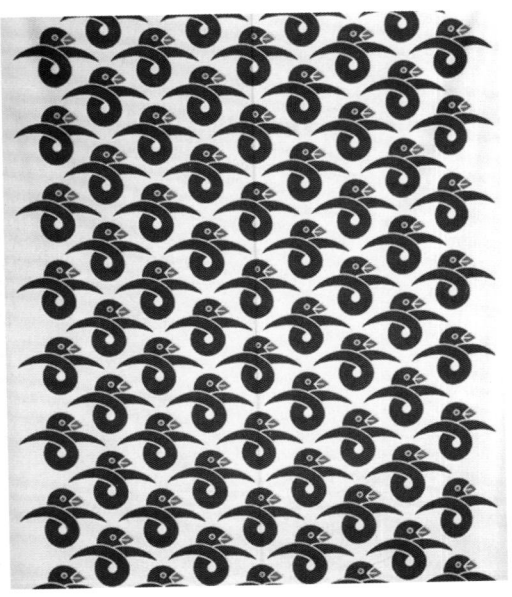

2.

3.

PIA WALLÉN

Like so many Scandinavian designers, Pia Wallén has always believed in the importance of preserving craft traditions that link the past to the present. Born in Umeå in northern Sweden, she moved to Stockholm in her early twenties and set up her eponymous fashion label in 1979. She studied fashion at Beckmans Designhögskola (Beckman's College of Design) in the city from 1980 to 1983. On graduating she began working with felt, a material she would make her own in terms of textile design over the coming decade. In 1991 she designed her Crux blanket for Element, which brought her widespread attention. She recalls, 'It's no coincidence that I designed my first felted wool blanket,

Crux, during the Kuwait invasion in 1991. The artist Joseph Beuys was also an influence … I've always been intrigued by the values that the cross represents. In Swedish folk art tradition, the cross is a strong symbol for hope, a meeting point of heaven and earth.' The following year Wallén was asked to participate in Cappellini's widely publicized Progetto Oggetto, which resulted in her Felt Programme and included her hugely popular felt slippers. In 1997 she established Pia Wallén AB and began designing for Asplund, producing carpets that were interesting in terms of shape and texture. Today Wallén's textiles are sold throughout the world by selected retailers and are represented in various permanent museum collections.

Below: Crux blanket by Pia Wallén for Element (Sweden), 1991 – later produced by Pia Wallén

1. Dot carpet by Pia Wallén for Asplund (Sweden), 2000

2. Felt slippers by Pia Wallén for Cappellini (Sweden), 1992 – later produced by Pia Wallén

3. Crux carpet by Pia Wallén for Asplund (Sweden), 1994

1.

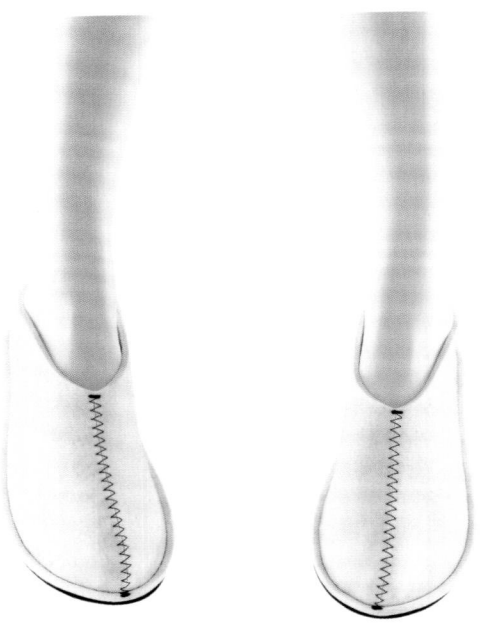

2.

3.

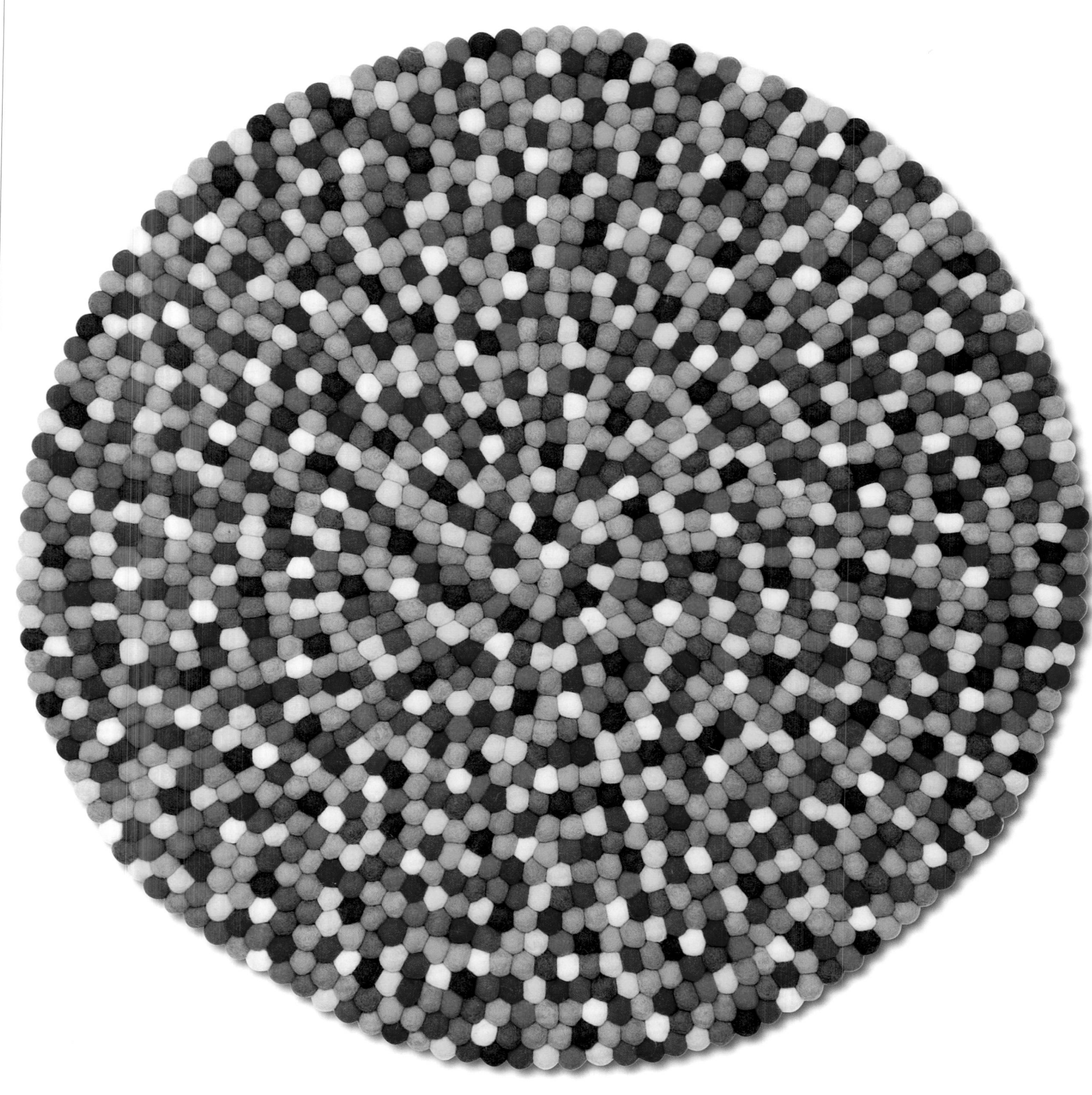

ASPLUND + HAY

The companies Asplund and Hay both produce rugs that perpetuate the long tradition of innovative rug design in Scandinavia. For more than 25 years Asplund, which is based in Stockholm, has been at the forefront of contemporary Scandinavian design with its manufacture of hand-tufted wool and wool-silk rugs, dhurries and kelims by world-renowned designers and design groups, including many from Sweden, namely Jonas Bohlin, Claesson Koivisto Rune, Thomas Sandell, Mats Theselius and Pia Wallén. Asplund's rug collection – which includes Sandell's stunning multi-hued Lapp and Pebbles rugs

(2010), shown below – accords with its belief that 'a product of good design is one that you can use and combine with almost any style, that looks good in any colour, and that seems to have been there forever.' The Danish company Hay is similarly committed to the ideals of good design, and likewise works with some of the world's leading designers, including a number from Scandinavia. However, its most famous rug, Pinocchio, was actually designed by Hay's in-house design team, and is made in local workshops by ingeniously stringing hand-rolled balls of felt together. The rug comes in a variety of colourways, and its name derives from a famous Danish brand of sugar-coated liquorice balls.

Opposite: Pinocchio carpet by Hay's in-house design team for Hay (Denmark), 2008

1. Pebbles carpet by Thomas Sandell for Asplund (Sweden), 2010

2. Lapp carpet by Thomas Sandell for Asplund (Sweden), 2010

2.

1.

MAIJA LOUEKARI + MARIMEKKO

The Finnish textile designer and illustrator Maija Louekari studied at the University of Art and Design in Helsinki and is now one of the main designers at Marimekko. Her career took off in 2003, when she won a competition organized by the company in conjunction with her alma mater. The pattern of her winning textile design, Hetkiä (Moments), took the form of a line drawing inspired by a vintage photograph of a street scene. It is, however, her Pakkanen (Frost) textile design of 2008,

with its lively hand-drawn bird perched on a tree branch with red berries, that best captures – in a lively, contemporary way – the fresh and cheerful spirit that has been synonymous with the Marimekko label since the 1950s (below). Louekari's Siirtolapuutarha (City Garden) cotton textile (2009; opposite) reflects the enduring connection with nature that has been characteristic of Finnish design since the 1950s. Over and above this, however, her work possesses a bold, eye-catching graphic confidence – yet another defining feature of Finnish design.

Opposite: Siirtolapuutarha (City Garden) cotton textile by Maija Louekari for Marimekko (Finland), 2009

1. Pakkanen (Frost) cotton textile by Maija Louekari for Marimekko (Finland), 2008

2. Puutarhurin Parhaat (Gardener's Best) textile by Maija Louekari for Marimekko (Finland), 2009

1.

2.

JEWELLERY

In the early twentieth century Scandinavian jewellery design was influenced by the British Arts and Crafts Movement, as well as trends from Germany and France. With the advent of Modernism in the late 1920s, however, a distinctively Scandinavian language of jewellery design evolved that reached its zenith between the 1950s and the 1970s.

Denmark's Georg Jensen is unquestionably Scandinavia's most renowned jewellery brand. Its eponymous founder trained as a goldsmith and later studied at the Kongelige Danske Kunstakademi (Royal Danish Academy of Fine Arts; KADK) in Copenhagen. After working as a silversmith for the artist-designer Mogens Ballin, Jensen opened his own silversmithy on Bredgade, Copenhagen, in 1904. Sales grew steadily, and in 1912 Jensen moved to larger premises and opened a shop, which was run by members of his wife's family. One brother-in-law, Harald Nielsen, worked as an engraver and later succeeded Jensen as the firm's artistic director.

By 1918 the firm's staff had grown to 125, and production expanded as the Danish economy flourished. Frederik Lunning, a gallery owner and salesman, opened a Georg Jensen shop in London in 1921 and two years later took the brand to New York, staging exhibitions for wealthy Americans at the Waldorf Astoria Hotel. Sales were phenomenal, and in 1924 he opened a Georg Jensen shop in New York.

In the 1930s the Skønvirke style (Danish Art Nouveau), which had been the mainstay of Georg Jensen's jewellery output, was increasingly supplanted by simpler Art Deco pieces. Danish jewellery firms that primarily worked in the Art Deco style included Edvald Nielsen, Anton Michelsen and Aage Dragsted. At Georg Jensen, the Art Deco style was exemplified in the designs of Oscar Gundlach-Pedersen and Arno Malinowski.

Sigvard Bernadotte began working for Georg Jensen in 1930, and his stark, geometric designs for the firm were unequivocally Modern. The biomorphic pieces designed by the artist Henning Koppel, however, received more attention. Indeed, the complexity of Koppel's designs pushed not only the physical properties of silver, but also the patience of Georg Jensen's silversmiths. Despite this, his perfectionism and vision inspired other designers, notably Hans Christensen, who became head of the model department in 1952. By the 1950s, biomorphism had been replaced by the so-called Scandinavian Modern style. In 1960 the Metropolitan Museum of Art in New York held an exhibition entitled 'Denmark: Viking to Modern', organized by the Danish Society of Arts and Crafts and Industrial Design. In addition to work by Georg Jensen, pieces by many of the designers who later worked for his firm were included in the show, most notably Nanna Ditzel, Arje Griegst, Edvard Kindt Larsen, Bent Gabrielsen and Erik Herløw.

Nanna Ditzel was the first woman to design for Georg Jensen. Her introduction to the company, with her first husband, Jørgen Ditzel, came in 1954 through Finn Juhl, who was designing Georg Jensen's 50th anniversary exhibition. Koppel felt that the company's product line could do with some more contemporary pieces, and the Ditzels' subsequent designs heralded the new 'Scandinavian Modern' look. Gabrielsen was also at the forefront of the expression of this emerging style; in 1957 his Model 115 necklace (1953), based on sycamore seed pods, won a medal at the 11th Milan Triennial. He often experimented with techniques gained during his travels, including a method of fire gilding that he had encountered during a trip to Egypt sponsored by his winning of the Lunning Prize in 1964.

Vivianna Torun Bülow-Hübe was the most famous designer working for Georg Jensen during the latter decades of the twentieth century. Raised in Sweden, she had studied in Stockholm under the jewellery designer Baron Erik Fleming. She also met Pablo Picasso on a beach in the French Riviera while gathering pebbles for her jewellery. This chance meeting resulted in her designs being shown at the Picasso Museum in Antibes. She designed jewellery for many famous performers, including Billie Holiday, Ingrid Bergman and Brigitte Bardot. Having begun designing for Georg Jensen in 1968, she remained one of the firm's key designers until her death in 2004.

In 1962 Søren Georg Jensen, the fifth son of the company's founder, succeeded Nielsen as the firm's artistic director. He also designed jewellery, which was distinctive for its use of delicately proportioned geometric shapes. Herløw and Othmar Zschaler experimented with similar angular forms in their designs for Georg Jensen. Other designers at the company in the 1960s were Griegst, who became known for his organic yet rough designs, and Ibe Dahlquist, who – in contrast to Griegst – used interlocking links with a strongly sculptural quality. In the 1960s, with the Scandinavian stainless-steel revolution in tableware and cutlery design in full swing, Georg Jensen focused increasingly on its jewellery production. By the 1970s, the restrained style of Danish jewellery had begun to fall behind as the USA and other countries forged ahead stylistically with more expressive designs. The firm was acquired in

Georg Jensen in his workshop in Bredgade in Copenhagen, ca. 1920

Model 159 Moonlight brooch by Georg Jensen for Georg Jensen (Denmark), 1914

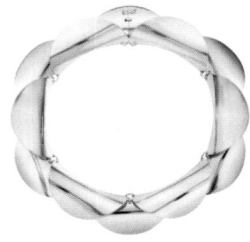

Silver necklace, Model 129, by Nanna Ditzel for Georg Jensen (Denmark), 1961

Daisy pendant by A. Michelsen (Denmark), 1940 – now re-edited by Georg Jensen

Necklace manufactured by Kalevala Koru (Finland), ca. 1950s – inspired by Viking designs

Opposite: Space Apple necklace by Björn Weckström for Lapponia (Finland), 1970

1972 by Royal Copenhagen, which merged with the Swedish companies Orrefors, Kosta Boda, Boda Nova, Höganäs and Venini to form the Royal Scandinavia Group. In 2001 the group was sold to the private equity group Axcel Capital, and in 2012 Georg Jensen was acquired by the Bahrain-based Investcorp. Since then the focus has been on the development of the firm's Living collection of homewares. New jewellery designs, however, have been added to the company's product line, while other 'classic' pieces from its illustrious past have been reintroduced.

The famous Danish firm of Anton Michelsen also shaped the development of Modern Scandinavian jewellery. In the 1850s Michelsen was commissioned to redesign the royal medals. The resulting expertise in enamelwork led to the most popular Danish jewellery of the twentieth century, the Daisy, created in 1940 to celebrate the birth of Princess (now Queen) Margrethe. The company was acquired by Royal Copenhagen in 1968 and eventually merged with Georg Jensen.

The Danish designer Hans Hansen opened a silversmithy in Kolding in the 1920s. His son Karl Gustav Hansen, who had begun working in the smithy in 1932, introduced Modernist jewellery of his own design to the company's product line, as well as designs by Gabrielsen, who was the firm's artistic director between 1953 and 1969. A number of other Danish Modernist silversmiths started their careers at Hans Hansen – among them Bent Knudsen, Eigil Jensen and Allan Scharff – and their designs were clearly influenced by the studio. One of Scharff's most famous pieces, the Alliance bangle, is now sold by Georg Jensen, although it was created for Hans Hansen. That firm was taken over by the Royal Scandinavia Group in 1991 and has since been incorporated into Georg Jensen.

Other noteworthy Danish jewellery companies and silversmiths include Volmer Bahner, Carl M. Cohr, Einer Fehrn, Niels Erik From, Bernard Hertz, Ole Lynggaard Copenhagen, Herman Siersbøl, Randers Sølvvarefabrik, W&SS Horsens Sølvvarefabrik and Algot Enevoldsen. Famously, the son of Algot Enevoldsen's founder went on to establish Pandora, one of the largest jewellery brands in the world, in 1982.

Finland also has a very strong history of innovative jewellery design. Its world-famous Kultakeskus (Gold Centre) was founded in Helsinki in 1897 by Nestor Westerback and moved to Hämeenlinna in 1918. Among the designs it produced were the medals and torches for the Summer Olympics held in Helsinki in 1952, and various sculptural silverware and jewellery by Tapio Wirkkala and Timo Sarpaneva. The designer Liisa Vitali also worked for Kultakeskus from the late 1960s, and some of her jewellery designs remain in production. Over the years the company has bought up a string of smaller manufacturers, and today it is the largest precious-metal company in Finland.

Another major name in Finnish jewellery design is Kalevala Koru (Kalevala Jewellery), which was established by Elsa Heporauta in Helsinki in 1935. Its foundation came from a plan to erect a statue dedicated to 'The Finnish Woman'. To fund it, Heporauta manufactured and sold copies of Viking jewellery that she had seen at the National Museum in Helsinki. The first collection was introduced in 1937 at a tea party held by Kaisa Kallio, the First Lady of Finland. When the Winter War started, in 1939, the charity helped by creating homes for refugees. Germund Paaer, who had designed for the company from the outset, became its head designer in 1950. He was succeeded by Börje Rajalin, who was in turn succeeded by Paula Häiväoja. Kaj Franck and Kirsti Ilvessalo also designed for the company, as did Eero Rislakki and Inger Lindholm. In 1989 Kalevala Koru acquired the jewellery manufacturer Kaunis Koru, and today it produces eye-catching contemporary jewellery with a very Finnish sensibility.

Lapponia is by far the most internationally celebrated Finnish jewellery company. It was founded by the silversmith Pekka Anttila in 1960, and three years later the highly talented Björn Weckström began designing for the firm, producing pieces that were unlike anything ever seen before in terms of sheer sculptural bravado. In 1965 Lapponia participated in the International Jewellery Contest in Rio de Janeiro, Brazil, where Weckström's golden necklace Flowering Wall won the Grand Prix. Weckström sometimes combined silver and acrylic in his designs, a practice that was then considered rather strange, but all that changed when John Lennon appeared on the *Dick Cavett Show* in 1975 with Yoko Ono wearing a Petrified Lake acrylic ring by Weckström. In 1977 Weckström's silver necklace Planetoid Valleys (1969) was worn by the actor Carrie Fisher in the closing scene of the first *Star Wars* film, having been personally selected by its director, George Lucas. Lapponia was acquired by Kalevala in 2005, and in 2013 the two companies merged.

The Finnish silversmith Bertel Gardberg worked in Copenhagen before setting up a studio in Helsinki in 1949. While he is better known for his cutlery and hollowware designs, he also created a number of noteworthy Modernist jewellery pieces, including some for Georg Jensen. Another pioneer of Finnish jewellery design was Elis Kauppi, who founded Kupittaan Kulta in 1945 and subsequently led the trend away from the popular mid-century floral patterns to more emphatically Modern pieces. Kupittaan Kulta exported much of its production to other Nordic and central European countries, but also to the USA and Japan. Modern Finnish jewellery, however, made its real breakthrough with an exhibition held in the Artek shop in Helsinki in 1958, which included work by Gardberg, Kauppi, Rajalin and Rislakki.

Pentti Sarpaneva (older brother of Timo Sarpaneva) was a noted Finnish jewellery designer, who created pieces that were as distinctive as they were innovative. He had studied graphic design at the Institute of Industrial Arts in Helsinki, and a major influence on his work was his childhood spent in the countryside with his father, a blacksmith. Pentti's designs were inspired by the bark of trees, weathered and dead pines, and Karelian embroidery, among other things. He initially worked in the 1960s for Kalevala Koru, but in 1967 was appointed head designer for Turun Hopea (Turku Silver). Sarpaneva worked mainly in bronze, and many of his large cast pieces were enhanced with the addition of amethyst, rose quartz and smoky quartz, all of which are found in Finland. His idiosyncratic designs were mainly exported to Sweden and Norway, but also sold in Denmark, the USA, Japan and the UK.

David-Andersen, Norway's leading silversmithy, was established in 1876 by David Andersen. The company gained fame through its production of enamel jewellery in the early twentieth century, when it was under the direction of the founder's son Arthur David-Andersen. After World War II the firm exported most of its production, with designs by Willy Winnaess based on butterflies and leaves being among the most successful. Later designers who created notable designs for the Oslo-based firm include Bjørn Sigurd Østern, Harry Søby, Marianne Berg, Unn Tangerud, Ben David-Andersen and Uni David-Andersen. Aksel Holmsen, who had worked for David-Andersen, founded his own firm in Oslo and produced Modern jewellery designs, many featuring enamelling; they were likewise of exceptional quality in terms of both design and execution.

Grete Prytz Kittelsen, daughter of the goldsmith Jacob Tostrup Prytz, also created striking jewellery designs, including large-scale enamelled silver brooches and unusual necklaces that incorporated Venetian glass segments by Paolo Venini. In a similar vein, the Stavanger jewellery designer Øystein Balle produced distinctive Modernist silver pieces during the 1950s and 1960s, incorporating abstract enamel work in vivid hues.

During the 1960s, the Norway Silver Designs workshop – an offshoot of the PLUS applied arts centre in Fredrikstad – won international recognition for its innovative silver jewellery designs by Erling Christoffersen and his wife, Anna Greta Eker, and by Tone Vigeland. When the business was closed, in the 1970s, Eker started her own workshop, making hand-hammered jewellery in both geometric and organic forms that incorporated semi-precious stones, hand-blown glass and wooden beads. Vigeland's international breakthrough came in 1981, when she exhibited her designs at the Electrum Gallery in London; that was followed by shows in New York, Tokyo and other major cities.

Swedish designers also contributed to the development of a distinctive Nordic Modern jewellery style. One of the pioneers was Baron Erik Fleming, who trained as an architect and engineer, but became a silversmith. He founded Atelier Borgila in Stockholm in 1921, and produced designs by Sigurd Persson, Birger Haglund and Stig Engelbert, among others. In 1948 Fleming sold the company to the Boliden Mining conglomerate, which ran the company until 1959, when Fleming's son Lars bought it back. The silversmith Henrik Ingemansson acquired Borgila in 2004, and to this day the workshop produces bespoke pieces as well as designs based on the 6,000 original drawings in its archive.

Wiwen Nilsson studied in Germany, Denmark and France, and also learned his trade in his father's Lund-based silversmithy, which he took over in 1927. He made a name for himself when he launched his designs at the Gothenburg Exhibition of 1923, and later showed Modern pieces in the geometric Art Deco style at the Stockholm Exhibition of 1930. Most of his jewellery featured large, boldly faceted stones in simple geometric settings, but he also designed highly stylized oriental-inspired brooches.

From the succeeding generation of Swedish designers, Sigurd Persson also followed in his father's footsteps, undertaking his apprenticeship in his father's goldsmithy in Helsingborg. He passed his journeyman's examination in 1938, and opened a studio in Stockholm four years later. During the war he designed for Atelier Borgila. Persson's jewellery always kept up with current trends and was formally inventive.

Theresia Hvorslev was a student of the goldsmith Sven Arne Gillgren, who was chief designer at the Swedish company Guldvaru G. Dahlgren in Malmö. After graduating from the Konstfack (University College of Arts, Crafts and Design) in Stockholm, she apprenticed with Georg Jensen and then worked for Bernadotte & Bjørn, as well as in Germany and Denmark. Hvorslev started her own workshop in 1964, and also designed jewellery for the firms Alton and Mema. In the 1970s her style evolved from the use

of precisely proportioned geometric lines into more sculptural voluptuous forms.

From 1930 to 1978 Guldsmedsaktiebolaget (GAB) produced Modern jewellery through its subsidiary, Guldvaru G. Dahlgren. Alton, in Falköping, in like manner manufactured interesting designs that fell within the Nordic Contemporary style. Its head designer from 1947 until the 1970s was Karl Erik Palmberg, who designed a number of innovative Brutalist pieces in silver and bronze. The firm also produced designs by Per Dåvik. In 1989 Alton purchased the Gothenburg firm of Ceson, whose head designer from 1943 to 1976 was Thore Eldh. Both Alton and GAB were bought by Svenskt Guldsmide & Design in 1996.

Flowering Wall gold and tourmaline pendant by Björn Weckström for Lapponia (Finland), ca. 1965

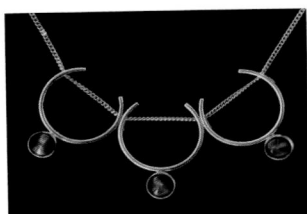

Silver and tiger's-eye necklace by Elis Kauppi for Kupittaan Kulta (Finland), ca. 1970s

Bronze necklace by Pentti Sarpaneva for Turun Hopea (Finland), 1970s

Silver collar and pendant by Theresia Hvorslev for Mema (Sweden), 1972

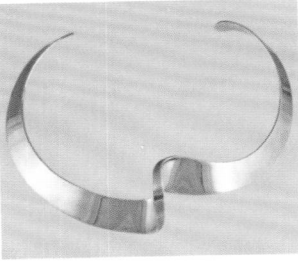

Silver collar by Karl Erik Palmberg for Alton (Sweden), 1978

WIWEN NILSSON

A Swedish designer born in Copenhagen, Wiwen Nilsson was an important and early pioneer of Modern Scandinavian jewellery design, whose work was astonishingly forward-looking. His father, Anders Nilsson, was the Danish court jeweller, and Wiwen learned his trade in his father's workshop in Lund. Later he studied at the Königlich Preußische Zeichenakademie (Royal Prussian Drawing Academy) in Hanau, Germany, and at the Académie de la Grande Chaumière in Paris. He rejoined his father's company in 1923, and that year he launched his own designs at the Gothenburg Exhibition. He subsequently took over the running of his family's workshop, and in 1930 exhibited his Modern silverware designs at the Stockholm Exhibition, to widespread acclaim. In the 1930s he created a number of jewellery pieces, such as the crystal and onyx cross shown right, that were equally innovative and possessed a strongly geometric Modern quality. Indeed, this bold and chunky look became his trademark, as can be seen from his later designs, and presaged the sculptural work of later Scandinavian jewellery designers.

1. Silver necklace with crystal and black onyx cross pendant by Wiwen Nilsson (self-produced) (Sweden), 1934 – this remarkably forward-looking design was shown at the Exposition Internationale des Arts et Techniques dans la Vie Moderne, Paris, in 1937

2. Silver and rock crystal pendant by Wiwen Nilsson (self-produced) (Sweden), 1946

3. Gold and citrine ring by Wiwen Nilsson (self-produced) (Denmark), ca. 1953

4. Gold and amethyst ring by Wiwen Nilsson (self-produced) (Sweden), 1966

5. Gold brooch by Wiwen Nilsson (self-produced) (Sweden), 1967

1.

2.

3.

4.

5.

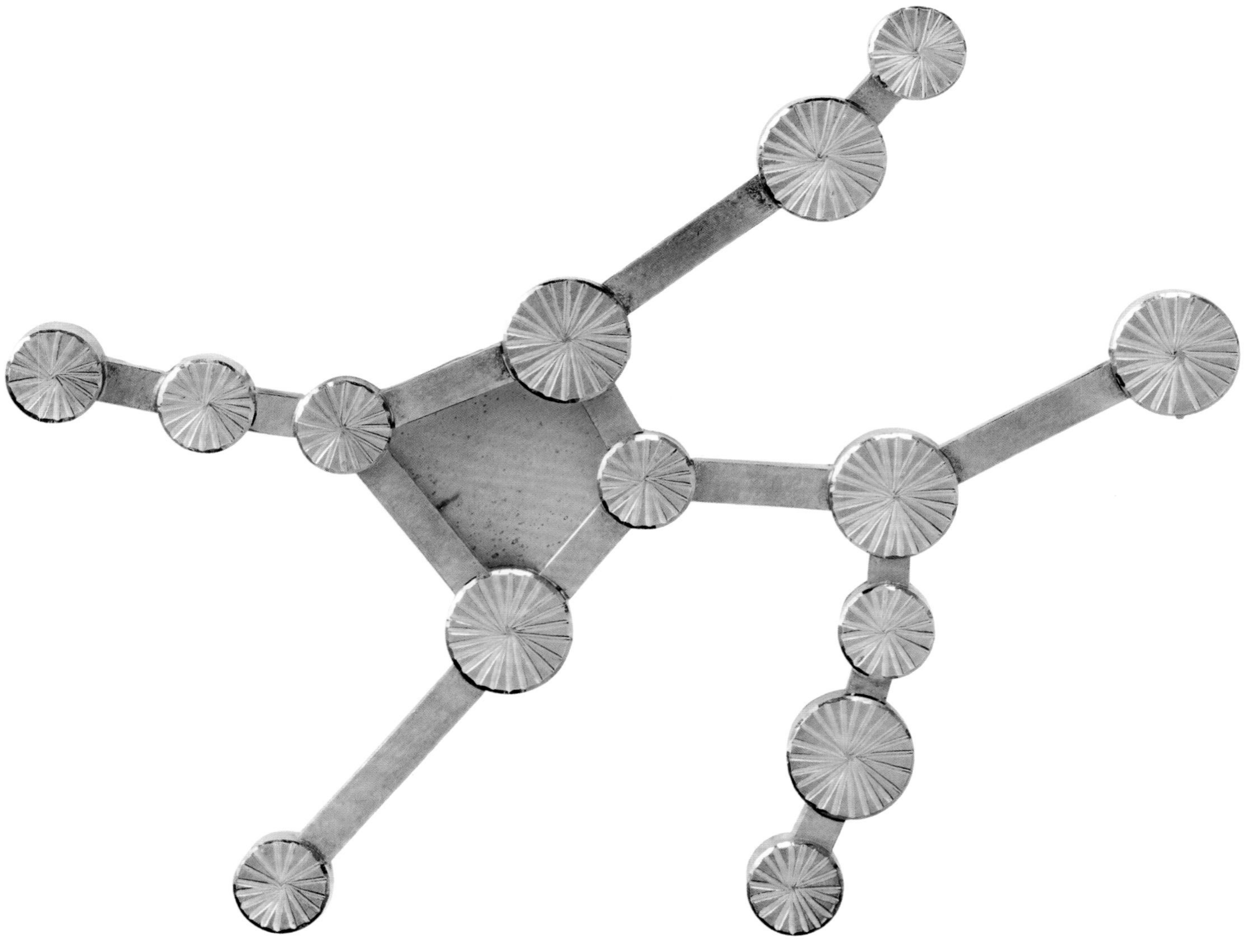

ARNO MALINOWSKI

A talented sculptor and engraver, Arno Malinowski trained at KADK in Copenhagen before embarking on a career as a designer. Although he is today best known for the jewellery designs he produced for the Georg Jensen silversmithy, he also created figurines and stoneware pieces for the Royal Copenhagen porcelain factory, as well as a dinner service that was awarded a Grand Prix at the Exposition Internationale des Arts Décoratifs et Industriels Modernes in Paris in 1925. Between 1935 and 1944 and again from 1949 to 1965 he worked as an in-house designer for Georg Jensen, creating various hollowware designs as well as numerous Art Deco-style pieces of jewellery, much of which featured highly stylized scenes and had a distinctive 'signature' geometric flatness. Among his best-known pieces are his Kneeling Deer and Moonlight Blossom brooches (both 1942). Malinowski also designed the silver and enamel Kingmark badge to commemorate the seventieth birthday of King Christian X in 1940; it was worn as a symbol of patriotism and resistance to German occupation by a great number of Danes during World War II.

1. Wheat gold cufflinks, Model 78C, by Arno Malinowski for Georg Jensen (Denmark), 1958

2. Moonlight Blossom brooch by Arno Malinowski for Georg Jensen (Denmark), 1942

3. Kneeling Deer brooch, Model no. 256, by Arno Malinowski for Georg Jensen (Denmark), 1942

4. Deer and Squirrel silver brooch by Arno Malinowski for Georg Jensen (Denmark), 1930s

5. Dolphin brooch by Arno Malinowski for Georg Jensen (Denmark), 1930s

6. Birds and Wheatsheaf silver brooch by Arno Malinowski for Georg Jensen (Denmark), 1939–1940

1.

2.

3.

4.

5.

6.

1.

2.

DAVID-ANDERSEN + SIGURD PERSSON

During the postwar period many jewellery designers in Scandinavia looked to the natural world for inspiration, and as a result produced highly stylized yet abstracted floral designs that had a strong organic quality and a sophisticated formal refinement. In Sweden, Sigurd Persson designed a very attractive necklace of interlocking leaf shapes, and also brooches and earrings that took the form of leafy sprigs. In Norway, meanwhile, the firm David-Andersen, a silversmith well known for its exquisite enamel work, manufactured designs that similarly incorporated leaf-like and petal-like forms. A suite of jewellery with a rhythmic double-leaf repeating motif, designed by Willy Winnaess in about 1950, was produced by David-Andersen in a number of colours and became one of the company's most commercially successful designs of all time.

1. Silver interlocking-leaf necklace by Sigurd Persson for Stigbert (Sweden), 1954

2. Silver brooch and matching earrings by Sigurd Persson (self-produced) (Sweden), 1945

Below: Silver and enamel necklace, bracelet and matching earrings by Willy Winnaess for David-Andersen (Norway), ca. 1950

NANNA + JØRGEN DITZEL

In 1949 Nanna and Jørgen Ditzel spent a month in Paris, where they sketched pieces of jewellery displayed in the museums they visited. The following year, at home with a new baby, Nanna began designing a matching ring, bangle, necklace and brooch for a competition held by the Danish goldsmiths' association, Guldsmedefagets Fællesråd, a contest that she won. The court jeweller, A. Michelsen, later produced her early prize-winning silver-gilt suite. Five years later, while working on the design of an exhibition for Georg Jensen,

Finn Juhl told Anders Hostrup-Pedersen, the silversmith's artistic director, that he needed to make something 'new' and should commission the Ditzels to come up with some contemporary pieces. The resulting body of work was impressively simple and expressive, and had a bold abstract quality that recalled the sculptures of Henry Moore and Jean (Hans) Arp. The Ditzels' beautiful jewellery designs for Georg Jensen embodied a new contemporary spirit in Scandinavian design and became a powerful symbol of Danish design excellence around the world.

Below: Necklace by Nanna and Jørgen Ditzel for A. Michelsen (Denmark), ca. 1960

1. Bracelet by Nanna and Jørgen Ditzel for Georg Jensen (Denmark), 1954

2. Bangle by Nanna Ditzel for Georg Jensen (Denmark), 1960

3. Bangle by Nanna Ditzel for Georg Jensen (Denmark), 1960

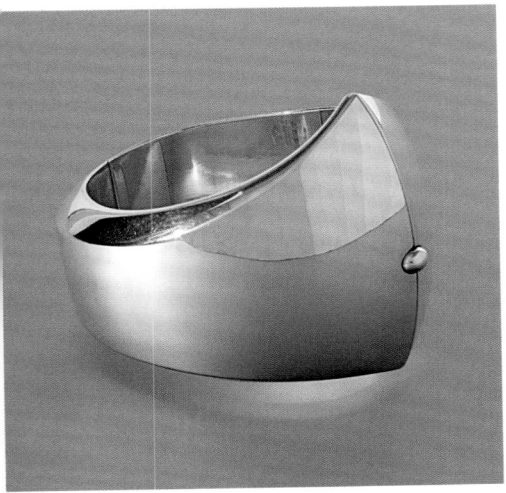

1.

3.

2.

HENNING KOPPEL

Of all the jewellery designed by Henning Koppel for Georg Jensen, the Model 88B necklace is surely the most distinctive, with its interlinking splash-shaped elements (opposite). This stunning design not only epitomizes the playful organicism found in Koppel's work, but also reflects the strong influence contemporary fine art had on the applied arts during the postwar period.

His free-form silver and enamel, fish-inspired brooch also channelled trends from the world of fine art, its abstracted bird-like motif recalling the work of Henri Matisse and Pablo Picasso. During the 1950s Koppel also created other jewellery pieces that were much more geometric, and these anticipated the fashion for such forms in jewellery design in the 1960s and 1970s, when the biomorphism of the 1950s had become passé.

1. Splash necklace, Model 88B, by Henning Koppel for Georg Jensen (Denmark), 1947

2. Stylized fish brooch, Model No. 307, by Henning Koppel for Georg Jensen (Denmark), 1959

Opposite: Bird pendant by Henning Koppel for Georg Jensen (Denmark), 1950s – produced by Georg Jensen in 2000 as its Annual Artist Pendant

1.

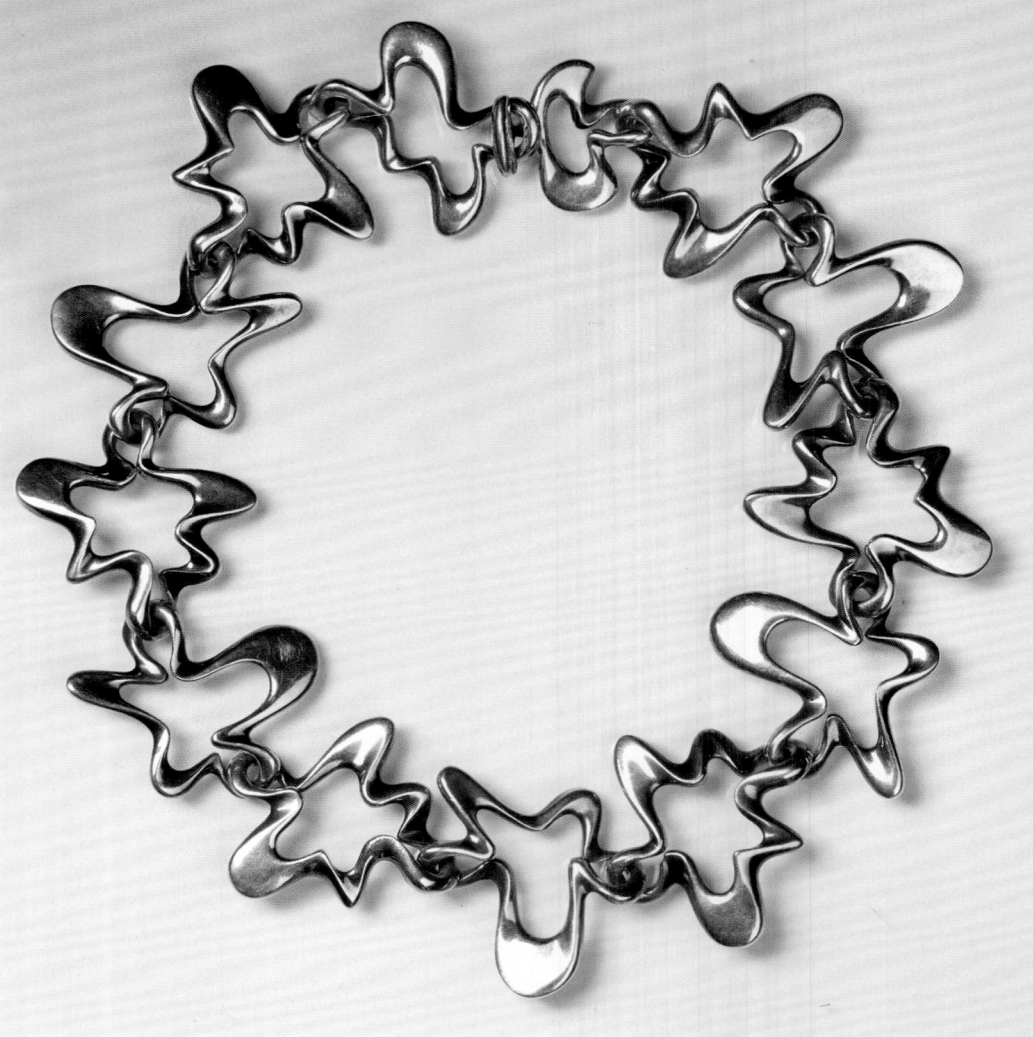

2.

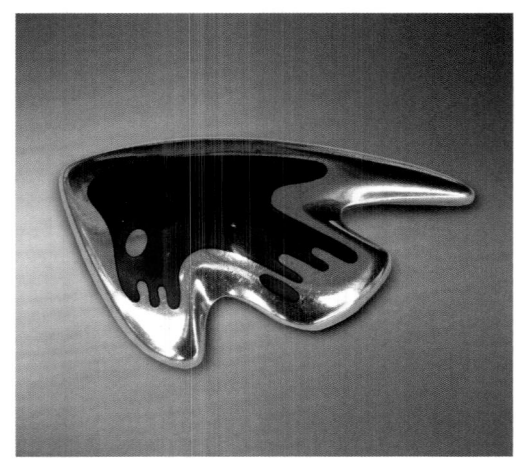

VIVIANNA TORUN BÜLOW-HÜBE: THE FRENCH CONNECTIONS

A legendary free spirit, Vivianna Torun Bülow-Hübe was one of the pre-eminent jewellery designers of her generation, and also the first female jewellery designer to enjoy widespread international recognition, thanks to her pioneering designs. Often referred to simply as Torun, she grew up in a highly creative family (her mother was a sculptor), and studied at the Konstfack in Stockholm. She was the first female silversmith in Sweden to establish her own workshop. She held her first exhibition when she was only 21 years old, and in 1948 she travelled to Paris and Cannes, where she famously met Pablo Picasso on a beach while searching for pebbles to include in her 'anti-status jewellery' designs. That year she married her second husband, a French architect, and in 1956 she moved to Biot in southern France with her third husband, the African-American artist Walter Coleman. There, she established another studio. The three necklaces shown here reflect Torun's desire to create wearable pieces that were strongly feminine and did not convey the ideas of wealth and status traditionally associated with high-end jewellery.

Below: Necklace with rock crystal drops by Vivianna Torun Bülow-Hübe (self-produced) (France), ca. 1954

1. Necklace with two stone pendants by Vivianna Torun Bülow-Hübe (self-produced) (France/Denmark), 1950s

2. Vivianna Torun Bülow-Hübe wearing her own jewellery, Paris, 1956

3. Necklace with quartz pendant by Vivianna Torun Bülow-Hübe (self-produced) (France), 1950s

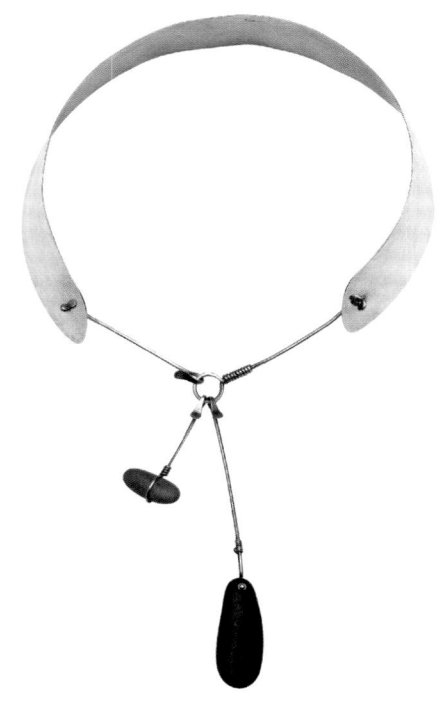

1.

2.

3.

'TORUN' + GEORG JENSEN

After Georg Jensen himself, Vivianna Torun Bülow-Hübe, often just known as 'Torun', is generally considered to be the highest-profile designer to have worked for his renowned silversmithy in Copenhagen. The reason is that her game-changing designs not only broke new ground both functionally and aesthetically, but also look as fresh today as when they were first introduced. This is no doubt because of their sculptural refinement and interesting symbolism. A case in point is her iconic Vivianna Bangle watch (opposite), which was designed as an 'anti-watch' for

the exhibition 'Antagonism II' at the Musée des Arts Décoratifs in Paris in 1962. Torun later explained that she chose to employ an open-ended bangle rather than a closed strap so that the wearer would not become 'a prisoner of time', and incorporated a mirrored face to remind one of 'the here and now'. The design was also unusual in that its dial was unnumbered, which added to its sculptural panache. Other key Torun designs for Georg Jensen were the Dew Drop necklace and earrings, and her eternal Mobius pendant and brooch, which revealed her ability to create instant classics that have remained impervious to the vagaries of fashion.

Opposite: Vivianna Bangle watch by Vivianna Torun Bülow-Hübe for Georg Jensen (Denmark), 1962

1. Vivianna Torun Bülow-Hübe wearing self-designed earrings and pendant necklace, 1950s

2. Mobius brooch by Vivianna Torun Bülow-Hübe for Georg Jensen (Denmark), 1968

3. Silver and pearl bracelet by Vivianna Torun Bülow-Hübe for Georg Jensen (Denmark), ca. 1968

1.

2.

3.

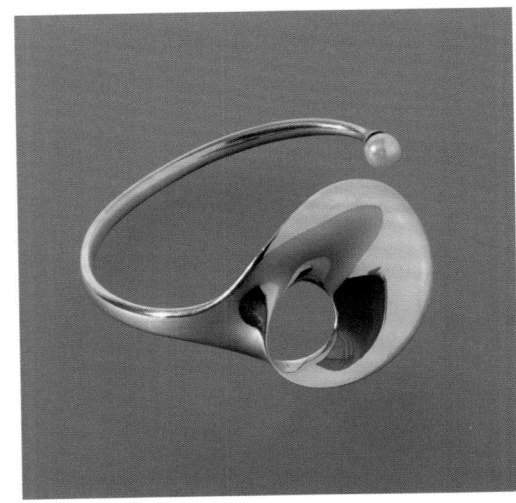

BJÖRN WECKSTRÖM

Drawing inspiration from the natural world, Björn Weckström has produced an impressive body of jewellery designs with a raw, sculptural, almost Brutalist aesthetic. For his gold pieces he was inspired by the irregular forms and matt surfaces of gold nuggets hewn from the Finnish landscape, while his silver pieces were influenced by winter in Finland, with its frozen lakes and epic snowy vistas. When Weckström began designing jewellery for Lapponia – a jewellery company he founded with Pekka Anttila in 1963 – he wanted to do, as he recalls, 'something totally new, totally different and to add three-dimensionality to jewellery design'. And that is exactly what he did by creating jewellery designs that function as 'sculptures in miniature' and evoke a sense of a 'complete landscape'. His Planetoid Valleys necklace (1969), which was famously worn by Princess Leia in the first *Star Wars* film (1977), is a perfect example of this rare ability to capture the ruggedness and beauty of the far North.

Below: Barbarella necklace from the Space Silver series by Björn Weckström for Lapponia (Finland), 1969 – this pendant was produced by Lapponia from 1973

1. Polaris cufflinks by Björn Weckström for Lapponia (Finland), 1973

2. Big Drop pendant necklace by Björn Weckström for Lapponia (Finland), 1970

3. Planetoid Valleys necklace by Björn Weckström for Lapponia (Finland), 1969

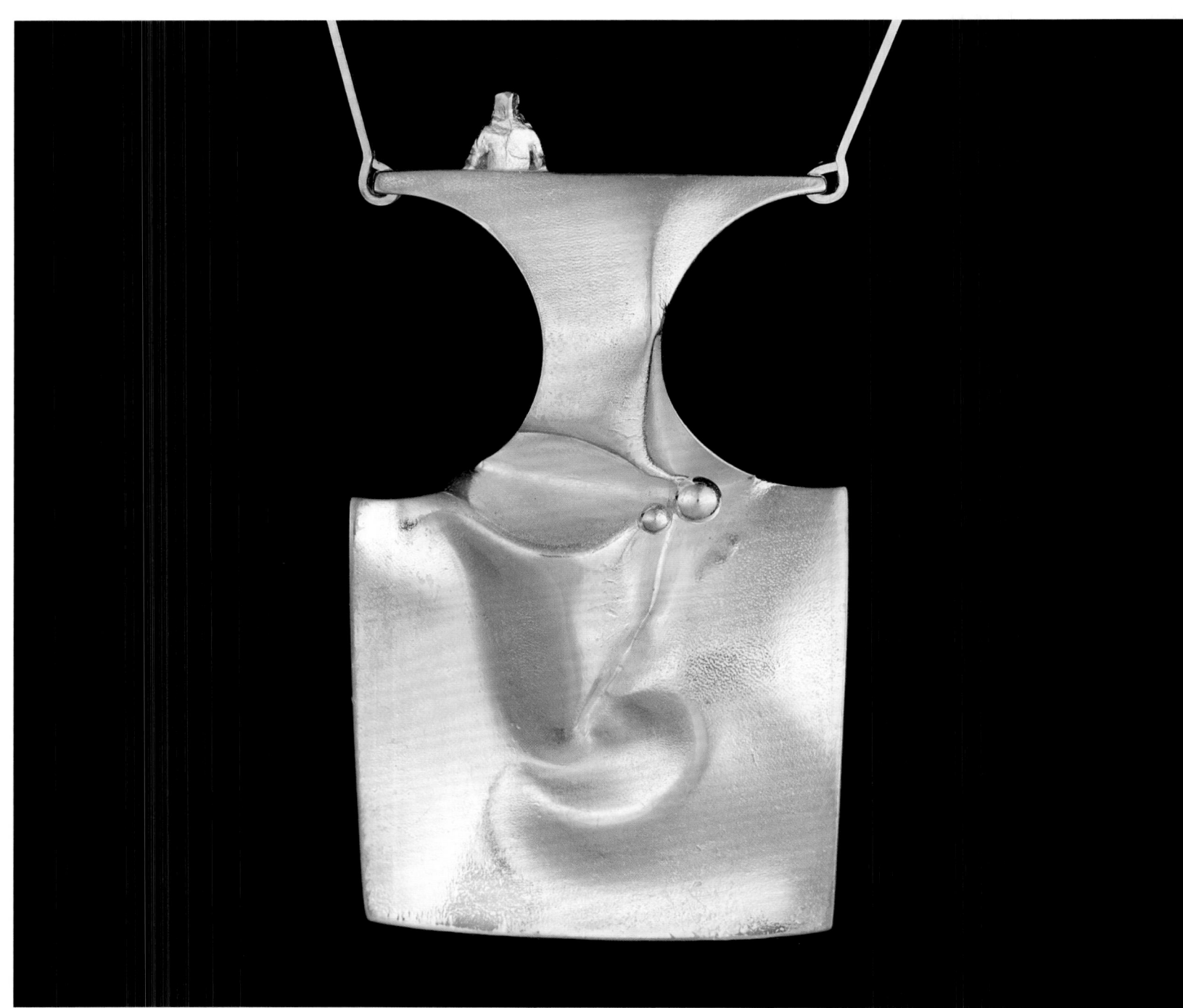

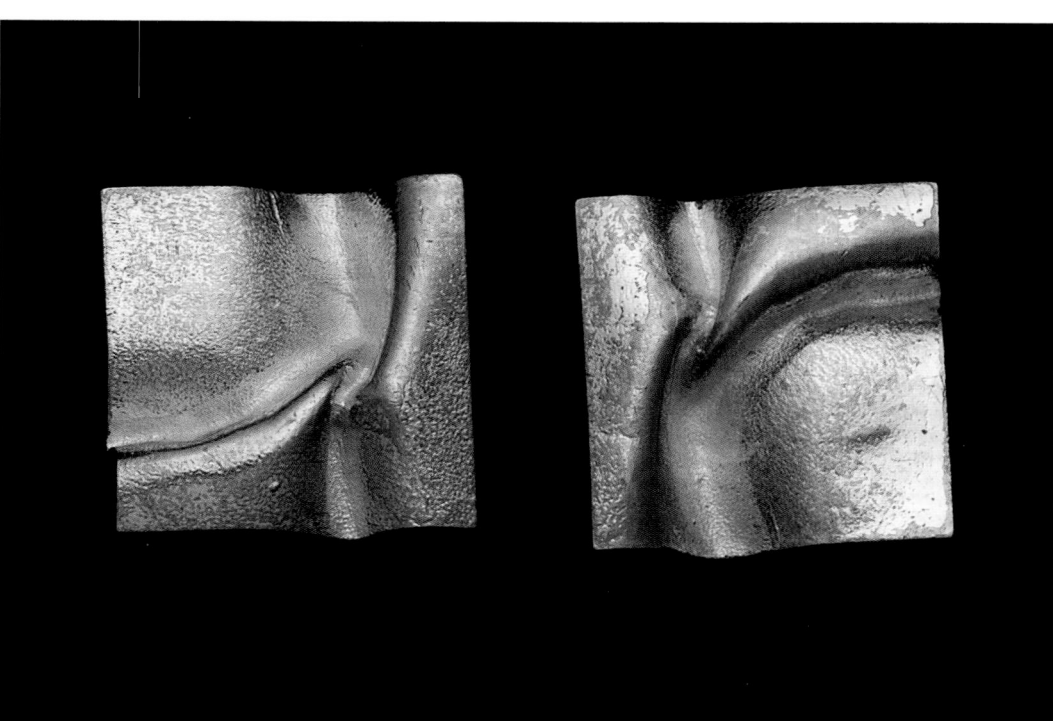

2.

1.

3.

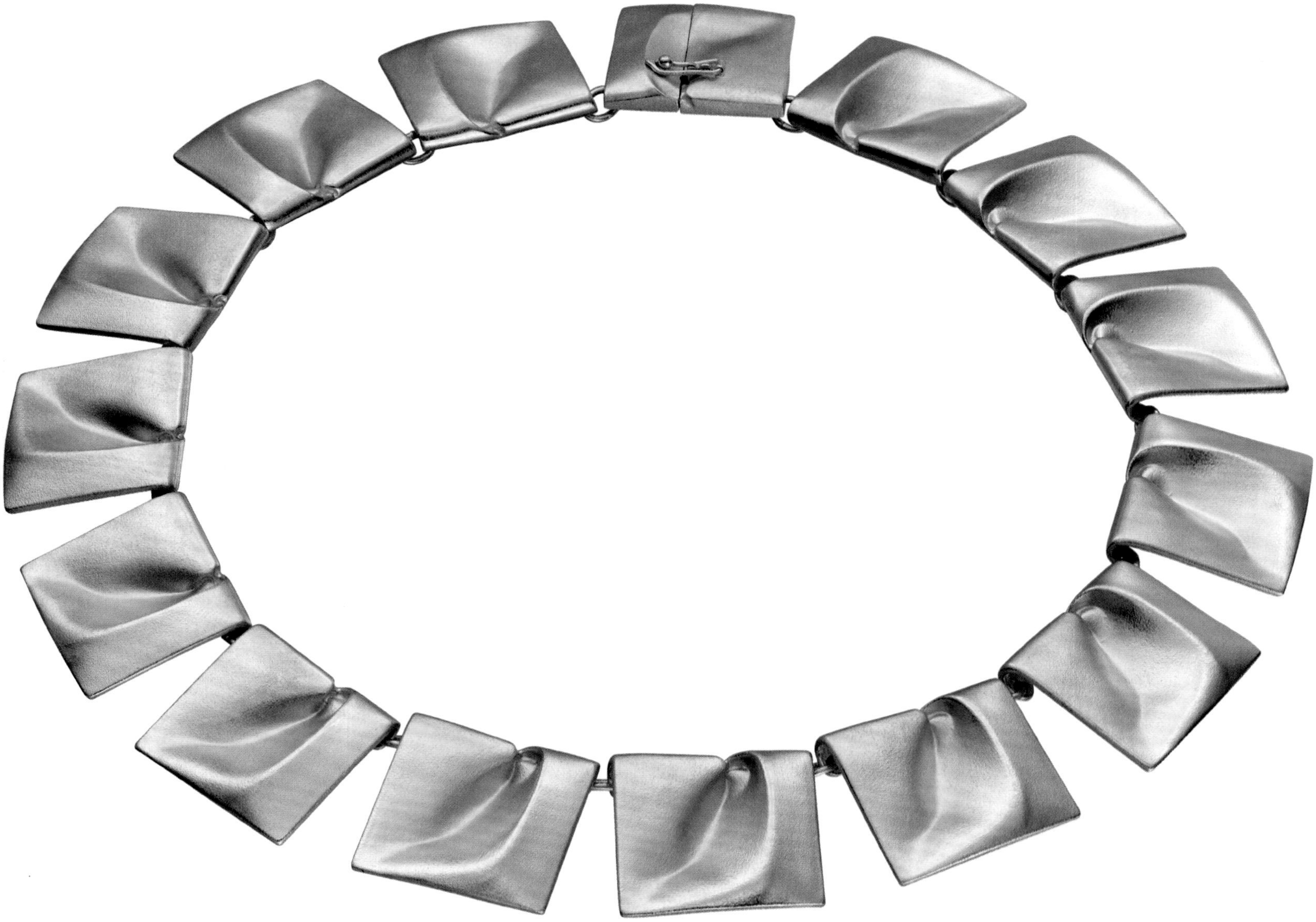

BJÖRN WECKSTRÖM – FINNISH GOLD

Having studied at the Kultaseppäkoulu (Gold-smith's School) in Helsinki, Björn Weckström travelled extensively throughout Europe, America, Mexico and the Far East before establishing his own jewellery workshop and gallery in Helsinki in 1958. Three years later a client commissioned him to create a piece of jewellery that incorporated raw gold nuggets panned from the Lemmenjoki River in Lapland. The resulting design had a sculptural ruggedness that reflected the landscape of the region, and, as Weckström observes, had a 'true, primordial nature'. This raw, nature-inspired aesthetic was then evolved and perfected in the many pieces of gold jewellery that Weckström subsequently designed as part of his Lappgold range for Lapponia – indeed, it became his signature style, which was copied by numerous design-ers but never equalled.

1. Kukkiva Muuri (Flowering Wall) necklace by Björn Weckström for Lapponia (Finland), 1970

2. White- and yellow-gold bracelet by Björn Weckström (self-produced) (Finland), 1965 – a unique one-off design

3. Bear's Tusk bracelet by Björn Weckström for Lapponia (Finland), 1975

4. Koskikivet (Stones in the Stream) bracelet, Model no. 27174, by Björn Weckström for Lapponia, 1964

5. Neptune's Cave necklace by Björn Weckström (self-produced) (Finland), 1969

1.

2.

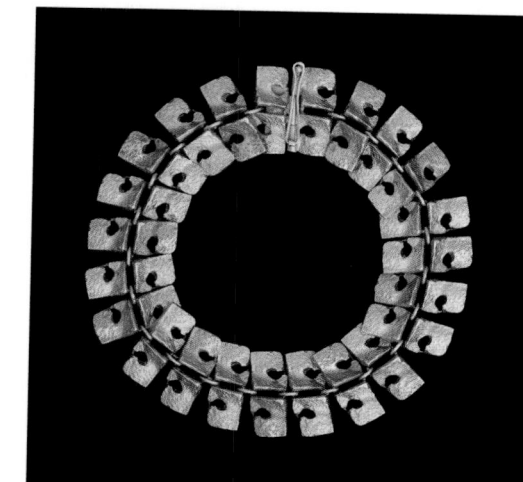

3.

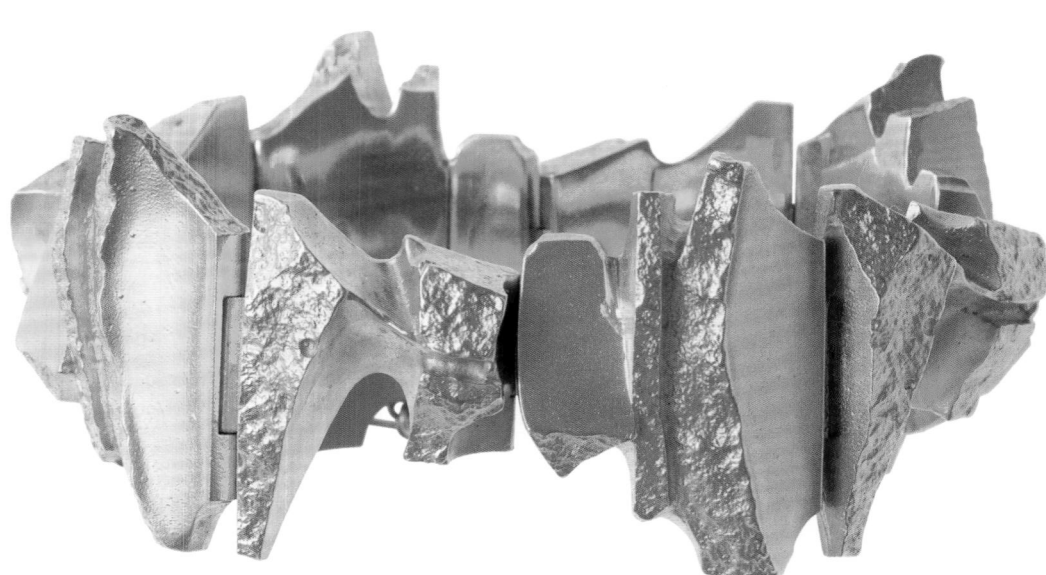

4.

5.

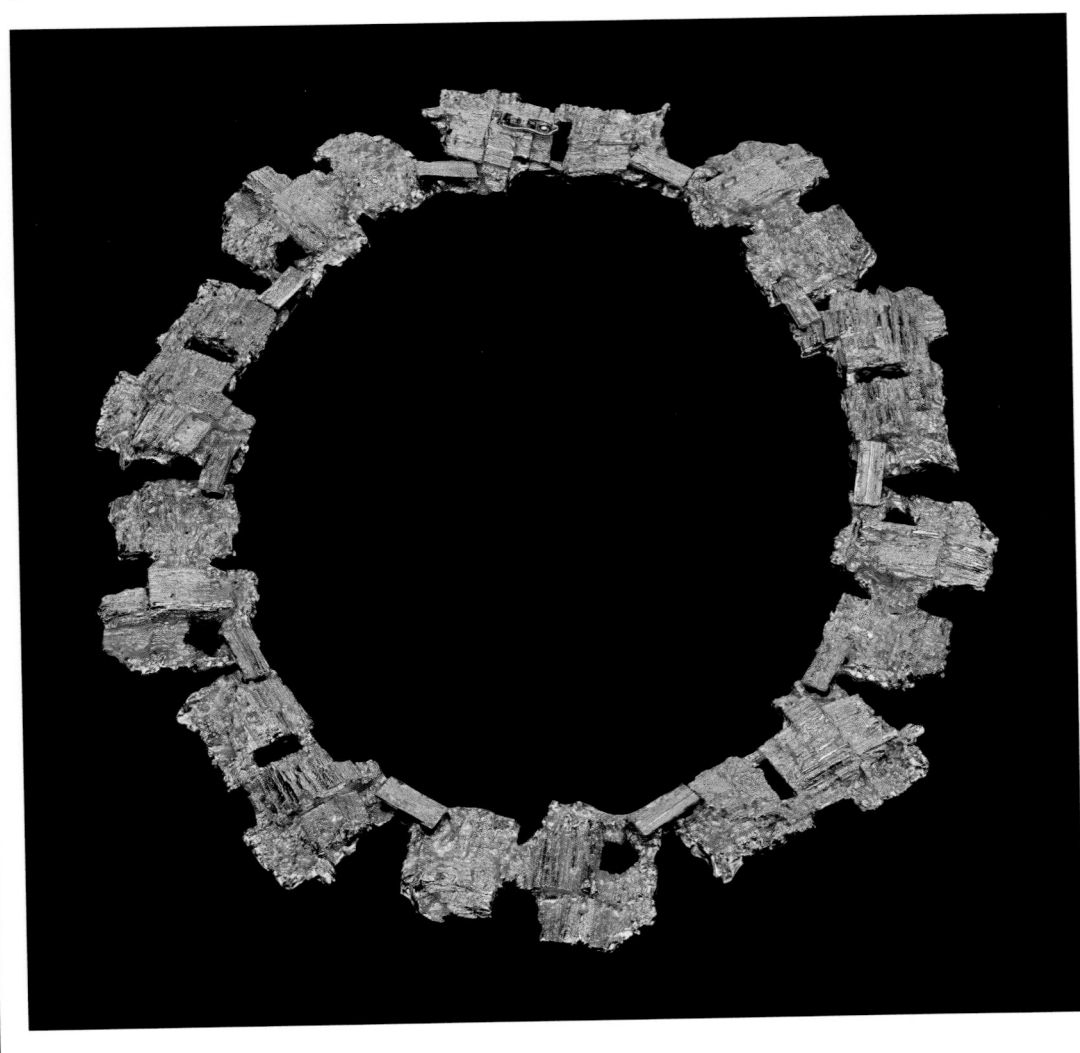

TAPIO WIRKKALA

The late 1960s and early 1970s are often regarded as the 'Golden Age' of Finnish design, thanks to a number of designers who were producing boldly contemporary work that was both experimental and innovative. Of this talented crop, by far the most accomplished was Tapio Wirkkala, a form-giver without equal. With a remarkable creative breadth that spanned craft and industry, Wirkkala worked in virtually all areas of design endeavour, from art glass to mass-produced packaging. The body of work he created in the field of jewellery design, however, was among his best, and he designed beautiful hand-beaten pieces for Kultakeskus and Nils Westerback in Finland, as well as for Tane Orfebres in Mexico. His glittering golden masterpiece, the Pirun Pää (Devil's Head) pendant, like much of his jewellery, has an ancient tribal quality, yet paradoxically was very much of its time.

1. Kuun Maisema (Moon Landscape) pendant by Tapio Wirkkala for Kultakeskus (Finland), 1966

2. Pirun Pää (Devil's Head) pendant/brooch by Tapio Wirkkala for Nils Westerback (Finland), 1966

3. Omena (Apple) pendant by Tapio Wirkkala for Kultakeskus (Finland), 1972

4. Viking bracelet by Tapio Wirkkala for Nils Westerback (Finland), 1969

Opposite: Hopeakuu (Silvermoon) pendant by Tapio Wirkkala for Nils Westerback (Finland), 1972

1.

2.

3.

4.

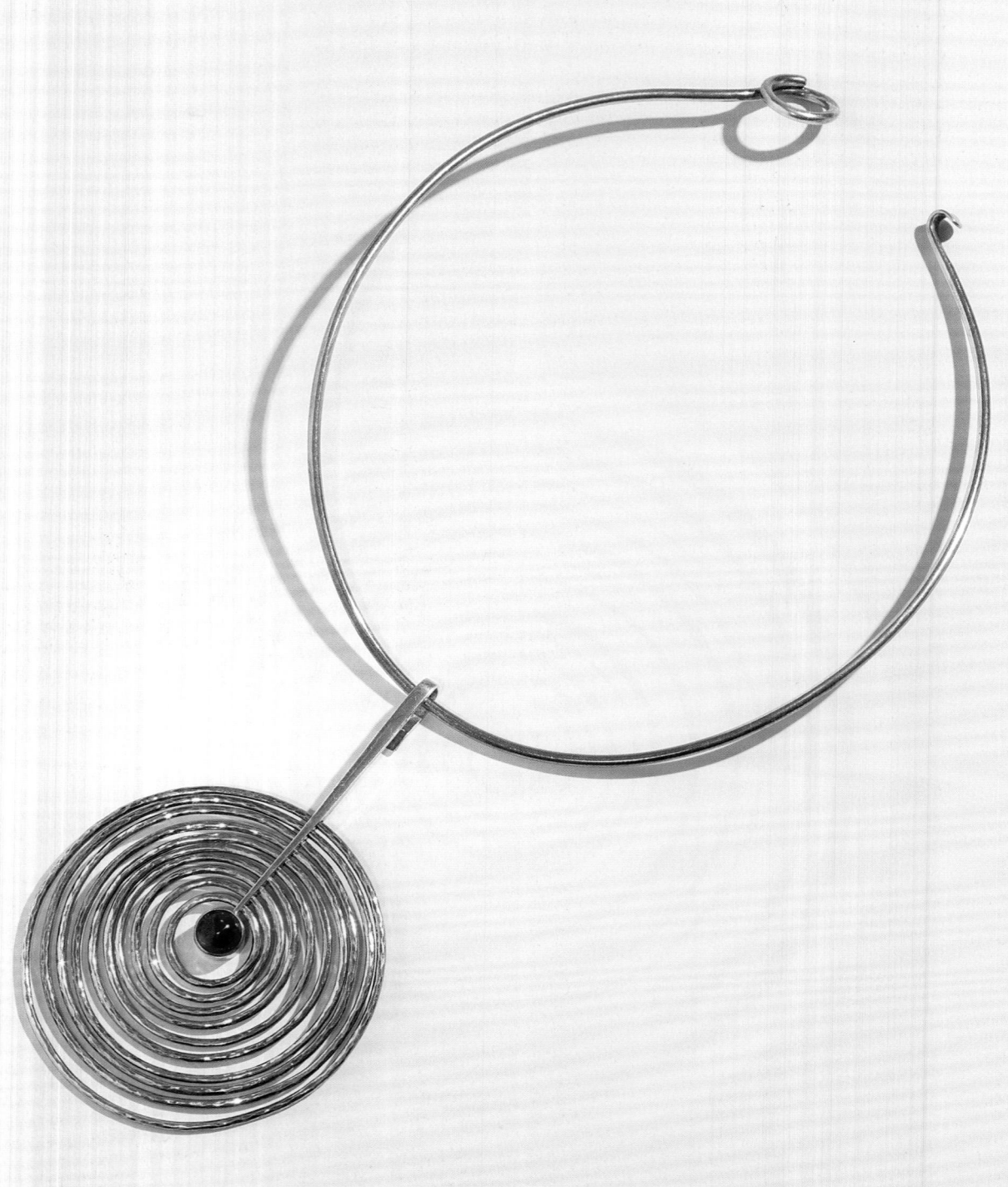

GEORG JENSEN IN THE 1960s

During the postwar period, Georg Jensen of Copenhagen firmly established its international contemporary design credentials with sculptural biomorphic jewellery pieces designed by Henning Koppel. On the advice of Finn Juhl, the famous silversmithy commissioned Nanna and Jørgen Ditzel to create even more forward-looking Modern pieces from the mid 1950s onwards (see pp. 514–15). By the 1960s, Georg Jensen had become a veritable design powerhouse of innovative contemporary jewellery, manufacturing in its workshops boldly sculptural, often chunky, silver and gold pieces by a host of talented young designers, including Vivianna Torun Bülow-Hübe (see pp. 518–21), Astrid Fog, Bent Gabrielsen and Ibe Dahlquist, to name but a few. These designs, which included various neck rings and armbands, were the very antithesis of traditional jewellery, functioning more as wearable sculpture. They also reflected the changing lifestyles of the 1960s and early 1970s, when women wanted less fussy pieces that could be worn casually.

Opposite: Model no. 143 necklace by Bent Gabrielsen for Georg Jensen (Denmark), ca. 1965

1. Neck ring by Astrid Fog for Georg Jensen (Denmark), 1971

2. Model no. 126 Heart necklace by Astrid Fog for Georg Jensen (Denmark), 1969

3. Model no. 123 necklace by Astrid Fog for Georg Jensen (Denmark), 1960s

1.

2.

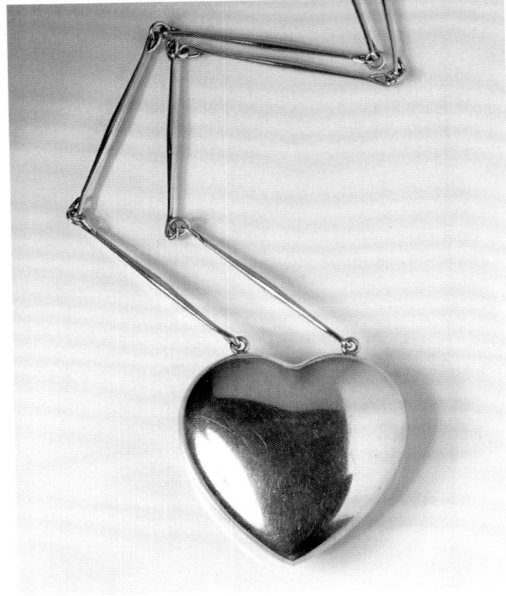

3.

1.

2.

3.

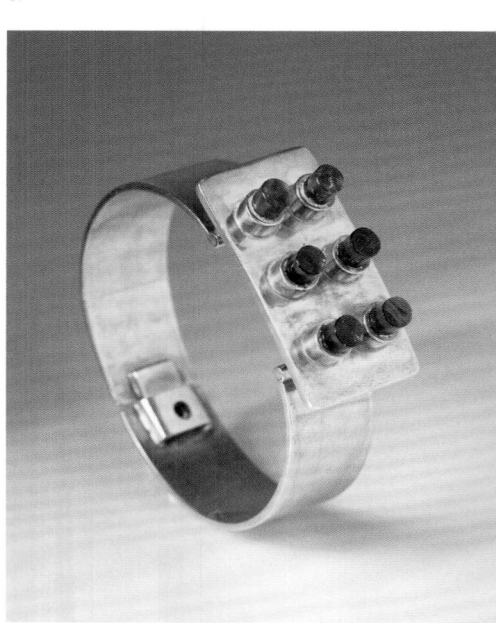

OTHER JEWELLERY DESIGNERS, 1950s + 1960s

Beyond the outstanding jewellery designs that have already been covered in this survey, there are many other pieces by Nordic designers that were every bit as innovative and pioneering, though less well known. For example, the pieces shown here by the Danish designer Bent Knudsen, the Swedish designer Sigurd Persson and the Finnish designer Paula Häiväoja share a strong and distinctive graphic quality – a characteristic that came to epitomize Nordic jewellery design of the 1950s and 1960s. This type of jewellery was not particularly expensive to produce or to buy, being generally made of silver and semi-precious stones, and as a result was more fashion-focused. Statement rings, bangles and necklaces such as these were intended to be worn casually with everyday clothes, unlike the high-end jewellery showpieces of earlier decades, which were traditionally reserved for wearing only on formal occasions. These were designs that conveyed not material status, particularly, but rather one's taste; and as such, this type of stylish yet affordable jewellery became very popular in Scandinavia, the rest of Europe and the USA.

1. Silver necklace with three pink topazes by Sigurd Persson (self-produced) (Sweden), 1965

2. Necklace with rock-crystal pendant by Paula Häiväoja for Kalevala Koru (Finland), 1965

3. Silver and amethyst bracelet by Bent Knudsen (self-produced) (Denmark), 1960s

Below: Silver and amethyst bracelet by Bent Knudsen (self-produced) (Denmark), 1950s

PENTTI SARPANEVA

During the 1960s and 1970s the Finnish designer Pentti Sarpaneva produced numerous distinctive jewellery designs that had a strong sense of creative expression and that often combined different materials. Using casting methods, his pieces were mostly left unpolished and were inspired by found objects, such as twigs, boat studs, traditional Finnish rope laces and even by-products of the manufacture of zips. Like a magpie, Sarpaneva collected these treasures and used them to create assemblages that he used as moulds for his pendants, necklaces and bracelets. Although he did work in gold and silver, his material of choice was bronze – which not only made his pieces more affordable, but also gave them a quasi-Brutalist aesthetic. Sometimes he would embellish his pieces with glass inserts or semi-precious stones. Although they were very much of their time, Sarpaneva's designs for Turun Hopea also possessed a strong sense of tribalism, which reflected the continuing influence of traditional Sami culture on modern Finnish design.

Below: Gold bracelet by Pentti Sarpaneva for Turun Hopea (Finland), 1968

1. Silver pendant and bronze pendant by Pentti Sarpaneva for Turun Hopea (Finland), 1960s

2. Bronze and amethyst pendant by Pentti Sarpaneva for Turun Hopea (Finland), 1970s

3. Bronze pendant by Pentti Sarpaneva for Turun Hopea (Finland), 1960s

1.

2.

3.

KRISTIAN NILSSON – POSTMODERNISM

The Swedish silversmith Kristian Nilsson created extraordinary Postmodern pieces that shook up Nordic jewellery design, which had relied for decades on the use of 'pure' silver or gold and refined forms. Instead, Nilsson, who enjoyed playing the role of a design *enfant terrible*, created exquisitely outlandish jewellery compositions often based on forms and motifs taken from the natural world, such as flowers, fish and birds. His pieces famously incorporated coral, black pearls and even a silver moulding of a lobster claw, which he sold to a small but wealthy clientele, including the

opera singer Birgit Nilsson and members of the Swedish and Danish royal families. Sadly, Nilsson died after a brief illness in 1989, when he was only 47 years old, yet despite his all-too-short career he left an impressive body of work that unequivocally defined Scandinavian Postmodern jewellery design. In 2004 a major retrospective of his work was held at Malmö Konstmuseum (Malmö Art Museum), in which his work was described as 'fascinating and unique … [its] expressive and opulent shapes and exclusive materials have few counterparts in the Swedish art of jewellery'.

Below: Gold, ivory and lapis lazuli arm ring by Kristian Nilsson (Sweden), 1972

Opposite: Gold and black-pearl collar by Kristian Nilsson (Sweden), ca. 1988

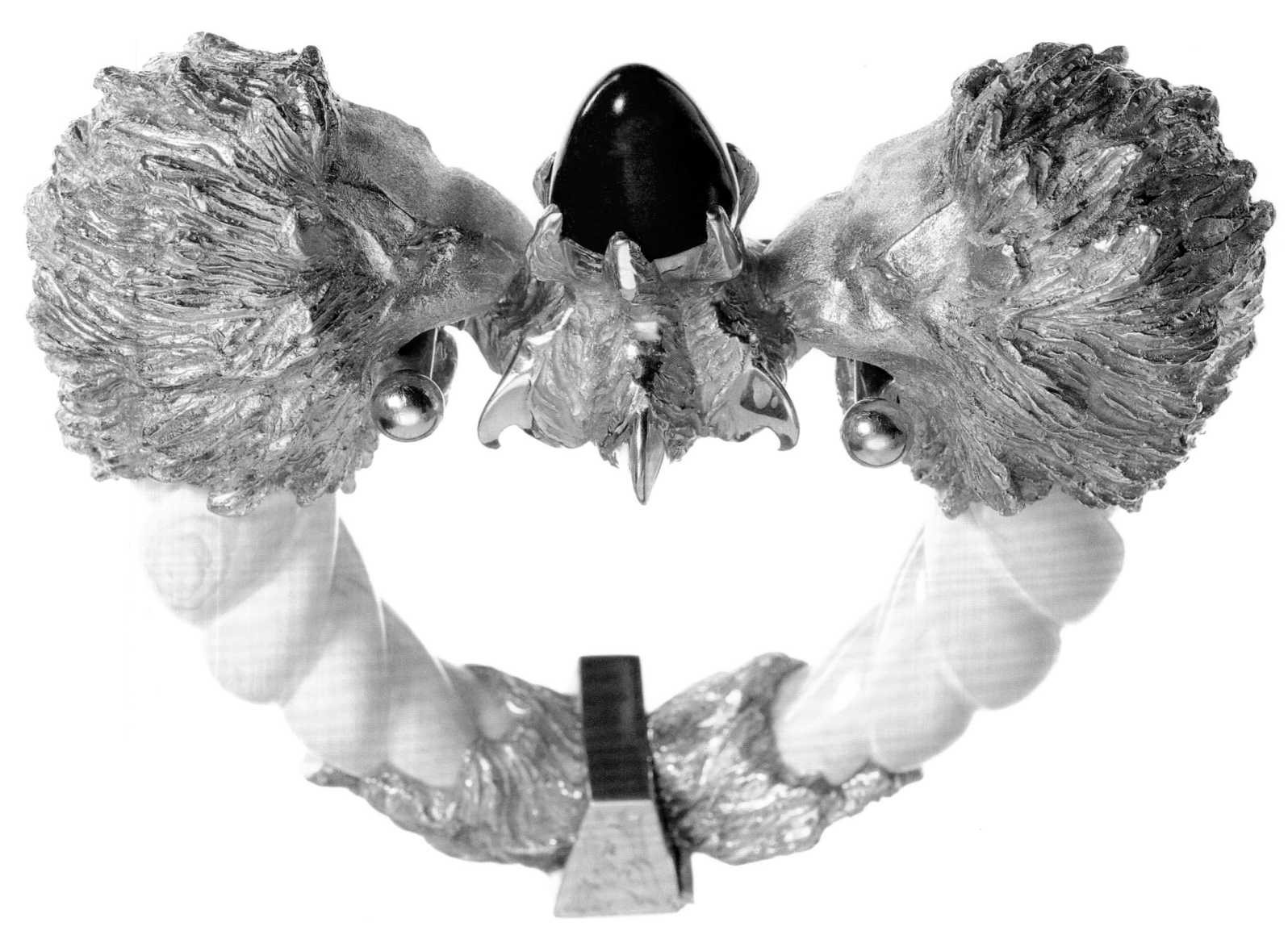

1.

2.

3.

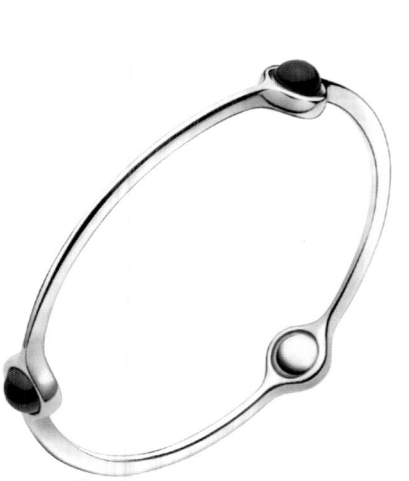

4.

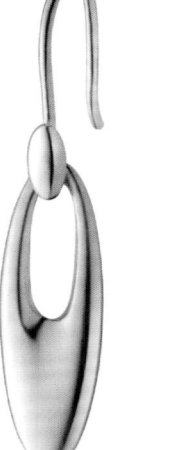
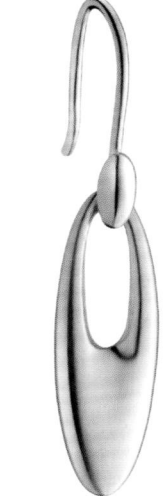

5.

GEORG JENSEN CONTEMPORARY

Today, Georg Jensen produces contemporary jewellery designs alongside classic pieces from its company archive. Yet these new pieces, which include those shown here, maintain the design DNA and jewellery philosophy of the firm, for they are not showy objects worn to impress, but rather beautiful, understated designs that are eminently wearable. Georg Jensen's contemporary jewellery collection defines what we have come to think of as 'Scandinavian luxury', which hinges on the idea of innovative designs that are beautifully crafted in high-quality materials. Above all, the firm's contemporary jewellery – ranging from the highly successful Magic ring series to the more recent Askill 'butterfly' collection (below) – are form-giving exercises of the highest order, functioning more as wearable sculpture than as traditional jewellery.

1. Magic ring by Regitze Overgaard for Georg Jensen (Denmark), 2001

2. Alliance bangle by Allan Scharff for Hans Hansen (Denmark), 1980s – recently reissued by Georg Jensen

3. Infinity necklace by Regitze Overgaard for Georg Jensen (Denmark), 2004

4. Sphere black agate bangle by Regitze Overgaard for Georg Jensen (Denmark), 2010

5. Zephyr earrings by Regitze Overgaard for Georg Jensen (Denmark), 2006

6. Askill oxidized silver bracelet by Jordan Askill for Georg Jensen (Denmark), 2015

7. Fusion rings by Nina Koppel for Georg Jensen (Denmark), 2000

6.

7.

DESIGN IN

SCANDINAVIA

GRAPHIC DESIGN

The most prolific area of Scandinavian graphic endeavour during the twentieth century was poster design. Posters were most often created to promote products, brands, films and travel, but they were also used as an important conduit for political propaganda and the dissemination of public information by Scandinavia's nascent welfare states. Despite this, poster design was not held in particularly high esteem for much of the twentieth century, being predominantly seen as the field of failed fine artists and regarded as far too commercial for serious cultural consideration. Over time, however, Scandinavia produced a number of visual communicators who would come to rival the very best working in Britain, France and the USA.

Thor Bøgelund studied at the Kongelige Danske Kunstakademi (Royal Danish Academy of Fine Arts; KADK) in Copenhagen from 1909 to 1914, and helped to develop commercial poster art in Denmark. His early posters were influenced by German Jugendstil designs, while later the Art Deco style and Modernism inspired his work. His early designs are both monumental and punchy, such as his 'Mother Denmark' poster of 1920, the subject of which was the reunification of Schleswig with Denmark after World War I. He designed many posters for the Tivoli Gardens in Copenhagen, the newspaper *Berlingske Tidende*, the automobile exhibition at Forum, the Danish Tourist Board and theatres. Another Danish designer who created bold Jugendstil posters was Sven Henriksen, a self-taught commercial artist. His poster for the Brandvaerns Udstilling (Fire Department Exhibition) held at the Tivoli Gardens has a characteristically Danish quirky, eye-catching humour.

Having studied in Aarhus and started out as a Cubist painter, Viggo Vagnby studied drawing in France and then started his own studio in Aalborg, specializing in advertising graphics and exhibition architecture. He moved to Copenhagen in 1943, and while living there created what is perhaps the most famous of all twentieth-century Danish posters, the *Wonderful Copenhagen* tourist poster of 1953. This colourful, humorous poster shows a policeman stopping pedestrians and traffic on a Copenhagen street in order to let a mother duck cross the road with her chicks (see also p. 407). That year, Vagnby moved to Skagen, in the far north of the country, and two years later he famously created for his new home town a tourist poster that depicted a plaice in the form of a painter's palette.

Henry Thelander was originally an advertising illustrator who worked in the advertising departments of various companies. He broke through as an independent poster artist in the mid 1930s with his posters for the Danish Tourist Board and the DSB (Danish State Railways). Thelander often used his own wife as a model for the young, smiling women in his posters.

The Danish illustrator and poster artist Aage Rasmussen was a graduate of the Tekniske Skole (Technical College) and the Kunsthåndværkerskolen (School of Applied Arts; now KADK) in Copenhagen. He is chiefly known for his many lithographic posters for DSB. Success came early in his career, when he won an award at the Exposition Internationale des Arts et Techniques dans la Vie Moderne in Paris in 1937. He also won a competition run by *Berlingske Tidende* for a new national tourist poster; the world-famous French-Ukrainian poster artist Adolphe Jean-Marie Mouron (Cassandre) was on the jury. The winning poster was printed only in 1948, owing to the outbreak of war. Rasmussen was also awarded a prize at the International Poster Exhibition in Japan in 1939. He continued after 1945 with designs for travel, transport, tourism and public information.

Ib Antoni was one of the most sought-after Danish graphic designers of his generation. He worked for over 150 companies and organizations worldwide, including *Life* magazine, Shell, Esso, Carlsberg, Volvo, UNICEF, Philips, Neiman Marcus and the Danish Ministry of Foreign Affairs. Many of his more than 300 posters are extremely memorable – Charlie Rivel the clown with a bird on his nose; the Danish guardsman marching with a gun loaded with flowers; the Little Mermaid with a tourist on her tail; a Tivoli lamp in the dark-blue twilight hour; and many more motifs that are forever associated with Copenhagen and Denmark. Birds and other animals appeared frequently in his drawings, but people were his real speciality, from Hans Christian Andersen, to children, to a distinguished British man in a bowler hat.

Antoni was never satisfied unless the right shading, line and detailing were in place, and he created hundreds of sketches during the design development of a single poster. He enjoyed royal attention; during her first visit to Denmark, in 1957, Queen Elizabeth II and the Danish royal family visited the Carlsberg headquarters to see the new Antoni graphics on the company's vans. Antoni also created the cover for the official wedding book for King Constantine and Princess Ann-Marie in Greece in 1964. In 1968 an exhibition of his work was held in London, and Queen Ingrid of Denmark was the official guest. Sadly, Antoni died in a hotel fire in 1973, but his designs are still widely reproduced and currently enjoying something of a popular revival.

Nu Kalder Danmark Paa sine Børn Farvel for Evigt du Tyske Ørn (Now Denmark Calls her Children: Goodbye Forever, German Eagle) poster by Thor Bøgelund (Denmark), 1920 – with its representation of 'Mother Denmark'

General Motors poster for the Forum exhibition by Thor Bøgelund (Denmark), 1939

Aarhus–Kalundborg poster by Henry Thelander for DSB (Denmark), 1935

Opposite: *Design in Scandinavia* exhibition catalogue by Tapio Wirkkala (Finland), 1954 – for a travelling exhibition in the USA and Canada, 1954–57

From the mid 1970s onwards the Danish artist and sculptor Per Arnoldi also came to prominence as a graphic designer. Best known for creating the logo and curtains of the Copenhagen Opera House, he also designed London's National Police Memorial with the British architect Norman Foster, and was responsible for the design of a monumental sculpture called *The V* in Videbaek. He has also designed numerous eye-catching primary-coloured posters for a long list of clients, including the Guggenheim Museum in New York, Louisiana Museum of Modern Art in Denmark, the Royal Danish Theatre, British Rail, DSB, Siemens, the Lincoln Center in New York and the Museum of Contemporary Art in Chicago. His distinctive Neo-Modern style epitomized Scandinavian graphic design during the Postmodern period – colourful, bold and, above all, artful.

Scandinavian graphic design was brought to a wider international audience through *Mobilia*, an international design journal published in Denmark from 1955 until 1984. The furniture designer Grete Jalk was an early editor of this square-format monthly magazine (1956–62), but it was her successor, the Danish architect Erik Møller, who oversaw the publication's golden period of graphic design, when each issue was innovatively designed to reflect its chosen theme. Importantly, *Mobilia* was conceived as a multilingual publication, with articles in Swedish, English, French and German, and for that reason it was influential in disseminating the work of Scandinavian designers abroad. (It did also feature the work of non-Scandinavian designers, notably Pierre Paulin and Robert Welch.)

The magazine's last editor was Per Mollerup, who oversaw its publication from 1974 until 1984. Mollerup later designed the visual identities for several public services and private companies. He was also an influential pioneer of wayfinding design – as he called it, 'wayshowing' – and even wrote a book on the subject in 2005. Crucially, he was also responsible for the visual identities and wayfinding signage of Copenhagen airport (1989), Oslo airport (1996), Stockholm Arlanda airport (1998), the Arlanda Express airport train service (1998) and the Copenhagen Metro (2002). In tribute to his graphic contribution to the distinctive look of Scandinavian public life, his studio, Designlab, has been given the Danish Design Award nine times.

Anders Beckman graduated in Industrial Design from the Tekniska Skolan (Technical College; now Konstfack, the University College of Arts, Crafts and Design) in Stockholm in 1930. That year he started his own advertising firm, working for organizations such as ABA Aerotransport, Svenska Europahjälpen and the Nationalmuseum in Stockholm.

During and after World War II he designed a number of posters on social topics, but he is perhaps best known for his graphic identity work for the legendary H55 exhibition held in Helsingborg in 1955. He was involved in several other exhibitions, including the Swedish Pavilion at the New York World's Fair in 1939, where he installed a traditional wooden Dala horse, 3 metres tall, by the entrance. He was fascinated by innovative exhibition technology and product presentations that combined word and image. With Nils Gustav Granath, he founded SAFFT, an organization for Swedish poster illustrators. In 1939 he started Beckmans Skola för Reklam Illustration Mode (Beckman's College of Advertising, Illustration and Fashion; now Beckman's College of Design) in Stockholm, with the textile designer Göta Trägårdh. After his death in 1967, his widow, Nunnie Beckman, ran the school for many years. Although the Konstfack is generally regarded as Sweden's most important design school, Beckmans comes a very close second, even to this day.

Olle Eksell was born in Kopparberg, Sweden, and declared at the age of 14 that he wanted to be an advertising illustrator. During World War II he studied graphic art in Stockholm, where his main teacher was professor Hugo Steiner-Prag, a Czech-Jewish émigré and illustrator. Eksell later worked for the Ervaco advertising agency, where he met his future wife, Ruthel Eksell, a fashion designer. In 1946 the newly married couple sailed on the liner SS *Drottningholm* to New York, in order to continue their studies at the Art Center College of Design in Los Angeles. It was during this period that Eksell first came into contact with some of America's leading graphic designers of the day, including Paul Rand, Alvin Lustig and Lester Beall. He developed a close friendship with Rand that would last throughout their lives. They visited each other frequently and often discussed new ideas, innovations and design processes.

The Eksells lived in a Modernist block of flats in Gärdet, Stockholm, for more than 40 years, and there, in his small home studio, Eksell created his well-known graphic programmes for Mazetti chocolate and Nessim carpets. Besides being an accomplished and innovative visual communicator, he was an influential writer, and his book *Design = Ekonomi* (1964) presents a clear, elegant argument about the important relationship between design practice and economics: 'Good design is not just aesthetic – it is also good economy. Good design is not just cool – it is bloody serious.' Eksell also participated in exhibitions at the Museum of Modern Art in New York, the Musée du Louvre in Paris and the Venice Biennale, which brought him even more international recognition. In 2001, in tribute

Nord-Express Skandinavien-Express poster by Aage Rasmussen for DSB (Denmark), 1946

Wonderful Copenhagen poster by Viggo Vagnby, printed by Jens Christian Sørensen (Denmark), 1953

Wonderful Copenhagen poster by Ib Antoni for Københavns Turistforening (Denmark), 1969

Save Energy poster by Per Arnoldi, printed by Gutenberghus Reklamebureau/Norup & Bramsted Offset (Denmark), 1978

to his talents, the Swedish government gave Eksell the title Honorary Professor for his significant contribution to the field of design.

In common with the rest of Western Europe, Sweden took a political step to the left with the outbreak of the Vietnam War. Although the Prague Spring of 1968 returned a Swedish Social Democratic government with its strongest mandate ever, the USA's bombing of Hanoi at Christmas 1972 hardened the voices of the Swedish left. This political shift is reflected in the posters, leaflets and books of the time. Sture Johannesson managed to cause upset with his poster *Pot Piggar Upp!* (Pot Cheer Up!) in 1965, and even more with his 'Hash Girl' poster of 1968. It was supposed to be part of the 'Underground' exhibition at Lunds Konsthall in Lund in 1969, but the show was forced to close before it had even opened, and its director was fired. Johannesson started Galleri Cannabis with his wife at about the same time, adding to the controversy surrounding him and his artwork.

A large number of Swedish artists contributed to the radical Socialist magazine *Puss* (Kiss), which was visually vocal in its promotion of sexual and political freedoms. It ran from 1968 to 1973, and among its contributors were Lars Hillersberg, Carl Johan De Geer and Lena Svedberg. Most of its associates had graduated from the Konstfack, which meant that although the magazine had a very strong rough-and-ready, underground quality, it packed a powerful graphic punch thanks to the formal training they had received.

Norway also has a proud tradition of innovative graphic design with a distinctively Nordic flavour. The painter Trygve Davidsen belonged to the first generation of Norwegian commercial artists. He opened his own studio in 1917, and went on a study trip to the USA in 1923. His best-known work is a poster of ca. 1926 for the Norwegian tourist board, featuring a naked sun-worshipping man holding skis; it was banned in the USA because of its depiction of nudity. As a design commentator, teacher and author, Davidsen did much to raise the reputation of advertising. He taught at the Oslo advertising school in the 1920s and at the Oslo Grafisk Institutt from 1920 to 1936, and published several textbooks on drawing. Later in life he illustrated many books and postcards, often with religious motifs or scenes showing goblins in Norwegian landscapes. He also wrote poems and, under the pseudonym Stein Striver (Printer), novels. Davidsen was a director of Norway's Advertising Association for a number of years, vice chairman of the Tegnerforbundet (Draughtsmen's Association) from 1945 to 1947, and a member of the government's council of experts involved in making preparations for the introduction of the Copyright Act of 1953.

In Finland, Tapio Wirkkala also worked in the field of graphic design, creating artwork for posters and packaging that was every bit as inventive as his glassware, furniture and ceramics. He was also responsible for designing the cover of the catalogue that accompanied the travelling exhibition 'Design in Scandinavia' in the USA between 1954 and 1957. Gunnar Forsström was another Finnish glass artist who also worked as a poster designer. He designed the windows of at least 22 Finnish churches – including those for Espoo Cathedral in 1942 – and was a business partner of the glass designer Göran Hongell. It is, however, his poster commemorating the 400th anniversary of Helsinki in 1950, with its flat colours and sans-serif lettering, that is his most iconic work.

No survey of Scandinavian graphic design is complete without mention of Erik Bruun, a prodigiously talented Finnish graphic designer who spent his childhood on the Karelian Isthmus. After the Soviet invasion in 1939 his family fled to Helsinki, where he later enrolled in the Taideteolliseen Keskuskouluun (Central School of Industrial Arts) and graduated as a graphic designer in 1950. After completing his studies Bruun worked as an exhibition designer and commercial artist. In 1953 he founded his own graphic-design studio, and over the next three decades he created numerous posters, logos, postcards, stamps and books. In the 1950s he made bold and colourful posters for Havi candles, Hackman metalware, Fazer sweets, Klubi cigarettes by Rettig, Nektar coffee and the soft drink Jaffa, made by Hartwall. From the 1960s, he also began producing highly detailed drawings of animals, one of which – of the endangered Saimaa ringed seal – was adopted by Suomen luonnonsuojeluliitto (Finnish Association for Nature Conservation) as its mascot (Bruun had already designed the association's logo). Such was his reputation that he was even charged with designing the last series of Finnish markka banknotes in 1986.

Featured over the coming pages is also work by various contemporary Nordic graphic designers and studios that builds on the visual communications legacy of their forefathers in order to forge their own national and international reputations. Aesthetically simple yet often boldly direct, ranging from the strident Neo-Modern to the charming Post-Folk, Scandinavian graphic design continues to distinctively reflect the socio-cultural values of the Nordic region.

Se Och Lyssna Förtag Varning (Listen for the Train at Crossings) printed by Bengtssons Litografiska (Sweden), 1952

Skrot blir Stål (Scrap Becomes Steel) poster by Anders Beckman for Skrotkommittén/Press & Propaganda (Sweden), 1952

H55 Helsingborg Sweden poster by Anders Beckman for Svenska Slöjdföreningen, published by Hälsingborgs Litografiska (Sweden), 1955 – reissued by Upplands Grafiska, 1984

Identity design by Stockholm Design for Akka Premium Water (Sweden), 2015

NATIONAL IDENTITIES –
TRAVEL POSTERS

Travel posters have always been an interesting window on how nations wish to depict themselves to the rest of the world, and this has been especially true in Scandinavia. The design of Trygve Davidsen's iconic *Norway: The Home of Ski-ing* poster of ca. 1926, for example, conveys with an abstracted male nude worshipping the sun an important theme that is common throughout the Nordic countries – profound reverence for nature. Likewise, Iwar Donner's bold *Stockholm* poster of 1936 communicates a friendly yet bold representation of Sweden's capital city – reflecting the desire of this socially progressive nation to express its modernity. A year later Henry Thelander designed his poster *Dänemark: Das Land des Meeres* (Denmark: The Land of the Sea), which imparted the growing interest in health and hygiene during the interwar years not only in Scandinavia but also in neighbouring Germany. During the postwar period many Scandinavian designers began infusing their travel posters with a touch of humour. Two charming examples are Osmo Oksanen's *Finland* poster (ca. 1949), featuring a characterful young skier, and Viggo Vagnby's *Hans Christian Andersen: Odense* (1962), with its plucky ugly duckling.

1. *Hans Christian Andersen: Odense* poster by Viggo Vagnby (Denmark), 1962

2. *Finland* poster by Osmo Oksanen (Finland), ca. 1949

3. *Stockholm* poster by Iwar Donner (Sweden), 1936

4. *Dänemark: Das Land des Meeres* poster by Henry Thelander (Denmark), 1937

5. *Norway, The Home of Ski-ing* poster by Trygve Davidsen (Norway), ca. 1926

1.

2.

3.

5.

4.

1.

2.

AAGE RASMUSSEN

The Danish illustrator and graphic design-er Aage Rasmussen got his first big career break in 1937 at the age of 24, when a poster he had designed for DSB (Danish State Rail-ways) advertising its express train service was accepted on the spot. Cleverly, the post-er used two railway tracks vanishing into the distance to draw the eye to its central motif – an express train hurtling down the tracks, with billows of smoke behind it symbolizing a steam train that it has left in the distance. The speedometer above not only clocks the express train's impressive speed (120 km/h), but also draws the viewer's eye towards the train. This impactful design was undoubted-ly influenced by the Swiss designer Herbert Matter's poster *All Roads Lead to Switzerland*, created two years earlier, which used a similar vanishing-point device. Rasmussen's design, however, also manages to capture the speed and excitement of this new form of transport by using bolder colours and more minimal ty-pography. He subsequently designed for DSB a number of other dynamically composed posters that similarly expressed the Machine Age zeitgeist of the 1930s.

1. *DSB* poster by Aage Rasmussen for Danske Statsbaner (DSB) (Denmark), 1950

2. *Storstrømsbroen* (Storstrøm Bridge) poster by Aage Rasmussen for DSB (Denmark), 1937

Right: *DSB: The Danish State Railways* poster by Aage Rasmussen for DSB (Denmark), 1937

ANDERS BECKMAN

Anders Beckman was a successful advertising executive who also enjoyed a prolific career as a poster designer. His pre-war work, such as the poster he designed to promote the film *Intermezzo* (1936; starring Ingrid Bergman), had a strong, dynamic layout that placed it firmly within the canon of International Modernism. His propaganda posters designed in the 1940s combined bold typography and eye-hooking imagery. It was, however, his poster promoting the H55 exhibition held in Helsingborg in 1955 that became his best-known design, with its clever background comprising an enormous black H. His exhibition poster of 1966 for Kontor 66 used a similar graphic device. Apart from his graphic-design work, Beckman famously founded (with the fashion illustrator Göta Trägårdh) the acclaimed Beckmans Designhögskola (Beckman's College of Design) in Stockholm in 1939. This private design college was established as an independent and creative alternative to the Konstfack, and it remains one of the Nordic region's most influential design teaching institutions.

Right: *Intermezzo* lithographic film poster by Anders Beckman, published by Ivar Haeggström (Sweden), 1936

1. Kontor 66 exhibition poster by Anders Beckman, published by Kopia Stockholm (Sweden), 1966

2. *Varning Mullvadsarbete Pågår* (Warning, Secretive Work in Progress) propaganda poster by Anders Beckman, published by Bengtssons Litografiska (Sweden), 1940s

3. H55 Helsingborg Sweden poster by Anders Beckman for Svenska Slöjdföreningen, published by Hälsingborgs Litografiska (Sweden), 1955 – Spanish language version

SVENSKA CIVILEKONOMFÖRENINGEN · KONTORSMASKIN OCH KONTORSMÖBELHANDLARNAS FÖRENING
INTERNATIONELL
UTSTÄLLNING
21-28 OKTOBER
KONTOR
66
S:T ERIKS-MÄSSAN
STOCKHOLM

1.

VARNING
mullvadsarbete pågår
spionen undergräver tryggheten

2.

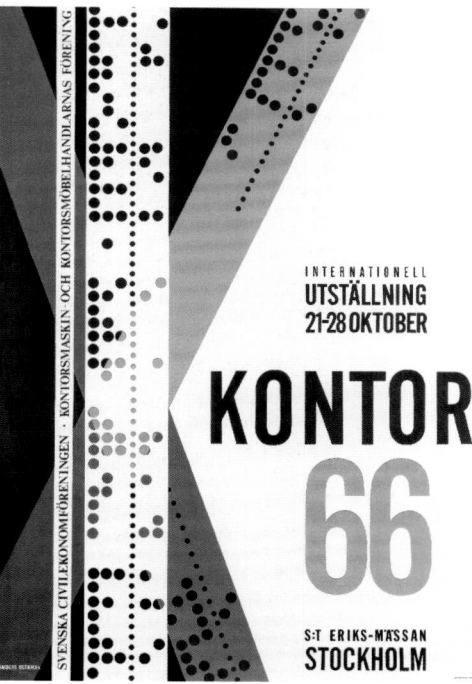

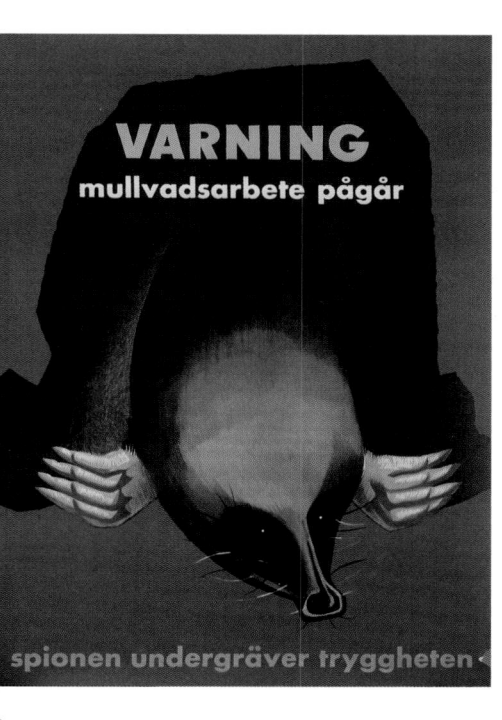

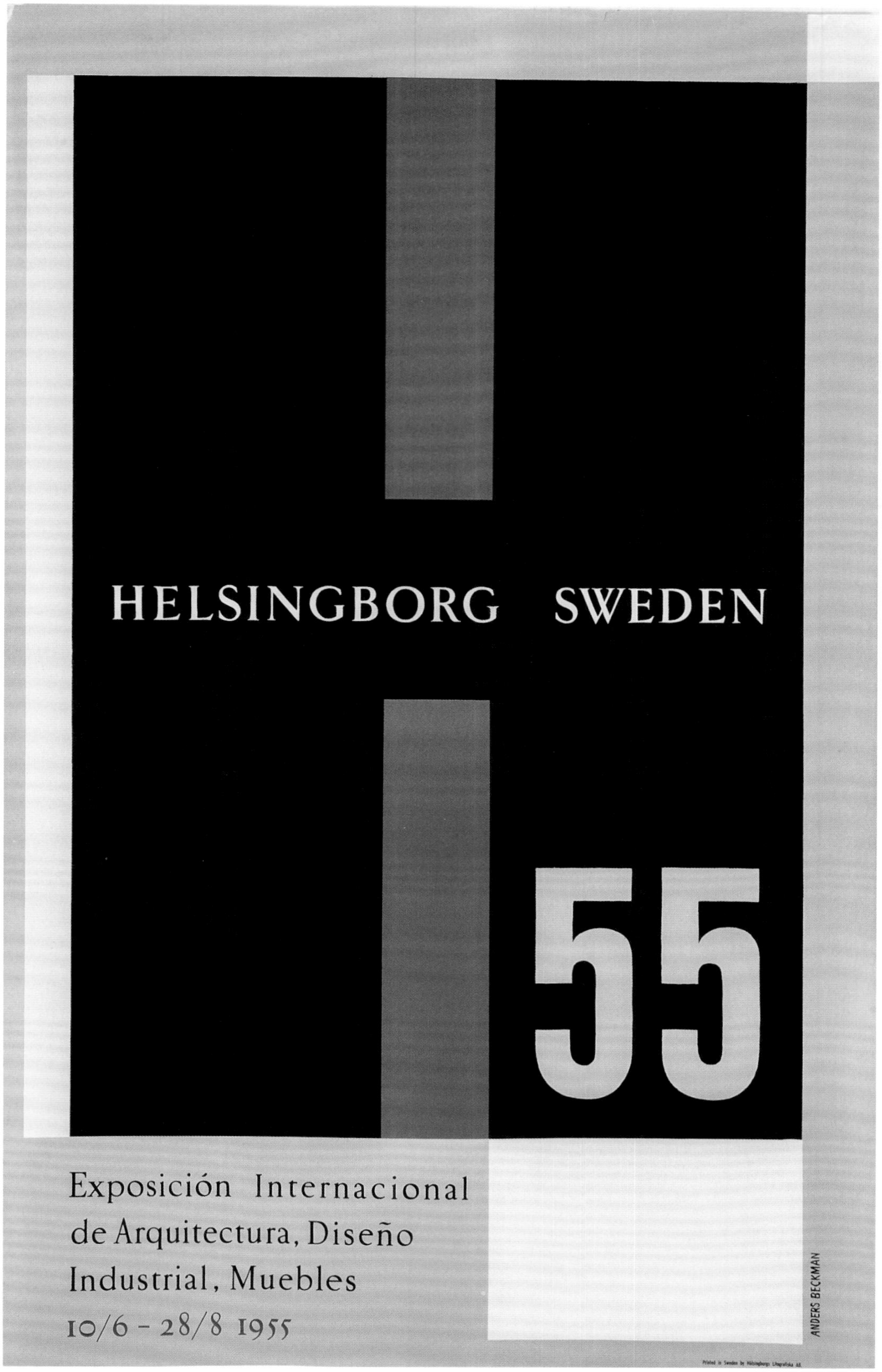
HELSINGBORG SWEDEN
55
Exposición Internacional
de Arquitectura, Diseño
Industrial, Muebles
10/6 - 28/8 1955
ANDERS BECKMAN

3.

FORM MAGAZINE, 1930s

The world's oldest design organization is to be found in Sweden – unsurprisingly, given how seriously Swedish society takes the notion of life-enhancing design. Founded in 1845, it was originally known as Svenska Slöjdföreningen (Swedish Society of Crafts and Industrial Design), but its name was changed to Svensk Form in 1976. As part of its design-reforming remit, the society founded its own magazine, *Svenska Slöjdföreningens Tidskrift*, in 1905. Its title was changed in 1932 to *Form* (Shape), and it remains the Nordic region's most influential journal of architecture and design. During

the 1930s it featured bold Modern covers, most of which incorporated black-and-white photographs of contemporary designs, such as ceramic vases by Sven-Erik Skawonius for Upsala-Ekeby, an engraved glass vase by Simon Gate for Orrefors, and a stand design used for a poster exhibition. *Form*'s covers tirelessly conveyed a forward-looking design agenda, and issue 7 (1936; below), showing a young woman with her arms outstretched under the banner line '*Fritiden*' (spare time), encapsulates the magazine's optimistic spirit, through which design was presented as a powerful tool for social change.

1. *Form* magazine no. 7/1936, published by Svenska Slöjdföreningens (Sweden), 1936 – 'Fritiden' means 'spare time'

2 & 3. *Form* magazine nos 9/1937 and 1/1939, published by Svenska Slöjdföreningens (Sweden), 1937–39 – featuring on their covers different aspects of contemporary Swedish design

1.

2.

3.

FORM MAGAZINE, 1950s

As the Nordic region's longest-running and most important journal of architecture and design, *Form* has over the decades tirelessly promoted Scandinavian design and its underlying values. The journal has always functioned as a vital mouthpiece for the influential design-reforming organization that founded it, Svenska Slöjdföreningen (Swedish Society of Crafts and Industrial Design; now Svenske Form). The 1950s were especially fruitful for the journal, coinciding with the worldwide cultural ascendency of Scandinavian design.

During those years *Form* featured many eye-catching covers designed by some of the leading Scandinavian graphic designers and illustrators of the day, including Staffan Wirén and Anders Beckman (see pp. 548–49). The stylistically diverse covers shown here, which date from 1952 and 1953, express the artistic inventiveness and intrinsic playfulness of postwar Scandinavian design, and stand in marked contrast to the journal's more sober covers from the interwar period; those mirrored the influence of International Modernism within Swedish graphic-design circles.

1. *Form* magazine no. 1/1953, published by Svenska Slöjdföreningens (Sweden), 1953

2. *Form* magazine nos 3 and 4/1952, published by Svenska Slöjdföreningens (Sweden), 1952 – cover designed by Staffan Wirén

3. *Form* magazine no. 2/1952, published by Svenska Slöjdföreningens (Sweden), 1952 – cover designed by Anders Beckman

1.

2.

3.

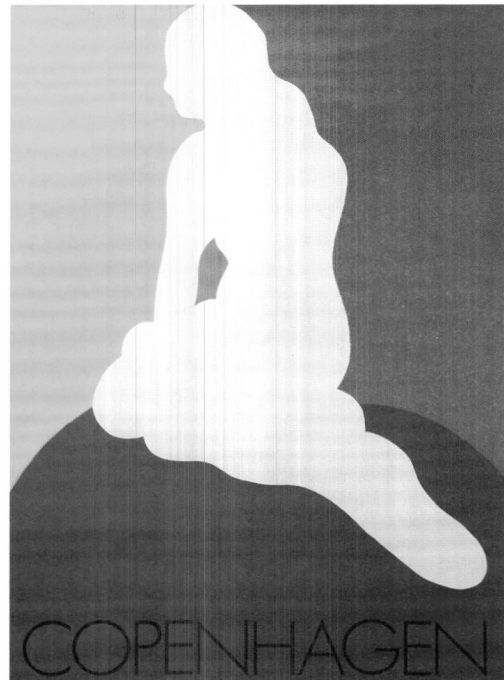

1.

2.

3.

PER ARNOLDI

Bridging the worlds of fine art and graphic design, the Danish artist-designer Per Arnoldi is well known for his bold, bright posters, which have very simple layouts, yet still pack a formidable visual punch. Over the years he has designed posters for numerous art institutions, including the Guggenheim Museum and Lincoln Center in New York, the Museum of Contemporary Art in Chicago and the Louisiana Museum of Modern Art outside Copenhagen. He has also designed posters for music events, including the Montreux Jazz Festival of 1994, as well as railway posters for both DSB and British Rail – again using his distinctive palette of primary hues. As a consummate rule-breaker both in his artwork and graphic design, Arnoldi tries to extract the essence of a subject and distil it into a bold composition that clearly communicates the intended message through the use of spare forms and vibrant colours.

1. *The Little Mermaid Copenhagen* poster by Per Arnoldi, printed by Kai Svendsen and A. C. Illum (Denmark), 1980s

2. *DSB Rainbow* poster by Per Arnoldi for DSB (Denmark), 1975

3. *The Chair* poster by Per Arnoldi for Nykredit (Denmark), 1980s

4. *Apple* poster by Per Arnoldi, printed by Weber & Sørensen and Alhof & Schrøder (Denmark), 1970s

5. *Den Kongelige Livgarde* (The King's Life Guards) poster for the 325th anniversary of the regiment (Denmark), 1983

4.

Ta'et dansk æble – så er du frisk

5.

OLLE EKSELL

A visionary designer, Olle Eksell played a vital role in the development of Modern graphic design in Scandinavia. He famously won an international competition to design a new logo for Mazetti in 1956. The resulting pair of stylized eyes was inspired by the confectioner's motto: 'You can see with your own eyes that you're getting quality.' The following year he designed for Mazetti Sweden's first Modern corporate identity programme, which in just one year increased the firm's market share from 40 to 70 per cent. It included packaging, display stands, print and billboard advertisements, and various other marketing media. After the success of his work for Mazetti, numerous companies and institutions commissioned Eksell to develop identities for them, including Nessim, Arjo, Handelsbanken and the Moderna Museet in Stockholm. In fact, it is safe to say that in this area of design Eksell had no equal in the Nordic region; he was essentially Sweden's equivalent of the American Paul Rand. Indeed, Rand was an idol of Eksell's, and in turn Rand had a huge respect for the Swede's work, ranking his Mazetti logo the number one trademark in the world in 1965. Interestingly, as a forward-thinking creative Eksell was also an early advocate of biodegradable packaging.

1. Ögon Cacao 'Eyes' logo by Olle Eksell for Mazetti (Sweden), 1956

2. Sketch of graphic design ideas for different chocolate and cocoa packaging by Olle Eksell for Mazetti (Sweden), late 1950s

3. Avanti luxury chocolate box by Olle Eksell for Mazetti (Sweden), 1956

4. Poster showing 52 logos designed by Olle Eksell during his career – published posthumously by olleeksell.se (Sweden), ca. 2016

5. Ögon Cacao – Glad Sommer (Happy Summer) poster by Olle Eksell for Mazetti (Sweden), 1956

1.

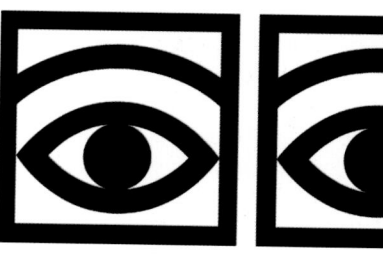

2.

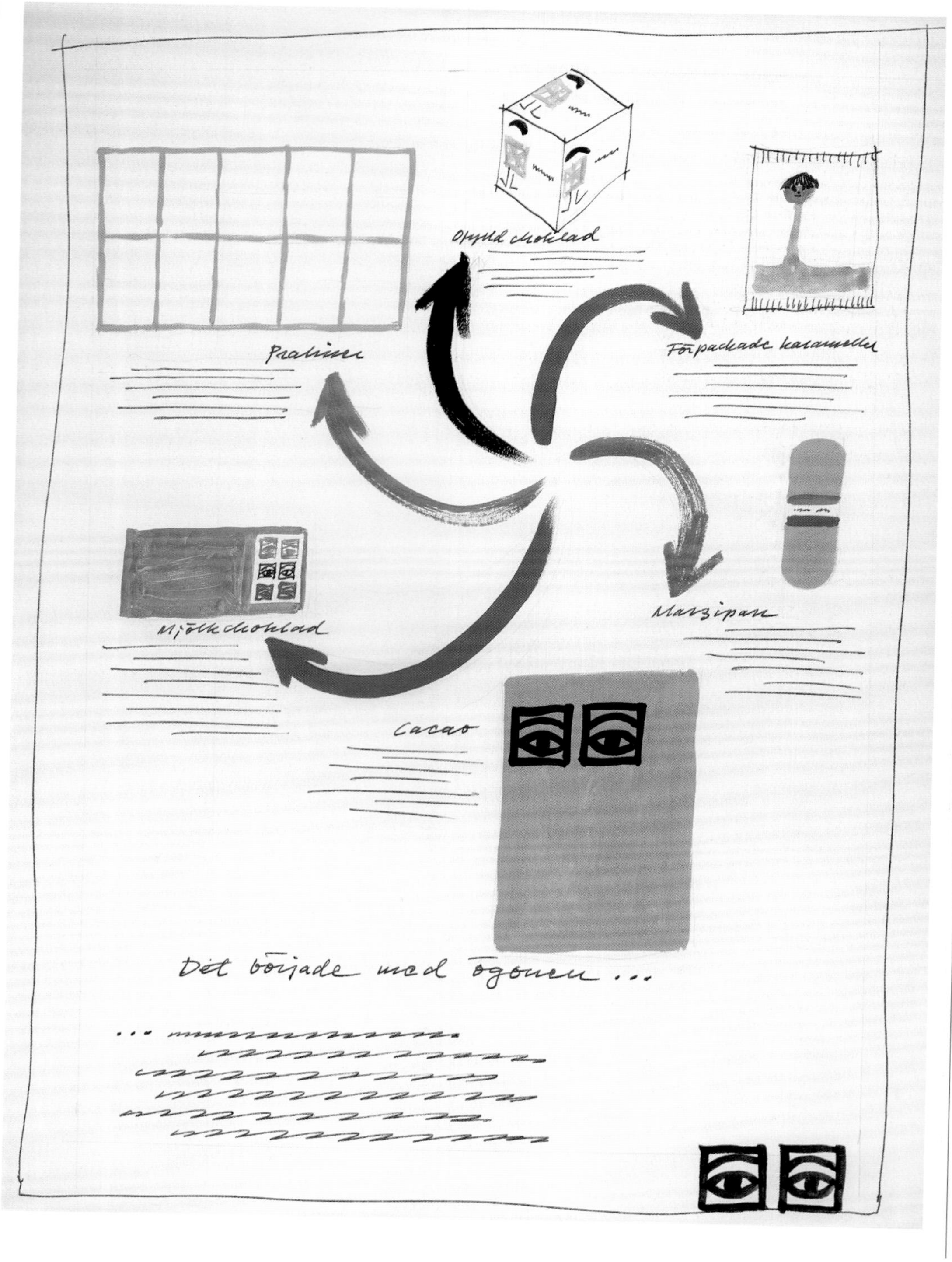

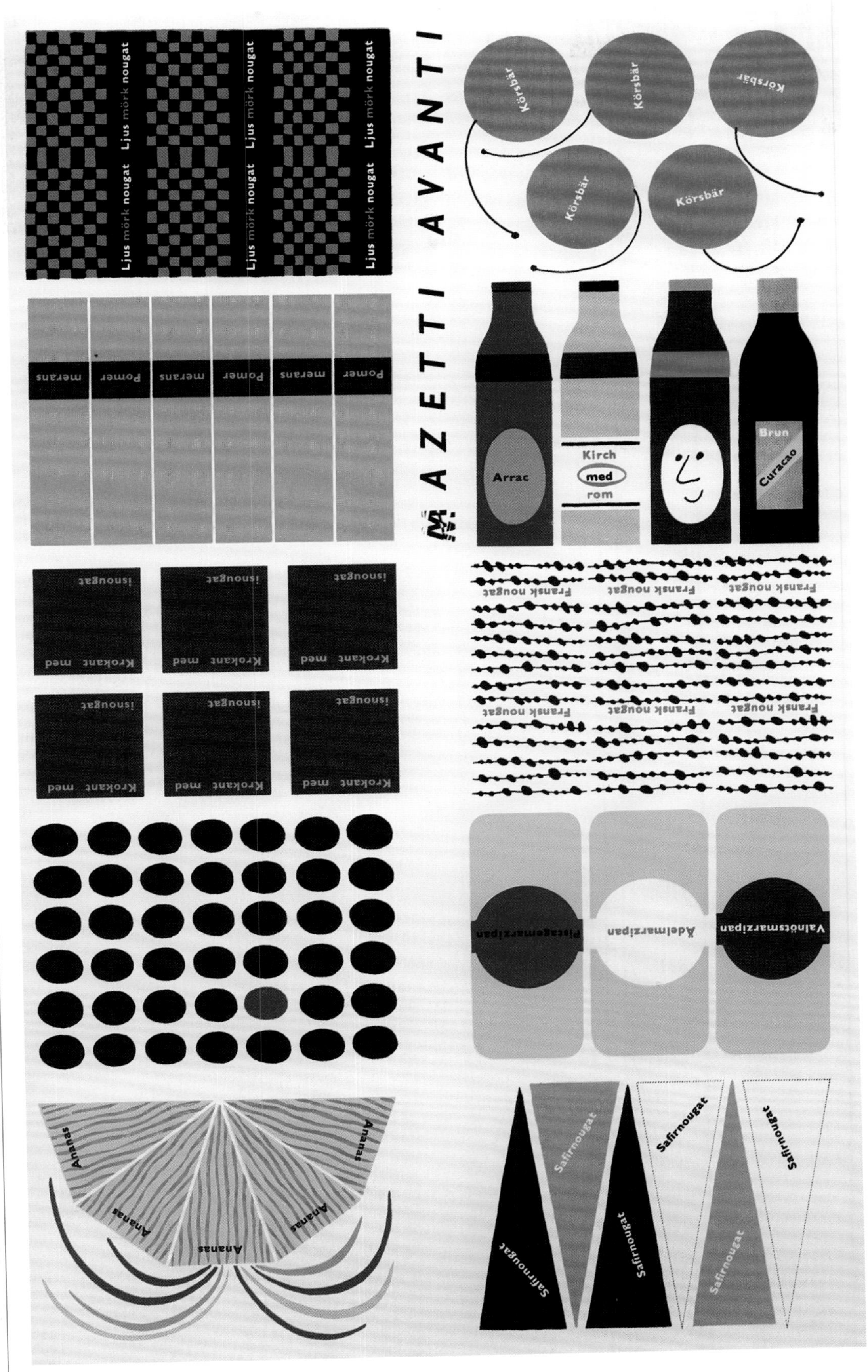
Ljus mörk nougat
AVANTI
MAZETTI
Körsbär
Pomerans
Arrac
Kirch med rom
Brun Curacao
Krokant med isnougat
Fransk nougat
Pistagemarzipan
Ädelmarzipan
Valnötsmarzipan
Ananas
Safirnougat

3.

52 logos by Olle Eksell

4.

5.

RONDO
Mazetti Småbröd
glad Sommar
mjölkcacao
GALA

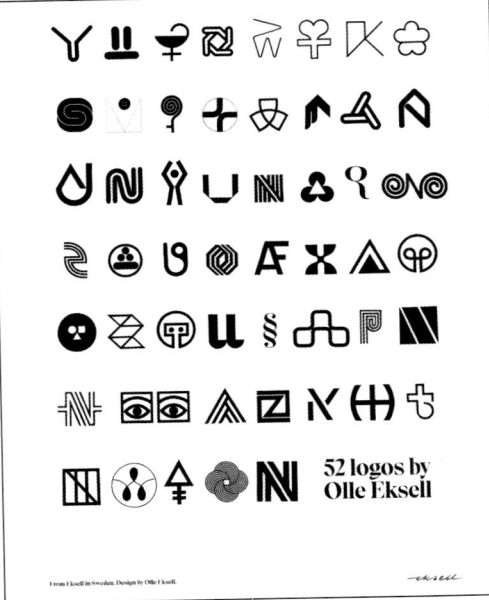

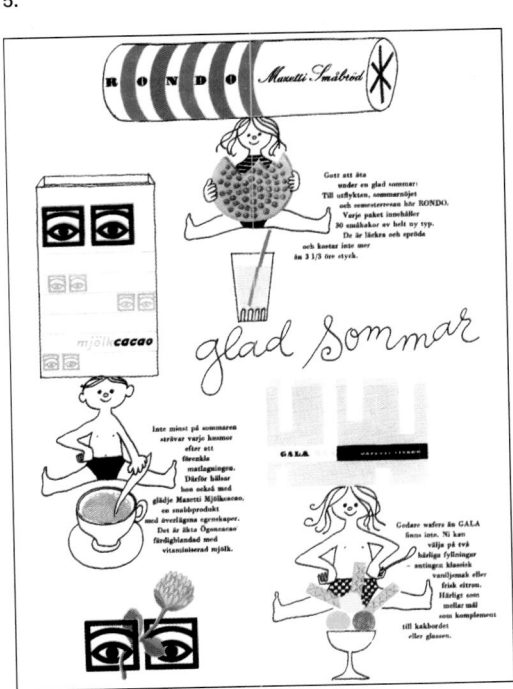

1.

2.

3.

ERIK BRUUN

Finland's most renowned graphic designer, Erik Bruun, graduated from the Central School of Industrial Arts in Helsinki in 1950. He subsequently worked as a commercial artist and exhibition designer, before establishing his own studio in 1953. During the 1950s he made a name for himself with advertising posters promoting various Finnish companies, including Fazer, Hackman, Kas Kas and Hyvon. He also famously designed a series of posters for Hartwall that launched the Jaffa drinks brand. During this period, Bruun also designed his well-known *Finland: Destination North* poster for the Finnish tourist board, which cleverly used three stylized fish to make up a simple aeroplane shape. In 1962 Bruun designed his *White-tailed Eagle* poster to highlight the threatened extinction of the species. This was the first of a series of posters spanning four decades that featured meticulously drawn representations of endangered native birds and animals. One of these posters, which featured a characterful Saimaa ringed seal, was later adopted by the Finnish Association for Nature Conversation as its mascot. As well as his poster designs, Bruun has over his long career also designed numerous logos, as well as postage stamps and banknotes. In 2008 he was awarded the Pro Finlandia medal for his immense contribution to Finnish graphic design.

1. *Finland: Destination North* poster by Erik Bruun for Finnair (Finland), 1950s

2. Pax Fazer advertising poster by Erik Bruun for Fazer (Finland), 1950s

3. Auri advertising poster by Erik Bruun for Auri (Finland), 1950s

4. Jaffa advertising poster by Erik Bruun for Hartwall (Finland), 1959

4.

IB ANTONI

A prodigiously talented graphic designer and illustrator, Ib Antoni was in high demand, with over 150 companies and organizations worldwide commissioning work from him. He was one of Denmark's leading visual artists, and his gently humorous drawing style became symbolic of his native country during the 1950s, 1960s and 1970s, instrumental in the way the nation's values were projected around the world. Indeed, his light-hearted and characterful posters for Copenhagen's Tourist Union, featuring royal guardsmen and mermaids, would become forever associated with the optimistic Danish postwar period. He was also highly regarded in the USA, where two leading advertising agencies – Young & Rubicam and J. Walter Thompson – both held exhibitions of his work, in 1957 and 1958 respectively. Over a 20-year period he produced in excess of 300 posters, which were infused with such engaging warmth and charm that they amused audiences around the world, regardless of age group or spoken language. As a creative ideas man who could so eloquently transmit his thoughts through the power of the poster, Antoni provided an enormous insight into twentieth-century Danish culture, and helped to shape it, too.

Opposite: *Altid Tør i Kawo Regntøj* (Always Dry in Kawo Rainwear) advertising poster by Ib Antoni for Aalborg Gummivarefabrik (Denmark), 1958

1. *Denmark* travel poster by Ib Antoni for Udenrigsministeriet (Danish Ministry of Foreign Affairs) (Denmark), 1964

2. *Denmark: Famous for Fine Furniture* poster by Ib Antoni for Udenrigsministeriet (Danish Ministry of Foreign Affairs), 1964 – this competition-winning poster was originally designed for the 'Danska Veckorna' (Danish Weeks) exhibition held in Stockholm, and reused for the New York World's Fair (1964–65)

1.

2.

STURE JOHANNESSON

The poster boy of the Swedish graphic underground movement, Sture Johannesson had originally worked as an assistant to the photographer Georg Oddner in the early 1960s. In 1965 Johannesson designed his first poster, *Pot Piggar Upp!* (Pot Cheer Up!), which had a nostalgic, almost Henri de Toulouse-Lautrec quality. It was the first of a number of pro-marijuana posters that Johannesson designed and published. The following year he designed a letterpress-printed calendar entitled *CIAO!*, the cover of which featured a dynamic typographic composition with a strong Dadaist flavour. It was, however, his *Revolution Means Revolutionary Consciousness!* poster of 1968 for the Underground I concert held the following year at the Lunds Konsthall art gallery that really revealed his talent for capturing the psychedelic zeitgeist. Provocatively featuring a naked pot-smoking siren, it is often just referred to as the 'Hash Girl' poster. Johannesson followed it with equally progressive posters that similarly packed a controversial political and visual punch in a nation that had for so long been dominated by classical Modernist ideals. Johannesson's skilful layering of imagery and typography presaged the use of similar techniques by the first wave of graphic designers working digitally in the early 1990s.

1. *Revolution Means Revolutionary Consciousness!* lithographic poster by Sture Johannesson, printed by Permild & Rosengreen for Underground I concert at Lunds Konsthall (Sweden), 1968 – often referred to as the 'Hash Girl' poster

2. *Find Out Yourself* lithographic poster by Sture Johannesson for Gallery Cannabis/Legal Visions (Sweden), 1969

3. *Andrée Will Take a Trip!* silk-screen poster by Sture Johannesson for Underground III concert at Lunds Konsthall (Sweden), 1969

4. *Modellen: En Modell för ett Kvalitativt Samhälle* (A Model for a Qualitative Society) poster by Sture Johannesson for Moderna Museet Stockholm (Sweden), 1968

1.

The one word 'frank' . . . is used . . . to express aught that is generous, straightforward, and free. The Franks . . . were a powerful German tribe . . . honorably distinguished by their love of freedom, their scorn of a lie.
TRENCH On the Study of Words lect. i, p. 10. [K. P. & CO. 1888.]
2. In the Orient, any European: so called from the French of the crusades. See FERINGEE. 3. [f-] A French coin, the franc. [< AS. Franca, < LL. Francus,
A POSTER TO EVERY CANDYMAN & HIS LEGAL VISION BUSINESS BY STURE JOHANNESSON · ©1969 BOX 4271 MALMÖ 4 SWEDEN · PHOTO: PER-ROLAND · PRINTED IN DENMARK BY PERMILD & ROSENGREEN

2.

!EXTRA!
ANDRÉE
WILL TAKE A TRIP!
ANYTHING WHICH CAN BE DONE CHEMICALLY CAN BE DONE BY OTHER MEANS
ON BEHALF OF LADY JANE & LUNDS STADS DRÄTSELKAMMARE
UNDERGROUND
LUNDS KONSTHALL

3.

4.

MODELLEN
EN MODELL FÖR ETT KVALITATIVT SAMHÄLLE
MODERNA MUSEET
POLISEN VISAR VÄGEN

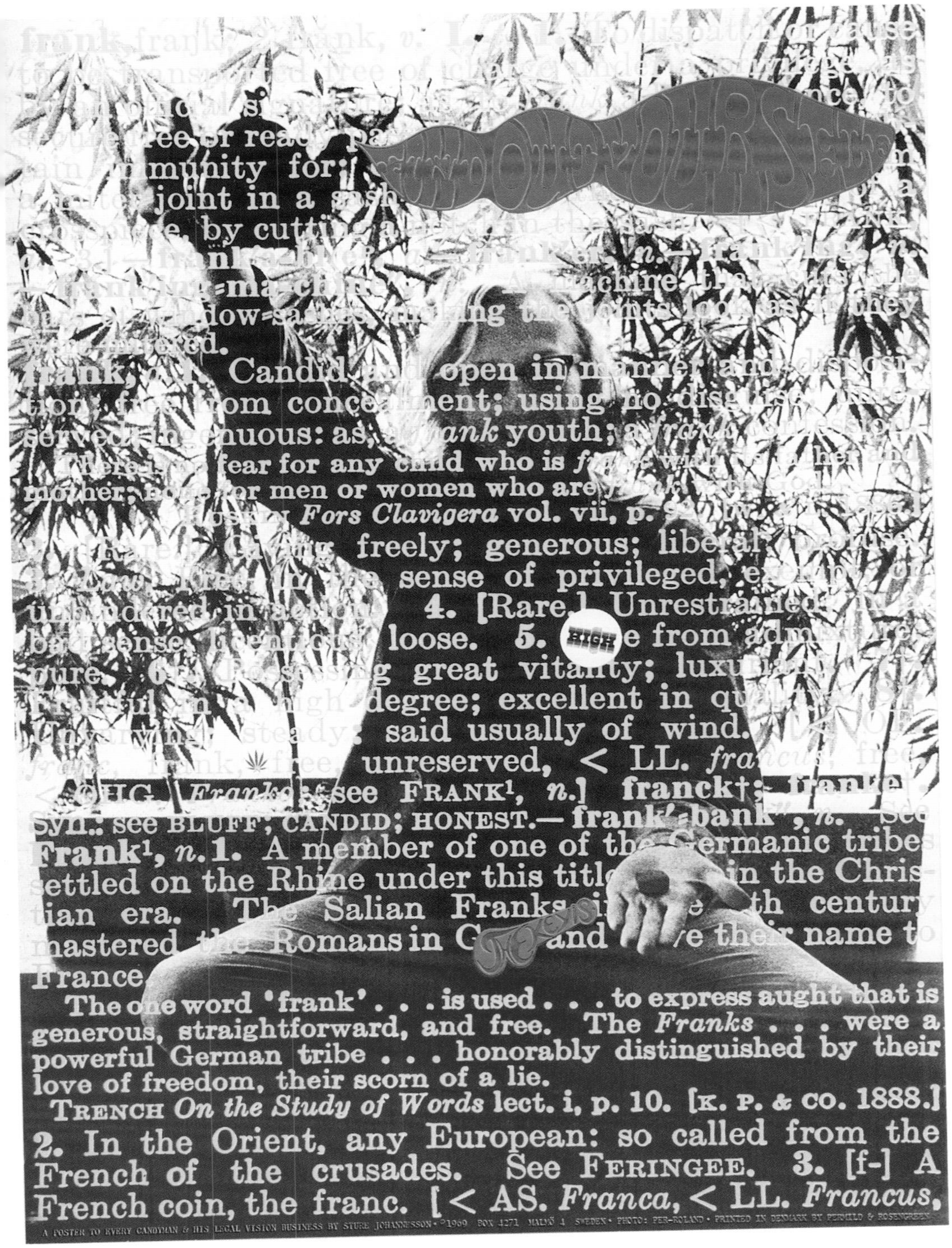

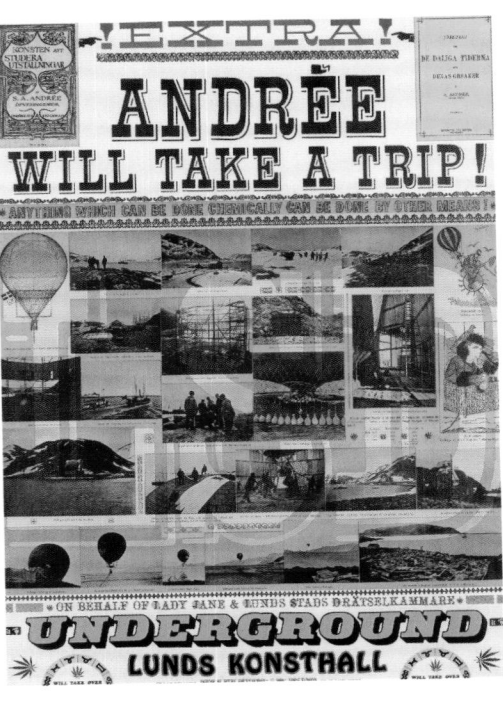

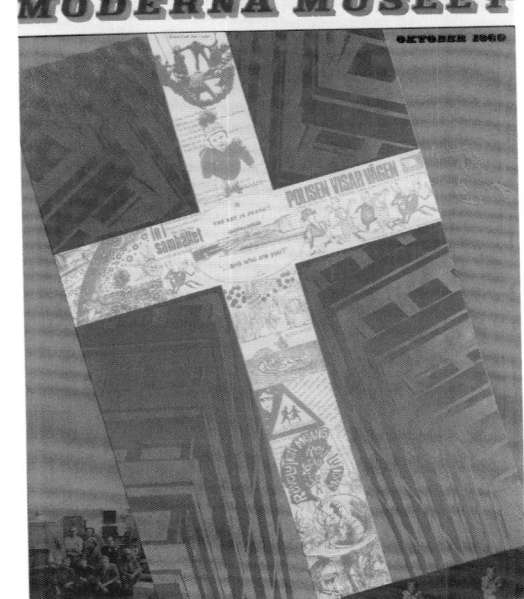

MOBILIA

From the mid 1950s to the mid 1980s *Mobilia* was Scandinavia's foremost international design journal, as notable for its innovative graphic design as for its superlative editorial content. Published in Denmark, each issue was dramatically different from the one that preceded it, and most were based on a single theme or designer. For example, one edition was dedicated solely to the work of Verner Panton, another to the output of Georg Jensen and another to designers who had won the prestigious Lunning Prize for design excellence. The editors of this influential monthly magazine included the furniture designer Grete Jalk, the architect Erik Møller and the wayfinding guru Per Mollerup. Crucially for its international success, this square-format magazine was published as a multi-language edition with articles appearing in Swedish, English, French and German. This enabled it to disseminate very widely knowledge of both Scandinavian and non-Scandinavian design.

1 & 5. Cover and internal pages of *Mobilia* magazine no. 236, published by Mobilia Press (Denmark), March 1975

2. *Mobilia* magazine no. 167/168, published by Mobilia Press (Denmark), June/July 1969

3. *Mobilia* magazine no. 208/209, published by Mobilia Press (Denmark), November/December 1972

4. *Mobilia* magazine no. 96, published by Mobilia Press (Denmark), July 1963

1.

2.

NO. 208/209 – NOVEMBER/DECEMBER 1972

3.

4.

5.

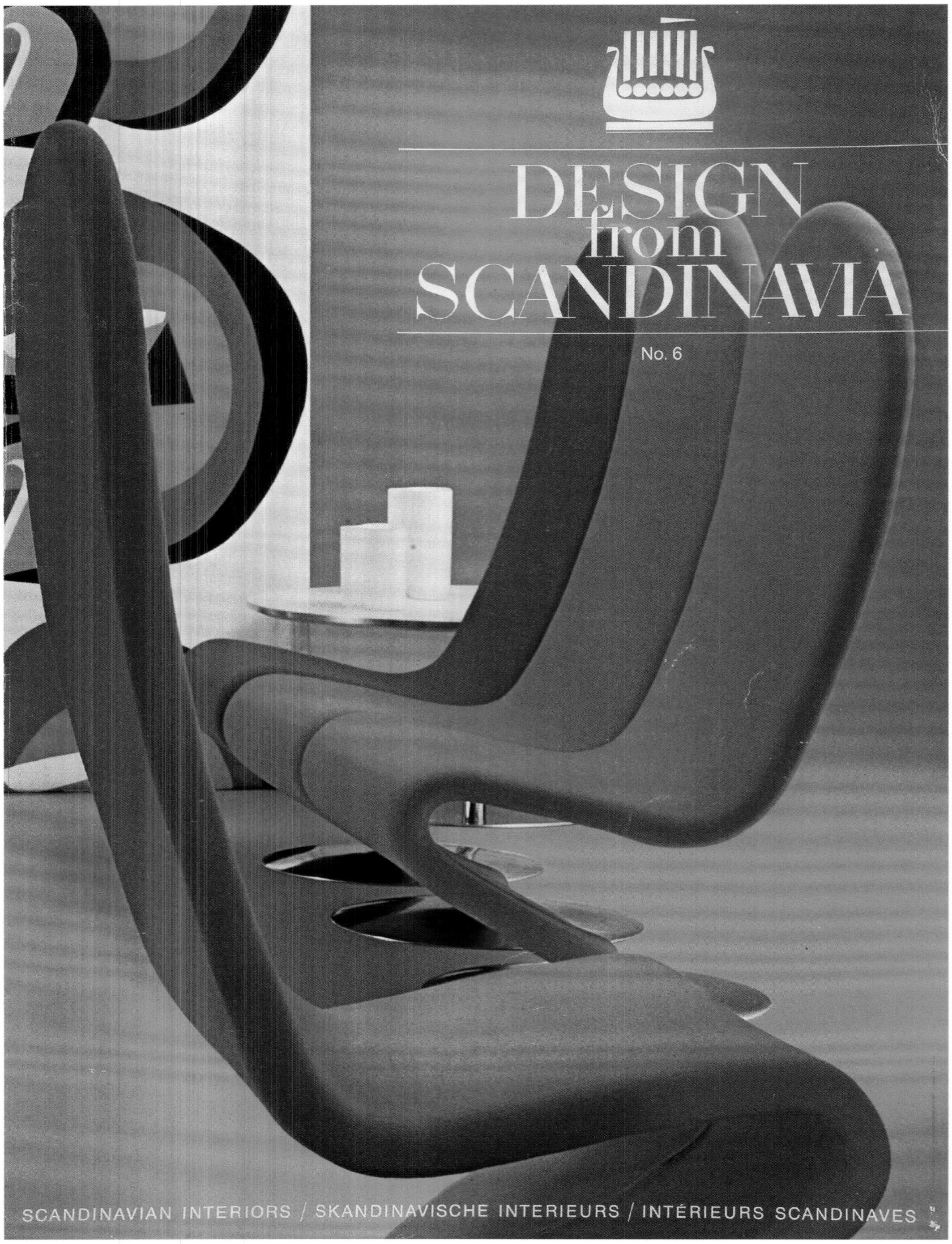
DESIGN
from
SCANDINAVIA
No. 6
SCANDINAVIAN INTERIORS / SKANDINAVISCHE INTERIEURS / INTÉRIEURS SCANDINAVES

1.

DESIGN
from
SCANDINAVIA
No. 7
SCANDINAVIAN INTERIORS / SKANDINAVISCHE INTERIEURS / INTÉRIEURS SCANDINAVES

2.

3.

SCANDINAVIAN INTERIORS / SKANDINAVISCHE INTERIEURS / INTÉRIEURS SCANDINAVES
DESIGN
from
SCANDINAVIA

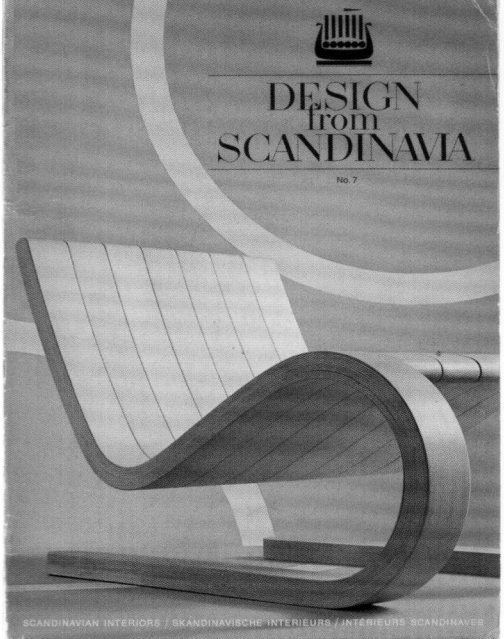

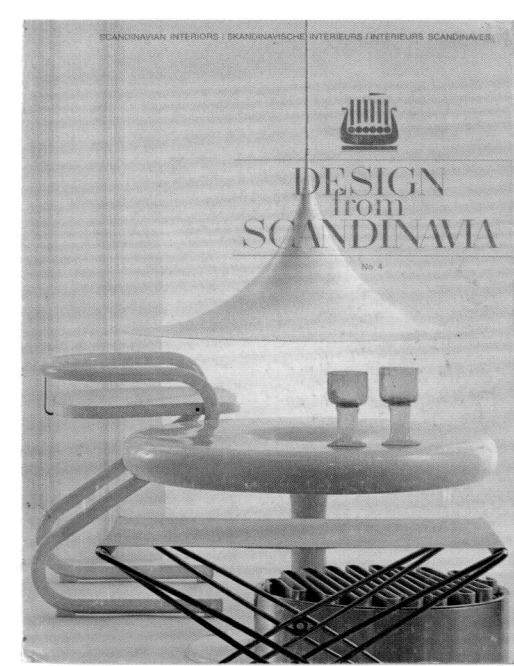

DESIGN FROM SCANDINAVIA

In 1967 Kirsten Bjerregaard launched a new annual magazine entitled *Design from Denmark* with the aim of producing a 'design exhibition in the form of a book'. Some 50,000 copies of this first design yearbook were distributed, and the following year the publication was renamed *Design from Scandinavia* to reflect its expanded remit, which now included contemporary designs from Sweden, Norway and Finland. While showcasing the latest currents in Scandinavian design, this trilingual journal – published in English, German and French – was itself on-trend when it came to page layout and cover design. From the outset it was art-directed by Ib Clausen, who incorporated opening pages featuring beautifully outline-drawn illustrations of various Scandinavian design classics. This large-format magazine also boasted bold covers, and the first few issues had a stylized Viking ship logo set atop the distinctive typographic title. Clausen's cover format remained virtually unchanged until the publication of the journal's 22nd edition in 2006, when it was given a light updating. Sadly, *Design from Scandinavia* is no longer published, but its back issues provide an outstanding insight into one of the golden periods of Scandinavian design.

1. *Design from Scandinavia* magazine no. 6, published by World Pictures (Denmark), 1973 – art-directed by Ib Clausen

2. *Design from Scandinavia* magazine no. 7, published by World Pictures (Denmark), 1974 – art-directed by Ib Clausen

3 & below: Cover and interior pages of *Design from Scandinavia* magazine no. 4, published by World Pictures (Denmark), 1971 – art-directed by Ib Clausen

TIVOLI POSTERS

Having visited various parks and pleasure gardens abroad, Georg Carstensen persuaded King Christian VIII of Denmark to grant him permission to open the Tivoli Gardens in the Vesterport (West Gate) area of Copenhagen in 1843, using the argument that 'when the people are amusing themselves, they do not think about politics.' The 8-hectare site, which now incorporates an extensive amusement park with various rides from carousels to rollercoasters, as well as exotic and fanciful landscaped gardens, has since its inception been advertised to the public with colourful, attention-grabbing posters. Indeed, there has been a tradition since the early twentieth century of leading graphic artists designing Tivoli posters, which happily continues to this day. Among the many posters devised for the gardens over the decades, the four shown here are among the most celebrated. Each conveys the playful spirit of the gardens with carefully balanced illustrative content and attention-grabbing typography, while also being in tune with the most progressive stylistic tendencies of its own time.

1. *Tivoli* poster by Ib Andersen for Tivoli Gardens (Denmark), 1943

2. *Tivoli 1843–1968* poster by Ib Antoni for Tivoli Gardens (Denmark), 1968

3. *Tivoli* poster by Bjørn Wiinblad for Tivoli Gardens (Denmark), 1981

4. *Summer in Tivoli* poster by &Co for Tivoli Gardens (Denmark), ca. 2011

1.

2.

TIVOLI

3.

4.

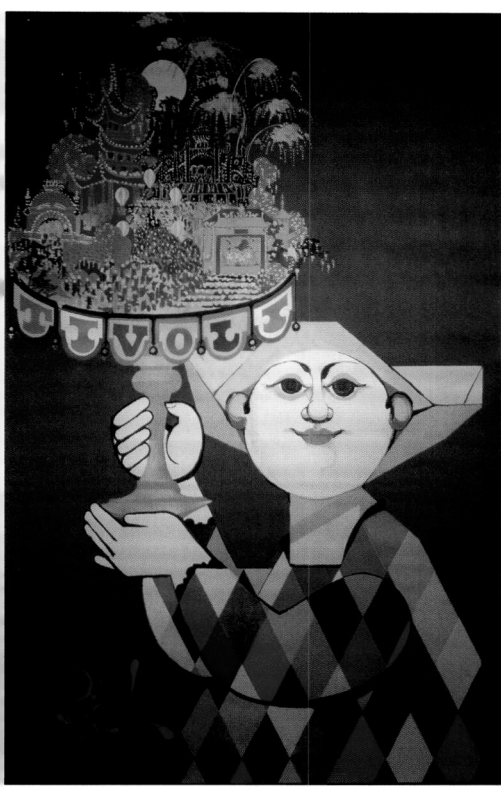

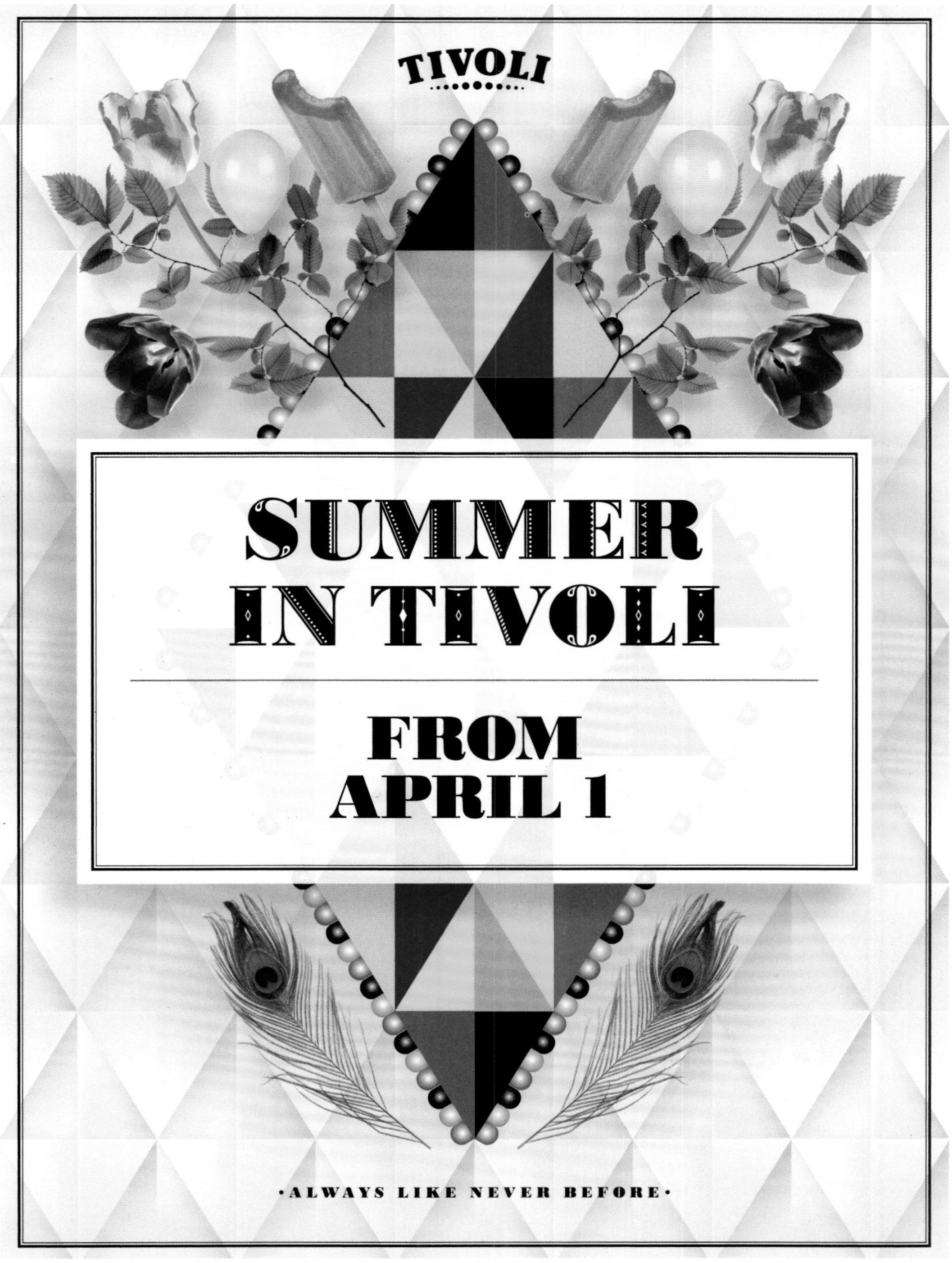
TIVOLI
SUMMER
IN TIVOLI
FROM
APRIL 1
·ALWAYS LIKE NEVER BEFORE·

SAS
Stockholm
abc
New York
06:25
08:40
20:05
Quick
Some travel in their minds
Some in their hearts
Welcome to the third choice
SAS Cargo
Beijing
737-600
TOKYO4345:-
LIKE A SWISS CLOCK, BUT SCANDINAVIAN.
Tokyo

Scandinavian
AaBbCcDdEeFfGgHhIiJjKkLlMmNnOoPpQqRrSsTtUu
VvWwXxYyZz1234567890(&.,:?!)§$£€™
SAS98/09/24
01
Boeing 737
Boeing 737
Boeing 737
ab

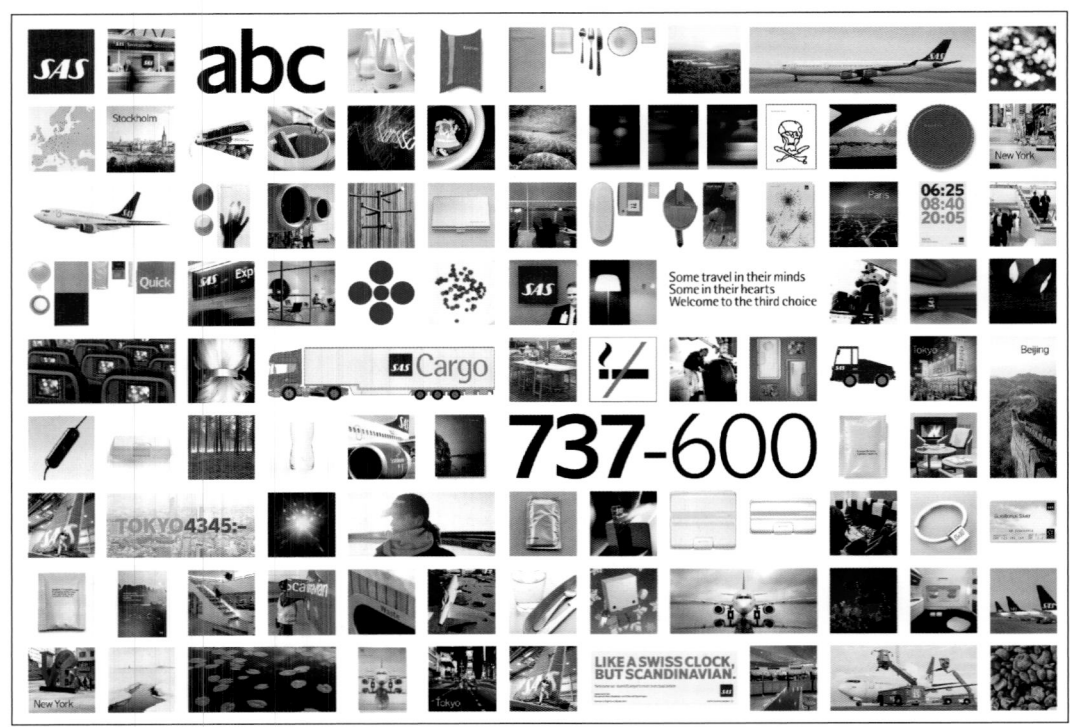

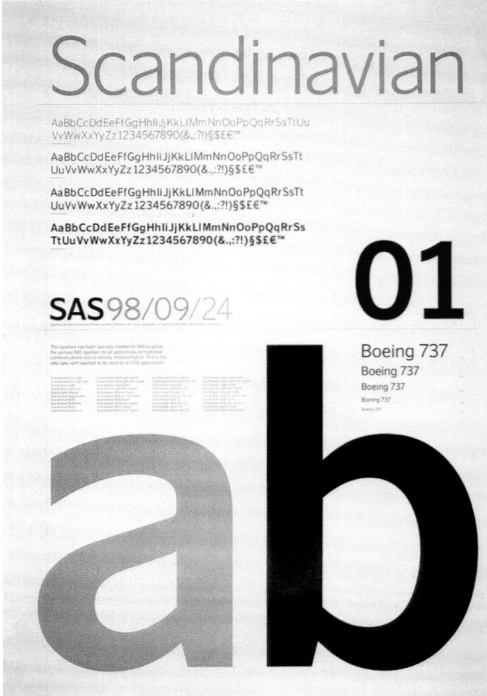

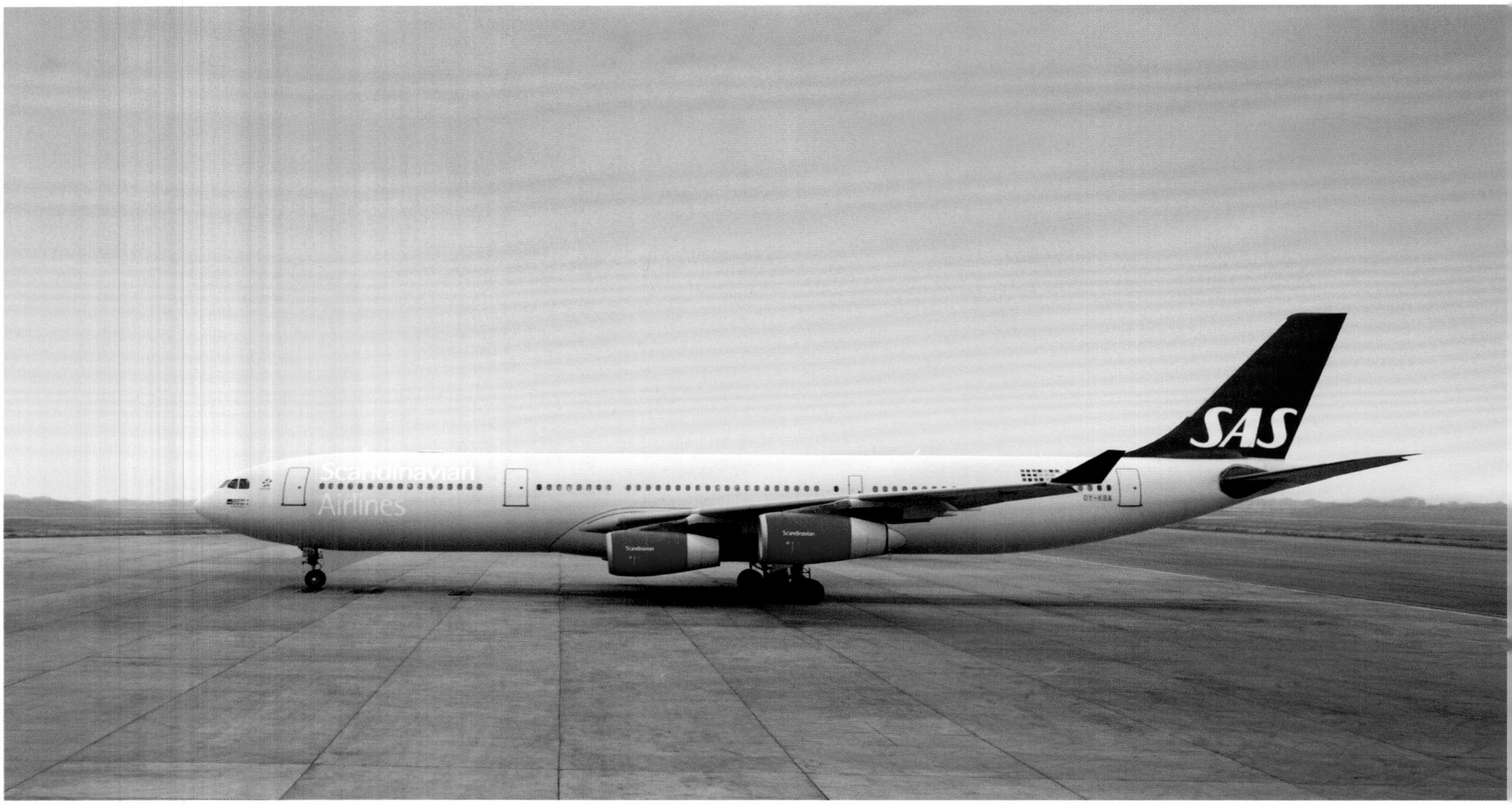
SAS
Scandinavian
Airlines

STOCKHOLM DESIGN LAB

Stockholm Design Lab (SDL) is one of Scandinavia's leading multidisciplinary studios and is especially acclaimed for its communications and branding work. Founded in 1998 by Björn Kusoffsky, Thomas Eriksson and Göran Lagerström – a creative director, an architect and a design strategist – SDL has since its inception focused equally on these three areas of expertise. Kusoffsky explains: 'Our design philosophy is rooted in Scandinavian tradition and based on the fundamental ideas of simplicity, clarity, openness and innovation.' The studio is best known for its comprehensive corporate identity programme for Scandinavian Airlines (SAS), which spanned 14 years and comprised 2,400 different applications, including aircraft livery, signage, uniforms, young-flyer packs and hand-wipe packaging. Other notable projects have included a house typeface and packaging for IKEA, and the distinctive graffiti-like identity of Stockholm's Moderna Museet.

Opposite: Identity design programme for Scandinavian Airlines (Sweden), 1998–2012 – included aircraft livery to airport signage, as well as a bespoke typeface, and was done in conjunction with project partner TEA Architects (Thomas Eriksson Arkitekter)

1. Logo for Åhlens (Sweden), 2011

2. Food-packaging design (sardine tin) for IKEA (Sweden), 2004 onwards – SDL has created numerous designs for IKEA, including its own corporate typeface (2004) and furniture-packaging system (1999)

3. Packaging design (batteries) for Askul (Sweden), 2005 onwards – SDL have designed packaging for over 200 Askul products

1.

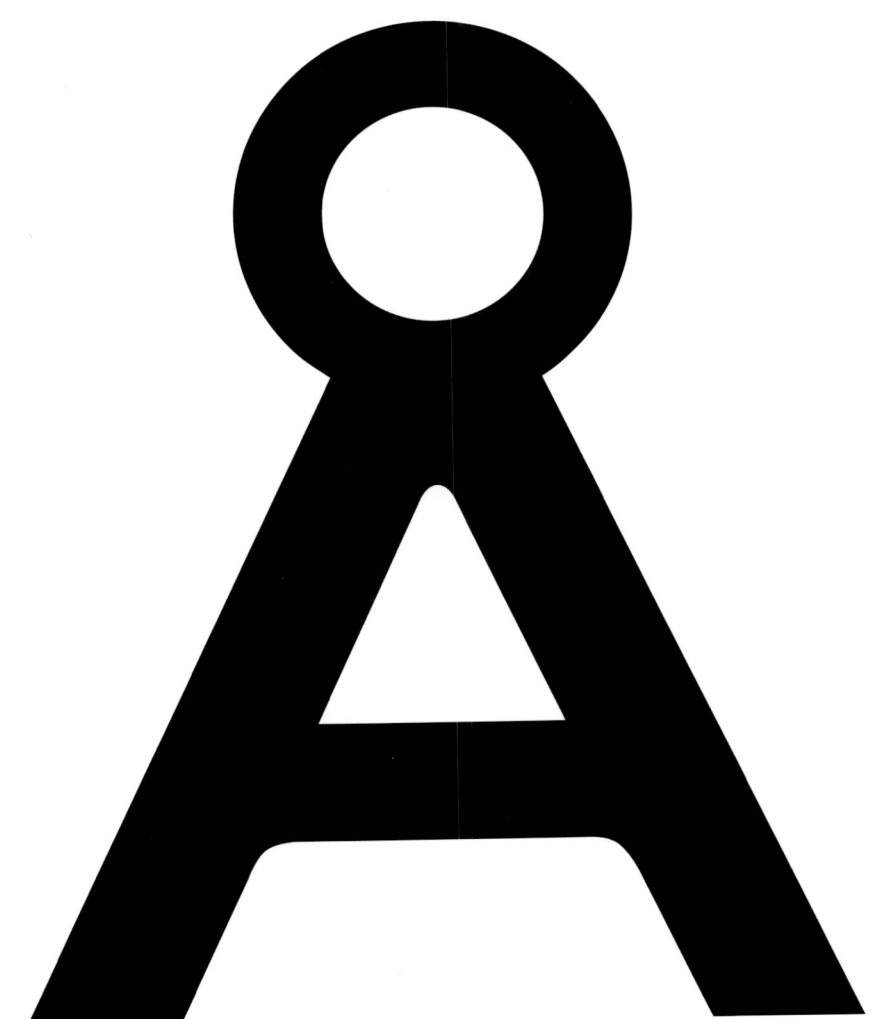

3.

2.

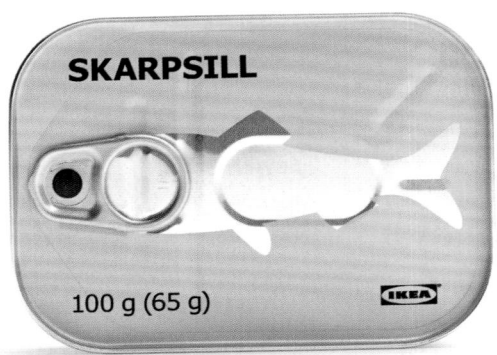

SWEDISH NEO-MODERNITY

Of all the Nordic countries, Sweden is probably identified the most with progressive visual communication design, thanks to the pioneering work of various Stockholm-based graphic designers and professional design practices during the latter half of the twentieth century, such as Vidar Forsberg, Melin & Österlin, Carl Fredrik Hultenheim, Tom Hedqvist and Per Mollerup. These graphic-design luminaries essentially laid the visual-communication foundations from which later designers were able to develop a very Swedish Neo-Modern graphic language, which emerged in the late 1980s with, for example, H. C. Ericson's eye-catching poster for Lammhults. Whether it is an exhibition catalogue by Malmsten Hellberg, a Karlsson's vodka bottle by Hans Brindfors, or even Gabor Palotai's iconic *Scandinavian Design Beyond the Myth* poster, each has evolved from a thorough grounding in Modern Swedish visual communications and has, therefore, a very distinctive Scandinavian clarity and directness, even if at times a touch of light-hearted subversion comes into play.

Below: *Grand Theory Hotel: Annika von Hausswolff* by Malmsten Hellberg for Hasselblad Center (Sweden), 2016

1, 2 & 3. *Scandinavian Design Beyond the Myth* exhibition posters by Gabor Palotai for the Nordic Co-operation/The Nordic Council of Ministers (Sweden), 2006

4. Vodka bottle packaging design by Hans Brindfors for Karlsson's (Sweden), 2008 – the potato-shaped bottle refers to the spirit's central ingredient

5. Poster by H. C. Ericson for Lammhults (Sweden), 1986

1.

SKANDINAVISCHES DESIGN
JENSEITS DES MYTHOS
7. NOV. 2003 – 29. FEB. 2004

S M
B Kunstgewerbemuseum
Staatliche Museen
zu Berlin

2.

SCANDINAVIAN DESIGN BEYOND THE MYTH
Röhsska museet 3.12.2005 – 26.02.2006
Vasagatan 37 – 39 www.designmuseum.se

3.

SKANDINĀVIJAS DIZAINS VINPUS MĪTA
24. marts – 5. jūnijs, 2005
11.00 – 17.00; Tr.: 11.00 – 19.00; Pirmd.- slēgts.
Dekoratīvi lietišķās mākslas muzejs. Skārņu iela 10/20
SCANDINAVIAN DESIGN BEYOND THE MYTH
March 24 – June 5, 2005
11 a.m. – 5 p.m.; Wed. 11 a.m.– 7 p.m.; Mon.- closed.
Museum of Decorative Applied Arts. 10/20 Skārņu St.

4.

5.

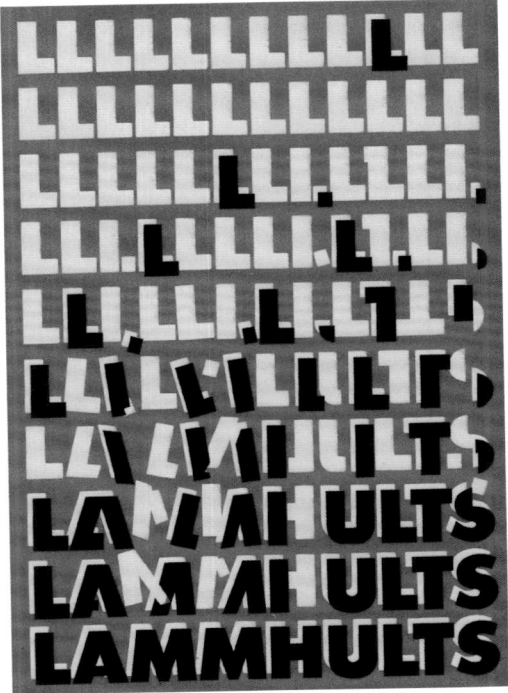

NEW NORDIC VISUAL COMMUNICATIONS

Since the mid 2000s, in reaction to the pervasive slickness of so much commercial graphic design, many of the more progressive designers have sought to infuse their work with a sense of authenticity by either producing work of a more illustrative nature or referencing handicraft skills. The designs shown here, ranging from subway maps and food packaging to book design and complete corporate-identity programmes, illustrate how this new arts-and-crafts direction has been developed and refined by graphic designers working in Sweden and Denmark. Indeed, the work has a definable Scandinavian look, a light-hearted poetic sweetness that pays homage to the rich folk traditions of the Nordic region. But, more than anything else, it transmits the long-held belief in Scandinavian design circles that thoughtful design can enrich our everyday lives.

1. Packaging design by Lundgren+Lindqvist for O/O Brewing (Sweden), 2015

2. Drink and popcorn packaging by Happy F&B for Liseberg (Sweden), 2012–2013 – part of a complete rebranding exercise undertaken for Gothenburg's historic amusement park

3. *Visual Identity Design* (exhibition catalogue) by Studio Claus Due for National Gallery of Denmark (Design), 2013–16

4. *Trädgårdsmästarens anteckningar* (Gardener's Notes) by André Strömqvist, book design by Lotta Kühlhorn for Norstedts (Sweden), 2016

5. Stockholm subway map by Fellow Designers for SL (Storstockholms Lokaltrafik) (Sweden), 2014

1.

2.

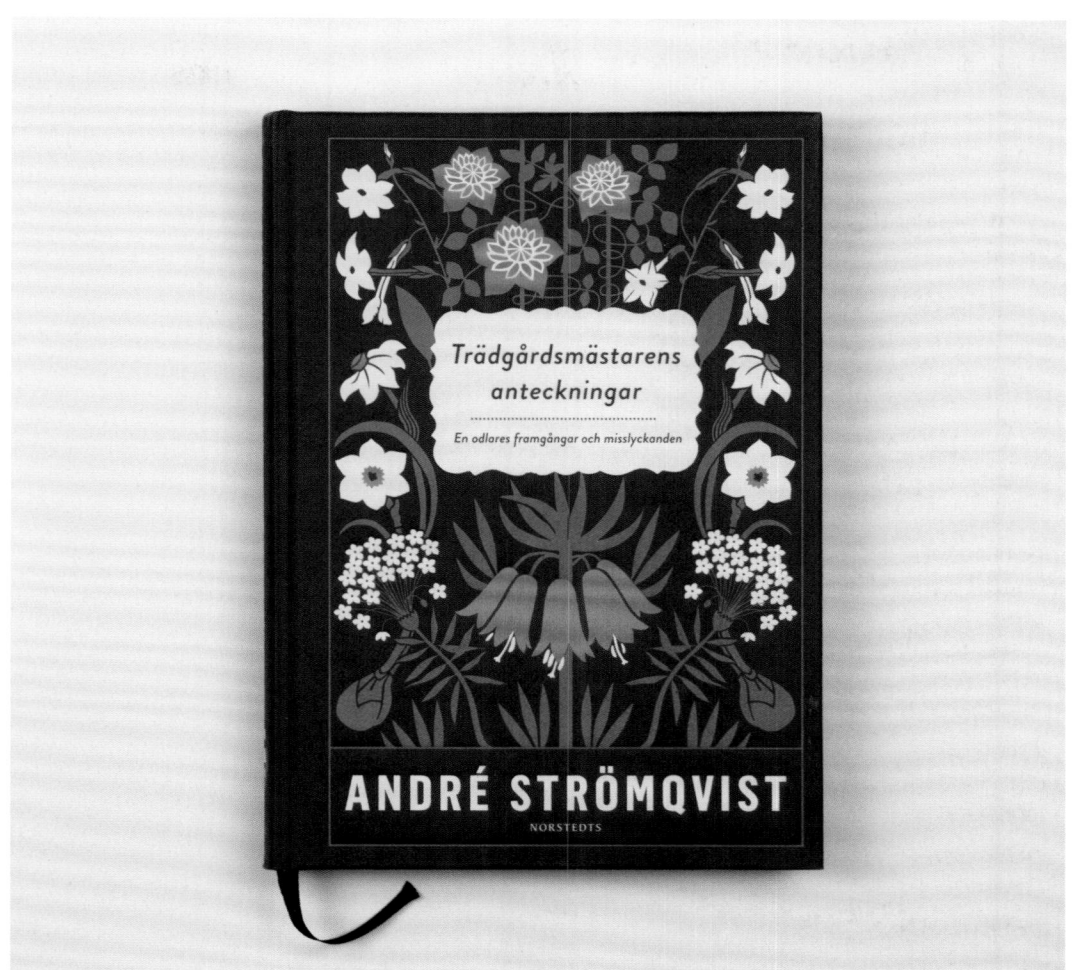

3.

4.

5.

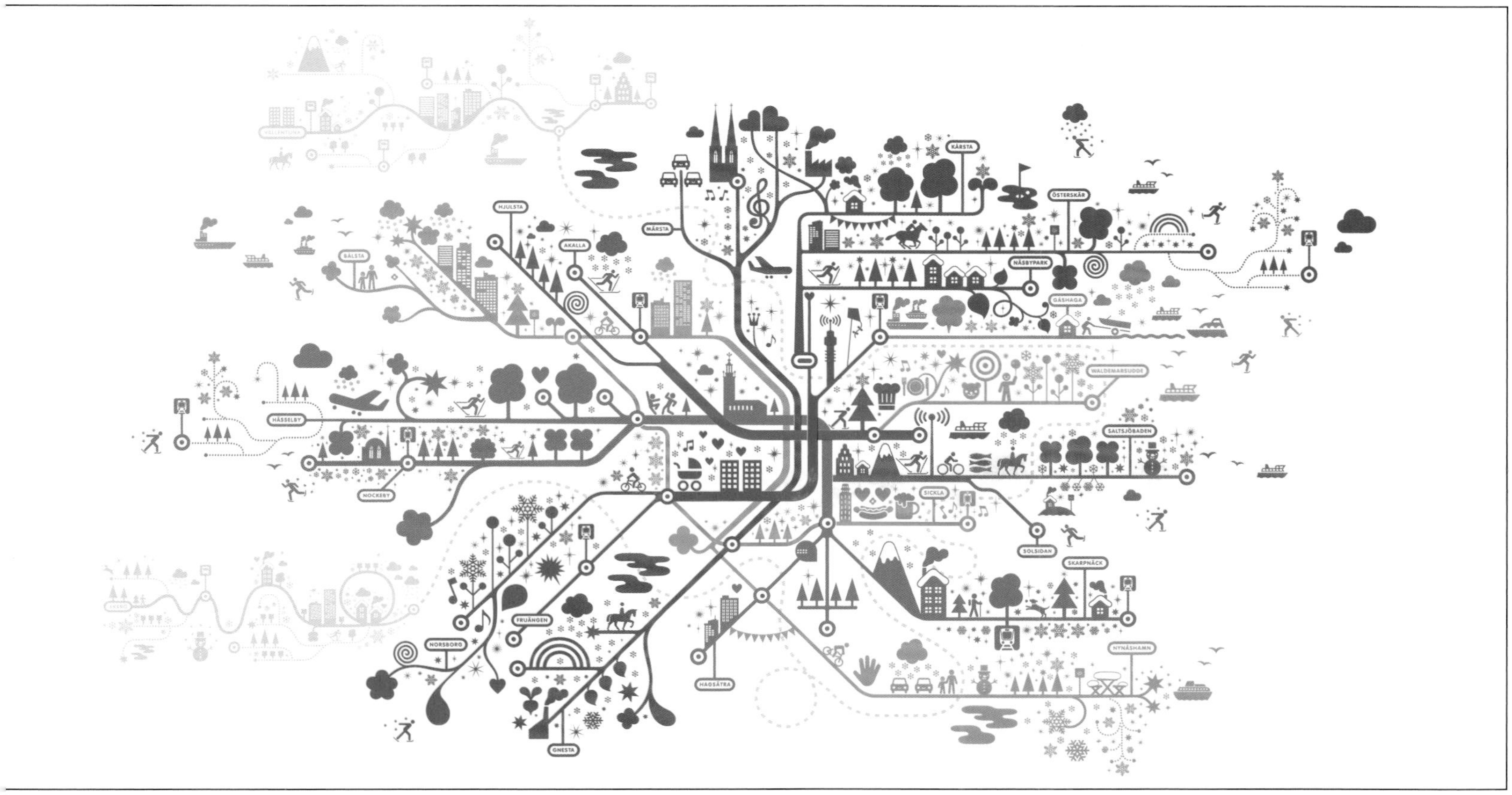

RESOURCES

AUCTION HOUSES

Bruun Rasmussen Kunstauktioner
A well-known Copenhagen-based saleroom specializing in mainly Danish design, which has set various world records for furniture and ceramics within this increasingly popular area of collecting activity.
www.bruun-rasmussen.dk

Bukowskis
This Stockholm-headquartered auction house is the largest in the Nordic region and has an impressive range of design-related sales throughout the year, as well as an excellent Internet-based 'market' site. It boasts showrooms in Stockholm, Gothenberg, Malmö, Norrköping and Helsinki, which accommodate a wide price-point range for all levels of collectors.
www.bukowskis.com

Dorotheum
Central Europe's largest auction house, this saleroom is headquartered in Vienna and holds regular design sales, which often include Scandinavian pieces. An especially good place to find rare and interesting pieces by Verner Panton.
www.dorotheum.com

Lauritz
Headquartered in Copenhagen, this auction house has salerooms in Denmark, Sweden, Norway, Belgium and Germany and holds regular sales offering an interesting range of Scandinavian design pieces across a very broad price point range.
www.lauritz.com

Pierre Bergé & Associés
This high-end auction room located in Paris and Brussels holds regular sales dedicated to Scandinavian design, which often feature rare examples of iconic Nordic classics. A firm favourite among the interior design cognoscenti.
www.pba-auctions.com

Phillips
This well-known international saleroom has a very strong 20th- and 21st-century design department that holds dedicated Scandinavian design sales. Often realizing world-record prices, Phillips predominately specializes in the very finest and often rarest examples of Scandinavian design classics.
www.phillips.com

Rago
Based in Lambertville, New Jersey, Rago holds regular Modern Design and Modern Ceramics and Glass sales, and occasionally has interesting Scandinavian pieces to be found within these auctions.
www.ragoarts.com

Stockholms Auktionverk
This Swedish saleroom is the world's oldest auction house having been founded back in 1674 and is now a leading marketplace for Nordic design pieces.
www.auktionsverk.com

Quittenbaum Kunstauktionen
This highly regarded Munich-based saleroom holds regular Design auctions throughout the year, and occasionally ones specifically dedicated to Scandinavian design. It is an excellent source for more obscure and unusual design pieces, including collectible Nordic items.
www.quittenbaum.de

Wright
This US-based saleroom is quite simply one of the best sources for interesting high-end design pieces and holds numerous sales throughout the year in Chicago and New York, including auctions specifically dedicated to Scandinavian Design. It also has its own excellent 'Wright Now' online shop with new collectibles posted weekly.
www.wright20.com

SPECIALIST DESIGN GALLERIES + DEALERS

AntikBar
Located on London's Kings Road, this gallery specializes in original vintage posters and always carries a very good selection of Nordic travel posters.
www.antikbar.co.uk

Bacchus Antik
This Stockholm gallery focuses on mid- to high-end Scandinavian Modern art glass, ceramics, lighting and furniture, while also offering a good range of Scandinavian Art Nouveau pieces, too.
www.bacchusantik.com

Dansk Møbelkunst Gallery
Established in 1992, this well-known Copenhagen-based gallery focuses on rare and original Danish furniture and lighting from 1920 to 1975 and has a satellite gallery in Paris.
www.dmk.dk

Gooday Gallery
London-based gallery selling designed artifacts and antiques from 1880 to present, with a special emphasis on interesting pieces of Scandinavian jewellery.
www.thegoodaygallery.com

Klassik Modern Møbelkunst
One of Copenhagen's largest design galleries, this elegant store specializes in top-end vintage furniture, lighting and ceramics, as well as fine art. Great for interior design inspiration as the pieces are so beautifully presented.
www.klassik.dk

L'Affichiste
Montreal's acclaimed L'Affichiste gallery sells original vintage posters reflecting a wide range of different periods and themes, while offering a good selection of Danish advertising and travel posters.
www.laffichiste.com

Jacksons
Based in Stockholm, this long-established design gallery specializes in the very best of Scandinavian design, with a special emphasis on sublime examples of the Scandinavian classics as well as early Nordic Modern pieces from the 1920s and 1930s – it also holds regular exhibitions and has a satellite gallery in Berlin.
www.jacksons.se

Modernity
Based in Stockholm, this highly regarded design gallery specializes in top-end Scandinavian furniture, glassware, lighting, textiles, ceramics and fine art, and always has very strong offerings of Nordic jewellery.
www.modernity.se

Out of Copenhagen
This online 'original vintage poster shop' offers a good selection of collectible Nordic posters, including various covetable Danish and Swedish travel posters and some iconic Tivoli posters, too.
www.outofcopenhagen.com

Rennert's Gallery
This New York-based gallery has an impressive stock of original vintage posters for sale, and also holds regular poster auctions, which sometimes feature rare and interesting Nordic posters.
www.rennertsgallery.com

Themes & Variations
One of London's leading specialists in postwar and contemporary design, Themes & Variations, though specializing in top French and Italian design, also stocks the occasional piece of high-end design from Scandinavia.
www.themesandvariations.com

SCANDINAVIAN DESIGN LIFESTYLE RETAILERS

H. Skjalm P.
www.hskjalmp.dk

Illums Bolighus
www.illumsbolighus.com

Pur Norsk
www.purnorsk.no

Skandium
www.skandium.com

MANUFACTURERS

Adelta
www.adelta.de

Arabia
www.arabia.fi

ArchitectMade
www.architectmade.com

Artek
www.artek.fi

Asplund
www.asplund.org

Ateljé Lyktan
www.atelje-lyktan.se

Brio
www.brio.se

Bruundesign
www.bruundesign.com

By Lassen
www.bylassen.com

Carl Hansen & Søn
www.carlhansen.com

Dale of Norway
www.daleofnorway.com

Dansk Plakatkunst
www.danskplakatkunst.dk

Design House Stockholm
www.designhousestockholm.com

Eeno Aarnio Originals
www.aarniooriginals.com

Erik Jørgensen
www.erik-joergensen.com

Fritz Hansen
www.fritzhansen.com

Finlayson
www.finlaysonshop.com

Fjordfiesta
www.fjordfiesta.com

Fuzzy
www.fuzzy.is

Gense
www.gense.se

Georg Jensen
www.georgjensen.com

House of Juhl
www.finnjuhl.com

Hay
www.hay.dk

Holmegaard
www.holmegaard.com

Ib Antoni
www.ibantoni.dk

Iittala
www.iittala.com

575.

IKEA
www.ikea.com

IQ Light
www.iqlight.com

Jobs Handtryck
www.jobshandtryck.se

Kähler
www.kahlerdesign.com

Källemo
www.kallemo.se

Karl Andersson & Söner
www.karl-andersson.se

Kay Bojesen
www.kaybojesen-denmark.com

Kosta Boda
www.kostaboda.com

Kvadrat
www.kvadrat.dk

Lammhults Möbel
www.lammhults.se

Lapponia
www.lapponia.com

Le Klint
www.leklint.com

LEGO
www.lego.com

Lightyears
www.lightyears.dk

Louis Poulsen
www.louispoulsen.com

Marimekko
www.marimekko.com

Muuto
www.muuto.com

Normann Copenhagen
www.normann-copenhagen.com

Northern Lighting
www.northernlighting.no

Olle Eksell
www.olleeksell.se

Orrefors
www.orrefors.com

Pandul
www.pandul.dk

Permafrost
www.permafrost.no

Pia Wallén
www.piawallen.se

Piiroinen Group
www.piiroinen.com

Playsam
www.playsam.com

PP Møbler
www.pp.dk

Rörstrand
www.rorstrand.com

Royal Copenhagen
www.royalcopenhagen.com

Secto Design
www.sectodesign.fi

Sigurd Persson Design
www.sigurdpersson.se

Skultuna 1607
www.skultuna.com

Stelton
www.stelton.com

Stokke
www.stokke.com

String
www.string.se

Svenskt Tenn
www.svenskttenn.se

DESIGN MUSEUMS, INSTITUTIONS + PLACES OF INTEREST

Denmark

Dansk Arkitektur Center – DAC (Danish Architecture Centre)
Strandgade 27B
1401 Copenhagen, Denmark
www.dac.dk

Dansk Design Centre
Bygning B, Fæstningens Materialgård
Frederiksholms Kanal 30
1220 Copenhagen, Denmark
www.danskdesigncenter.dk

Designmuseum Danmark (Danish Museum of Art and Design)
Bredgade 68
1260 Copenhagen, Denmark
www.designmuseum.dk

Finn Juhls Hus (Finn Juhl's House)
Kratvænget 15
2920 Charlottenlund, Denmark
www.ordrupgaard.dk/finn-juhls-hus/

Finland

Arkkitehtuurimuseo/Finlands Arkitekturmuseum (Museum of Finnish Architecture)
Kasarmikatu 24
00130 Helsinki, Finland
www.mfa.fi

Designmuseo (Design Museum)
Korkeavuorenkatu 23
00130 Helsinki, Finland
www.designmuseum.fi

Hvitträsk (Studio Home of Herman Gesellius, Armas Lindgren and Eliel Saarinen)
Hvitträskintie 166
Luoma (Kirkkonummi), Finland
www.kansallismuseo.fi/en/hvittrask

Suomen Lasimuseo (Finnish Glass Museum)
Tehtaankatu 23
11910 Riihimäki, Finland
www.suomenlasimuseo.fi

Iceland

Hönnunarsafn Íslands (Museum of Design and Applied Art)
Garðatorg 1, Garðabær
Reykjavik, Iceland
www.honnunarsafn.is

Hönnunarmiðstöð Íslands (Iceland Design Centre)
A promotional organization that organizes the annual DesignMarch and various exhibitions and talks throughout the year.
www.icelanddesign.is

Norway

Nasjonalmuseet (National Museum of Art, Architecture and Design)
Universitetsgata 13
0164 Oslo, Norway
www.nasjonalmuseet.no

Norsk design- og arkiektursenter – DOGA (Norwegian Centre for Design and Architecture)
Hausmanns Gate 16
0182 Oslo, Norway
www.doga.no

Sweden

Form/Design Centre
Lilla Torg 9
203 14 Malmö, Sweden
www.formdesigncenter.com

IKEA Museum
Ikeagatan 5
343 36 Älmhult, Sweden
www.ikeamuseum.com

Nationalmuseum
Södra Blasieholmshamnen 2
111 48 Stockholm, Sweden
www.nationalmuseum.se

Nordiska Museet (Nordic Museum)
Djurgårdsvägen 6-16
115 93 Stockholm, Sweden
www.nordiskamuseet.se

Svensk Form (The Swedish Society for Crafts and Design)
Svensksundsvägen 13
111 49 Stockholm, Sweden
www.svenskform.se

SELECT BIBLIOGRAPHY

Aars, F., *Norwegian Arts and Crafts/ Industrial Design*, Dreyers Forlag, Oslo c.1963

Aav, M. and N. Stritzler-Levine, *Finnish Modern Design; Utopian Ideals and Everyday Realities 1930–1997*, The Bard Graduate Center for Studies in the Decorative Arts & Yale University Press, New Haven & London 1998

Abrecht, B., *Arkitektúr á Íslandi*, Mál og Menning, Reykjavik 2000

Bang, J., *Bang & Olufsen: From Vision to Legend*, Vidsyn 1. edition, Copenhagen 2000

Castenfors, D., *Olle Eksell – Of Course!*, IKEA of Sweden, Älmhult 2015

Christiansen, P. and H. Stephensen, *40 – Håndvaerket viser vejen (The Craftsmen show the Way)*, Uffe Petersen Schmidt, Copenhagen 1966

Creagh, L. and H. Kaberg, *Modern Swedish Design: Three Founding Texts*, The Museum of Modern Art, New York 2008

Daun, Å., *Swedish Mentality*, Pennsylvania State University Press, Pennsylvania

Drucker, J., *Georg Jensen: A Tradition of Splendid Silver*, Schiffer, Atglen 1997

Fiell, C. and P. Fiell, *Design of the 20th Century*, Taschen GmbH, Cologne 1999
— *Industrial Design A–Z*, Taschen GmbH, Cologne 2000
— *Plastic Dreams: Synthetic Visions in Design*, Fiell Publishing, London 2009
— *Scandinavian Design*, Taschen GmbH, Cologne 2002
— *The Story of Design*, Goodman Fiell, London 2013

France, J., *France & Søn: British Pioneer of Danish Furniture*, Forlaget VITA, Stadil 2016

Hald, A. and S.E. Skawonius, *Contemporary Swedish Design*, Nordisk Rotogravyr, Stockholm 1951

Hard af Segerstad, U., *Modern Scandinavian Furniture*, Bedminster Press, Totowa, New Jersey 1963
— *Scandinavian Design*, Lyle Stuart, New York 1961

Harlang, C., K. Helmer-Petersen and K. Kjaerholm (ed), *Poul Kjaerholm*, Arkitektens Forlag, Copenhagen 1999

Harrison Beer, E., *Scandinavian Design, Objects of a Life Style*, Farrar Straus Giroux/The American-Scandinavian Foundation, New York 1975

Helgeson, S. and K. Nyberg, *Svenska Former*, Stockholm 2000

Hiort, E., *Finn Juhl – Furniture, Architecture, Applied Art*, The Danish Architectural Press, Copenhagen 1990

Holmsted Olesen, C., *Wegner: Just One Good Chair*, Hatje Cantz, Ostfildern 2014

Holte, E., *Living in Norway*, Flammarion, Paris 1993

Huldt, A.H. and E. Bendikts (eds.), *Design in Sweden Today*, Swedish Institute in collaboration with Svenska

Slojdforeningen (Swedish Society of Industrial Design), Stockholm 1948

Ikea, *Democratic Design*, IKEA of Sweden, Älmhult 1995

Jalk, G. (ed.), *40 Years of Danish Furniture Design*, The Copenhagen Cabinet-Makers' Guild Exhibitions 1927–1966, Teknologisk Instituts Forlag, Copenhagen 1987

Jørstian, T. and P.E.M. Nielsen, *Light Years Ahead: The Story of the PH Lamp*, Louis Poulsen, Copenhagen 1994

Karlsson, G., *A Brief History of Iceland*, Mál og Menning, Reykjavik 2000

Kent, N., *The Soul of the North – A Social, Architectural and Cultural History of the Nordic Countries 1700–1940*, Reaktion Books, London 2000

Kristoffersson, S., *Design by IKEA: A Cultural History*, Bloomsbury Academic, London 2014

Lammhults, *The Collected Works of Lammhults*, Lammhults, Sweden 1998

Lindblad, T., *Bruksföremål AV Plast*, Bokförlaget Signum, Lund 2008

Madestrand, B., *Ingegerd Råman: It's Nothing, but it's still Something*, IKEA of Sweden, Älmhult 2015

Marimekko, *Phenomenon Marimekko*, Marimekko, Helsinki 1986

Møller, H.S. (ed.), *Danish Design*, Det Danske Selskab, Copenhagen 1974
— *Motion and Beauty, The Book of Nanna Ditzel*, Rhodos, Copenhagen 1998

Nordstrom, B.J., *Scandinavia Since 1500*, University of Minnesota Press, Minneapolis 2000

Oda, N., *Danish Chairs*, Korinsha Press, Kyoto 1996

Opie, J., *Scandinavian Ceramics & Glass in the Twentieth Century*, Victoria & Albert Museum, London 1989

Pallaasmaa, J., *Hvitträsk – The Home as a Work of Art*, Otava Publishing Company& Museum of Finnish Architecture, Helsinki 2000 (5th Edition)

Papanek, V., *Design for the Real World: Human Ecology and Social Change*, Pantheon Books, New York 1971

Polster, B., *Design Directory Scandinavian*, Pavilion, London 1999

Poutasuo, T. (ed.), *Finnish Industrial Design*, Kirjayhtymä, Helsinki 1987

Remlov, A. (ed.), *Design in Scandinavia: An Exhibition of Objects for the Home*, Kirstes Boktrykkeri, Oslo 1954

Rømer, M., *25 Years with Cylinda-Line Design: Arne Jacobsen*, Stelton A/S, Hellerup 1991

Schildt, G., *Alvar Aalto, The Decisive Years*, Rizzoli, New York 1986

Sieck, F., *Contemporary Danish Furniture Design – a short illustrated review*, Nyt Nordisk Forlag Arnold Busck, Denmark 1990

Solaguren-Beascoa, F., *Jacobsen*, Santa & Cole Ediciones de Diseno SA, Spain 1991

Thau, C. and K. Vindum, *Arne Jacobsen*, The Danish Architectural Press, Copenhagen 2001

Thomsen Brits, L., *The Book of Hygge: The Danish Art of Living Well*, Ebury

Press, London 2016

Turner, B. (ed.), *Scandinavia Profiled*, St. Martin's Press, New York 2000

Weston, R., *Alvar Aalto*, Phaidon, London 1995

Wiking, M., *The Little Book of Hygge: The Danish Way to Live Well*, Penguin Life, London 2016

Wollin, N.G., *Modern Swedish Decorative Art*, The Architectural Press, London 1931

Zahle, E. (ed) *Scandinavian Domestic Design*, Methuen, London 1963

EXHIBITION CATALOGUES

Amos Anderson Art Museum, *Oiva Toikka, Glass from Nuutajärvi*, Helsinki 1996

Art Gallery of Western Australia – Perth Cultural Center, *Scandinavian Crafts and Design*, Perth 1987

Bard Graduate Center for Studies in the Decorative Arts, *Utopia and Reality – Modernity in Sweden 1900–1960*, published in association with Yale University Press, New Haven & London 2002

Cooper-Hewitt Museum, *Scandinavian Modern Design 1880–1980*, New York 1982

Copenhagen Cabinet-Makers' Guild, *Håndvaerket viser vejen*, Copenhagen 1966

Cosmit, *Alvar Aalto*, Milan 1998

Cosmit, *Impulsi dalla Svezia/Swedish Inspiration*, Milan 1993

Danish Design Center, *Arne Jacobsen, Architect & Designer*, Copenhagen 1999

Danish Design Center, *Hans J. Wegner on Design*, Copenhagen 1994

Danish Design Center, *Innovation via Design*, Copenhagen 1990

Danish Society of Arts & Crafts and Industrial Design, *The Arts of Denmark, Viking to Modern*, America 1960–61

Danske Møbelkunst, *Møbeldesign; Danske Klassikere 1930–1965*, Copenhagen 2000

Danske Møbelkunst, *Møbeldesign; Danske Klassikere 1925–1975*, Copenhagen 2000

The Design Council, *Svenska Form, A Conference about Swedish Design*, London 1981

Design Forum Finland, *Finnish Design 125*, Helsinki 2000

Det Danske Kunstindustrimuseet, *Børge Mogensen – Møbler, Lis Ahlmann – Tekstiler*, Copenhagen 1974

Det Danske Kunstindustrimuseet, *Dansk Design 1910–1945, Art Déco & Funktionalisme*, Copenhagen 1997

Det Danske Kunstindustrimuseet, *Marie Gudme Leth*, Copenhagen 1995

Det Danske Kunstindustrimuseet, *Mestervaerker 100 års dansk møbelsnedkeri*, Copenhagen 2000

Det Danske Kunstindustrimuseet, *Små Størrelser, Børns Møbler*, Copenhagen 1999

Haslam & Whiteway, *Alvar Aalto,*

Furniture 1929–1939, London 1987

Iittala Glass Museum, *Alvar and Aino Aalto as Glass Designers*, Iitala 1996

Kaupungin Taidemuseo (Helsinki), *Antti Nurmesniemi*, Helsinki 1992

Kjarvalsstadir (Reykjavik), *Design in Iceland*, Reykjavik 2000

Musée des Arts Decoratifs, *Tapio Wirkkala*, Paris 1983

Museum of Art & Design (Helsinki), *Annika Rimala 1960–2000*, Helsinki 2000

Museum of Art & Design (Helsinki), *Kaj Franck – Muotoilija, Formgivare, Designer*, Helsinki 1992

Museum of Art & Design (Helsinki), *Tapio Wirkkala – Eye, Hand and Thought*, Helsinki 2000

Museum of Finnish Architecture, *The Language of Wood: Wood in Finnish Sculpture, Design and Architecture*, Helsinki 1987

Nationalmuseum Stockholm, *A Swedish Legacy, Decorative Arts 1700–1960*, Nationalmuseum & Scala Books, Stockholm/London 1998

Nationalmuseum Stockholm, *The Lunning Prize*, Stockholm 1986

Nuutajärvi Glass Museum, *Kaj Franck, Theme & Variations*, Heinolan Town Museum Publications, Lahti 1997

Renwick Gallery of the National Collection of Fine Arts, *Georg Jensen Silversmithy: 77 Artists – 77 Years*, Smithsonian Institution Press, Washington 1980

Röhss Museum of Arts & Crafts, *1900-tal*, Götenborg 1987

Röhss Museum of Arts & Crafts, *From Ellen Key to Ikea*, Götenborg 1991

Stedlijk Museum, *The Nordic Transparency*, Amsterdam 1999

Suomen Lasimuseo, *Make Glass Not War*, Riihimaki 1991

Suomen Lasimuseo, *Tapio Wirkkala, Venini*, Riihimaki 1988

Tada Architectural Studio, *Finn Juhl Memorial Exhibition*, Osaka 1990

The Swedish Institute, *Design in Sweden*, Uddevalla 1985

Vitra Design Museum, *Verner Panton, The Collected Works*, Vitra Design Museum, Weil-am-Rhein 2000

JOURNALS

Design from Denmark, World Pictures, Copenhagen

Design from Scandinavia, World Pictures, Copenhagen

Kontur (No. 3), Svenska Slojdforeningen (Swedish Society of Industrial Design), Ake H. Huldt, Stockholm, 1953

Mobilia (No. 131/132), *Georg Jensen 1866–1966*, Copenhagen 1966

Scandinavian Design Council, *Scandinavian Design 1990 – Towards 2000*, Malmö 1990 (Conference Papers)

Scandinavian Journal of Design History, Volumes 1–10, Rhodos International Science and Art Publishers, Copenhagen 1991–2000

INDEX

Illustrations are indicated in *italic*
Main entries are <u>underlined</u>

THANK YOUS

We would like to offer our enormous gratitude to the numerous people involved in the successful completion of this beautiful great tome of a book. Firstly, we would like to thank our co-author Magnus Englund for writing the opening essays for each chapter, which reveal such a broad insider's knowledge of the subject, and for his insightful suggestions along the way. We would also like to offer very big thanks to Henrik Nygren for his excellent graphic design work and all the members of his team for its implementation including: Emelie Hannebo, Joel Wennström, Johannes Lilahti, Keun Kim Roland, Marek Nedelka, Märta Andrén, Oskar Key, Petter Dybvig and Simon Wallhult. Many thanks must also go to Andy Stammers for his wonderful new photography, which was specially taken for this project.

Likewise, we are grateful to everyone who has worked in-house on this project at Laurence King Publishing, especially Melissa Danny for her good-natured editorial management of the project, Sophie Drysdale for coming up with the initial idea for the title and then commissioning us to undertake it, Felicity Awdry for skilfully overseeing its production and Angus Hyland for providing valuable creative direction throughout its design development. In addition, we would also like to thank Rosanna Fairhead for her painstaking copy-editing, Angela Koo for her exacting proofreading and Pauline Hubner for her careful indexing. And lastly we would like to acknowledge the immense contribution made by all the designers, manufacturers, auction rooms, design galleries, picture libraries, museums and institutions who have so kindly loaned us imagery – without whose contribution, this title would simply not be the book it has turned out to be, so special thanks to, among others:

10 Gruppen – Ingela Hakansson-Lamm
&Co – Louis Rasmussen
Antik Bar
Arabia
Architectmade
Artek
Adelta
Asplund – Madeleine Gillgren
Atelje Lyktan – Hanna Strömbäck
Bacchus Antik – Michael Strömquis
BIG-Bjarke Ingels Group – Daria Pahhota
Board of National Antiquities, Finland/ Museum Virasto – Soile Tirilä
Brio – Sophie Elvefors
Bruun Rasmussen – Lene Søbo
Bukowskis – Eva Seeman
By Lassen – Søren Lassen + Lars Østergaard Olsen
Cappellini

Carl Hansen & Søn – Pernille Ehlert Florentz
Carlton Publishing Group – Steve Behan
Daniel Rybakken
Dansk Plakatkunst – Claus Friberg
Design House Stockholm – Petra Stenvall
Designmuseo/Design Museum Helsinki – Johanna Luhtala
Digitalt Museum
Dorotheum – Dr. Gerti Draxler
Eero Aarnio Design
Ericsson Archives/Centre for Business History, Stockholm – Lina Wiberg
Erik Bruun – Peter Bruun
Erik Jorgensen
Fellow Designers – Paul Kühlhorn
Filip Henley
Finlayson – Julia Vierros
Fiskars – Marika Orkamo
Fjordfiesta
Fritz Hansen – Kalina Kalarus
Fuzzy Iceland
Gabor Palotai
Gense – Mikaela Jannering
Georg Jensen – Ida Heiberg Bøttiger
Gooday Gallery – Debbie Gooday
Gunnar Cyren
Hans Brindfors
Happy FB – Rebecca Einarsson
Hay – Lene S. Hermansen
Holmegaard – Bente Fallinge
House of Juhl
Ib Antoni – Mikael Hauberg
IKEA – Josefin Thorell
IQ Light
Iittala – Siru Nori
Jacksons – Paul and Carina Jackson
Jobs Handtryck – Åsa Jobs
Kahler – Trine Rasmussen
Karl Andersson & Söner – Sara Wadskog
Kay Bojesen – Bente Fallinge
KiBiSi – Jens Martin Skibsted
Källemo – Sofia Enocson
Knoll – Maya Sorabjee
Kosta Boda
Lammhults – Ulrika Johansson-Ståhl
Lapponia – Hautanen Raili
Le Klint – Søren Andersen
LEGO – Kathrine Bisgaard Vase
L'Affichiste – Karen Etingin
Lightyears
Lotta Kuhlhorn + Fabian Kühlhorn
Louis Poulsen – Sarah Lærke Stevens
Luke Anderson
Lundgren+Lindqvist – Andreas Friberg Lundgren
Luxo
Malmsten Hellberg – Stefania Malmsten
Marimekko – Maarit Heikkilä
Modernity – Andrew Duncanson + Isaac Pineus
Nanna Ditzel Studio – Dennie Ditzel
Normann Copenhagen – Vibe Høst
Northern Lighting
Olle Eksell – Johan Andersson
One Collection
Orrefors – Thomas Hagstrom
Out of Copenhagen – Morten Hoffmeyer
Pandul
Permafrost – Tore Vinje Brustad
Peter Opsvik
Phillips – Ekaterina Tyumentseva
Pia Wallén
Piiroinen
Playsam – Carl Zedig

Posters Please/Rennarts Gallery – James McCobb
PP Møbler – Katja Kejser
Quittenbaum – Arthur Floss + Kalan Konietzko
Rago Auctions – Anthony Barnes
Rörstrand – Marika Orkamo
Skultuna 1607 – Jenny Ericsson
Snøhetta – Julie Skogheim
Stelton
Stephen Morris
Stockholm Design Lab – Lisa Fleck
Stockholms Auktionhaus – Hanna Meijer + Daniel Wahlberg
String
Studio Claus Due – Claus Due
Studio Granda – Steve Christer
Svenskt Tenn – Vicky Nordh
Stokke
Themes & Variations – Liliane Fawcett
The Futuro House
Theo de Haan
Thomas Eriksson
Valvomo – Markus Nevalainen
Verner Panton Design/Panton Archive – Rina Troxler
Wright Auctions – Richard Wright + Todd Simeone

PICTURE CREDITS

Images are listed by page number followed by picture number (13.4 = page 13, picture number 4). Where the pictures are not numbered on page, they are referenced here either from the top down (1 being the top image) or clockwise from top left.

All images credited to Fiell/LKP were photographed by Andy Stammers.

LEGO disclaimer: All information is collected and interpreted by its authors and does not represent the opinion of the LEGO Group.

4 Louis Poulsen, Copenhagen, Denmark
6 Fiell/LKP
9 Republic of Fritz Hansen/photo: Ditte Isager
10–11 Felix Odell/Link Images
12 Snøhetta/photo: Ketil Jacobsen
13.1 Scanrail1/Shutterstock
13.2 out of copyright/WikiCommons
13.3 out of copyright/WikiArquitectura
13.4 Dorling Kindersley Ltd/Alamy
14.1 Dainis Derics/Shutterstock
14.2 Arcaid Images/Alamy
14.3 C+P Fiell Design Archive
14.4 out of copyright/Digitalt Museum (Sweden)
15.1 FP Collection/Alamy
15.2 Rose-Marie Murray/Alamy
15.3 Alexey Seafarer/Shutterstock
16.2 Ivan Vdovin/Alamy
16.2 Ivan Vdovin/Alamy
16.3 FP Collection/Alamy
17 C+P Fiell Design Archive
18, 19.1, 19.2, 19.3 out of copyright/ Digitalt Museum (Sweden)
20 FP Collection/Alamy
21.1 laurentui iordache/Alamy
21.2 Guy Brown/Alamy
22.1 out of copyright/Digitalt Museum (Sweden)
22.2 sellinmedia/Shutterstock
22.3 Wiki Commons
23.4 Stefan Holm/Shutterstock
23.5 Digitalt Museum (Sweden)
24, 25.1, 25.2 Arcaid Images/Alamy
26 Museovirasto/Museiverket/National Board of Antiquities, Archives and Information Sevices, Picture Collections, Finland/photo Soile Tirilä
27.1 WikiCommons
27.2 Lasse Ansaharju/Shutterstock
27.3, 28.1 WikiCommons
28.2 Harryfn/Dreamstime
29.3 WikiCommons
29.4 Peter Forsberg/Europe/Alamy
30.1, 30.2, 31.3, 31.4, 31.5, 32.1 WikiCommons
32.2, 32.3, 33.1, 33.2 Digitalt Museum (Sweden)
34.1 Alastair Philip Wiper/VIEW Pictures Ltd/Alamy
34.2 Republic of Fritz Hansen/photo: Jørgen Strüwing
34.3 SAS/WikiCommons
35 VIEW Pictures Ltd/Alamy

36.1 Republic of Fritz Hansen/photo: Jørgen Strüwing
36.2, 37 VIEW Pictures Ltd/Alamy
37 VIEW Pictures Ltd/Alamy
38 Republic of Fritz Hansen/photo: Egon Gade
39.1 Chris Mattison/Alamy
39.2 FP Collection/Alamy
40, 41.1, 41.2, 41.3 Republic of Fritz Hansen/photo: Egon Gade
42.1, 42.2, 42.3 FP Collection/Alamy
43 John Peter Photography/Alamy
44, 45.1, 45.2 Niels Quist/Alamy
46, 47.1, 47.2, 47.3 House of Finn Juhl/ Onecollection A/S
48.1 Panton Archive
48.2 ullstein bild/Getty Images
49.3, 49.4, 50, 51.1, 51.2 Panton Archive
52.1, 52.2 VIEW Pictures Ltd/Alamy
53.3 Ville Tuomola/Alamy
53.4, 54.1 WikiCommons
54.2 FP Collection/Alamy
55 Lauren Orr/Shutterstock
56 WikiCommons
57.1 42pix Premier/Alamy
57.2, 57.3 The Futuro House.com (from the collection of www.thefuturohouse.com)
58.1 Markku Vitikainen/Shutterstock
58.2 Dmitry Nikolaev/Shutterstock
59.3 Mmartin/Shutterstock
59.4 Dmitry Nikolaev/Shutterstock
60.1, 60.2, 61.3, 61.4 Filip Henley
62 Susana Guzman/Alamy
63.1 Lars Johansson/Alamy
63.2 Lphoto/Alamy
64.1 Wiki Commons
64.2 Kevpix/Alamy
65 Mikhail Markovskiy/Fotolia
66 Yadid Levy/Alamy
67 kimson/Shutterstock
68.1, 68.2, 69.1, 69.2, 69.3, 69.4, 70.1, 70.2, 71.1 BIG/Bjarke Ingels Group
71.2, 71.3 © 2017 The LEGO Group, used with permission
72, 73.1, 73.2 Snøhetta/photo: Gerald Zugmann
74, 75.1, 75.2 Snøhetta/photo: Ketil Jacobsen
76, 77.1, 77.2, 77.3 Studio Granda (architects: Studio Granda/structural and environmental engineers: Viðsjá/ electrical engineers: VJÍ/photo: Sigurgeir Sigurjónsson)
78–79 Felix Odell/Link Images
80 Hay Studio
81.1, 81.2 Bukowskis
81.3 Modernity
81.4 Jackson Design AB – www.jacksons.se
81.5 IKEA
82.1 Bukowskis
82.2 IKEA
82.3 Thomas Ericksson/Cappellini
82.4 Carl Hansen & Søn
82.5 House of Finn Juhl/ Onecollection A/S
83.1 Republic of Fritz Hansen/photo: Egon Gade
83.2 Bukowskis
83.3 Karl Andersson & Söner/photo: Jonas Sällberg
83.4 Modernity
83.5 Courtesy of Knoll, Inc
85.1, 85.2 Bukowskis

85.3 Eero Aarnio/Eero Aarnio Originals/photo: Otso Pietinen 1970
85.4 Bukowskis
85.5 Peter Opsvik AS/photo: Tollefsen (www.opsvik.no/www.stokke.com)
86.1 C+P Fiell Design Archive
86.2, 87 Modernity
88 Bruun Rasmussen Auctioneers of Fine Art
89.1 Modernity
89.2 Bruun Rasmussen Auctioneers of Fine Art
90 Bukowskis
91.1 Jackson Design AB – www.jacksons.se
91.2, 91.3 Bukowskis
91.4 Digitalt Museum (Sweden)
92 Modernity
93.1 Jackson Design AB/ www.jacksons.se
93.2, 93.3 Modernity
93.4 Phillips
94.1 Modernity
94.2 Fiell/Carlton archive
95.3, 95.4, 96.1 Modernity
96.2 Fiell/LKP
96.3 Artek
97 Modernity
98.1 Wright/Courtesy of Wright, Chicago
98.2, 99.3, 99.4 Modernity
100.1, 100.2, 100.3 Bukowskis
101, 102 Modernity/photo: Åsa Liffner
103.1 Modernity/photo: Modernity
103.2 Bukowskis
103.3 Jackson Design AB/ www.jacksons.se
104.1 Bukowskis
104.2 Modernity
105.3 Wright/Courtesy of Wright, Chicago
105.4 Modernity
105.5 Bukowskis
106 Bruun Rasmussen Auctioneers of Fine Art
107.1, 107.2 Bukowskis
107.3 Phillips
108, 109.1 Wright/Courtesy of Wright, Chicago
109.2, 109.3 Modernity
110.1, 110.2, 111, 112, 113.1 Wright/ Courtesy of Wright, Chicago
113.2 House of Juhl
113.3 Phillips
114, 115.1, 115.2, 115.3, 115.4 Wright/ Courtesy of Wright, Chicago
116 Jackson Design AB – www.jacksons.se
117.1 Wright/Courtesy of Wright, Chicago
117.2 Modernity
118.1 Fiell/Carlton archive
118.2 Modernity
119.3 WikiCommons
119.4 Wright/Courtesy of Wright, Chicago
120.1 Bukowskis
120.2, 120.3 Archival (from earlier publication)
121 Modernity
122.1 Jackson Design AB/ www.jacksons.se
122.2 Phillips
123.1, 123.2, 124.1, 124.2 Modernity
125, 126, 127.1, 127.2, 127.3, 127.4, 127.5,

128.1 Bukowskis
128.2 Fritz Hansen
129 Modernity
130.1 Bukowskis
130.2 Wright/Courtesy of Wright, Chicago
131, 132 Modernity
133.1 Bukowskis
133.2, 133.3 By Lassen
134 Modernity
135.1, 135.2 Wright/Courtesy of Wright, Chicago
135.3 Fritz Hansen
135.4 Wright/Courtesy of Wright, Chicago
136.1 Fiell/Carlton archive
136.2, 136.3, 137.4, 137.5 Wright/ Courtesy of Wright, Chicago
138 PP Møbler
139 Bruun Rasmussen Auctioneers of Fine Art
140 PP Møbler
141, 142.1, 142.2, 142.3, 142.4 Bukowskis
142.5 Fritz Hansen
143.6 Phillips
143.7 Carl Hansen & Søn
143.8 Bukowskis
143.9 Wright/Courtesy of Wright, Chicago
143.10 Bukowskis
143.11 Wright/Courtesy of Wright, Chicago
143.12 Bukowskis
144.1 Fritz Hansen
144.2 Wright/Courtesy of Wright, Chicago
145.3 PP Møbler
145.4, 145.5 Wright/Courtesy of Wright, Chicago
146.1, 146.2 IKEA
147.3, 147.4, 147.5 Bukowskis
148 Wright/Courtesy of Wright, Chicago
149.1 Fjordfiesta/photo: Espen Istad
149.2 Wright/Courtesy of Wright, Chicago
149.3 Bukowskis
150.1, 150.2 Fiell/Carlton archive
151 Fuzzy (Iceland)
152 Jackson Design AB/www. jacksons.se
153, 154, 155.1, 155.2 Wright/Courtesy of Wright, Chicago
155.3 C+P Fiell Design Archive
156 Bukowskis
157.1 Nanna Ditzel Design/photo: K. Helmer-Petersen
157.2 Bukowskis
158.1 Wright/Courtesy of Wright, Chicago
158.2 Bukowskis
159.3, 159.4 Wright/Courtesy of Wright, Chicago
160 Bukowskis
161.1 Wright/Courtesy of Wright, Chicago
161.2 Bukowskis
162.1 Bruun Rasmussen Auctioneers of Fine Art
162.2 Wright/Courtesy of Wright, Chicago
162.3 Jackson Design AB/ www.jacksons.se
163.4, 163.5 Bukowskis
163.6, 164 Wright/Courtesy of Wright, Chicago

165.1 Bukowskis
165.2 Erik Jørgensen Møbelfabrik
165.3 Stockholms Auktionsverk
166.1 Modernity
166.2 C+P Fiell Design Archive
167 Quittenbaum Kunstauktionen GmbH
168.1 Panton Archive
168.2 Phillips
168.3, 169 Wright/Courtesy of Wright, Chicago
170 Phillips
171.1, 171.2 Wright/Courtesy of Wright, Chicago
171.3 Fiell/Carlton archive
171.4 C+P Fiell Design Archive
172.1 Rago Auctions (www.ragoarts.com)
172.2 Fiell/Carlton archive
172.3 C+P Fiell Design Archive
173 Fiell/Carlton archive
174.1 Archives of String Furniture AB, Sweden
174.2, 174.3, 175 Bukowskis
176, 177.1 Wright/Courtesy of Wright, Chicago
177.2 Bukowskis
177.3 Eero Aarnio/Eero Aarnio Originals/photo: Kuvakiila 1967
177.4, 178 Bukowskis
179.1 C+P Fiell Design Archive
179.2 Wright/Courtesy of Wright, Chicago
180 Piiroinen
181.1, 181.2, 182 Wright/Courtesy of Wright, Chicago
183.1 Lammhults/photo: Pelle Wahlgren
183.2 Bukowskis
183.3 Lammhults/photo: Pelle Wahlgren
184 Peter Opsvik AS/photo: Tollefsen (www.opsvik.no/ www.varierfurniture.com)
185 Peter Opsvik AS (www.opsvik.no)
186, 187.1, 187.2, 187.3 Modernity
188, 189.1 Källemo AB/photo: Johann Bergenholtz
189.2, 189.3 Källemo AB/photo: Curt Ekblom
190, 191.1, 191.2, 191.3, 191.4 IKEA
192.1 Modernity
192.2 Asplund
193 Fiell/LKP
194.1 Asplund
194.2 KiBiSi
195.1 Hay Studio
195.2 Design House Stockholm
195.3 Normann Copenhagen
196–197 Felix Odell/Link
198 Secto Design/photo: Lasse Keltto
199.1 Modernity
199.2 Le Klint A/S
199.3 Pandul/photo: Lennart Soegaard-Hoeyer
199.4 IQ Light/Holger Strøm
199.5 Lightyears
200.1 Ateljé Lyktan
200.2 Ateljé Lyktan/photo: Johan Jansson
200.3 Luxo
200.4 Northern Lighting
200.5 Daniel Rybakken/photo: Kalle Sanner & Daniel Rybakken
201.1, 201.2 Bukowskis
201.3 Design House Stockholm
201.4 Snowcrash/Valvomo Ltd./courtesy of Markus Nevalainen

202.1 Jackson Design AB/ www.jacksons.se
202.2, 203, 204 Louis Poulsen, Copenhagen, Denmark
205.1 Phillips
205.2 Louis Poulsen, Copenhagen, Denmark
206.1, 206.2, 206.3, 207.4, 207.5 Modernity
208, 209.1 Wright/Courtesy of Wright, Chicago
209.2, 209.3 Bukowskis
210 Wright/Courtesy of Wright, Chicago
211.1 Bukowskis
211.2, 211.3 Wright/Courtesy of Wright, Chicago
212, 213.1, 213.2, 213.3, 214.1, 214.2, 215.3, 215.4, 215.5 Le Klint A/S
216.1 Wright/Courtesy of Wright, Chicago
216.2 C+P Fiell Design Archive
216.3, 217.4, 217.5 Wright/Courtesy of Wright, Chicago
218.1, 218.2 Fiell/Carlton archive
219, 220.1 Bukowskis
220.2 Designmuseo/Design Museum, Helsinki
221.3, 221.4, 222 Wright/Courtesy of Wright, Chicago
223.1, 223.2 Quittenbaum Kunstauktionen GmbH
223.3 Wright/Courtesy of Wright, Chicago
224.1, 224.2, 224.3, 225 Louis Poulsen, Copenhagen, Denmark
226 Quittenbaum Kunstauktionen GmbH
227.1 Wright/Courtesy of Wright, Chicago
227.2 Dorotheum GmbH & Co KG/from Dorotheum Vienna, auction catalogue 4 November 2015
228 Phillips
229.1, 229.2 Wright/Courtesy of Wright, Chicago
230.1 Quittenbaum Kunstauktionen GmbH
230.2, 231 Wright/Courtesy of Wright, Chicago
232 Design House Stockholm
233.1 Bukowskis
233.2 Le Klint
233.3 Design House Stockholm
234.1, 234.2, 234.3, 235 Louis Poulsen, Copenhagen, Denmark
236–237 Brendan Austin/Link Images
238 Fiell/LKP
239.1, 239.2 Orrefors
239.3 Bukowskis
239.4, 239.5 Orrefors
241.1, 241.2, 241.3 Bukowskis
241.4 IKEA
241.5, 242.1, 242.2, 243, 244, 245.1, 245.2, 245.3 Bukowskis
246.1 Fiell/LKP
246.2 Bukowskis
246.3 Iittala archival/out of copyright
247 Fiell/LKP
248 Iittala
249.1, 249.2 Bukowskis
249.3 Iittala (archival)
250.1 Iittala
250.2 Fiell/LKP
251 Phillips
252.1 Wright/Courtesy of Wright, Chicago

252.2, 253, 254, 255.1, 255.2 Bukowskis
256 Holmegaard
257.1 Wright/Courtesy of Wright, Chicago
257.2 Holmegaard
258 Jackson Design AB/ www.jacksons.se
259.1, 259.2, 259.3 Bukowskis
260.1 C+P Fiell Design Archive
260.2 Fiell/LKP
261.3, 261.4 Bukowskis
261.5 Jackson Design AB/ www.jacksons.se
262 Fiell/LKP
263.1 Bukowskis
263.2 Quittenbaum Kunstauktionen GmbH
264 Wright/Courtesy of Wright, Chicago
265.1 Jackson Design AB/ www.jacksons.se
265.2 Wright/Courtesy of Wright, Chicago
266.1, 266.2, 267.3, 267.4 Phillips
268 Phillips
269.1 Bukowskis
269.2 Phillips
269.3 Iittala (archival)
270.1, 270.2 Bukowskis
270.3 Arabia
271 Phillips
272 Bukowskis
273.1 Wright/Courtesy of Wright, Chicago
273.2, 274.1 Phillips
274.2 Jackson Design AB/ www.jacksons.se
275 Quittenbaum Kunstauktionen GmbH
276.1, 276.2 Iittala
277 Fiell/LKP
278.1, 278.2 Holmegaard
279 Fiell/LKP
280, 281.1, 281.2, 282 Bukowskis
283.1 Gunnar Cyrén AB – © Birgitta Cyrén, Mårten Cyrén, Henrik Cyrén, Gustav Cyrén through Gunnar Cyrén Aktiebolag
283.2, 284, 285.1, 285.2, 285.3 Bukowskis
286.1 Designmuseo/Design Museum, Helsinki
286.2 Bukowskis
287 Phillips
288 Bukowskis
289.1 C+P Fiell Design Archive
289.2, 290 Bukowskis
291.1 Jackson Design AB/ www.jacksons.se
291.2 C+P Fiell Design Archive
291.3, 292.1 Bukowskis
292.2 Stockholms Auktionsverk
293 Fiell/LKP
294, 295.1 Bukowskis
295.2 Jackson Design AB/ www.jacksons.se
296.1 Fiell/LKP
296.2 Luke Anderson
296.3 Luke Anderson
297 Fiell/LKP
298.1 Bukowskis
298.2 Kosta Boda/photo: Jonas Lindstrom
299.3 Fiell/LKP
299.4 Bukowskis
300.1, 300.2, 301.3 Fiell/LKP
301.4 Iittala
302.1, 302.2, 303 Bukowskis

304 Fiell/LKP
305.1, 305.2, 305.3, 306.1, 306.2, 307 Bukowskis
308.1 Fiell/LKP/Courtesy of Magnus Englund Collection
308.2 Iittala/photo: Timo Junttila
308.3, 309 Fiell/LKP
310, 311.1 Orrefors/photo: Jonas Lindström
311.2 Orrefors/photo: Micke Persson
312–313 Felix Odell/Link Images
314 Kähler Design
315.1 Fiell/LKP/Courtesy of Magnus Englund Collection
315.2, 315.3 Bukowskis
315.4 Jackson Design AB/ www.jacksons.se
315.5, 317.1 Bukowskis
317.2 Arabia
317.3, 317.4 Bukowskis
317.5 Fiell/LKP
317.6 Bukowskis
318, 319.1, 319.2 Rörstrand
320.1 Arabia
320.2 Bukowskis
321 Designmuseo/Design Museum, Helsinki
322 Jackson Design AB/ www.jacksons.se
323.1, 323.2, 323.3 Bukowskis
324.1 Bruun Rasmussen Auctioneers of Fine Art
324.2 Bukowskis
325 Bruun Rasmussen Auctioneers of Fine Art
326.1, 326.2, 326.3, 327 Jackson Design AB/www.jacksons.se
328.1 Phillips
328.2, 329 Bukowskis
330.1 Jackson Design AB/ www.jacksons.se
330.2, 330.3 Luke Anderson
331 Bukowskis
332.1 Stephen Morris/Courtesy of The Ken Stradling Collection, Bristol
332.2 Bukowskis
333.3 Designmuseo/Design Museum, Helsinki
333.4 Bukowskis
334.1 Rörstrand
334.2, 334.3 Bukowskis
335 Fiell/LKP/Courtesy of Magnus Englund Collection
336 Bruun Rasmussen Auctioneers of Fine Art
337.1 Bukowskis
337.2 Luke Anderson
338.1 Bukowskis
338.2 Modernity
338.3 Arabia
339 Jackson Design AB/ www.jacksons.se
340 Arabia
341.1 C+P Fiell Design Archive
341.2 Fiell/Carlton archive
341.3 Arabia
342.1 Bukowskis
342.2 Rörstrand
343.3, 343.4 Wright/Courtesy of Wright, Chicago
344, 345.1, 345.2, 346, 347.1, 347.2 Bukowskis
347.3 Rörstrand
348 Bukowskis
349.1 Designmuseo/Design Museum,

Helsinki
349.2 Fiell/LKP
350 Wright/Courtesy of Wright, Chicago
351 Fiell/LKP/Courtesy of Magnus
Englund Collection
352.1 Jackson Design AB/
www.jacksons.se
352.2, 352.3, 353 Bukowskis
354 Fiell/LKP/Courtesy of Magnus
Englund Collection
355.1 Bukowskis
355.2, 356, 357 Fiell/LKP/Courtesy of
Magnus Englund Collection
358.1, 358.2 Bukowskis
359.1 Luke Anderson
359.2 Fiell/LKP
360 Bukowskis
361.1 Modernity
361.2 Bukowskis
362 Luke Anderson
363.1 Designmuseo/Design Museum,
Helsinki
363.2 Bukowskis
364 Fiell/LKP
365.1 Design House Stockholm
365.2 Iittala
365.3 Design House Stockholm
366–367 Felix Odell/Link
368 Stelton
369.1 Modernity
369.2 Svenskt Tenn/photo: Svenskt Tenn
369.3 AP Press on behalf of TT
Nyhetsbyrån, PrB/TT – photo: DEX
369.4 Wright/Courtesy of Wright,
Chicago
369.5 Skultuna
371.1, 371.2 Bukowskis
371.3 Fiell/LKP
371.4 Brooklyn Museum Creative
Commons
371.5 Bukowskis
372.1, 372.2 Jackson Design AB/
www.jacksons.se
373, 374.1, 374.2, 375.3, 375.4 Bukowskis
376, 377.1 Fiell/LKP
377.2 Gense
378.1, 378.2 Fiell/LKP
379.1 Stadsmuseet, Stockholm (The City
Museum of Stockholm)/photo:
Lenart af Petersens
379.2 Bukowskis
380.1 Jackson Design AB/
www.jacksons.se
380.2 Fiell/LKP
381.1, 381.2 Modernity
382 Wright/Courtesy of Wright, Chicago
383.1 Jackson Design AB/
www.jacksons.se
383.2 Wright/Courtesy of Wright,
Chicago
383.3 Bukowskis
384.1, 384.2, 385 Wright/Courtesy of
Wright, Chicago
386.1, 386.2, 387 Georg Jensen
388.1 Wright/Courtesy of Wright,
Chicago
388.2 Bukowskis
389 Wright/Courtesy of Wright, Chicago
390, 391.1 Bukowskis
391.2 Quittenbaum Kunstauktionen
GmbH
392.1 Bukowskis
392.2 Gense
393.3 Stelton
393.4 Gense

394.1, 394.2 Georg Jensen
395.3 Fiell/LKP
395.4 Bukowskis
396 Iittala
397.1, 397.2, 398 Fiell/LKP
399.1, 399.2 Bukowskis
399.3 Modernity
400 Designmuseo/Design Museum,
Helsinki
401.1, 401.2 Bruun Rasmussen
Auctioneers of Fine Art
402 Stelton
403.1 Design House Stockholm
403.2 Iittala
403.3, 403.4 Iittala (Hackman)
404–405 Felix Odell/Link
406 Fiell/LKP
407.1 Bacchus Antik
407.2 Kay Bojesen Denmark
407.3 Modernity
407.4 Architectmade
408.1 Phillips
408.2 Bukowskis
408.3 Fiell/LKP
408.4 Fiell/Carlton archive
408.5 Permafrost/photo: Johan
Holmquist
409.1 Theo de Haan
409.2 Bacchus Antik
409.3 Playsam/photo: Jonas Lindstrom
409.4 Jackson Design AB/
www.jacksons.se
409.5 Modernity
410, 411.1, 411.2, 411.3, 411.4, 412, 413.1,
413.2, 413.3 Kay Bojesen Denmark
414 Modernity
415.1, 415.2, 416.1 Modernity
416.2 Jackson Design AB/
www.jacksons.se
417 Phillips
418.1 Quittenbaum Kunstauktionen
GmbH
418.2, 419 Fiell/LKP
420 Bruun Rasmussen Auctioneers of
Fine Art
421.1 Designmuseo/Design Museum,
Helsinki
421.2, 421.3 Bukowskis
421.4 Modernity
422, 423.1, 423.2 Bukowskis
424, 425.1, 425.2, 425.3 Brio
426.1, 426.2, 426.3, 427 Playsam – photo:
Jonas Lindstrom
428 Fiell Archive/Carlton Publishing/
photo: Paul Chave
429.1, 429.2 Iittala
429.3 Fiell/LKP
429.4 Iittala
430–431 Gerry Johansson/Link
432 Stelton/photo: Brian Buchard
433.1 Fiell Archive/Carlton Publishing/
photo: Paul Chave
433.2 WikiCommons
433.3 Digitalt Museum (Sweden)
433.4 Bukowskis
433.5 C+P Fiell Design Archive
435.1 Fiell/LKP
435.2 Designmuseo/Design Museum,
Helsinki
435.3 Fiskars
435.4 Fiell Archive/Carlton Publishing/
photo: Paul Chave
435.5 Normann Copenhagen/photo:
Jeppe Sørensen
435.6 © 2017 The LEGO Group, used

with permission/photo: Palle Peter
Skov
436.1, 436.2 Ericsson Archives/Centre
for Business History, Stockholm
437 Tekniska museet/National Museum
of Science and Technology, Sweden/
photo: Truls Nord
438.1 Fiell/LKP
438.2 Archival (out of copyright)
439.3 Fiell/LKP
439.4 Fiell Archive/Carlton Publishing/
photo: Paul Chave
440.1 Ericsson Archives/Centre for
Business History, Stockholm
440.2 Fiell/LKP
440.3 C+P Fiell Design Archive
441 Fiell/Carlton archive
442 Fiell/LKP
443.1, 443.2, 444 Fiell Archive/Carlton
Publishing/photo: Paul Chave
445.1 Wright/Courtesy of Wright,
Chicago
445.2 Fiell Archive/Carlton Publishing/
photo: Paul Chave
445.3 Designmuseo/Design Museum,
Helsinki
446 Fiell/LKP/Courtesy of Magnus
Englund Collection
447 Fiell Archive/Carlton Publishing/
photo: Paul Chave
448.1, 448.2 © 2017 LEGO/photo: Palle
Peter Skov
448.3 © 2017 The LEGO Group, used
with permission
448.4 © 2017 LEGO/photo: Palle Peter
Skov
449 Ekaterina_Minaeva/Shutterstock
450.1, 450.2, 451 Fiell/LKP
452.1, 452.2, 453 Normann Copenhagen
454–455 Felix Odell/Link
456 Marimekko
457.1 Jackson Design AB/
www.jacksons.se
457.2 Bukowskis
457.3 IKEA
457.4 Finlayson
457.5 Marimekko
459.1, 459.2 Fiell/LKP
459.3 Bukowskis
459.4 Dale of Norway
459.5 Design House Stockholm
460.1, 460.2, 461.1, 461.2 Jackson Design
AB/www.jacksons.se
462.1 Phillips
462.2 Wright/Courtesy of Wright,
Chicago
463 Bukowskis
464 Phillips
465.1 Wright/Courtesy of Wright,
Chicago
465.2 Phillips
466.1, 466.2 Bukowskis
467 Wright/Courtesy of Wright, Chicago
468.1, 468.2, 469 Bukowskis
470 Svenskt Tenn/photo: Lennart
Nilsson, Svenskt Tenn
471, 472, 473.1, 473.2, 474.1, 474.2, 475
Svenskt Tenn
476 Jackson Design AB/
www.jacksons.se
477.1 Bukowskis
477.2, 478, 479.1, 479.2 Jackson Design
AB/www.jacksons.se
480.1, 480.2, 481 Jobs Handtryck
482, 483.1, 483.2 Fiell/LKP

484 Jackson Design AB –
www.jacksons.se
485.1, 485.2 Bukowskis
486.1, 486.2, 486.3, 487 Marimekko
488 Quittenbaum Kunstauktionen GmbH
489.1, 489.2, 489.3 Bukowskis
490, 491.1, 491.2, 492, 493.1, 493.2, 494
Fiell/LKP
495.1 10 Gruppen
495.2 Fiell/LKP
495.3 10 Gruppen
496 Pia Wallén/photo: Frederik
Lieberath
497.1 Pia Wallén/Asplund
497.2 Pia Wallén/photo: Frederik
Lieberath
497.3 Asplund
498 Hay Studio
499.1, 499.2 Asplund
500, 501.1, 501.2 Marimekko
502–503 Brendan Austin/Link
504 Bukowskis
505.1, 505.2, 505.3, 505.4 Georg Jensen
505.5, 507.1, 507.2, 507.3, 507.4, 507.5,
508.1, 508.2, 509.1, 509.2, 509.3
Bukowskis
510.2, 510.1, 510.3 Georg Jensen
511.4, 511.5, 511.6 The Gooday Gallery/
www.thegoodaygallery.com
512.1, 512.2, 513 Bukowskis
514, 515.1 Wright/Courtesy of Wright,
Chicago
515.2 Georg Jensen
515.3 Wright/Courtesy of Wright,
Chicago
516.1 Modernity
516.2 Themes & Variations
517 Fiell/LKP
518 Wright/Courtesy of Wright, Chicago
519.1 Bukowskis
519.2 Georg Jensen
519 Bukowskis
520 Fiell/LKP
521.1, 521.2 Georg Jensen
521.3 Wright/Courtesy of Wright,
Chicago
522, 523.1, 523.2 Bukowskis
523.3 Lapponia Jewelry/Kalevala Koru
524.1, 524.2, 524.3 Bukowskis
525.4, 525.5 Phillips
526.1 Bukowskis
526.2, 526.3, 526.4 Phillips
527 Bukowskis
528 Wright/Courtesy of Wright, Chicago
529.1 Georg Jensen
529.2, 529.3 Modernity
530.1 Bukowskis
530.2 Phillips
530.3, 531 Modernity
532, 533.1, 533.2, 533.3, 534, 535
Bukowskis
536.1, 536.2, 536.3, 536.4, 536.5, 537.6,
537.7 Georg Jensen
538–539 Felix Odell/Link Images
540 C+P Fiell Design Archive
541.1 C+P Fiell Design Archive
541.2 Antik Bar
541.3, 542.1 Dansk Plakatkunst
542.2 Poster Photo Archives, Posters
Please Inc., New York
542.3 Hauberg Design & Ib Antoni/
Ib Antoni (1929–73), www.ibantoni.dk
542.4 Out of Copenhagen
543.1, 543.2 Antik Bar
543.3 Bukowskis

543.4 Stockholm Design Lab (SDL)
544.1, 544.2, 545.3 swim ink 2 llc/Getty
    Images
545.4, 545.6 David Pollack/Getty Images
546.1 Antik Bar
546.2, 547 swim ink 2 llc/Getty Images
548, 549.1 Bukowskis
549.2 Stockholms Auktionverk
549.3 Bukowskis
550.1, 550.2, 550.3, 551.1, 551.2, 551.3
    Fiell/LKP/Courtesy of Magnus
    Englund Collection
552.1 Out of Copenhagen
552.2 L'Affichiste
552.3, 553.4 Out of Copenhagen
553.5 L'Affichiste
554.1, 554.2, 555.3, 555.4, 555.5 Olle
    Eksell/courtesy of Ruthell Eksell
556.1, 556.2, 556.3, 557 Erik Bruun
    represented by Bruun Design Oy
558, 559.1, 559.2 Ib Antoni
560, 561.1, 561.2, 561.3 Bukowskis
562.1, 562.2, 563.3, 563.4, 563.5, 564.1,
    564.2, 564.3, 565 Fiell/LKP
566.1 Antik Bar
566.2 Ib Antoni
567.3 C+P Fiell Design Archive/Tivoli
    Gardens
567.4 &Co/NoA & Tivoli
568.1, 568.2, 568.3, 569.1, 569.2, 569.3
    Stockholm Design Lab (SDL)
570 Malmsten Hellberg
571.1, 571.2, 571.3 Gabor Palotai/Gabor
    Palotai Design
571.4 Hans Brindfors
571.5 Lammhults
572.1 Lundgren+Lindqvist (design:
    Lundgren+Lindqvist/artwork:
    Lundgren+Lindqvist, Alexander
    Palmeståhl, Ferik Åkum/photo: Kalle
    Sanner/post-production: Carl Ander)
572.2 Happy F&B
573.3 Designbolaget
573.4 André Strömqvist & Norstedts
    Förlag, Stockholm/design: Lotta
    Kuhlhorn/photo: André Strömqvist
573.5 Fellow Designers – design: Fellow
    Designers, Eva Liljefors & Paul
    Kühlhorn (www.fellowdesigners.com/
    represented by www.agentbauer.com/
    illustrators/fellowdesigners)

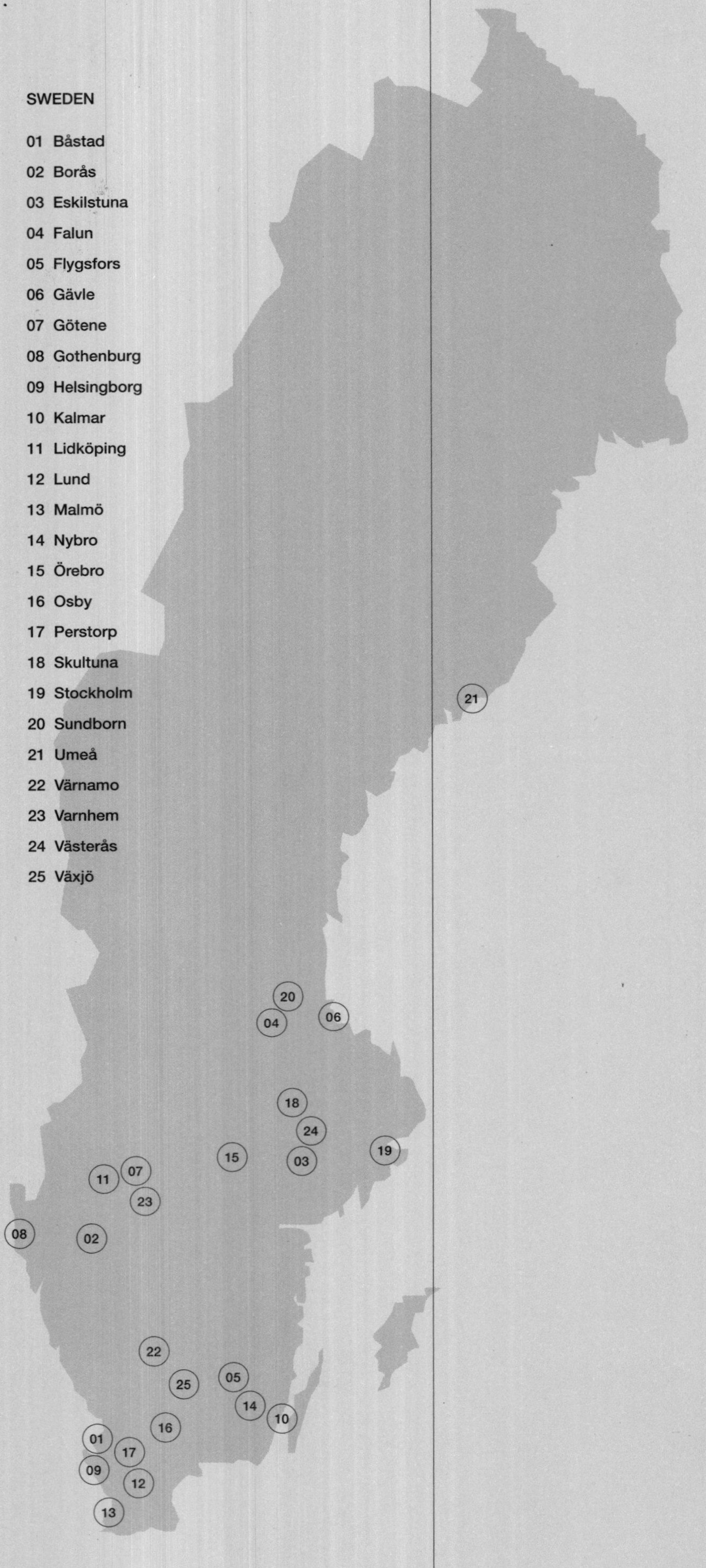

SWEDEN

01 Båstad
02 Borås
03 Eskilstuna
04 Falun
05 Flygsfors
06 Gävle
07 Götene
08 Gothenburg
09 Helsingborg
10 Kalmar
11 Lidköping
12 Lund
13 Malmö
14 Nybro
15 Örebro
16 Osby
17 Perstorp
18 Skultuna
19 Stockholm
20 Sundborn
21 Umeå
22 Värnamo
23 Varnhem
24 Västerås
25 Växjö

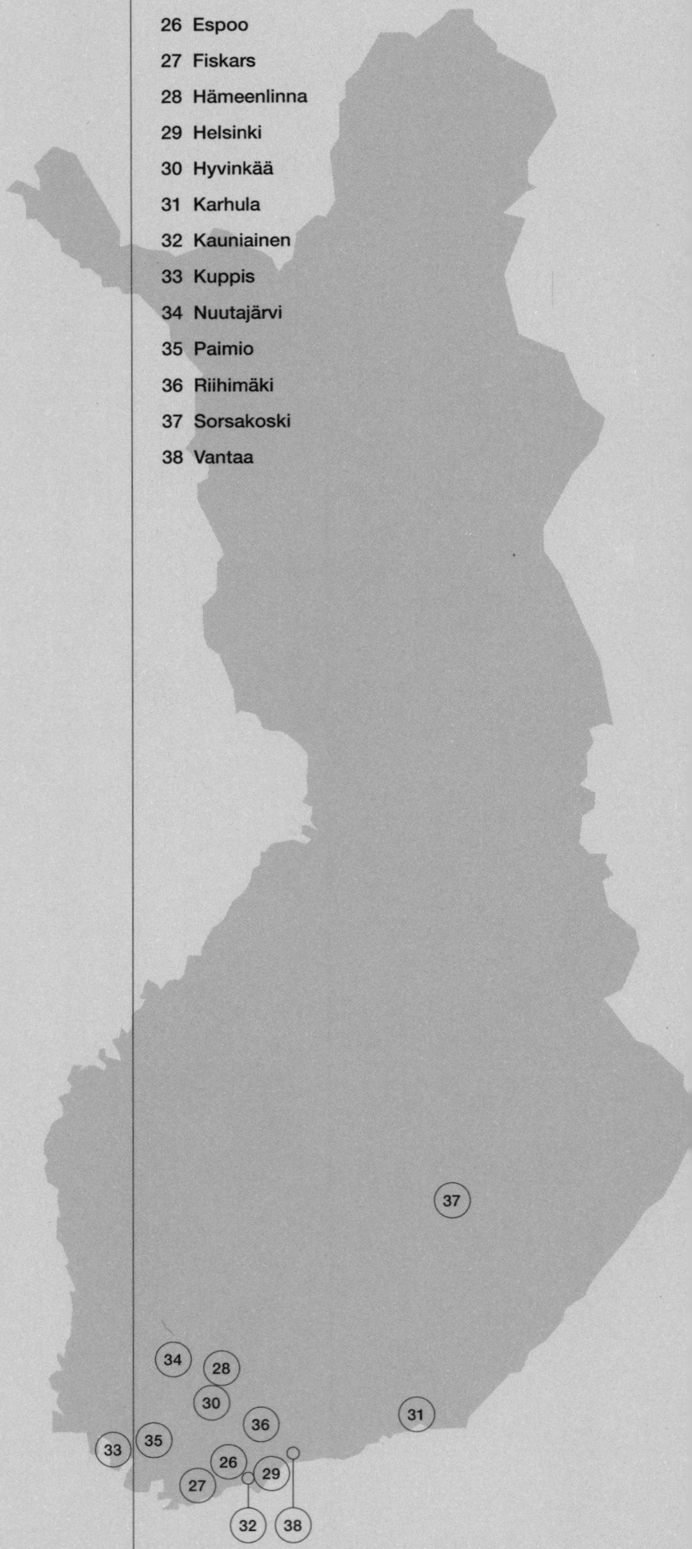

FINLAND

26 Espoo
27 Fiskars
28 Hämeenlinna
29 Helsinki
30 Hyvinkää
31 Karhula
32 Kauniainen
33 Kuppis
34 Nuutajärvi
35 Paimio
36 Riihimäki
37 Sorsakoski
38 Vantaa